The Deptford royal dockyard and manor of Sayes Court, London

Excavations 2000–12

MOLA Monograph Series

For more information about these titles and other MOLA publications visit the publications page at www.mola.org.uk

The Deptford royal dockyard and manor of Sayes Court, London

Excavations 2000–12

Antony Francis

MOLA MONOGRAPH 71

Published by MOLA (Museum of London Archaeology)
Copyright MOLA 2017

The Ordnance Survey mapping included in this publication is
© Crown copyright 2017, Ordnance Survey 100049883. All rights reserved.

A CIP catalogue record for this book is available from the British Library

Production and series design by Tracy Wellman
Typesetting and design by Sue Cawood
Reprographics by Andy Chopping
Copy editing by Simon Burnell
Series editing by Sue Hirst/Susan M Wright

Printed in the United Kingdom by the Lavenham Press,
an ISO 14001 certified printer

MIX
Paper from
responsible sources
FSC
www.fsc.org   FSC® C010693

*Front cover: panoramic view of the Deptford royal dockyard by Joseph Farington,
c 1794 (Fig 140)*

CONTRIBUTORS

Principal author	Antony Francis
Additional text	Damian Goodburn (wooden structures), Duncan Hawkins (iron slip cover roofs), Susan M Wright (historical background)
Documentary sources	Antony Francis, †Christopher Phillpotts, with Julian Bowsher, Mark Latham
Building material	Ian M Betts
Clay tobacco pipe	Jacqui Pearce
Medieval and post-medieval pottery	Nigel Jeffries
Plaster mouldings	Simon Swann
Glass	Lyn Blackmore
Accessioned finds	Lyn Blackmore, with Julian Bowsher
Archaeological woodwork	Damian Goodburn
Wood species identification	Karen Stewart
Animal bone	Alan Pipe
Tree-ring dating	Ian Tyers
Graphics	Hannah Faux (finds), Juan José Fuldain, Carlos Lemos (plans)
Site photography	Maggie Cox
Studio photography	Andy Chopping
Project managers	David Bowsher (post-excavation), David Divers, Robin Nielsen (fieldwork)
Academic advisor	Jonathan Coad
Editor	Susan M Wright

CONTENTS

**The late Georgian and Victorian dockyard
(period 5, 1774–1869)** **7**

FIGURES

TABLES

SUMMARY

The largest-ever excavations of a British naval dockyard are the subject of this publication. The archaeological fieldwork was undertaken at the *c* 16.6ha site of Deptford royal dockyard and Sayes Court in the London Borough of Lewisham in 2000–12. The excavations by MOLA (Museum of London Archaeology) and others were carried out before and after the demolition of warehouses and other buildings on the site, then known as Convoys Wharf. A wealth of documentary and pictorial evidence, maps and even a model contribute to and enhance our understanding of the complex structures and material revealed by the archaeology.

Royal yards and a standing navy were the creation of the first two Tudor monarchs, and especially of Henry VIII; Deptford, a Thames anchorage, and Deptford Strand were a short boat ride from his palace at Greenwich. There were structures, including a possible barge gutter, on the site earlier, but the royal dockyard began with Henry VIII ordering the construction of a storehouse in 1513. The bases of the walls of this scheduled building were recorded along with those nearby of the Treasurer of the Navy's house, hitherto unknown. Other early structures included the double or great dock and the wet dock, which made use of a pre-existing pond. No archaeological traces of the earliest forms of these docks were identified, but an indenture of 1517 commissioning the wet dock's construction is published here in full for the first time. The indenture names ships such as the *Mary Rose* that were to be housed afloat in the dock. A succession of timber waterfronts was also recorded archaeologically. Deptford was the most important Tudor dockyard in England; it was the last resting place for Francis Drake's ship the *Golden Hinde*, and the privateer was knighted by Elizabeth I at the yard.

The first maps of the dockyard appear in the Stuart period (1603–1714) and show how the site had grown to include more storehouses, offices, a smithy, slipways where ships were repaired, built and rebuilt, and a mast dock to season mast timbers. The wet dock was rebuilt in 1658–61, and its timber sides and the east side of the timber gate arrangement were exposed, braced by land-ties. The remains of a slipway (the great slip) survived, as well as more humble boathouses and pitch houses.

Inland, in the south of the site, some remains were identified of Sayes Court, home to John Evelyn, who wrote *Sylva* and *Fumifugium* and entertained friends such as Samuel Pepys here. No features associated with Evelyn's famous gardens were identified, apart from the base of his garden wall. The Russian Czar Peter the Great stayed here in early 1698 and caused much damage. Sayes Court was demolished in the mid 18th century and replaced by a workhouse.

Although the early Georgian period (1714–74) saw a relative decline in the dockyard's importance, this was offset by the increasing demand for ships for wars with France and Spain. Appointment to Deptford was still considered the pinnacle of success for a naval officer. These conflicts prompted sharp increases in work for the dockyard against a steady background of repair and maintenance of the navy's warships.

The excavations uncovered the foundations of the huge quadrangle storehouse, built in the early 18th century, as well as evidence of the piecemeal rebuilding of the wet dock in brick. The layout of the yard was broadly determined by this storehouse and the main docks, but within this outline adaptation and rebuilding of the yard structures and new construction were continuous. The dockyard expanded in size, swallowing land to the east and south, and a second, much larger, mast dock was created. Documents shed light on the yard's troubles and disasters, from fires to failing dock gates, while some of the most visually striking remains excavated were the three riverfront slipways, the floors of two excavated fully in plan. Many of these structures can be seen in maps of the period and in a remarkable scale model of the yard constructed for George III in 1774.

One historical source says that Deptford was of 'none estimation' before the yard was established. What is beyond doubt is that the development of the town was bound up closely with the yard. Deptford's streets were paved in advance of a visit by Edward VI. Part of the site lay outside the dockyard, and this provided the opportunity to recover and examine the discarded domestic belongings of people with access to items from overseas who were either directly employed by the dockyard or at least subject to its influence.

Ironically, the growth of the town blocked further expansion in the final stages of the yard's life in the late Georgian to Victorian period (1774–1869). The yard's up-river location also became a problem, with ships having to labour up the Thames, and the tendency for silting preventing the launching, and so construction, of the ever-larger ships that were now required.

Despite major changes to the wet dock by the engineer John Rennie in the early 19th century, the dockyard was stuttering to an end. After the Napoleonic Wars the yard was a key depot for stores but built only smaller ships; it closed for all but ship breaking in 1830. An apparent reprieve in 1843 was only temporary and the yard closed for good in 1869, many of its buildings being pulled down and bricks and timber carted away for use elsewhere. The yard was bought by the Corporation of the City of London and turned into the Foreign Cattle Market, with animal sheds built on top of its backfilled slipways.

ACKNOWLEDGEMENTS

MOLA (Museum of London Archaeology) would like to thank Convoys Properties Limited for their generous funding of the archaeological work, including this book, and in particular (the late) Andy Maton who was the archaeological team's main contact on site. We also wish to thank the London Borough of Lewisham for their input. Thanks also are due to Mark Stevenson of English Heritage (now Historic England) and Jonathan Coad for their invaluable advice during the archaeological work. Particular thanks go to Archaeological Consultant Duncan Hawkins of CgMs whose knowledge of Royal Navy dockyards and of the Deptford yard, and whose support during and after the excavations, were essential to the success of the project.

The excavation was directed by Antony Francis, and particular thanks go to the supervisory staff Steve White, Greg Laban, Kasia Olchowska, Jess Bryan, Bruce Ferguson, Hana Lewis, Aaron Birchenough, Mark Ingram and Ruth Taylor, without whom it would have been impossible to run this complex and demanding site. Thanks are also extended to the scores of MOLA and seconded Pre-Construct Archaeology (PCA) staff for their dedicated efforts, particularly through the especially hard winter of 2011–12. The site team of archaeologists consisted of Coralie Aitcheson, James Alexander, Veyrel Apaydin, Rick Archer, Homa Badr, Vesna Bandelj, Emily Bates, Nicola Bennett, James Best, Matthew Blewett, Charlotte Bossick, Kari Bower, Tanya Bowie, Samantha Boyle, Ian Bright, Joe Brooks, Howard Burkhill, Patrick Cavanagh, Juan Chacon, Clare Chapman, Will Clarke, Andrew Cochrane, Guy Cockin, Greg Crees, Charlotte Crowson, Umberto Crupi, Michael Curnow, Callum Davey, Sarah Deacon, Shelley Dootson, Matt Edmonds, Tom Eley, Rachel English, Vicki Ewens, Aidan Farnan, Phil Frickers, Pawel Galant, Vince Gardner, Lucy Garnsworthy, Peter Girdwood, Malcolm Gould, Val Griggs, Laura Green, Phredd Groves, Stacey Harris, Danny Harrison, David Harrison, Lee Harvey, Neil Hawkins, Dan Heale, Jim Heathcote, Phil Henderson, Sam Hogsden, Stuart Holden, Tina Holloway, Simon Holmes, Kim Hoskins, Annette Hughes, Nicky Humphrey, Owen Humphreys, Peter James, Tim Johnson, Gemma Jones, Phil Jefferies, Dan Joyce, John Joyce, Michael Joyce, Matt Juddery, Patrick Kavena, Leanne Kendall-Corps, Michael Kernow, Dougie Killock, Richard Krason, Myrto Kritikou, Paul McGarrity, Natasha McIntosh, Sheryl MacKimm-Watt, Michael McLean, Karl Macrow, Roberta Marziam, Roddy Mattinson, Lucy May, Tom Mazurkiewitz, Charlotte Mecklenburgh, Shayna Meyers, Jeremy Moore, Tomasz Moskal, Adela Murray-Brown, Deborah Nadal, Sam Oates, Chris O'Brian, Fergal O'Donoghue, Nina Olofsson, Victoria Osborn, Paul Owens, Phil Parker, Chris Pennell, Sam Pfizenmaier, Sasathorn Pickering, Claudia Pinci, Tom Pinfold, Steve Price, Emma Prideaux, Jonathan Rampling, Serena Ranieri, Sam Riley, Ruth Rolfe, Guy Seddon, Chris Spence, Rachel Stacey, Toria Standfield, Karen Stephens, Simon Stevens, Jason Stewart, Karen Stewart, Aiden Turner, Rob Tutt, Elena Valtorta, Helen Vowles, Nigel Ward, Jake Warrender, Jonathan Whitmore, Mark Wiggins, Mornington John Woodall, Tom Woodley, Emily Wright and James Wright. Damian Goodburn's unrivalled and detailed knowledge of London waterfront sites was an immeasurable help to the site team. Geoarchaeological support was provided by Mary Nicholls, Graham Spurr and Virgil Yendell, and surveying was carried out by MOLA geomatics, in particular Raoul Bull, Mark Burch, Catherine Drew, Sarah Jones and Gideon Simons.

We would also like to thank Keltbray who undertook groundworks for MOLA, and its site manager Jimmy Clarke, together with Martin Crees, Tim Fitz, Florian Igna, Frank O'Donnall, Gus Smith and Eamon Walsh.

Steve White and Greg Laban helped extensively with the post-excavation work. The late Christopher Phillpotts wrote almost all of the medieval historical section, and his work in identifying sources formed the foundation for further research into the history of the yard, while Mark Latham researched the Sayes Court part of the site, building on Chris's work, and transcribed the 1517 indenture, published here in full for the first time; Julian Bowsher researched King Street and Orchard Place outside the yard, to the east. We are grateful to Sally Eaton, archivist at Lewisham Local History and Archives Centre, Len Reilly, Archives and Library Manager at Lambeth Archives, and Elizabeth Scudder, Principal Archivist (Access) at London Metropolitan Archives, for their assistance in identifying certain manuscripts referenced in the documentary research. Thanks also go to Brian Philp for the archive of site works undertaken by the Kent Archaeological Research Unit (KARU) in the 1990s. And lastly, but by no means least, we are indebted to Royal Museums Greenwich, in particular to the staff of the Caird Library (National Maritime Museum) and to Pieter van der Merwe (General Editor and Greenwich Curator), for their assistance.

1

Introduction

The archaeological investigations reported on here at the former Royal Navy Dockyard Deptford, Lewisham, consititute the largest-ever excavations on a British naval dockyard site (Fig 1; Fig 2). The dockyard closed in 1869 and the site thereafter was put to various uses – as a foreign cattle market, warehouses, military and paper depot – and bombed in the Second World War. The Tudor storehouse, for example, was revealed during the removal of bomb-damaged buildings in 1952 (*ILN*, 1 March 1952) and demolished shortly afterwards. Proposed redevelopment at the beginning of the 21st century brought about renewed interest in and a re-examination of the history of this naval dockyard.

Also known as Convoys Wharf, the *c* 16.6ha site lies on the south bank of the River Thames, *c* 4km south-east of the City of London and *c* 1km west of Greenwich (Fig 1). It is bounded by the Thames to the north-east and by Watergate Street to the east, Prince Street to the south and Sayes Court and the rear of properties in Dacca Street and Grove Street to the south-west; Leeway bounds the site to the west (Fig 3; Fig 4). The Ordnance Survey National Grid Reference for the centre of the site is 537000 178200.

All the archaeological interventions on the site will be referred to here as 'the excavations' to avoid confusion, including the previous unpublished evaluations (Divers 2000; Francis 2010; 2013) and the results described in an interim publication (Hawkins 2015). There were also a series of desk-based assessments, and a Scheme of Archaeological Resource Management (SARM: Hawkins 2009). The detailed evidence recovered for the topography and geoarchaeology of the site and for prehistoric and Roman activity is reported elsewhere (Francis 2013).

The excavations were financed by Convoys Properties Limited and took place in 2000 (Pre-Construct Archaeology (PCA)), 2010 and 2011–12 (Museum of London Archaeology (MOLA)), with a much smaller recording project in the 1990s by the Kent Archaeological Research Unit (KARU). The purpose of the main part of the excavations was to examine, record and interpret archaeological deposits, features and structures, and, as appropriate, retrieve artefacts, ecofacts and other remains within the site. The objective of this exercise was to plot the archaeological remains so that these could be preserved *in situ* in the context of future development.

Two major evaluations took place on the site in advance of the larger excavation. In 2000 an evaluation was undertaken by PCA (under the site code CVW00) and in 2010 by MOLA (CVF10). For all phases of work the archaeological consultant was Duncan Hawkins (CgMs) and the monitor for English Heritage (now Historic England) was Mark Stevenson.

These two evaluations constituted the stage 1 evaluations. The 2000 evaluation consisted of 19 trenches (Divers 2000). The work showed that major dockyard features and post-medieval elements of a building in the location of Sayes Court survived. Trenches from this evaluation are prefixed with 'CVW00' (eg

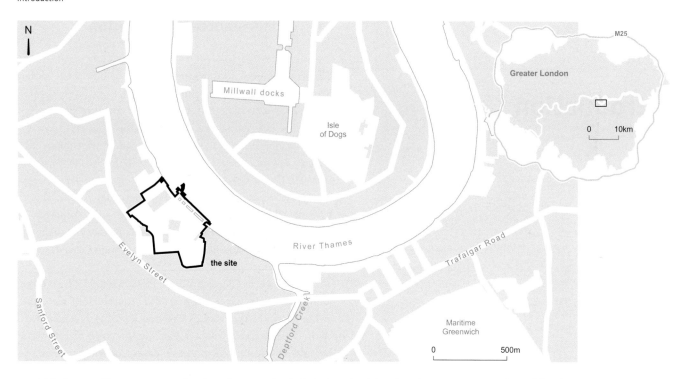

Fig 1 The location of the site superimposed on the modern street plan (scale 1:25,000) and (inset) in relation to Greater London and the Thames (scale 1:1,250,000)

Fig 2 Aerial view of the site in 1993 from the south-west (LLHAC, A/15/31/30)

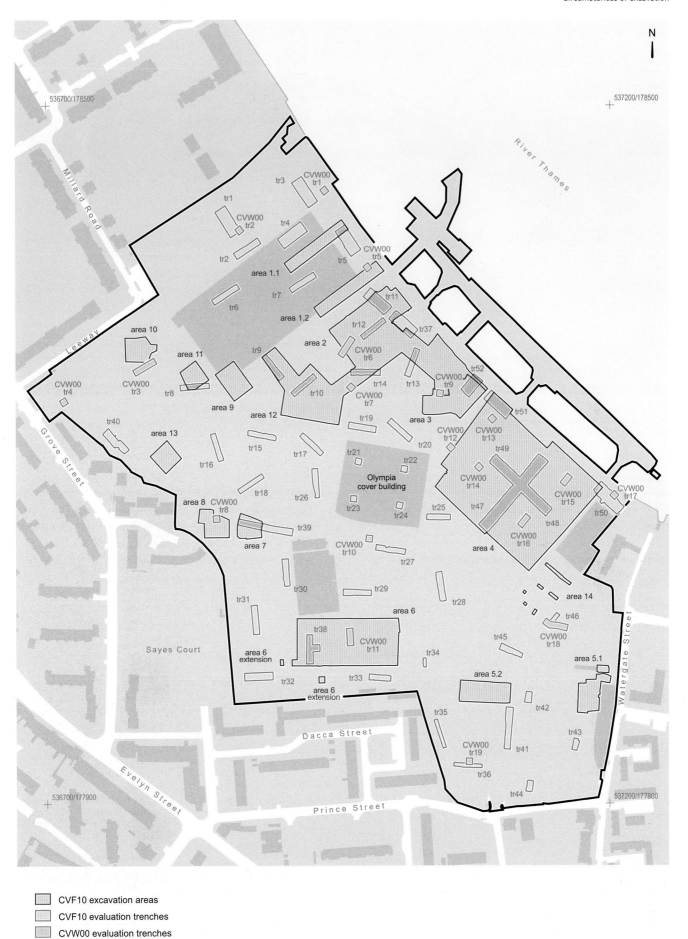

N

Fig 3 The location of the evaluation trenches and excavation areas within the site (scale 1:3250)

CVF10 excavation areas

CVF10 evaluation trenches

CVW00 evaluation trenches

0   100m

Fig 4 Aerial view of the site during excavation from the south-east (copyright Historic England)

CVW00 tr1) in Fig 3. The 2010 evaluation consisted of 52 trenches (Francis 2010). Many of the stage 1 evaluation trenches coincided with the subsequent excavation areas which formed stage 2.

Stage 2 consisted of a much larger excavation of 14 areas, the largest measuring 126m × 100m (Francis 2013) (Fig 5). It

should be noted that site north was taken as running at right angles to the riverfront (ie north-east of true north (Fig 3)).

The excavations investigated the Georgian quadrangle storehouse, into which an earlier Tudor storehouse (a Scheduled Ancient Monument) had been incorporated; the Treasurer of the Navy's house; the yard's wet dock (known as the 'basin' in

Fig 5 View of the excavations in 2011, looking north; in the foreground is the timber water tank (S33; Chapter 7.3) under excavation

the 19th century); slipways where ships were built and launched, including those under the only standing historic structure investigated archaeologically, the Grade II-listed slip cover roof of the 'Olympia' building; the small and large mast docks or ponds where masts were stored; the officers' quarters; the smithy; and other ancillary structures and multiphase buildings. Also investigated were buildings on the site of Sayes Court, the home of the diarist and horticulturalist John Evelyn, lying immediately south-east of the yard.

1.2 The Royal Navy dockyards, Deptford and the workings of the navy: introduction and background

The Royal Navy and the dockyards

To the young King Henry VIII, a standing navy was a symbol of royal authority and an instrument of power (Coad 2013, 1). Wars with France and other kingdoms (1511–16), including Scotland, had seen the number of English ships increase from seven or eight to more than 20 by 1513 (Rodger 1997, 476). Henry had inherited a basic dockyard facility at Portsmouth and a single official, the Clerk of Ships, a role he augmented by appointing a Clerk Controller (or Comptroller), while the Lord Admiral had general oversight (Loades 1992, 72; Knighton and Loades 2011, xxvii). He also began appointing the more experienced shipwrights to take charge of the royal dockyards, including James Baker at Deptford (MacDougall 1982, 39), and ordered the construction of storehouses at Deptford and at Erith (east of Woolwich).

Southampton had been used briefly as a base by Henry V in 1420, but Portsmouth is the oldest naval base still in operation. A dry dock was built there in 1492 and the yard remained important largely because of its sheltered harbour. Deptford and Woolwich were founded in the early 16th century, in 1513. A short-lived dockyard at Erith, created a year later in 1514, was abandoned in the 1540s. As the Tudor navy expanded, the Medway became attractive as a safe anchorage and Chatham grew in importance from its founding in 1547, superseding Portsmouth. Sheerness guarded the mouth of this river from the Dutch from 1665. In the late 17th century naval operations were shifting westwards into the Atlantic and beyond, resulting in the establishment of Plymouth (later Devonport) dockyard with a wet and a dry dock in the 1690s. Conflict with the French in the 18th century saw Portsmouth regain its importance. Much later, in 1809, 13 building slips and a graving dock (a dry dock for 'graving', ie cleaning accretions off ships' hulls) were built to form Pembroke dockyard, the only royal dockyard in Wales. From c 1700 well into the 20th century, the three home dockyards of Plymouth, Portsmouth and Chatham were pre-eminent: all had the advantage over the other home yards of being sited next to large and relatively safe anchorages and thus received the major share of government funding (Coad 2013, 1–4).

By the 18th century, naval administration had developed from Henry VIII's two officials in a haphazard, perhaps eccentric, way. Even so, the administrators managed to maintain what became the largest industrial organisation in the western world, the most complex of all the government services and the largest fleet in Europe (Rodger 1988, 29, 36). The job of the Admiralty was to coordinate the work of other departments, while the Treasurer of the Navy was responsible for the finance of the navy as a whole. The Admiralty staff was small, numbering only 30 in 1759. Below them, the Navy Board, set up in 1546, was responsible for all aspects of the dockyards – their construction, maintenance, operation and management. The officers of the yards, who dealt with day-to-day business concerning the construction and repair of ships, reported to the Navy Board (Rodger 1997, 225–8; 1988, 33–51; Morriss 2011, 138–41; Knight 2013).

The Deptford yard and its workforce

Deptford thus was one of a number of Royal Navy dockyards or 'royal dockyards'. In the early 16th century, the Deptford yard consisted of storehouses, a wet dock (the 'pond' or 'basin') and a dry dock (the 'great dock') (Chapter 3.1). By the end of the 17th century it had grown to include several building slips, a mast dock and mast house, a mould loft, sawhouses, a smithy, a sheathing board house, a pitch house, a wheelers' shop, boathouses and stables (Chapter 4). The storehouses, wet dock and dry dock had been much enlarged and the yard's officers were comfortably lodged in houses along the south-east perimeter. The Treasurer of the Navy lived in a separate house at the yard from the 1540s, convenient for London. In the following years, the yard acquired a second dry dock, other slipways and a second (much larger) mast dock, while other buildings were much enlarged or rebuilt.

As the dockyards grew in the following centuries to a great size, the problems of managing them grew too, in particular managing the regular workforce (Rodger 2004, 298). The repair of ships went on routinely and continuously. Of the five principal officers, the Master Shipwright (also known as the Builder) was in practice the pre-eminent one, in charge of all building and repair and of most of the workforce (see also eg Chapter 3.1, 'The Elizabethan dockyard'); the Clerk of the Cheque saw to accounts and wages, the Clerk of the Survey surveyed all yard transactions, while the Master Attendant supervised yard operations not controlled by the Master Shipwright, including the ships afloat and in reserve ('in Ordinary'), docking, launching, graving or careening, caulking, replacing damaged or worn timber, repainting, fitting and refitting; and the Storekeeper was responsible for naval stores and supplies (Morriss 1983, 168–70; Rodger 1988, 34–5). The Surgeon looked after the health of the men; his salary was paid from the men's wages (Linebaugh 2003, 375), supplemented by 30s for every man he cured of venereal disease (TNA, ADM 106/2537, 21 July 1742, np). Commissioners of the dockyards were members of the Navy Board, but they were not actually in charge of the yards (Rodger 1988, 34). Full-time permanent resident Commissioners were introduced into the dockyards not long before *c* 1660, but for most of the 17th and 18th centuries there was none at Deptford (or Woolwich), leaving the Master Shipwright as the pre-eminent officer (Ehrman 1953, 101, 104; Baugh 1965, 289). The Clerk of the Survey (although less senior because his was a newer role) was expected to check the issues and accounts of his fellow principal officers, but especially to check the activities of the Storekeeper, who could issue nothing without the Clerk of the Survey's signature. In 1778 Deptford's Clerk of the Survey told the Navy Board that he 'cautiously avoided intermeddling with any Expence arising from the Hulls Masts & Yards of Ships either building or under Repair', which was just what the role had been created for in the 17th century (Knight 1987, xxxvi).

The principal officers were assisted by clerks. In the 18th century salaries for dockyard clerks were low, promotion prospects limited, and in wartime the hours of work were long, encouraging slackness, inefficiency and dishonesty (Knight 1987, xlii). The Deptford officers told the Navy Board that a substantial premium and years of low salary ensured that the clerks were 'Sons or Relations of People in its Neighbourhood who have acquired some Fortune in Trade or by Family Connexions … without which in the Junior Clerkships from the small Salary allowed by Government it would be impossible to subsist, much more appear decent' (ibid). Reform of the salary and career structure was needed (ibid). In 1815 there were 32 clerks at Deptford to assist the five principal officers and newer offices: the Commissioner and Master Shipwright each had two; the Master Attendant one; the Clerk of the Cheque and the Clerk of the Survey six each; the Storekeeper seven; and the Timber Master and Master Measurer each had four (Morriss 1983, 130).

Workers were attracted to the dockyards by a combination of wage rates, perquisites and the other advantages of working in a large state establishment, principally greater security of employment. Navy accounts for August and October 1544 show that the then Master Shipwright, James Baker, received 1s a day, his son Matthew 2d, and the other shipwrights and caulkers (in total 80–90) varying amounts in between; the men were also paid lodging money of three halfpence a week, and were expected to sleep two to a bed (Oppenheim 1926, 340). In the Elizabethan yard, the Master Shipwright's 1s a day was usually supplemented by a fee of £4–8 per annum and a pension from the Exchequer of another shilling per day; building many of the ships on contract would also have been to their profit (ibid, 342). In the 17th century Master Shipwrights were being paid 2s a day in addition to their allowances, but some were allegedly absent for months from the royal yards, busy in their own yards (ibid, 345). In Charles II's reign the Deptford Master Shipwright was paid £114 10s per annum, and his assistants £70 per annum (ibid, 353). In 1696 officers' salaries were raised but the old Exchequer fees abolished, so that Deptford's Master Shipwright was to be paid £200 per annum; the day wages of the men varied from 1s 6d to 3s, paid quarterly (ibid, 365).

John Evelyn gives a description of one of the Master Shipwrights at the yard in the late 17th century. Jonas Shish (1605–80) was 'a plain, honest carpenter, master-builder of this dock, but one who can give very little account of his art by discourse, and is hardly capable of reading, yet of great ability in his calling … It was the custom of this good man to rise in the night, and to pray, kneeling in his own coffin, which he had lying by him for many years'. Evelyn stated that Shish's family had been ship carpenters at the yard 'above 300 years' and although this is not borne out by any evidence available to us today, his comment does illustrate how shipwrights' skills were passed down the generations. In fact, Shish's son succeeded his father as Master Shipwright at the yard (*Evelyn diary*, 3 March 1668; 13 May 1680; 17 April 1683). However, in 1668 Thomas Harper, the Storekeeper, urged the Navy Board to send no barge to the yard without proper documents. Many barges were arriving without details of the timber, 'very disorderly', especially as 'Mr Shish and his instruments being overhasty to receive and convert some of it before any account can be taken' (*Cal S P Dom*, 1668, 265–7, 18 April).

Of course the Deptford yard employed not only shipwrights but also house-carpenters, bricklayers and their labourers, smiths, scavelmen (who removed mud and debris from docks, slips and other waterways), caulkers, pitch heaters, quarterboys, oakum boys, joiners, wheelwrights, plumbers, block makers, sailmakers, riggers and their labourers, armourers and compass makers (below, 1.3, 1.4). Each trade could consist of several grades of worker. There were some 240 men at Deptford in the mid 17th century in peacetime (Oppenheim 1926, 350, 352). Yard employees included, for example, watchmen, some 18 in the mid 17th century at Deptford (ibid, 351). The yard's wartime establishment was larger, often considerably, than in peacetime (Morriss 2011, 160).

The navy contracted for some manufactured items – especially more specialised items – on standing contracts, selected by tender, as well as for all its supplies of raw materials. In *c* 1670, at the beginning of the French war, there began a system of supplying a particular dockyard with items required 'for one year certain', with six months notice on either side. By 1688 Deptford had standing contracts of this type with a small group of tradesmen – anchor smith, ironmonger, glazier and plasterer, brazier, plumber, sailmaker, cooper, compass and watch glass maker, painter, tanner, turner, and tile maker – and for colours (ie flags), handscrews, and lead and solder. Deptford and Woolwich shared some of the same tradesmen; one sailmaker handled the work for the whole navy (Ehrman 1953, 67–8). By 1698 most of the standing contracts were handled by either a single London trader who monopolised one trade in all the yards or a local trader who monopolised all the remaining trades in one yard. Their local workshops were part of the yard but the workers were not naval employees (ibid, 69; for eg the 18th-century compass maker's and glazier's workshops, see Chapters 6.2 and 7.2). Sailmaking was firmly established in all the major yards following a decision in 1716 made with the aim of better-quality, and cheaper, sails (Coad 2013, 112–13). As a result, canvas soon provided plentiful business for the small marine dealers outside the walls (Linebaugh 2003, 377).

Daniel Defoe compared a dockyard to 'a well order'd city;

and tho' you see the whole place ... in the utmost hurry, yet you see no confusions, every man knows his business' (quoted in Ashton 1955, 113). The work in a dockyard was hard and could be perilous: 'William Cowdry a shipwright belonging to his Majesty's Yard here was drowned yesterday' (TNA, ADM 106/3313, 16 September 1760, np).

Master shipwrights and other officers were well placed to be able to carry out many kinds of malpractice in the 16th and 17th centuries and later (below, and Chapters 3.1 and 4.1), but it was what the Navy Board saw as the abuse by the dockyard workers of the right to collect 'chips' that became notorious (Oppenheim 1926, 347; Rodger 2004, 299). Dockyard workers supplemented their wages with 'chips', the scraps of waste wood produced during the work of hewing, chopping and sawing ship and building timbers; they were used for construction or furniture or as fuel, providing between a third and a half of weekly earnings (Linebaugh 2003, 378–9; Morriss 2011, 167). A contemporary estimate was that only a sixth of the timber entering the Deptford yard left it afloat (Sutherland 1711, 7). The men argued that they could not live without the perquisite. In 1650 wages were raised all round to try to stop the practice but the men took both the extra money and chips (Oppenheim 1926, 348). In 1662, the Navy Board issued sometimes contradictory instructions that only 'lawfull ones may be carried away once a week', only at 'noon and night', and 'every Saturday at night' superintended by the Master Shipwright and his assistants (TNA, ADM 106/2537, 10 May 1662, np; 20 June 1662, np; 11 October 1662, np). In 1673 an informer stated that the chips at Deptford, Woolwich and Chatham might be estimated at a 'load' of timber (ie 50ft^3) a day and that many other things went out with them (Oppenheim 1926, 358).

The yard workers frequently had a genuine grievance in that wages could go unpaid for long periods of time: in 1686 wages were a year in arrears, and in 1693 15 months in arrears when the navy debt included £107,000 for yard wages (Oppenheim 1926, 363; Ehrman 1953, 326). The Deptford yard officers advised the Navy Board in 1749 that 'the people employed in his Majesty's yards by the day at low wages are seldom paid in less than twelve but often not 'til eighteen months after their work has been performed' whereas it was 'the constant practice of the merchant builders to pay the men they employ on task work every fortnight or three weeks at farthest' (Morriss 2011, 166).

Collectively the yard men resisted attempts by the Navy Board to impose changes and 'efficiencies', a pattern which continued as their numbers grew, and the officers were often in sympathy with them (Rodger 2004, 298–9). By the 18th century the yard as a whole might employ 900 men and boys in peacetime and 1100 to 1200 during wartime (Linebaugh 2003, 374; Coad 2013, 6 table 1.2). In 1711, employees at Deptford numbered 1102, surpassed only by Chatham (1309) and Portsmouth (2022) (ibid). The workforce at Deptford on 14 September 1755 totalled 1066 (including 536 shipwrights, 170 labourers, 51 sawyers and 46 smiths), larger than at Woolwich (995) and Sheerness (389) but smaller than at Plymouth (1314), Chatham (1671) and Portsmouth (1836) (Morriss 2011, table 4.4). On 12 February 1814 (in the era of the Napoleonic Wars) 2084

was the figure recorded for employees at Deptford, on a par with Woolwich (2070) but fewer than at Chatham (2474), Plymouth (3914) and Portsmouth (4133), reflecting the relative importance of these home yards at that date (Coad 2013, 6 table 1.2; cf Morriss 2011, table 4.5, 2 April 1814).

Working hours were not surprisingly also a source of much dispute. The working hours of the Deptford yard were 'between six and six' (TNA, ADM 106/3309, 7 April 1753, 105) but when there was much to do, and the light and the Navy Board would allow it, 'extra' was worked. Overtime was basically measured in periods of an hour and a half, a 'tide', which earned just under a third of a day's pay (Knight 1987, xliii; Linebaugh 2003, 374). Holidays – such as Easter or Whitsun – were often worked (eg TNA, ADM 106/3313, 23 May 1760, np). Major building works were almost always undertaken in spring and summer when the weather was better (and daylight longer); a general order allowed all the men to work one tide extra during the summer to supplement the basic wage. At particularly busy times a 'night' could be worked, a five-hour period that earned a full day's pay. There was friction over what the men saw as their right to work overtime at the higher rates, not just in a crisis or wartime when night and day working was a necessity (Knight 1987, xliii; Rodger 2004, 299). Occasionally, the men refused extra work: the Deptford men had mutinied in February 1665 when it was proposed to work the breakfast half hour (Oppenheim 1926, 352–3), and in April 1742 they again declined 'to work their breakfast time' despite being threatened with loss of pay (TNA, ADM 106/3305, 22 April 1742, 104).

There was thus considerable variation in the men's income depending on the number of hours of daylight, the urgency of the work or whether it was peace- or wartime. For example, in 1774 a shipwright at the yard earned £35 a year but was earning £52 in 1778 (Knight 1999, 6). In 1762 the wages at Deptford were 'fifteen months behind', causing unrest (Linebaugh 2003, 375). During the American War of Independence, in 1775, there was a widespread shipwrights' strike when the Admiralty introduced piecework in an attempt to reform wage rates. The Deptford men did not join in but the Portsmouth men, among others, did strike (Oppenheim 1926, 379; Morriss 1983, 100; 2011, 168–9). The correspondence from this period between Portsmouth's officers and the Navy Board illustrates the arguments, as well as pay and conditions, and alternating labour shortages and discharges as the yard work available fluctuated (Knight 1987, 33–64). Reductions in the workforce were understandably unpopular; security of employment in the royal yards offset the generally higher wages in merchant yards (Morriss 1983, 98–9; Knight 1987, xliii n32).

Many contemporaries in the 18th century thought the men worked well, but not hard (Rodger 2004, 299). Embezzlement and security were constant and linked themes at all the royal yards (eg Portsmouth: Knight 1987, 65–72). In 1702 the men maintained their right – and that of their families – to take chips out of the Deptford yard (and Woolwich) three times a day (Oppenheim 1926, 363–4; Linebaugh 2003, 378). In practice this meant usable pieces of some size and quantity, not infrequently concealing more valuable items like ironwork and, later, copper (Rodger 2004, 299). Informers were paid: in 1711 two Deptford labourers who had informed about abuses in the yard asked the Navy Board for 150 guineas; the Board said £25 was sufficient (Oppenheim 1926, 363). The Navy Board sought to restrict chips to only that timber that could be carried on a shipwright's shoulders (TNA, ADM 106/2537, 31 August 1739, np) and later 'under one arm unbound', defining chips as only those that 'fall from the axe' (ibid, 4 May 1753, np). 'Poor people [were to be] allowed the sweepings' under the watchful eye of the officers at the gate (ibid, 9 January 1759, np). The attempt by the Navy Board to suppress the collection of chips in 1739 led to strikes, including at Deptford. There were disturbances in 1742, troops were called to the yard in 1744, and there was a further strike in 1758 when some 30 of the leaders of the 'riotous' men were discharged (Oppenheim 1926, 370, 374; Knight 1999, 9; Linebaugh 2003, 375, 381).

After the end of the American War of Independence in 1783, the Navy Board unsuccessfully again attempted to dispense with this 'extremely expensive method of supplementing the mens' wages' by suggesting to the Admiralty that the custom of retaining chips be commuted to a money allowance. The Navy Board said that the men left off work half an hour early to cut up good timber, and suggested that an allowance be paid of 4d a day to the shipwrights and 2d a day to house-carpenters and servants (Knight 1987, xliii).

To tighten up security, the Navy Board ordered that only one gate should be kept open (TNA, ADM 106/2537, 20 October 1696, np) and any other 'back doors' should be paled or bricked up (ibid, 4 May 1715, np). As well as keeping trespassers out of its dockyards, the Navy Board strove to keep Crown property in. Dockyard workers were to be 'searched frequently' (ibid, 20 February 1743, np). (The Navy Board and dockyard commissioners also at times feared arsonists.) The dockyards had been patrolled by watchmen drawn from the workmen. From 1764 these watchmen were replaced by marines who themselves were subsequently replaced by a new police system based on the old one; at Deptford there were then seven day and 30 night watchmen (Oppenheim 1926, 377).

The copper sheathing of vessels, introduced in the late 18th century, provided additional material to steal. In early 1800, three workmen were caught with copper, the thefts being reported to the Navy Board on the very day the officers bemoaned shortages of the metal. Two of the men had stashed 'two sheets of old copper weighing about sixteen pounds' stripped from the bottom of a troop ship, and a scavelman was caught at the gate with an 8lb sheet (TNA, ADM 106/3325, 7 April 1800, np). All types of naval stores were stolen, from the stores and from ships under repair or moored in ordinary; hemp and cordage were the materials most commonly detected as being stolen, but precautions and punishment had little effect (Morriss 1983, 94).

Theft and corruption were not restricted to the lower orders. The officers of the Royal Navy yards often managed their own private yards or supply houses. At Deptford they were in a position to requisition the labour of the yard for their own purposes (Linebaugh 2003, 375). Their malpractice and

corruption on a massive scale were in effect a public scandal (below, Chapters 3.1 and 4.1). Dockyard artisans including the shipwrights became property owners in Deptford. The Slade family, for example, had been dependent on the dockyard as shopkeepers and employees (Benjamin Slade was probably the dockyard's purveyor in 1792–3 and a 'B. Slade' was the yard's master boat builder in 1802–5), and turned to property speculation in the late 18th century in the area of what came to be known as Deptford High Street (Guillery and Herman 1998, 29, 32, 121).

Dismissals were not uncommon. Usually this was for theft, but not always. In 1715 a watchman, Owen Edwards, was dismissed for 'returning saucy language' to the Storekeeper (TNA, ADM 106/3297, 19 October 1715, 6). In November 1716, seven shipwrights 'expressed themselves in an unbecoming and disrespectful manner towards his Majesty' and were discharged (ibid, 19 November 1716, 77). Examining the two-year period of 1766–7, selected more or less at random, there were a number of misdemeanours, some typical and some not. These included a shipwright, Charles Smith, who was discharged for 'neglect of duty' (TNA, ADM 106/3315, 14 March 1767, 141); a watchman, James Bamber, caught at the gate with 'two old bolts of his Majesties weighing sixteen pounds, value two shillings concealed under his great coat' (ibid, 21 June 1766, 92); Morgan Jones, also caught at the gate with 'a piece of an old bolt five old nails and a broken forelock', who was discharged immediately (ibid, 3 February 1766, 78); while Edward Linton and Joseph Cuff 'were confined on suspicion of embezzling copper' (ibid, 14 August 1766, 99). Less typical was the case of Benjamin Orrell, a pitcher's assistant, who stole a watchman's gun (ibid, 5 December 1766, 125). Five men, including three shipwrights, were discharged in 1767 for keeping public houses (ibid, 1 October 1767, 165).

There was a sense of community in the yards (Rodger 2004, 299). The artisans and labourers of the Deptford dockyard formed a food cooperative, and the shipwrights of the yard combined with those of Woolwich and Chatham in the 1750s to form a retail society open to all those employed within these yards (MacDougall 1999, 55). The dockyards employed men on quarterly wages from apprenticeship to old age: in 1744 the Deptford yard officers reported that 'here are indeed many persons belonging to the yard who have behaved well that are grown old in the service but are capable of performing several light works upon which they are employed to the advantage of the Crown' (Rodger 2004, 298). Allowance was made for ageing artisans in 1810 when the Navy Board directed that 'the oars shall be made by the old and infirm shipwrights' (although the officers objected that there were no such shipwrights in the yard 'capable of making oars') (TNA, ADM 106/3336, 19 November 1810, 43).

Dockyard workers were not always protected from being pressed into the navy. There was general anxiety about this in the 18th century and particularly during the Napoleonic Wars; after 1815, although not abolished, impressment was no longer used. In March 1719, the smiths sought reassurances that they would not be 'prest' (TNA, ADM 106/3298, 13 March 1719,

92). When an artificer at the yard was pressed in 1790, 'a large mob consisting principally of shipwrights belonging to Deptford Yard' found the lieutenant in charge and 'with horrid imprecations, threatened him and his gang with death, and tore down his colours which they carried off in triumph' (Morriss 1999, 27 n6; 2011, 243). The yard workers were formed into regiments at times, as in the 1740s when France threatened, and in the late 1750s with the Seven Years War (Oppenheim 1926, 370–1, 372, 374).

The major dockyards were individual working units, managed as parts of one centralised organisation by the Navy Board at the beginning of the 19th century, when Britain was dominant at sea, as it had been since the 16th century (Morriss 1983, 167; 2011, 182, 396–403). Reforms imposed on the navy, in the Navy Office and in the dockyards during the period of the Revolutionary and Napoleonic Wars were part of a wider transformation affecting the whole of government, continuing an earlier, more gradual process towards achieving greater efficiency and economy in the management of men and resources, and greater professionalism on the part of officers particularly. Since the 17th century the Navy Board had issued warrants empowering yard officers to act as part of a system which had become very confused. A huge number of standing orders had been issued since Samuel Pepys and the Duke of York issued permanent instructions in 1662, designed to suit the particular circumstances of each yard and 'to meet each present difficulty as it arose, perhaps without having the least reference to the general principle on which they had been at first established' (Knight 1987, xxii; Morriss 2011, 147). By 1806 the yard officers all possessed comprehensive printed instructions which remained the basis on which the yards operated for half a century (ibid, 148). The principal officers were affected not only by the revision of standing orders but by the removal of anomalies, gratuities and some allowances, compensated for by increased pay and superannuation schemes (Morriss 1983, 128–30, 157–8; 2011, 139–48, 167, 182 and *passim*). As to the yard workforce, chips were finally commuted to daily allowances in 1801 (Morriss 1983, 104); in 1805 weekly subsistence money was introduced (the payment of three-quarters of usual earnings weekly) and beginning in 1813 all earnings were paid in full each week (Morriss 2011, 168).

1.3 Cartographic and other pictorial evidence

Cartographic evidence for the yard is particularly rich. The earliest map of the yard is the 1623 sketch map of Deptford annotated by John Evelyn in 1698 (Fig 14; Fig 50), and there is a detailed survey of the yard of 1698 (BL, Kings MS 43, fos 66–88 [Deptford]) including a map and panorama (Fig 23), as well as maps of 1725 (Fig 57), 1753 (Fig 58), 1802 (Fig 95), 1858 (Fig 98; Fig 121; another version at UKHO, D4624) – and an amended version of the 1858 survey dated 1878 (ICE, 623.81(422) M) –

and others (eg Fig 55; Fig 128; Fig 129). Using some of these key cartographic sources, Fig 6 illustrates the expansion of the Deptford dockyard: extending the yard to the south-west in the 1720s into John Evelyn's land; leasing and then buying the Red House estate and building a large complex of victualling stores and mills in the mid 18th century; the Admiralty taking in an area to the south in the mid 19th century while the dockyard lost some land to the victualling yard; and, throughout the life of the dockyard, piecemeal small-scale expansion eastwards.

It is a lucky archaeologist who has a scale model of their site, built for a king (in this case, in 1774: Fig 7). Although many now consider these models of the royal dockyards to have been made at least partially for political purposes to encourage greater naval spending by the monarch, George III, the models of all the royal dockyards ordered by the Earl of Sandwich, First Lord of the Admiralty, seem originally to have been made to give members of the Navy Board a clearer idea of the size and complexity of the yards and to help with their replanning (Coad 2013, 60–1).

Another source of evidence are the numerous paintings, views (eg of *c* 1794: Fig 140) and sketches (eg Fig 57; Fig 64; Fig 113) of the yard, often made when a ship was launched. The paintings by John Cleveley the elder (*c* 1712–77), one of the yard's shipwrights, are particularly notable and useful, as well as being accomplished works of art in their own right (eg Fig 61; Fig 72) (van der Merwe 2010; 2013).

1.4 Historical sources and their citation

There is a wealth of documentary evidence relating to the yard, and only part of it was sampled for this project. The targeting of one year in ten of the material held in the National Archives was devised by the late Christopher Phillpotts, but this strategy did not restrict the historical research to these years and leads were followed up by examining further documents in these classes. Some of the most useful written evidence is to be found in the yard officers' letter books, which contain copies of messages by the officers, mostly to the Navy Board. The letters could be terse: 'We pray leave to acquaint you that we have discharged John Haynes a joyner for neglect of duty, and that this morning Henry Gardner a rigger dropt down dead in the Yard' (TNA, ADM 106/3309, 17 April 1753, 106). Others contain useful details of building work, ship construction and repair. The names by which structures were known changed over the yard's 350-year history. Only in the 19th century is the 'Wet' or 'Wett Dock' referred to as the 'Basin' (eg TNA, ADM 106/2516, 28 August 1805, order no. 169). The dry dock – the 'Great Dock' – became the 'Double Dock', and at the turn of the 18th and 19th centuries it is even referred to as the 'Long Dock' (eg TNA, ADM 106/3325, 17 April 1799, np). Slipways were named after their position, for example 'the East Slip on the River' or by the ship that was being built in the slip at that time. The slipways were only numbered (nos 1–5, from west to

1659 (see Fig 26)

1753 (see Fig 60)

1774 (see Fig 71)

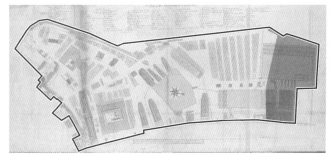

1802 (see Fig 95)

1858 (see Fig 98; Fig 121)

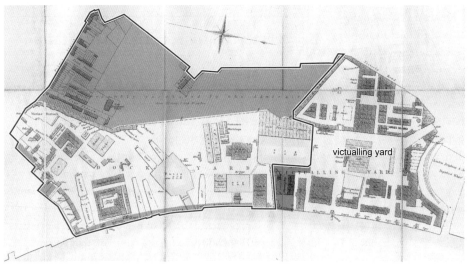

victualling yard

—— perimeter of dockyard

area extended

area subtracted

1870 (see Fig 129)

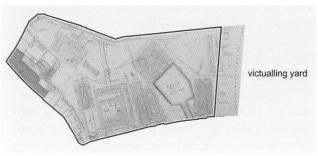

victualling yard

Fig 6 The sequence of dockyard expansion as illustrated by the cartographic sources, with the dockyard perimeter overlain on an historic map of the date indicated; the dockyard closed in 1869 and stores were moved to the victualling yard

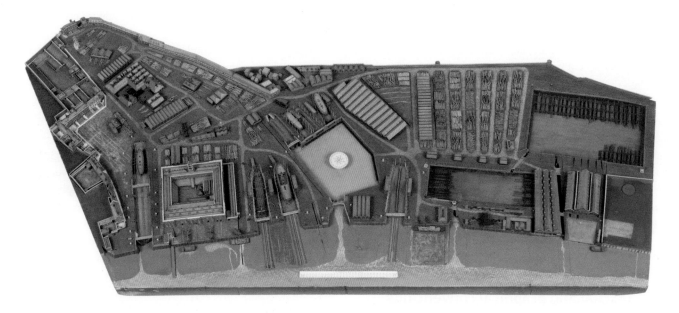

Fig 7 The 1:576 scale model of Deptford dockyard, c 1774, looking 'south': the wet dock (the basin) is in the centre, the small and large mast docks to the west (right) of this and the storehouse complex to the east (left); note ships at various stages of construction or repair in dock and on the slipways, and the extensive areas used to stockpile timber (National Maritime Museum, Greenwich, L0459-001)

east) from the 1840s. The gate at the south end of the yard was called the 'South Gate' in 1698, the 'Sailfield Gate' in 1715 and the 'Upper Gate' in 1726, and so on. For the sake of clarity, it has not always been possible to keep to the names of the structures as given at the time.

For most of its history, the yard had one mast dock or pond where masts were seasoned – or rather, they were kept in workable fresh or 'green' condition by soaking in ponds to reduce splitting and decay in the finished masts. From 1770 a new mast dock, much larger, was built and the two mast docks were referred to in different ways – for example, the 'Old Mast Pond' and the 'Great Mast Pond' in 1802, or the 'Small Mast Pond' and the 'Large Mast Pond' in 1878. To avoid confusion, before 1770 we refer to the 'mast dock' and after 1770 to the 'small mast dock' and the 'large mast dock', unless in a direct quote, which is qualified if necessary.

The officers' letter books have yielded valuable information about the development of the yard. In quoting from these sources, original capitalisation has been retained to highlight the fact that this is direct quotation, and to be consistent with the unavoidable retention of antiquated or obsolete terminology, orthography, punctuation and syntax; an exception to the latter principle is that 'ye' is rendered as 'the'. Because of the frequency of references to the letter books (TNA, ADM 106) in sections where they occur, to save space 'ibid' is used for consecutive references to the same volume within a paragraph, but followed by the specific date and (if applicable) page number of the letter.

When referring to page numbers in the letter books here, the left-hand page is consistently numbered the same as on the right-hand page where there is no page number on the left-hand page. Sometimes this practice is followed in the letter books, sometimes not, and there can be variations within a single volume (eg TNA, ADM 106/3305). Some pages in the letter

books are wrongly numbered, for example in TNA, ADM 106/3296. In such cases, we have reproduced the original (wrong) page number followed by the correct page number in square brackets (eg TNA, ADM 106/3296, 4 April 1715, 146 [246]). In another volume (TNA, ADM 106/3315) the pages bear two numbers, one printed and one handwritten. Since it is the handwritten page numbers that correspond to the index in this volume, these are used here. No page number is indicated by 'np'. All dates are expressed in New Style (post-1751 calendar), with the year beginning on 1 January.

Some terms that are no longer familiar are used in the officers' descriptions. 'Tarras' was used for waterproofing brickwork and was a forerunner of the Roman cement that was developed by James Parker in the 1780s and patented in 1796. 'Tarras' or 'terras' are 18th-century spellings of the material now known as 'trass', a volcanic deposit or tuff of a pozzolanic character, used in combination with lime to form several of the early types of cement (E Trout, Concrete Society, pers comm). 'Treenails' were carefully made wooden cylindrical pegs normally wedged at both ends like a rivet. 'Wales' are thicker, strengthening longitudinal outer hull planks with bevelled edges. 'Oakum' is the tarred fibre used for 'caulking' or packing ships' joints. Building and repair work for timber buildings was usually done by house-carpenters; shipwrights built the ships.

Ships are described here principally in terms of tonnage. Tonnage up to 1873 is the builder's measurement (bm), a capacity measurement arrived at from perhaps the 15th century by calculating the number of tuns (casks) of wine the ship could carry. Figures for tonnage calculated as bm (quoted here as, eg, 200bm-tons) are taken from Colledge and Warlow (2010, *sub* ship), and usually represent just the as-built tonnage (ibid, ix); armament figures (eg 406-pounder) and dimensions (length, ie that of the gundeck for sailing vessels, and beam in ft) also derive from Colledge and Warlow (2010) unless otherwise stated. Figures in simple 'tons'/'tonnage' for early (after 1510) naval ships over 100 tons are, unless otherwise stated, taken from Rodger (1997, 475–83). Both sources also give further details, including the type of ship, date built (as in the hull launched from the dockyard) and number of guns. English warships were classified into five or six 'rates' from the late 16th century. The classification as standardised by Pepys in the late 17th century, and which continued until 1817, was: 1st rates 90–100 guns; 2nd rates 64–90 guns; 3rd rates 56–70 guns; 4th rates 38–62 guns; 5th rates 28–38 guns; 6th rates 4–18 guns. The first four, with three or two gun decks, were fit for the 'line of battle', or 'ships of the line' (Rodger 2004, xxvi–xxvii).

1.5 Textual and graphical conventions

This book divides the yard's history into six broad periods: period 1, pre-dockyard (dealt with largely in Francis 2013); period 2, Tudor (1513–1603); period 3, Stuart (1603–1714); period 4, early Georgian (1714–74); period 5, late Georgian to early Victorian (1774–1869); and period 6, post-dockyard (1869 to the present). Any such division is artificial in some way, but a division largely on the basis of the reigns of monarchs may seem particularly anachronistic. However, it is justified in this case – it was a royal dockyard after all – and the division serves as well as any other for this particular establishment.

The basic unit of reference throughout the archive that supports this report is the context number. This is a unique number given to each archaeological event on site (such as a layer, wall, pit cut, road surface, etc). Context numbers in the text are shown within square brackets, thus: [100]. Land-use entities are described as Buildings (B), Open Areas (OA), Roads (R), Structures (S) and Waterfronts (W). The site divided into two parts geologically – the south and east part formed a gravel headland (OA1) while the rest of the site was alluvium (OA2) (Chapter 2.1). The influence of the underlying geology became less important as the dockyard's history progressed; yards and other recorded surfaces are identified by their own separate (OA) numbers.

Accession numbers given to certain artefacts from the site are shown within angled brackets, thus: <1>. Smaller glass items were given individual accession numbers; larger items (bottles etc) were recorded in bulk. Some finds have been given catalogue numbers, with a prefix denoting their category, thus:

<CP1> clay tobacco pipe no. 1;
<G1>   glass object no. 1;
<P1>   pottery vessel no. 1;
<S1>   'small' or accessioned find no. 1;
<T1>   tile/brick no. 1;
<WP1> wall plaster item no. 1.

The prefixes AO (for Atkinson and Oswald 1969) and OS (for Oswald 1975, 37–41) are used to indicate which typology has been applied in the classification of the English clay tobacco pipe bowls (Chapter 10.2).

MOLA publications employ standard codes for ceramics and give expansions of the codes at the first mention in a text section. These codes were originally developed by the Museum of London (MOL) for recording purposes. A fabric number system is used to record building materials (tile and brick); these numbers relate to detailed fabric descriptions. Pottery is recorded using codes (alphabetic or a combination of alphabetic and numeric) for fabrics, forms and decoration. Detailed descriptions of the building material fabrics and complete lists of the pottery codes, their expansions and date ranges are available on the MOLA website at http://www.mola.org.uk/resource-library. Pottery is quantified by sherd count, estimated number of vessels (ENV) and weight (in g, or occasionally kg for very large groups), as appropriate. (Reference to '[number of] vessels' in the text always means the same as ENV, in contrast to the actual numbers cited for sherds.) The following abbreviations are used in catalogue entries:

D   depth;
Diam diameter;
H   height
L   length;
Th   thickness;
W   width;
Wt   weight.

Sums of money quoted in the text are as cited in £, s and d, where 12 pence (d) made one shilling (s) and 20 shillings (or 240d) a pound (£). A guinea is 21s. A mark is 13s and 4d; 3 marks equal £2. County names in the text refer to historic counties.

The field records, finds and other details pertaining to the excavation will be archived by the Museum of London under the site codes CVW00 (PCA) and CVF10 (MOLA). The archive may then be consulted by prior arrangement at the Museum of London's Archaeological Archive, currently at Mortimer Wheeler House, 46 Eagle Wharf Road, London N1 7ED.

The graphical conventions used in this report are shown in Fig 8.

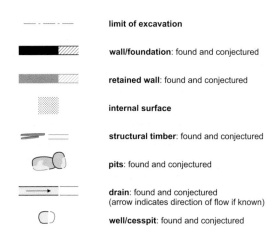

— · — · —	**limit of excavation**
	wall/foundation: found and conjectured
	retained wall: found and conjectured
	internal surface
	structural timber: found and conjectured
	pits: found and conjectured
	drain: found and conjectured (arrow indicates direction of flow if known)
	well/cesspit: found and conjectured

Fig 8 Graphical conventions used in this report

2

Before the dockyard

2.1 The topography and geoarchaeology of the site

Large sites such as this are rarely studied as a whole, and the breadth of topography and landscape settings (eg terrace, flood plain, tributary channels and the Thames foreshore) leads to a considerable complexity that is only touched on here (it is explored in detail in Francis 2013). The underlying pre-Quaternary bedrock of the site consists of Thanet sands with an area of surviving chalk bedrock to the centre of the site. The present flood plain of the wider Thames valley was formed by the River Thames down-cutting from an earlier flood plain (represented by the Kempton Park Gravels) as a result of the low sea-level and the large influx of meltwater into river channels which occurred after the Last Glacial Maximum of the Devensian Glacial period (*c* 18,000 BP). These high-energy fluvial conditions deposited coarse-grained sediments across the valley floor (the Shepperton Gravel) and these sediments underlie the alluvium in the present flood plain. South of the site, the gravels rise up to form the nearby Kempton Park terrace with a surface recorded between +1.50m OD and -0.50m OD. To the north of the site the gravel surface also appears to rise and may form a remnant island of Kempton Park Gravels similar to the eyots recorded in Southwark (Sidell et al 2000).

The centre of the site lies on lower flood plain gravels or Shepperton Gravel. The surface of these gravels lies between -1.00m and -5.00m OD and is indicative of a Late Glacial to Early Holocene channel running west to east across the site (Fig 9). This west to east channel perhaps exploited an area of erosion in the bedrock that dated to the Devensian cold stage or resulted from Holocene fluvial activity. The channel may have been a precursor to the later and northern *Orfletediche*, first recorded in 1279, or the medieval tidal basin recorded on site by Hawkins (2000) (also below, 2.2). Thus, the earlier Late Glacial and Early Holocene natural evolution of the landscape contributed to the later human activity that took place in the area, specifically the use of the site as a dockyard.

2.2 The medieval history of the site and its environs (AD 964–1485)

Deptford's name is thought to derive from the Anglo-Saxon for 'deep ford', a crossing point over the River Ravensbourne to the east of the site (the 't' only appears in the 15th century) (Wallenberg 1931, 2). The name 'Deptford Strand' may indicate a beach where boats could be landed, while 'Greenwich' may be the Anglo-Saxon for 'green port' (Field 1980, 53). Greenwich first appears as part of the estate of Lewisham, granted to the abbey of St Peter at Ghent by King Edgar (959–75) in 964, a grant confirmed by Edward the Confessor (1042–66) and William the Conqueror (1066–87) (Kemble 1846, 80–4, no. 771; Birch 1887, 337–9, no. 661; Round 1899, 500–2, nos

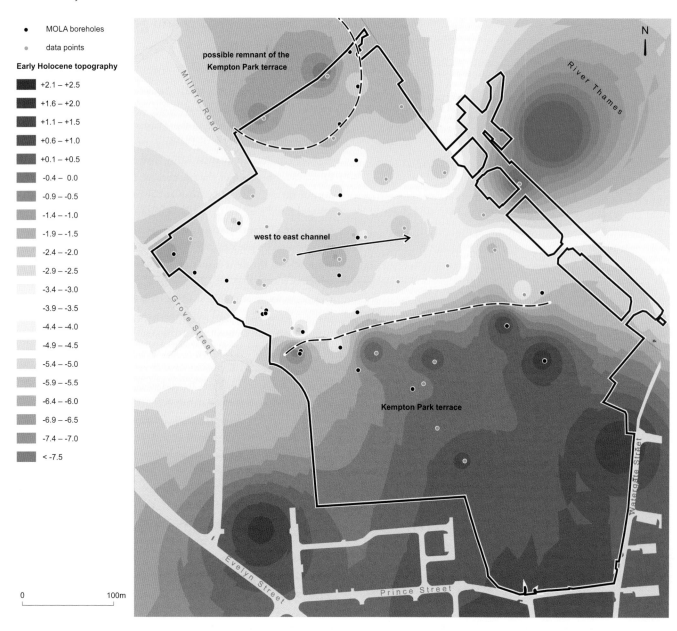

Fig 9 *The topography of the site showing the Early Holocene channel running west–east across the site, superimposed on the modern street plan (Fig 3) (scale 1:4000)*

1373–5; Martin 1927, 104–5; Grierson 1941, 86–95; Sawyer 1968, 236, no. 728; 299, no. 1002). There have been few Anglo-Saxon finds from near the site, although there are some from further south (Hawkins 2000, 13).

In the Domesday survey of 1086, the present Deptford was not mentioned by that name, but was referred to as the manor of *Grenviz* (ie West Greenwich), held by Gilbert de Magminot (or Maminot), Bishop of Lisieux, from Bishop Odo of Bayeux, half-brother of William the Conqueror. Before the Norman Conquest, *Grenviz* had been held as two manors, one by Earl Harold Godwinson and the other by Brixi Cild (or Beorhtsige), perhaps corresponding to two settlement centres at Deptford Broadway and St Nicholas's church. In 1086 the manor had a population of 24 villeins, four bordars and one cottar (all unfree peasants), and five slaves, with their families, and comprised arable, meadow, pasture and woodland. The presence of a few bordars (who had less land than villeins) and an increase in

annual value from £8 to £12 between 1066 and 1086 suggest that there was some expansion of the area of farmland in progress, probably by the reclamation of marshland (Hasted 1797; Watson 1987, 9–10; Williams and Martin 2002, 16).

Gilbert de Magminot, the Domesday Book tenant, was said to have built a castle at Deptford. Evidence for its location is not good, but in the 17th century it was thought to be represented by 'some remains of stony foundations' close to the mast dock on the Thames bank near Sayes Court (Philipott 1659, 160). According to Dunkin, the sub-manor of Hatcham was described in an inquisition post mortem of 1323 as the manor of 'Hatche in Deptford castle', but in fact the reference was to land in Dartford (Dunkin 1877, 111; *Cal Inq PM*, vi, 321, no. 518). The construction of Magminot's castle therefore remains enigmatic, but its influence may perhaps be seen in the settlement history of the area. The draw of the castle may have resulted in a shift of settlement away from St Nicholas's church to the area of Deptford Strand and Sayes Court.

The chief manor of West Greenwich was passed on by Gilbert de Magminot to his descendants the Maminots, several of whom bore the Christian name Walkelin. Several other Walkelins were involved in 13th-century land transactions in Deptford. The manor remained in the Maminot family until the late 12th century, and then passed to their descendants the de Says, apart from two short intervals when half the manor was granted to Bermondsey Priory, later Abbey (although the grant was apparently never implemented), and when the whole manor was held by the Order of Knights Templar. The Say family gave the manor its alternative name of Sayes Court. The medieval manor house of Sayes Court, constructed of wood, was located at about National Grid Reference TQ 36970 78038. It was certainly in existence by 1405. In the 15th century the manor was held by the de la Pole earls of Suffolk, and was confiscated by the Crown in November 1487. In the late 15th and early 16th centuries it was held for several short intervals by royal courtiers, including the St John family, Charles Brandon, Duke of Suffolk, and Cardinal Wolsey. It passed back to Henry VIII in 1535 and has been held by the Crown ever since (Dews 1884, 17–22; Drake 1886, 2–5; *Cat Anc D*, iii, 101, nos A4754–5; *Cal Inq Misc*, i, 494, no. 1786; *Cal Inq PM*, i, 281, no. 813; iii, 169, no. 271; vi, 192, no. 327; x, 403, no. 517; xiv, 213, no. 207; xv, 331, no. 846; xviii, 366–8, nos 1069, 1076; xx, 112, no. 364; TNA, E 40/6483; E 41/270).

There was another small manor in Deptford Strand held by the Badelesmere and Mortimer families in the 14th century, and by their descendants the dukes of York in the 15th, before it passed to the Crown with the accession of Edward IV in 1461. In 1327 this consisted of land and rents in West Greenwich, Rotherhithe and Camberwell, held as a tenancy of Sayes Court manor, and only later was it regarded as a distinct manor. This manor was therefore subordinate to Sayes Court, to which the king was paying a customary rent for the manor in 1464–5. In the 14th and 15th centuries it had a bailiff and other manorial officers, a manor house, a dovecote, a rabbit warren and a grange. Edward IV granted the manor to his mother Cicely Neville, Henry VII to his queen Elizabeth of York, and Henry VIII to two of his queens, Catherine of Aragon and Jane Seymour (Drake 1886, 3 n13, 6–7; *Cat Anc D*, iv, 183–4, no. A7551; *Cal Inq PM*, vii, 90, no 104; viii, 131, no. 185; xiii, 133, no. 167; BL, Add MS 6693, p 57; TNA, SC 6/1113/12; /1114/9, 10, 12, 13, 15). In the 16th to 18th centuries it was part of the manor of Bermondsey and Deptford Strand, and had its own manorial court (LA, Class VI 67–222, 261; LLHAC, A66/4).

The geographical extent of this manor is unclear, but it certainly included some land in Rotherhithe and most of it probably lay in the north-west part of Deptford parish, including the great or dry dock, king's storehouse and wet dock areas of the later royal dockyard. It also included some land by the River Ravensbourne (Deptford Creek). In 1393 and 1429 the Mortimers' manor house, a toft and other lands lay in the north-west corner of *Cherchefeld* in the Watergate Street area (Fig 3), and another of their tenements lay further to the west (Jones 1972, 37; LMA, CLA/007/EM/02/H/019, /H/077, /I/018).

The basic division of land use in the vicinity was between arable upland and pasture marshland. In 1272 the manor of *Westgernewich* (Sayes Court) included 173 acres in the uplands outside the marsh (*Cal Inq PM*, i, 281, no. 813). Surviving deeds from the 13th century onwards, principally deriving from the possessions of the Bridge House estate and the hospital of St Thomas the Martyr in Southwark, permit a fairly complete reconstruction of the layout of the fields, marshes and roads of late medieval Deptford. Houses and settlements are also represented, but less frequently (Parsons 1932, 131–51, after BL, Stowe MS 942; LMA, CLA/007/EM/02). Further to the west beyond the Deptford Strand settlement, the marshes of *Cranmede*, *Saltmede* and *Tounmannismershe* were bordered by the dyke of *Orfletediche* to the north and the demesne lands of Sayes Court, including *Pottemede*, to the south. A pond at West Greenwich, or Deptford, is referred to in 1278–9 in a lawsuit relating to fishing; the fishery was preserved although it was open to the Thames and, while no mention was made of it being of any use to receive shipping, this (tidal) pond is presumed to have later become the dockyard basin or wet dock (Oppenheim 1926, 337; above, 2.1; Chapter 3.2).

On the fields of the manor of Lewisham and Greenwich the main crops raised until the mid 14th century were wheat and barley. After 1350 these gave way to sheep farming and corn (Mills 1993, 26). The same changes probably occurred in the demesne lands and tenant holdings of Sayes Court manor, but the evidence of the accounts no longer survives. A property transaction of 1393 specified that none of the meadow lands conveyed was to be converted into arable land, except the meadow of *Tounmannismershe* for three years only (LMA, CLA/007/EM/02/I/018).

On the Bridge House lands at Deptford Strand there was tile and brick making for the London market from 1418 onwards, for which a Dutch craftsman was hired to test the qualities of the local clay. A small dock was dug to assist in the transport of the products. Brick making continued at Deptford, which supplied nearly two million bricks to Henry VIII for his new manor house at Dartford (Jones 1972, 36; Smith 1985, 21, 27, 28, 49).

A shipbuilding industry was certainly established at Deptford in the early 15th century, and possibly before. The people of Deptford possessed shipping at least a century earlier: in 1326 it was recorded that the men of Greenwich had set out ships to serve with the king's admiral. Several of Henry V's ships are documented as being rebuilt or repaired at Deptford: in 1420 the *Thomas of the Tower* or *Thomas* (a four-gun, 180bm-ton vessel) was brought from Wapping to be put on the 'stokkes' at Deptford and rebuilt; the *Katherine* or *Katrine* (210bm-tons) was brought from Greenwich to be put on the stocks in a 'dook' at Deptford and rebuilt; and the *Trinity Royal* (540bm-tons, built in 1398 and rebuilt in 1416), was recorded as lying in a dock at Greenwich, possibly in Deptford Creek, while under repair (Oppenheim 1926, 337). At this date, 'dock' implied only a 'mud dock': the vessel was beached or hauled on to the foreshore, with a temporary brushwood fence perhaps puddled with clay around her stern to keep out the tide while work was carried out, or a channel was dug in the shore for the ship and a watertight, earth dam or dockhead created for the duration of the work (ibid; Rodger 1997, 70–1).

The accession of Henry VI in 1422, however, began a period of neglect of the royal fleet. In the 1450s naval affairs became an intensely political issue as Lancastrian–Yorkist rivalries escalated, and the naval policies of Edward IV and Richard III, and even of Henry VII, were modest. Only six ships of all sorts are known to have been built for the Crown between 1422 and the death of Henry VII in 1509 (Rodger 1997, 146–56). Towards the end of the century, shipwrights and caulkers were sent from Deptford to rig and repair Henry VII's ships, and some of the king's ships were laid up in the Thames off Erith, necessitating the hire of a storehouse at 'Greenwich' for their gear (Oppenheim 1926, 337–8). Only with the accession of Henry VIII did a new naval era begin.

2.3 Archaeological activity on the site before the dockyard (period 1)

The founding of Deptford dockyard is generally dated to the establishment of the Tudor storehouse by Henry VIII in the early 16th century (Chapter 3.1). Although there is evidence for prehistoric and Roman activity on the site before this (described in Francis 2013), there were a number of other structures and

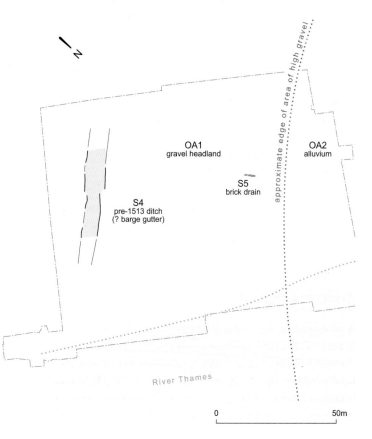

Fig 10 Plan of the ditch (? barge gutter) (S4) pre-dating the dockyard (period 1) (scale 1:1500)

remains that were more immediate precursors of the dockyard and these are described below.

Ditch (S4), ? barge gutter

One intriguing feature was a ditch (S4), running roughly north–south but at an angle to the Tudor storehouse built around 1513 (Fig 10). It seems likely that this ditch ran down to the river. If so, its route would have taken it under the walls of the Tudor storehouse, suggesting a pre-1513 date for the ditch. Unfortunately this could not be tested as the ditch in this area had been completely removed by modern truncations, and the Tudor storehouse was exposed only in plan and not excavated fully. A trench excavated on the riverward side did not reveal the ditch and it may have been removed here also.

The ditch was certainly earlier than the walls of the quadrangle storehouse dating to the early 18th century – some of the latter's foundations were deeper on the softer ground where the ditch passed under the walls. The south end of the ditch was cut by the foundation trench of the rigging and sail loft (B40) built in the late 18th century.

The ditch Structure 4 survived 34+m long and up to 8m wide, sufficient to accommodate small vessels, particularly barges. The sides of the shallow U-shaped surviving profile had been partially backfilled and the backfill then revetted with timber; the distance between the simple pile and plank revetments was *c* 3m (Fig 11). The revetments were made of small oak vertical piles and up to two pit-sawn oak sheathing planks survived, wedged horizontally on-edge behind them. These planks were rather thick, with some sapwood, and were probably planks from the outside edges of the parent sawn baulk. (Dendrochronological analysis of the revetments did not produce a date.) This was low-value material often sold on from the east London post-medieval shipyards for local drain revetments (Goodburn 1999, 173). The use of pit-sawn plank seen *in situ* is very rare in the Thames region before the early 15th century, being rather more common from the 16th to 18th centuries. The line of small oak retaining piles was rather irregular. The ditch's original function is uncertain. A drainage use is likely but the width and revetting also suggest another possible function, that of a small navigable channel or 'barge gutter' (Bond 2007, 153). These were widely used in wetland zones of England and were often dug to move heavy items such as building materials; many survive in the Fenland areas (where they are known as 'lodes'). The width of 3m and depth of over 1m would have been adequate for small shallow barges and punts in the late 15th to early 16th centuries. Potential cargoes would have been agricultural produce, reeds and just possibly bricks and tiles which are known to have been made nearby (above, 2.2).

Part of the ditch backfill yielded medieval pottery of *c* 1170–1350 as well as building material compatible with this date; another early fill yielded medieval pottery dating to *c* 1270–1500. The ditch backfills contained chalk rubble, peg roofing tile, ridge tile and grey roofing slate, one fragment of which is complete (<775>, Fig 12), two iron objects, one

Fig 11 View of timber revetment of the west edge of the ditch (? barge gutter) (S4) (1.0m scale)

<775>

Fig 12 Roofing slate <775> from the backfill of the ditch (S4) (scale 1:4)

the ditch is likely to have continued to the river, it suggests that it pre-dated the Tudor storehouse (although, as mentioned above, there was no evidence for it on the riverward side). Similarly, the ditch is not shown on the 1623 map (Fig 50), nor does it feature on the pre-1688 map (Fig 23), and it must have been filled in by then as its location is occupied by a building.

If the *c* 1640–60 pipe bowl is indeed intrusive (modern vibropiles extended into the ditch and may have carried later material into the fills), the ditch may have been opened as early as the 12th century and backfilled by the 16th century, in advance of the construction of Henry VIII's dockyard. It may have been a medieval barge dock, perhaps serving Sayes Court. Alternatively, if the clay pipe was not intrusive, the ditch may have been partly backfilled to allow construction of the Tudor storehouse while elsewhere it was left open until the mid to late 17th century.

Gravel headland (OA1)

A pit dug in the area of the gravel headland (OA1) yielded fragments of Kentish ragstone and oolitic limestone rubble and three iron objects, one of which is possibly a large D-shaped handle (<S36>, Fig 195) in corrosion, the rounded side of which is more substantial than the straight side. The others comprise a complete clench bolt used on a timber *c* 28mm thick, and a rove nail or larger clench bolt (<134>). The latter object hints at the breaking up and burning of late medieval clinker-built boats nearby.

(<554>) possibly part of a window, and fibrous caulking material (<41>). The remarkably intact grey-coloured slate (length 259mm, width 149–116mm, thickness 8mm) has a 10mm-diameter round nail hole to allow for nailing to the roof and may have come from the West Country. The possible window comprises a pair of narrow strips of thin sheet metal (width 8–9mm, thickness 1mm) between which are the remains of a thin sheet of mica. A single clay pipe bowl dating to *c* 1640–60 was recovered from one of the basal fills and is likely to have been intrusive.

All of the finds assemblages from the ditch fills were small, but the combined evidence seems to point to a pre-1513 date. As

Brick drain (S5)

An east–west brick drain (S5) was identified during the
excavations (Fig 10; Fig 13), in part apparently rebuilt. Its east,
presumably original, end was built of small pink and cream
bricks measuring 172–178 × 83–91 × 38–43mm, probably Low
Countries imports of the 14th to late 15th centuries. The west
end, presumably a rebuild, comprised bricks of a *c* 1550–
1666/1700 date. The earlier part was 1.65m long, 0.56m wide
and survived 0.24m high. Although it is difficult to say whether
this was a 14th- to late 15th-century drain altered in the 16th to
17th centuries, or a 16th- or 17th-century drain partly made
with medieval bricks, the former seems more likely as there is a
clear break between the two areas of brickwork. The drain ran
under the later Treasurer of the Navy's house immediately
adjacent to the west. Its east end appeared to have fed into a
channel (largely obscured by walls of the quadrangle
storehouse) that was revetted in the Stuart period (S11) (Chapter
4.2, 'The storehouse and brick drain').

Fig 13 View of brick drain (S5), looking west (1.0m scale)

3

The Tudor dockyard (period 2, 1513–1603)

3.1 Historical introduction

The Henrician dockyard

The young Henry VIII's (1509–47) desire to take centre stage internationally ushered in a new naval era. To operate overseas, Henry had to develop the navy's administration and support services, and to expand the small fleet he inherited by buying and building ships, an urgent necessity when he went to war with France in 1512, and again in 1522 (Rodger 1997, 164–75). In the interim, war with France having (temporarily) ended, in 1516 Henry inventoried and decommissioned 13 of his ships and retained a number of smaller vessels to patrol the North Sea and the Channel (Knighton and Loades 2011, xxvii). Peace with France was concluded again in 1525 and the English fleet mostly continued to consist of a few big ships (carracks) and a larger number of smaller and faster caravels or carvels and other vessels (Rodger 1997, 210). New shipbuilding was stimulated by attack from the sea by Scotland in the 1530s (and the Scots alliance with France), which culminated in war being declared against Scotland in 1542. In all, Henry was to build about 40 warships over 50 tons during his reign, some 27 of which were over 100 tons, but where they were built is largely unknown or uncertain (Banbury 1971, 26; Loades 1992; Rodger 1997, 475–8; Knighton and Loades 2000).

Deptford had long been an anchorage with yards, and its proximity to the favourite palace of the young King Henry VIII would also have been a factor in its development as a shipyard. The building of Greenwich Palace (the Old Royal Navy College now occupies its site) on the south bank of the Thames from 1447 may be seen as the beginning of large-scale development of this area. Henry VIII's father had also rented storage facilities there (Chapter 2.2). There was a storehouse in 'Deptford Strond' (the latter marked on the 1623 map: Fig 14, top right) used by the Crown by 1511. In September of that year, John Carpenter was paid 36s 6d for conveying 'oars by water from London to Deptford Strond, to the storehouse there, for repairing the said house and for 2 hanging locks for the same' (*L and P Hen VIII*, i, 1496). The royal household's requirements, for example for meat, were catered for by the king's slaughterhouse which was established by the River Ravensbourne (Deptford Creek) in the 16th century (John Bagley 'of the Boiling House' is referred to in 1548: TNA, E 315/68).

Deptford, however, 'was of none estimation at all until King Henrie the eight advised (for the better preservation of the Royal fleete) to erect a storehouse, and to create certaine officers there' (Lambarde 1596, 386). The Crown's decision to build a storehouse on the site at Deptford in 1513 and a 'pond' or wet dock at Deptford Strand at the west end of the storehouse in 1517 provided a major boost to the economy of the town (Oppenheim 1926, 339–40; below). The great or dry dock was probably built at around the same time as, and immediately east of, the storehouse (both are shown on Fig 14); the dock was repaired for 6s 8d in 1520 (*L and P Hen VIII*, iii, 369–81).

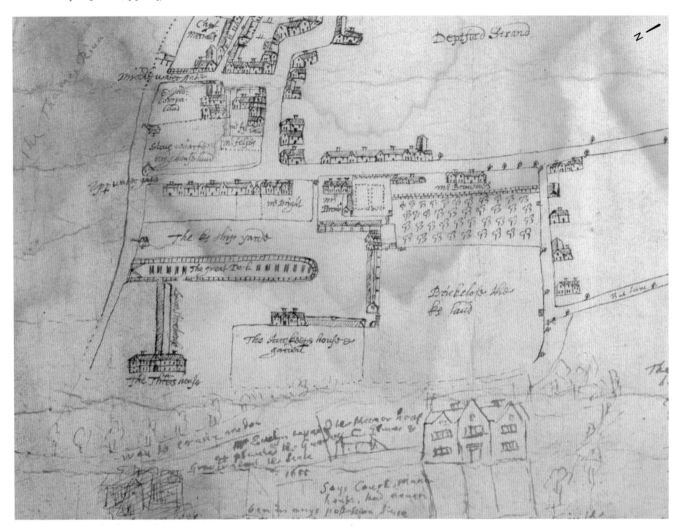

Fig 14 Detail of the dockyard ('The k[ing]'s ship yard') on a 1623 map of Deptford (with Sayes Court added later) (The British Library Board, Add MS 78629 A)

In 1513, £52 7s 5d was paid to John Myllot for wages of men at the storehouse at Deptford (*L and P Hen VIII*, ii, 1458–63). The construction of the storehouse was under way by this date: a carving below a brick niche that was originally part of the storehouse reads 'AX HK 1513' (Anno Christi, Henry's first initial entwined with that of his first queen Katherine of Aragon, and the date) (Fig 15); the design is similar to those on the king's armour at the time (Rimer et al 2009, 330). However, the storehouse (Fig 16) does not seem to have been completed until the following year. In December 1514, a receipt was issued by John Guillyot, from Sir John Daunce, for 'wages of workmen making a new wharf at Erith and finishing the King's storehouses there and at Deptford' (*L and P Hen VIII*, i, 1483–5). A shed was added in 1516 to the storehouse 'for keeping dry the king's ordnance' and for drying ropes and cables (Loades 1992, 70). About 22 ships were on a 'care and maintenance' basis in the Thames estuary by October 1517 (ibid, 69, 70). In 1539, the Deptford storehouse was suggested as a place for the king to keep 'cordage which he has ordered from Dansik [Danzig, now Gdańsk, Poland]' at a cost of about £200 (*L and P Hen VIII*, xiv(1), 51–77).

The king's Deptford shipyard may have been equipped to build, and not just repair, ships from an early stage, but there

were other private yards in the Deptford area and caution is needed about which yard is being referred to (Loades 1992, 91). The 100bm-ton *Kateryn Plesaunce* was constructed in 1518, at a cost of £324, 'for transporting the King to Calais'; the expenses of this itemised in 1519 include various payments to individuals for transporting timber to 'Deptford' and to 'Deptford Strond', as well as the wages of 15 carpenters working on the ship, from 22 February to 19 March 1518, paid by John Hopton at 2d to 8d a day. When the vessel was launched in 1519 a stable had to be partially demolished to allow it to reach the river (*L and P Hen VIII*, iii, 183–99; Friel 1995, 57; Wilkins 2010, 174).

The contract for the construction of the 'pond' (the wet dock) survives as an indenture of 1517 between Thomas Howard, Earl of Surrey and Great Admiral of England, and John Heron, Treasurer of the Chamber, on the one part, and John Hopton on the other. The indenture (transcribed by Mark Latham and not previously published in full) reads as follows:

This endenture made the 9th Day of Juyn the 9th yeare of the reign of oure moste Drade Sov'aign Lorde Kyng Henry the 8th Byween Thomas earl of Surrey Grate Admiyrall of England and John Heron Treassurer of said Sov'aign Lorde the kynge most honorable Chambre for and in the name and by

the comanndement of oure said Sov'aign Lorde the Kyng on
the oon ptie [party] and John Hopton Clerke Comptroller of
the Shipps of our said Sov'aign Lorde the kyng on the other
ptie Witnessith that it is conemited [an insertion suggests this
word has been misspelt; possibly 'covenanted'] condistendid
[probably 'condiftended'] and agreed bytween the said pties
the Day and year aforesaid of and for the makying of a pond
Wheryn certayn Shipps of the same oure Sov'aign Lorde
herafter exp'ssd [illegible insertion above the text, probably
'expressed'] shall ride aflote The same John Hopton knon [?]
lachith [?] and confessith hymself by thise pties to have
reecyved and had of oure said Sov'aign Lorde the kyng by the
handis of the said Earl and John Heron the sume of six
hundreth -arkis ['marks'] stelinge redy money of and for the
full contentacyon and payment of the same ponde The
Whiche ponde the forsaid John Hopton concenntith promysith
and granntith and hym and his executors by thise pties
byndith that he his executors or Assignes at their own -re
[?'pre'] coste and expensis by byfore the feaste of Cristemas
next comyng after the date of thise endenture shall wele
surely sufficyently and substancyally cause to be made and
cast in a medow next addoynyng unto the storehouse of oure
said Sov'aign Lorde at Deptford Strand at the westend of the
said storehouse a good and an hable ponde Whereyn shall ride
at all tymes and on flote these shipps ensuyng that is to say the
great Galey the Mary Rose the Peter Pomegarnet the great

*Fig 15 View of the north wall of the Tudor storehouse (B1), exposed in 1952
during demolition, with the brick niche in the left part of the image; (lower)
detail of the brick niche in the north wall, in 1952 (Getty Images/Hulton Archive,
156993168, 156993169)*

21

Fig 16 View of a four-light mullioned window of the Tudor storehouse (B1), in 1952 (Getty Images/Hulton Archive, 156993167)

Bark and the lesser Bark and also the said John Hopton conemitith and granntith by thise pdtes that he his executors or Assignes at their lyke cost and charges byfore the same fest shall wele and substanncyally make or cause to be made a good hable and suffycient hed for the same ponde and also certeyn hable Slewsis thurgh the which the water may have entre and course into the foresaid ponde as well at Spryng tydes as at nepetydes Moreover the forsaid John Hopton conemitith and granntith by this pdtr that he his executors or Assignes at their own -re [?'pre'] costs and expensis byfore the forsaid fest shall wele and sufficyently enclose all the same ponde with good hable and suffycient pale of tymbre of Oke of the stanteton in thicknes of oon [?'one'] ynche [inch] of assyse every boarde therof and that the same pale shall conteyn in heith Sevyn foote of assyse provided alwey that if the said fyve Shipps cannot be conveyed and brought into the same ponde and there to ride on flote as is aforsaid then the forsaid John Hopton conemitith promyttith and granntith and hym and his executors by thise pdtr byndith wele and truly to restore and repay orders to be restored and repayed unto the said Earl and John Heron their executors or Assignes the forsaid some of Six hundred markes Stelinge unto thise of oure said sov'aign Lorde the kyng without any delay in any wyse In witnesse wherof the pties aforesaid to thise endentures sundirly have sett their Seall yovyn the day and yere abovesaid. (BL, Add Ch 6289 (1517))

The indenture contains a number of important details. John Hopton (d 1524), Clerk Controller of the Ships since 1512 and appointed also 'keeper' of the storehouses 'lately erected' at Deptford and Erith in 1514, was responsible for building the wet dock (Oppenheim 1926, 339; Loades 1992, 69; Rodger 1997, 222–3). He was paid 600 marks sterling to build the structure by Christmas 1517; otherwise the money would have to be returned (either by him or his heirs). The dock was to be built in the meadow to the west of the storehouse – the location of all subsequent wet docks at the yard – although there is no mention of a pre-existing pond (Chapter 2.1 and 2.2). 'Deptford Strand' evidently covered a greater area than shown in the map of 1623 (Fig 14) for example. The dock had to be large enough to admit and house afloat five of Henry's ships – the *Great Galley*, the *Mary Rose*, the *Peter Pomegranate*, the *Great Bark* and the *Small* or *Less Bark*, built between 1510 and 1515 (ibid, 476–7) (Fig 17). The wet dock is likely to have been earth-cut; the 7ft long, 1in thick oak pales referred to in the indenture would not have been long enough to revet the sides sufficiently to allow for the draft of the ships, and there is no reference to land-ties to brace such a revetment. Instead, the pales are more likely to have been intended for a fence around the dock. The water was to be retained in the wet dock by a head, with sluices ('Slewis') to admit the spring and neap tides. The head, large enough to admit the 800bm-ton galleasse, the *Great Galley* (built in 1515), would have been a considerable engineering undertaking; whether it still had to be dug out in the traditional fashion of a dock to allow ships in and out or had gates above a dam, making the structure a permanent one, is not certain (Oppenheim 1926, 339–40; Loades 1992, 70–1; Rodger 1997, 223–4). The wet dock was evidently completed by 1520, when John Hopton was paid £40 'for bringing divers of the King's ships into the Pond at Deptford' (*L and P Hen VIII*, iii, 1539–43).

There seems to have been a marked increase in activity at the Deptford dockyard in 1520. Two further sheds were built in that year, and the storehouses at Erith and Deptford fitted with new locks (Loades 1992, 72). The 180bm-ton *Mary and John* was put 'out of dock at Deptford' in the same year (*L and P Hen VIII*, iii, 369–81). This may be a reference to the wet dock, but perhaps more likely the dry (great) dock. The *Mary Rose* was caulked and seven men were paid 2s 8d to 'plumpe' (ie pump out) the ship for a day and a night (ibid). The 60-gun *Mary Rose* was back in the dock 'beside the storehouse' in October 1525, needing to be caulked 'from the keel upward, both within and without', and so certainly in the dry dock (*L and P Hen VIII*, iv, 762). This 500bm-ton ship was joined by the 800bm-ton *Great Galley*, the 400bm-ton *Peter Pomegranate*, the 200/400bm-ton *Great Bark*, the 160/240 ton *Small* alias *Less Bark* and two row barges of 60 tons each in the pond or wet dock, all requiring considerable repair (ibid; Rodger 1997, 476–7) (Fig 17). By 1520, then, 'the standing navy had come into existence' (Loades 1992, 72). John Hopton had looked after 21 ships at Deptford and Woolwich 'aswell in their dockes as aflote' between October 1518 and March 1522 at a cost of £1481 (ibid, 79). Ships needed to be grounded and caulked once a year, and are documented moving in and out of the Deptford and Woolwich

anchorages throughout the 1520s (ibid, 111, 153).

The king's yards and facilities were administered by two permanent officials, the Clerk Controller, based at Deptford, and the Clerk of the Ships, based at Portsmouth (Loades 1992, 72). Hopton, the first Clerk Controller and keeper of the storehouses at Deptford and Erith, died in 1524 and the offices were separated. By 1526, William Gonson was the keeper of the storehouses, paid £18 5s a year (*L and P Hen VIII*, iv, 852–78); Gonson was (among other offices) Vice-Admiral of Norfolk and Suffolk, and one of London's wealthiest citizens (Rodger 1997, 223). Over the next dozen or so years, the practice evolved of paying warrants for naval expenditure to Gonson, concentrating control of the navy in his hands. By 1540, he was generally called 'treasurer' or 'paymaster' of the king's ships (Knighton and Loades 2011, xxviii). When he died in 1544, his son Benjamin was appointed 'to act as treasurer of sea causes' (ibid, xxix).

The yard's workforce is recorded in the 1540s (Loades 1992, 150–1). Benjamin Gonson's accounts of 1544–5 as Treasurer of Marine Causes show payments to 'shipwrights, caulkers, sawyers, anchorsmiths and other artificers and labourers at Deptford Strand', and that Lincolnshire merchants Thomas

a

b

c

d

Fig 17 Four of Henry VIII's ships housed at Deptford: a – the Mary Rose *(built 1510); b – the* Peter Pomegranate *(1510); c – the* Great Bark *(1512); d – the* Lesser Bark *(?1512) (from the* Anthony roll: *Pepys Library 2991, Magdalene College, Cambridge)*

Trollop and William Browne had been paid £100 by the Crown for cordage to be deposited in the storehouse (Knighton and Loades 2011, 168, 414–15). In August and October 1544, some 80–90 shipwrights and caulkers were being paid at Deptford (Oppenheim 1926, 340) (Chapter 1.2). The 160bm-ton ship *Greyhound* was built at Deptford in 1545 (Banbury 1971, 26; Colledge and Warlow 2010). In 1546, Richard Howlet was paid £32 13s 4d as 'keeper of the King's storehouse at Deptford Strand' (*L and P Hen VIII*, xxi(1), 252–69). The war with France had evidently involved the hire of more storehouses at Deptford: during 1547, £17 18s 8d was paid for them, compared to only £1 6s 8d at Woolwich (Oppenheim 1926, 340).

In August 1546, the French Admiral Claude d'Annebault arrived for the ratification of the treaty ending Henry VIII's last French war. The king's ships lined his route up the Thames as far as Deptford 'richly decked with streamers and banners', saluting with 'great and terrible shots' from guns that a few months earlier had been aimed at the admiral's compatriots (Knighton and Loades 2011, 142 n1).

Edward VI (1547–53)

By the time Edward VI acceded to the throne, aged nine, Deptford was the most important royal dockyard for the construction and repair of warships. Total expenses for Deptford for 1547 were £18,824, compared to £3439 and £1211 for Woolwich and Portsmouth respectively (Oppenheim 1926, 340). Edward's short reign was turbulent: Protector Somerset initially continued the war with Scotland, was himself overthrown and peace made in 1550 (Rodger 1997, 184–9). Just six ships of 60–300 tons were commissioned during Edward's reign (Banbury 1971, 27; Rodger 1997, 478). A well and a building for the clerks of the new naval administrative body, the Chief Officers of the Admiralty, or Navy Board as it was later known, 'to write therein' were constructed at the yard, in addition to two new kilns for furnaces in the 1000bm-ton *Edward* (which may have caused this flagship's accidental destruction by fire in 1553 at Woolwich), at a total cost of £88 6s 2d (ibid, 225–6; Knighton and Loades 2011, 157 nn1–2, 158). The innovations in navy administration during Edward's reign continued until the early years of Elizabeth I (ibid, xii).

The young king was not uninterested in maritime affairs, and was delighted with the elaborate naval tournament staged for him on 10 June 1550. The centrepiece of the mock battle was 'a fort made on a great lighter afloat in the River of Thames before the great storehouse at Deptford Strand', manned by John Basing, William Southwick, Roger Irland, Hugh Tolley, William Wood and other captains (Knighton and Loades 2011, 166). The 12-year-old wrote in his diary that sailors 'with clods, squibs, canes of fire, darts made for the nonce, and bombards assaulted the castle; and at length came with their pieces and burst the outer walls' (*Chron Edw VI*, 36–7). The captains received £13 for their trouble while £61 8d was paid to 'Robert Vyot and 11 other drums and fifes' (Knighton and Loades 2011, 166). Edward returned to the yard in July the following year to witness the launch of the 240bm-ton discovery vessel *Primrose*

and the rebuilt 160bm-ton ship *Mary Willoughby* (ibid, 9).

Edward's visits were a bonus for the town as the Admiralty paid for its streets to be paved to keep excrement off his shoes (Oppenheim 1926, 341; Loades 1992, 154–5; Rodger 1997, 231). Payments were made in 1548 to 15 men at 'Deptford Strand' for wages, victuals, 'shipkeeping' and other goods and services, including to William Holstock, Thomas Morley, John Clarke (a clerk), Richard Willson (a victualler), shipkeepers and watermen (Knighton and Loades 2011, 107). In 1548–51, £22 5s 4d was paid for 'hire of docks and storehouses' at 'Deptford Strand' (ibid, 165). In 1551 a payment of £26 13s 4d was made to 'Christopher Spender, mariner, for one old barge of the King's Majesty's called the *Maidenhead*, which lay sunk in the great dock at Deptford' (ibid, 154).

Englishmen were not the only nationality at the yard. Payments of £94 16s 1d were made to two 'Bretons serving the King's Majesty', Francis Ordraye and Peter Tort, and three others for making sails; a further £1798 0s 1d for 'cables, hawsers and other tackling'; £199 10s 2d for masts; £224 5s 7d for 'timber, boards and planks'; £254 1s 7½d for 'iron and ironwork'; £115 4s 6d for 'pitch, tallow and rosin'; £56 18s 3d for 'lime and sand'; £256 9s 1½d for 'oakum of divers sorts'; 63s 4d for lead; and £208 12s 2d for other 'necessaries' (Loades 1992, 155; Knighton and Loades 2011, 157–8).

The merchant navy was also becoming established, with the first of the great chartered companies, the Muscovy Company for trading with Russia, incorporated during Edward's reign (1552). London became the primary centre of naval shipbuilding and fitting-out, and some of the ocean-going ships of the 16th-century trading companies may have been built in the royal dockyards (Banbury 1971, 27, 31).

Mary I (1553–8)

The galleons *Mary Rose* (600bm-tons) and *Philip and Mary* (550bm-tons), and the 406-pounder *Lion* (also *Golden Lion*), were all probably built on the Thames during Mary's reign (Banbury 1971, 27; Rodger 1997, 478–9). Repairs to the 'storehouses' at Deptford Strand cost £74 4s 9d in 1554–5 (Knighton and Loades 2011, 421–2) and the yard's storehouses were repaired, while others nearby were rented (in one case for ships' provisions at a cost of £7 4s 10d) in 1555–6 (ibid, 430).

Deptford was still the most important dockyard and the biggest spender, but largely on materials rather than wages (Loades 1992, 160, 166). In 1554–5, large sums were transferred to the yard for shipbuilding, including £752 11s 9d for 'timber, planks, quarters, deal, fir, wainscot, oars, shores, rafters and other kinds of wood and timber', £1676 2s 1¼d for 'cables, hawsers, with cordage and tackoning', £384 16s 4¾d for 'pitch, tar, rosin and tallow', £549 5s for anchors and metal, £10 13s 10¼d for masts, and £15 19s 9d for 'reed, dry and seasoned' (Knighton and Loades 2011, 418–19). £649 5s was paid in 1554 to William Watson for delivery to Deptford of various masts and spars 'brought out of Dansk' (Danzig, modern Gdańsk, Poland), including three 31 yards long and seven 30 yards long, suitable for the largest ships (Loades 1992, 159). Dockyard expenditure rose sharply at the end of Mary's short reign in 1557–8, a time when she lost Calais in the war with France while at home there was a sustained attempt to depose her (Rodger 1997, 191–5, 228–9, 237). The bulk of the money was spent at Deptford (£22,120), almost twice that spent on Woolwich and Portsmouth combined (Banbury 1971, 27). The Navy Board was placed under the control of the Lord Treasurer in 1557, where it remained into the 1590s (Rodger 1997, 228).

The Elizabethan dockyard

Elizabeth I (1558–1603) inherited a small fleet of about ten ships of 160–600 tons, some rebuilds by Mary of ships commissioned by their father (Rodger 1997, 478). A large proportion of royal ships were built and repaired by the 200-plus men employed at the Deptford yard (Banbury 1971, 26). Five ships were under repair at Deptford ('on the Ordinary') in 1559, worked on by 170 shipwrights and other artificers at 12d per man per day for wages, victuals and lodging, and 25 labourers for wages alone of 7d per day, with timber, ironwork and so on budgeted at £880, at a total estimated cost of £1816 13s 4d for three months' and six days' work (Loades 1992, 180). Between 1559 and 1570, the galleons *Hope* (403/500bm-tons), *Triumph* (741bm-tons) and *Elizabeth Bonaventure* (600bm-tons), the 42-gun *Victory* (565bm-tons; purchased by the navy in 1560), the 18-gun *Aid* (300bm-tons), 40-gun *White Bear* or *Bear* (729bm-tons) and 36-gun *Foresight* (306bm-tons), together with the ships *Primrose* (800bm-tons) and *Minion* (600bm-tons), both purchased by the navy in 1560, were built, most likely at Deptford or Woolwich with a few at private yards (Banbury 1971, 28; Loades 1992, 185–7, 193–4; Rodger 1997, 479; Colledge and Warlow 2010). The queen is reported as visiting Deptford and Woolwich in 1559 and 1560 respectively (Oppenheim 1926, 341). These two yards on the Thames with their working docks were the most important of the dockyards serving the Navy Royal in Elizabeth's reign, although Chatham increased in importance in this period. Chatham dockyard first appears under that name in 1567, a mast pond, storehouses and so on being constructed to enable it to maintain ships moored in the Medway, and it built its first ship (actually a 'boat', the *Sonne* pinnace) in 1586 (Oppenheim 1926, 341–2; Rodgers 1997, 336; May 1999; Coad 2013, 1–2; J Coad, pers comm 2015).

Although relatively little money was spent on ships in the 1560s and into the 1570s and the fleet stayed small, the queen's ministers were planning for full-scale mobilisation against Spain (Rodger 1997, 327–30, 238–96). English galleons could be characterised as fast men-of-war with little stowage, and Spanish warships in contrast as armed merchantmen; by the late 16th century, English ships may also have been technologically more advanced (ibid, 217–20). The queen was fortunate to have able master shipwrights at her disposal. Not least of these was Mathew Baker (c 1530–1613), the son of James (a master shipwright to Henry VIII) and author of *Fragments of ancient English shipwrightry* (Johnston 2005, 107–65). Baker exemplified the role of a royal Master Shipwright, a title not officially used until 1572 when he was appointed to Woolwich (MacDougall

1982, 39). Similarly, the Pett family was associated with Kentish dockyards for a century or so: Peter Pett was Master Shipwright at Deptford in Edward VI's reign and stayed there until his death in 1589; a son, Joseph, was subsequently Master Shipwright at Deptford, with five assistants (Oppenheim 1926, 342–3). Master shipwrights were not humble artisans, but were versatile figures who managed resources and dockyard workers, and supervised the construction and repair of ships and of the dockyard itself. In constructing a ship, master shipwrights oversaw the entire process, from the selection of timber from living trees in woods whose shapes and sizes were most appropriate for the projected vessel, to the successful launch of the completed vessel. Master shipwrights also had work outside the royal yards and built most of the queen's ships under contract (Rodger 1997, 232, 336–7; Johnston 2005, 115); for example, Peter Pett had a private yard at Harwich, his son Joseph one at Limehouse and Richard Chapman a yard at Deptford (Banbury 1971, 30–1).

During this period, ships built at Deptford in the dockyard but also in private yards included the 41-gun, 450bm-ton *Dreadnought* (1573, by Mathew Baker) and a number of galleons: the 360bm-ton *Swiftsure* (1573, by Peter Pett), the 580bm-ton *Revenge* (1577), the 600bm-ton *Nonpareil* (1584, a rebuild of the *Philip and Mary*), the 384bm-ton *Rainbow* (1586, by Peter Pett) and the 694bm-ton *Ark Raleigh* (1587, by Richard Chapman; subsequently Lord Howard's flagship the *Ark Royal*) (Banbury 1971, 28; MacDougall 1982, 34; Rodger 1997, 329–30, 479). These ships were part of the fleet – possibly 40 big ships in all – that engaged the Spanish Armada in 1588, with 18 smaller ships built or rebuilt before then, mostly at Deptford or Woolwich (Banbury 1971, 29; Rodger 1997, 255). Later ships built or rebuilt at Deptford included the galley *Adventure* (343bm-tons, 1594, by Mathew Baker), the galleons *Repulse* (also *Due Repulse*, 622bm-tons, 1596) and *Warspite* (also *Warspight*, 648bm-tons, 1596, by Edward Stevens), and the galleys *Superlativa* (1601) and *Volatillia* (1602), both 100bm-tons. Other large ships were undoubtedly built at Deptford, but precise information is hard to find (Banbury 1971, 31; Loades 1992, 188, 193–5, 279; Rodger 1997, 480).

In 1575 the office of clerk and keeper of the stores and storehouses at 'Deptford Strond' and other yards was granted to Christopher Baker 'in reversion after the death or surrender of Henry Gilman' (*Cal S P Dom*, 1547–80, 508–13). The storehouse was surveyed in 1582 (*Cal S P Dom*, 1581–90, 557–62), although there is no record of ensuing repairs at this time. Cordage, sail canvas, masts, oars and other stores were regularly delivered out of the storehouse for navy use, for example in 1568 (from the Muscovy Company to the value of £4000: *Cal S P For*, 1566–8, 457–72), 1577 (*Cal S P Dom*, 1547–80, 478–80), 1588 (by 'Mr Allen': *Cal S P Dom*, 1581–90, 562–71) and 1590 (ibid, 677–83). Forty-six spruce masts were delivered to the yard in August 1589 by Thomas Allin, 'Her Majesty's merchant for Dantzic' (ibid, 612–14), and in June 1590 John Burnell petitioned Lord Burghley for payment of £876 19s 10d due to him for cordage delivered to the yard in 1588–9 (ibid, 669–76).

Small-scale building work and maintenance were constant

features of the dockyards. In 1574 Deptford's dry dock underwent considerable repair, but the old method of closing the dock with a gravel dam apparently remained in use (Oppenheim 1926, 341; Rodger 1997, 335). In 1578 Mathew Baker supervised the construction of wooden ways in the dry dock, and a pair of gates of a more modern type at the head of the dock were also to be fitted at this time; in the early 1580s the yard accounts cease to include payments to marshmen for digging out the dockhead when a ship was launched, implying that the gates were watertight and could open at will (Oppenheim 1926, 341; Rodger 1997, 335; Johnson 2005, 115). The constant building and repair work at Deptford from 1585 necessitated additional wharfs: some 500–600ft of new wharf was constructed in 1588–9, which probably implies an enlargement of the yard by the addition of marshland (Oppenheim 1926, 343; MacDougall 1982, 34). There were repairs to the yard in 1600 (*Cal S P Dom*, 1598–1601, 430–9).

Sir John Hawkins (Hawkyns) and William Holstock (Holstok) wrote to Lord Burghley for payment of £2000 in February 1589 towards the expense of repairing four ships in the dry docks at Deptford and Woolwich (*Cal S P Dom*, 1581–90, 577–82). The latter dockyard had been equipped with a dry dock since the 1570s (MacDougall 1982, 35). The 26-gun, 343bm-ton ship *Bull* (built in 1546) was to be rebuilt (apparently as the galley *Adventure*) at Deptford in March to September 1594, at a cost of £1594 14s 4d according to an estimate by Lord Admiral Howard (*Cal S P Dom*, 1591–4, 559–62; Colledge and Warlow 2010). A note of March 1598 records that Sir Edward Carey received £2500 for the repair of the 680bm-ton galleon *Elizabeth Jonas* at Woolwich and the 41-gun, 709bm-ton *Merehonor* at Deptford dry docks, upon a warrant of September 1597 (*Cal S P Dom*, 1598–1601, 33–8).

Valuable as they are, such details convey little of the day-to-day burden of naval administration. A letter from Sir John Hawkins to Lord Burghley of January 1594 is an exception. Hawkins despaired at the processes of the Exchequer; the auditors had retained four years' accounts for a long time. Only nine of the 15 years' worth of accounts Hawkins had sent to Burghley had been approved. Hawkins's wife was ill and could not leave Deptford. He was badly paid. He remarked ruefully that Mr Gonson (his predecessor as Treasurer of the Navy) had told him that the office was of great care and charge, with no benefit for the holder. Gonson had remarked, 'I shall pluck a thorn out of my foot and put it into yours.' Hawkins said he had not believed him at the time, but he did now (*Cal S P Dom*, 1591–4, 406–21).

In 1581, the dockyard found itself the setting for an extraordinary piece of Elizabethan theatre. The previous year, Francis Drake had sailed into Plymouth after becoming the first Englishman to circumnavigate the world (Rodger 1997, 244–5). On his three-year voyage (1577–80), he had plundered Spanish ships, particularly the rich *Nuestra Señora de la Concepción* (known colloquially as the *Cacafuego*). On his return, he presented the queen with half the spoils, more than the rest of the Crown's income for that entire year. The Spanish demanded the loot back and for the pirate to be punished. Instead of complying, in

April 1581 Elizabeth had Drake knighted at the dockyard on the deck of the *Golden Hinde* (formerly the 18-gun, 100bm-ton *Pelican*, his privateer, renamed in 1578). As every detail of this event seems to have been choreographed to enrage the Spanish as much as possible (including allowing a Frenchman to perform the actual ceremony with a golden sword), it is perhaps fitting that the best account comes from Spain's ambassador Bernardino De Mendoza in a letter to his king:

> On the 4th instant [April] the Queen went to a place a mile from Greenwich to see Drake's ship, where a grand banquet was given to her, finer than has ever been seen in England since the time of King Henry. She knighted Drake, and told him there she had there a gilded sword to strike off his head. She handed the sword to M. de Marchaumont, telling him she authorised him to perform the ceremony for her, which he did. Drake, therefore, has the title of 'Sir' in consideration of the lands he has purchased, and he gave her a large silver coffer, and a frog made of diamonds, distributing 1200 crowns amongst the Queen's officers … . (*Cal S P Spain*, 1580–6, 91–103)

The *Golden Hinde* had been ordered to be preserved in a dock at Deptford yard and put on display. The plan was for the brick dock to be roofed over and filled with earth to support the hull. However, although an estimate of £370 was arrived at for this work, it is uncertain whether it was ever carried out in full. In the navy accounts only £67 7s 10d appear for the ship's repairs, £35 8s 8d for a wall of earth and £14 13s 4d for the queen's visit (Oppenheim 1896a, 168 n6, citing *Cal S P Dom*, 1598–1601, 35). 'Captain Drackes Schip' is shown near 'Ditfort' in a schematic *c* 1606 map by Benjamin Wright (NMM, G218:9/22).

The ship probably fell into disrepair in the 17th century. There is a reference by Pepys to a ship in the wet dock that is generally thought to be the *Golden Hinde*. Pepys reports that he

> … heard (which I had before) how, when the [wet] docke was made, a ship of near 500 tons was there found; a ship supposed of Queene Elizabeth's time, and well wrought, with a great deal of stone shot in her of eighteen inches diameter, which was shot then in use: and afterwards meeting with Captain Perriman and Mr. Castle at Half-way Tree, they tell me of stone-shot of thirty-six inches diameter, which they shot out of mortar-pieces … . (*Pepys diary*, 28 April 1667)

3.2 Archaeological evidence for the Tudor dockyard

Introduction

The 'great dock', a dry dock, was probably built around the same time as the storehouse (under way in 1513) (above, 3.1) and is also shown on the 1623 map (Fig 14). However, no traces of the Tudor dock were found during the investigations and it is likely to have been completely removed by later versions.

The construction of the Henrician 'wett dock' (above, 3.1) made use of the *Orfletediche* and the natural water-filled pond near the Thames (Chapter 2.1). The route of the *Orfletediche* followed a shallow arc across the site, passing just north of the location of the wet dock. The convenience of this pond as a dock may have been a determining factor in the selection of the site for the dockyard. Any trace of the Tudor wet dock also eluded the excavations and it may have been wholly displaced by later modifications. A short section of on-edge planking, supported on both sides by piles, was initially thought to be part of the structure, but closer investigation revealed that it was more likely part of a revetment against the river (below, 'Thames frontages'). In addition to revetments, archaeological evidence was recovered for the storehouse (B1) (a Scheduled Ancient Monument) and associated activity on the gravel headland, and for the Treasurer of the Navy's house (B2) (Fig 18).

Thames frontages

Timber riverfront pile and plank revetment and land-ties (S6)

A simple pile and plank revetment (S6, Fig 18; Fig 19) running roughly east–west and to a depth of approaching 1m was partially exposed (over a length of 3m). Six small, round or minimally trimmed oak log piles retained a mix of pit-sawn oak and elm planks wedged on edge behind them. The planks lay on the landward side to the south. This was indicated by the fact

that all the log piles were set on the north side to resist landfill thrust from the south, indicating that the water (ie the tidal Thames) lay to the north. Similar clay/silt alluvium lay on both sides of the structure. Structure 6 could not be fully exposed and had been truncated by later activity, but an interpretation as a small riverfront revetment, possibly at the base of a truncated mud wall, seems most likely. Pile and plank waterfront revetments of the Thames have frequently been archaeologically excavated in the London area (eg the late Saxon to 12th-century waterfronts described by Ayre and Wroe-Brown (2015a; 2015b) but the use of pit-sawn elm and oak planking suggests a late 15th- to 16th-century date or later. However, a date later than the early 16th century seems very unlikely on stratigraphic grounds. Initially thought to be part of the Tudor wet dock, this structure is probably instead the earliest Thames frontage revetment found on the site. It could just pre-date or just post-date the founding of the yard in 1513.

A loose collection of land-tie assemblies seen to the north-west of the Tudor storehouse once supported the timber revetment Structure 6 (Fig 18). Later timbers and foundations also partially obscured these timbers, making the precise sequence of construction difficult to unravel. The varying

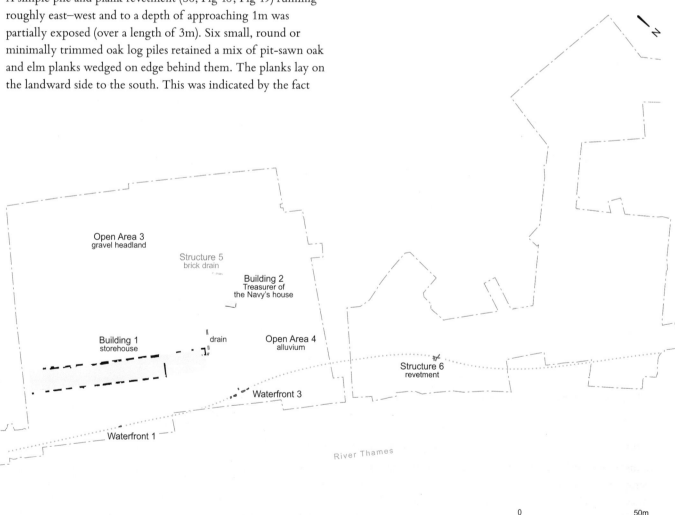

Open Area 3
gravel headland

Structure 5
brick drain

Building 2
Treasurer of
the Navy's house

Building 1
storehouse

drain

Open Area 4
alluvium

Structure 6
revetment

Waterfront 3

Waterfront 1

River Thames

0   50m

Fig 18 Plan of principal archaeological features in the Tudor dockyard (period 2) (scale 1:1500)

Fig 19 View of early timber riverfront pile and plank revetment (S6), looking south (0.5m scale)

alignments suggest that there may even have been more than one phase of these early river wall revetments. The basic form of these structural assemblies of timber included pairs of anchoring small piles (or stakes) that held in place a lock-bar of timber set in a through-socket or lap-joint in the main north–south land-tie beam. These assemblies are distinctive elements of waterfront archaeology and were used from the Roman period to the 19th century in the Thames region (eg Ayre and Wroe-Brown 2015a; 2015b). However, close recording of woodworking technology features such as tool marks and fastenings can provide broad dating, which is usually tightened by association with finds and tree-ring dating.

None of these timber assemblies could be dismantled but they were exposed on three sides in most cases. Land-tie assemblies consisting of timbers [6122], [6123] and others, and probably also timbers [6144] and [6130], can be grouped as roughly north–south land-tie beams. North–south beam [3717] and lock-bar [3739] just to the west were also probably part of this 'ghost' timber river wall. As the northern parts of the frontage had been removed it is not certain whether this was simply a river wall revetment or part of a working wharf frontage just to the north of the Tudor storehouse (B1). The oak land-tie assembly including north–south main beam timber [6122], anchor piles [6123] and [6124] and lock-bar [6127] was the most exposed example with the most detailed record. Timbers [6122] and [6123] were not recorded as having clear evidence of previous use, but anchor pile [6124] had clear traces of cream-coloured paint indicating that it was second-hand. This was probably white lead paint, a common naval material. Although the sister anchor pile [6123] appeared to have been a freshly cut timber from a sawn quarter of a squared beam, the possibility of previous use for a short time before its last use must be acknowledged. This timber [6123] has a tree-ring

felling date range of 1554–89 (Chapter 10.9; Fig 199) and hence a date in the mid to late 16th century for this land-tie assembly seems very likely.

16th-century Waterfront 1

A Thames frontage was identified in this area (W1, Fig 18). This structure was only very partially exposed due to considerations of access and safety, and extensive damage and masking by recent building foundations. However, enough was exposed running east–west for *c* 1.5m and vertically extending nearly 1m for it to be clear that it was a Thames frontage revetment with squared oak uprights, set *c* 0.5m apart on the north, riverward, side of sawn oak planking set on edge. Two round log piles were also driven just to the south of the plank sheathing. One of these planks ([2926]) was lifted and a tree-ring felling date range of 1493–1538 obtained from it (Chapter 10.9; Fig 199). This plank was of through-sawn oak including what was probably the boundary between heart- and sapwood (a plank sawn through nearly all the thickness of the parent log, with the perishable sapwood removed). It survived 385mm wide and 40mm thick, and a section 1.03m long could be lifted. An iron nail was found used to fasten the planking to one of the log piles to the south, and traces of a 10mm through-hole were also found that might possibly suggest a phase of previous use. It could well be that the squared oak uprights on the north side were repairs to what had been another simple pile and plank revetment originally, later reinforced.

The location of the timber frontage (W1) *c* 8m north of the Tudor storehouse (B1) and broad tree-ring dating evidence (above) suggest that it was a relic of the working wharf frontage facing the Thames against which barges would probably have unloaded naval supplies. However, the presence of later frontage timbers hard up against the north side of this frontage prevented very detailed examination of the structure. No land-tie assemblies survived that could be very clearly associated with this structure. Given the tree-ring dating (above), this frontage (W1) could be contemporary with the documented new wharf construction in 1588–9 (above, 3.1).

16th- to early 17th-century Waterfront 3

A few metres to the west of the Tudor (W1) and the 17th-century (W2, W4, W6; Chapter 4.2) timber river frontages, a similar timber river frontage was exposed, running east–west for *c* 5.3m (W3, Fig 18). This consisted of several rectangular-sectioned uprights that were exposed in plan lying to the north of planking set on edge. Although it was not possible to expose much depth of the structure, two sheathing planks were found, with others buried. The layout of the sheathing planking echoes that of Thames frontage Waterfront 1 to the east (Fig 18), and it may be the case that this river frontage was of a similar period. Timber [3297] lay horizontally on a north-west to south-east line and may have been part of a land-tie for the frontage.

Waterfront 3 displayed a clear pattern of apparently alternating oak uprights, with slightly varying cross sections, on the south, landward side of the frontage, similar to the pattern observed in Waterfront 4 (below). The plank sheathing was of oak *c* 50mm thick and around 250mm wide. Although decayed at the top, the planking was better preserved lower down and clear pit-saw marks were visible on the plank faces. In this case the planking was fastened by a mixture of iron spikes and oak treenails *c* 34mm in diameter. The combination of oak treenails and iron spikes resembles fastening patterns used in some carvel-built ships. The spikes had to be driven through bored pilot holes in the hard oak timber but would have held the planking in place, rapidly pulling all the timbers closely into line. Then the task of driving the treenails into large pre-bored holes could have been delegated to less skilled workers. The oak uprights were *c* 170–180mm thick by *c* 250mm wide and two, timbers [2613] and [2614], were extracted as a sample with a mechanical excavator.

The alternating uprights were found to be original tenoned posts and shorter repair piles with axe-cut points on their bases. This evidence clearly indicates that originally the frontage was a timber-framed structure with posts tenoned into a morticed sill beam that could not be exposed in the excavation. The tenoned post timber [2613] was extracted with little damage and had a fully preserved tenon which may imply that the locking peg used to hold it in the mortice had not actually been driven, possibly due to awkward tidal access for the erection on-site (Fig 20). The post was hewn out of a moderately small 'parent oak log' *c* 0.35m in diameter at the mid length, a rather knotty but straight oak log similar to those used for the straighter frame timbers in contemporary shipbuilding; this was quite a small log by the standards of the modern native hardwood timber yard.

The alternating piles were evidently the result of a major repair. At some point after this repair was achieved, sloping

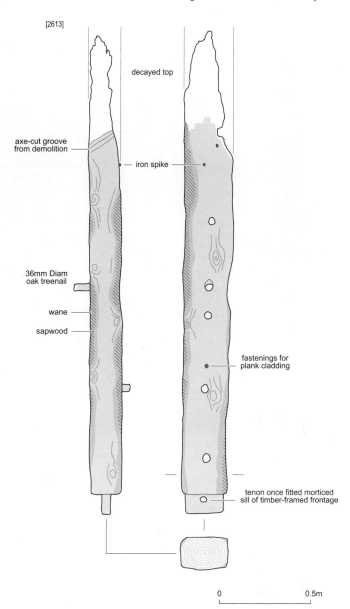

Fig 20 *Tenoned post (timber [2613]) from Waterfront 3 (scale 1:20)*

front brace timbers were set at an angle of *c* 30° down into the foreshore to the north. While strong land-tie assemblies must have been used, these had not survived later disturbance. Again, although the timber frontage was probably originally a working wharf, once the front braces were *in situ* unloading craft alongside would have been impossible here in front of the storehouse. This meant that unloading barges at that time would have had to have taken place elsewhere along the frontage. Both the survival of the structure to an OD level of *c* 2.79m and its character might suggest an early 17th- rather than late 16th-century date for the original construction.

The Tudor storehouse and activity on the gravel headland

The remains of the Tudor storehouse constitute a Scheduled Ancient Monument that was only exposed in plan, with no further excavation (Fig 21). The storehouse (B1, Fig 18) was

Fig 21 View of the Tudor storehouse (B1, in foreground) as exposed in the excavation, looking south

founded on the gravel headland (OA3, Fig 18). The main axis of the 52.30m × 9.50m rectangular building runs approximately east–west, parallel to the river nearby. The truncated remains of the original north, south and west walls of the storehouse survive to current ground level. The east wall is not original and appears to have been a replacement for the original wall to bring the east end of the storehouse in line with the rest of the storehouse complex in the early 18th century. A stub of wall that would have carried the north wall further east was identified in the excavations. As well as being longer to the east, the storehouse may also have originally extended 17m further west. Three short lengths of wall – of the same build as those in the main part of the building – were identified in the excavations, in line with the south wall. The westernmost of these returned north, suggesting that this was the original gable end to the building. This westernmost part seems to have been demolished by 1688. Taking these extra parts of the building into account, west and east, the Tudor storehouse may therefore have been at least 73m long originally.

The Tudor walls survived to a height of *c* 3.90–4.15m OD and were exposed up to 0.74m high. They are built of orange bricks of probable fabric 3033/3046 (length 217–223mm, width 100–107mm, thickness 50–55mm) set in cream-coloured mortar, suggesting a date of *c* 1450/70–1550. Typically, the walls are built in English bond (with alternating courses of headers and stretchers), but occasionally two courses of stretchers were noted between header courses. The walls are typically 0.71m wide, although in the south wall a 1.50m

length of wall at the east end and a 3.00m length in the central part are wider at 1.10m wide. Flat areas cut into both these wider walls may have been the bases for alcoves.

The walls survived to ground-floor level. A possible opening, which may have been a doorway, was recorded in the central part of the south wall; a tile abutting a stopped end seemed to be the base of this opening. The opening was at least 0.90m wide, and had been partially blocked with reused yellow stock brick and concrete in the 20th century (Chapter 8.3); the other side of the opening had been removed by modern concrete. No internal features relating to the Tudor phase of the storehouse survived.

The north and south brick walls were cut by ten north–south concrete walls at *c* 2–4m intervals (seen in Fig 21). These modern concrete walls were 1.5–2.0m wide, their tops at the same level as the surviving tops of the Tudor walls. The concrete walls were not excavated in the area of the Scheduled Monument, but excavation immediately to the north showed that they were up to 3m deep. In places, the Tudor walls were also truncated at regular intervals by vibropiles. The line of the south wall of the Tudor storehouse continued as a number of fragmentary walls, returning north.

While no floor levels survived in the building, vertical slots along the internal faces of the north and south walls were identified that would have supported substantial timber floor joists. The four best-surviving slots were at the west end of the north wall (Fig 22), and seem to have been modified during the Tudor period (as a partial blocking consisted of Tudor bricks).

Inspection revealed that parts of the slots were integral to, and built with, the wall, while other, lower, parts had been carefully cut into the wall face. The timber floor joists had probably been replaced during the long life of the building, but all traces had decayed away. However, the slots provided an unexpected insight into the primary carpentry of the building, matched in some other high-status Tudor buildings elsewhere in south-east England.

In medieval buildings floor joists were rectangular in cross section and laid with their widest faces horizontal, unlike those of recent buildings which have a narrow plank-like form and are set on edge with the greatest dimension set vertically. During the 16th century the form of floor joists in many buildings was changing and they became mainly sawn out, rather than hewn and sawn half or whole logs. The 'Great Standing' (popularly known as 'Queen Elizabeth's Hunting Lodge') in Epping Forest (Chingford, Essex), commissioned by Henry VIII in 1543 and renovated in 1589 (Seddon and Moxey 2003, 28; Weir 2008, 470), is one of the earliest surviving buildings to have these new deep, narrow, sawn joists made by pit-sawing. There, large square, axe-hewn baulks of oak were sawn into plank-like slabs which were then used as floor joists.

Presumably the same method was used for the joists of the Deptford storehouse floor which must have had to bear the weight of heavy naval stores. The shape of the voids (Fig 22) indicated that the joists had tenons set in the middle of the depth of the timber, and the bottom of the joist also protruded further than the upper shoulder so that it would have carried much of the weight of the timber and materials on the floor above. This form of jointing floor joist ends is known in the

Great Standing and several other timber buildings of the mid 15th to 16th centuries (Hewett 1980, 280–1). The joist end voids were clearly c 380–400mm deep and c 110–120mm wide, which is probably slightly larger than the original timbers as they would have been bedded in mortar. The spacing of the joists would have been c 0.45m (18in) edge to edge or c 0.6m (2ft) centre to centre. The joists were also supported a little way above an underfloor void so as to keep them reasonably dry and to reduce rotting and the spread of damp into the material stored on the floor. Clearly the joists would have been very robust and capable of bearing the weight of such items as large full casks of tar and oil, ironware, heavy timber, oars, masts and sails.

The fact that the voids clearly had impressions of the original tenons is important as it implies that the brickwork was assembled around floor timbers left *in situ* from a timber-framed building set on a low brick dwarf wall. The tenon also indicates that originally the joists were jointed into large sill timbers that would have rested on the brick foundation wall. This suggests that the original building was timber-framed and would also have had timber-framed walls, with posts tenoned into the same sills as is typical of many Tudor buildings.

This early structure, then, was later underpinned and rebuilt in brick in the 16th century, although the timber floor was left *in situ*; it may have been that this work was done in stages. Alternatively, the rebuild in brick may have been relatively rapid and carried out to make the building more secure, especially as many naval stores, such as tar barrels, were both highly flammable and very valuable. Fig 24 illustrates the development of the brick Tudor and Stuart storehouse complex.

The evidence for a timber-framed structure presents

joist
tenon
void

Fig 22 The south face of the north wall of the Tudor storehouse (B1), showing the later brickwork that was assembled around floor joists left in situ *from the original timber-framed building set on a low brick dwarf wall: above – view looking north, showing the joist end voids (0.5m scale); far left and left – conjectural reconstruction of a tenoned joist and an original timber wall (not to scale)*

problems for the hitherto accepted dating of this building, which relies on the carving of 'AX HK 1513' below a brick niche in the north wall (Fig 15). If the foundations are earlier than this wall, it means that the storehouse was also originally built before 1513. Other references to a storehouse in the area include one of 1511 at 'Deptford Strond' (above, 3.1). Alternatively, the inscription might simply record the date of 1513 when the storehouse was originally built or at least begun, and the brick niche and the north wall were built afterwards – although presumably only shortly afterwards.

Indeed, while the carving 'AX HK 1513' indicates that construction was under way in 1513, the work does not seem to have been completed until 1514 when a receipt was issued for wages for workmen finishing the building (*L and P Hen VIII*, i, 1483–5, 22 December). Locks for the storehouse were purchased in 1520, with 2s paid for 'a portall lock for the hall door' and 20d for 'a platt lock for the middle door' (*L and P Hen VIII*, iii, 369–81), and two new sheds were constructed by Geoffrey ap Fluellyn, house-carpenter, 'on the north side of the storehouse' for 'the King's iron and brass guns' (ibid).

The Treasurer of the Navy's house

Other sections of probable Tudor walls included those seen in a narrow building to the west of the Tudor storehouse on a very distinctive north-east to south-west alignment. This was likely to have been the Treasurer of the Navy's house (B2, Fig 18), probably in existence by the 1540s. The house had been rebuilt by the late 16th to 17th centuries (B3, Fig 25). These later walls were not removed during the excavation, so the original walls were only seen where the later ones had been truncated. Where observable, the original walls of the building were constructed of the same smaller red and orange bricks as the Tudor storehouse (B1), measuring 217–223 × 100–107 × 48–55mm and probably of *c* 1450/70–1550 in date. The original house may perhaps have been timber-framed on brick foundations. Apart from these bricks, finds and dating evidence were scarce. Both the Tudor storehouse (B1) and the Treasurer of the Navy's house (B2) were founded on the gravel headland (OA3), but only scattered finds and features were identified (see Chapter 9.3, OA8, pit [5972]).

4

The Stuart dockyard (period 3, 1603–1714)

4.1 Historical introduction

James I (1603–25)

James I's peaceful accession was soon followed by peace with Spain, but piracy was a serious problem in the first two decades of his reign (Rodger 1997, 347–53). James had 37 warships in 1607, but some were 'old and rotten and barely fit for service' (MacDonald 1982, 44); by 1617 he had 27. He commissioned 21 ships of over 500 tons in 22 years, about half rebuilds of Elizabeth's ships. Deptford was James's principal dockyard, building or rebuilding 13 of these, including the 41-gun *Dreadnought* in 1614 (a rebuild as 552bm-tons), and the 30-gun *Happy Entrance* (404/540bm-tons) and the 42-gun *Constant Reformation* (725bm-tons) in 1619. A proposal in 1611 to sell Deptford, at which time the value of the yard was estimated at about £5000, came to nothing (Oppenheim 1926, 344). The *Trades Increase* and the *Peppercorn* were also built at Deptford, in 1609–10, for the East India Company (Banbury 1971, 33; Rodger 1997, 480–1). The East India Company's own Deptford yard (east of the royal dockyard, close to Deptford Creek, known later as Deptford Green yard) was being expanded: in 1614 a new dock was to be begun at Deptford, a crane fitted for the timber yard, and a stone wharf and a foundation for a storehouse built (*Cal S P Col*, 267–74; Barnard 1997, 50–1). The 1623 Evelyn plan of Deptford shows the Company's buildings, a dock and slipway (Fig 14, top left, between 'Middle water gate' and 'Upper water gate'), but the Company had leased out its entire yard by the 1630s, deserting it in favour of that at Blackwall (Oppenheim 1926, 349; Divers 2004, 22, 46–8).

Corruption and inefficiency in government administration including naval administration, already a problem in the 1590s, worsened rapidly under James (Rodger 1997, 364–78). Sir Robert Mansell, a royal favourite, was appointed Treasurer of Marine Causes in 1604, joining Sir John Trevor, Surveyor since 1598; unscrupulous and unpleasant, together they intimidated colleagues and others, and embezzlement and corruption escalated (McGowan 1971, xiv–xv). A commission of enquiry into the state of the navy reported in 1608 on Deptford and the other yards. Depositions recorded bribery of officers, price fixing and price inflation (where official bills were increased above the rates actually paid, for instance for timber or nails, to the supplier, allowing the officers to claim from the king the higher rates, with the profit going to Trevor and others) (ibid, 7, 22–3, 28–9, 35, 82–91, 104, 136, 143). The king was paying, for example, for 'a greater weight and number [of brass sheaves] than were demanded to go for the king's use' and 'for bigger masts and greater measure than are in his store' (ibid, 104). Officers were accepting green and rotten timber, whereas unfit timber should have been rejected out in the woods (ibid, 51–3). Wastage was significant: 'And by reason of the glutting of the store with masts … and for that there is no dock for the convenient keeping of them at Deptford where the greatest stores remaineth, there be divers masts which cost the King betwixt £20 and £30 a mast, and a multitude of other of lower price, very much decayed and wasted to the King's exceeding loss' (ibid, 48). The stores at Deptford in 1604 included 210 masts, 322 loads of timber, 41,000 feet of plank, 171 cables, 499 hawsers, 15 serviceable and 28 unserviceable anchors, 24 compasses, 40 bolts of canvas, 24,000 treenails and many other articles (Oppenheim 1896a, 211). In 1608 a shipwright at the king's store at Woolwich and Deptford reported 'a great part of the store of the king's provisions for the navy to be very much decayed, windshaken and rotten' (ibid, 53).

The theft of materials and provisions was systematic and on a large scale, committed by officers and subordinates alike, with cordage, masts, timber, planks, board and treenails going out of the yards to merchants and to individuals for private use:

And being demanded whether the Officers use not to command the King's provisions out of the store for their own use, he answereth that Sir Robert Mansell hath commanded such for the King's own house at Deptford for the making of a wash-house, a pheasant house and a pale the length of the whole moat with a great gate, and some other planks for his house at Westminster; and Sir John Trevor some 300 foot of 3-inch plank for his own use at his own house, also at Westminster. And he sayeth further that in *anno* 1605 he received a warrant from Sir John Trevor for the delivery out of four brass cases of one-hundred-weight or thereabouts from the stores at Deptford to Phineas Pett, which were laid there in Mr Borough's time and now said to be meant for sheaves of brass, and were never brought into the store again. (McGowan 1971, 104–5)

Thomas Buck was rewarded in July 1609 for 'discovering abuses', including theft from Deptford storehouses; officers were to be required to account for the provisions in their charge (*Cal Cecil P*, xxi, 78–88). The yard was enclosed with an oak paling in 1610, presumably for added security (Oppenheim 1926, 343). However, the commission was to little avail: King James in 1609, for example, found for Phineas Pett, Master Shipwright at Woolwich, accused of waste and fraud; and the officers carried on as before (McGowan 1971, xv; Rodger 1997, 367–8). The Deptford storehouses were said a decade later, in 1618, to be 'full of rotten wood and bad cordage', the scales light by one pound per hundredweight, and with bad materials knowingly being received while the good were sold to boatswains and other ships' officers at low prices (Oppenheim 1896a, 211).

In 1618 a new commission into the state of the navy, appointed by the new Lord High Admiral, the Duke of Buckingham, had more success than that of 1608; it replaced the Navy Board with the new Navy Commission and set about a programme of reform of naval administration (Oppenheim 1926, 344; McGowan 1971, xxiv; Rodger 1997, 368–70). The commission resulted in Chatham being further expanded in the next few years, with new docks, mast ponds, storehouses, wharfs and so on. It was again suggested that Deptford be abandoned because of the cost of moving vessels to and from the Thames from the Upnor anchorage. Despite this, Deptford was enclosed with a brick wall in 1619 and the commissioners recommended that the building of new ships should be restricted to Deptford

where two could be worked on at the same time in the long (double) dry dock. As a result, ten large men-of-war were built at Deptford in five years. A member of the new Navy Commission, William Burrell, formerly of the East India Company, became Master Shipwright at Deptford in 1618 (Oppenheim 1926, 344–5, 346; Rodger 1997, 370).

Evelyn's plan of Deptford in 1623 shows '[the king's] great Dock' (Fig 14), and other dry docks between 'Upper water gate' and Deptford Creek, as fitted with gates. Private yards nearby were expanding, with one – the Blackwall yard – matching the capacity of the royal dockyards (Banbury 1971, 34).

Charles I (1625–49), Parliament and civil war

In 1625 England went to war with Spain, and in the following year with France, necessitating endless work repairing and fitting ships. Navy debt in 1626 was £100,000, much of it due to workmen in the yards; in 1627 the workmen were owed 18 months' pay, materials could only be got on credit and at ruinous prices, and the yards became utterly disorganised (Oppenheim 1926, 345). Peace was concluded in 1630, at which point Charles needed to make the navy once again a force to be reckoned with in the eyes of his European rivals, but his financial resources were very limited. Ship Money fleets were the result, in which can be seen the beginnings of a regular naval service (Rodger 1997, 379–94, 401–10).

The Deptford yard seems to have declined slightly in importance in the second quarter of the 17th century. In October 1628 there were 37 men at Deptford compared to 224 at Chatham (Oppenheim 1926, 345) and the Deptford yard constructed only three of the ten large ships built during Charles I's reign. The 42-gun *Henrietta Maria* (594/792bm-tons) was constructed at the yard in 1633 and the following year the 48-gun *James* (660/870bm-tons) was built, designed by Peter Pett (Banbury 1971, 34; Rodger 1997, 482). Charles visited the Deptford yard in 1633 (Oppenheim 1926, 346). Chatham was the pre-eminent repairing yard, carrying out three times more repairs than Deptford in 1635 (ibid, 344, 346).

Fraudulent practices and corruption continued to be rife. Master shipwrights had their own private yards to attend to, and they and other officers abused their positions in the royal dockyards, while the workmen had escalated the custom of taking home broken pieces of wood ('chips') to scandalous levels (Chapter 1.2). The storekeepers and some other officers at Chatham and Deptford were suspended in 1634 for malpractice in the sale of cordage. About the same time, a lighter was seized at Deptford which contained some 9000 treenails, 1–2ft in length, which the offender maintained were a lawful perquisite; the intended recipient was a government shipwright with a yard of his own (Oppenheim 1926, 345, 347).

The English Civil Wars (1642–51) saw London, the navy, the royal dockyards and much of south-east England declare for Parliament against the king. Parliament introduced a new moral standard to the yards (Oppenheim 1926, 348). In December 1644, the Lord Admiral, Robert Earl of Warwick, wrote to the Clerk of the Cheque at Deptford instructing that the officers and men should attend a forenoon (morning) lecture every Wednesday and so 'be improved in knowledge and practice of saving truths'. They were to lose no wages for attendance: '... the time lost in their work will, I doubt not, be abundantly recompensed by a greater blessing from God upon their labours, besides the prevention of many disorders that may be committed by neglect of this opportunity' (*Cal S P Dom*, 1644, 177–8, no. 66).

No ships were built until 1646 when Parliament instituted a steady building programme. The 34-gun *Nonsuch* (400/500bm-tons) and 42-gun *Assurance* (456bm-tons) were built in that year at Deptford, the latter by Henry Johnson, and the following year the 32-gun *Tiger* (457bm-tons) and *Elizabeth* (474/643bm-tons) were built (Banbury 1971, 35; Rodger 1997, 483).

In 1648 (during the 'Second Civil War' of 1648–9), Deptford was briefly in the hands of Royalists and local people were able to plunder the naval stores (Oppenheim 1926, 348). John Evelyn recorded the gathering of Royalist supporters in the Broomfield 'next my house at Sayes Court'. The troops were part of a rising in Kent, led by George Goring, 1st Earl of Norwich, and soon departed for Maidstone where they were defeated that June by Parliamentary forces under Sir Thomas Fairfax. Evelyn reported that some then made their way to Colchester, which was besieged for 11 weeks (*Evelyn diary*, 30 May 1648; Trevelyan 2002, 274–5).

The Commonwealth (1649–60)

Both Parliamentarians and Royalists had learnt the cost of not having an effective navy, and a permanent sea power was now seen as essential (Rodger 1997, 434). Over the preceding century and more, an 'extensive and sophisticated naval administration had grown up ... with docks and slips, stores and offices, smithies and ropewalks, foundries and powder mills; with a numerous staff of long experience, backed by advanced and prosperous private industry' (ibid; Rodger 2004, 33–49). Deptford continued under the control of the Navy Commissioners in London and the beginning of the Deptford victualling yard may be seen in the use of a slaughterhouse, formerly attached to Greenwich Palace (Chapter 3.1), for the navy from about 1649 (Oppenheim 1926, 348; Chapter 5.1). Besides shipbuilding, Deptford was a foremost distribution centre of naval stores. The Admiralty invested in the 1650s in infrastructure at the dockyards; the mast yard and dock at Deptford were surveyed, noting repairs and alterations required (*Cal S P Dom*, 1653–4, 492), and a dock was repaired or constructed and new wharfs built (Oppenheim 1896b, 76; 1926, 350–1; Rodger 2004, 46).

In its 11-year period of power, the republican government of the Commonwealth commissioned 45 ships of over 500 tons, ten of them from Deptford, according to Banbury (1977, 35). War with the Dutch began in 1652 and in that year John Evelyn 'saw the *Diamond* and *Ruby* launched in the Dock at Deptford, carrying forty-eight brass cannon each; Cromwell and his grandees present, with great acclamations' (*Evelyn diary*, 15 March 1652). With the First Dutch War at an end in 1654, the

number of men employed in all the yards was to be limited to 980 (Oppenheim 1926, 350). In March 1655, it was reported that the number of men working at the Deptford yard had been reduced to 240; there were only six caulkers and eight more were requested (*Cal S P Dom*, 1655, 441, no. 65).

Poor organisation, malpractice and corruption remained serious issues. A Greenwich waterman allegedly made £5000 by purchases from workmen at the Woolwich and Deptford yards, while in September 1658 all merchantmen afloat between London and Deptford were searched for stores stolen from the yards or men-of-war (Oppenheim 1926, 350).

In December 1658, the Navy Commissioners asked their superiors (the Admiralty Commission) what coat of arms should be placed in the stern as part of the carved works of a ship being built at the yard – 'whether the Protector's quartered or those of the Commonwealth' (*Cal S P Dom*, 1658–9, 482, no. 16). Oliver Cromwell had died three months earlier and these were febrile political times. Cromwell's son Richard took power, only to resign in 1659, and the Commonwealth was briefly reinstated before the restoration of Charles II in 1660. In August 1659, Captains Packwood and Greene reported that they had enlisted 100 men each to guard the magazines and ships at Deptford and Woolwich and asked for arms and provisions (*Cal S P Dom*, 1659–60, 471, no. 112).

Charles II (1660–85) and James II (1685–8)

Charles II visited the yard only months after the Restoration (*Pepys diary*, 15 October 1660). He would have been anxious to consolidate the support of the navy, his hold on power not yet being secure. Guards had to be set at the royal dockyards, including Deptford, early the following year (ibid, 11 January 1661) against an attempt to seize London by the nonconformist Fifth Monarchists; one of their number had recently been hanged for regicide (Burrage 1910, 743–4).

Charles's new naval administration included confirming his brother James, Duke of York (later King James II) as Lord High Admiral, as well as appointing Samuel Pepys, aged just 27 in 1660, as Clerk of Acts of the Navy Board (Rodger 2004, 94–111). Pepys was determined on 'seeing into the miscarriages' at the royal dockyards, despairing at the difference between 'the King's new Captains' and 'the old Captains for obedience and order'. He visited the Deptford yard's storehouse to view the stores and the records, concluding of the officers, 'I do not perceive that there is one-third of their duties performed' (*Pepys diary*, 2 July 1662; Oppenheim 1926, 351–2).

Charles had inherited a £1 million debt and a 150-strong fleet. He laid up the ships and sold off navy stores (overseen by Pepys) which cut the cost of the fleet by almost two-thirds between 1659 and 1663 (Banbury 1971, 36; MacDougall 1982, 54). In July 1663 there were 238 men at Deptford and 324 at Chatham (Oppenheim 1926, 352). The cost of the navy rose again sharply in 1664 as the Second Dutch War broke out. On 12 June 1667 the Dutch were able to seize the *Royal Charles* from the Medway and tow it away (Banbury 1971, 36; Lavery 2003, 120), a national embarrassment. In 1667 the yard was busy repairing ships damaged in the war: Jonas Shish estimated the cost of repairing damage to three hired fireships at £188 15s 8d (*Cal S P Dom*, 1667, 499, no. 82).

In the summer of 1667 a fire in the Deptford yard led many people to believe that the Dutch had attacked the Tower of London. John Evelyn blamed the blaze on 'some chips and combustible matter prepared for some fire-ships' that had caught light (*Evelyn diary*, 17 June 1667). The yard's watchmen on duty that night were gaoled in Southwark's notorious Marshalsea prison, protesting their innocence. One of them, Thomas Eaton, said that there was no watchman where the fire broke out – a point the officers confirmed. Other men were so tired out by hard labour that they had refused to accept the place of the watchman, who was ill (*Cal S P Dom*, 1667, 292–3, nos 91–2). This was the second major blaze the yard's workmen had tackled in less than a year. During the Great Fire a few months previously, they had been sent to the City to blow up houses to create fire-breaks (*Pepys diary,* 5 September 1666).

Immediately after the capture of the *Royal Charles* guns were installed in the yard to guard against the Dutch (*Pepys diary*, 14 June 1667). In November 1667 a number of sailors were punished for cowardice in the face of the Dutch, the sentences – including one execution – being carried out on the *Victory*, 'riding at anchor before Deptford Yard' (*Cal S P Dom*, 1667–8, 17).

Sheerness was established at the mouth of the Medway in 1665, and hardly any additions were made to the older Kent yards in the 1660s and 1670s (Oppenheim 1926, 353–5, 359–60). In July 1667, Edward Rundells asked the Navy Office for a warrant for six labourers to clear the ground at Deptford for the bargehouse (*Cal S P Dom*, 1667, 293, no. 94); this suggests that the bargehouse was built around this time. Maps of 1688 and 1698 (Fig 23) identify 'Boat-houses &c' as number '32' (below, 4.2, B7) but do not name a bargehouse as such. Boats were an essential part of a ship's equipment in the 17th century (viz longboats, barges, pinnaces, shallops, jollywatts) and later (May 1999).

The response to the wars with the Dutch was to build more 1st-rate ships. The first of these giant three-deckers, the 1129bm-ton, 163ft × 42½ft *Charles*, built by Jonas Shish, was launched at Deptford in 1668 (MacDougall 1982, 54; Colledge and Warlow 2010). The launch was attended by the king and queen and their court, as well as Evelyn and Pepys, who remarked of the ship 'God send her better luck than the former!' (*Evelyn diary*, 3 March 1668; *Pepys diary*, 3 March 1668).

When the Third Dutch War broke out in 1672, the fleet of almost a hundred warships had largely been built or refitted at Deptford, Woolwich and Chatham (Banbury 1971, 36). Investment at Deptford included a new mast dock early in the 1670s (below, 4.2). The war ended in 1674 and it was proposed to discharge 1616 men from Deptford, Woolwich, Chatham and Portsmouth, retaining just 424 in pay; £31,600 was owed in yard wages (Oppenheim 1926, 356). In May 1677 there were 113 shipwrights and caulkers at Deptford (ibid, 356–7). However, in 1677 war with France was anticipated and a huge increase in shipbuilding was largely due to Pepys who had been promoted to a senior position in the Admiralty in 1672. Deptford built

two 2nd-rates and six 3rd-rates (MacDougall 1982, 65). By 1678 the fleet (which was actually not used) consisted of 89 warships, 13 fireships and 15 auxiliaries; three of the eight ships over 1000 tons were built at Deptford (Banbury 1971, 37).

Following the Exclusion crisis and Popish Plot, and a shift in power over the navy to Parliament, in 1679 a new Admiralty dismissed Pepys (Rodger 2004, 108–9). He was accused of various misdemeanours and imprisoned in the Tower (*Evelyn diary*, 4 June 1679). Charles took back the Admiralty and appointed Pepys 'Secretary of the Marine' in 1684, in which capacity he then drove forward a restoration of the navy (Rodger 2004, 109–10). Ships were increasing in size and new works were required in the yards (Oppenheim 1926, 360). An increase in expenditure at the end of Charles II's reign and the beginning of James II's (ie *c* 1685) resulted in improvements generally, and at Deptford the wet dock was extensively repaired at a cost of £2430 and six new mast houses were built (ibid, 361), as well as work begun on new boathouses and the rebuilding of the officers' quarters and other buildings (below, 4.2). Demolition of the Treasurer of the Navy's house and the inclusion of the ground and garden in the Deptford yard did not do much to relieve the pressure on space (ibid; below, 4.2).

The period 1660–88 was altogether marked by a struggle to make naval administration more efficient, alongside the contest between Parliament and the king for control of the navy (Rodger 2004, 110). However, lack of money throughout this period meant that abuses and corruption were endemic in all the yards (Oppenheim 1926, 355–8). In 1688, Deptford was valued at £15,760 and Woolwich at £9669, Sheerness at £5393 and Chatham at £44,940; in March 1688, 171 shipwrights and caulkers were employed at Deptford and 96 at Woolwich, but 479 at Chatham (ibid, 362; MacDougall 1982, 71). The Deptford and Woolwich yards did heavy repair work and the new warships they constructed tended to be sent into the Medway for completion (ibid, 70–1).

William III (1689–1702)

William, Prince of Orange, who in February 1689 supplanted James II as William III in a bloodless revolution, also knew the importance of sea power and maintained the high level of naval spending, as the new, uneasy, Anglo-Dutch alliance immediately went to war against France (MacDougall 1982, 66). The previous naval system was ended: Pepys resigned in 1689, the Admiralty lost most of its responsibilities, and the Navy Board lost status (Rodger 2004, 155, 181–8). The Board's last major shipbuilding programme had been in 1677. Over the next 25 years, however, the numbers of 1st- to 4th-rate ships increased from 100 in 1688 (the year of mobilisation) to 131 in 1714, and 5th- and 6th-rates from eight to 66, an expansion beyond the capacity of the naval dockyards and necessitating much building elsewhere by contract (Rodger 2004, 188). Investment and major construction work was required in the dockyards themselves, and in 1691 work began on a new dockyard at Plymouth (Rodger 2004, 188).

This spending does not seem to have trickled down as it

might have done to the dockyard workers themselves, and the ordinary working of the dockyards continued to present considerable problems (Rodger 2004, 189–92). Obtaining materials was seen as more pressing than paying wages by the Navy Board: in 1693 yard wages owed totalled £107,000, and the men had 15 months' wages due (Oppenheim 1926, 363). At the end of 1694, the shipwrights and other workmen of Deptford and Woolwich yards petitioned the Admiralty to complain that their wages were a year in arrears (*Cal Treasury P*, i, 407–21). This problem had still not been resolved some years later; in 1697 (the year of peace, and hence seeing demobilisation and cuts) a letter from the Deptford and Woolwich men was sent to the Treasury about their 'extreme want of pay' (*Cal Treasury P*, ii, 37–58). The men supplemented their income as best they could, through chips and not uncommonly outright theft (Chapter 1.2; Oppenheim 1926, 363–4).

In 1684 and 1687 the Navy Board had undertaken surveys of both shores of the Thames. Deptford lay in a shallow reach, which shoaled noticeably throughout Charles II's reign; there was only 1ft to spare at low water for a 1st-rate ship riding at anchor off the waterfront. The river was generally more crowded as private wharfs and warehouses expanded, more piers and steps were created and the river silted up off the new walls and landing stages (Ehrman 1953, 82–3). Space at the Deptford yard was constrained: its waterfront measured approximately 1370ft (418m) in length and the greatest depth of the yard was 1050ft (320m) (ibid, 86); on the map of 1698 (Fig 26) these dimensions correspond to the waterfront measured from the east side of the dry (double) dock to the west perimeter wall, and the depth measured from the south gate to the waterfront in front of the north-west corner of the quadrangle storehouse. In 1691–4 some new ground, formerly occupied by the house of the Surveyor of the Navy, was added to the yard and workhouses, storesheds and cranes were erected there (ibid, 429). The dry dock was just wide enough to take the small 1st-rates with a few inches to spare, while the older-style wet dock could accommodate only the smaller rates (ibid, 88). By 1689 Deptford and Woolwich were effectively 'minor yards', increasingly used for refitting of smaller ships, while the building of great ships, and the majority of all rates, took place at Chatham and Portsmouth (ibid, 90). In 1691 it was said that at a time of normal activity Deptford could build two rated ships at once whereas Chatham could build five and Portsmouth four (ibid, 88). Deptford had built 23 of the English fleet in 1698 out of 111 ships whose origins are known: just two 1st-rates and two 2nd-rates, five 3rd-rates, eight 4th-rates and two 6th-rates, plus a bomb-vessel, a ketch and a smack (ibid, 629). When at demobilisation the majority of the fleet was distributed among the dockyards for repair, Deptford received no 1st- or 2nd-rates, just one 3rd-rate and four 4th-rates (ibid, 621).

Major works at Deptford in this period included the completion of the officers' quarters (below, 4.2) and the 'Great New Storehouse' abutting the west end of Henry VIII's storehouse. On the 1698 map (Fig 23, 'B' right) the 'Great New Store house' (no. 42) is shown at the west end of, and at right angles to, the Tudor storehouse (ie aligned south-west to north-

east), and the 'New Store-house' (no. 37) is shown to the east abutting the south wall of the Tudor storehouse. Both are absent from the 1688 map (Fig 23, 'A' left) so were constructed between 1688 and 1698. However, in May 1688, bricklayers had finished the 'outsides' of a building 'at the end of the Long Storehouse' (TNA, ADM 106/3289, [?15] May 1688, np), which is likely to be a reference to the 'Great New Storehouse'. The 1698 panorama (Fig 23) shows the half-hipped gable end of the 'Great New Store house' to the right of the two earlier building ranges fronting the river, the 'Additional Store-house' and to its left the 'Store-keeper's Office', both shown on the 1688 map. Fig 24 uses the evidence of the 1698 survey to illustrate the development of the Tudor and Stuart storehouse complex.

Queen Anne (1702–14)

The War of the Spanish Succession continued the demands on the royal dockyards, but under Anne naval administration did become more efficient and government financial operations were also improved (Rodger 2004, 164–200). By 1711 the navy yards employed a total of 6488 officers and men, 1092 of whom were at Deptford; in October 1711, however, wages at the yards were over 18 months in arrears (ibid, 189). Construction and repair at Deptford included major work on the dry dock and gates (below, 4.2).

The 1709 survey of the dockyard

The officers undertook a major survey of the yard's wharfs, storehouses and other buildings in November 1709 (TNA, ADM 106/3295, 24 November 1709, np; 10 December 1709, np). They concluded that extensive repairs were required to the following:

the dry dock, its apron, wings and most of its wharf – one wing of the wharf needed to be replaced completely, about 130ft of the wharf requiring to be rebuilt, the other wharf could be repaired, and its apron 'requires to be shifted' – presumably entailing a major rebuild (at an estimated cost of £876);

the wet dock, its gates and apron needed repair, its wharf being in good condition (£103);

the mast dock was in need of cleaning out, its bridges and locks 'very much decayed' and a small part of its wharf needed repair (£760);

the 'wharfing to the river' – 'that of brick [is] in good condition; that of timber about 150ft in length requires to be new, and the other part about 600ft long wants a great repair' (£646);

the 'wharfs fence along the ditch to the marshes' – in other words, the fence along the west perimeter of the yard and the wharfing to the ditch – and other fences (£143);

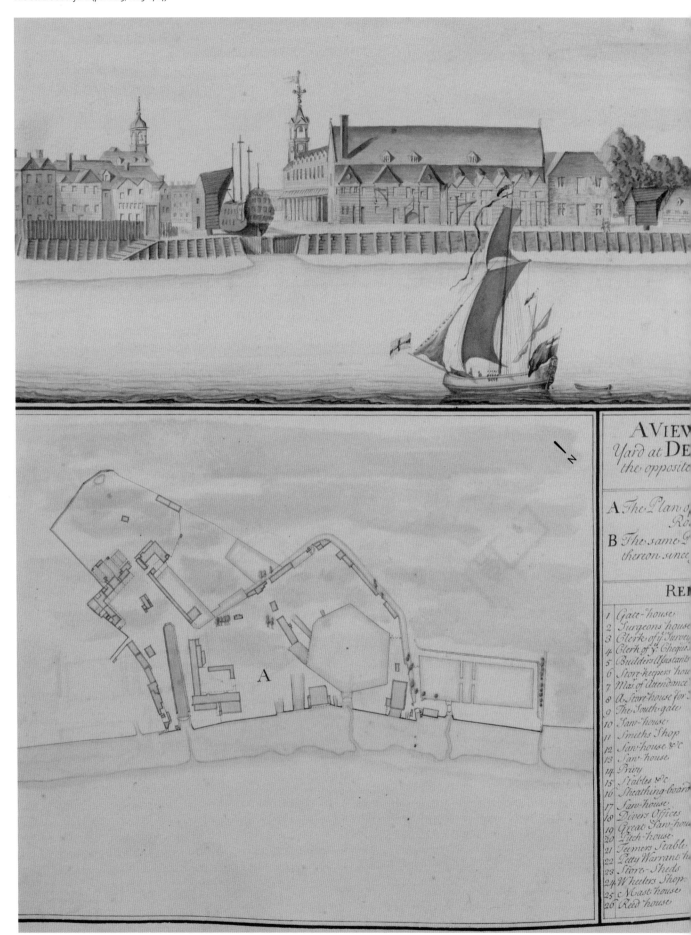

Fig 23 *The yard in the late 17th century: panorama and (below) maps of 1688 ('A', left) and 1698 ('B', right) from the 1698 survey (The British Library Board, Kings MS 43, fos 65v–66)*

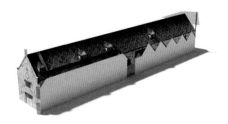

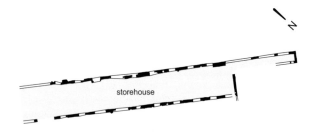

storehouse

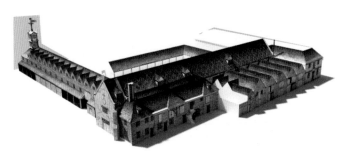

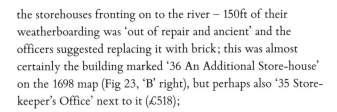

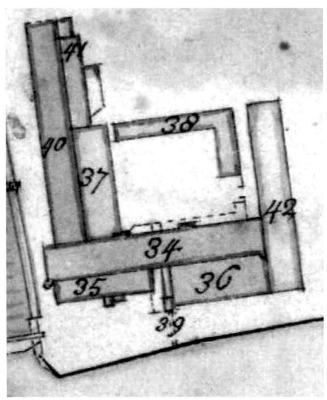

Fig 24 The Tudor and Stuart storehouse complex: upper – three-dimensional reconstruction and plan of the archaeological remains of the Tudor structure; lower – three-dimensional reconstruction of the storehouse complex based on the 1698 survey (BL, Kings MS 43, fo 82) and the complex on the map of 1698 (Fig 23, 'B' right) (scale 1:1000)

0   25m

the storehouses fronting on to the river – 150ft of their weatherboarding was 'out of repair and ancient' and the officers suggested replacing it with brick; this was almost certainly the building marked '36 An Additional Store-house' on the 1698 map (Fig 23, 'B' right), but perhaps also '35 Store-keeper's Office' next to it (£518);

other storehouses and the officers' houses – tiling, plastering and gutters (£315);

the mast house (to the west of the wet dock) required to be 'new plated' – presumably with weatherboard – and underpinned, and the boathouse, rigging house, smithy 'and other workhouses' required some small repair (£290);

the 'Great Slip' 'near the Boathouse' – undoubtedly the larger slipway opening on to the river shown on the 1698 map (Fig 23, 'B' right) immediately east of the boathouses and wet dock – 'wants a large repair or to be new' (£86).

The other slips, the cranes and the 'Great and New Storehouses' (the former being the Tudor storehouse) were in good condition. The officers also suggested that an extra storey be added to the washhouse in the back yard of the Clerk of the Survey's house, at a cost of £52 10s (TNA, ADM 106/3295, 18 November 1709, np).

Expanding the yard eastwards, and to the Isle of Dogs, 1710

There were also plans to expand the yard. Early in 1710, the officers reported to the Navy Board that they had carried out a survey of land adjoining the yard belonging to a Mr Hollis, including his wharf. The house on this land (referred to as 'the mansion') was a substantial building of brick, divided into two tenements. The land also included the 'Royall Ann Tavern' and two further tenements ('their first storeys brick and the other timber'), a brandy shop, a newly-built summer house in timber and a still-house newly built in brick. The land and the premises were worth £800, and could be let to the yard for £50 per annum. As well as being useful for receiving stores from the river, the advantage of the yard acquiring the land would be to eliminate the threat of fire from the still-house (TNA, ADM 106/3295, 3 February 1710, np).

A Mr Wright also had a piece of ground, adjoining the Master Shipwright's house (and so lying immediately east of the yard), with an old house divided into three tenements (TNA, ADM 106/3295, 3 February 1710, np), worth £250 (ibid, 15 February 1710, np). The officers wrote to Wright at Great Marlow in Buckinghamshire (ibid, 10 March 1710, np), but despite his agreeing to meet the Navy Board – presumably to discuss the yard acquiring his land or the use of it – he did not turn up, much to the officers' irritation (ibid, 29 April 1710, np).

Negotiations with Hollis were more successful. He had sold his land by autumn 1710, when the officers were considering the cost of demolishing the old house and clearing the ground, estimated at £60. '[R]epairing the brick wharf belonging to the said premises next the water gate, and making a brick wall for inclosing the Yard' would cost another £34. The Master Shipwright Joseph Allin subsequently requested that part of Hollis's land be used for a garden for his house and a 'brewhouse in lieu of my present conveniencys to be taken down', at an estimated cost of £123 (TNA, ADM 106/3295, 26 January 1711, np). (For the Master Shipwright's house see below, 4.2, 'The Master Shipwright's house, 1708'.) This suggests that Hollis's land also lay to the east of the yard, either to the north of Wright's (and fronting the river here), or – more likely – to the east of Wright's.

By November 1710, then, the Navy Board was actively exploring the possibility of further expansion and was even considering land opposite the yard on 'the Isle of Doggs' for a new mast dock, a wharf and anchor crane. The officers went as far as surveying 'the creek and land about it' and spoke to the aptly-named Mr Crane, the 'proprietor of the land without the marsh wall' by early 1711. The problems were too great, however, and the plans were abandoned. The officers concluded that although 'the creek itself will admit of the reception of masts' the crane could not be made 'without a very great charge'. The remoteness of the land was also a problem as 'it will require the transporting men and horses over the river too frequently' (TNA, ADM 106/3295, 8 January 1711, np). Some 150 years later this area was to be the location of the Millwall Iron Works and Napier Yard where the *Great Eastern* was built.

There was further correspondence with neighbours to the east of the yard. In May 1711 the officers complained to Richard Grew, referred to as a 'wine cooper' and a 'wine merchant' in London, who owned houses adjoining some of the officers' lodgings, that his chimneys were 'much decayed' and a fire risk to the yard (TNA, ADM 106/3296, 31 May 1711, 6). Grew failed to respond (ibid, 12 June 1711, 10) and the following year the officers' fears were realised when a fire broke out in one of his chimneys (ibid, 18 April 1712, 81). This may have prompted a review of the yard's firefighting capability. One small and two large fire engines required repair in 1713 (ibid, 14 September 1713, 154). They had been sent from Sheerness and were repaired by a Mr Sam Newton (ibid, 3 November 1713, 161).

4.2 Archaeological and documentary evidence for the Stuart dockyard

Introduction

Important new buildings in this period for which no archaeological evidence was recovered included the 'Great New Storehouse' (Fig 23, 'B' right, no. 42; above, 4.1), but there was

evidence for the repair of the existing Tudor storehouse. This section discusses the archaeological remains identified on site: the rebuilt (and then demolished) Treasurer of the Navy's house, officers' quarters and wet dock, the new mast dock, and other buildings and works (Fig 25; Fig 26).

The storehouse and brick drain

There were some repairs to the Tudor storehouse (B1, Fig 25) in this period, comprising red and reddish-orange bricks measuring 222–239 × 103–110 × 59–66mm, probably dating to the late 16th to mid 17th centuries. Fig 24 includes a three-dimensional reconstruction of the complete Stuart storehouse complex incorporating it, with clock tower, which is also shown from the river on the late 17th-century panorama (Fig 23).

South of the Tudor storehouse, a building (B4, Fig 25) survived only as a foundation of flint rubble, chalk and brick bonded with lime mortar, 1.70m long and 0.42m wide. The foundation ran east–west but was so fragmentary that it is impossible to say what it might have belonged to. Buildings are shown on the 1688 and 1689 maps in this area (Fig 23), but there can be no certainty that the foundation related to these. If it did, this foundation may have been part of the storehouses here.

The brick drain (S5, Fig 25), apparently pre-dating the foundation of the yard, continued in use into the Stuart period. Its west end, some 1.32m long, 0.46m wide and 0.30m high, was rebuilt with bricks of a *c* 1550–1666/1700 date. The drain fed into a channel to the east (S11, Fig 25). Only the west edge of this channel was visible, the rest being obscured under the later walls of the quadrangle storehouse, but this west edge was revetted in timber.

The Treasurer of the Navy's house (16th/17th century to 1684–8)

The Tudor Treasurer of the Navy's house (B3, Fig 25) was rebuilt entirely in brick in the 16th or 17th century, the new walls reusing the earlier, Tudor, walls/footings (Chapter 3.2) as foundations (Fig 27). The building measured 50.50m north–south by 5.70m east–west and contained a number of *in situ* floor levels, including tiled floors. The Treasurer's house is shown on the map of 1623 (Fig 14) as 'The Threr's house', apparently a three-storey (or possibly two-storey) building. In July 1633 the Admiralty required of the officers that the Surveyor of the Navy (whose house was in the yard at Deptford) be allowed to use the old coachhouse at the yard, 'heretofore in the use of the Treasurer of the Navy', for a stable, with the loft above it (*Cal S P Dom*, 1633–4, 139). The Treasurer of the Navy's house is not shown on the 1688 map (Fig 23, 'A' left) and so must have been demolished by this date.

Samuel Pepys visited the Treasurer of the Navy at his house at Deptford several times (eg *Pepys diary*, 30 July 1663; 24 January 1666; 4 March 1669). The last occasion suggests that the Treasurer of the Navy's house was standing until at least early 1669. John Evelyn dined with the king, the Duke of York and

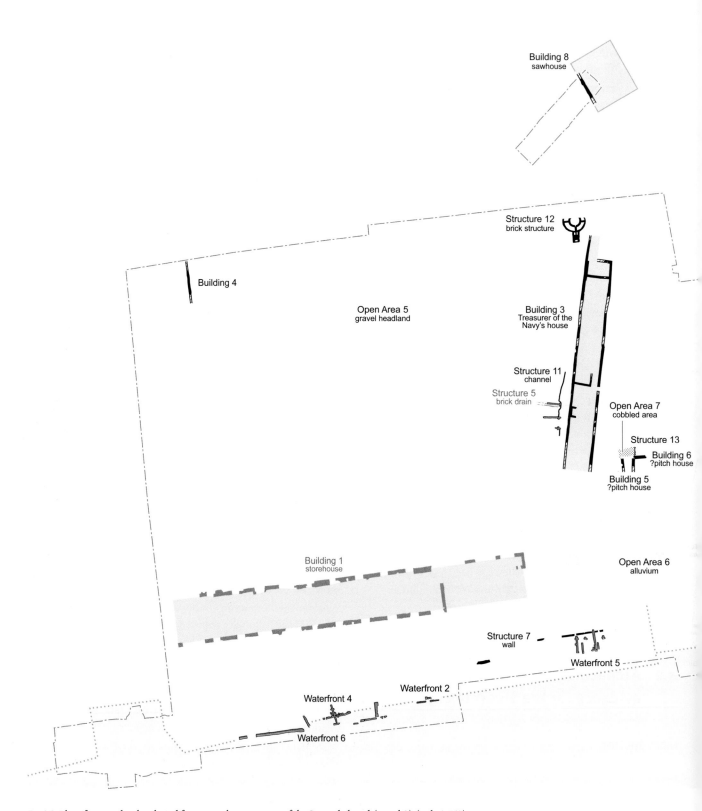

Building 8
sawhouse

Structure 12
brick structure

Building 4

Open Area 5
gravel headland

Building 3
Treasurer of the
Navy's house

Structure 11
channel

Structure 5
brick drain

Open Area 7
cobbled area

Structure 13

Building 6
?pitch house

Building 5
?pitch house

Building 1
storehouse

Open Area 6
alluvium

Structure 7
wall

Waterfront 5

Waterfront 2

Waterfront 4

Waterfront 6

Fig 25 Plan of principal archaeological features in the eastern part of the Stuart dockyard (period 3) (scale 1:750)

revetment

land-ties

Structure 10
perimeter wall

Structure 8
land-ties

wet dock

Structure 8
land-ties

revetment

Structure 8
land-ties

Structure 24
ay tie-backs

Structure 9
gate

Structure 10
perimeter wall

Building 7
?boathouses

apron

Waterfront 8

terfront 7

River Thames

0   25m

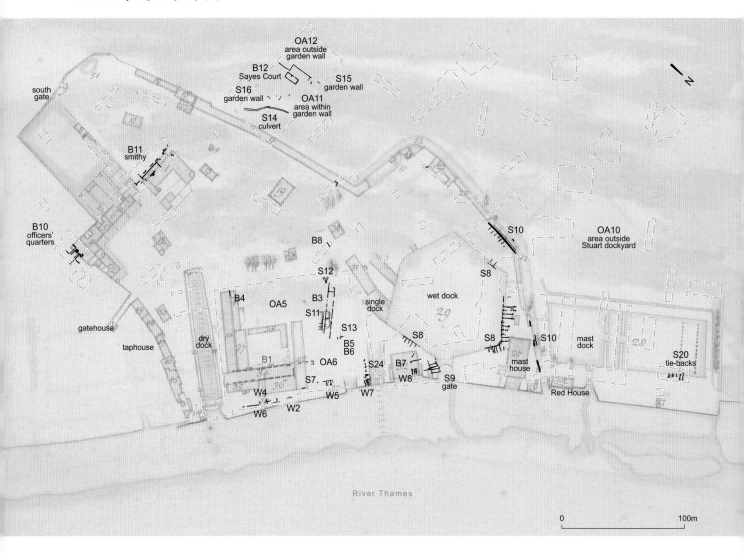

Fig 26 Plan of principal archaeological features in the Stuart dockyard (period 3) overlain on the 1698 map (Fig 23, 'B' right) (scale 1:3000)

other lords at the Treasurer of the Navy's house in 1662 – almost certainly in Deptford as they also visited Evelyn's grounds (*Evelyn diary*, 16 January 1662), but a later entry suggests that the building may have been standing even later than 1669. In the summer of 1684, Evelyn records dining 'at Lord Falkland's', then the Treasurer (ibid, 25 July 1684), but does not specify where. However, the following year Evelyn records the death of Falkland's wife, who he refers to as 'our neighbour' as Falkland was Treasurer of the Navy (ibid, 10 March 1685). Falkland was Treasurer from 1681 to 1689 (Mosley 2003, 1382), which suggests that his house was a neighbouring one to Sayes Court until at least 1681 and perhaps until at least 1684 when Evelyn dined with him.

The Treasurer of the Navy's house, therefore, seems to have been demolished some time between 1684 and 1688, apparently to make way for the 'Great New Store house' constructed at some point between 1688 and 1698, but probably soon after 1688, which formed part of the much enlarged Tudor and Stuart storehouse complex (above).

The tiled floor in the rebuilt Treasurer of the Navy's house consisted of plain unglazed Low Countries imports measuring 245–259mm square (Fig 28). Similar-sized Low Countries floor

tiles were used in a tiled surface along with stone paving cut from a shelly white limestone, probably a type of Purbeck limestone from Dorset.

Further fragments of Low Countries floor tiles were found in dumping associated with the Treasurer's house, along with brick, peg roofing tile and three mid to late 17th-century Dutch tin-glazed ('delftware') wall tiles. One of the latter shows part of a sea creature while another bears a ship design (<T4>, <T5>, Fig 29). It seems reasonable to assume that delftware wall tiles were installed in this building (B3) in the mid to late 17th century, probably set in fireplace surrounds, and images with a nautical theme would be fitting for the Treasurer of the Navy's house. Also present in dump/demolition debris was an earlier plain white tin-glazed floor tile, probably of late 16th- to mid 17th-century date.

Of particular interest are a number of brown-glazed pantiles, almost all of which were associated with the rebuilt Treasurer of the Navy's house. Black-glazed pantiles have been recorded from a number of sites in London, but these are the first examples glazed brown. They would almost certainly have been seen as prestigious items, hence their use in the rebuilt property. The pantiles are almost certainly Dutch, so may well

Fig 27 View of the 16th-/17th-century Treasurer of the Navy's house (the long narrow building in the centre) during the excavations, looking north

Fig 28 View of tiled floor at the north end of the rebuilt Treasurer of the Navy's house, looking south

<T4> <T5>

Fig 29 Dutch tin-glazed wall tiles showing a sea creature <T4> and a ship design <T5> (scale 1:2)

have arrived with the Dutch wall tiles (above) in the mid to late 17th century (Chapter 10.1). Such brown-glazed pantiles were very likely used for a new roof on the rebuilt Treasurer of the Navy's house.

A large quantity of pottery was spread among the various make-up and levelling layers associated with the rebuilt Treasurer of the Navy's house (161 sherds, 68 ENV, 7779g). While this material may not be directly derived from the use of the dockyard and could have been brought on to the site in the make-up, taken as a whole the pottery shares a number of characteristics with other maritime assemblages of the period (Chapter 10.3). Firstly, there are the Iberian (Seville, Spain or Merida, Portugal) olive jars (OLIV: 30 sherds, 7 ENV, 2353g), with four jars found in the fill of a posthole. This broken up 'amphora' material would have been well suited to provide packing and bedding for the timber. Fragments of a green-glazed bowl (SPGR), also thought to be of Sevillian origin, were retrieved from the same feature. The remaining imported pottery comprises ubiquitous Frechen stoneware (FREC) *Bartmann* jugs with their characteristic medallions (Gaimster 1997), here featuring the rosette design (Hurst et al 1986, 220, pl 44 (left)) which, together with the arms of the city of Amsterdam, is the most common medallion type found on archaeological excavations in London.

As is usual for the medieval and later periods, most of the pottery was sourced from pothouses in London or those in its local environs. London-area post-medieval red wares (PMR: 19 ENV, 4259g) feature in a range of bowl and cauldron/pipkin forms; of note are large-sized fragments from two storage jars found in a make-up spread and dump. Excavations in Spitalfields, London, have shown that these vessels were also used as 'pot sinks' in the brick floors of a number of 17th-century properties and their cellars (Harward et al 2015, 53, 54, 333, figs 35–6). A possible clue to their function is offered by the later two-handled stoneware jars of similar shape and size made at the Fulham pothouse, referred to as 'pickling pots' in late 17th-century price lists (Green 1999, 116, 123; 118, fig 95 nos 197–8). A small amount of decorative tableware was also present, comprising fragments of both chargers and plate forms made in London delftware (largely TGW C, D and F: 12 ENV) and dated to the second and third quarters of the 17th century.

A total of 70 clay pipe bowls and 12 stem fragments were recorded. The majority of the pipes recovered date to *c* 1660–80, with a small number of earlier types present; pipes gave a latest date of *c* 1680–1710 for posthole fill [2749] and *c* 1700–70 for dumped deposit [2024]. The tile, pottery and clay tobacco pipe from these various features combine to suggest that the house went out of use in the second half of the 17th century, reinforcing the documentary and cartographic evidence for its demolition in the period 1684–8.

The various make-up layers and external deposits associated with the rebuilt Treasurer of the Navy's house yielded eight other objects, of which one is an oak treenail. The four iron objects comprise a small knife (<S8>, Fig 30), an incomplete tanged ?chisel (<S29>, Fig 30), a mooring ring (<635>) and half a washer (<140>). Also present were two lead window cames (<212>, <213>) and some lead waste (<215>). The destruction debris contained a copper-alloy farthing <516>, possibly dating to 1613–49, and two small lead weights (<S33> and <S34>, Fig 193), along with copper alloy and lead waste (<515> and <537> respectively). In addition there are three pieces of green bottle glass, two of shaft-and-globe form, and 14 pieces of window glass, ten of which came from the posthole (above).

An unusual brick structure (S12, Fig 25; Fig 31) of unknown function is also likely to date from this period. The purpose of this structure (only partially excavated) is unclear but one possibility is that it was the base of an ice house serving the Treasurer of the Navy's house alongside. This would explain the lack of any residues on this 'industrial' building. A brick

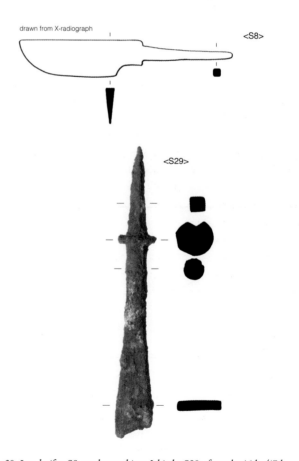

drawn from X-radiograph

<S8>

<S29>

Fig 30 Iron knife <S8> and tanged iron ?chisel <S29> from the 16th-/17th-century Treasurer of the Navy's house (scale 1:2)

Fig 31 View of brick structure (S12), looking north

culvert, square in cross section and leading north from the central part of the structure, would have acted as a drain or sump.

A later ice house survives in the Commissioner's garden at Chatham, but its design is the classic one of an egg-shaped brick structure, mostly below ground and covered with an earth mound; this design seems to have been far more common in England. The *Gardener's Chronicle* for 26 February 1842 does, however, illustrate a largely above-ground circular ice house in the centre of a circular cold store for fruit, the brick structure covered with an earth mound. A common feature in all these designs is the provision of a drain or substantial sump to take away the melt water, essential for an ice house to function effectively (J Coad, pers comm 2015).

The 17th- to early 18th-century timber Thames frontages

Waterfronts 4, 2 and 6 (Fig 25) excavated in front of the storehouse indicate a shift of the river frontage north into the river compared to the earlier 16th-century waterfront (W1, Fig 18; cf Chapter 3.2, 'Thames frontages'). Thereafter the position of the riverfront indicated by these structures and Waterfronts 5, 7 and 8 to the west (Fig 25; Fig 26) seems to have changed relatively little, advancing only slightly (eg W6) between that

shown in 1698 (Fig 23) and in 1725 (Fig 57) compared to the mid 18th-century waterfront (Fig 58).

The 1698 panorama (Fig 23) shows a timber river wall with vertical timbers which look like large 'fenders' (rubbing posts), rather than sloping front braces which would have prevented craft from coming alongside. The frontage shown appears to be of large timbers with the main posts hidden behind shuttering planks. Broadly similar structures with large fender posts were also recorded at the Woolwich royal dockyard, where rectangular-sectioned uprights were set at *c* 2.1m intervals in front of plank sheathing fastened to uprights on the landward side (Goodburn et al 2011). The 1774 model of Sheerness dockyard – on display in Chatham Historic Dockyard – clearly shows these timber wharfs with planking on the 'inside' of the upright posts (J Coad, pers comm 2015).

Waterfronts 2, 4 and 6

WATERFRONT 2

Approximately 0.3m to the north of the Tudor timber riverfront revetment (W1, Fig 18), a later timber revetment was partially exposed (part of W2, Fig 25; Fig 26). This timber frontage also ran east–west and was exposed for a length of *c* 2m where it had survived later damage. Three courses of 30mm thick, sawn oak planking set on edge as sheathing were identified. These lay on the riverward side of four squared oak uprights. Safety considerations prevented the full exposure of the frontage, but at the west end the remains of the top of what was probably a small sloping shoring timber (or 'front brace') were found on what would have been the riverward side. This could have been one of several timbers added to resist the landfill pressure from the south as a repair. As the later river frontage (W6, below) set to the north of the east end of this structure also had a set of front braces extending out into the foreshore, it too may have been a continuation of Waterfront 2, rather than post-dating it.

With a front brace timber added, the riverfront here could not have been a working wharf, although it may have been one when first built. The fact that the sheathing planking was set on the riverward side of the posts reflects typical river or wharf frontage construction on the Thames familiar from other sites from the 17th century onwards (Heard 2003, 35; Divers 2004, 51). This formed a flush frontage that could be repaired piecemeal at low tide. In the many earlier, 16th-century and later medieval, waterfront structures excavated in the region the sheathing planking has always been found on the landward side, that is the posts were set on the riverward or 'water' side. This reversal of basic procedure in revetment building for some post-medieval timber revetments may have been influenced by carvel ship construction, where the sheathing planking was robustly fastened to the water side of the ship's upright frame timbers.

WATERFRONT 4

Lying slightly further north than the river frontage represented by Waterfront 2, Thames frontage Waterfront 4 (Fig 25; Fig 26) extended eastwards for over 5m and comprised sawn oak planking *c* 50mm thick, set on edge on the riverward side of oak uprights. The oak uprights were substantial, with slightly varying rectangular cross sections centring on *c* 200 × 200–250mm, although some were thinner. The uprights were mainly hewn to shape and clearly installed in two phases or 'sistered'. Although the revetment could only be exposed for a total height of *c* 1m, it could be seen that the planking was fastened to the posts with large iron nails or 'spikes'. The uppermost plank had some redundant fastening holes and was probably a reused ship wale plank. A post-*c* 1600 date would be most likely on woodwork technology grounds (samples from the planking unfortunately could not be tree-ring dated).

It was possible to extract a sample of two uprights, timbers [2629] and [2619], from the structure to examine why they appeared to alternate and were set exceptionally close. The upright [2629] was found to have survived 2.53m long with a truncated top and a tenon on its foot which clearly showed that it had once been jointed into a morticed sill beam as part of a prefabricated, timber-framed frontage wall, like Waterfront 3. This timber-framed structure is interpreted as the first phase of timber frontage in this position and would have functioned as a wharf frontage north of the Tudor storehouse (B1). It appears that a group of damaged land-tie assemblies found just to the south-east of the frontage were probably also part of this structure. The timbers of this group were of oak, including a

virtually untrimmed oak log land-tie beam [2615]. A simple lap-joint for the lock-bar survived but no anchor stakes remained. This land-tie log was tree-ring dated with a felling date range of 1636–81 (Chapter 10.9; Fig 199). The original height of the structure must have been *c* 3m so that it required extra support from the land-tie assemblies, which were perhaps installed subsequently.

The second upright timber extracted, [2619], showed that this timber frontage then required substantial repair. An alternating set of oak piles with pointed feet were driven into the landfill between the original tenoned-in posts – a repair technique seen in Waterfront 3 (Chapter 3.2) and also in the 17th-century timber wet dock walls (below). Timber [2619], an example of these later repair pile uprights, survived only 1.18m long, having only been driven to a depth commensurate with the repair of the upper, more damage-prone parts of the structure. Additionally, assorted sloping front braces were set in the foreshore to help prop up the frontage which was being pushed northwards towards the river by the landfill pressure. These front braces included minimally trimmed round oak logs, such as timber [2617], and more squared timbers, and seemed to be ad hoc phases of work. Clearly, once the front braces were installed the frontage functioned principally as a river 'wall' rather than as the front of a working wharf where barges could easily unload.

The two, or possibly three, phases of construction of this section of river frontage as found may well have spanned a half-century or more, reaching well into the 18th century.

WATERFRONT 6

The fragmentary remains of a waterfront revetment (W6, Fig 25; Fig 26), comprising a set of front braces extending out into the foreshore, were also recorded slightly north of Waterfront 4 and Waterfront 2 (of which it perhaps was a continuation), in front of and parallel to the storehouse. The river frontage represented by these three revetments (W2, W4, W6) appears to fit broadly with that shown in both 1698 (Fig 23) and 1725 (Fig 57); Milton's map of 1753 clearly shows how much further into the river the waterfront and wharfs had reached by that date (Fig 58).

Waterfront 5

To the west of Waterfronts 2, 4 and 6, Waterfront 5 (Fig 25; Fig 26) consisted of five land-tie beams whose north ends extended into the northern limit of excavation. The longest beams [3288] and [3285] were respectively 3.85m and 3.20m long, with better-preserved land-tie [3285] anchored in place by two sets of lock-bars held by posts with chamfered tops. The land-ties cut across earlier Waterfront 3 and would have extended the face of the river frontage north by at least 1.9m.

Waterfront 7

To the west of Waterfront 5, adjacent to the east side of the western slipway (below, S24), a fragmentary structure (W7, Fig 25; Fig 26) survived as a pair of north–south aligned land-tie assemblies and an east–west line of six rectangular-sectioned posts. Although the post line was barely exposed, the land-tie assemblies were more fully uncovered. The western example was made of a slightly crooked oak log *c* 200mm in diameter fitted with one lock-bar and had one surviving anchor pile. This land-tie overlay two timbers of the adjacent slipway (S24). The eastern example, which appeared to have been repaired, was secured with a double lock-bar and four squared anchor piles. In both cases the lock-bars were held in place with lap-joints and fastened with an iron spike; neither survived to join the post line of the probable frontage. The slipway and waterfront structure may have been in use together.

Waterfront 8

Continuing to the west, between the western slipway (S24) and the wet dock, several north–south land-tie assemblies (W8, Fig 25; Fig 26) were exposed that were quite distinctive as the main north–south beams were made from hewn baulks of a coniferous timber (Fig 32). The corners of the baulks were left slightly rounded as they would have been naturally under the bark. The main beam baulks were large at *c* 400mm square and it is possible that they were left-over imported baulks ordered for mast making, although such timber was also used for

dockyard buildings and secondary ship structures by this period. Long, straight, relatively light coniferous timber was sought after for such work in large English dockyards from at least the 17th century. Each of the land-tie beams was fitted with a pair of oak lock-bars made of shipyard offcuts and originally had four squared oak anchor piles also of sawn oak offcuts. The assemblies clearly once extended to the north but had been sawn off during later building work (B55; Chapter 7.3).

The 17th- to early 18th-century western slipway (S24)

To the west, part of a slipway (S24, Fig 25; Fig 26) survived, consisting of a revetment of planks braced by tie-backs and extending north beyond the limit of excavation. The revetment had been backfilled with chalk and in places the planks had degraded, leaving only iron nails embedded in the edge of the chalk. This revetment is probably related to the western and larger of the two slips shown in 1698 and 1725, extending on to the foreshore, and could have formed the east side of the slipway. This must be the slip referred to in the 1709 survey as the 'Great Slip' 'near the Boathouse' which was in need of repair or renewal (above, 4.1) and a predecessor to a slipway (S30) rebuilt between 1753 and 1774 (Chapter 6.3).

Fig 32 View of land-tie assemblies associated with Waterfront 8, truncated (right, ie north) by the construction of the brick storehouse (B55), looking west

The wet dock rebuilt, 1658–61, and repaired, 1686

A note that the 'dock' was being cleaned in 1658 (*Cal S P Dom*, 1658–9, 403) is certainly a reference to the wet dock. In addition, there is supporting evidence that the wet dock was rebuilt at this time, as was often the case when it had been drained to clear the accumulated silt.

Deptford's wet dock was rebuilt not long before 1662 when there were urgent discussions about making a wet dock at Chatham. Sir John Mennes, Sir W Batten and Peter Pett urged the Navy Commissioners in a letter of 1 October to arrange a meeting at Chatham involving Captain Badily, Master Attendant at Deptford, Jonas Shish, the assistant, Mr Johnson, the Master Shipwright at Blackwall, and Mr Castle at Redruth to 'resolve the matter and estimate the charge'. 'Mr Randle, the house carpenter at Deptford that made the dock there', was also to be invited (*Cal S P Dom*, addenda 1660–85, 79). The wet dock was certainly in use and large enough to test John Evelyn's diving bell in summer 1661 (*Evelyn diary*, 19 July 1661; Chapter 9.2). This suggests that the wet dock was rebuilt in 1658–61.

A few years before, Sir Nicholas Crisp had proposed making a 'great sasse' on Evelyn's land, a giant wet dock capable of holding 200 ships. Evelyn met Crisp and viewed his designs in late 1655 (*Evelyn diary*, 30 September 1655; 27 November 1655). However, the wet dock rebuild is not Crisp's 'sasse', which had not been built by 1662, even in a scaled-down form. In 1662, Evelyn wrote that he dined with the king, the Duke of York

and other lords who 'viewed some of my grounds' about the project, but it was 'laid aside as a fancy' (ibid, 16 January 1662). Samuel Pepys records that Evelyn's father-in-law, Richard Brown, was against the idea: 'the ground, it seems, was long since given by the King to Sir Richard' (*Pepys diary*, 25 January 1662). Still on the drawing board, the plans were debated at Trinity House (ibid, 15 February 1662). It is difficult to say what influence Crisp's unrealised project – opposed by the Navy Board – had on the rebuilding of the wet dock at the yard, or even whether the new-built dock influenced his own thoughts (cf Oppenheim 1926, 355).

In his diary of 1667 Pepys records speaking with yard officials about the wet dock: 'To Deptford, and there I walked down the Yard, Shish and Cox with me; and discoursed about cleaning of the wet docke, and heard (which I had before) how, when the docke was made, a ship of near 500 tons was there found' (*Pepys diary*, 28 April 1667). It seems to be the case here that the wet dock was repaired or even rebuilt when the accumulated soil was being removed, Pepys's 'cleaning of the wet docke' coinciding with 'when the docke was made [ie rebuilt]' in 1658–61.

The wet dock (S8) was the largest of the timber structures recorded during the excavations (Fig 33). The woodwork record (Chapter 10.7) includes structural assemblies, raw materials, jointing, fastenings, constructional procedures and parallels. The basic structure was a polygonal, timber-revetted, watertight wet dock, with the gateway to the tidal Thames to the north.

Fig 33 View of the timber wall of the east side of the wet dock (S8) under excavation, looking north

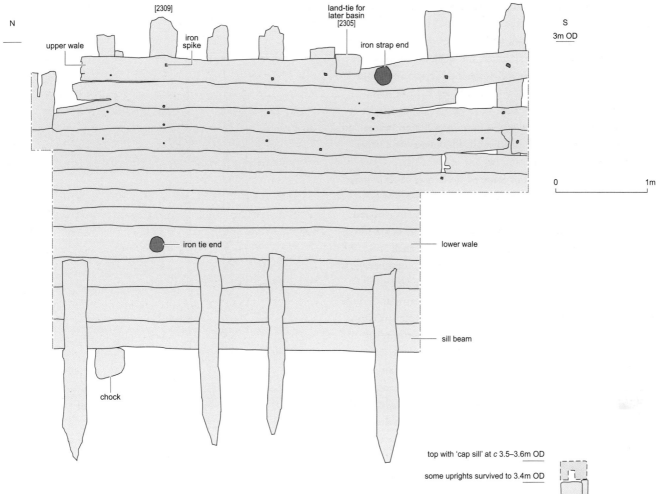

N

S
3m OD

upper wale
[2309]
iron spike
land-tie for later basin [2305]
iron strap end

iron tie end

lower wale

sill beam

0   1m

chock

top with 'cap sill' at c 3.5–3.6m OD

some uprights survived to 3.4m OD

iron strap end

upper land-tie

landfill

lower land-tie

However, this deep lining, erected in often wet and unstable deposits, could only resist the pressure of the ground behind it with the help of an extensive system of land-tie assemblies, or 'back braces' (Fig 33; Fig 34), resembling the front or back braces used for the river frontage revetments described above (W2–W4). This means that the footprint of the wet dock lay at least 10m beyond the more visible timber frontage of the basin itself, all around the perimeter.

The full depth of the walls of the wet dock could not be fully exposed due to logistical constraints and the risk of collapse, but it appears to have been at least 4.5m deep towards the south-east corner where briefly exposed in a very wet, machined test trench. Near the west side of the wet dock gateway a dock wall post was extracted that was 4.70m long, implying a depth of very roughly c 5m on that side. The highest upright top survived up to 3.40m OD, implying a minimum height of 3.50m OD or more (below). From other excavations of waterfront and shipyard sites just east of London we know that in the 1660s, when the timber dock seems to have been rebuilt, waterfront yard surfaces were typically built between c +3.0m and c +3.5m OD (eg Heard 2003, 48). The greater depth of the dock bottom on the north side towards the river would have aided drainage and the cleaning of the dock of silt, and also allowed slightly deeper-draft vessels to moor on the north side of the dock. This change in depth was probably accomplished by overlapping the sill beams of the dock wall

Fig 34 The 17th-century timber wet dock structure, on the east side of the wet dock (S8): upper – elevation of the exposed waterside west face; lower – partial cross section of the land-tie assembly bracing the frontage (scale 1:40)

frame in several steps with the highest to the south. The limited archaeological evidence for the variation in depth of the dock is supplemented by brief documentary sources. A letter of August 1668 reported that the 'depth of the wet dock is 13 foot water on the North side, or better, when the mud is out, and about 11 or 12 on the South side' (*Cal S P Dom*, addenda 1660–85, 273). The water-depth of 13ft (3.96m) and a greater depth of 14ft or more 'when the mud is out' might fit quite well with a total depth of roughly 5m to the dock wall, allowing a little height above the water level.

Variations in the layout of some of the details of the timber dock wall construction, raw materials used and levels of key features suggest that it was built in stages, possibly by different work gangs. Possibly about half of the structure was exposed in plan during the excavations but only a relatively small area along part of the east side and north-west corner, together with the east side of the gateway (below), could be exposed to perhaps half its surviving depth. In two small areas within those zones, small sections were machine-dug and the full surviving depth and form were observed and recorded in outline.

One key question was whether the early wet dock was a piled structure or made as a series of jointed timber frames like the walls of a large building. Using a mechanical excavator, it was possible to extract an original wet dock wall upright timber (5666]) from the northern edge of the structure. This timber was clearly a post tenoned into a sill beam (Fig 35). In other words, the wet dock wall was originally an enormous prefabricated timber-framed structure comprising substantial posts tenoned into sill beams anchored in place with location piles on the waterside and two tiers of land-tie assemblies on the landfill sides. It is also likely that the frontage would have terminated vertically in a top plate beam, but the uppermost tops of the posts had decayed or been truncated by later building activity. The original posts were all oak and appeared freshly-made for the job. They were square to rectangular in cross section, between c 200–225 × 250–275mm, and spaced at c 0.6m (2in) between the centres. The extracted post [5666] appears to have been typical; it survived c 4.7m long, having been originally c 5m or so, not including the 140mm long tenon at the base. It was made by sawing an axe-squared log into four 'box quartered' sections, leaving some sapwood and bark edge on one corner. The parent tree was slightly knotty, around 90 years old and c 0.7m in diameter when felled. Such a moderately fast-grown oak was probably of hedgerow or more likely open woodland origin and similar to those used in contemporary timber-framed buildings. We might hazard a general observation here that the style of woodworking used in this structure was more one of 'carpentry' than of shipwrightry, except perhaps for details of the fitting of some irregular sheathing planking noted below. This is unsurprising given that 'house-carpenters' were a separate part of a dockyard workforce from the shipwrights and seem to have been employed on fitting out accommodation in warships, as well as building and maintaining dockyard structures (Coad 1989, 151).

The timber wet dock wall was sheathed with sawn oak planking, c 35–55mm thick and of varying relatively narrow

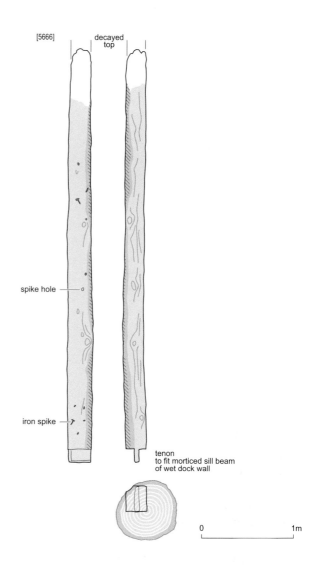

Fig 35 Timber upright [5666] from the 17th-century wet dock wall (S8) (scale 1:40)

widths of c 150–200mm and moderate lengths. The planks were fastened to the water- rather than landfill side of the posts with single iron spikes. These fastenings were staggered towards the upper then lower edges, with a pair at some but not all of the ends. No treenails were used. Some of the planks observed had notched edges like some ship 'anchor stock planking'. This use of notched edge planking was also found in some of the river and slipway walls at the Woolwich royal dockyard (Goodburn et al 2011, 320). Two bands of thicker waling planks were also found being used to bind together the posts; these were up to nearly 150mm thick and had bevelled corners to reduce chafe. The sheathing planking was surprisingly thin, bearing in mind that it would have had to withstand the impact of ships moving around in the wet dock. The sparing use of alternating iron fastenings gives the impression of efforts to economise. The inner face of the dock wall would have resembled the side of a small carvel-built ship as these usually also had thicker wales that protruded beyond the main planking at intervals.

The planking of the wet dock was repaired in places, such as at the north-west corner where a short section of carvel ship planking (timber [5635]) was fitted late in the life of the

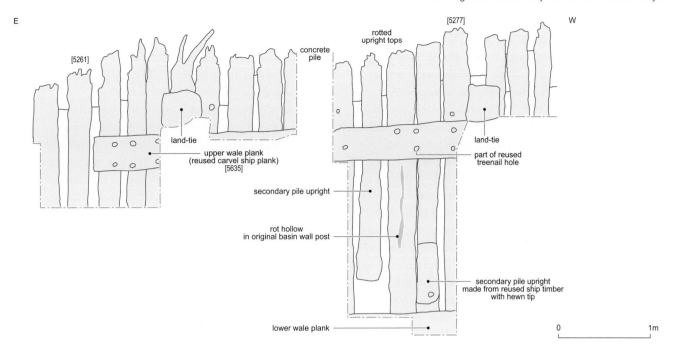

E

[5261]

concrete
pile

land-tie

upper wale plank
(reused carvel ship plank)
[5635]

[5277]

rotted
upright tops

W

land-tie

part of reused
treenail hole

secondary pile upright

rot hollow
in original basin wall post

secondary pile upright
made from reused ship timber
with hewn tip

lower wale plank

0   1m

Fig 36 The north-west corner of the 17th-century timber wet dock wall (S8) showing repairs: elevation of north (landward) face (scale 1:40)

structure to the back (landward) side (Fig 36). It could be
identified as such from the relict treenail holes and traces of
white lead paint. The planking was bent from its ship use and
this allowed it to be adventitiously used to fit a change in angle
of the wet dock wall.

Apart from the iron spikes used to fasten the sheathing,
large wrought-iron tie straps were also used at staggered
intervals, 'dogged' (stapled) to the sides or top faces of the large
land-tie beams; one example was retained (<S26>, Fig 37). This
technology allowed for a stronger and more easily fitted
connection than was normally achieved by the joints used in
late medieval waterfront carpentry. The use of iron tie straps
for this purpose dates from as early as the 1580s on the London
waterfront (Tyler 2001, 76). The land-ties were used at two
levels to retain the wet dock frontage, spaced *c* 2.4–3.0m apart.
The waterside ends of the iron ties were attached to the wale
beams in several ways: some had been forged into large domed
bolt heads while others were in the form of a strap. In a few
cases the straps had angled ('knee-shaped') ends with 'forelock
bolts' passing through the main posts and wales. Forelock bolts
were long or through-bolts with expanded heads, smooth
round shanks and a slotted tip through which an iron 'forelock'
wedge was driven against a washer to tighten them. The ends of
the land-ties near the posts were supported by sections of
planking nailed to the backs of the posts, and in some cases the
land-ties were lapped around the posts.

The land-tie beams were varied in shape, some being
minimally trimmed logs and others more carefully squared,
c 250–300mm in diameter. They were set in two tiers,
a system also employed at another wet dock of similar date at
Poplar Dock (archaeological fieldwork by AOC, site code
NPV07: D Goodburn, pers comm 2016). Most of the land-tie
beams were new and of oak. However, behind the north-west

<S26>

*Fig 37 Large iron dog or staple <S26> from the 17th-century timber wet dock
wall (S8) (scale 1:2)*

corner a group of much larger land-tie beams were identified, c 420–450mm square, made from a tough species of elm (given the date, probably native-grown). It is possible that these large timbers were used because the dock was built deeper at this point, nearer the entrance channel, but this is not entirely certain. Most of the land-tie beams were anchored in the landfill of estuary clay silt behind the dock frontage; where exposed in the west, two oak lock-bars spiked into lap housings were found. Each lock-bar had two or more anchor stakes, mainly made of sawn oak offcuts.

A detailed specification exists for the construction of a similar large wet dock at Blackwall yard, a short distance away at Poplar (Survey of London 1994). The specification was part of a contract of 1659 between the shipbuilder Henry Johnson senior (who had served his apprenticeship at Deptford) and local master carpenter George Sammon of Wapping (BL, Add Ch 13686). The timber dock wall was to be 16ft or 17ft (5+m) deep and sloping slightly outwards; the uprights were specified as piles rather than jointed posts, c 10in × 8in (250 × 200mm) set c 2ft (c 0.6m) apart. Only one tier of land-tie assemblies was specified, all to be fitted with large iron tie straps each weighing about 25lb (11.3kg). Although many of the dimensions of these timbers are rather similar to those of the Deptford wet dock, the piled rather than timber-framed frontage construction was quite different.

In July 1668, John Cox and J Uthwat wrote to the Navy Commissioners that 'the wet dock here is grown up with mud, having not been cleared since its making, so that, whereas it would have formerly receive fourth-rates of the greatest draft, a fifth-rate cannot now be taken in but at spring tides and, when in, they cannot wind in it' (Cal S P Dom, addenda 1660–85, 271). By 14 September, William Coll (also Cole or Coles), who had contracted to 'clear the wet dock of the slob, has nearly done half of it and may soon dispatch it', and by 24 September it was reported that 'by the end of next week [he] will finish' and that he had asked for an interim payment of £100 (ibid, 273, 275). The dock is likely to have been cleared of mud by the end of the autumn.

A 'new sluice' for the wet dock seems to have been built in the early 1670s. In August 1671, Jonas Shish sent the Navy Commissioners the estimated costings for a new sluice, also stating that 'the elm for the wet dock has come, but there is a great want of other elm' (Cal S P Dom, 1671, 454). In October that year, Shish sent the Navy Commissioners details of 'William Wood's beech timber, which will be useful for the new sluice', and suggested that the sluice should have 'three channels for the water to run out' (ibid, 523). No beech was found in this area of the excavation.

Both in the walls of the wet dock and the remaining eastern wet dock gateway (S9, below) a pattern of alternating oak uprights of slightly larger and smaller cross section could be seen. This indicated the possibility of an original build and a later phase of extensive repair, possibly also including raising the timber walls. From clay levelling deposits [4635] associated with the wet dock in this period came four clay pipe bowls and one stem fragment with a date of c 1680–1710; these include

part of a pipe with moulded 'mulberry' decoration, which is probably not London-made (<CP2>, Fig 178). A make-up layer contained a copper-alloy token <383> with the initials 'JV' under a crown on one side, but of unknown date; lead waste <214> and painted wood <751> were also found.

Just west of the wet dock entrance it was possible to excavate a deeper trench to explore the possibility of a secondary repair phase and examine the lower parts of the structure facing the landfill side (Fig 36). The smaller secondary uprights were found to have axe-cut pointed tips, that is, they were piles driven down to about half the depth of the wet dock timber wall. The timbers also had notches to allow them to be driven down to slot between the established frontage planking and thick planks fastened to the landward faces of the original posts used to support the land-tie ends. Many of the piles had redundant treenail holes in them and had clearly been cut down from old carvel ship frame timbers. Given that this rebuilding seems to have happened after considerable use of the wet dock over perhaps 20 years or so, it is likely that this work took place towards the end of the 17th century.

This interpretation is supported by documentary evidence. In May 1686 a royal warrant was issued authorising Pepys to sell 'several decayed and unserviceable ships and vessels', including seven at Deptford (below), 'for finishing the wet dock and gates at Deptford' as well as for works at Chatham and Portsmouth (Cal Treasury B, viii, 418–19). A letter from the officers to the Navy Board also refers to the wet dock being cleaned out and repairs made, including to its gates and apron, in the summer of 1686, aided by house-carpenters from Woolwich (TNA, ADM 106/3296, 13 September 1711, 43–4).

The wet dock entrance (S9) underwent extensive repair, or was rebuilt. In essence the construction of the entrance channel and gate area walls was very similar to that of the main dock walls. On the east side of the entrance gateway the channel to the dock basin survived and featured some very neatly fitted, oak lining planking similar to that of the rest of the dock. A deeper area of excavation to the east of the entrance revealed a complex intercutting jigsaw of land-tie assemblies where there were three timber frontages to retain the wet dock wall, the entrance channel and the Thames frontage not far to the north. As might be expected, a 'cat's cradle' of large land-tie assemblies had been built.

Due to the multiple phases of rebuilding and repair, the later, upper timbers of this area were difficult to associate clearly with tightly phased building campaigns. However, those lying on the large internal bolted beams (timbers [6410] and [3742]) do seem to date to a late phase of repair but one probably dating to somewhere after 1700. The majority of the timbers were of minimally trimmed oak but some were second-hand ship timbers, including parts of a large ship rudder post [3720] as well as a stern post [3718], both of which date to the 18th century (Chapters 9.2 and 10.7; Fig 196; Fig 197). Two lengths of copper-alloy strip/binding pierced by complete copper-alloy nails (<608>) were found together with structural timber [3720] in the wet dock entrance. Documentary and archaeological evidence attests the repair or rebuilding of the wet dock and its entrance channel at various times in the first half of the 18th century, before the failure of the wet dock gates in 1751 (Chapter 6.2, 6.3). The evidence for copper sheathing is interesting as it may well hint at a date in the later 18th century for this timber. Copper sheathing was proposed as early as 1708 but was not officially trialled until the 1760s; it was recognised as the only viable protection against shipworm and weed from 1775 and adopted for the fleet from 1779 (Cock 2001; J Coad, pers comm 2015). It may thus provide evidence of quite a later rebuild of the wet dock gateway area where it was found (Chapter 6.3).

It is possible that the reused, trimmed, carvel vessel frame timbers found in the rebuild of the dock may derive from some of the vessels Pepys was instructed to sell in May 1686 (above), particularly those at Deptford itself. Local ship-breakers at this time might break up naval vessels and then sell back usable timbers to the navy (Saxby and Goodburn 1998, 176). The vessels to be sold that were moored off the yard were listed as the fireships *Providence* (175bm-tons) and the *Thomas and Katherine*, the yachts *Anne* and *Deale* (100bm-tons and 28bm-tons), the sloops *Hound* (50bm-tons) and *Walwich*, and the 20-gun *David* (76bm-tons), a prize from the Scottish navy, captured and sold in 1685 (*Cal Treasury B*, viii, 418–19).

Building and repairing the mast dock, late 17th and early 18th centuries

Richard Browne sold part of Great Crane Mead to the Crown for the mast dock in the 1670s (BL, EP 39, 41, 46), and the mast dock seems to have been built early that decade. In May 1671, the Navy Commissioners sent the Duke of York the estimated cost of construction of a 'New mast dock at Deptford', a figure of £4114 (*Cal S P Dom*, 1671, 268). The mast dock was complete by 1688, when it is shown on the map dated to that year (Fig 23, 'A' left; Oppenheim 1926, 362). It was undoubtedly built in timber; its 0.06m thick timber lining (S20) was seen during the excavations in plan in a limited sondage near the north-east corner of the mast dock (Fig 38). It was braced by land-tie beams consisting of minimally trimmed oak logs *c* 300mm in diameter. The timber wharfs of the mast dock were repaired in 1700 (below) and also probably after 1709 (above, 4.1, 'The 1709 survey of the dockyard'), but the lining seen in the excavations seemed to date from earlier as the land-ties were very similar to those used in the timber wet dock rebuild of 1658–61 (above), with similar lapped and spiked-on lock-bars. The latter were retained with oak stakes, many of which appeared to be shipyard offcuts.

By March 1690, the wharfing of the mast dock was in very bad repair and needed to be made good with 'bricks or wood'; the officers asked the Navy Board for an order to carry this out (TNA, ADM 106/3289, 26 March 1690, np). Repairs were also under way on the mast dock in 1700, which required clay to be rammed. The officers recommended that this work be done by Deptford resident George Halsy who had supplied the yard with clay in the past (TNA, ADM 106/3292, 3 May 1700, 125). At around the turn of the 17th and 18th centuries, the river wall

Fig 38 View of the remains of timber lining and an associated degraded land-tie (S20) of the late 17th-century mast dock, looking north-east (0.5m scale)

near the mast dock was built, by contract, in brick (TNA, ADM 106/3301, 19 April 1727, 47).

Boathouses, a new oar maker's shop and other buildings, late 17th century

By June 1688, the yard officers reported that master bricklayer Thomas Shoor had completed the brickwork for three 'new boathouses where the old boathouses stood'. These had pantile roofs (TNA, ADM 106/3289, 30 June 1688, np). By August, Shoor had completed a further building 'with a brick wharf on the bank of the Mast Dock', also with a pantile roof (ibid, 7 August 1688, np). William Reynold was also paid for work on this building (ibid, 10 August 1688, np).

The panorama accompanying the 1688 and 1698 maps (Fig 23) shows a large rectangular three-gabled building fronting the river, with an additional building or annex to each side, between the wet dock (west) and a large slipway (east), keyed on the 1698 map as no. 32 'Boat-houses &c' and labelled no. 32 'Three Boat:houses' in the detailed survey of 1698. Fragmentary remains in this area may relate to these boathouses. A building (B7, Fig 25; Fig 26) was identified comprising three brick walls on timber baseplates, *c* 0.3m wide, that formed the south-east corner of a room surviving 8.6m+ long east–west by 2.3m+ long north–south. A series of related construction cuts and deposits suggested that there may have been two to three phases of building.

The room contained a number of surfaces. A tiled surface was constructed of plain floor tiles and brick. Two sizes of Low Countries floor tiles were present: green-glazed tiles measuring 176–177mm square (thickness 21–23mm) and larger tiles measuring 206–208mm square (thickness 31mm). One larger tile has an area of brown glaze, but this only covers part of the top surface so it is uncertain if this was deliberate or accidental; the other larger tiles are too worn to indicate whether they were glazed or unglazed. The tile surface also reused a number of small pink-coloured late medieval bricks, almost certainly imports from the Low Countries. Two brick types are represented, one measuring 183–187 × 86–90 × 41mm (fabric 3043), the other ? × 86 × 39mm (fabric 3208); the latter are from the same brick-making area as the bricks used in the pre-dockyard drain (S5) (Chapter 10.1). Another floor, made largely of brick, reused unglazed Low Countries floor tile, 205mm in breadth by 31–32mm in thickness, and peg roofing tile. Patches of very degraded timber floor also survived; the best-preserved consisted of 0.35m wide planks up to 1.40m long, supported on joists. A complete iron ring-headed spike (<S24>, Fig 39), several nails, and two clay pipe bowls dating to c 1640–60 were found in association with the timber floors. Boathouses were generally used for storing, repairing and maintaining warships' boats and, as only hand tools were used, few traces of such a building's use survive the departure of the craftsmen (J Coad, pers comm 2015).

In 1690, plans were made to 'take down the old Boat House, and erect it in another place'. Shoor had agreed to undertake the work. Old material was to be reused, including that from the 'workhouses and old Pitch House adjoining' – these buildings also presumably to be, or already having been, demolished (TNA, ADM 106/3289, 29 May 1690, np).

A more difficult building to interpret was located near the three putative boathouses (B7) in the north-west part of area 3 (Fig 3). This consisted of a small patch of tile and brick floor, the tile of 17th-century date and the bricks forming the edging reused from the medieval period. It is unclear if this was an internal or external surface as the areas that surrounded it had all been heavily truncated by later features. The remains of another small rectangular brick building were recorded in area 2

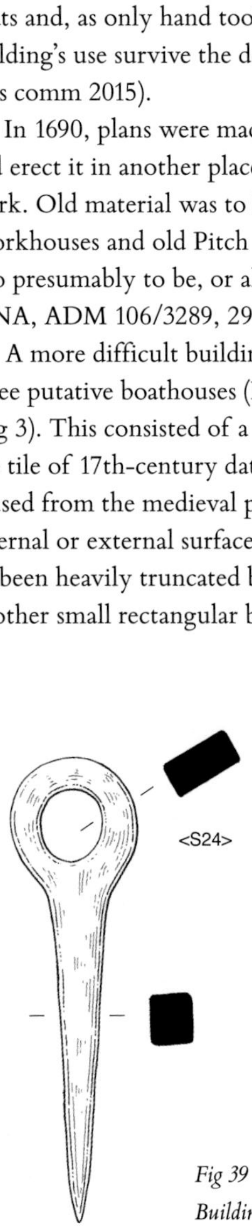

Fig 39 *Iron ring-headed spike <S24> from Building 7 (scale 1:2)*

<S24>

(Fig 3), largely truncated by the eastern edge of the 19th-century slipway. It appears to be a building shown on the 1698 map, but not identified in the key (Fig 23).

In May 1697, the Navy Board had given permission for the construction of a 'house for the Oarmaker over the ditch' (TNA, ADM 106/3292, 22 May 1697, 32). This is probably the 'Oar-makers shop' at the end of the range of 'Divers Offices' (no. 18 on Fig 23, 'B' right) on the 1698 survey, at the re-entrant angle of the yard's west perimeter wall.

Rebuilding the officers' quarters, late 17th century

The documented works

A major rebuilding and refurbishment of the yard officers' dwelling houses, including the Clerk of the Survey's, Clerk of the Cheque's and Surgeon's houses, was carried out in the late 17th century, with the internal fittings and roofing being carried out in 1689–90. The officers' quarters were situated on the east side of the yard, adjacent to and south of the gate (the lower gate) and gatehouse in the east wall of the yard (no. 1 on the 1698 map, Fig 23, 'B' right). The documented works and repairs here were complemented by the excavation, which revealed a number of building phases (shown on Fig 26; Fig 60; Fig 98) (below).

The 1698 map (Fig 23, 'B' right) shows this doglegging terrace while the 1698 detailed survey (Fig 40) shows the buildings in both plan and elevation. At the south-east corner of this terraced housing, walls (B10) corresponding to the Clerk of the Cheque's house on the map were recorded (below, 'Archaeological evidence'), together with sections of the yard/garden wall to the east (presumably parts of the brick wall between the Clerk of the Cheque's house and the yard gate blown down in 1703: below, 'Enclosing and paving the yard, late 17th to early 18th centuries'). The survey drawing shows a compact rear garden or courtyard area (and similarly to the rear of some of the other houses), apparently with an arrangement of paths/paving and beds or low hedging suggesting a parterre design (cf the garden parterres of this terrace shown on the 1774 scale model: Fig 66; Fig 96). This was a much more modest garden than, for example, the contemporary elaborate terraced garden of the Commissioner himself at Chatham dockyard (Coad 2013, 156–8). Nonetheless, the Clerk of the Cheque, the yard's accountant, was a senior dockyard official (Chapter 1.2). Official accommodation inevitably meant a transient resident population, although some officers might stay for years (ibid, 156). The size alone of the officers' terrace houses indicates that they were built with ample accommodation, not just for families but also for live-in servants (J Coad, pers comm 2015). Although there are few 'female' objects from inside the Deptford dockyard (Chapter 10.6), a variety of finds from the Royal Navy victualling yard at East Smithfield suggests that Deptford too would not have been an exclusively male establishment (Stevenson and Goffin 2010).

By November 1688, Shoor and Reynolds (*sic*) had built 'the framing of the 2nd floor to the houses … for the Clerk of

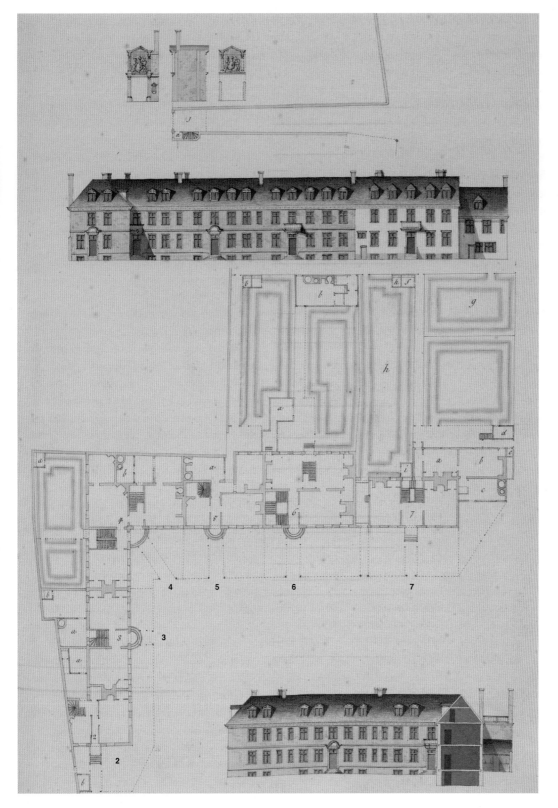

N

Fig 40 *The officers' quarters from the detailed survey of 1698: 2 – Surgeon's house; 3 – Clerk of the Survey's house; 4 – Clerk of the Cheque's house; 5 – Builder's (ie Master Shipwright's) assistant's house; 6 – Storekeeper's house; 7 – Master Attendant's house; north is to the bottom of the page (scale 1:500) (The British Library Board, Kings MS 43, fo 68r)*

Cheque, Survey and Chirugeon [ie Surgeon]'. Their contract evidently was for these buildings to be in the same style as earlier ones that were part of the same terrace, as the officers noted that the contract for the new buildings should be of 'the same form of Mr Barney built the Storekeepers House by

contract of 10th August 1686' (TNA, ADM 106/3289, 3 November 1688, np). A payment was due to Shoor and Reynolds early the next year (ibid, 25 January 1689, np) and the officers' houses were still under construction in February, with the Surgeon's house mentioned by name. A wall was also required to be built from the Surgeon's house to the yard gate – likely the east gate, the other gates being some distance from the houses. This was not in Shoor's contract, but he offered a price for a wall 'at what height your Honours [of the Navy Board] shall order' (ibid, 5 February 1689, np).

In March 1689, the yard officers were considering what stonework, paving and other works were still required for their new houses, including the internal fittings. The Clerk of the Survey's and the Clerk of the Cheque's houses (nos 3 and 4, Fig 23; Fig 40) were to have their washhouse and front passages laid in Purbeck stone, which was also to be used in the Clerk of the Cheque's kitchen. Wall pipes and chimneys were to be laid, and partition walls and ovens built. The rooms were to be 'wainscotted and painted' and both passages and yards laid with Purbeck stone. The officers suggest that 'there may be old stone enough, and indeed marble that belonged to the old houses to lay about ½ in these places' (TNA, ADM 106/3289, 6 March 1689, np). Wooden steps were to be made going up to the Surgeon's house (no. 2, Fig 23; Fig 40) and a wall built from the Surgeon's house to the yard gate. The door cases and window frames were to be built of 'Palisado' rails (ibid, 5 and 6 March 1689, np). The emphasis was on a uniformity of elegant design. 'Window shutters' were to be 'thrice primed and painted plain colours' (ibid, 14 March 1689, np). The houses were ready for the 'masons works' by August (ibid, 6 August 1689, np). The glazing was to be carried out by John Austin, who 'for several years past hath done all such work' (ibid, 14 August 1689, np), and the joinery was done by Richard Jonson for the 'new wainscoting of four rooms in the Clerk of Cheques House, two in the Clerk of the Surveys house and one in the Churgeons house' (ibid, 29 January 1690, np). The roofs of the new houses were being tiled with pantile in March 1690 (ibid, 19 March 1690, np).

In summer 1712, the officers reported that the timber fence between the gardens from the Master Attendant's house to the Clerk of the Survey's house (nos 7 and 3, Fig 23; Fig 40) needed to be replaced. Their preference was clearly for a brick wall; the cost to replace in brick at £15 was £1 10s cheaper than wood. To aid the Navy Board in their decision, the officers pointed out that brick is 'more durable' (TNA, ADM 106/3296, 24 June 1712, 97).

Archaeological evidence

Walls corresponding to those of the officers' quarters were identified during the excavations. The 1698 map shows this terrace of buildings running along the east boundary of the yard, running north–south and then doglegging west (Fig 23). The excavations uncovered walls (B10, Fig 26; Fig 41) that appear to match the building labelled '4' in 1698 (Fig 40), referred to in the map key as the 'Clerk of the Cheque's house', together with sections of wall running north which correspond to the yard perimeter wall (Fig 144). A Frechen stoneware (FREC) *Bartmann* jug, complete except for its handle, was found beside a truncated wall ([5428]). The jug shows the mid 17th-century 'pear'-shaped (Noël Hume 1970, 56–7, fig 5)

development of this form, with a medallion displaying a four-petalled flower (<P1>, Fig 42), and is apparently an uncommon design. A George III penny <610> found in another wall ([5436]) of the building must be intrusive or part of a rebuild as it dates from 1806.

A number of distinctive, very fine sandy 17th-century bricks (fabric 3257) had been used in the construction of the officers' quarters (B10). These were probably made in brick clamps in New Cross to the south-west of Deptford (Proctor et al 2000, 187), in common with some bricks in the tar house (B6, below). Five clay pipe bowls and one mouthpiece were recovered, giving a date of c 1680–1710 for context [5872], although the mouthpiece (in context [6438]) could come from a late 18th- to early 19th-century form of pipe. Part of the stem of a glass ?candlestick <621> and a sherd from an octagonal wine bottle were present in the backfill of soakaway [6526] in the officers' quarters.

A large dump of domestic waste in the area of the officers' quarters was also identified ([6013], OA5), providing a fragmented picture of the material culture of those in control of the yard. This dump contained 257 sherds of pottery from up to 112 vessels (4963g), together suggesting a mid 17th-century date for discard. The condition of this material suggests frequent redeposition: few profiles could be reconstructed and most vessels survived as a few cross-joining sherds only. London-made tin-glazed wares (TGW) (28 vessels) comprise up to 15 tableware dishes or chargers decorated in styles common in the second to third quarters of the 17th century (TGW D: decorated with eg blue-dash rims, intersecting arcs, fruit and flowers: cf Orton and Pearce 1984). Pottery sourced from Continental Europe accounts for the remaining decorative tableware, with vessels from Portugal and Italy, including joining sherds of a Montelupo maiolica polychrome (MLTG POLY) tazza with 'fruit and foliage' decoration (cf Hurst et al 1986, 15, fig 2.4), north Italian marbled slipware (NIMS) bowls (ibid, 36–7, fig 14.30) and a north Italian (Pisa) sgraffito ware (NISG) dish decorated in a floral style (ibid, 32, fig 13.25). Storage vessels are represented by olive jars (OLIV) from Seville or Merida and a Midlands purple stoneware (MPUR) butterpot. No overall picture otherwise emerges from the remaining pottery, which mainly comprises highly fragmented household wares (mostly bowls and dishes) in Surrey-Hampshire border wares (BORDB, BORDG, BORDY, RBOR) together with London-area post-medieval red wares (PMR, PMSRG) and some Essex red wares (METS, PMBL, PMFR).

Perhaps the most significant ceramic find from the entire site was made in this layer of domestic waste, namely the right paw of a London-made tin-glazed ware (TGW) 'cat jug' (<P2>, Fig 43). Fourteen complete delft 'cat jugs' are recorded in museum and private collections, with eight dated examples ranging between 1657 and 1677 (R Massey, pers comm 2015). These include one in the Museum of London (MOL acc no. 6236: Britton 1987, 126, fig 79). Another whole example, bearing the date 1672 and initials 'EL', is in the Chipstone Foundation in the United States (acc no. 1985.5), while the third, bearing the date 1669 and initials 'WP', is displayed in the

Fig 41 Views of walls of the officers' quarters (B10) revealed during the excavations: upper – looking north, with a modern concrete base in the foreground (right) and the angled dockyard perimeter wall; lower – looking south-east

Fitzwilliam Museum in Cambridge (object no. C.1330-1928). Privately sold by the auction house Christies in 2008 (sale 7561, London, 18 June 2008, lot 128), a fourth complete example bears the date 1659 and the initials 'L/^{W}/I' in a triangular arrangement (Sainsbury 2008). A complete cat jug in the collection of Lady Charlotte Schreiber in the Victoria and Albert Museum (acc no. 414:821-1885) bears the date 1676 (Fig 43). Part of a cat jug was also found on the site of the William Drummond Plantation near Williamsburg, Virginia (Austin 1994, 17). The only other find from a London archaeological

<P1>

Fig 42 17th-century Frechen stoneware Bartmann jug <P1> found in association with the officers' quarters (the Clerk of the Cheque's house) (scale c 1:4)

<P2>

Fig 43 Right paw of a 17th-century London-made tin-glazed ware 'cat jug' <P2>, from a dump of domestic waste in the area of the officers' quarters (OA5) (period 3) (scale c 1:2); (right) a complete example with a heart-shaped cartouche with the initials 'LTM' and date '1676' on the cat's chest (V&A, acc no. 414:821-1885)

clustered between 1657 and 1677, suggesting that they were made towards the end of the Commonwealth and during the reign of Charles II. Other than the cat jug figures, London and Bristol delftware potters in the late 17th century only made male and female images (eg Archer 1997: V&A C.225-1991), and it was not until the 18th century that other animals, such as the lioness (eg ibid: V&A C.80A-1796), were added to their repertoire of (occasional) products. The making of cat jugs appears peculiar to the London pothouses and does not follow a tradition in Dutch delftware, which instead produced ornate and skilfully made monkeys, parrots, dogs and squirrels.

The same dump of domestic waste contained a small copper-alloy ring <404> (diameter 17mm), a glass lid <771> and fragments of glass from three wine bottles, a case bottle, two bell-shaped phials and three windows. Two of the bottles are of shaft-and-globe and onion form and are consistent with the mid 17th-century date of the pottery (above), but one rim with bulbous neck appears to be from an early cylindrical bottle dating to the later 18th century. A Victorian halfpenny dated 1887 (<207>) and a flint brick <692> recovered from a pit are certainly intrusive. Most of the total of 45 clay pipe bowls, 50 stem fragments and seven mouthpieces found in features associated with the gravel headland (OA5) came from this dump of domestic waste and date to c 1660–80. One unusual example (<CP1>, Fig 178) has fleur-de-lis stamps all over the bowl (a type AO18). A small fragment of tin-glazed floor tile with the fashionable 'Tudor rose' pattern in blue and white (<T1>, Fig 174) was also recovered from Open Area 5.

Rebuilding the smithy and other works, late 17th century

In autumn 1699, the officers were reporting that the smithy was 'much out of repair'. The work on 'the greatest part of the roof', building the forge chimneys and other repairs was more than the yard's own bricklayers could manage and needed to be done before winter (TNA, ADM 106/3292, 14 September 1699, 105). Most of the bricks used in the walls of the smithy (B11, Fig 26; Fig 44) in this period would seem to be a mixture of

excavation, surviving as two upper breast fragments, is from the site of Shakespeare's Globe theatre in Southwark (site code ACT89, context [368]). No biscuit-fired examples have been identified from the numerous London delft pothouses that have been excavated (Bloice 1971; Tyler 2001; Tyler et al 2008).

Cat jugs have a number of features in common when found whole. Firstly, they appear to be commissioned pieces that carry the initials of their owner. The jug sold at auction by Christies deviates slightly in that the triangular arrangement of three initials follows the convention used on objects such as glass bottle seals, lead trade tokens and, on delftware, for displaying the initials of a married couple. Secondly, the dated jugs are

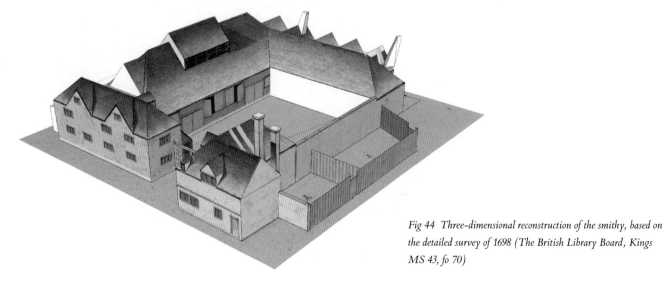

Fig 44 Three-dimensional reconstruction of the smithy, based on the detailed survey of 1698 (The British Library Board, Kings MS 43, fo 70)

pre- and post-1666 (Great Fire) types, including a particularly long (292mm long) brick in one wall in an unusually fine clay (fabric 3224), which possibly dates to before 1600 and may have been brought in from outside the London area (Chapter 10.1). An area of masonry incorporated a plain green-glazed Low Countries floor tile dating to *c* 1480–1600. Part of a glass jar <685> was found in structural feature [5586] in the smithy, while an iron structural fitting <669> and a piece of lead <683> were found in a wall.

The main backfill [6405] of a cesspit associated with the rebuilt smithy (B11) was filled with a range of pottery dated *c* 1630–50, recovered in a fragmented and poor condition, with few joining sherds. It was found alongside five clay pipe bowls and 16 stem fragments, dating to *c* 1680–1710, whose later date could suggest that much of the ceramic material had been broken and discarded elsewhere before being finally dumped in this pit as fill, perhaps sourced from a midden or from yard or building cleaning episodes. Alternatively, the ceramics may simply have continued in use into the later 17th century. Cooking vessels make up most of this pottery group, with tripod pipkins in Surrey-Hampshire border white ware with green and clear (yellow) glaze (BORDG, BORDY) and cauldrons/pipkins in London-area post-medieval red ware (PMR, probably from Deptford). Tableware is restricted to a single sherd from a London tin-glazed ware (TGW D) charger, with Wan-Li panel border and central daisy pattern (cf Noël Hume 1977, 45, pl 45). The range of imports is similar to that from the Stuart dockyard generally, with fragmented Frechen stoneware (FREC) jugs, Iberian amphorae/jars (SPOA) and, for the first time, starred costrels (STAR, three upper profiles). The cesspit also contained two small coins, one of Charles I dated to 1625–49 (<535>) and the other a 17th-century token or farthing (<773>), and two small pieces of copper-alloy strip (<734>). A Portland stone internal moulding with traces of two layers of

grey paint covering the outer decorated surface (<754>, Fig 45) may be from a door or window; such stonework became popular after the Great Fire of 1666.

Other works carried out in the late 17th century included repairs to a crane, repairs to the Storekeeper's house and the installation of a weighing machine for cables (ie anchor ropes). In October 1662, the Navy Commissioners issued a warrant for the crane to be repaired and for 'making a pair of stairs' at the yard (*Cal S P Dom*, addenda 1660–85, 79–80). In November 1662 Jonas Shish and Edward Rundells estimated that this crane repair and making stairs down to the water at the yard would cost £66 9s 11d (*Cal S P Dom*, 1661–2, 543). In April 1664, Thomas Harper, the Storekeeper at the yard, sent an estimate of £27 for repair of his house (*Cal S P Dom*, 1663–4, 543). In 1665 there was a 'King's beam' at the yard that was used to weigh cables (ie anchor ropes) (*Cal S P Dom*, 1664–5, 342). At the same time, Jonas Shish also recommended to the Navy Commissioners the construction of 'a house crane, to go with a wheel of 14 feet, by the new launch in the plank yard' at an estimated cost of £217 10s 8d; the crane would be 30ft long, 13ft wide and 30ft high (ibid, 343).

Enclosing and paving the yard, late 17th to early 18th centuries

In the 17th century, most of the yard perimeter is likely to have been a timber fence. Reference was made in September 1634 (apropos the keeping of the gates and keys by the porters and (at Deptford) the Clerk of the Cheque) to the Lords of the Admiralty having ordered that the fences should be repaired and doors kept locked (*Cal S P Dom*, 1634–5, 213–14). Brick began to replace timber in the perimeter, but this was not without problems. The brick wall between the Clerk of the Cheque's house and the yard gate – presumably the one built by Shoor in

<754>

Fig 45 Portland stone moulding <754> from the late 17th-century fill of a cesspit associated with the smithy (B11) (scale 1:2)

the late 1680s (above) – blew down in a storm in November 1703. The gap was blocked with old materials as there was some uncertainty about the ownership of the wall and the ground it stood on, but the owner of the adjoining land, Mr Vittelles, now 'disclaimed all right thereto', and the officers asked the Navy Board about erecting a new wall of '3 Rodd of brickwork' (TNA, ADM 106/3295, 18 November 1709, np).

By March 1711, there were plans to build a brick wall, some 823ft (250m) in length, to enclose what is described as the north-west side of the yard, but 'the ground is so loose and soft that it is incapable of bearing the intended wall, unless a timber foundation be made'. 'Piled and planked foundations' would

cost £674, planked only £415 8s, and building the wall itself £1017 10s (TNA, ADM 106/3295, 29 March 1711, np).

A ditch ran along the north-west perimeter of the yard, annotated on the 1698 map as 'A lake of water to wash the Docks' (Fig 23, 'B' right, no. 52). In addition, this waterway would have served to channel the *Orfletediche* and any flood water away from the dockyard (Chapter 2.2). At this time, the area outside the dockyard boundary here would have been marsh and is labelled as 'The Ten Acre or Great Meadow' in a map of 1712 (BL, Add MS 78629 K). The ditch was revetted in timber associated with a timber fence (S10, Fig 25; Fig 26; Fig 46; Fig 47) that formed this part of the perimeter until it

Fig 46 View of timber ditch revetment (S10), seen here below the later dockyard perimeter wall, looking north

Fig 47 View of timber ditch revetment (S10), with a land-tie passing through the built-in arch of the later dockyard perimeter wall (behind), looking south

was replaced in brick in 1714–15 (TNA, ADM 106/3296, 19 February 1714, 174). The later wall had probably removed all traces of the fence (it was not identified in the excavations). Fragments of the revetment, however, were recorded on both sides of the later wall in excavation area 12. On the east (inside) side of the wall the remains consisted of simple oak log land-tie assemblies at regular intervals. These assemblies were made up of east–west aligned log beams with lap housings holding lock-bars anchored by two small round oak piles. The log land-tie beams were relatively small (*c* 150–200mm diameter) and their west ends were truncated by the later brick wall. They were clearly intended to retain a north-west to south-east aligned revetment along the east edge of the ditch, fragments of which survived as a line of three rectangular-sectioned oak uprights on the west (outside) side of the later wall recorded in area 2 of the excavations. An east–west wall (S7, Fig 25; Fig 26) parallel to the river, but set slightly back from it, may have marked a boundary.

In February 1700, several places in the yard needed repaving. Loose stone was collected for this purpose (TNA, ADM 106/3292, 4 February 1700, 117) and the 'paveiour' was ready to begin this work in the summer (ibid, 17 July 1700, 129).

The Master Shipwright's house, 1708

The Master Shipwright's house in the north-east corner of the yard was probably built in 1708 as its windows were being fitted with glass in the spring of the following year (TNA, ADM 106/3295, 3 May 1709, np). John Ryalls had carried out the mason's works on this house 'lately built' (ibid, 9 May 1709, np). The Master Shipwright's house is depicted in Fig 61 in 1747; the surviving Grade II★ listed building, which has been extensively remodelled since 1708, together with a north-east range of brewhouse and offices (dating to *c* 1710 and 1809), is clearly visible on Fig 4 photographed in the mid 1990s (Historic England listing designation: https://www.historicengland.org.uk/listing/the-list/list-entry/1213984, last accessed 27 May 2016). In January 1711, the Master Shipwright requested a new garden out of land acquired east of the yard, and the replacement of his brewhouse if taken down (above, 4.1, 'Expanding the yard eastwards, and to the Isle of Dogs, 1710'). The cost of a wharf from the Master Shipwright's garden to the wharf at the river, and a brick wall to enclose it, was estimated to cost £834 14s (ibid, 31 March 1711, np).

Possible pitch houses and a 'sawhouse'/slipway wall

Building 5 (Fig 25; Fig 26) survived as a 1.70m long brick wall, 0.45m wide, and a separate brick rubble foundation, both running north–south, between the storehouse (B1) and the wet dock. It was associated with a surface made of angular stone (OA7, Fig 25) which survived in two areas (4.20m × 3.10m and 3.50m × 1.70m in size), presumably representing some sort of yard. The cobbles included mottled coarse white and creamish-brown granite and what appeared to be black, fine-grained

limestone; fibrous caulking material <645> was recovered from this stone surface. An adjacent structure (S13, Fig 25; Fig 26) on the west side of the cobbles consisted of a rectangular block of bricks, measuring 0.50m × 0.30m, attached to a curved structure of brick and mortar, 0.92m long and 0.18m wide. A large midden, 2.00m × 1.70m in size and consisting of concretions of pine tar, hair, shredded wood, pebbles and ceramic building material lay next to the structure. This striking feature seems to be a deposit of waste pine tar. Tar was heated to remove impurities; there was, however, no surviving fireplace or hearth in either Building 5 or Structure 13. The tar midden and the proximity of these buildings to a dock and slipway where pitch would be needed for caulking the ships might suggest that they were associated with the process of making pitch, but these were very fragmentary remains. A demolition deposit over the cobbles (OA7) yielded part of a large straight-sided screw bolt (<558>) derived from a construction of some size (Chapter 10.6).

Building 5 was demolished and backfilled, and was succeeded by a further fragmentary building (B6, Fig 25; Fig 26). This latter building survived as a 3.10m east–west length of brick wall, 0.47m wide and 0.28m high, which had been extended by a later addition, an east–west aligned wall 2.20m long. The building contained a number of distinctive, very fine sandy 17th-century bricks (fabric 3257) like those used in Building 10 (above, 'Rebuilding the officers' quarters, late 17th century – Archaeological evidence') and which were probably made in brick clamps in New Cross (Proctor et al 2000, 187; Chapter 10.1). Backfill over the walls yielded two clay pipe bowls and nine stems, dating to *c* 1680–1710, a (plain) lead cloth seal (<S17>, Fig 48), lead window cames <216>, two small fragments of glass from a phial and a window, and part of the neck of an onion bottle. There is no direct evidence that Building 6 was a pitch house, but as the building succeeded Building 5 in the same location this is a possibility. Ancillary royal dockyard industrial buildings like these no longer survive but are documented; by the mid 18th century pitch houses were generally brick-vaulted, like that at Chatham, to contain the spread of fire (Coad 2013, 144).

Both buildings had been considerably truncated for the construction of the floor of slipway Structure 27 in the late 18th century (Chapter 6.3). A large square-headed clench nail (<556>; length 130+mm, head *c* 37 × 37mm) was found in one of the levelling deposits for this construction, together with six clay pipe bowls, 17 stems and one mouthpiece, dating to *c* 1660–80, in another.

<S17>

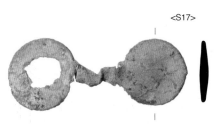

Fig 48 Lead cloth seal <S17>, from backfill over the demolished walls of ?pitch houses (B5/B6) between the wet dock and the storehouse (scale 1:1)

A brick wall (B8, Fig 25; Fig 26) seen south of the wet dock corresponded to the location of a building on the 1688 and 1698 maps, keyed as a 'Sawhouse' on the latter (Fig 23, 'B' right, no. 30). However, the deep, sloping wall seems more likely to have been the east wall to a slipway or dock. Such structures nearby would include the single dock or the slipway before it, although the position of the wall does not correspond to these structures where they are shown on maps; yard plans are not, however, always accurate.

The west part of the site, consisting of alluvium (OA6), yielded a number of finds, among them clay pipe bowls (including a single type AO15) and stem fragments giving a date of *c* 1660–80. A number of very worn, glazed floor tiles made from an undiagnostic, slightly fine sandy clay (fabric 2324) were found in dump deposits. Part of a copper-alloy chain attached to an iron fitting (<S37>, Fig 195) and a bone counter (<S13>, Fig 187) were recovered from a make-up layer.

Rebuilding the dry dock and its gates, 1711–13

The Navy Board ordered the widening of the wharf by 4ft on 'the northwest side of the dry dock gates' in 1699. The officers reported that this would take six months to complete, but warned that the gates were 'extraordinarily defective' and could not be trusted; they asked for a new pair to be built (TNA, ADM 106/3292, 26 May 1699, 94). The gates were not the only problem with the dry dock. By October the officers were reporting that they had had to 'cut some of the wharf down' to widen the entrance, presumably to allow a ship into the dock. The rest of the wharf was decayed and needed 'to be made new' and the apron was also 'very bad' (ibid, 15 October 1699, 44).

A major rebuild of the dry dock was proposed in late summer of 1711, its wharfs having 'been a considerable time under decay' (TNA, ADM 106/3296, 11 August 1711, 36). Part of the wharf had been taken down, in fact, to allow the easier launch of the ship then in the dock, revealing the 'mud cells [as the lower sill beams (the mudsills) of the wharf wall were then known] and groundways of the apron to be unserviceable'. The officers estimated the cost of 'inlarging the Dock to 49ft broad' and 'to lengthen it to 32ft making a return wharf to the river, taking down and so fixing the crane, and removing the stair of the Watergate for the more convention placing of the capston' to be £2145. Alternatively, a simple repair, with new gates, apron and wharf, would cost £1515.

The Navy Board opted for the more ambitious scheme as the officers requested the loan of 'the Woolwich lighter' to help 'take away the soil and rubbish made by inlarging the Dry Dock', Deptford's own 'small lighter' being insufficient (TNA, ADM 106/3296, 10 September 1711, 40). The gates were taken into the upper part of the dock to be rebuilt (ibid, 23 September 1713). With an eye to the completion of the dry dock work before the onset of winter, the officers asked the Navy Board for Trinity House carpenters to be engaged and to work extra time (ibid, 20 August 1711, 38). The 'dirty and difficult' work prompted the house-carpenters to ask for extra allowances – they had received these last in 1686 when repairing the wet dock (ibid, 13 September 1711, 43–4). The extra money was forthcoming to encourage the work, which was 'near at end' by the close of the year (ibid, undated but almost certainly December 1711, 61).

The rebuild had to be suspended to allow work on the 2nd-rate, 158ft × 42½ft ship the *Shrewsbury* (1257bm-tons) to go ahead and the dry dock was not fully complete until 1713. When this ship, rebuilt as 1314bm-tons, was put out, all that remained was work on the bottom of the dock which was done in late 1713. The officers could report that 'by laying a new apron we gained 18 ins more water at the stern of the dock than before and 15 ins in the middle'. The groundways in the bottom of the dry dock were lowered so that the next ship for rebuilding, the 2nd-rate, 163ft × 46½ft *Barfleur* (1476bm-tons), could be accommodated (TNA, ADM 106/3296, 23 September 1713, 157).

5

Sayes Court (16th to 19th centuries)

5.1 Historical introduction

Sayes Court before Evelyn, 16th century to 1652

In 1528, the manor of Sayes Court was awarded to William Capon, Dean of Ipswich, by Thomas Wolsey (*L and P Hen VIII*, iv, 1987–2002). The pastures of Sayes Court were in the charge of Edmund Peckham, the Cofferer of the King's Household, from 1535 onwards, while John Johnson, the bailiff of the manor, had been appointed by the Duke of Suffolk in 1516. He held manorial courts at the manor house once or twice a year. Stray sheep within the manor were seized by Peckham for the royal court's table (BL, EP 36; TNA, SC 6/HenVIII/6024, /6025, /6026). In 1537–8 the barn at Sayes Court was repaired and a new pinfold (enclosure) was made (TNA, SC 6/HenVIII/6025). In 1578–9 the manorial account was drawn up by Richard Bull, deputy to the queen's bailiff of the manor, Sir George Howard, and the demesne lands were still held by the cofferer (BL, EP 36).

In the late 16th and early 17th centuries, as clerks of the Board of Green Cloth (the main instrument of organisation and accounting for the royal household, presided over by the Lord Steward), the Browne family of Sayes Court supplied the slaughterhouse with cattle, sheep and other animals grazed on their fields at Broomfield nearby. The buildings at Sayes Court included 34 bays of ox-stalls, eight of which were reserved for the monarch's cattle. These structures were in need of repair in 1599 and 1608 and had been demolished by 1649 (BL, EP 37; TNA, LR 2/196, fo 166v; TNA, E 317/Kent/56, fo 2). A survey of 1660 noted that the ox-stalls and stables were formerly 300ft (92m) long (BL, EP 38).

In the 16th century a gateway was added to the manor house. An undated survey of the second half of the century, made by the queen's auditor John Ashton, mentions 'a meane house and a barn' as belonging to the lordship of Sayes Court (BL, EP 36). The whole house was rebuilt on the same site in 1568. Late in the 16th century the manor house was separated from the manor and estates were attached to it, taken from the demesne lands of the manor. In 1585 it passed by lease to the Browne family, and eventually to their descendants the Evelyns in the 17th century (Drake 1886, 7–9).

It is clear from a later survey that the demesne lands of the manor (in the hands of the cofferer and later the Brownes) all lay to the south, west and north of the manor house. They comprised Broomfield, Broadmarsh (alias Mould Meadow), Barn Close, New Marsh (alias Neale's Marsh or Eight Acres), Bottom Mead (alias Five Acres), Twenty-Six Acres, Potte Mead and Great Crane Mead. Only the northernmost field, Great Crane Mead, had a frontage on the River Thames, stretching as far north as Earl's Sluice (TNA, E 317/Kent/56, fos 2–3). This was in the area of the large mast dock and the victualling yard, west of the dockyard. The bailiff of the manor was obliged to maintain and repair the river bank within the manor as part of his office, in return for his daily fee of 2d (TNA, SC 6/HenVIII/6025). The river bank or marsh wall was 160 perches (804.67m) long and included a sluice gate called King's Sluice or

Crane Sluice (TNA, E 317/Kent/56, fo 10). The embankment and sluice within the manor between the royal dockyard and Earl's Sluice were repaired in a series of campaigns by Christopher Browne in the period 1627–36, using royal money advanced by the Cofferers of the King's Household (TNA, E 351/3402).

A survey of the Crown manor of Sayes Court was made in July 1608 (surviving in several versions), and found that Christopher Browne held it with the keeping of the king's cattle under a 40-year lease which had begun in July 1603 (TNA, LR 2/196, fos 166–8; /198, fos 152v–153v; /219, fos 246–58v; Dews 1884, 286–98). He was married to Thomasine Gonson, a descendant of Henry VIII's and Elizabeth's Treasurers of the Navy, William and Benjamin Gonson (Chapter 3.1). Christopher Browne restored the buildings of the manor at his own expense, and planted its gardens and orchards. In recognition of this, in January 1611 he received a new grant of the office of bailiff of the manor, with the manor house of Sayes Court, its stables, gardens and orchards, for a term of 41 years, with the right to pasture 12 cows, one bull and two horses of his own throughout the year. In November 1635 he obtained a 24-year extension of the lease of the manor house, and passed it on to his grandson Richard Browne (BL, EP 37; TNA, E 317/Kent/56, fos 7–9). In 1647 Richard's daughter and heiress Mary married John Evelyn, who took possession of Sayes Court in October 1648 (Drake 1886, 7). Browne was the king's ambassador in France, and remained there during the Commonwealth (1649–60).

In July 1649 the manor was seized with other royal estates by the Parliamentary government and surveyed for sale in the following December and January. The survey was submitted to the Surveyor General (BL, EP 38; TNA, E 317/Kent/56). The manor house and its appurtenances were in the hands of William Prettyman (as executor of Christopher Browne), who sold them on to William Somerfield of London in April 1650. Following correspondence between Prettyman and Richard Browne in 1650–2 (BL, EP 38), the diarist and horticulturist John Evelyn moved into Sayes Court on behalf of his father-in-law in 1652, and purchased it in a series of complicated transactions that were completed in February 1653 (de la Bedoyère 1997, 13) for £3500 (*Evelyn diary*, 22 February 1653).

Evelyn's Sayes Court, 1652–94

John Evelyn (Fig 49) settled somewhat despondently into life at Sayes Court: 'I made preparation for my settlement … there being now so little appearance of any change for the better, all being entirely in the rebels' hands'. The estate was 'very much suffering for want of some friend to rescue it out of the power of the usurpers' (*Evelyn diary*, 9 March 1652). Visitors to Sayes Court included the 'wonderful genius' Sir Christopher Wren (ibid, 5 May 1681), the king (ibid, 30 April 1663), the queen (ibid, 28 April 1676), Samuel Pepys (*Pepys diary*, 5 May 1665) and the poet laureate John Dryden (*Evelyn diary*, 27 June 1674).

The manor and its demesne lands were bought by Sir Nicholas Crisp. Following the restoration of the monarchy in

Fig 49 John Evelyn (1620–1706), painted in c 1687 by Godfrey Kneller; Evelyn is holding in his hand a copy of Sylva, *written at Sayes Court (The Royal Society, RS.9268)*

1660, a survey was made of what had happened to the demesne lands during the Interregnum, and was submitted to the Board of Green Cloth in December. Much of the cattle pasture and meadow land had been ploughed, dug and planted; 7 acres of Great Crane Mead had been dug out to provide ballast for ships, which had created a dock to house ships, linked to a canal intended to convey lighters to Hatcham Barn (BL, EP 38). In May 1663 the restored Charles II granted Evelyn a lease of the manor house, gardens, orchards and the adjacent fields for 99 years. The bulk of the demesne lands were returned to the custody of his father-in-law Sir Richard Browne in October 1662, and leased to him by the Crown in 1671 (Drake 1886, 8–9; BL, EP 29, 30, 38, 39, Deptford Charters box 2).

As described in 1608, the house was nine bays long, two storeys high and contained 18 rooms (Dews 1884, 294–5; TNA, LR 2/196, fo 166v; /219, fo 254). In an uncertainly dated inventory made by Christopher and Thomasine Browne for letting the house to Sir Thomas Smith in 'year 13' (ie either 1617–18 or 1637–8), the 'capital messuage' comprised the courtyard next to the street, the hall, the parlour, the inner parlour, the buttery, three cellars, the entry between the hall and the kitchen, the kitchen, the back yard next to the kitchen, the wet larder, rooms over the coalhouse, the chamber over the parlour, the chamber over the hall, the chamber over the porch, the chamber over the buttery, the entry at the stair head over the still house called the brushing room, the entry over the passage out of the hall into the kitchen, two chambers over the kitchen, the entry at the stair head leading into the chamber over the inner parlour, the closet adjoining this entry, the little chamber over the inner parlour, the hot house, the entry between the little chamber over the inner parlour and the chamber over the wet larder, the chamber over the wet larder, the staircase leading up into the garret, the great garret, and the chamber at the end of the garret. There was also a brickhouse in the garden, a stable in the orchard, and the garden and orchard with fruit trees (BL, EP 37, Deptford Charters box 1). In 1649 the house was described as timber-built, and comprised three cellars, a hall, a parlour, a kitchen, a buttery, a larder with a dairy-house and a chamber on the ground floor; eight chambers with four closets in the second storey; and three garret rooms at the top. The courts leet and courts baron for the tenants of the manor were held at the house (TNA, E 317/Kent/56, fos 6, 11). John Evelyn found that the house had some long-term structural problems (de la Bedoyère 1997, 13). In April 1652 he had repairs carried out to it, and in December 1653 made an agreement with a bricklayer to build two new chimneys (BL, EP 38, 39). In 1664 he paid tax on 19 hearths in Sayes Court manor house (LLHAC, PT69/62).

In c 1698, Evelyn sketched a view of the manor house at Sayes Court on to an earlier map of Deptford dating to 1623 (BL: Add MS 78629 A, formerly EP 42; Fig 50; Darley 2006, 17). It shows the south front with three gables (of which the central gable is the tallest), two chimneys and a central doorway opening on to a straight approach path. A 19th-century drawing derives from this sketch (BL, Add MS 16945, fo 71). The house appears with an irregular outshot rear wing to the north on Joel Gascoigne's plan of 1692 (BL, KTOP xviii.17.2), a dockyard plan of 1725 (TNA, CRES 6/34, fos 80v–81; different version at LLHAC, A88/8/6) (Fig 57) and Milton's plan of the dockyard in 1753 (Fig 58).

In 1608 there was a stable at the west end of the storehouse, with a hayloft over it, and a four-bay granary (TNA, LR 2/196, fo 166v). In 1649 there were two stables and a small stable

adjoining the manor house; the great barn was eight bays long (TNA, E 317/Kent/56, fos 6, 7). The survey of 1660 stated that the barn had been 140ft long and 26ft wide (42.67m × 7.92m), but had been completely demolished (BL, EP 38).

The survey of 1649 measured the outbuildings, courtyards, gardens and orchards around the house at 2 acres 2 rods 16 perches (TNA, E 317/Kent/56, fo 6). Evelyn found the manor house largely surrounded by pasture land, except for some old hollow elms in the stable court and next to the watercourse; he developed his famous gardens around the house. In February 1653 he planted the orchard with 300 mixed fruit trees. He had visited Pierre Morin's garden in Paris in 1644, and the design of his original oval parterre was based on this. He planted groves in 1656 and 1660, and the Lower Grove in 1662. In spring 1664 he planted the home field and west field around Sayes Court with elms. He established a holly hedge 160ft long, 7ft high and 5ft thick (48.77m × 2.13m × 1.52m); by 1679 it was a 300ft (91.44m) long hedge (Dews 1884, 31–2, 206; Laird 2003, 117–18, 127, 139; de la Bedoyère 1997, 68, 338; BL, EP 39). Evelyn was presented with a glass apiary by Dr John Wilkins which he installed in his garden at Sayes Court (*Evelyn diary*, 13 July 1654) and which was admired by Pepys (*Pepys diary*, 5 May 1665). Pepys's view of Evelyn was that he 'must be allowed a little for a little conceitedness; but he may well be so, being a man so much above others' (ibid, 5 November 1665), but later that 'the more I know him the more I love him' (ibid, 29 April 1666). As for Evelyn's opinion of his friend, Pepys was 'a very worthy, industrious and curious person, none in England exceeding him in knowledge of the navy' (*Evelyn diary*, 26 May 1703) (Chapter 4.1).

In 1668 Evelyn obtained a Crown lease of a small piece of ground in Brick Close on the east side of the house, which allowed him to enlarge the forecourt of the house and build a stable. It also had the effect of distancing the house further from the dockyard, and a new boundary wall was probably built. At this time Evelyn was involved, with others, in the speculative manufacture of bricks, but complained to Pepys that he had lost £500 in the venture. Pepys confided to his diary, 'I see the most ingenious men may sometimes be mistaken' (*Pepys diary*, 23 September 1668; Dews 1884, 31–2, 206; Laird 2003, 117–18, 127, 139; de la Bedoyère 1997, 68, 338; BL, EP 39).

The gardens included bowling greens, eight walnut trees, a carp pond and glass beehives; plots for melons, peas and beans; a kitchen garden, a nursery garden and a walled private garden; a moated island for raspberries and asparagus; and a banqueting house, a pigeon house, a laboratory, a brewhouse, a woodhouse, a cart-house and sawpits. All these buildings and garden spaces appear on John Evelyn's map of c 1652–4 (Fig 55).

Evelyn's home was particularly exposed to the elements. A great storm in 1658 'threw down my greatest trees at Sayes Court' (*Evelyn diary*, 18 August 1658). Another storm three years later again damaged his gardens and also 'miserably shattered' Evelyn's house, including bringing his parlour chimney down (ibid, 17 February 1662; 20 February 1662). Frost destroyed many of his rare plants in 1684, his 'oranges and myrtles very sick, the rosemary and laurels dead to all appearance, but the

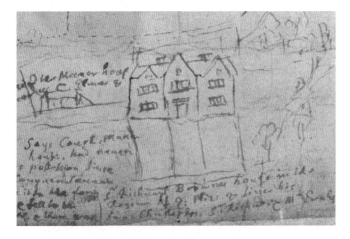

Fig 50 Detail of 'Says Court' manor house added by John Evelyn in c 1698 to a map of 1623 (cf Fig 14) (The British Library Board, Add MS 78629 A)

cypress likely to endure it' (ibid, 4 February 1684) and Evelyn redesigned his parterre in a semicircular shape and planted part of an orchard (Laird 2003, 117). There was a 'hurricane and tempest of wind, rain, and lightning' in November 1703 in which 'Sayes Court, suffered very much' (*Evelyn diary*, 26–27 November 1703; 7 December 1703).

It was during his time at Sayes Court that Evelyn produced works such as *Sylva*, the first publication of the recently formed Royal Society, *Fumifugium*, his treatise on air pollution, and his revolutionary plan for the rebuilding of London after the Great Fire of 1666. *Sylva* is a book dedicated to the king that gives advice on how forests are best managed 'for the benefit of His Royal Navy' (Evelyn 1706, lxxxvi).

Access from the manor house to the river was by a track running northwards around the then western perimeter wall of the royal dockyard to a causeway and river stairs, where Evelyn, his family and visitors disembarked. Because the dockyard staff needed access across this causeway to reach the mast dock on its north side, it was agreed that the watchman of the gate at the north end of the dockyard should keep the causeway and stairs clear of mud deposited by the floods of high tides. On several occasions Evelyn wrote to Pepys to remind him of this obligation, as in September 1672, June 1686 and October 1687 (de la Bedoyère 1997, 168, 178–9). The Crown purchased the land for the mast dock (part of Great Crane Mead) from Richard Browne in the 1670s (BL, EP 39, 41, 46).

Evelyn also discovered the great woodcarver Grinling Gibbons while walking 'near a solitary thatched house, in a field in our parish, near Sayes Court' (*Evelyn diary*, 18 January 1671). Gibbons had moved to Deptford some time in the late 1660s, apparently to earn a living from ship carving. Both Christopher Wren and Samuel Pepys visited Gibbons at his cottage soon after, and a few months later Evelyn was presenting Gibbons and his work to Charles II at Whitehall Palace (Esterly 2013, 40).

The eastern extremity of the Sayes Court estate – the north-western part of Deptford High Street (known as Butt Lane until 1825) – was developed from 1654 onwards. The nine conjoined houses that stood on the site by 1692, and probably sketched by the steward of the estate, John Strickland, in 1706 (BL, Add MS 78616), each had frontages of approximately 15–16ft. They were possibly early forms of the type of housing now described as town houses (Guillery and Herman 1999, 62). These early houses no longer survive, but no. 227 was rebuilt in 1791–2 for a baker, Thomas Palmer, and is still standing (ibid, 64).

By 1662 the Deptford estate was generating £72 per annum in rent (BL, Add MS 78614). The Evelyn family undertook various schemes to generate further income from the estate, including signing an agreement with the Dutchman Sir John Kiviet and Sir Samuel Morland to manufacture bricks – up to 30,000 per day – on the estate (ibid). From the 1660s Evelyn leased ground west of the dockyard to Sir Denis Gauden, victualling contractor for the navy, where Gauden built the Red House (Oppenheim 1926, 362; Rodger 2004, 105) (Fig 26). Evelyn also received income from the 99-year lease he signed with the Crown in 1676 for the mast yard that the navy

constructed in the Thames-side meadow leased to Gauden (ibid). The yard measured 529ft along the Thames, by 220ft. Evelyn included several covenants in the lease, including retaining control over the sluice gate which fed the ditch that led up to his house and which sat between the mast yard in the west and the 'Kings master yard' in the east. A few years later Evelyn wrote to the Comptroller of the Navy to complain about 'the very great damage which my meadow has sustained by the perpetual freezing of the water thro the bank of your new mast dock' (ibid). This episode, along with several other disagreements between the Evelyn family and the navy – such as over the enlargement of the docks in 1725 (BL, Add MS 78616) – indicates that the relationship between the two was slightly fractious at times.

Because the severe winters of the late 17th century often made the road between Deptford and London impassable, Evelyn began spending the winters in central London. In 1694 he finally gave up Sayes Court to rent-paying tenants and moved to the family seat at Wotton, near Dorking, inherited from his older brother. Initially Sayes Court was in the hands of Evelyn's daughter Susannah and her husband William Draper, and their artistic entourage. In May 1694 Evelyn wrote to Samuel Pepys from Wotton to urge him to visit 'the young Housekeepers at Says-Court' when he went down-river, describing them as 'a family of 21 – Mrs Tuke is library-keeper, and the rest painters, embroiderers, carvers, gardener, etc' (*Evelyn diary*, 4 May 1694). Evelyn did not move the last of his goods from the house to Wotton until 1700 (ibid, 24 May 1700; de la Bedoyère 1997, 14, 244, 269 n7).

The visit of Czar Peter the Great, February–April 1698

Peter the Great and his 15-strong retinue visited England between January and April 1698, arriving at Sayes Court on 9 February after a stay in London. The czar had met William III in the Netherlands a few months earlier and the visit was planned then. The king was keen to improve trade with Russia, and the czar saw England as a useful ally against the Ottoman empire and wanted to improve his own knowledge of western technology, particularly the shipbuilding of the Dutch and English (Loewenson 1962, 432, 439; MacGregor 2004, 116, 118).

The idea that those of noble birth should study a trade or, more specifically, shipbuilding, was not a new one. Sir Robert Dudley (1574–1649), the illegitimate son of the Earl of Leicester, had been a pupil of Mathew Baker and published a treatise on shipbuilding before he fled England in 1605 (Johnston 2005, 134).

Sayes Court seemed the ideal place for the czar to base his embassy. John Evelyn's tenant, Vice Admiral John Benbow (*Evelyn diary*, 1 June 1696; Dews 1884, 32), moved out, 'supposing it might be a pleasure to his good master the King' (*Cal Treasury P*, ii, vii–xlv). While residing at Deptford, the czar was visited by Anglican clergy, including Gilbert Burnet, Bishop of Salisbury, and Quakers (Peter later repaying the visit to the local Quaker meeting house) including the founder of

Pennsylvania, William Penn. A female giant was one of his more unusual guests (MacGregor 2004, 122). The czar may also have received a visit from William III, or one was planned at least. 'The King is expected there this day, the best parlour is pretty clean for him to be entertained in' one of Evelyn's servants wrote to him (quoted in Bray 1819, 60; the date of the visit is not given). While based at Sayes Court, the czar visited Windsor Castle, Hampton Court Palace, the Tower of London, the Royal Mint, Greenwich and Oxford, as well as the naval dockyards of Chatham, Portsmouth and Woolwich where elaborate maritime displays were staged for him (MacGregor 2004, 122, 123, 128).

The sources are divided on how much manual work Peter did in the dockyard (Phillips 1995, 173 n44). Evelyn's servant stated that the czar 'is very seldom at home a whole day, very often in the King's Yard, or by water' (quoted in Bray 1819, 60). A 19th-century source quotes 'an old man, a workman of Deptford yard some forty years ago [1790s], that he had heard his father say, the Tzar of Muscovy worked with his own hands as hard as any man in the yard' (Barrow 1832, 93). The czar was particularly interested in the systematic way the ships were made. The yard's shipwrights 'showed him their draughts and the method of laying down by proportion any ship or vessel of what body soever required, with the rules for moulding and building a ship according as laid down in such a draught, which extremely took with and pleased His Majesty' (Perry 1716, 164). The czar concluded that the shipbuilding methods he had seen in Holland were 'inferior to the English way of building' (ibid, 165).

The czar left Sayes Court on 21 April (*Evelyn diary*, 21 April 1698) and returned home in the 6th-rate, 90ft × 23½ft *Royal Transport* (220bm-tons), a gift from the king, with as many shipwrights as would go with him (MacGregor 2004, 125–6). His visit was important for the development of Russian engineering, mathematics, navigation and instrument making as well as shipbuilding (ibid, 132–7). Ironically, relations cooled by the 1720s because of the growing power of the very Russian navy which English shipbuilding skills had helped create (ibid, 136–7).

Back in Deptford, it was discovered that the czar had done considerable damage. Evelyn had been warned: his servant had written that the czar's 'people' were 'right nasty' (quoted in Bray 1819, 60). Not only had Evelyn's house been damaged, but also that of a Mr Russell, ruined by the czar's 'guards' (*Cal Treasury P*, ii, vii–xlv). Evelyn's gardens were also wrecked: 'It is said that one of Czar Peter's favourite recreations was to demolish the hedges by riding through them in a wheelbarrow' (Bray 1879, xi n1). Evelyn got Sir Christopher Wren and his gardener Mr London to consider Benbow's petition for recompense. Wren decided in May 1698 that £158 2s 6d should go to the Vice Admiral, £30 to Russell and £162 7s to Evelyn. The claim for damage included £50 for 'several fine draughts and other designs relating to the sea, lost', £10 for 'twenty fine pictures very much torn and the frames all broke' and £1 for wheelbarrows. The Treasury ordered that the Office of Works should pay (*Cal Treasury P*, ii, vii–xlv, 158–72).

Sayes Court after Evelyn, 18th to 19th centuries

In 1700 John Evelyn was renting Sayes Court House to Lord Carmarthen for £73 per annum (BL, EP 28; *Evelyn diary*, 18 March 1701). On the death of John Evelyn in 1706, both the Browne and Evelyn leases of Sayes Court and its lands passed to his grandson Sir John Evelyn (d 1763). He was able to convert the leases into a grant in fee in trust to himself and his heirs in 1726 (Drake 1886, 9; BL, EP 29, 30). A valuation was made of the Deptford estate of Sir John Evelyn in February 1725 (BL, EP 41). The documentation associated with this grant records that by 1725 the 'capital messuage' – Sayes Court – sat in about 64 acres of land. The estate accounts indicate that the 56 plots on the estate were generating £951 in rental income (BL, Add MS 78616). The plots were numbered according to a plan and survey of the estate undertaken by John Grove in *c* 1712 (BL, Add MS 78629 K). In 1725 the royal dockyard was extended into the lands of Sayes Court manor by 6 acres (BL, EP 41; Oppenheim 1926, 367). The Evelyn estate was also mapped by Joel Gascoigne in 1692 (BL, KTOP xviii.17.2) and John Dugleby in 1777 (LMA, O/267/1, 2). In 1720 the tenant of Sayes Court house and gardens was William Lee esquire (BL, EP 29).

Despite claims that the house was 'pulled down in 1728 or 1729' and a workhouse built in its place (Lysons 1796, 364), this seems unlikely. From at least 1728 until 1740 the estate account books record that Sayes Court and its gardens were leased out to Captain William Newland at a rent of £28 per annum (BL, EP 30, 33; BL, Add MS 78621). In 1727 a carpenter, a smith and a plumber were paid for work on the pump at Sayes Court, and the grounds of the barn were fenced (BL, EP 29). In 1755 payments were made for work on asparagus beds and hedges (BL, EP 31).

The parish of Deptford did build a workhouse for its poor in 1726 on the east side of Church Street, adapting the building of the Deptford Bridewell prison, on part of the Gravel Pits estate by Deptford Creek. The workhouse served both the parishes of St Paul and St Nicholas until 1740, and thereafter St Paul's only. It was in 1740 that the parish of St Nicholas transferred its poor to the old manor house of Sayes Court, held on lease from the Evelyn family. It appears that in 1740–1 the family had 'Sayes Court house' surveyed and repaired before it was leased to the parish (BL, Add MS 78621). The estate account books record that St Nicholas's parish was paying the Evelyn family rent on the property from 1744 (£13pa) to 1757 (£18pa). The accounts also record that the family was intermittently paying the Crown a small rental charge in relation to the 'capital messuage of Says Court'. The last of these payments was also made in 1757 (BL, Add MS 78622).

In 1759 the old house was demolished and a new workhouse built which continued to house the poor until 1848 (BL, Add MSS 16945, fo 46; 32360, fo 111; Dunkin 1877, 96–7; Dews 1884, 38; Drake 1886, 28–9, 35; Sturdee 1895, 46). The old barn was demolished in the mid 18th century as part of this process, £3 being received for its materials. The rebuilt workhouse appears as a rectangular block on Dugleby's map of

1777, surrounded by the remnants of Evelyn's gardens (LMA, O/267/1, 2). According to the 1777 Parliamentary report on the workhouse, the institution could accommodate 130 people (Phillpotts 2011, citing *Abstracts of the returns made by the Overseers of the Poor*, 1777). A view of the workhouse appears on a lease plan of 1789: it appears to be similar to the 17th-century mansion house, but with different fenestration, a pillared central doorway and a central cupola (BL, Add MS 16945, fo 72). Writing in the late 19th century, Walford described it as 'a large brick-built house of two storeys, oblong in shape, and with a tiled roof. The rooms are low-pitched, and about a dozen in number; some of them are about thirty feet long, and those on the ground floor are paved with brick' (Walford 1878, 156–8).

Housing development again occurred on the Sayes Court estate in 1770–2 during a period of enlargement of the dockyard, when 40 brick houses were constructed on King Street, later Prince (Princes) Street (Guillery and Herman 1999, 64). By the end of the 18th century, according to Lysons, there was 'not the least trace' remaining of the house or gardens of Sayes Court, save 'some of the garden walls' and 'some brick piers' (Lysons 1796, 364), and the site had clearly become fairly run down by the early 19th century. Walford lamented that, thanks to the expansion of the naval yard, parts of Evelyn's once beautiful garden were now sites where 'oxen and hogs were slaughtered and salted for the use of the navy' (Walford 1878, 156).

The parish of St Nicholas became part of the Greenwich Poor Law Union in 1834, with the new union workhouse situated in Woolwich Road completed in 1840. The opening of the Greenwich Union Workhouse, along with the fact that the building itself had apparently become 'too decayed and confined' for continuing use as a workhouse, meant that in September 1848 the parish surrendered the workhouse to Mr W J Evelyn of Wotton. It was used as a factory, then an emigration depot until 1852. In 1853 it was used as a factory to make clothing and bedding for emigrants (Drake 1886, 29). In 1856, Mr W J Evelyn sold about 15 acres to the Admiralty; on the closure of the royal dockyard in 1869 he bought back more than 11 acres, including the site of Sayes Court (ibid, 18). By this point the building was probably being used as some kind of police station and salary office associated with the yard (Walford 1878, 156). From the 1840s the Metropolitan Police had provided security for the Thames yards, and in 1860 they took over security at all the home dockyards (Coad 2013, 375 and n). The building was a pension pay-office by 1869 (*London Journal*, 1 March 1869, 136).

In 1881 the house became the Evelyn Almshouses, Sayes Court, for 21 residents (Dews 1884, 40). The site consisted of about 14 acres of open ground; 4 acres formed a new garden for the house while 10 acres were given over to a public garden which contained trees, shrubs and flowers imported from the Evelyns' house at Wotton, a bandstand, and a large building in one corner which was to serve as a library and museum. The preparations for all this were described by Walford (1878, 158).

In 1884, Mr W J Evelyn suggested to Octavia Hill that he wished to gift the property to the newly formed Society for the Protection of Ancient Buildings. The subsequent feasibility study conducted by the society concluded that the only existing methods for holding and retaining the property for the enjoyment of the public – conveying the property to local authority ownership or trusteeship – were unsuitable. The opportunity to place Sayes Court in public ownership was thus lost. However, as a direct result of the discussions over Sayes Court, Octavia Hill and Robert Hunter conceived the idea of the National Trust (Murphy 1987, 103).

5.2 Archaeological evidence for Sayes Court and other buildings

Sayes Court and the later workhouse

The excavations identified the ground plan of a building (B13, Fig 60) in area 6 whose location corresponded to that of Sayes Court, the home of John Evelyn from the 1650s. However, Building 13 was not Sayes Court; its plan matched instead the workhouse that was constructed on the site of Evelyn's home when that building was demolished in 1759 (above, 5.1).

Only overburden was removed during the excavation, and walls and floors were left intact. Where not obscured by the later workhouse building (B13), the remains of an earlier building (B12, Fig 26) were recorded which may be those of Sayes Court. A fragment of wall and a tile floor, at 3.11m OD, formed part of this earlier building (Fig 51). The tiled surface comprised very worn Low Countries floor tiles whose size (247–256mm square) suggests that they are of unglazed type dating to *c* 1580–1800. It is therefore possible that they could originally have been part of Sayes Court.

The cellar at the west end of the building was more problematic. Few bricks in the cellar walls could be dated with any accuracy, but those that could seemed to date to the late 16th to mid/late 17th century. It is difficult to reconcile the cellar with maps of the Stuart period, and it may have been built reusing earlier bricks (Fig 52).

Reuse of earlier brick also made dating Building 13 (Fig 53) from its fabric alone problematic – many of its bricks are remarkably similar in colour, fabric, size and date to those of the late 16th to 17th centuries. Similarly, it is difficult to reconcile the layout of Building 13 with that of the building shown in this location on maps pre-dating the mid 18th century (eg by Evelyn (Fig 50) or on Milton's 1753 map (Fig 58)), whereas the building is a good match for that depicted on maps after the mid 18th century (eg Dugleby's 1777 map: LMA, O/267/1, 2). It seems certain, therefore, that Building 13 relates to the 1759 workhouse, its fabric composed in part of bricks reused from the demolished earlier building.

The main axis of the workhouse building (B13, Fig 60) ran roughly east–west. The building was 25m long and 12m wide, with walls surviving about a metre high in places (eg to *c* 3.89m OD); floors had been robbed out. The building faced south,

Fig 51 View of the remains of a tiled floor, possibly of Sayes Court (B12), looking west

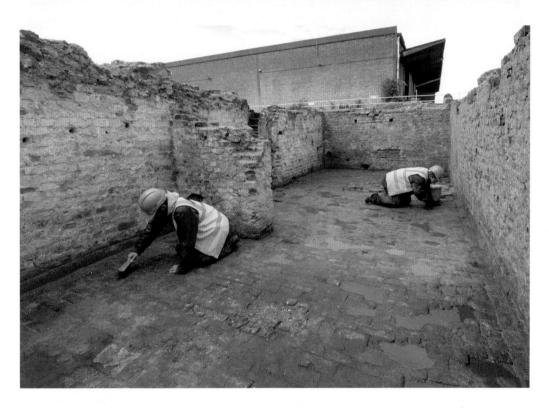

Fig 52 View of the cellar of the earlier, pre-workhouse, building (B12), which incorporated late 16th- to 17th-century brick, looking north

with a central opening in the south wall forming the main door; a threshold stone was probably not original. The front door opened into a central hallway, with a room either side. The east and west walls forming the hallway were built of yellow stock brick and are therefore also likely to be additions in the 19th century. The east wall of the hallway had been pushed over into the eastern room. At the back of the building (ie the north half), a series of rooms were evident, linked by a narrow east–west corridor. Stone thresholds still survived in places, marking the former position of internal doorways. Wings to the west and east flanked the central part of the building, set back slightly from the frontage. The east wing

comprised two rooms, with the foundations of a later bay window, while the cellar occupied the west wing. The cellar floor (at 1.41m OD) was built of a mixture of yellow London stock, red and orange type bricks, and dark red brick with cream bands, and was therefore a replacement, probably dating to the 18th to 19th centuries (I Betts, pers comm). Recesses cut into the north and west walls are likely to have been for timbers to support a stair that was replaced by stone steps in an extension to the west wall of the building in the 18th to 19th centuries. Two rooms at the south-west corner of the building are likely to have been latrines, probably also dating to the 1759 rebuild or later. The workhouse and its yard were pictured from

Fig 53 View of the 18th- to 19th-century workhouse building (B13) under excavation, looking west

the south in 1869 (Fig 54).

A fragment of brick wall (B35, Fig 60), which survived 4.25m long and 0.23m wide, was recorded east of the workhouse (B13) that replaced Sayes Court. A buttress was recorded at its south end. This wall seems to correspond to part of the perimeter wall of the workhouse as depicted in Fig 54. A nearby well 0.61m in diameter, built in yellow stock brick and capped with a stone, was probably also associated with the workhouse and was 19th-century in date. A brick base measuring 1.15m × 0.75m × 0.60m high, recorded in the north-west corner of the excavation trench, was probably part of a late 19th-century warehouse or similar building (B48, Fig 130).

Further modifications to the workhouse (B13) are shown on Fig 130. Its buildings are shown on a plan of the Supply Reserve Depot of 1935 (LLHAC, A/15/31/10) but had been demolished by 1949 (the Ordnance Survey map of 1949, 1:1250, shows the site as 'Sayes Court, site of' with no building: Fig 134).

Garden features

John Evelyn designed and laid out an important experimental garden, famous in its day (shown on his map of *c* 1652–4: Fig 55). Garden features were identified neither in area 6 nor in

Fig 54 The workhouse in 1869, looking north towards the dockyard and the slip cover roofs (cf Fig 118) (ILN, Supplement, 24 April 1869, 421) (Look and Learn)

targeted test pits immediately to the west and south, nor in trenches further away to the north, south, east and west (trenches 29–34). Disappointingly, when exposed more fully in subsequent excavations, a feature identified as a 'terrace' turned out to have been made by a tree throw or burrowing animal.

A garden wall (S15, Fig 26; Fig 56) to the west of Building 13 survived up to a height of *c* 4.14m OD, with a fragmentary

return east in the north part of area 6. Further fragmentary wall remains (S16, Fig 26) to the east of the building are also likely to have been garden walls. These walls do match the Evelyn map of *c* 1652–4 (Fig 55) and are likely to date to the time of the earlier Sayes Court building (B12). The position of the southernmost wall to the east of the building corresponds to a gate on Evelyn's map, referred to in the key as 'The door into

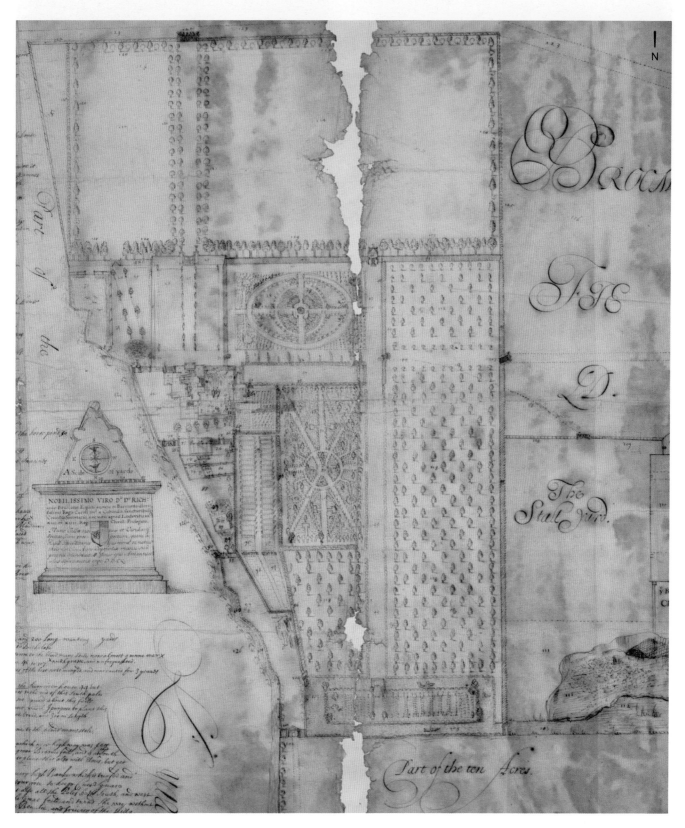

Fig 55 Detail of John Evelyn's map of gardens at Sayes Court, c 1652–4, with the dockyard wall east (left) of the gardens (The British Library Board, Add MS 78628 A)

Fig 56 View of brick garden wall (S15) belonging to Sayes Court, looking east

the Milking Close'.

Further east, the bricks in a culvert (S14, Fig 26) suggested a date of the late 16th to mid/late 17th centuries, although the addition to its south end of several smaller culverts (S49) was later. A stretch of wall matched the position of the dockyard perimeter wall shown on the *c* 1652–4 map. Elsewhere in the garden area (OA11), pits, drainage features and plough marks dated to the 19th or 20th century (Fig 130).

6

The early Georgian dockyard (period 4, 1714–74)

6.1 Historical introduction: Deptford's role in the early to mid 18th century

Whereas Deptford had been the leading dockyard in the 16th century, by the late 17th century it (and Woolwich) had been superseded by Chatham (Baugh 1965, 263; MacDougall 1982, 70). From the beginning of the 18th century and for the following 250 years, Portsmouth and Plymouth on the English Channel and Chatham on the Medway were the pre-eminent naval dockyards (Chapter 1.2; Coad 2013, 1–6). For much of the 18th century conflict was focused on France and Spain; the Spanish War of 1739–48 and the Seven Years' War of 1756–63 put enormous pressures on both the navy and its bases (Rodger 2004, 226–90). The century saw a massive growth in naval power, with the size of the navy increasing four-fold. As the size of the individual warships also increased, there were obvious consequences for the yards and their approaches (Coad 2013, 4). The royal dockyards were at the very heart of British foreign policy and were the largest industrial complexes, responsible for generating numerous additional industries (MacDougall 1982, 81). Key figures at the Admiralty in the mid 18th century and up to 1782 were Anson and the Earl of Sandwich, who both understood the importance of finance and of infrastructure onshore, with Sandwich considered the most effective naval administrator of the 18th century. From 1749 Sandwich pioneered visitations, or tours of inspection, of the royal dockyards, and in the second half of the century the Admiralty and Navy Board were much concerned with modernising and enlarging the main yards, including (to a limited extent) Deptford (Oppenheim 1926, 372–7; Rodger 2004, 291–301, 310; Morriss 2011, 138–41; Coad 2013, 5–10, 59–65).

By the 1740s, there was a broad division of the royal dockyards between Portsmouth, Plymouth and Sheerness which dealt with the immediate needs of the home fleet, and Deptford, Woolwich and Chatham which mainly undertook shipbuilding, minor repairs and the preparation of naval stores (Baugh 1965, 263; Rodger 2004, 297–8). Deptford was the furthest upriver; it built smaller ships and served as the headquarters of the naval transport service, as well as a depot from which naval stores were distributed to yards and the fleet (ibid, 297). Despite its decline relative to other yards, by the mid 18th century appointment to Deptford was considered the pinnacle of success for an officer, offering prospects of promotion to the Navy Board for the Master Shipwright and Clerk of the Cheque (Baugh 1965, 301).

Although Deptford was considered one of the best royal yards in 1717 (MacDougall 1982, 88), that year saw another petition from the men complaining that their wages had been unpaid for 19 months, that they were being denied further credit and so 'cannot subsist', and that many had been arrested (*Cal Treasury P*, v, 279–94; cf Chapter 4.1). Yard wages were frequently in arrears, for example by 15 months in 1762 (Oppenheim 1926, 376). Private shipbuilders were busy and could afford high wages in wartime, but dockyard jobs were still desirable for their privileges and potentially long-term employment (Rodger 2004, 298–9; cf Oppenheim 1926, 376–7; Chapter 1.2). A circular of

1715 to all the yards had highlighted the irregularities lately discovered at Deptford, for which the Master Shipwright had been dismissed, such as 'the shameful practice' of taking money for entering and promoting workmen, entering servants under the names of persons who were not entitled to the privilege, favouritism, and other evils. Officers were forbidden to employ the king's workmen or to use the king's stores for their own purposes. Such abuses were still flourishing a century later (Oppenheim 1926, 365, 367). A pamphlet of 1717 reveals the enormous waste of timber there (ibid, 366).

The role of the Deptford yard, however, was changing. The victualling establishment on Tower Hill was closed in the 1740s and the Deptford victualling yard (to the west of, and outside, the excavation site) became the principal manufacturing establishment as well as the place from which stores were distributed to other yards, home and overseas (Cock and Rodger 2008, 236; MacDougall 1982, 83). Since the 1660s, storehouses on the property which became known as the Red House had been used by victualling contractors (Chapter 4.1), but in July 1739 the Red House storehouses burnt down (Oppenheim 1926, 369). In 1743 the Victualling Board leased the Red House estate and was able to build a large complex of stores and mills

(Rodger 2004, 306); the Board purchased the property in 1756 (Oppenheim 1926, 372).

During the 18th century it was impossible to find a mooring of sufficient depth for any large warship at Deptford. Even though launchings only took place at high tide, the river still had to be dredged: in 1739 the 2nd-rate, 80-gun *Boyne* (1160bm-tons) was ready for launching, but dredging in front of the slip was needed to create sufficient depth (Oppenheim 1926, 369, 375; MacDougall 1982, 88). One of the major drawbacks of Deptford was becoming increasingly apparent. A report in 1774 stated that the yard 'is useful for building both large and small ships there being a sufficient flow of water for landing them, although not a sufficient depth at low water to lay the large ships on float … after such are launched they are moved at the first opportunity … [to] other ports' (MacDougall 1982, 130). Deptford still had only the two main docks, three slips opening on to the wet dock and three on to the river; the slips on the river had 12–14ft of water in front of them, the double (dry) dock 16–18ft, so ships of any size had to be launched light (Oppenheim 1926, 379). In 1779, mud needed to be cleared from in front of the storehouse wharf (TNA, ADM 106/3319, 23 August 1779, 54) so that stores could be offloaded. By the last quarter of the 18th century, and

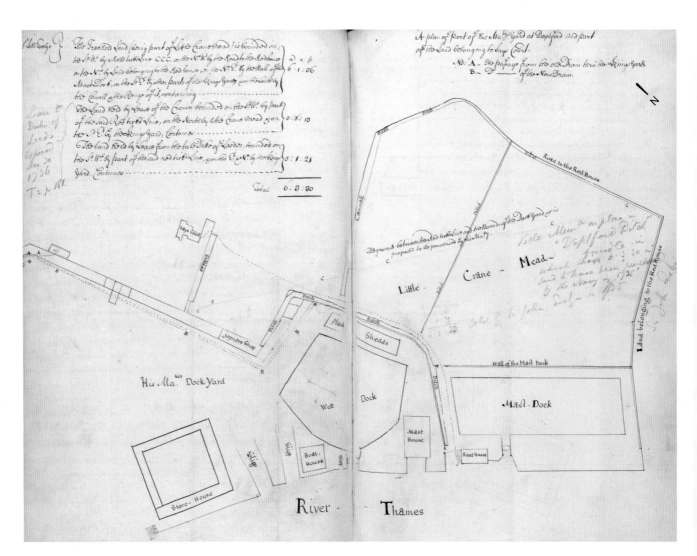

Fig 57 *A sketch map of the dockyard, 1725, with the Evelyn estate of 'Little Crane Mead' and Sayes Court to the south, before the dockyard expansion westwards (TNA, CRES 6/34, fos 80v–81)*

as ships increased ever more in size, it was clear that the Deptford yard was becoming obsolete.

6.2 Rebuilding and upgrading the yard: archaeological and historical evidence for the dockyard in the early to mid 18th century

Following on from the major survey of the yard's wharfs, storehouses and other buildings in 1709 and its recommendations for extensive repairs (Chapter 4.1), the storehouse was replaced, the mast dock and wet docks renovated and much other work undertaken, together with the extension of the yard into Sir John Evelyn's land agreed in 1725 (Chapter 5.1). A sketch map of 1725 of the dockyard (Fig 57) shows the new storehouse, two slips between the storehouse and the boathouse complex (square in plan) and the wet dock (but omits its subsidiary slips/dock, cf 1698: Fig 25; Fig 26), and to its west the yard perimeter wall and external ditch separating the mast dock (and Evelyn's access) from the rest of the yard, with Evelyn's ground to the south of the mast dock and Sayes Court to its east.

Milton's map of 1753 (Fig 58) illustrates in greater detail changes to the yard buildings, docks and slips since 1698, for some of which archaeological evidence was recovered (below). In addition, a comparison of the 1698 map (Fig 23, 'B' right) and the 1725 sketch with the map of 1753 clearly illustrates the new 'basin' (wet dock) constructed within the footprint of the timber wet dock and the general advance into the Thames of the waterfront and wharfs (Fig 59; Fig 60). From the middle decades of the 18th century brick was increasingly frequently used in construction work in the dockyard.

The new storehouse (the 'quadrangle storehouse')

The officers had proposed in May 1713 the 'thorough repair' of the 'Old Storehouse fronting the river' (TNA, ADM 106/3296, 28 November 1713, 165). Thorough indeed, the repairs consisted of taking the building 'wholly down' and constructing 'a brick front raised to correspond with the Cable House adjoining'. The cost was estimated at £750, reduced to £600 by using 'some of the materials of the old structure and old ship materials' (ibid, 5 December 1713, 165). The plans for demolition seem to have been modified later, with plans for only 'some part of the Storehouse fronting the river … taken down and rebuilt' (ibid, 1 February 1714, 173). By the end of February 1714, the officers had prepared 'a draught of the

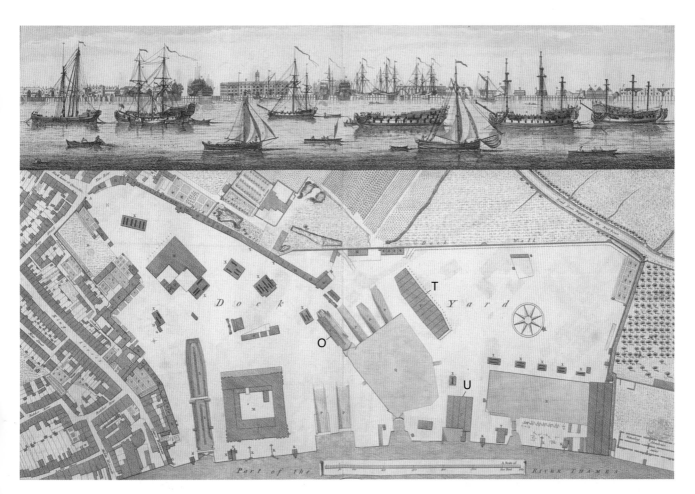

Fig 58 Milton's map of 1753: lower – plan of the dockyard and environs, with Sayes Court top centre; upper – view of the dockyard waterfront from across the Thames (The British Library Board, KTOP xviii.17.1)

N

cobbled
surface

Open Area 15
area of
dockyard expansion

Building 42
? later addition

Building 20
E–W walls

slipway

wet dock

Structure 17
dock wall

Structure 9
gate

0   25m

River Thames

Fig 59 Plan of principal archaeological features in the eastern part of the dockyard in the early to mid 18th century (to 1753) (period 4), with (inset) the new (quadrangle) storehouse as first built in the 1710s (scale 1:750)

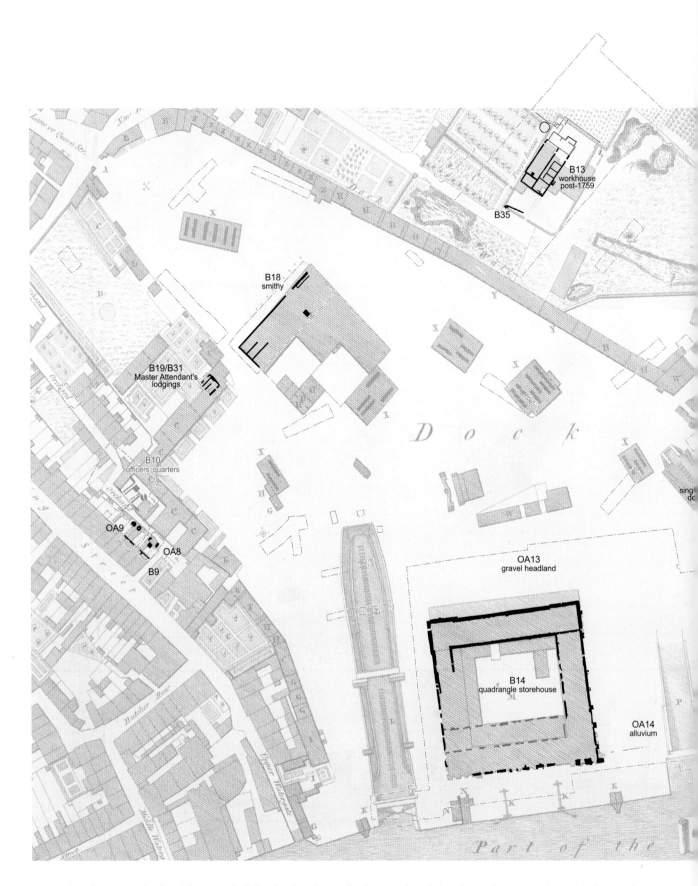

Fig 60 Plan of principal archaeological features in the dockyard in the early to mid 18th century (period 4) overlain on the 1753 map (Fig 58) (scale 1:1500)

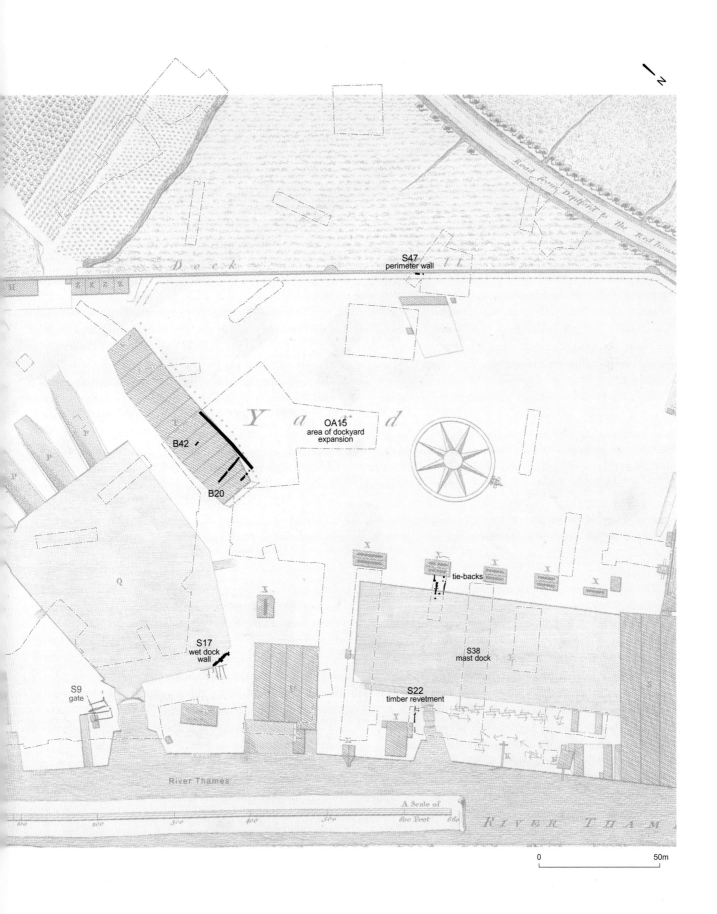

Storehouse designed to be built in the Yard in room of the old one fronting the water side between the cablehouses and the crane which is to be taken down'. The new storehouse was to be 98ft (29.9m) long and 42ft (12.8m) broad. The wall from the foundation to the first floor was to be three bricks thick, two-and-a-half bricks thick from there to the second floor and from the second floor to the 'raising pieces' two bricks thick. The 'ornamental mouldings' were to be 'answerable with those of the Cable House' and the roof was to be of plain tiles (ibid, 19 February 1714, 177).

The 'Cable House' referred to by the officers is likely to be the 'Great New Store house' (no. 42) shown on the 1698 map and panorama, immediately west of the Tudor storehouse (Fig 23, 'B' right; Fig 24). The river-facing gable end of the 'Great New Store house' (albeit of only two storeys) is in a similar position to that of the quadrangle storehouse whose facade projects north here (cf Fig 59; Fig 60; Fig 93). If this is correct, then the 'Great New Store house' built between 1688 and 1698 was incorporated into the new storehouse and the old storehouse planned for demolition is the 'Additional Storehouse' (no. 36) shown on the 1698 map, its long axis parallel with the river. The 'Store-keeper's Office' (no. 35) next to it to the east would also have been demolished to make way for the new building (Chapter 4.1).

Work on the new storehouse may have started in summer 1715. The officers wrote to the Navy Board in September that labourers could be spared over autumn and winter (TNA, ADM 106/3297, 28 September 1715, 3); these labourers may have been involved in digging the foundations for the storehouse. However, 'the works of New Storehouse' were certainly under way by the summer of the following year, when the officers requested more workmen (ibid, 11 June 1716, 48). Progress was not helped by 'Mr Goodwin the contractor for serving this his Majesty's Yard with bricks neglecting to send these' (ibid, 16 July 1716, 52).

The officers were keen to appropriate whatever materials they could. They wrote to the Navy Board, 'I pray your honours will order them [the ships] about as soon as possible; knowing their old beams, clamps etc will be of great service in rebuilding the Storehouse, repairing slips and other works in the Yard' (TNA, ADM 106/3297, 16 March 1716, 34). (The ships in question were the the 2nd-rate, 1202bm-ton *Torbay* and the 4th-rate, 914bm-ton *Medway*, rebuilt respectively at Woolwich in 1719 and at Deptford in 1718.) In April the following year, the officers sent out another urgent request for 'as much old serviceable stuff as you can spare toward rebuilding our Storehouse' (ibid, 5 April 1717, 103). Getting rid of the soil dug out for the foundations was a problem, and the officers asked the Navy Board if this could be 'carried away by any person so inclined', in their own boats or the yard's if necessary (ibid, 29 August 1716, 61).

Construction was delayed by a lack of bricklayers (TNA, ADM 106/3297, 23 November 1716, 78) and by work on ships at the yard. In March 1717, the officers requested an extra 60 shipwrights (ibid, 28 March 1717, 102). By April 1717 the foundation 'of the Old Storehouse rebuild' was complete, its

walls over 5ft high. The officers requested permission 'to take down the end of the Cordage House which answers with the front of the said Storehouse, believing it will conduce very much to its strength and uniformity' (ibid, 20 April 1717, 104). This seems to refer to the shortening of the east end of the Tudor storehouse to bring it into line with the rest of the quadrangle storehouse. The officers asked to employ six extra house-carpenters in February 1718 'for rebuilding the east side of the Old Storehouse' (TNA, ADM 106/3298, 26 February 1718, 3).

By July 1718, the new building was ready for stonemasons to do their work. A John Hudson was supposed to provide four masons, but they had refused as the pay offered was too low (TNA, ADM 106/3298, 25 July 1718, 32). In September the officers asked Woolwich dockyard for the loan of bricklayers 'so many as you can spare' for work on 'our Storehouses' (ibid, 22 September 1718, 47), and again the following year, the construction having been delayed by other work (ibid, 26 August 1719, 131).

In October 1719, the officers estimated that the construction of the south-west side of the 'Quadrangle of the Storehouse' would cost £717 8s (TNA, ADM 106/3298, 27 October 1719, 153). The turret for the yard's clock was 'near finished' in spring 1720, indicating that this southern range of the quadrangle storehouse was complete. However, the clock itself was old and 'much out of order' (TNA, ADM 106/3299, 14 May 1720, 6) and the officers were considering 'Mr Bradley's proposal for making a new clock', able to strike the quarter hour (ibid, 15 July 1720, 9). Bradley operated from Fan Church Street (modern Fenchurch Street) and the clock had been out of order for some years (TNA, ADM 106/3298, 15 May 1718, 19). Four bricklayers were discharged at the end of 1720, suggesting that the work on the storehouse had ended or was coming to an end (TNA, ADM 106/3299, 31 December 1720, 29).

The remains of the quadrangle storehouse (B14, Fig 59) dominated excavation area 4 (Fig 3). A series of dumps may have been an attempt to level up the ground before construction began. Some of the dumps contained brick that may have derived from earlier buildings on the site, demolished to make way for the quadrangle storehouse. However, given that the officers of the yard were asking for material from other dockyards for these works, this is uncertain. The level was increased to *c* 2.81–2.85m OD.

The storehouse was 66.10m (217ft) square externally and its four ranges enclosed a yard 43.70m (143ft) (north-west to south-east) by 30.00m (98ft). For ease of description, the four ranges of the quadrangle storehouse are described as the north, south, east and west ranges (Fig 59). The 1753 map (Fig 58) shows each corner of the storehouse offset from the main wall, and this was clear in the surviving walls found in the excavations. Foundations for the clock tower (visible in contemporary paintings and drawings: eg Fig 61; Fig 64) were identified in the south range. The north-eastern corner of the quadrangle storehouse and much of its courtyard were heavily truncated by a series of modern concrete foundations. The north (waterfront) range had fared worst and little of it survived beyond its fragmentary

Fig 61 The St Albans (a 4th-rate, 60-gun, 1207bm-ton, 150ft x 43½ft ship) being floated out of her dock – the dry (double) dock – 'light' (ie with little ballast) and not yet fitted out in 1747 between two sailing cargo barges and (right) the quadrangle storehouse and clock tower and (left) the Master Shipwright's house built in 1708, in a painting by John Cleveley the elder (National Maritime Museum, Greenwich, BHC1046)

north wall. This range was wider than the others as it incorporated the Tudor storehouse (B1). A substantial brick platform in the north-west corner of this range may have supported a stair. The contemporary, early 18th-century waterfront may be represented by the fragmentary remains of a timber revetment (W6, Fig 25). The storehouse is depicted from the river in 1747 in Fig 61.

The east wall of the east range was increasingly fragmentary to the north. At the south end a series of narrow walls formed the foundations to two small rooms. The north wall of the south range (the wall facing into the central yard) had been strengthened with inverted brick arches, a process that would have required at least its partial demolition. The foundations in the west range survived better than the others but showed how much modification had occurred during the quadrangle storehouse's life. As the storehouse developed, there were attempts to strengthen the upper floors, as represented by a line of pillars in the east range. Internal buttresses were also added to walls. Generally, part of the wall was cut away to receive the buttress, so often there was no butt-joint visible.

Further ranges of buildings were constructed along the internal sides of the south and east ranges by 1753 (shown on Fig 58; Fig 59) and along the west range by 1774; the 1774 model shows these as single-storey structures (Fig 7; Fig 93). A narrow wall survived of the southern internal range, with an integral set of stone steps into what would have been a cellar (only a fragment of a later concrete floor survived), as well as the base of a 0.89m wide stone chute. The eastern end of the

narrow wall returned north to form a 2.40m length of wall that was all that remained of the eastern internal range. Other buildings were also constructed in the central yard by 1774, but traces of these had mostly been removed by modern activity. The further works and building construction around the storehouse complex known from the period 1753–74 are described below (6.3).

The building in the south-west corner of the courtyard involved the construction of a set of three north–south aligned cellars (Fig 62). These vaulted cellars were each 3.20m wide and 2.13m high with rough concrete floors. What survived of the brick vaulted ceilings of the western and central cellars ran north–south. The use of varying materials – concrete, cement, red and yellow stock brick – in conjunction with abutting walls suggested that the cellars had been considerably modified over time, but that they were no later than 19th-century in date. In the eastern cellar a scar on the west wall indicated that the vaulting had run east–west. Coal debris in this eastern cellar revealed what had last been stored there before the cellar went out of use; the coal would undoubtedly have been used for the engine house immediately north, alongside the west range, built between 1753 and 1774 (below, 6.3). An iron hatch (subsequently bricked up) opened into the western cellar from the west.

Finds were sparse, considering that this was the main place of storage for the whole dockyard, but numerous iron nails were recovered from a make-up layer, in addition to a copper-alloy buckle (<S1>, Fig 185). Two curved and tapering iron

Fig 62 View of brick vaulted cellars in the quadrangle storehouse (B14), looking north-west

forelock wedges <106> and <107> and the shanks of 15 small copper-alloy nails <39> (length 18–31mm) were also found, together with seven clay pipe stems dating broadly to *c* 1580–*c* 1910.

The mast dock rebuilt, 1714–15

The Navy Board had asked for a survey to be made of the mast dock in the yard. The officers reported that the wharf was 1138ft (347m) long and that to build it new would cost £2333 (TNA, ADM 106/3296, 13 June 1712, 96). This length must relate to the total length of the wharfs forming the internal edge of the mast dock. However, 'the wharfing in the Mast Dock does not require to be wholly new framed', the officers said. Six additional house-carpenters and four additional bricklayers would need to be employed to complete the necessary work in a season (ibid, 1 February 1714, 173).

The accumulated soil in the mast dock also required cleaning out, although 'several masts are lodged in' that would hamper this work. Thirty additional scavelmen – the labourers who cleaned and maintained waterways and ditches – would be required (TNA, ADM 106/3296, 1 February 1714, 173). Disposal of the soil was a recurrent problem. The officers suggested using it 'for the breach down the river' (ibid, 15 February 1714, 173). They also proposed taking down the 'much decayed … old sheds on the Ditch side between the Petty Warr[ant's] House and Mast Houses' and dumping '1500 loads' there, with the rest stored 'on the Anchor Wharf'. The block maker and the wheelwright were using the sheds, but they could be moved into the 'Oarmakers Workhouse … the

upper room being sufficient for the Oarmaker's affairs' (ibid, 19 February 1714, 176). A shed is shown on the 1688 and 1698 maps (Fig 23) behind the mast house (no. 25) and is also shown in the panorama above them, in the background between the wet dock (with ships) and the three-gabled mast house right (ie west) of the wet dock. It is possible that this is the 'old sheds' mentioned, although it is on the yard side rather than the 'ditch side'. In any case, the area referred to seems to lie just to the east of the mast dock.

In April 1714, Nicholas Sampson was contracted to do the work clearing the accumulated soil from the mast dock (TNA, ADM 106/3296, 31 May 1715, 152 [252]). By June 1714 the yard had run out of space to store this soil and there was no space at Woolwich dockyard either (ibid, 16 June 1714, 192). The soil was used later 'to raise the ground' of the yard (TNA, ADM 106/3297, 29 August 1716, 61). The cleaning operation had developed into a major rebuild. Sampson's men were to dig down and replace the 'mud cells' (ie the lower sills of the wharf). He would be paid more for the additional work, and have the use of the yard's labourers, if necessary, and 'pumps and scoops' to keep the water down (TNA, ADM 106/3296, 6 July 1714, 197). About 300ft of the wharf needed to be made good and other works included removing 'the old locks and bridges' and replacing them with new locks, for which 20 extra scavelmen and 30 extra labourers were needed (ibid, 23 February 1715, 238). Water ingress hampered the work, but the 'framing of the locks' was complete by April (ibid, 7 April 1715, 146 [246]). The works were still ongoing in May (ibid, 20 May 1715, 151 [251]), when Sampson had 'finished two of the said locks' (ibid, 31 May 1715, 152 [252]). The works were to be piled: 130 piles 19ft long, 11½in square at the lower end and 9½in at the head, could be supplied from the yard's stores, but many more than this were needed (ibid, 31 May 1715, 153 [253]). The work was drawing to a close by the end of summer and the officers told the Navy Board that the works would be finished by the end of August (ibid, 27 July 1715, 161 [261]).

Despite having been substantially rebuilt thus in 1714–15, there were ongoing problems with the mast dock. 'The land tyes in the wharf at the further end of the Mast Yard being old, occasions the water to break through into the sluice ditch which runs along side the Red House' was one such that needed to be dealt with. The officers suggested extending the new brick wall 'at the further end of the Mast Dock' to the river, some 260ft, 'which will wholly enclose the Yard' at a cost of £642 12s (revised down in a subsequent – near duplicate – letter to £542, with the additional estimate of £502 'if wharf with timber fenced upon' the wall, presumably to address the problem of the ingress of water). The officers also suggested that a new compass maker's shop be built for £77 7s 3d, but this suggestion is absent from the second letter (TNA, ADM 106/3301, 28 November 1728, 102, 103).

During the excavations a timber revetment (S22, Fig 60) was identified which is likely to have been the west side of the entrance channel to the mast dock, through which the mast logs could be floated into the dock from the Thames. The woodwork that survived in this trench, which was not excavated to any great depth, was very decayed but some features of the structure could be discerned. A form of revetment ran north–south for c 5m, with closely-set rectangular oak uprights to which planking had once been fastened on the east side with iron spikes. The uprights were c 180 × 110mm in cross section, and the planking was over 35mm thick.

The wet dock and a new dry dock, 1716

In March 1716, the officers proposed 'cleansing of the Wet Dock that ships, yachts etc may be taken out, and that the gates may be turned outward for the better keeping out the water, which may be easily done' (TNA, ADM 106/3297, 16 March 1716, 34). This work had started by the summer, but the silt was 'more than can be dispensed with in the Yard' and the officers proposed offering it to the local 'country people' (ibid, 5 July 1716, 51).

The empty wet dock would allow the 'slip in the Wet Dock' to be rebuilt. Its sides were rotten and it needed to be deeper to accommodate the 5th-rate *Gosport* (530bm-tons, 118ft × 32ft), built at Woolwich in 1707 and presumably in for repair and maintenance (TNA, ADM 106/3297, 20 March 1716, 35). This slip is shown on the 1698 map (Fig 23, 'B' right). Somewhat confusingly, it is referred to later as 'the slip next the boathouse', although it is clear that it is the slip on the wet dock that is being referred to, not a slip on the river. By the end of April the slip had been 'sunk so low that we are ready to plank the sides'. The project soon developed into a major conversion of this slip into a dry dock; this is the 'single dock' at the north-east corner of the wet dock on the 1753 map (Fig 58; Fig 60). The officers

suggested that they fit 'a small pair of gates at the stern' and build a drain 'to one of the slips launching into the river'. This would make the slip 'a commodious dock for 5th rates' (ibid, 24 April 1716, 39). The cost of the gates and an apron to the new dock would be £400 (ibid, 8 May 1716, 41). This 'New Dry Dock' would require '23 beachways of 39ft long and 30ins by 18ins' (ibid, 25 July 1716, 52). By November 1716, the wharfing at the head and sides of the new dry dock had been framed (ibid, 23 November 1716, 78). There was some minor water ingress from 'springs' and leaks from the wet dock into the new dry dock, but the officers were not overly concerned (ibid, 7 January 1717, 83). The cost of completing the new dry dock was estimated at £200 (ibid, 22 January 1717, 87). The planking of the sides of the new dry dock was almost complete by the end of January 1717 and the focus switched to the base of the dock (ibid, 1 February 1717, 92). By March 'the New Dry Dock is so near finished as to be capable of receiving' the *Gosport* (ibid, 9 March 1717, 102). (The maximum internal width of the much-altered 19th-century double dock, as the dry dock came to be known, was 15.40m.)

The construction of the brick culvert (or 'dreane') was 'an absolute necessity' by August 1716. This was to run from the stern of the new dry dock 'into the next launching slip down the river [?S24]' (TNA, ADM 106/3297, 30 August 1716, 61; 23 October 1716, 70). The officers suggested Nicholas Sampson, who had cleaned the silt out of the mast dock and almost certainly the wet dock. He was 'used to do such work after an uncommon manner by digging under ground (without opening it a top)' for sewers and other water courses in the City of London. Sampson's method of tunnelling was cheaper and could not be done by the men of the yard (ibid, 30 August 1716, 61). This 'water course of the Dry Dock to the river' would be 280ft long, 10ft wide and 18½ft deep, costing £64 4s 6¾d (ibid, 30 August 1716, 62).

Work was under way by autumn 1716, when six extra bricklayers and their labourers were required (TNA, ADM 106/3297, 5 November 1716, 72). The 'dreane' was to be equipped with a sluice, the screw for which (weighing 60lb) and its 'fine brass' nut were to be made by 'the contractor for hand screws', a Mr Bails (or Bayles). The 'brazier contractor', Mr Johnson, had also been approached about the work (ibid, 29 January 1717, 91; 31 January 1717, 91). Bails also supplied 4½in diameter iron screws 'cut with an engine' (ibid, 5 June 1717, 109).

The yard had problems finding bricklayers because of the low wages offered, and asked to borrow four bricklayers from Woolwich (TNA, ADM 106/3297, 23 October 1716, 70). Bad pay may not have been the only reason, as a year later dockyard workers were petitioning for wages not paid for a year. By the end of October 1716, the officers requested that 20 labourers be kept on 'a fortnight longer' for the work on the new dry dock, the storehouse and 'repairing the slips' (ibid, 30 October 1716, 70).

One early brick wall (S17, Fig 63) was identified in the excavation 'cutting off' the north-west corner of the wet dock. The wall, which was mortared into the timber wall at either end, may have been a repair that was made by 1725, as the

Fig 63 View of the junction of the earlier timber and later brick wall (S17) of the wet dock, looking north-west (1.0m scale)

sketch map of this date shows the 'cut-off' corner of the wet dock (that nearest the mast dock on Fig 57).

In 1726 the timber sides of the wet dock required repair (TNA, ADM 106/3301, 14 June 1726, 19). The wet dock was probably cleaned out in 1731 when a rate for the work had been set, the work contracted to 'Mr Nicholas [Sampson]', as in 1716 (TNA, ADM 106/3305, 3 June 1741, 24; 7 July 1741, 26), and it is likely that the repairs were made then if not before.

The wet dock is depicted in 1739 from the west in a drawing attributed to John Cleveley the elder (Fig 64). By 1741 it required emptying again. The contractor had since died and his widow was unsuccessful in winning the contract, which was awarded instead to Christophers Hewitt and Wells (TNA, ADM 106/3305, 3 June 1741, 24; 31 July 1741, 35). The officers calculated the cost of the work on the 1731 rate as £237 10s. The soil was to be dumped 'into the new ground purchased of Sir John Evelyn on the south side of the Mast Dock' (ibid, 7 July 1741, 26). The opportunity was used to repair 'fenders round the wet dock fence' (ibid, 10 November 1741, 57), indicating that at least some of the sides of the structure were timber at this time. The wet dock was drained and by June 1741 the mud was dry enough for the contractors to start work.

The yard perimeter, painters' shop and wharfs in the early 18th century

The officers estimated the cost of replacing a part of the 'old paling fence' on the perimeter of the yard with 'a brick wall with a wood wharf to the ditch'. The new wall would run from 'the Painters Shop where the old brick wall at the upper side of the Yard ends' and continue to the mast dock, returning 'all along the

Fig 64 'Launch of a 60-gun ship at Deptford, 1739', depicted in a view downstream across the wet dock towards the quadrangle storehouse and clock tower, with assorted timber stacks and the perimeter wall visible on the right and two small ships in frame on the slips on the right-hand side of the wet dock (drawing attributed to John Cleveley the elder) (Ministry of Defence, crown copyright 2015, MOD, 4153)

bankside at the extent of the ground lately bought to the Reddhouse so as to enclose the Yard, making a pair of doors for the passage to Says Court and a brick arch across the ditch'. The wall foundation was to be 3ft deep 'in the present ground', presumably the land outside the perimeter that was lower than the level of the yard as the foundation would be '6ft into the Yard'. The length from the painters' shop to the mast dock was 559ft (170m) (TNA, ADM 106/3296, 19 February 1714, 174). Work on the wall started after March 1714 (ibid, 31 March 1714, 182).

The painters' shop identified in the 1698 survey is shown as occupying the near-right-angled turn of the perimeter on the west side of the yard (Fig 23, 'B' right). From here, the wall ran north–south along the south-west perimeter, turning north-east to south-west near the wet dock for a short distance and then parallel to the edges of the mast dock. The wall was identified in area 12 and area 2. The 1.35m wide red brick wall (S10 retained) was stepped and had brick arched openings every few metres along its entire length to allow horizontal land-ties to pass through (Fig 65). These land-ties supported a new revetment on the dockyard side of the ditch. In area 2, the wall was seen in a sondage excavated through the southern end of the 19th-century slipway. Both this and the wall seen in area 12 were constructed of similar bricks, namely post-1666 bricks measuring 215–224 × 97–105 × 60–62mm. Like the earlier revetment, this revetment consisted of timber piles with timber planks nailed in place from the west side. The revetment was slightly shorter than the brick boundary wall and ran significantly deeper. The considerable thickness of this perimeter wall (Fig 46; Fig 65) compares with the surviving early 18th-century brick dockyard wall at Portsmouth which measures *c* 2m thick above ground.

Two slots were excavated to the west of the brick boundary wall and timber revetment, at either end of area 12. These

revealed a red-brick stepped foundation wall that appeared to run parallel to the similarly constructed boundary wall. The stepped foundation was a metre deeper than the boundary wall and lay on a timber baseplate. Along with the revetment, this wall was probably intended to help channel the *Orfletediche* around the yard's perimeter. The marshy area outside the yard at this time was probably susceptible to erosion and would have provided a poor foundation for the wall. The perimeter wall was listing alarmingly to the west when uncovered by the excavation.

The work on the drift wharf and the construction of the brick wall by the side of the ditch would cut off the water supply to 'Mr Andrews of Says Court', and the officers considered how this might be addressed. The solution, they suggested, was to build a drain from 'the Wet Dock slip by side of the Mould Loft to the little ditch by the Oarmakers Shop' (TNA, ADM 106/3296, 12 May 1714, 187). The mould loft (no. 31) and wet dock slip are both shown on the 1698 map, and indeed on the 1688 map (Fig 23), so these structures were still extant in 1714. The oarmakers' shop is not shown, but it was presumably located in the range of buildings on the perimeter of the yard, over the ditch, on a rough line between the slip and Sayes Court.

By August, the piers for 'the gateway in the brickwall', built by Henry Hester, 'for enclosing the Yard and Mast Dock' were ready for the masons' work (TNA, ADM 106/3296, 18 August 1714, 208). This gateway is almost certainly the 'pair of doors' to preserve the access from Sayes Court to the river. Early the next year, Hester had finished the brick wall 'from the Mast dock Gate to the extent of the ground to the Thames returning to the Mast House Slip'. The wall was 165ft long, its face 'wrought with stock bricks, laid the length of a brick or nine inches in Terrass to High Water Mark' (ibid, 22 January 1715, 228). Hester was paid £600 for 'building a brick wall at Deptford' (*Cal Treasury B*, xxviii, clxx–clxxxviii). The mast

Fig 65 View of the yard's brick boundary wall (S10) and timber revetment, looking east towards later slip no. 1 (S27)

house slip was probably the small (east–west) slipway shown on the west side of the wet dock on the 1753 map (Fig 58).

Elsewhere, timber fences were being replaced in brick. 'The fence from the Master Attendants Lodgings to the Sailfield Gate', 67ft in length, was decayed and the officers suggested replacing it with a 9ft high brick wall (TNA, ADM 106/3296, 4 April 1715, 146 [246]). The 'sailfield', which is shown on the 1753 Milton map (Fig 58), occupied the south-eastern corner of the yard to the east of the south gate (Fig 66). The lodgings (house), shown on the 1698 map (Fig 23, 'B' right, no. 7), lay at the west end of the officers' quarters well inside the perimeter, and the gate referred to must be the south gate shown on the map. The timber fence must therefore be the one running north–south along the *west* side of the sailfield, not the yard perimeter that formed the east side.

This wall was probably built by 1722; there is a reference to part of a wall by the south gate and around the sailfield blowing down in that year. The following year, the officers suggested taking it down altogether and building a new one (TNA, ADM 106/3300, 29 March 1723, 23; /3301, 28 April 1726, 13). In 1726 the officers wrote to Woolwich asking for the loan of bricklayers, having had orders to complete this wall (ibid, 21 April 1726, 13).

In 1726 the 'wharfs of the Wet Dock, by the Wet and Mast Docks and fronting the river' needed repair. The officers asked that five house-carpenters be employed (TNA, ADM 106/3301, 14 June 1726, 19), indicating that these wharfs were timber at this time. Other repairs were either not carried out or not identified, because in April 1727, 150ft of the river wall by the

mast dock collapsed (ibid, 17 April 1727, 47). The wall had been 'built by contract about thirty years ago and in the opinion of the Master Bricklayer not well performed'. A further 150ft of the wall was also in a very bad condition and the officers proposed taking this part down and rebuilding it all, at an estimated cost of £435 (ibid, 19 April 1727, 47). Initially the Navy Board agreed to a rebuild of the collapsed part only and to the building of a new perimeter wall to enclose the land bought from Sir John Evelyn (below). The officers asked for four bricklayers and ten labourers to be employed (ibid, 21 April 1727, 48) and for the yard's scavelmen to work extra time (ibid, 24 April 1727, 48). A further two bricklayers and six labourers were soon required for the new perimeter wall 'and the brick wharf by the Mast Dock Crane', presumably the river wall (ibid, 31 May 1727, 53).

The officers asked for an additional six bricklayers and ten labourers in August 1727 to be employed to complete 'the new wall and repairing the wharf by the Mast Dock before the frosty weather comes on' (TNA, ADM 106/3301, 9 August 1727, 63). In July 1728, they asked that the bricklayers and labourers be allowed to work extra 'for finishing the wall and drien [presumably drain] before winter' (ibid, 26 July 1728, 94). In spring 1729, the officers proposed construction of 'the two arches, for a water course for the Common Sewer from the Painters Shop to the corner of the Red House' and asked for three extra bricklayers and their labourers to be employed (ibid, undated, but probably 10–12 March 1728, 114).

The costs of recent works in the yard were detailed in a letter of February 1728. For 'finishing the wall to enclose the west end of the Yard from the Redhouse Road to the old wall of the Mast Dock 394ft [long] height 14ft mean thick 2½ bricks, containing 34¾ rods of brickwork', the cost was £260 12s 6d; for 'digging the trench and laying two pipes to carry the water … oak pipes of 6in bore 30ft [long, presumably] … two plugs with iron hoops and handles, fixing and planking them', the cost was £19 17s 6d; total cost £280 9s 6d. For 'building a brick wall against the bank, between the Mast Dock and Redhouse, length 260ft[,] depth below the surface 14ft, height from thence 12ft[,] from the foundation to the surface mean thickness 4 bricks; from thence 2½ bricks mean thickness; to be wrought 200ft long 5ft high, from the foundation ½ brick thick with Tarras', total cost £636 14s 6d. For 'building a brick wall from the Painters Shop to the Block Loft, length 348ft[,] height to the surface 4ft[,] mean thickness 4½ bricks, from thence 18ft high, mean thickness 2½ bricks', total cost £486 9s 6d. For 'making a brick arch for a water course for the Common Sewer from the Painters Shop to the corner of the Redhouse 700ft[,] 2ft high from the brick paving at the bottom of the underside of the arch, and 1ft 6ins broad, the inside and bottom to be

Fig 66 The sailfield and (left) perimeter wall, as shown (upper) on the 1774 scale model (Fig 7), with (lower) part of the officers' quarters, looking 'south-east' (National Maritime Museum, Greenwich, L0459-016)

wrought with Tarras 4ins' including 'digging and clearing the ditch for the foundation' and 'planking and making the foundation', total cost £302 8s ½d. For 'making another brick arch of the same dimensions to convey the water from the river to Sir John Evelyn's ground', cost £302 8s ½d. For 'filling up this ditch over the arches 700ft long; 15ft broad, 4½ft deep', cost £131 10s. Discounted for use of old bricks, the total cost was £2081 19s 7d (TNA, ADM 106/3301, 16 February 1728, 83).

Extending the yard in the 1720s

A plan to extend the yard into John Evelyn's land was being considered in the mid 1720s. The diarist had died in 1706 and his grandson, Sir John Evelyn, Bt (1682–1763) had inherited. '[I]t would be a great advantage and convenience to join and lay open to the rest of the Yard the piece of ground at present purchased of Sir John for a mast dock as likewise another piece of ground of about 9 acres lying between the Mast Dock wall and his garden.' Evelyn had use of a path from Sayes Court 'through the Mast Dock to the waterside' (ie to the east of the mast dock) (shown on Fig 57). The officers suggested that this be moved to the other end of the mast dock (ie the west) to make the yard 'more private'. Sayes Court had been let 'to a gentleman who has set up a manufacture' employing a hundred people, 'and great numbers of them are frequently passing to and fro through the mast dock' (TNA, ADM 106/3300, 11 March 1724, 67; undated, but almost certainly 9–18 May 1724, 75).

The officers also highlighted the problem of the mast dock being cut off from the rest of the yard by the brick wall (Fig 57). The workmen were 'out of sight' during the day and at night the watchmen were separated from their colleagues (TNA, ADM 106/3300, 11 March 1724, 67).

The addition of the 9 acre meadow 'will afford room to enlarge the Mast Pond', currently too small. The officers had been obliged to lay masts out in the river, where 'they frequently in stormy weather break loose and drive away' and had to be recovered. This land could also be used to build a new smithy, mast house and boathouse, the current ones 'inconveniently situated … old and under a necessity of being rebuilt' (TNA, ADM 106/3300, 11 March 1724, 67; 18 May 1724, 75). The officers wanted no buildings to be erected by the Evelyn estate within 40ft of the yard walls and for the yard's workmen to have access to his land, with due notice, for repair of the yard (ibid, undated, but probably 9–18 May 1724, 75).

Sir John agreed to the sale the following April (TNA, ADM 106/3300, 16 April 1725), and this meadow land corresponds to Open Area 15 (Fig 59). Sir John was concerned about the water supply to Sayes Court and the officers suggested that a ditch be made leading from his pond 'by the intended new wall of the Yard' and fed by water from a drain from the river via Little Crane Mead (ibid, 28 April 1725, 113). This pond is likely to be one of those shown on the 1753 Milton map near the re-entrant angle between the old yard wall and the new one (Fig 58; Fig 60).

A number of cobbled surfaces to the west (Fig 59; Fig 67) represent the original surface level of the dockyard during the 18th century after it had expanded into the land acquired from Sir John Evelyn. Despite this expansion, a section of the pre-1725 south-west perimeter wall (immediately east of the plank sheds) still seems to have been standing in 1739 when it is shown in a drawing (Fig 64, bottom right). A brick wall (S47, Fig 60) south-west of the plank sheds (B20 (Fig 59; Fig 60) and B17) corresponds to the new yard perimeter on the 1753 map (Fig 58); it may have survived because it was reused as part of one of the buildings near the yard perimeter shown on the 1774 model (Fig 7) and map (Fig 71). An associated cobbled surface may have been part of this building or the yard.

Offices, officers' quarters and lodgings

Domestic and official buildings were also being constantly repaired and rebuilt. The wooden fence between the Storekeeper's and the Builder's (Master Shipwright's) assistant's gardens was rotten and needed to be replaced in brick at a cost of £4 10s 'as the rest of the gardens here are secured' (TNA, ADM 106/3297, 22 November 1717, 153), and the Storekeeper's washhouse needed to be similarly rebuilt (ibid, 14 February 1718, 169). The Navy Board ordered that a 'brewhouse' be erected for Mr Janeway 'in the same manner as the Storekeepers' and the officers estimated that this would cost £76 (TNA, ADM 106/3298, 26 August 1719, 131).

The relations with neighbours could be fraught. In September 1718, the owners of the property behind the Master Shipwright's house (Fig 23, 'B' right, no. 45 'Builders Dwelling house') cut off part of his lead gutter and dug a foundation close to his wall, with the intention of erecting timber tenements overlooking his house. The new building was to include an alehouse, and the officers worried about the fire hazard (TNA, ADM 106/3298, 18 September 1718, 44). It was completed by the end of the following year, the Master Shipwright complaining that his back parlour was 'entirely darkened' by it (ibid, 11 December 1719, 181).

In June 1720, the officers were reporting that 'the Master Attendant, Master Shipwright, Clerk of the Survey and Master Shipwrights Assistants Offices' were very rotten and needed replacing. These buildings were 'from the end of the Master Shipwrights house and the Porters Lodging'. The Storekeeper's office, which was by the Water Gate, was also to be taken down and replaced with 'new offices of two storey high'. The cost for this work was estimated at £350 (TNA, ADM 106/3299, 27 June 1720, 8; 30 June 1720, 8).

Parts of the 'Master of Attendance's house' or lodgings (Fig 23, 'B' right, no. 7) were identified in the excavations (B19/B31, Fig 60). These are keyed as the 'Wash-house' and 'Kitching' on the 1698 detailed survey (Fig 40), although their function may have changed when the lodging was rebuilt. A number of phases of building were identified. The earliest phase consisted of an east–west aligned wall, exposed 0.29m deep and built of red-purple bricks set in white lime mortar; its foundation consisted in part of reused stone, including an ashlar block measuring 0.53m × 0.16m. It was not clear what structure this wall might relate to. It had been partially destroyed by the construction of the north, south and west walls of a room built

Fig 67 View of cobbled surfaces of the 18th-century dockyard and, beyond, the brick boundary wall, looking east towards the 19th-century slip cover roof structure 'Olympia'

of red brick, with some yellow brick, set in white lime mortar. This room corresponds to the walls of the Master Attendant's washroom to the north and his kitchen to the south. External surfaces identified to the north and west also correspond to the layout of this part of the Master Attendant's lodgings, the surfaces consisting of brick paving and flattish stones respectively. The width of part of the west wall suggested that it might have supported a structure, such as a stair. An internal east–west aligned wall had been added; later still, the south wall had been rebuilt in red brick set in cement, suggesting a 19th-century date for the rebuild.

The officers suggested enlarging the Clerk of the Cheque's office by expanding into the adjacent guardroom, removing a chimney and enlarging a room adjoining the pay office (TNA, ADM 106/3300, 6 August 1723, 40). Among other works proposed, in June 1722 the officers wrote to Chatham asking for 'chalk rubbish … of the largest sort, and as free from dirt as possible' for raising parts of the yard (TNA, ADM 106/3299, 22 June 1722, 94).

The porter's lodging was much decayed by summer 1726, and the officers suggested taking it down and building a new house 'near the upper gate for the better security of the gate, [and] to join to the wall of the Yard'. The new house was to be three storeys high, with a washhouse and chamber over the two small rooms in front, at a cost of £350. The officers explained that the present lodging was a considerable distance from both gates, and there was no room near the lower gate for the new building. The upper gate was 'the only gate where timber can pass' (TNA, ADM 106/3301, 13 August 1726, 23). The lower gate was almost certainly the gate and gatehouse in the east wall of the yard, just north of the officers' quarters, and the upper gate the 'south gate', both indicated on the 1698 map (Fig 23, 'B' right, nos 1, 9). The new porter's lodge is likely to be that marked on the 1753 map, to the west of the south gate (Fig 58). It was built and inhabited by 1741 (TNA, ADM 106/3305, 9 November 1741, 56).

6.3 Changes and problems in the mid 18th century (c 1740–70): archaeological and historical evidence

The smithy rebuild of 1741

In 1723, the smithy contained five sets of single bellows, ranging in size from 6ft 4in long by 2ft 6in broad to 8ft 9in long by 3ft 2in broad, and three sets of double bellows, the largest 6ft long by 3ft 2in broad. Other tools in use by the smiths included gang hammers, tools for making anchors, gauges, callipers, hoops, tongs, cast-iron weights and anvils. The reason for the survey was that John Crowley, a well-known figure in the local area (Francis and Bowsher 2013), was 'leaving the Smiths contract'. The smithy was to be run more directly by the dockyard and the officers recommended to the Navy Board the numbers of men that should be employed: a master smith, three 'servants', foremen of the 1st, 2nd, 3rd, 4th and 5th fires, and five 'hammersmen'. A Mr Dummer acquired the foremen: Robert Smith, Joseph Ripington, J Beddard, Thomas Booth and George Morgan (TNA, ADM 106/3300, 20 May 1723, 26–31; 19 June 1723, 33–4).

The smithy was 'much enlarged with several additional large fires', the rebuild completed by the end of July 1741 (Fig 68). There were now 26 fires 'which will be constantly at work' and the number of men would have to be increased from 62 to 80 (TNA, ADM 106/3305, 21 August 1741, 41). Four hundred chaldrons of coal were required by the smithy for 1742, compared to 25 for the offices (ibid, 6 April 1742, 99). The work of the smithy showed a steady increase. In 1756, 362¼ chaldrons of coal were used; in 1757, 453¼ chaldrons; 417½ chaldrons in 1758; and 453¼ chaldrons in 1759 (TNA, ADM 106/3313, 22 April 1760, np).

Only the south end of the smithy was excavated, but this showed that the rebuild (B18, Fig 69) was extensive. The smithy

Fig 68 The smithy, as shown on the 1774 scale model (Fig 7), looking 'south-east' (National Maritime Museum, Greenwich, L0459-013)

Fig 69 View of the walls of the smithy rebuilt in 1741 (B18), looking west

was extended south, its 28.70m long south wall returning to form the 12.80m long east wall. Both walls were 0.56m wide and built of red bricks measuring 240 × 115 × 65mm. The walls of the earlier smithy were demolished, and in one case used as the foundation for a new internal wall.

A make-up layer [5755] in the rebuilt smithy contained one fragment from a small case bottle made of natural blue glass, while the infill of a furnace [5756] contained an iron forelock wedge <657> and iron slag. A dump [5769] yielded a post-medieval peg roofing tile with a single round nail hole 9mm in diameter (normally two holes would be present). Medieval peg tiles with a single hole are occasionally found in London, but post-medieval examples are extremely rare and it is possible that the single hole was accidental. A similar peg tile was found nearby, in Open Area 9.

Other renovations and repairs in the 1740s

In 1740, £538 2s was spent on the Surgeon's lodgings, a major rebuild; £264 17s 8d on paving the yard; and £33 on the single dock (TNA, ADM 106/3305, 26 February 1741, 5). By 1741 there had been a number of further changes to the yard: 'an addition to the wharf in front of the Storehouse ranging from its east end to the east slip and middle crane'; a new crane had been built 'at the Masthouse' – probably the crane shown to the north-west of the mast houses marked 'U' on the 1753 map (Fig 58) and '25' ('Mast house') on the 1698 map (reproduced here as Fig 23, 'B' right); and the rebuilt smithy (B18, above) and new sawhouses (below). There was now an ambitious plan to pave these parts of the yard, together with the 'Carriage Road' linking the new crane with the new sawhouses, using '70 Tuns of Ragg Stones [delivered] by Mr Morgan Hall', although this on its own would not be sufficient. The additional cost was estimated at £625 (ibid, 8 July 1741, 26; 15 July 1741, 28). The officers also proposed that the yard's single landing place on the river be equipped with an iron gate – purchased from 'Messrs Crowley' and built for £25 – and a hard way made for men and stores to land, costing £91 6s 8d (ibid, 28 December 1741, 69). The iron gate can be seen on the 1774 model near the north-east corner of the storehouse (Fig 93).

The necessity for paving was demonstrated by the contractor's method of removing mud from the wet dock. Previously the soil had been barrowed out, but now they 'do it by carts and horses', tearing up the roads and ground (TNA, ADM 106/3305, 31 July 1741, 35). Although the mud had been cleared by November 1741 (ibid, 10 November 1741, 57), the officers reported to the Navy Board in some panic that the wet dock could still not be used. The wing wharfs of the single (wet) dock (marked 'O' on the 1753 map) were still under major renovation and allowing in water would make this work impossible. The cause of the panic was clear – the winter was hard and the yachts and small vessels in the river needed a harbour to avoid risking damage if 'the Thames freezes'. The officers suggested that these vessels be sent to Greenwich (ibid, 30 December 1741).

The clockhouse and clock needed painting in summer 1741

(TNA, ADM 106/3305, 19 August 1741, 39). Repairs were also ongoing in autumn 1741 to the boatswain's house, painters' shop and 'sheds in the Deal Yard' (ibid, 10 November 1741, 57).

A shed between the stables and the painters' shop in the range of buildings on the west perimeter wall of the yard was rotten and the officers proposed taking it down and putting up a small shed at the east end of the painters' shop instead. They also suggested running 'a grating fence' from the pond to the stables from which large pieces of canvas could be attached for painting and to enclose the area. Part of this fence would be 70ft long and 24ft high, the rest 60ft long and 14ft high. The estimate for the cost of the shed was £32 6s and that for the fence £116 15s 8d (TNA, ADM 106/3305, 12 March 1741, 6; 14 May 1741, 15).

'[T]he old Porters Lodging' had not been used since the new one had been built, and the officers suggested that it be used as lodging for the boatswain, a Mr Landen. To put the lodging into 'habitable repair' would cost £64 (TNA, ADM 106/3305, 9 November 1741, 56). The porter's lodging may be that mentioned in 1720 as near the Master Shipwright's house and reported as 'much decayed' and ready for demolition in 1726. As for Mr Davies, the porter, the officers proposed that he be built a washhouse 'at the west end of his garden adjoining to the brick wall of the Yard' for £36 10s. Davies had been using his cellar, but this was damp, 'occasioned by the Common Sewer running under it' (ibid, 18 November 1741, 57). (This problem had still not been resolved some ten years later when repairs to the porter's lodging, to prevent his cellar from flooding, were estimated at a cost of £31 11s 6d (TNA, ADM 106/3309, 24 April 1752, 64).) Work on the old porter's lodging had revealed that its foundations were rotten, and the officers proposed taking it down and building 'a small brick house ranging in front with the Offices' instead, at a cost of £195 (TNA, ADM 106/3305, 23 November 1741, 59).

'[T]he shed which covers the pitch kettles' burnt down in March 1742, despite the pitch heater insisting that 'he withdrew the fire and quenched it' (TNA, ADM 106/3305, 27 March 1742, 97). In July 1739, a serious fire had destroyed thousands of barrels of pitch tar and turpentine being stored (Oppenheim 1926, 369; Baugh 1965, 279).

The clock was repaired by February 1751 at a cost of £23 (TNA, ADM 106/3309, 2 February 1753, 21). This was evidently a major undertaking as the clock had to be removed from the turret above the storehouse (Fig 61) for repair. Gravel was used for 'the New Pavement' of the yard (ibid, 22 April 1752, 64). The king's coat of arms over the 'Old Gateway' was 'very much decayed and ready to fall down', and it was proposed to take it down in 1753 and replace it with brickwork (ibid, 5 March 1753, 100).

Building in the east part of the yard, c 1740–53

This area of the yard became the focus of building activity in the 1740s. The sum of £722 2s 1d had been spent repairing what was described as the double dock in 1740 (TNA, ADM 106/3305, 26 February 1741, 5), evidently a major rebuild of the dock known previously as the dry dock. (The dock entrance is pictured in 1747 in Fig 61.) However, there were problems with the gates of the double dock in the summer of 1752. The 'decayed parts' of the timber gates and wing wharfs failed and at high tide water forced its way in. As an emergency measure, the officers proposed making a dam outside the gates 'for the greater security of the ships in the Dock' as the gates and wing wharfs were being repaired (TNA, ADM 106/3309, 31 July 1752, 75). In April 1754 it was decided to enlarge the double dock: the new work was to include piers of stone and two-leaf gates, instead of wicket gates (Oppenheim 1926, 374).

Repairs were necessary to 'the Causey of the Upper Watergate' (presumably the gravel hard outside the watergate just to the east of the yard) due to damage by the yard's lighter and storeship grounding on it. The arrangement was that its timber frame be repaired at the king's expense, with the Deptford watermen supplying the gravel infill which formed the 'support to the Dock wall' (TNA, ADM 106/3309, 30 March 1751, 26).

In 1753 work began on a 'new brick wharf at the east side of the Double Dock Gates' (TNA, ADM 106/3309, 5 March 1753, 100). The foundation, of 'one hundred and sixty solid yards', could only be dug at low water, and the scavelmen agreed to work extra time (for more pay) to do this (ibid, 7 April 1753, 105). The specification included 'fender piles 12ins by 14ins [in cross section]', 'landtyes 12ins square at inner and 14ins square at outer end', 'needles 9ins by 6ins', 'templets 14[ins] by 12[ins] to lay under the landtyes' and 'piles 9ins by 6ins'. The total cost was estimated at £515 13s 5½d (ibid, 25 June 1753, 112). This difficult building work involved reclaiming land from the Thames, bringing the new wharf 'so far into the river as to range with the wharf above it on the west side of the Double Dock' (ibid, 30 April 1753, 106); this difference in alignment between the wharfs on the the east and west sides of the double dock is evident on the map of 1753 (Fig 58). The officers warned that the wharf could not be completed before winter because of the restrictions imposed by the tide (ibid, 6 June 1753, 109).

The officers took the opportunity of work on the wharf to suggest moving the crane 'on the larboard side of the Dock' (shown to the east of the double dock gate on the 1753 map, Fig 58). This crane, whose timber foundations were rotten, so 'often obstructs the repairs of ships carrying on in the Double Dock in war time' that 'the workmen have been obliged sometimes to lay down their tools, in order to let the timber pass and repass on the carriages'. Additionally (and somewhat in contradiction), the crane was 'sometimes not used for three months together'. A location 'to the side of the West slip' would be better; a new crane would cost £242 12s (TNA, ADM 106/3309, 19 December 1753, 87).

Plank sheds in the west part of the yard, 1750s

In the west of the yard, the 1753 map (Fig 58) shows a long building, subdivided into 13 bays, immediately west of the wet dock and labelled 'T' for plank houses. The west wall of this building (B20, Fig 59) corresponds to the perimeter of the yard before the acquisition of the Evelyn land in 1725 (above, 6.2),

which would account for its odd alignment. The original building (B20) then was formed of two brick walls running roughly east–west that used the yard perimeter wall as its west wall. The walls survived at best only a few courses high, the northern wall [5002] being 13.30m long by 1.00m wide and the southern wall [5105], more fragmentary, being 5.75m long by 0.74m wide. Both walls sat on timber plank foundations. The walls probably correspond to the subdividing bays. Another short length of brick wall (B42, Fig 59; Fig 60), surviving one course high and measuring 2.00m long by 0.60m wide, may also have been part of this building, perhaps a later addition. Subsidence makes the decision to incorporate the yard wall a questionable one; the instability of the perimeter wall may have been a factor in the decision to demolish it, after which an extension to the plank sheds (B17) was built to the west.

The 1774 and 1802 maps show this second building (B17) along the west side of Building 20, but with its south gable stopping short so that this structure was subdivided into only 12 bays (Fig 71; Fig 95). This western building or extension (on the other side of the (former) perimeter wall) is not shown on the map of 1753 (Fig 58), although tree-ring dating (below) suggests that it utilised timber felled in 1746. The map of 1858 (Fig 121) shows that these buildings had been replaced by two 'plank sheds' further west (B26, B27).

The eastern and western sides of the extension (B17) used two further types of timber foundation (Fig 70; Fig 71). A series of oak trestle frames were set to run east–west across the perimeter ditch, now filled in, which appear to have supported the east side of the extension (B17) and presumably the west side of Building 20. The trestles comprised a simple short sill beam timber morticed for a short vertical post and having a short curved brace timber on the east side. The tenons were not pegged as they would normally have been in earlier work, nor were the trestles supported on piles or any other foundations. Presumably the design was intended to rely on the area of the plank-like sill beams to resist downward pressure. Trestle foundations appear to have been used where it was inconvenient to set up a pile-driving rig. The western side of the extension (B17) appears to have been set on a line of large oak piles which were only minimally exposed but had clearly been made by a combination of hewing and sawing. These load-bearing points were widely set and any building above them would also have had to have had strong lateral beams supporting it.

A representative trestle consisted of a sill beam [5640] comprising a pit-sawn oak plank, surviving 2.15m long by 380mm wide and 100mm thick. The post [5638] was tenoned into the west end of the sill but it was not secured with a peg, possibly due to the difficult access after erection. The post was hewn to a rectangular cross section 310mm square and was 0.83m long below a rotted top. The slightly curved oak brace timber [5639] was hewn to a rectangular section measuring 300 × 230mm, leaving some of the curved ('waney') edge of the parent log under the bark.

A similar oak brace timber [5632] was slice-sampled and successfully tree-ring dated, giving a felling date of spring 1746 (Chapter 10.9; Fig 199). Technologically speaking there is no

Building 29

Open Area 18
yard

Building 30
workshops

Building 16

Open Area 13
gravel headland

Open Area 14
alluvium

Building 15
storehouse/boathouse

Building 14
quadrangle storehouse

south range

courtyard

engine
house

west
range

east
range

Building 1
Tudor storehouse

north range

Structure 31
slipway no. 5

timber
posts

Building 17

trestles

Building 20

land-ties

slipway

wet dock

Structure 18
brick dock wall

Structure 18
brick dock wall

land-ties

land-ties

Structure 9
gate

walkway

Structure 30
slipway no. 4

Structure 27
slipway no. 1

River Thames

0   25m

Fig 70 Plan of principal archaeological features in the eastern part of the dockyard in the mid to later 18th century (1753–74) (period 4) (scale 1:750)

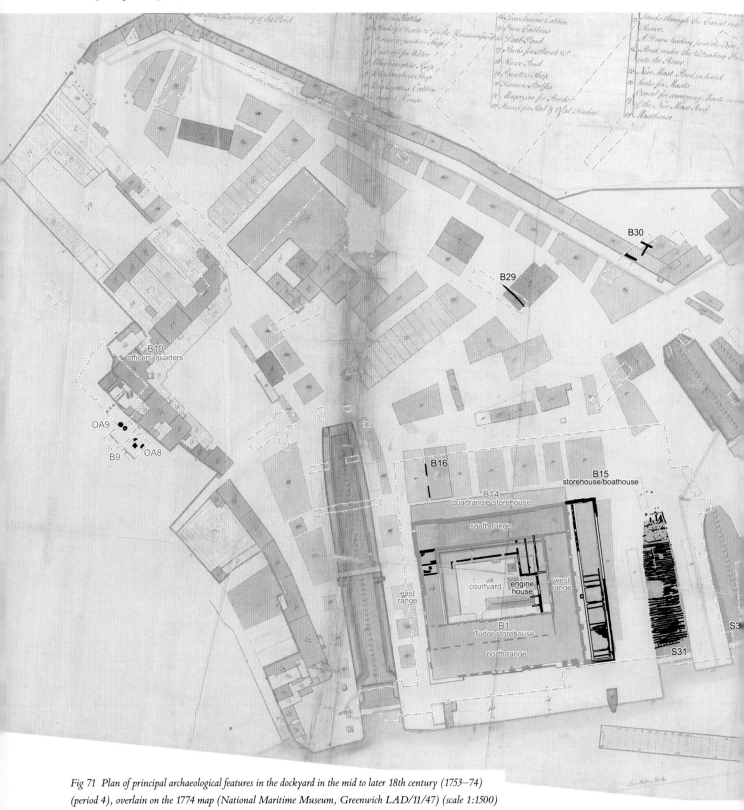

Fig 71 Plan of principal archaeological features in the dockyard in the mid to later 18th century (1753–74) (period 4), overlain on the 1774 map (National Maritime Museum, Greenwich LAD/11/47) (scale 1:1500)

reason to reject this date and the sapwood was well preserved, so we might presume that these foundations were probably erected in 1746 or possibly 1747, rather than that these timbers were being reused or stockpiled. There would have been no reason to season any of these timbers as they were set in wet ground. However, the fact that this western extension is not shown on the map of 1753 (Fig 58) suggests that the building was at most under construction at that date.

Repairs to the wet dock and the failed dock gates, 1751 onwards

The failure of the wet dock gates, 1751, and the aftermath, as reported

On the night of 6 December 1751, the gates of the wet dock failed. As the tide receded, water started to rush out into the

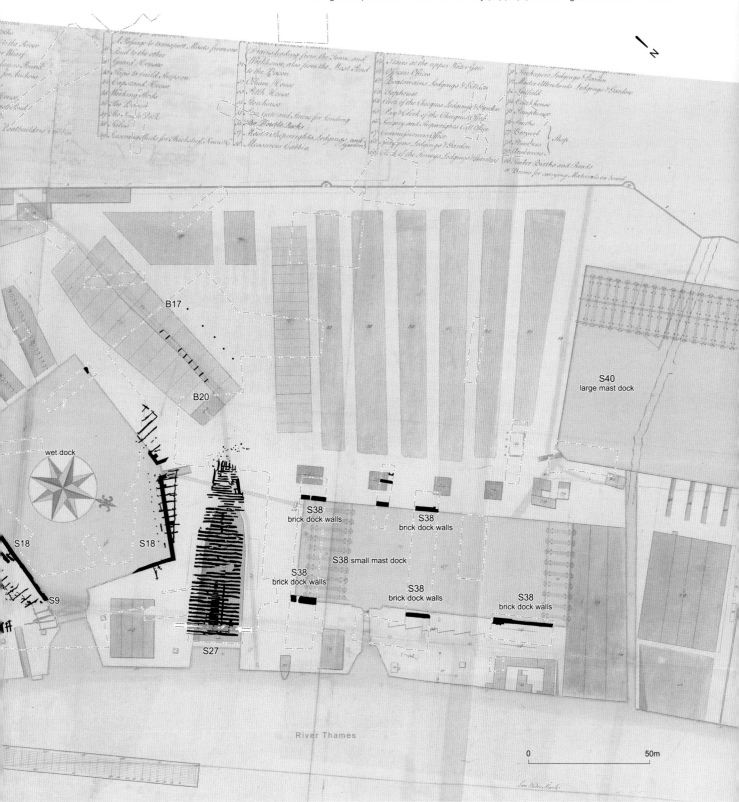

river. The water level sank and the ships in the dock, the sloop *Royal Caroline* (232bm-tons, built at Deptford in 1750) and two 6th-rate ships, the *Wager* (511bm-tons) and the *Winchelsea* (441bm-tons), were all in danger of grounding on the base of the wet dock. One hundred and thirty shipwrights were kept for up to three hours to 'shore and secure these ships', while a team of six house-carpenters and eight scavelmen attempted to stem the leak. Disaster was only narrowly averted (TNA, ADM 106/3309, 10 December 1751, 47). It is safe to assume that the gates were extensively repaired after this event.

The launch of the 3rd-rate, 70-gun, 160ft × 45½ft *Buckingham* (1436bm-tons) was delayed because it was not yet painted. The Navy Board had ordered that ships should be 'compleat and painted' before being launched, and the officers asked for a delay in the *Buckingham*'s launch because the master painter had not been able to finish as 'the weather has been so wett for some weeks past' (TNA, ADM 106/3309, 25 March 1751, 26). There were further delays for the 'spring tydes' and the 'full moon' (ibid, 11 April 1751, 28; 19 April 1751, 28) before the *Buckingham* could be launched 'from the East Slip on the River' on the 30 April (ibid, 30 April 1751, 28; Fig 72). The wet dock entrance and dock wall were still timber-faced at this time, as Fig 72 shows.

In March 1760, the officers suggested making a drain 'between the Wet Dock and Mast Pond … by which communication we conceive the water will contribute greatly to the scour and keep the said Docks much longer clean from soil and sullage, and thereby prevent their being so frequently cleaned'. The cost would be £1200 (TNA, ADM 106/3313, 27 March 1760, np). Cleaning the docks was a major expense, and an inconvenience as it put them out of action for a considerable period.

The wet dock had already been drained for cleaning and this provided an opportunity to inspect the sides. 'The wood wharfing of the side of the Wet Dock from the gates to the Mast House being decayed', the officers proposed 'to build a brick wall in their room' at a cost of £595 1s (TNA, ADM 106/3313, 2 April 1760, np). This was probably the brick lining running west from the wet dock gates. The work of building the drain and the brick wall were approved by the Navy Board on 28 March and 2 April respectively, and the officers listed the materials required. These included: 'Plain piles out of elm or

oak 6ft long and about 9ins square, to be shod with iron or not as may be directed'; 'Do. [ditto] with the heads to be Tennanted'; 'Ground ways … sawed to about 12ins square morticed on the heads of the piles'; 'Bearers on piles … sawed to about 12ins by 8ins and secured on the heads of the piles with two bolts or spikes in each length of bearer'; 'Plank of 4ins' and of '3ins' 'to be secured on the bearers or ground ways'; 'Ground and capsills … sawed to about 14ins square'; 'Fenders Do. 14ins square'; 'Landties'; 'Crosspieces and piles thereto [ie for the land-ties]'. The brickwork was to be set in tarras and mortar. Parts of the wet dock sides were already built in brick as the yard's workmen were to be employed 'cutting down the old brickwork' (ibid, 4 April 1760, np). These materials seem to relate mostly to the replacement of the timber wet dock wharf in brick, including the foundations of the wharf (ibid, 8 May 1760, np).

Modifications to the wet dock were ongoing in May 1760. The dock was being cleaned, the mud deposited in the 'Meadow' (TNA, ADM 106/3313, 8 May 1760, np), the land bought from Sir John Evelyn some years previously and now enclosed within the dockyard perimeter wall. The officers requested more bricklayers, labourers and house-carpenters. A new apron was being built as well as 'two side wharfs' – that is, the wharfs forming the channel from the wet dock to the river. The work also included 'hanging the gates the contrary way to open into the said Dock' (ibid, 8 May 1760, np). This indicates

Fig 72 The Buckingham *on the stocks, ready for launch, painted by John Cleveley the elder (possibly the figure drawing the scene on the corner of the river wall) in 1752. The wet dock gates and entrance are to the right, with sawpits in the background; in the centre can be seen an overhanging privy to the left of a small (half-) slip, with a wherry or water-taxi in the foreground; to the left of the* Buckingham *(shown with only minimal elements of cradling and support) are the sheer legs for raising the stern post, transom and lower frame timbers of another large ship and, to its left, an 'upriver' or West Country timber barge next to a house or donkey crane, showing a team of four horses drawing a baulk of timber which has just been unloaded (National Maritime Museum, Greenwich, BHC3762)*

that before 1760 the wet dock gates opened outwards, although reversing the direction of the gates did not happen until two years later (ibid, 25 August 1762, np). The 1774 model shows the gates opening inwards (Fig 7). This change made sense as the weight of water in the wet dock would seal the gates shut at low tide. The gates would only have to hold off the pressure of water from the river when the wet dock was drained, usually only when repairs or cleaning were necessary.

Problems were also revealed with the south-east part of the wet dock, where 'the foundation is sunk and the wall cracked in several places and bulges into the Dock'. Workmen shored the wall and dug away the ground at the back of the wall to relieve the pressure. 'We also find a small crack in the north part of the wall next the Mast house'. The officers needed to borrow 20 scavelmen from the contractor George Collard (TNA, ADM 106/3313, 10 July 1760, np). Further digging revealed that the foundation was 'entirely decayed' and the officers recommended that the wall be taken down and rebuilt by contract. Despite there being 80,000 bricks that 'may be saved from the old wall', the cost of this unforeseen work was still an enormous £1427 11s (ibid, 19 July 1760, np).

There is the sense from the officers' letters that the scale of the work was beginning to overwhelm them. In August, the officers reported that there were not enough labourers 'to carry on the other works and pump and bale the water out of the Wet Dock' and they proposed that this be done 'by the Contractors people' (TNA, ADM 106/3313, 18 August 1760, np). The heavy rains in September would not have helped (ibid, 26 September 1760, np), but by November Collard had almost finished 'the new wall at the southeast part of the wet dock'. The officers asked the Navy Board for £207 4s 9d for him to finish the job and listed the work outstanding. This included ramming in 'chalk rubbish' behind the new wall, pumping water out of the wet dock, removing 'the stages and brows' (ie the barrow and cart runs), and 'clearing the brick rubbish from the bottom'. Also still to be done was 'spreading chalk rubbish on the bottom of the Dock about 6ins thick between the two aprons' (ie in the channel linking the wet dock with the river), and ramming this down 'to make an hard for the better clearing away the mud that may settle' there (ibid, 19 November 1760, np).

While the wet dock was empty of water, major repair work was also taking place on the single dock at its south-east corner (Fig 73). The yard did not have enough scavelmen to 'prepare and ram the clay between the punchins and fill the ground thereof' at the single dock and requested that Collard's labour be used (TNA, ADM 106/3313, 19 May 1760, np). By the summer, 'the gates of the little Dock' (ie of the single dock) were found to be 'much decayed' and needed replacing with a new pair at a cost of £417 18s (ibid, 22 July 1760, np). By November, Collard had finished the base of the single dock with oak, of 'greater thickness' than allowed in his contract (ibid, 8 November 1760, np).

The wet dock was still not entirely fit for use. On an occasion the following summer when the tide withdrew and the gates were closed, water 'forced its way under the timber foundations of the new wall and round the wing wharf of the gates and thereby blow'd some small part of the outer apron', lifting it off its piles 'about 6¾ins'. The officers proposed 'taking up some small part of the ground at the end of the wing wharf adjoining the new brick wall' and to 'draw down the ground ways to the shoulder of the pile heads and secure them with iron straps and bolts' (TNA, ADM 106/3313, 30 April 1761, np).

Problems persisted. The following summer, 'the wall at the west side of the Wet Dock' had given way 'in the angle next the Slip' (ie the mast house slip), with a further 187ft cracked and

Fig 73 The wet dock (top left) with (centre) building slips and ramps, and (right) the single dock, as shown on the 1774 scale model (Fig 7), looking 'north' (National Maritime Museum, Greenwich, L0459-037)

bulging inwards. Soon this part had also fallen, the officers blaming 'the badness of the foundation'. This whole side of the wet dock seemed to be collapsing: 'We are of the opinion that the other part of the wall next the Masthouse will not stand.' The foundation of this other part of the 123ft long wall had given way, and the wall was 'cracked and broke' (TNA, ADM 106/3313, 23 August 1762, np).

The officers suggested taking 'the remnants of the wall down and rebuild[ing] it', filling the back with 'chalk rubbish'. This work was to be done by contractors 'and taken in hand as soon as the Wing Wharfs of the Wet Dock are completed, which we hope will be in a month's time so as to turn and shut the gates the other way to keep the Dock dry the time the wall shall be building'. The officers estimated the cost to be £3564 15s 2d (TNA, ADM 106/3313, 25 August 1762, np).

The remains of the wet dock recorded in the excavations

Brick walls (S18, Fig 70) that formed the lining of the wet dock were recorded during the excavations, the brick wet dock lying within the footprint of the earlier timber wet dock, as is evident from a comparison of the 1753 and 1774 maps (Fig 60; Fig 71). The brick walling was built in several stages, with four different brick building styles in evidence along the wet dock walls; one early (probably pre-1725) brick wall (S17) was identified 'cutting off' the north-west corner of the wet dock (above 6.2; Fig 59; Fig 63).

The wall's battered frontage was similar to that of the later phases of mast dock brick walls and other 18th-century brick dock structures elsewhere in the capital. The use of sloping-

back or 'battered' dock and river walls on the Thames is currently known from as early as the 17th century; earlier walls were vertical (Heard 2003, 10). Presumably the battering was thought to make the walls more stable. Built inside the earlier timber dock wall, the brick walling was connected to the timber dock gate which continued in use. The junction of the brick wall with the timber gate is shown on the 1774 model (Fig 74).

The wall was the most visible element of a composite structure anchored and reinforced with timber (Fig 75; Fig 76). A very similar and near-contemporary arrangement of land-ties in the Camber Wharf at the Portsmouth dockyard is shown in a drawing of 1786 (Coad 2013, 59 fig 3.5; J Coad, pers comm 2015).

Nowhere was it possible to fully excavate a trench at right angles to the wet dock wall to expose a whole timber land-tie assembly; they extended *c* 10–11m back from the landward side of the brick dock walls and the section would have had to have been over 4.5m deep in dangerously unstable wet deposits. However, a combination of controlled machine and hand excavation was able to expose most elements of the huge and elaborate structure, although the lower ends of the timbers could not be safely examined closely (Fig 76). A diagonal bracing beam of squared oak of *c* 200mm on the faces linked the two roughly horizontal land-tie beams. The lower end could not be closely examined but either rested on or more likely was jointed to some form of sill beam running around the base of the wall on the landfill side. At least two squared upright oak posts (timbers [5098] and [6031], Fig 76) were also used within the lower part of the assembly apparently to hold up the first level of land-tie beams. These varied in dimensions, with the larger (*c* 400mm square) towards the brick wall and the smaller

Fig 74 The wet dock and gates (centre left) and slipway no. 1 (right), as shown on the 1774 scale model (Fig 7), looking 'south' (National Maritime Museum, Greenwich, L0459-028)

Fig 75 View of the west part of the timber and brick wet dock under excavation, looking east

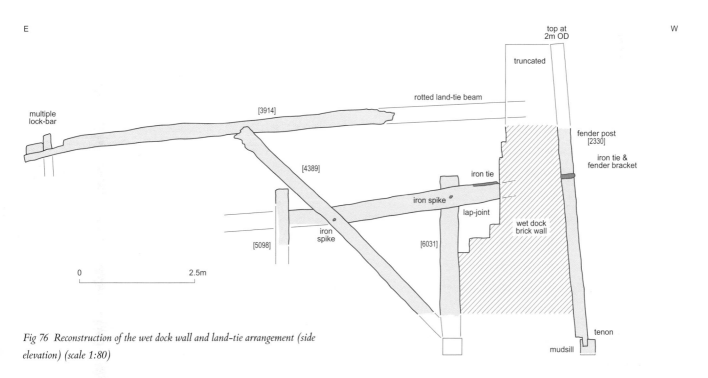

Fig 76 Reconstruction of the wet dock wall and land-tie arrangement (side elevation) (scale 1:80)

(c 220mm square) set c 3.6m landward. All the joints used in the vertical and diagonal timbers that could be examined closely were simple lap-joints secured by large iron spikes; however, at the bases of these timbers some form of mortice-and-tenon joint was probably employed. The use of these simple but strong joints would have made it easier to assemble the heavy timbers than the more complex jointing used in medieval waterfront structures. It could be seen as a step towards the simple jointing and ferrous fastenings used in more recent waterfront carpentry. It is unclear how much prefabrication was used in making these assemblies, and some of the joints must have been measured in and cut as the carpenters worked around the polygonal shape of the dock and the slowly rising brickwork and landfilling.

The upper tier of land-tie assemblies was exposed over quite a large area, and although some were a little decayed it could be seen that they were varied in form. Most were fairly straight, modest-sized oak logs in the round, but many examples were also made of two timbers joined together with simple end-to-end or 'scarf' joints secured with iron spikes or 'drift bolts' (pointed-headed rods and spikes with a rectangular-sectioned shank; see Chapter 10.6 for examples). Some of these composite land-tie beams included softwood (imported coniferous wood, with some examples being identified as of the pine family). One of the land-tie beams [5162] proved to be a currently unique example of the structural use of sweet chestnut (*Castanea sativa*) (Stewart 2013) which may have been among a mixed supply of modest-sized logs from local woods which still often include both oak and sweet chestnut, both also being rot-resistant species. By the late 17th century increasing quantities of coniferous timber were being imported into London for general, land-based use (Chapter 9.1). Some of the softwood was in the form of trimmed round spar sections ('spar' being the general nautical term for any wooden support used in the rigging of a ship, including all yards, booms and the like). The

landward ends of the land-tie beams were generally linked with beams that functioned as lock-bars for several land-ties at once. These timbers varied, including examples of softwood and oak both in the round and squared, mostly 150–200mm in greatest dimension. These multiple lock-bars were in turn anchored by small, mainly oak piles made from offcuts.

The heavy land-tie beam sections nearest the brick wall were mainly of slightly trimmed oak logs *c* 300mm in diameter (Fig 77). They were squared towards the wet dock wall where their ends fitted in cavities in the landward side of the brickwork. The two tiers of land-tie beams clearly lined up with vertical rubbing posts (or 'fenders') of *c* 0.3m square softwood set on the inside of the dock walls (Fig 76). Clasping straps of wrought iron were fitted around the fender posts and ran back into the brick walls to connect with the ends of the timber land-ties (Fig 76). These fender posts helped reduce collision damage between the wet dock wall and ships. Ingress of water permitted only brief glimpses of the base of one of the fender posts in a machine-dug slot, but enough to show that the fender was tenoned into a sill beam set on the water side of the brick wall frontage. The fenders could have been replaced at regular intervals, hence it is likely that the softwood fenders found *in situ* were later replacements of originals. Beyond the bottom of the dock wall the base of the dock seems to have been made mainly of rammed chalk with some clayey alluvium.

Dating this phase of the brick wet dock is difficult on archaeological grounds due to sparse finds in the landfill deposits. Make-up layer [5459] in the brick dock contained part of an iron eyelet <236>, possibly from a sail, bulk iron nails and

Fig 77 View of land-ties for the west wet dock walls, looking east

four fragments from two sheet glass windows. However, a tree-ring date obtained from what seems to have been a freshly used oak timber links the archaeological and historical evidence together. The timber in question ([5389]) was a multiple lock-bar log on the west side of the brick wet dock wall. It was minimally flattened on the face and set in the lap-joints with a 'D' section of c 330 × 240mm. It was a relatively slow-grown timber with 114 annual rings and full sapwood, and provided a secure tree-ring felling date of the winter of 1756 (Chapter 10.9; Fig 199). This timber showed no signs of previous use and it is very likely that it indicates a construction date in 1757 or a year or two later, which corresponds with the historical date of 1760–2 for extensive work on this dock.

As described above, the side wharfs of the channel linking the wet dock with the river were being rebuilt in May 1760, including 'hanging the gates the contrary way' so that they opened into the wet dock (TNA, ADM 106/3313, 8 May 1760, np). This rebuild was not completed until two years later (ibid, 25 August 1762, np). Evidence seen during the excavations for a major rebuild of the surviving east side of the timber gateway (S9 retained, Fig 70) probably dates to this time (Fig 78). The timber gateway was still in use after the wet dock had been re-lined with brick. Where the hinge side of the eastern leaf of the gate would have pivoted was a massive oak post [3771] with a neatly carved concave south-west corner; this was an addition which probably dates to the use of the timber channel with the brick-built dock.

The channel side was straight to the north but had a zone to the south that was built with a concave curve. This concave area

must have been made to accommodate the convex southern (ie internal) face of the eastern leaf of the wet dock gate, the better to withstand the water pressure of a full wet dock at low tide. The concave and channel areas were more robustly built than the rest of the dock wall and were fitted with c 220mm thick horizontal oak beams which held up the ends of the land-ties and firmly braced the posts. These horizontally set beams were secured with iron forelock bolts to all the uprights. Again the evidence of a major rebuild was suggested by the alternating size grouping of the slightly varying oak uprights, similar to that seen elsewhere in the timber walls of the wet dock. The curved section must have been built as a curved frame and joined to the straight sections (although the lower levels could not be examined during the excavations).

The substantial posts along the entrance channel frontage must relate to a rebuild of this area and are not just the result of the need for reinforcement. The immediate area around the pivot point of the eastern leaf of the gate was clearly stressed by the operation of the huge gate. The complex angles at which some of the timbers joined and the use of iron ties and grown oak knees meant that the work of ship smiths was much in view, as tie-bolts and brackets had to be forged to fit individual locations. Two types of iron bolt were also seen used side by side: the more numerous 'forelock bolt' secured by a tapering wedge against a washer, and a small number of what must have then been very new-fangled threaded bolts with large square nuts (Fig 79). Use of the heavy threaded bolts dates the rebuild to the mid 18th century (or a little earlier); they may have been some of the very earliest employed in heavy woodworking in

Fig 78 View of the internal (water-side) face of the east side wharf (S9) of the timber gate to the wet dock, rebuilt in 1760–2, looking east

*Fig 79 Views of iron threaded bolt with large
nut in situ in the wet dock, end-on (upper)
and lengthways (lower) (0.5m scales)*

the yard. Grown oak knees were also used alongside iron ties, and would have been recycled from ships being repaired or broken up in the yard.

Roman numeral depth marks, made out of copper-alloy sheet, were found still attached to sheathing planks just inside the gate pivot at the entrance to the dock. The highest surviving mark read 'XII' (ft) or 3.66m at a height of +2.53m OD. However, originally the depth of water must have been much greater as 'XIIII' (<S21>, Fig 80) was also found (detached from the gate). XIIII (ft) or 4.27m would have represented a height of +3.14m OD, but large tides would have been reaching well over + 3.50m OD. To withstand such a tide, the gate would have had

to have been at least 4.60m high. This also suggests that the lowest exposed part of the gate lay at -1.13m OD, not including its foundation. Detached marker 'XI' (<704>) was also recovered.

The large land-tie assemblies excavated on the east side of the wet dock entrance channel and gate area were complex structures and the upper timbers in particular were difficult to associate definitively with specific building phases. Among the later timbers recorded as part of the later 17th-century building phase (period 3; Chapter 4.2; Fig 25) were some which on closer examination were clearly part of a late phase of repair, after *c* 1700. Two reused ships' timbers – parts of a large ship

<S21>

Fig 80 Copper-alloy depth mark 'XIIII' <S21> from the depth gauge of the timber wet dock gate (scale 1:4)

rudder post [3720] and a stern post [3718] – both date to the 18th century (Chapters 9.2 and 10.7; Fig 196; Fig 197); the copper sheathing <608> found with reused timber [3720] in the wet dock entrance may suggest a date in the later 18th century for this timber (Chapter 4.2).

Maintenance and repairs, early 1760s

At the end of January 1761 there was a serious fire in 'the Red Lyon alehouse near the upper Watergate' that 'butted to the back of the Boatswain's House and adjoined to the Taphouse [beer house] and offices'. The bell was rung and it was only with 'great difficulty' that the blaze was kept from the yard's buildings, helped because 'there was no wind'. The fire 'raged so violently that nothing could be saved out of the alehouse' although the inhabitants escaped alive (TNA, ADM 106/3313, 31 January 1761, np). In a subsequent letter to the Navy Board, the officers stressed that disaster had only narrowly been averted. Had there been a wind, not only could the lodgings and offices along the east side of the yard and the ships in the double dock have gone up in flames, but also 'the Magazine would have been in very great danger' too. As the remains of the alehouse smouldered (as they continued to do for a further 12 days), the officers weighed up the risk posed by other buildings near the yard. Two public houses, a private house, a ruined house and various outbuildings 'run up to the back of the Master Shipwrights lodgings and office and the Clerk of the Surveys office'. Other houses nearby were let to 'mean and indignant' people and included an 'Oil Shop'. Not including King Street (which is marked on the 1753 map), the houses and outbuildings nearby were part brick and part weather-boarded. The officers listed three public houses (presumably one did not directly adjoin the yard) – the Mansion House, the Three Jolly Sailors and the Duke of Cumberland – and a tavern called the Globe. There were also a draper's and a chandler's shops (ibid, 3 February 1761, np; 9 February 1761, np; 11 February 1761, np).

In the spirit of never letting a good crisis go to waste, the officers said that the nearest properties would be 'a useful acquisition to the yard, particularly that (called the Orchard) at the back of the Clerk of Cheque's Lodgings', and could be added to the area now used 'to dry and air sails', that is, the sailfield at the south end of the yard (TNA, ADM 106/3313, 3 February 1761, np). The Orchard was a narrow street running parallel to the east perimeter wall of the yard, west of King Street (Fig 58; Chapter 9.3, 'On the east side of the dockyard: King Street and Orchard Place'). Cesspits and other features excavated in the yards and outbuildings on the east side of the Orchard (OA8, Fig 144; Fig 146) yielded discarded artefacts and faunal remains; these assemblages are examined in detail in Chapter 9.3 for what they potentially reveal about the material culture and lifestyle of those occupying these properties in the mid 18th (and 19th) century.

The officers were not the only ones taking advantage of the fire for their own purposes. The blaze had brought down 72ft of the dockyard perimeter wall and £7 worth of ring-bolts went missing, despite a guard at the breach. The warder and several watchmen were dismissed for the theft. The officers estimated that rebuilding the collapsed wall, 10ft high with a 6ft deep foundation, would cost £35 (TNA, ADM 106/3313, 3 February 1761, np; 4 February 1761, np; 5 February 1761, np; 11 February 1761, np).

Ongoing maintenance and further works were also urged by the officers at this time. A gale blew down 'a great part of the fence enclosing the Painters Shop' and the officers proposed rebuilding it in brick and constructing 'four bays' for painting 'canvas, oars, arm chests, colour chests, hencoops' (TNA, ADM 106/3313, 10 March 1760, np). The 'four bays' was in fact a building to be put up 'with great dispatch'. A description of the materials used suggests that it was weather-boarded with a tiled roof (ibid, 24 March 1760, np). The work was under way by April (ibid, 4 April 1760, np). The storehouse roof, being 'very leaky and bad', also required repair (ibid).

The officers proposed building a 'small wash-house' near Mr Landen the boatswain's lodgings (TNA, ADM 106/3313, 3 March 1761, np). It was also suggested that the Master Shipwright's lodgings be 'painted and whitewashed' (ibid, 13 August 1761, np), and there was a further proposal to replace 'the wood fence before the Master Attendant, Storekeeper, Clerks of the Cheque and Survey, Master Shipwrights Assistant and Surgeons Lodgings' with 'an iron Pallisado fence fixed on a stone kerb' at a cost of £257 19s 10d (ibid, 6 November 1761, np).

The base of the dry (double) dock was 'greatly out of repair', and the officers laid out a specification of what was required to fix it. They proposed using 9ft long, 12in square piles and 6ft long, 9in square piles of elm or oak, their heads 'shod with iron … drove in tiers or otherwise'; groundways 'saw'd to about 20ins by 13ins' and '12ins by 8ins' and 'halved on the heads of the piles and secured with bolts'; and mudsills and capsills 'saw'd to about 14ins square' and morticed on the piles (TNA, ADM 106/3313, 30 April 1761, np).

The mast dock also required extensive repair to the locks, apron, wing wharfs, fenders and mud- and capsills. As well as repairing these by contract, the officers proposed a new pair of gates to fit a channel to the river widened from 9ft to 12ft 'which will give better room for taking in and putting out masts and other stores'. The level of the apron was to be raised by 15in to be level with the new drain leading from the mast dock to the wet dock (TNA, ADM 106/3313, 24 July 1761, np). By November the following year, 'the locks capsills and fenders' were finished and only the wing wharf and apron gates 'or hatch' needed to be done. '[T]he penstock at the Boathouse adjoining' also required repair 'to render the Pond fit to receive masts'. The officers suggested 'an hatch instead of gates' for the mast dock (pond) (ibid, 10 March 1762, np).

The walls of the mast dock are also likely to have been rebuilt in brick (S38, Fig 71; Fig 81) at this time, as part of what seems to have been a general move to replace timber structures and wharfs. The redundant timber tie-backs were sawn off and replaced by a later set of land-ties consisting of minimally trimmed logs, each extending through a 1.50m wide red-brick wall to connect to a corresponding vertical fender on the inside of the small mast dock, the connection being made with an iron bracket. The trenches showed that the mast dock was 37m wide and *c* 5m deep to the base of the brickwork. Early brick walls were exposed at the west end of the dock: the earliest was visible in the north (landward) face and was built of orange, yellow and red bricks set in white lime mortar; this wall had been extended west by a later wall of yellow brick in brown sandy mortar. These walls were modified and heightened in the 19th century (Chapter 7.4). Finds were scarce: a single type OS11 clay pipe bowl <575> in context [4877] was found in association with the mast dock and is dated to *c* 1730–60, and a wooden wedge <749> was found in a make-up deposit associated with the walls.

In summer 1762, the officers reported that the 'wood wharf between the Albion [a ship] and the new 74 Gunships Slips to the river here and wood drain that leads from thence to the Single dock being decayed and the piers of the penstock thereto at the head of the Albion's slip broke', and proposed building 'a brick wharf in a direct line, with the Storehouse wharf and wharf on the west side of the Albion's slip, also a brick drain in their room, and to remove the penstock to the stern of the said slip'. The yard's house-carpenters and scavelmen could do the work, rather than it being done by contract (TNA, ADM 106/3313, 25 June 1762, np). The *Albion*, a 168ft × 46ft, 74-gun, 1662bm-ton 3rd-rate, was under construction in 1762 and launched in May 1763 (Colledge and Warlow 2010).

The 'elm or oak' piles in the new brick wharf were to be 11ft and 9ft long and 12in square, and 6ft long and 9in square, shod with iron and 'drove in tiers or otherwise'; the bearers were to be 'about 20ins by 12ins' and '12ins by 8ins halv'd on and bolted on the heads of the piles'; the planks were to be 'of elm or oak'; the mudsill '8ins by 12ins halv'd on the bearers and secured with treenails or bolts'; while the uprights were to be 12in square and 'tenanted onto the mudsill below and let into the sides of the land-ties'. The land-ties were to be 'about 14ins square, let into the Bond timber, to have an iron strap fastened to each side of it and left beyond the face of the wharf to receive the fenders'. The capsill and the fenders were to be about 14in square, the latter 'tenanted into the mudsill below'. A penstock was also to be built, its 'sill post

Fig 81 View of the landward side of the brick south wall of the small mast dock (S38), looking north

and partners … saw'd to about 14ins square'; the ground was to be dug away for the foundation and clay rammed in, presumably to ensure that the penstock was watertight. The workmen were also to 'rip up and clear away the old materials of the decayed drain and part of the Old Slip, making dams and bale and keep down the water' (TNA, ADM 106/3313, 25 June 1762, np).

However, this work had still not been done by 1765 when the officers were reporting that 'the wood wharf fronting the river here between the slips of the Magnificent and Marlborough are decayed and require to be new, also the drain that leads from the front wharf to the river from the single Dock'. (The *Magnificent* (1612bm-tons) and the *Marlborough* (1642bm-tons) were both 3rd-rate, 74-gun, 169ft × 47ft ships, completed in 1766 and 1767 respectively.) The work was proposed to be taken in hand by the yard's workmen at a cost of £861 6s (TNA, ADM 106/3315, 24 January 1765, 18).

Fire was a recurrent problem. In May 1765 a fire broke out in the tar house. The building itself suffered little damage, being 'built with bricks the walls so thick and arched over with brick and so well fortified against fire', but £13 16s 10d worth of rope was destroyed and three workmen badly burned (TNA, ADM 106/3315, 7 May 1765, 33).

A new mast house and slipway, 1765–70

By the end of 1765, the officers sent the Navy Board a design for a new mast house, consisting of four bays with a mould loft 'over the two middle ones'. This would cost £3337 11s 5d and would be located on 'land belonging to the Victualling Wharf adjoining to the Boathouses' (TNA, ADM 106/3315, 2 December 1765, 55). The boathouses in question were those at the far west end of the mast dock, and the mast house and mould loft were built west of these by 1774 when they can be seen on the dockyard model and map of that year (Fig 7; Fig 71). This is a decade later than a similar mast house and mould loft constructed at Chatham in response to the growing size of warships (Coad 1973).

The ground-plate foundations of the new mast house were to rest on piles 'of oak or elm from five to seven feet long', and the windows were to consist of 'sashes of twelve lights' and be 'fixed with iron bars'. The roof was to be tiled with 'plain tiles' and feature 'dormer windows'. The soil dug out for the foundations was to be dumped not more than 53 yards away (TNA, ADM 106/3315, 14 January 1766, 74; 14 August 1766, 99). There were also to be 14in square land-ties 'secured with iron dogs or straps', 'needles about 12ins square' and 7ft long piles, 12in × 8in in cross section. Evidently, these land-ties were for 'building the wall of the canal leading to the intended mast pond' (ibid, 6 March 1766, 81) – a reference to the large mast dock that was to be built to the north of the new mast house, also on ground provided by the victualling yard. The Navy Board approved the plans on 30 January and 7 April 1766, including the transfer of land from the victualling yard, and construction was under way on the new mast house by the spring when the officers asked for the loan of three

bricklayers from Woolwich (ibid, 5 March 1766, 82; 6 March 1766, 81; 14 August 1766, 98).

The officers had also sent in 1765 a design for 'building a principal slip on the place where the Masthouses now stand for ships of the largest class' at a cost of £3818 7s (TNA, ADM 106/3315, 2 December 1765, 55), and this was approved by the Navy Board on 18 January 1766 (TNA, ADM 106/3316, 6 April 1770, 72). The new slip was to be a replacement for 'the Old Masthouses Slip' which was to be ripped up, its 'groundways land-ties &c' removed and the ground cleared for £7 (TNA, ADM 106/3315, 4 May 1767, 152). Work on the construction of the new slip was delayed by the masts of the *Magnificent* and *Marlborough* (above) occupying the old mast houses where the slip was to be sited. The officers suggested sending these by raft to Chatham so that work could begin. They assured the Navy Board that the old mast houses would be taken down carefully to ensure maximum reuse of their tiles, bricks and timber. The cost of demolition would be £76 (ibid, 23 March 1767, 145), although the Navy Board ordered that this be reduced (ibid, 30 March 1767, 147).

The materials required for the construction of this 'Third Principal Slip' were detailed by the officers:

'plain piles … about 12ins square … 10 to 14ft long to be shod with iron or not and drove in tiers or otherways as directed, to receive the groundways';
the groundways 'about 14ins thick and breadth as may be directed and scarph'd together with a plain scarph and morticed from the heads of the piles';
'thickstuff of 6 by 5ins thick and wrought on the bottom of the slip or else where it may be directed';
mudsills 'about 14 by 18ins and let down on the ends of the groundways and bolted thereto and rabbitted [*sic*] to receive the plank';
capsills 'about 12 by 15ins and morticed on the heads of the puncheons and rabbitted to receive the plank';
puncheons 'about 10 by 12ins and tenanted for mud and capsills';
backbends 'about 16 by 9ins and properly let into the puncheons and bolted thereto';
land-ties '12 by 14ins and about 10ft from one end and let down to the upper edges of the backbend and secured with an iron dog or strap';
wale pieces '16 by 9ins and properly let into the puncheons and bolted thereto';
needles '10ins square and let down and secured on the ends of the land-ties';
piles for needles '10ins square at the head and about 7ft long';
braces '10ins square and bolted under the lower edges of the back bend and tenanted in to the end of the groundways';
uprights '10ins square and tenanted in to the end of the groundway and secured to the underside of the land-ties';
timbers 'sawn and wrought into bollards, shovels and braces';
'plank of 4ins and 3ins';
bearers '14 by 9ins and secured to the sides of the puncheon'.

The dimensions of the timber were mostly qualified by 'about', and so were approximate measurements allowing some latitude to the workmen on the ground. Where specified, all the timber was to be 'sawn out of oak or elm' (TNA, ADM 106/3315, 4 May 1767, 151).

The officers also proposed 'to drive dove-tail piles at the aft sides of the groundways at the aft part of the stern brow and to ram in clay at the sides of the slip from thence to the end next the river, and to fix gate pannels or a dam to keep the tide out the time which the 74 Gunships are building' (ie the primary reason for the slip). The dove-tail piles were to be 'about 5ft long' and '7ins by 10 or 12ins'. The bricklayers' work was to include 'cutting down and taking away the old brickwork', and the scavelmen were to dig out the ground and wheel it away 'not exceeding 60 yards' and 'to unload fill in and well ram with chalk rubbish' (TNA, ADM 106/3315, 4 May 1767, 151–2).

The slip (S27, below) was built by April 1770, when the officers proposed 'making a launch at the end of the said slip to the river'. It would be built of 12in square plain piles, '10 to 14ft long' and 'drove in regular tiers to receive the groundways' which were to be '14ins square' and 'morticed on the head of the piles'; clay was to be well rammed in (TNA, ADM 106/3316, 6 April 1770, 72). This feature is shown on the foreshore on the 1774 model (Fig 7).

The excavated slipways, third quarter of the 18th century

The slipways opening on to the river are referred to as Structure 27 (the westernmost slip, west of the wet dock), Structure 30 and Structure 31 (east of the wet dock, between the wet dock and the quadrangle storehouse) (Fig 70). From the 1840s, these were numbered respectively as slipways no. 1, no. 4 and no. 5.

Single slipway (S27) (slipway no. 1)

The slipway Structure 27 (Fig 70; Fig 82), dating to 1767–70 (above) and visible on the 1774 model (Fig 74), was excavated in area 2. It was aligned north–south, its timber floor sloping towards the river, and was exposed over a length of c 60m. It would originally have been a timber-lined structure, but only the floor survived; the lining was replaced in brick in the 19th century. However, in places traces of what might have been its earlier lining could be seen, and voids that had once held timber uprights were visible along the edges. Measured from the south (bow) end as indicated by the surviving timbers to the conjectural line of the waterfront in 1774 (Fig 71), the slip was a maximum of c 18.46m (60ft 6in) wide at the waterfront by c 68.39m (224ft) long.

The base of the slip was best preserved towards the river

Fig 82 View of slipway no. 1 (S27), looking south

where it was deepest. The higher southern end was far more decayed, the sleepers surviving as voids with decayed piles seen under them at intervals. The slipway floor was made of assorted oak sleepers, mainly in three lengths crudely scarfed and spiked ('end-jointed') together. Much of the timber had been hewn and sawn to produce two broad parallel faces and regular thicknesses (ie it was 'sided') but with curving sides. This seems to have been the sort of raw material shipwrights would lay templates or 'moulds' on to find the best fit for ship framing. The features of the parent trees used to produce the timbers were recorded for sample areas of better-preserved sleepers. These features included major knots, where they could be seen, and sapwood. A selection of the timber sleepers were also recorded in more detail and were very similar in general to those found in slipway Structure 31 (below); timber sleepers are discussed in more detail in Chapter 9.1 ('The dimensions and size range of some typical large oak trees used by the navy'). Some of the timbers were very large and mostly over 400mm (c 1ft) wide, with a few up to 900mm (c 2ft 6in) wide.

Previous investigations of large dockyard slipways on the Thames have revealed construction of slipway bases broadly similar to that of Structure 27. At the large dockyard complex a short distance to the east, originally founded by the East India Company, the slipway bases were also made of partially prepared ('sided') shipyard timbers and second-hand nautical timbers (Divers 2004, 51). These large oak timbers were used mainly as crosswise sleepers to which lengthwise decking planks were spiked. However, the excavations in the area of the Woolwich dockyard revealed both similar and rather more elaborate slipway floor structures. There, the westernmost slipway base was of timber set on a gridwork of brick walls with the spaces between the brick dwarf walls filled with sand (Courtney 1974, 25). The decking of the slipway base there was fastened with very large iron spikes.

Part of the slipway floor of Structure 27 was dismantled to reveal widely spread oak piles, some of which were iron-shod and had tenoned tops that engaged with mortices on the underside of the largest sleepers. This corresponds to the officers' specification of groundways morticed on to the heads of iron-shod piles. The largest sleepers formed the groundways, the other timbers of the floor the 'thickstuff'. The fitting of the mortice-and-tenon assemblies would have been very tricky.

A small number of the timbers had relict fastenings such as oak treenails in the sides and erratic patterns of iron spikes, indicating previous use. Most of the sleepers were separated by short, horizontal, north–south oak blocks or 'noggings' (noggins) and rammed cobbling. Noggings were also used in warehouse flooring from the late 18th century onwards to provide stability, by preventing the joists tipping sideways.

Blobs of tar and woodchips were not the only evidence for use of the slipway. The crosswise sleepers were trimmed to receive blocks of timber to support the keels of ships being built or repaired, although the blocks had been removed. In other places screw-threaded iron ring-bolts had been left in place or broken off (Fig 83); these would have served to secure rigging used to hold timbers in place as ship frameworks were assembled with ropes, tackle and winches. The base of the slipway was clearly long in use and would have been clad with planking that was removed and replaced as required, which accounts for the multiple spike holes. In a few places small sections of tropical timber probably dating from the 19th century were found set in the slipway bottom, while the vast majority of sleeper timbers appeared to be original, preserved by waterlogging at the north end.

Near the middle of the slipway on the west side, a timber that was probably a mobile capstan foot block was also found; it was probably used to anchor the base of the vertically set winch-type tool used to raise heavy ship frames. This was a

Fig 83 View of screw-threaded iron ring-bolts in situ in slipway no. 1 (S27) (1.0m scale)

plank of oak 260mm long by 130mm wide and 70mm thick. It was pierced with a central worn hole 36mm in diameter, and had a 12mm spike hole at each end. This fixed pivot point could be moved as required to place the windlass spindle in the best location. These tools were essential, backed up by block and tackle, for lifting timbers into place in a ship's frame, which might often weigh as much as 1 ton (1016kg). Evidence of the use of larger capstans was found just to the east of the north end of the slipway in the form of large timber bearings set in brick matrices. These human-powered winches were crucial parts of the dockyard infrastructure, used to manoeuvre ships and handle heavy materials. Sloping recesses or 'scutches' were also found in the tops of some sleepers where struts used to support stacks of vertical blocks were once fitted. A small number of neatly made wooden wedges were also found, used for supporting shoring timbers pushing planking into place.

Towards the northern, deeper end of the slipway, an east–west line of paired mortices was found that almost certainly supported posts of a temporary walkway crossing the slip. Such walkways saved a long walk all around the ship sitting on the slipway. A group of three squared oak timbers with tenons at one end, laid between major sleepers at the north end of the slip, may have been relict posts from this walkway. The 1774 model includes a walkway across the slip in this general location (Fig 74).

Twin slipways (S30 and S31) (slipways no. 4 and no. 5)

Map evidence indicates that the twin slipways shown on the 1753 map (Fig 58) between the wet dock and the quadrangle storehouse were substantially rebuilt between 1753 and 1774 (S30 and S31, Fig 70; Fig 84). The east edge of Structure 30 truncated an earlier slipway (S24) (Chapter 4.2, 'The 17th- to early 18th-century timber Thames frontages'; Fig 25; Fig 26).

Like Structure 27, the original timber linings to slipways Structures 30 and 31 had been replaced with brick and concrete in the 19th century (Fig 97; Fig 98). Two sleeper timbers from Structure 31 (timbers [2705] and [2730]) gave tree-ring felling date ranges of 1754–99 and 1745–90 respectively (Chapter 10.9; Fig 199); it is possible that the former was a timber set in as a repair. The similarity in design of the floors to Structure 27, which dated to 1767–70 (above), suggests a similar date range for Structures 30 and 31.

Much less of slipway no. 4 (S30) was exposed in the excavation, but the dimensions of the two slipways were probably very similar; slipway no. 5 (S31), measured from the southernmost surviving timbers to the conjectural line of the waterfront in 1774 (Fig 71), was a maximum of c 15.43 (50ft 6in) wide at the waterfront by c 72.62m (238ft) long, and slipway no. 4 (S30) a maximum of c 15.86m (52ft) wide by 72.16m (236ft 9in) long.

SLIPWAY NO. 4 (S30)

In slipway no. 4 (S30), the base was founded on crosswise timber sleepers, with widely spaced squared oak piles set underneath (Fig 85). One of the lifted piles was found to have had a rough tenon on the top, implying that some of the

Fig 84 Slipways no. 5 (S31, left) and no. 4 (S30), ramps and ships under construction, with (top right) the edge of the wet dock, as shown on the 1774 scale model (Fig 7), looking 'south' (National Maritime Museum, Greenwich, L0459-008)

sleepers were morticed underneath to engage with at least some of the piles as in slipway Structure 27.

A small exploratory trench was dug through the north-west corner to investigate evidence for the earlier phases of construction. In that trench traces of the earlier timber-framed western side wall were found, in the form of a large oak sill beam ([3083]) c 300mm deep by c 400mm wide (Fig 86; Fig 87). It was sawn from a whole log but the internal face sloped outward at 10–15°. Large unpegged mortices c 200mm wide were also found in the upper face, cut parallel to the sloping face (Fig 87). This implies that posts at least 200mm square would originally have been tenoned into the mortices and supported the side sheathing planking.

Along the western edge of area 4 the eastern timber side wall was partially exposed. There, four land-tie assemblies ([3082], [3279], [3276], [3061]) were exposed, aligned east–west, that would have supported the eastern north–south timber wall of the early phases of Structure 30. The very eastern edges of the squared uprights of that wall were also exposed along the extreme edge of area 4. They were so closely set that they may well be evidence of a partial rebuild of the timber wall. It is also clear that the sheathing planking must have been fastened to the western, internal face of the posts so that the slipway wall would have presented a flush face internally.

Fig 85 View of the western exposed part of slipway no. 4 (S30), looking south; the upstanding trestles are post-dockyard (Chapter 8.2)

Fig 86 View of slipway no. 4 (S30), looking south, with (centre) the earlier sill beam [3083] from the original timber-framed lining (0.5m scale)

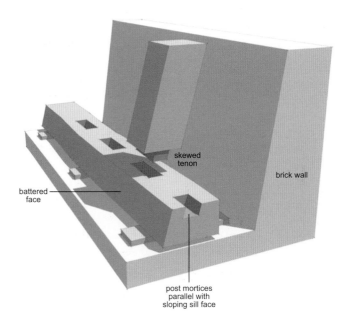

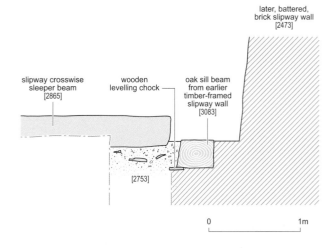

Fig 87 Details (section and reconstruction) of the western side wall of slipway no. 4 (S30), including the earlier oak sill beam [3083] (scale 1:20)

The land-tie assemblies found on the east side were similar to those of the timber wet dock, with main east–west land-tie beams *c* 200–300mm wide and *c* 4m long, set between 2.40m and 2.60m apart. They were equipped with one lock-bar timber (or 'needle') retained by two anchor piles and had the addition of a pile at their eastern ends. This feature was peculiar to these land-ties and was probably intended to resist thrust from the shores or props set against the slipway walls to support ships lying on the slipway. The location and survival of the relict timber Structure 30 eastern wall indicates that there was a slight shift to the west when the slipway was rebuilt in the 19th century.

SLIPWAY NO. 5 (S31)

Slipway no. 5 (S31, Fig 70; Fig 88) was the easternmost large slipway opening into the river. Two east–west sections were recorded through the north–south structure as found. As in slipways Structures 27 and 30, its original timber lining had been replaced by later brick walls. A brick phase, intermediate between the timber lining and the 19th-century wall, may be represented by a thin surviving wall (S23, not illustrated) that ran along the western edge of the slipway, largely truncated by its later 19th-century wall. At the north end the base of the slipway was found to be *c* 14.5m (47½ft) wide, tapering down to *c* 12.2m (40ft) towards the south end, just before the extreme

tapering-in of the very end. The shape of all the slips broadly mirrored that of the typical form of ships, with less depth and width needed at the bow than to accommodate the hull.

The timber floor of the slip incorporated a wide variety of irregular oak sleepers, set crosswise (Fig 89) as found in the other two slip structures (S27, S30). Most were formed of two to three timbers simply overlapped with ends cut to a splay rather than a clear scarf joint. These sleepers were also a mixture of roughed-out 'sided' oak timber in the condition in which much of it entered the yard (eg [2720] and [2727]) and second-hand nautical timbers. The larger sided oak timbers provided rare outlines of what oak trees the 18th-century shipwrights were actually receiving for shipbuilding at the yard, bearing in mind that many of these timbers did not make the grade for use in ships (Chapter 9.1). In some cases the wider ends of the timbers had clear felling cuts, with one axe-cut 'back cut' or 'gob' and a slightly higher, straight cut made with a saw (eg [2727]). The nautical timbers included curved ship frame timbers of oak with relict treenails, which were laid on their sides to provide a flat upper face (eg [2825], [2890]). Some straighter ship frame timbers were also reused, including a few with notches typically once used to hold horizontal timbers framing gun port openings in the sides of warships (eg [2824]).

In several areas large iron spikes were found bent over on

Fig 88 View of slipway no. 5 (S31), looking south

Fig 89 View of the timber floor of slipway no. 5 (S31), looking east

the upper faces of the sleepers. The space between the spike heads and the sleepers was *c* 100mm (4in), showing that slipway base planking of that thickness, or a little more, had once been laid there to provide the working surface. A smaller number of oak treenails *c* 30–40mm in diameter were also used to fasten this sheathing or other temporary structures such as keel blocks, shores and windlass bases. Presumably the sheathing was levered up for reuse or fuel after the yard was sold off. Shallow adze-cut recesses were found running through several areas of the sleeper base, and these must have been where blocks used to support the keel of ships being worked on fitted; there were also shorter parallel sets of blocks for supporting part of the bottom of the ships on either side. Wide support for the bottom of heavy ships (designed to be evenly supported by the water when they were afloat) was essential to reduce distortion.

It was possible to excavate a narrow cross section through the slipway base by machine which revealed fairly widely set lines of beech and oak piles under two layers of horizontal oak timbers. These lower layers were set north–south, with east–west aligned sleepers on top. The mix of oak and beech piles *c* 200mm square, converted by a mixture of axe hewing and pit sawing, may possibly hint at two phases of construction. The use of beech suggests an effort to save money as it was generally a cheap material, only used sparingly well below the waterline in shipbuilding and waterfront construction as it has limited rot resistance otherwise. Several beech piles were sampled for dendrochronological analysis but it did not prove possible to tree-ring date them.

A new mast dock, 1770–4

The Navy Board had first ordered that a new mast dock be built

in January 1766, but it was only some four years later that the officers were in a position to provide a detailed estimate of the cost. The new mast dock was sorely needed. The officers complained that since there was 'a great want of room to keep the large masts under water there has been a necessity of using a great part of the Wet Dock for some years … although they float on the surface of the water exposed to the injury of the weather which greatly hastens their decay'. The new mast dock was to be located 'on the ground adjoining to the Victualling at the Redhouse'. The total cost was estimated at £16,943, of which £9573 was the cost of making the mast dock itself. The other work required included making a drain leading from the new mast dock to the river, the construction of locks, 'building the canal leading from the Old into the New Mast Pond [ie dock]' (£1590), and building a 'New Fence wall next the Road leading to Grove Street' and 'from the north angle of the wall already begun to the corner of the Old Cooperage' (TNA, ADM 106/3316, 22 December 1769, 47). A total of £3887 of the estimated cost had been spent by June 1771 (ibid, 24 June 1771, 126), which gives some idea of how the work was progressing. It was proposed to take down a watch cabin in the way of the new drain (ibid, 23 July 1770, 82) and erect a new one 'at the corner of the cordage shed joining the Storehouse' at a cost of £9 6s (ibid, 10 September 1770, 85). The large mast dock was completed by 1774 when it is shown on the model and map of that year (Fig 7; Fig 71).

The large mast dock (S40, Fig 71) was built in the west of the dockyard and lay only partially within the site. It evidently underwent much modification. A later wall forming the north wall of the large mast dock was exposed in the excavations; a stone capstan base (S42) had been inserted into the wall (Fig 90). Built-in openings corresponded to fenders on the inside of the

Fig 90 Views of the north wall of the large mast dock (S40): upper – the exposed wall, looking north, with the inserted capstan base (S42) visible in the centre of the wall; lower – detail of the capstan base (S42), looking south

wall, but any connecting tie-backs supporting the wall had either been removed or had decayed. The removal of such supports had caused the wall to subside into the 20th-century backfill of the mast dock.

A second wall in the south corner of the trench, built of red and orange brick (Fig 91), is likely to have been the opening of the canal (S41) connecting the large mast dock to the small mast dock, as shown on the map and model of 1774 (Fig 92). A stone base (S43) behind the large mast dock wall is likely to have been for a crane base.

Fig 91 View of the opening of the canal (S41) linking the large mast dock (S40) to the small mast dock, looking north

Fig 92 The mast docks as shown on the 1774 scale model (Fig 7): upper – the large mast dock in the foreground with the canal leading to the small mast dock (top right), looking 'north'; lower – the small mast dock and its entrance, seen from the waterfront, looking 'south' (National Maritime Museum, Greenwich, L0459-038 and L0459-022 respectively)

Repairs and building (plank sheds etc), 1765–71

The first assistant's lodging required repairs that were deemed 'absolutely necessary', including 'a new cistern in [the] back yard'. The work would cost £78 12s 6d (TNA, ADM 106/3315, 24 July 1765, 39). The Storekeeper's lodging needed repair in late 1765, at a cost of £22 13s (ibid, 11 November 1765, 54). The porter's lodging required repair in early 1767, at a cost of £18 (ibid, 20 February 1767, 141). The fronts of the Clerk of the Cheque's and pay offices were 'much decayed' and in need of repair in summer 1768, at a cost of £29 9s 2d (ibid, 26 June 1768, 202). At around the same time, the 'Capstand house between the New Slip and the Wett Dock gates' required demolition, and the officers proposed building a new one 'at the northernmost part of the Plank Houses', at a cost of £50 18s (ibid, 5 July 1768, 205).

In summer 1767 the officers suggested building a 'shed with old materials joining the Painters Shop, on an angle upon piece of ground [sic]'. This shed was to be used to store 'thickstuff' (ie timber), much of which was 'exposed to the weather'. The shed would have lattice doors and a pantiled roof and would cost £27 16s 3d (TNA, ADM 106/3315, 19 June 1767, 156). In February 1769, the Navy Board ordered that a shed be built 'for the shipwrights to work under (particularly in bad weather)'. The officers asked for old ships' timbers to be supplied from other yards for this. It was not a small structure: the 14 oak beams required were to be 30ft long and the 21 posts 15ft long (TNA, ADM 106/3316, 6 March 1769, 22).

In April 1769 the Navy Board ordered that the wall separating the yard from the land recently acquired from the victualling office be taken down and a new wall built around the recently acquired land. The bricks were to be reused in the new wall and its foundation was to consist of 'plank of 3in', '6in thick bearers' and 12in square piles '8 to 10ft long' (TNA, ADM 106/3316, 29 April 1769, 24).

In July 1769 the officers proposed that the yard's house-carpenters build 'a shed about 11ft from the SW side of the Smiths Shop' out of old ships' beams, at a cost of £503 4s 4d (TNA, ADM 106/3316, 10 July 1769, 30). They asked for the timber to be supplied from other yards. The purpose of the shed was to protect from the weather 'the English and German thickstuff' (ibid, 28 July 1769, 33). This is probably the building of 11 bays to the south of the smithy, seen on the 1774 model (with louvered sides to admit the air) and map (but there with ten bays) (Fig 7; Fig 68; Fig 71).

In March 1771 the officers sent a design for 'the shed near the Double Dock proposed to shelter thickstuff, plank etc from the wet and sun but exposed as much as possible to the air', at a cost of £807 5s (TNA, ADM 106/3316, 20 March 1771, 117). The following month, the Navy Board directed that the officers consider what length of sheds would be required to contain this timber (including 'sided knees'), 'placed edgeways equal to one years expense calculated from an average of the last 7 years'. In addition there was to be 3ft 6in clearance 'between the supporter of each bay and middle supports to be so place as to ship and unship that knees or thickstuff may be put in discriminately

under the said sheds'. Using these criteria, the officers estimated that such sheds would need to be 444ft long and 45ft wide (ibid, 22 April 1771, 122). This must have been part of the drive initiated by the Earl of Sandwich to provide seasoning sheds in all the yards (Coad 2013, 117).

In August 1771 the Navy Board ordered that the sheds be built, and the officers asked to be supplied with 'old ships timber … from other Yards … [and] merchant yards' to be used in the construction (TNA, ADM 106/3316, [probably 17] August 1771, 136). The officers proposed using '3in oak plank' for the foundation, '12in square' oak posts, 'weather boarding' and 'loover board', brickwork and tiling (ibid, 21 November 1771, 154). These sheds are likely to be those to the north of the smithy, consisting of 12 bays and also shown with louvered sides on the 1774 model (Fig 7; Fig 68; Fig 71).

In the south-east part of the yard, the walls of workshops (B30, Fig 70) shown on the 1774 (Fig 71) and later mapping were exposed, as well as a north–south aligned wall (B29, Fig 70) which may correspond to the northern of two timber sheds also appearing on the 1774 and subsequent maps.

In early 1771, the officers proposed urgent repairs to 'the slip next the plank houses in the Wet Dock', although the materials required – including piles, groundways, mudsills, capsills and land-ties – suggest a major rebuild (TNA, ADM 106/3316, 25 February 1771, 115). This is likely to have been the westernmost slip on the south side of the wet dock, shown on the 1774 model (Fig 73).

A range of building materials and a few clothing items were among the material recovered from excavation in the northern and western parts of the site, that is around the wet dock, in the area of the yard where the underlying deposits were alluvium (OA14). Peg and pantile roofing and brick, along with a small fragment of plain white tin-glazed wall tile, were found, as well as two short lace chapes (length 21–22mm), one plain and the other with horizontal ridges <37>, and a longer lace chape <38> (length 33mm). Two clay pipe bowls and 13 stems dating at the latest to c 1700–70 were found, although most of the pipes date to c 1660–1710 and were presumably residual from the previous period.

Other work and buildings around the quadrangle storehouse, 1753–74

A building was constructed in the north-west corner of the courtyard of the quadrangle storehouse between 1753 and 1774, on map evidence (Fig 71; Fig 93; cf Fig 60), and the west range of the quadrangle storehouse underwent significant modification to accommodate it. What survived of the west end of the Tudor storehouse (B1) would have been demolished to make way. The west range's east wall was partially demolished and machine bases inserted, one with two 55mm diameter iron rods inset, anchored by short flanking walls. This building would appear to be an 'engine house', but for what sort of engine is uncertain, as is the date of installation of an engine. Possibilities suggested for the building's use include for a horse gin powering a hoist for shifting stores, for a weighing machine/

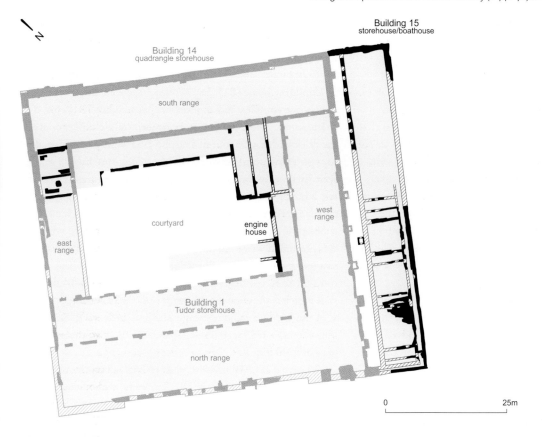

Fig 93 The quadrangle storehouse (B14) in 1774: upper – plan of the archaeological remains (scale 1:750); lower – the storehouse as shown on the 1774 scale model (Fig 7), looking from the waterfront 'south-east', with (top left) the dry dock (National Maritime Museum, Greenwich, L0459-004)

engine, or for a fire engine – manually operated and perhaps using water from the courtyard tank (below) (J Coad, pers comm 2015). The steam engine installed in the wood mills at Portsmouth in 1797 is generally considered to be the first in a royal dockyard; until James Watt invented the rotary motion in 1783, steam engines could only be used for pumping (Coad 2013, 76, 118; J Coad, pers comm 2015).

In the 19th century this was clearly an engine house, presumably steam-powered: the chimney and part of the east wall of the engine house can be seen in an illustration of 1869 (*London Journal*, 1 March 1869, 136, erroneously titled 'Exterior of Old Monastery'), and it is marked 'Engine House' on the 1870 Goad map (Fig 129). A second engine house, marked on a map of the 1930s (LLHAC, A/15/31/11) as 'Old CS Eng. Ho.' in the location of a concrete platform at the north end of this wall, may have been installed after the yard closed.

The internal yard of the quadrangle storehouse was metalled with gravel until 1776 when the officers complained that this surface was 'perpetually breaking up' as stores were moved in and out 'so that it is impossible to preserve a level, in wet weather is full of ponds … in dry weather with dust'. Bad drainage meant that standing water 'stinks under the foundation of the House'. They proposed paving the yard with 'Purbeck Square Stone' and to have 'a tank sunk in the center of the area of 12ft diameter and 12ft deep which will contain 33 tons of water'. The tank could also act as a reservoir for water to fight fire. There would be a '2in lead pipe with a stop cock laid to fill it occasionally' or to drain it. The tank would cost £207 9s 6d (TNA, ADM 106/3315, 6 February 1766, 78). Fortuitously, this tank survived the considerable later

truncation in the yard and was identified during the excavations. It was built of brick, rather like a soakaway, with several drains feeding into it.

Other major changes in this period included the construction of a building range (B15, Fig 70) along the west side of the storehouse complex and another smaller building (B16, Fig 70) to the south. These buildings can be seen on the 1774 model of the dockyard (Fig 93) but not on the 1753 Milton map (Fig 60), so were constructed between 1753 and 1774. Building 15 to the west survived as a series of three phases of structures. The first was a north–south aligned wall abutted by patches of a roughly cobbled surface. Internal east–west aligned walls which cut the cobbled surface but butted against the first-phase wall, which was presumably still standing, represent the second phase. These east–west walls subdivided the building into narrow bays. The third phase is represented by a wall parallel to the first-phase wall which is presumably the outer wall that can be seen on the 1774 model. This building range (B15) is labelled as a 'Store house' on the 1858 map (Fig 121) and as a 'Boat store' on the map of 1870 (Fig 129).

The smaller building to the south (B16) survived only as a thin north–south aligned wall, 0.36m wide, which would have formed the outside wall on the east side (Fig 94). The wall was built on a timber raft foundation and consisted of two parts, truncated centrally by a modern concrete pile cap and 14.00m long in all. With its main axis aligned north–south, Building 16 is shown on the 1774 model as consisting of two bays. It was probably used as a timber store. The building would have been demolished by 1791 to make way for the rigging house (B40; Chapter 7).

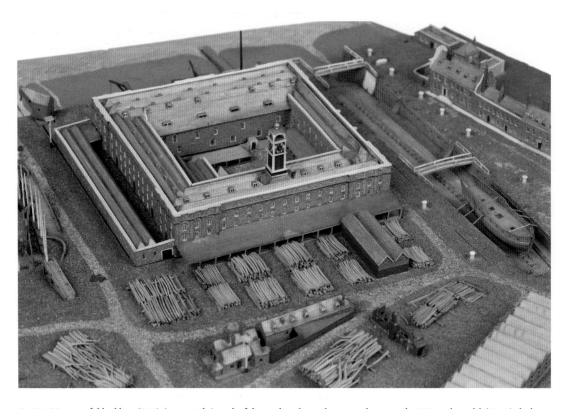

Fig 94 Twin-roofed building (B16) (centre right) south of the quadrangle storehouse, as shown on the 1774 scale model (Fig 7), looking 'north'; the dry dock is to the right (National Maritime Museum, Greenwich, L0459-035)

7

The late Georgian and Victorian dockyard (period 5, 1774–1869)

7.1 Historical introduction: 'British maritime ascendancy' versus Deptford's long decline

The navy had grown faster in the decades between 1690 and 1763 than the capacity of the dockyards: the number of ships had doubled and the tonnage tripled, whereas the number of men employed at the height of each successive war had not quite doubled and the infrastructure – docks, slips and buildings – had grown much less (Rodger 2004, 368). The Seven Years' War (or Austro-Prussian War) of 1756–63 had drawn in all the major powers of Europe but had also involved overseas colonial struggles between Britain and France, as they vied for control of North America and India. After 1763 Britain's strategic perspective altered; she turned away from Europe and towards her colonies. The American War of the 1770s meant maintaining a large army 4000 miles away, supported by the navy and overseas bases; naval war in the Americas continued into the 1780s, with Britain saving only half (13) of its American colonies, together with Gibraltar and India. In the years that followed, Britain looked to replace its lost transatlantic trade and naval facilities (ibid, 327–57, 365; Morriss 2011, 131–82 and *passim*; Coad 2013, 209–16). Logistical capability and a more competent state bureaucracy were combined with a thriving maritime economy, and the result, argues Morriss (2011, 396–403), was British maritime ascendancy in the period 1755–1815.

Between 1755 and 1814 the British navy more than tripled in size but dockyard manpower only doubled (Morriss 2011, 160). In the late 18th century there was substantial investment in Portsmouth, Plymouth and Chatham (Coad 2013, 4–10). Productivity in the yards needed to increase and the ships had to be built to last longer; the Earl of Sandwich attempted to tackle both issues, introducing piecework for shipwrights and ensuring that ships were built of seasoned timber (Morriss 2011, 141). Pitt the younger, Prime Minister (1783–1801, 1804–6) during the French Revolutionary and Napoleonic Wars, took care to look after the navy and carried forward much of Sandwich's work in rebuilding the fleet. Prompted by concerns about defending Gibraltar, several gunboats were built at Deptford and trialled in 1787–9 (Knight 2013, 8). Maintaining both ships and men was vital, but moves to reform naval administration and yard management had mixed success at this time, and later (Rodger 2004, 358–79, 473–88; Morriss 2011, 139–48). The Navy Board moved to Somerset House, making the navy's administration more integrated, with paintings of the yards hung for reference in the boardroom. That of Deptford (Fig 140) was done by Joseph Farington by July 1794, at least in part from a perspective drawn by William White, the master mast maker at Deptford; Farington first requested payment (£63) on 12 July 1794 (Cordingly 1986, 66–9). A new Transport Board was responsible from 1794 for transporting the army by sea, striving for greater efficiency and turning down potential charter ships in poor condition. In 1794 the master of the *Lady Juliana* transport vessel told the owner that his ship had been subject to a very strict survey and that the Deptford dockyard officers 'behaved with as much Friendship as I could expect from men of long acquaintance put under a new and perhaps troublesome Board'; the master circumvented some of the trouble, paying 'a small fee in a proper place' in order not to have to take his mast out for repair and spending £6 9s on wine for the Deptford Master Attendant and Clerk of the Survey (Knight 2013, 179–80). Previously, ships were chartered largely through brokers, and these transports were inspected and measured by Deptford officers (Morriss 2011, 326, 332).

Merchant builders played a vital part in meeting the navy's demand for ships, particularly 3rd-rates and below, in the 18th century and up to the defeat of Napoleon in 1815 (Barnard 1997, 71; Morriss 2011, 132–7). The Barnard family dockyards at Grove Street (leased from 1763 by William Barnard, William Dudman and Henry Adams), immediately west of the Deptford victualling yard, and from 1779 at Deptford Green to the east of the royal dockyard, next to Deptford Creek, built naval vessels from the 1760s to 1810 and, most importantly in business terms, East Indiamen. Royal yards loaned shipwrights to merchant yards on occasion, and in 1771 the Deptford officers were ordered to assist the Grove Street partnership with personnel and the chain boat to lift a 6th-rate naval vessel into wet dock to finish her inside work so that Grove Street could dry-dock an East Indiaman (Barnard 1997, 37, 39, 45–6). In the decade 1780–90, Grove Street and Deptford Green launched 42 ships, comprising 13 naval vessels (3rd-rates, 5th-rates and a lighter) and 29 East Indiamen (ibid, 52; for these yards, see also Ellmers 2013a).

Supply – of ships, munitions and stores – was critical during the Napoleonic Wars; due to the conflict's duration and scale, the contribution from the private sector was many times greater from 1803 than it had been during the wars of the 18th century. The six home royal dockyards reached a maximum combined workforce of nearly 16,000 artificers and labourers by 1813, but still could not meet demand (Knight 2013, 357–8). Completing a ship of the largest size and in the shortest possible time would have taken the full-time labour of 40 shipwrights for a 1st-rate, 30 for a 3rd-rate, 16–20 for a frigate depending on size, and 12 for a sloop, but there were not enough shipwrights to allow these numbers to be employed on new construction in wartime (Morriss 2011, 133, 165, 170). The recruitment of artificers (who served apprenticeships) and of labourers, 'extra men' and riggers were all problematic for periods in the 1800s (Morriss 1983, 105–9). Gangs of shipwrights and caulkers were sent from Deptford and Woolwich to Portsmouth in 1797 and to Sheerness in 1803 (ibid, 108). Of 518 warships built between 1803 and 1815, British merchant shipyards built 436 (84%) and the royal dockyards 82, with a further 52 built abroad (Knight 2013, 363). Royal yards were building the largest ships, but their priority, certainly in wartime, was maintenance – docking, repair and refitting – so that ships could be sent back to sea (ibid, 367). During this period Britain's domestic economy thrived and overseas trade was only intermittently disturbed by the war. New docks were established on both sides of the river, with the West India, London and East India docks opening in 1802–6 on the north side (ibid, 352–3).

Growing criticism of the inefficiencies of the royal dockyards by the late 18th century (MacDougall 1982, 131) was undoubtedly a factor in the decline of the Deptford yard, and there was a push for economies of scale. On top of this, the yard was also too far upriver, on a meandering channel prone to shoaling: by the 1760s, warships were being delayed at Deptford for up to two months while waiting for suitable winds and tides (Coad 2013, 11; Knight 2013, 381). The increasing difficulty of reaching the eastern yards was reflected in the reluctance to build more docks, leaving Deptford with just one dry (double) dock (able to accommodate two smaller 1st-rates) and one single dock on the wet dock throughout the 18th century. The largest rate of ship that each building slip at Deptford could accommodate was as follows: slip no. 1, a 74-gun 3rd-rate; slips nos 2 and 3 (on the wet dock), a 1st-rate; slips nos 4 and 5, a 32-gun frigate (Morriss 1983, 44–5; 2011, 132–3). However, ships had to reduce their draught to reach Deptford, for example by offloading their guns at Northfleet Hope or Gravesend; spring tides provided only 19ft of water and neap tides 2ft less (Morriss 1983, 41).

The First Lord of the Admiralty from 1801, the unpopular St Vincent, wanted an enquiry into the running of the navy and imposed stringent economies in an attempt to make the dockyards more productive. Following an unusually large reduction in the Deptford workforce in 1802, involving the discharge of numerous able-bodied men, St Vincent and the Admiralty Board inspected the yard and 'experienced much abuse from the enraged families of the workmen', were 'pelted with mud by the women and boys' and 'with some difficulty escaped from worse treatment' (Morriss 1983, 99; 2011, 168; Knight 2013, 222). Despite the need for warships in the Napoleonic Wars, in 1806 St Vincent suggested that Deptford dockyard could with profit be given over completely to the victualling office; in 1810 Admiral Berkeley wrote to the First Lord that Deptford and Woolwich were 'almost useless' (ibid, 381). John Rennie the elder drew up improvement plans for a number of dockyards, including Deptford (Fig 95), and wrote a report on all the dockyards for the Commission of Naval Revision; in 1807 Rennie recommended that Deptford (and Woolwich) not be developed but rather be closed, an opinion expressed by Samuel Bentham earlier, in 1800, as Inspector General of Naval Works. Not only were there problems of silting and location, but Rennie also argued that both yards suffered from a lack of space. Government decided to allocate money to expand existing facilities at all the eastern dockyards except Deptford (MacDougall 1982, 134; Morriss 1983, 53; Knight 2013, 381).

Nonetheless, at the beginning of the 19th century Deptford retained its importance, alongside Portsmouth and Plymouth, because of its proximity to the London boards; Navy Board couriers could reach Deptford in half an hour (Morriss 1983, 143). As well as building new and repairing, Deptford and Woolwich acted as depots for stores – for the other yards, for the fleet at sea and for foreign bases – and Deptford had a high turnover (ibid, 1, 14, 86). Naval stores were a significant part of the cost of maintaining the navy and there was ample scope for much less waste and greater efficiency (ibid, 86, 89, 91–4). The first Inspector of Canvas was appointed in 1804, to assist the

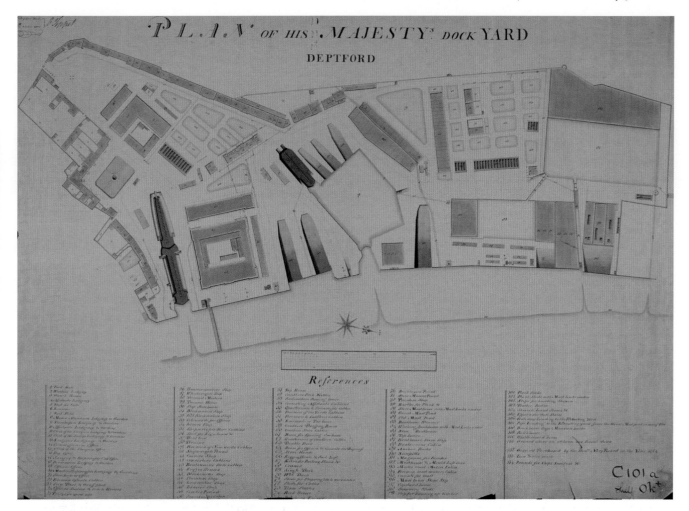

Fig 95 Map of the dockyard, 1802 (UK Hydrographic Office, UKHO, C101a-Ok)

Navy Board regarding contracts, prices and quality, and to supervise the receipt of canvas mainly at the Deptford and Woolwich yards (ibid, 89).

The effects of the Industrial Revolution were increasingly felt in the royal dockyards: in the growing use of outside experts like the Rennies, Samuel Bentham and James Watt; in the introduction of machinery such as blowing engines; in the greater use of iron in ships; and in the introduction of steam-powered warships and then all-metal warships that finally killed off the Thames yards (Coad 2013, 65–79 and *passim*). Steam was used increasingly in the naval dockyards from *c* 1800: at first for pumping out docks, and from 1802 in the new bucket-ladder steam dredgers invented by Samuel Bentham, which were far more efficient than the hand-operated Trinity House dredgers and yard scavelmen could be. Deptford built the second steam dredger in 1807, for use in the Thames at Woolwich (Morriss 1983, 54). Steam also began to be applied to manufacturing in the 1800s, as in the steam-driven block or pulley mills, designed by Brunel and implemented by Bentham (ibid, 46–53; Knight 2013, 376–8). The navy's first steam vessel, the paddle survey schooner *Congo* (83bm-tons), was launched at Deptford in January 1816, but was never used under steam and its engine was removed the same year (Colledge and Warlow 2010; Coad 2013, 25).

In the first two decades of the 19th century, Deptford built several 60-gun warships which were converted to steam in the 1840s and 1850s – the Blenheim-class *Blenheim* (1813) and *Hogue* (1811) and the Cornwallis-class *Russell* (1822) (Lambert 1984, 139). Despite the advent of steam dredgers providing a temporary solution for the silting problem, Deptford closed in 1830 to all but shipbreaking. The yard reopened for shipbuilding in 1843 (Fig 121) and made some significant final contributions to the fleet before permanent closure in 1869.

7.2 Works documented in the last quarter of the 18th and early 19th centuries

A new taphouse, repairs and other building works, 1774–*c* 1820

In March 1774, the officers sent the Navy Board an estimate for building a new taphouse (TNA, ADM 106/3318, 18 November 1775, 13). This was completed by November the following year when the porter removed his 'utensils' from the old taphouse. The glazier, compass maker and others were still occupying the floor over the old taphouse, and the officers proposed moving the glazier and others to the first floor of the braziers' and plumbers' shops after 'altering the end (now a high roof) into a gable end' at a cost of £25. The compass maker was to be moved to the treenail house where 'a small chimney' would be built for him. Once the old taphouse was unoccupied, the officers proposed taking it down and reusing its old materials (ibid, 16 November 1775, 11). In April 1776, the Navy Board ordered that a 'Call Office, Surgery, first Assistant and Sawyers Measurers Cabins, Compass makers and Glaziers shops etc' be built 'where the Old Taphouse stood' (ibid, 8 April 1776, 31). The officers reported that repairs to the Master Attendant's lodgings would cost £26 (ibid, 25 November 1776, 69).

In late 1788 repairs were ongoing on the anchor wharf, and the officers proposed that the wharf be paved with the 'more durable … Guernsey Squared stones (in stead of the Scotch Pebbles usually made use of)' (TNA, ADM 106/3322, 17 December 1788, 28). In September 1789 the officers suggested that the cost of various works should be included in the following year's estimate of expenditure. These included completing the new anchor wharf, as well as repairing the apron and piers of the 'Wet Dock's new gates' and laying a new floor in the mast house (ibid, 3 September 1789, 57). The new pair of gates had been completed and the piers of the wet dock finished by late 1791, at a cost of £560 (ibid, 2 November 1791, 141).

There was a dispute over a shed in the sailfield in the south-east corner of the yard. The officers reported that 'like most of the other partition fences, and erections in the Sailfield', it sprang originally from encroachments (TNA, ADM 106/3322, 9 December 1789, 67).

The officers sent an estimate for the cost of rebuilding the stone piers of the dry (double) dock in late 1788 (TNA, ADM 106/3322, 8 October 1788, 17). Work was under way by the next summer, when the mason, Mr Dent, found the existing stones 'more perished than he expected' (ibid, 2 July 1789, 5). The house-carpenters were also busy making and fixing the gates of the dry dock and erecting a new crane – referred to as 'Coles Crane' – on the anchor wharf (ibid, 13 January 1790, 71).

In 1790 the 'causeway at the Iron Gate' (ie in front of the storehouse) was being repaired (TNA, ADM 106/3322, 12 October 1790, 104). The officers also suggested that six windows be glazed in the 'range of the Treenail house', the snow and fog admitted by the current openings being 'hurtful to the Treenails in their seasoning' (ibid, 27 October 1790, 106).

Warrants for repairing the upper water gate and stairs by the yard's labourers were issued in September 1730, April 1751, April 1764 and December 1781, and there was a proposal to make a further repair in November 1795 for £65. This work was done 'for the security of the foundation of the Yard wall' (TNA, ADM 106/3324, 10 November 1795, 52).

In late 1796, the officers sent the Navy Board a model and drawings 'of a weigh bridge agreeable to directions from Sir John Henslow' that would cost £185 (TNA, ADM 106/3324, 10 October 1796, 140; 14 November 1796, 153); the proposed location was said on 14 November 1796 to be indicated on a separate plan (not included in the letter book). This 'weighing engine, capable of weighing ten tons (with iron and brass weights properly marked)' was installed in early 1797 (ibid, 27 February 1797, 187).

In 1799, the officers estimated that 'forming piers and making a pair of swing gates for separating the Long Dock' would cost £4179. This work seems to have been imminent as they asked for ten extra house-carpenters to be employed (TNA, ADM 106/3325, 17 April 1799, np). The reference to 'the Long Dock' is certainly to the dry (double) dock (ibid, 25 April 1799, np). The gates were part of a major rebuilding of this dock, including reducing the height of the apron that would extend 'the full length of the ways … backing the piers and sides of the Dock with clay' and building a piled cofferdam (ibid, 19 April 1799, np). The rebuild seems to have been focused on the 'head dock' (ie the part of the dry dock furthest from the river), as there was a ship in the 'stern of the Long Dock' (ibid, 29 August 1799, np). Good progress had been made by the summer, when more house-carpenters were required (ibid, 8 June 1799, np), although by autumn the pace had slowed due to 'the difficulty in driving the bearings and cofferdam piles' into the hard gravel (ibid, 14 October 1799, np).

In 1805, the Navy Board issued a warrant for a substantial rebuild of the single dock on the wet dock basin. The dock was to be enlarged 'to receive a 38-gun frigate' by deepening it '2ft below the present bottom', moving the gates 'three feet further aft' to make it longer, and widening it by 'alteration on each side'. The steps at the head of the dock were to be moved 'ten feet further in' to increase the working room (TNA, ADM 106/2516, 28 August 1805, order no. 169). Maps show that between 1802 (Fig 95) and 1810 (NMM, ADM/Y/D/6) the number of slips on the wet dock was reduced from three to two; two slips are also shown on the the plan of 1813 (TNA, ADM 7/593).

The construction of a 'new Sloproom' was almost finished by summer 1820, when the building was 'nearly ready to receive the Hydraulic Machine for the purpose of pressing and packing Slops' (TNA, ADM 106/3342, 18 July 1820, 39). The slate roof was being built in August (ibid, 31 August 1820, 47). The 'Press' had been installed by the autumn (ibid, 19 September 1820, 50; 22 September 1820, 51) when, presumably, the building was complete. Hydraulic machinery is generally thought to have become widespread in the royal dockyards in the 1850s (J Coad, pers comm 2015).

The mast docks, 1778–1815

In July 1778, the officers suggested enclosing a piece of ground 'joining to the SE end of the back of the Guardhouse, at the New Mast Pond' (ie the large mast dock built in 1770–4) for working on masts and storing 'Tarr, Turpentine etc'. This would cost £54 17s (TNA, ADM 106/3318, 9 July 1778, 158). Four new saw pits 'on the spare ground near the head of the New Mast Pond' would cost £226 8s 6d (ibid, 16 September 1778, 162).

In October 1778, the officers told the Navy Board that the 'Old and New Mast Ponds' were not sufficient to contain the *New England*, *Riga* and other masts in store. More masts were expected and the officers warned that these 'will be exposed to a succession of wet and dry weather' leading to 'speedy decay' unless they were in the mast docks' locks or under cover. They asked for sheds 'to cover the locks of the new Mast Pond and on the west side and to be continued to the wall next the road leading to Grove Street' at an estimated cost of £3216 4s (TNA, ADM 106/3319, 15 October 1778, 3). The Navy Board approved this in November. The officers asked for more house-carpenters to be employed, the current complement of 30 being too few (ibid, 29 March 1779, 37). Later, more bricklayers were needed (ibid, 22 September 1779, 58). This work was still ongoing in spring 1780, when further house-carpenters were requested (ibid, 19 April 1780, 95).

The Navy Board had approved further work on the small mast dock (the 'Old Mast Pond'), but in October 1788 the officers reported that a 'misfortune' had befallen 'the New Wall building for inclosing the sluiceway into the Old Mast Pond. Two feet of its thickness from the outside for half its length … separated and fell into the river.' The bricklayer blamed 'the land-ties and backbands having trip'd it', while the house-carpenters said 'the cause proceeded from the water every tide flowing over it and getting between the brickwork set in tarras … and that part of the wall which was built with sand mortar'. The foundation mudsills would have to be rebuilt (TNA, ADM 106/3322, 8 October 1788, 18).

A 'Mast Pond' was being cleaned in summer 1789. This is more likely on balance to be the small mast dock, as repair work was often done at the same time as such structures were being cleared of mud. The work was hampered by 'lumps of masts' in the soil at the base of the mast dock, so much so that the officers asked that 'the 52 extra labourers with the 3 teams of horses' be kept on for three further months. Such rotten masts were being stored in 'the Meadow' bought from Sir John Evelyn, although this was also causing problems as the masts were getting in the way of work to raise the level of this area in advance of paving (TNA, ADM 106/3322, 17 June 1789, 51). Later that year, the officers requested that these men be kept on for an additional three months (ibid, 23 September 1789, 57).

By early 1814, so much mud had accumulated in the mast docks that there was no room to store all the masts underwater. The officers suggested cleaning out the 'great Mast Pond', the masts in 'the lower locks' being completely covered in mud (TNA, ADM 106/3338, 18 May 1814, 192). But there were problems. The entrance to the large mast dock was too narrow to admit barges to take away the soil. Instead, the officers suggested hiring the 'Marsh Land that lies to the westward of the meadow in this Yard for the purpose of stowing timber' and disposing of the soil there. The 'landlord (Lady Evelyn) would have no object to the measure' (ibid, 25 May 1814, 196). In the summer of 1814, the officers took possession of the land (ibid, 8 July 1814, 218). The yard asked for extra labourers (ibid, 8 August 1814, 8) who had been employed by the following spring to clear soil from 'the New Mast Pond'. This was to be

deposited on Lady Evelyn's land, although the contractors Jolliffe and Banks would also have to dispose of some as the land was too small to take all '1500 cubic yards' (ibid, 10 April 1815, 169). The 'great Mast Pond' was clear of mud by the summer and the officers proposed transferring masts into it from 'the small Mast Pond' so that it too could be emptied. The soil would be taken away by a Mr Mills in barges (ibid, 8 July 1815, 215), as he had done with that from the large mast dock (ibid, 29 July 1815, 223).

'[T]he piece of Mud Land opposite the Yard' was also being used for storing masts. The marshland having been acquired, the officers told the landlord in late 1814 that it was no longer needed (TNA, ADM 106/3338, 21 November 1814, 73). The yard's timber was cleared from his land (ibid, 31 January 1815, 123), but the landlord, Richard Flanks of Brixton, Surrey, refused to accept the notice to quit (ibid, 24 January 1815, 120).

The officers' quarters and offices, 1778–1820

The boatswain's lodgings required £9 17s worth of repairs in late 1778 (TNA, ADM 106/3319, 9 November 1778, 11). In 1791 the cost of repairing the Surgeon's lodgings was estimated at £118 (TNA, ADM 106/3322, 12 January 1791, 116) and for the porter's lodgings at £93 (ibid, 18 March 1791, 123). The officers estimated that repairs to the Master Shipwright's lodgings, including repairing the windows and the roof of the kitchen outhouses, would cost £127 (TNA, ADM 106/3324, 27 August 1795, 19), repairs to the Storekeeper's lodgings £104 10s (ibid, 30 September 1795, 30) and to the Clerk of the Survey's lodgings £100 (ibid, 30 May 1796, 106). Repairs later to the Master Shipwright's lodgings were estimated at £102 (TNA, ADM 106/3325, 19 December 1799, np), and there were other repairs to the Surgeon's lodgings (ibid, 12 February 1800, np) and to the Clerk of the Survey's lodgings (ibid, 14 May 1800, np) (Fig 96; cf Fig 40; Fig 98).

The officers asked for 'the square at the front' of their quarters to be turfed, at a cost of £8. There was a central sundial in this area. They suggested that the turf be laid by a labourer at the yard, Edmund Major, who had done similar work 'for gentlemen in this neighbourhood' (TNA, ADM 106/3322, 2 December 1791, 143).

A fence wall and engine house by the Clerk of the Cheque's office and the 'Rear Guard Room' had been erected by early 1800 (TNA, ADM 106/3325, 29 January 1800, np). A fire in 1783 was reported as penetrating 'to the Engine House by the Old Gate, the roof of which was entirely destroyed; the officers lodgings were in great danger and it was found necessary for their preservation to remove the Books & Papers &c from the Clerk of the Cheques office …' (Chapter 9.3; cf Chapter 6.3, 'Other work and buildings around the quadrangle storehouse, 1753–74', for the use of steam-powered engines).

In the early 19th century the Clerk of the Survey's lodgings were to undergo proposed repair at a cost of £101 (TNA, ADM 106/3342, 21 March 1820, 4), and likewise the Surgeon's lodgings (ibid, 19 May 1820, 23).

Fig 96 Offices and accommodation along the east side of the yard, from the Master Shipwright's house on the waterfront (upper left) to the officers' quarters (lower right) (cf Fig 40; Fig 98), with the dry (double) dock to the left, as shown on the 1774 scale model (Fig 7), looking 'east' (National Maritime Museum, Greenwich, L0459-036)

7.3 Archaeological and historical evidence for the late Georgian and Victorian dockyard

The yard may have been experiencing difficulties and restrictions in this period but repairs and maintenance were ongoing. As well as the documented work on the dry (double) dock and single dock on the wet dock (above, 7.2), major building projects in this period included the construction of a new wet dock entrance, designed by John Rennie, which was exposed in the excavation. Archaeological evidence was also recovered for some of the early 19th-century roofs or covers erected over slipways and docks, as well as other structures (Fig 97; Fig 98).

Shaping timbers: sawpits, a saw mill and a steam kiln

Sawpits were very important parts of any dockyard, and their importance increased in the London yards with time as more timber conversion and secondary shaping was done with pit-saws rather than by 'hewing' with axes (Goodburn 1999,

173; Goodburn et al 2011, 315). Straight saw cuts were used initially to make planks and some beams, and to cut the sides off some curved timbers. Later, narrow-bladed pit-saws were used to cut out curved shapes. After they had been marked, trimmed logs or baulks of timber were sawn on movable cross-bars and rollers set on beams laid around the edge of a sawpit (or occasionally a raised timber gantry). The pits were often deep and had to be revetted to stop the sides collapsing. The more experienced sawyer stood on top of the timber and another sawyer pulled the saw down into the pit following the carefully marked line. The pit-saw only cut on the downstroke unlike the cross-cut two-man saw which cut in both directions. It was repetitive, hard work, but without many teams of sawyers the dockyard's shipwrights could not have functioned. Some standardised plank elements were clearly sawn elsewhere and imported; for example, Pepys recorded '... down to Deptford first and there viewed some Deales, lately served in at a low price' (*Pepys diary*, 11 July 1662), deals being imported, thick (usually 3in thick), sawn softwood planks. The bulk, however, had to be converted in the yard itself. Archaeological work at the sister royal dockyard of Woolwich showed that navy yard sawpits were timber-lined before being rebuilt in brick (Courtney 1974, 54). There the sawpits were *c* 5–7m long and *c* 1.0–1.3m across, with a probable depth of *c* 2m.

In this period, two sawpits were to be taken down 'near the Old Call Office' and the officers suggested building two new ones in that location. In addition, they proposed that two further sawpits be built 'near the Pentstock of the New Mast Pond' to replace 'those thought to be too near the area of the tarr cellars' (TNA, ADM 106/3318, 3 July 1777, 100). In January 1778, the officers proposed taking down 'the old Surgery and Shipwrights Call Office and roofs of the sawpitts joining' which were in disrepair, and to build a new single sawpit. The proposal included digging new foundations, 'ground cells [ie ground sills] of oak framed to posts' and weather boarding (ibid, 27 January 1778, 137).

The officers asked the Navy Board for two sawpits 'at the easternmost end of the New Mast Pond' at a cost of £90 19s. The sawpits were to be built of oak, fir and brick, weatherboarded and with tiled roofs (TNA, ADM 106/3319, 11 November 1779, 68; 13 November 1779, 69). New sawpits were being built in 1791 (TNA, ADM 106/3322, 24 January 1791) and more sawyers and sawpits were required in 1813 when the officers suggested dividing the current 'Double Pitts' to make three (TNA, ADM 106/3338, 3 September 1813, 55) at a cost of £46 (ibid,15 September 1813, 59).

Just south of the central part of the site, in trench 15 (Fig 3), and south of the wet dock, the brick linings of two sawpits (S46, Fig 98), built of stock bricks, were uncovered. Two new sawpits in the meadow had been proposed by the officers in 1789 (TNA, ADM 106/3322, 3 September 1789, 57), and may have been these. One of the sawpits was excavated to its base (Fig 99). In contrast to the Woolwich examples, it had a full surviving depth of 2.10m to the base of the brickwork. A ledge set 400mm higher may have supported a raised timber floor, since robbed. Surprisingly, no sawdust residues were found. The sawpit was rather wide at 2.10m and had a length of over 3.08m. The internal width of the pit was wider than in many examples found, but this would have allowed for the sawing of very wide timbers while still admitting air and light. In any pit-sawing work the bottom sawyer needs room for his arms and shoulders to move up and down. This requirement means that a pit would have been *c* 0.7m wider than the widest straight timbers typically to be sawn. Once curved cuts were being sawn out of large timbers, perhaps from the late 18th century, a wider working pit would have been needed. This suggests that the excavated pits could have been used to cut large curved timbers.

Elsewhere, there were other structures relating to shaping timbers. Two parallel walls built of stock brick and connected by a shorter wall of the same build (B28, Fig 98) corresponded to walls of a sawmill shown in the angle between the large and small mast docks on the 1858 map (Fig 121) and the 1868 Ordnance Survey map (Fig 128). A north–south brick wall on a timber baseplate ([268], Fig 100) is likely to have been part of the steam kiln(s) shown on the maps of 1858 and 1868, situated between the plank/timber sheds and the wet dock.

Fighting fire and a water tank

In a dockyard largely comprising timber buildings packed with flammable stores such as rope, tar and turpentine for work on wooden ships, fire was an understandable concern. The smoking of tobacco was forbidden in the dockyards, including their workhouses and storehouses, according to Navy Board standing orders from the early 1660s (TNA, ADM 106/2537, 15 March 1663, np; 5 August 1679, np). Despite this, and other precautions, there were several major fires at the yard during its working life, one of the most famous being that in the summer of 1667 which caused many to believe that the Dutch had attacked the Tower of London (Chapter 4.1). In January 1761 there was a serious fire in the Red Lyon alehouse adjoining the yard (TNA, ADM 106/3313, 31 January 1761, np); only luck saved the yard from more serious damage than part of the perimeter wall being brought down (Chapters 6.3 and 9.3). Because of the constant danger posed, fire engines were a feature of the yard (eg Chapter 4.1); by the 19th century, the fire engines were inspected four times a year (TNA, ADM 106/3338, 18 May 1814, 193).

There was a serious fire in 'one of the Mills' at the victualling office in 1776. Fire engines from the yard attended, but the mill was destroyed. The cause of the blaze was unknown (TNA, ADM 106/3318, 9 January 1776, 21). The following summer, the officers proposed to make a tank for '60 tons of water' near the back of the smithy for firefighting (ibid, 3 July 1777, 100). A pitch kettle caught fire in 1778 (as had occurred in 1742: Chapter 6.3), but was extinguished before the building could be damaged (ibid, 1 October 1778, 162). There was another large fire in 1793 (MacDougall 1982, 122).

Various incidents prompted the Admiralty in 1777 to order proper provision in all the royal yards (Oppenheim 1926, 379–80). The officers drew up elaborate plans for coordinated measures to fight fire at the Deptford yard. They proposed the construction of buildings near the dock gates, at the Clerk of the Cheque's office, 'where the wooden fence now is, adjoining the Measurers Cabbin, at the East corner of the Yard', at the deal yard, and 'at the back of the Guard house, near the Boathouse'. These would contain 11 large and 11 small fire engines, as well as 'lanthorns', saws, 'tubbs', cordage and over 170 leather buckets, with more buckets in the officers' lodgings. In the event, only the building near the boathouse was approved and was being built in August 1778, although 'four ladders and four fire poles with hooks' were placed around the yard. The officers also asked for 'two additional tanks', one to be supplied by a reservoir and the other to hold 'forty tons' of water 'supplied from the river at high water by a drain' (TNA, ADM 106/3318, 23 December 1777 with notes in margin, 128). Although these two tanks were not ordered at this time, the description of the latter tank bears a striking resemblance to a timber tank (S33) found near the south end of slipway no. 5 (S31) and the west end of the rigging and sail loft (B40) (Fig 97; Fig 98), and which may be one of the officers' proposed alterations to the rigging house as 'security against fire' (ibid, 2 June 1777, 100). The rigging and sail loft would have been

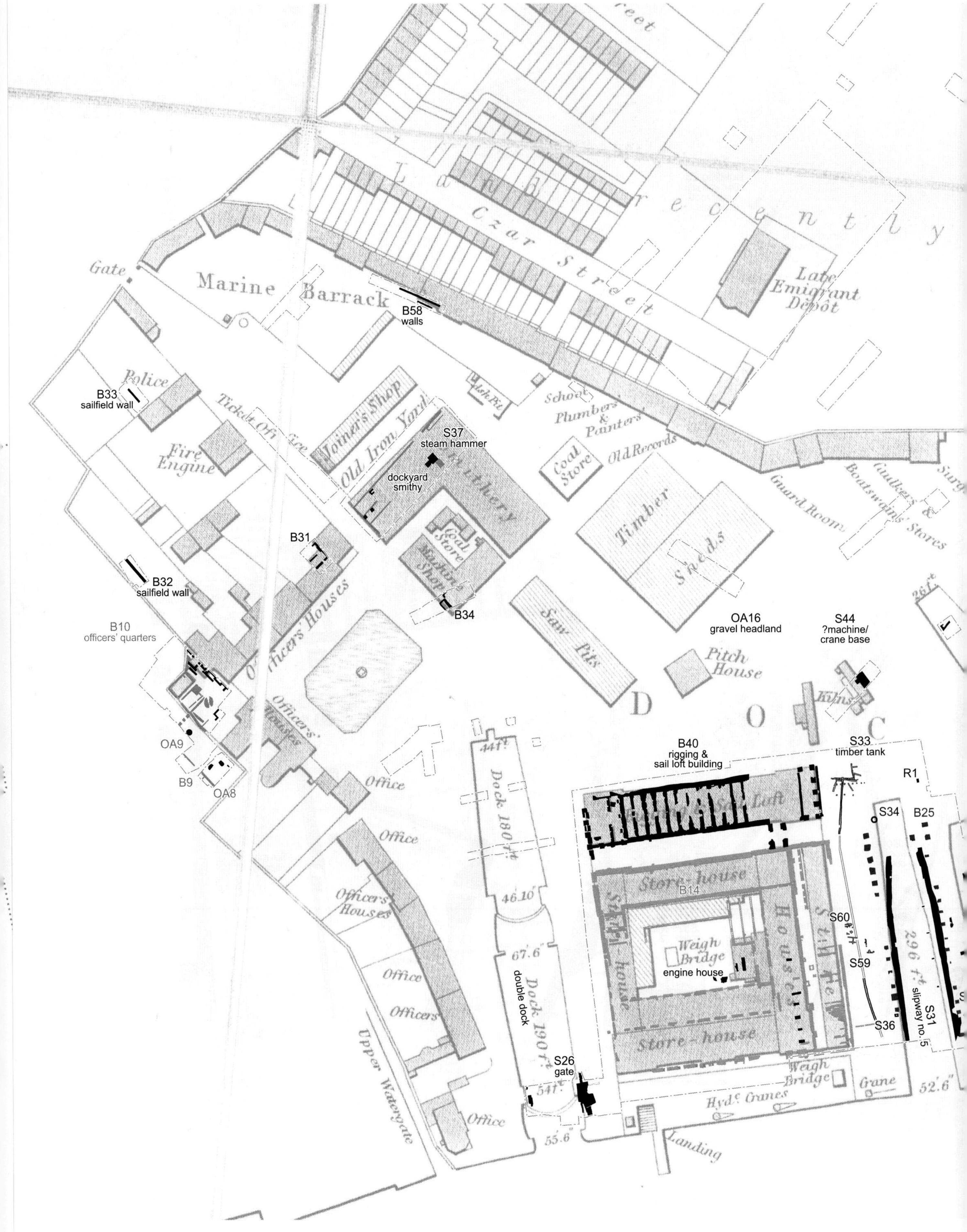

Gate

Marine Barrack

B58
walls

Late Emigrant Depot

Police

B33
sailfield wall

Ticket Off.

Joiner's Shop

Fish Pit

School

Plumbers & Painters

Fire Engine

Old Iron Yard

S37
steam hammer

Coal Store

Old Records

dockyard smithy

Guard Room

Caulkers & Boatswains' Stores

B31

Coal Store

Machine Shop

Timber

Sheds

B32
sailfield wall

B34

B10
officers' quarters

Officers' Houses

Saw Pits

Pitch House

OA16
gravel headland

S44
?machine/
crane base

Officers' Quarters

D   O   C

Kilns

OA9

Office

B40
rigging &
sail loft building

S33
timber tank

R1

B9

OA8

441'

Dock 180 ft

Sail Loft

S34   B25

Office

Store-house

B14

296 ft slipway no. 5

46.10'

Sail-house

S60

Officers Houses

Weigh Bridge

engine house

Sail-house

S59

67.6'

Dock 190 ft
double dock

Office

Store-house

S36

Officers

S26
gate

Weigh Bridge

S31

Upper Watergate

Office

54'

55.6'

Hydc Cranes

Landing

Crane

52'6"

Fig 98 Plan of principal archaeological features in the late Georgian to Victorian dockyard (period 5) overlain on the 1858 map (Fig 121) (scale 1:1500)

Fig 99 View of one of the brick-lined sawpits (S46), looking east

Fig 100 View of remains of the steam kiln (the brick wall is to the left) and adjacent cobbled yard, looking south-east

Fig 101 View of timber tank and box-drains (S33), looking north

particularly prone to fire which could spread to the quadrangle storehouse nearby, with disastrous consequences for the yard.

The tank (S33, Fig 101) was located at the edge of the excavation trench, so that only partial excavation was possible, but this revealed it to have been built in two phases. The earliest phase consisted of a sawn oak plank lining nailed to small oak piles set on 0.40m centres. A set of small softwood piles were driven just inside this original lining to which knotty, sawn softwood planking 300–400mm wide and 25mm thick was nailed, close-fitting and on edge. Towards the top edge of the lining a nailed plank box-drain or culvert of oak and elm ran to the nearest section of Thames frontage, as described in the officers' request for a water reservoir. An interesting and unusual innovation, not mentioned in the documentary evidence, was located in the corner at the bottom edge of the lining. This was a tight-fitting, sliding, planked sluice gate connected to a similar box-drain *c* 420mm wide, made mainly of elm planks that also ran to the Thames frontage (Fig 102). The lower sluice and drain arrangement must have worked as a drain at half or low tide, while the upper timber box must have acted as a pipe bringing river water to the tank. Part of the lid of the upper timber box ([3485]) was tree-ring dated to after 1618 (Chapter 10.9; Fig 199). Both the upper and lower boxes were edge-nailed with iron spikes and the seams packed with tarred hair ('blair' or 'setwork') in the manner used in the 18th century to waterproof river barge planking in the London region (Goodburn 2002, 85). The ends of the elm or oak planks were cut to a bevel to fit over each other and sealed with tarred hair. Surprisingly, the planks were overlapped in an alternating pattern rather than so as to aid the liquid flow in one direction.

The tank contained what appeared to be a large, crudely fashioned wooden paddle in its fill (<S35>, Fig 194). Just to the south was a large oak log set vertically earthfast, which may possibly have been used as part of a simple crane used to raise and lower buckets in and out of the tank. Alternative interpretations of the tank and box-drains (S33) are that they

Fig 102 View of lower timber box-drain running from the timber tank (S33), looking south

were used to flush out parts of the yard (although it is difficult to see how enough 'head' would have been generated), or provided a water supply for steam chests and for washing ships' decks and timbers such as masts.

In late 1788, the officers proposed 'to line the purlins etc in the Anchor Shop with Mr. Hartley's Copper Fire plates, to guard against any accident from fire' (TNA, ADM 106/3322, 19 December 1788, 29). There was a further fire in summer 1791 'to the eastward of His Majesty's Yard between the lower and upper Watergates … which burnt with great violence'. The yard's engines were used and the fire did no damage to it (ibid, 25 August 1791, 136). In 1800, a fire 'in the Bakehouse belonging to the Sailmakers, [was] occasioned by a candle … knocked into a bin of rope', but was quickly extinguished (TNA, ADM 106/3325, 26 February 1800, np).

A half-slip on the wet dock, 1788

The officers sent the Navy Board a proposal to build a slipway 'fronting the Top and Boathouses'. The slip was 'to be framed with ground sills, fitted on pileheads athwart, and bond timber to be laid with Portland ashlers'. Mr Dent would provide the stone for £200 and build the slip. Work 'rebuilding the Painters Shop' and the construction of 'temporary sheds for covering the births of timber' had been postponed, and the officers suggested that the money for these projects be used for the slip instead (TNA, ADM 106/3322, 1 October 1788, 16; 8 October 1788, 17). (Early the following year, the officers sent details of the new painters' shop to be built 'in room of the old one' (ibid, index and 20 January 1789, 35).) The slipway is referred to as 'the Boathouse Slip', its 'pavement' to be built of 'cube … purbeck Ashlar' (ibid, 29 October 1788, 22; 5 November 1788, 23). This slipway may have been a rebuilding of slipway no. 1 (S27) between the wet dock and the small mast dock, although the description of a stone base fits better with the much smaller half-slip (S19, Fig 98; Fig 103) found on the west side of the wet dock itself. A half-slip is shown in this location on the 1753 map

(Fig 58; Fig 60) and maps up to and including 1858; the slip is not shown on the 1868 map, so it seems to have been removed some time in the last decade of the yard. The 1788 slip may therefore have been a rebuild of the half-slip located on the wet dock since c 1753.

The half-slip's base of stone and brick was laid on a timber raft which was not exposed. In total the slip measured 12.00m × 7.50m (39ft × 24½ft). This half-slip only extended a little way down the brick wall of the wet dock. The location and depth were ideal for launching and retrieving boats and timber such as softwood spars. Several such small slips were built around the yard and are shown in historic paintings and on the 1774 model. When the slip went out of use, the end that opened into the wet dock was blocked with stone taken out of the base of the slip (below, 7.4; Fig 97).

The rigging and sail loft, constructed 1791–6, rebuilt by c 1880

At the beginning of 1791, the officers sent the Navy Board the design of 'a building proposed to be erected on a parallel with the South West front of the Storehouses for the use of the storekeeper to hold Oakum, junk etc in the room of those to be taken down which are in the way of the new sawpits now building'. The initial estimated cost was £486 (TNA, ADM 106/3322, 24 January 1791), rising to £1222 later that year, presumably to reflect more ambitious plans for the construction of this 'brick building one storey high' (ibid, 29 March 1791, 125). This is almost certainly the building range (B40, Fig 97; Fig 98; Fig 104) south of and parallel with the south range of the quadrangle storehouse. The 'New Rigging House' seems to have been finally completed in 1796 when the discharge of seven bricklayers and their labourers engaged for its construction

Fig 103 View of stone half-slip (S19) on the wet dock, looking north-west

Fig 104 View of the rigging and sail loft (B40) (converted to a cold store in the 20th century), looking west; the alley and quadrangle storehouse are to the right

was proposed (ibid, 15 April 1796, 92). There is also a reference later in 1796 to this building being 'ready to receive the gratings for enclosing ... the stone work round the area of the Pitch and Tar Cellars' (TNA, ADM 106/3324, 8 August 1796, 124). The building is referred to as the 'Rigging House & Sail Loft' on the map of 1802 (Fig 95).

The space between Building 40 and the south wall of the quadrangle storehouse was used as an alley. Map evidence shows that a gateway was installed at the east end by 1802 and existed until the end of the yard's life. A 2.70m × 1.10m brick foundation may have supported a pier for this on the north side. At the west end a set of double gates was built by 1802. The foundations for these were identified in the excavations, each *c* 2.2m × 1.1m in size. The alley was roofed over, with slots carefully cut into the walls for (presumably) vertical timber supports, although this does not seem to have happened until after the yard closed in 1869.

This one-storey building (B40) seems to have been rebuilt some time before *c* 1880 when it is shown in a photograph as having two fenestrated upper storeys (Fig 105). The photograph shows that the south wall of the building was punctuated at ground-floor level by at least 20 arched door openings (more are obscured by other structures). Excavation of this building

suggested that its gable ends also featured openings. At the east end, 1.40m square blocks of brick foundation cut through the earlier continuous brick wall which was 0.50m thick. At the west end, the same blocks of foundation were recorded, although the building seems to have been slightly shortened at this end as the earlier wall lay just to the west. The building is referred to as a 'rigging and sail loft' on the Goad map of 1870 (Fig 129).

Only the cellars of Building 40 survived and are likely to have been part of the earlier phase. The cellars consisted of a series of north–south aligned bays, each 3.60m wide. The springing of the brick vault survived in some of the bays. Full excavation was not possible due to safety restrictions.

Cranes and capstans

Several features relating to cranes and capstans were identified during the excavations, including around the edges of the brick-lined wet dock (Fig 97; Fig 98). They are diagnostic relics of how the dock was used, that is, they were probable or known crane bases, capstan bases or just possibly strong posts used in 'careening' vessels. Cranes clearly needed strong foundations to avoid being tipped over by their loads. Capstans were a widely used form of winch, on land and aboard vessels; they had a

Fig 105 View of the south facade of the rigging and sail loft (B40, left) and the south end of the double dock slip cover building (B21, right) in a photograph of c 1880; the cover structure to slipway no. 5 (B25, extreme left) can be seen in the distance (LLHAC, Thankfull Sturdee Collection PH87-13391 SS63)

vertical shaft rotated powerfully by men using bars set into sockets running at right angles to the shaft. The length of the bars provided mechanical advantage and the men walking in a circle were traditionally entertained by shanty singers. Capstans were crucial parts of the established dockyard infrastructure, and they were extensively used for warping vessels into and out of docks and basins. The bases of the capstan shafts on land had to be well supported below ground due to the pressures exerted. The methods for achieving this at the yard varied considerably, possibly mainly related to the scale of work intended. Careening was the process of controlled hauling-over of a floating vessel, by pulling on the masts and rigging and attaching them (on the opposite side) to strong anchor points, such as major posts. This was a way of getting access to the below-the-waterline parts of the hull without using a slipway or dry dock.

A substantial subrectangular composite brick and timber capstan base (S25, Fig 97) was situated between slipways nos 4 and 5 (S30 and S31). The brick base supported an east–west aligned plank 450mm wide and fitted with a central worn rounded socket *c* 140mm in diameter (Fig 106). This plank had a redundant treenail hole, indicating that it was originally a ship plank of some form. It is likely that there was once a shaft of some type above the brick base to provide access for lubrication. A 2.23m square brick crane base (S36, Fig 97) was located on the east side of slipway no. 5 (S31). It survived nine courses high and its walls were 0.34m wide. A 1.93m diameter brick crane base (S34, Fig 97) stood six courses high near the south end of slipway no. 5 (S31). Its walls were 0.35m wide and the remains of a brick internal floor survived.

Another composite brick and timber circular capstan base

(S64, Fig 97) lay to the west of the middle of the brick wet dock near the stone-lined half-slip (S19, above). A small circular brick shaft was *c* 1.6m in diameter and had a tropical hardwood plank in the base *c* 400mm across. It had a central circular hole of *c* 15mm diameter which would have taken the base of the capstan shaft. Redundant holes in the plank indicate that it was originally a thick ship's hull plank. The timber appeared to be of teak, which is known from another early shipyard context nearby where it was thought to date from *c* 1800 (Pitt and Goodburn 2003, 202). The Deptford example is likely to be of similar date.

A simple plank capstan base (S65, Fig 97) lay just east of the pivot point of the eastern leaf of the wet dock gate (S9). It survived as a simple plank of oak *c* 1m long, *c* 0.5m wide and 170mm thick. It had a central worn hole *c* 140mm in diameter for the capstan shaft, and its location suggests that it was used for hauling vessels into the dock.

Another capstan base (S66, not illustrated) was found not *in situ* but displaced sideways in alluvium as a result of later disturbance. It was recorded by the trench edge (area 4) near the waterfront between the quadrangle storehouse and slipway no. 5 (S31), and was found to have been made of three substantial sawn oak beam offcuts fastened together with four large iron drift bolts. The assembly of three beams [3351] measured 1.85m long by 910mm deep and 620mm wide in total. A central iron-lined circular socket 310mm in diameter was found in what must have been the upper face. This would have held a very substantial windlass shaft, so that the capstan must have been used for very heavy work.

In 1790 the officers proposed building a 'New Crane on the

Fig 106 View of brick and timber capstan base (S25, foreground) positioned between slipways nos 4 and 5 (S30 and S31), looking south

Anchor Wharf', referred to as 'Coles Crane' (TNA, ADM 106/3322, 13 January 1790, 71). The Anchor Wharf lay between the north edge of the old (ie small) mast dock and the river.

Later a crane broke down and the officers proposed erecting 'one of Mr. Lloyds cranes' as a replacement (TNA, ADM 106/3336, 21 May 1811, 130). In the event, three of Lloyd's cranes were built at the yard; as they were 'for landing timber and other stores', they must have been on the riverfront. The cranes needed repair in 1814 (TNA, ADM 106/3338, 14 March 1814, 164). In 1815, chains on two cranes had broken and the officers invited Lloyd to the yard 'to inspect the apparent inefficiency of the workmanship' and 'evident signs of defect' (ibid, 23 February 1815, 140; 29 April 1815, 174).

Other cranes consisted of long timbers set on the ground with a timber upright and diagonal bracing. An example of such an arrangement was Structure 63 (Fig 97; Fig 107), consisting of a 3.35m long reused timber aligned east–west, with the surviving one of two diagonal timbers ([5701], a reused small ship deck beam or 'ledge') and an upright ([5540], a reused ship stern post broken at the top, with chiselled Roman numeral depth marks) set in a mortice secured by a wooden wedge. This trestle assembly was probably a crane base and was found set close to the junction of the west wall of the wet dock and the northern edge of the small stone half-slip (S19, above). The horizontal timber was supported on two timber sleepers; several redundant mortices and peg holes were from an earlier

use. Four small copper-alloy nails (<611>, <612>) and a larger one (<613>) were associated with timber [5540]. Another crane (S52, Fig 97) was also of this design, although less complete. The basal reused timber [4307], also aligned east–west and 3.35m long, rested on two sleepers. The upper end of the diagonal timber [4390] was broken.

Several crane bases (including S52, above) were apparently related to the construction of the new wet dock entrance in 1814–19 (below). Structure 50 (Fig 97) consisted of a 0.93m post slotted into a timber base measuring 0.86m × 0.52m × 0.27m. A 6.42m long plank, with a small chock and a 0.50m long post nearby, were all that remained of crane Structure 51 (Fig 97).

Structure 53 (Fig 97) survived only as a timber platform 3.70m × 2.00m in size. Finds from demolition debris associated with this crane include glass fragments from two windows, three bottles and one or two glass inkwells (<238>, <239>). One of the bottles has dosage lines and was used for medicine or poison, while another bore relief-moulded lettering; the third is in natural green glass and of plain cylindrical form. Iron objects comprise a large iron nail <561>, a smaller iron nail with lengths of wire <562>, possibly from a hawser, and a small length of heavy iron chain made up of oval links and partly covered in a tar-like substance (<S39>, Fig 195).

On the west side of slipway no. 4 (S30), a circular crane base (S54, Fig 97), built of red brick, had an external diameter of 2.20m and an internal diameter of 1.74m. It survived eight

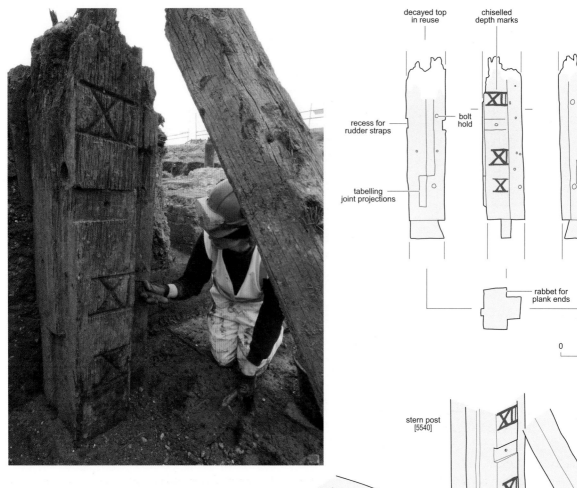

Fig 107 View (above, looking north), elevations and isometric reconstruction (right, scale 1:40) of timber crane (S63) employing reused ship stern post [5540], with depth marks in Roman numerals, and deck beam or 'ledge' [5701]

courses high, to 0.60m. A squarish stone (S55, Fig 97), 0.25m × 0.22m × 0.14m in size, may have been the base for a post or a hoist. West of slipway no. 1 (S27), crane Structure 58 (Fig 97) was cruder, consisting of a 1.02m × 0.48m baseplate, 0.08m thick, with a number of short, vertically-set truncated timbers.

Several vertical earthfast, large oak log uprights were scattered across the yard. These were minimally trimmed oak logs around 450mm in diameter, set in substantial post pits cut within the landfill behind the brick wet dock frontage. They would appear to have been used as anchor points for careening (above) or possibly as the bases of simple cranes. One of these simple earthfast posts was found adjacent to the large timber-lined tank (S33, above) near the rigging and sail loft (B40) and probably functioned as a simple timber crane base.

Two rectangular brick crane bases were constructed respectively on opposite, west and east, sides of the 18th-century brick wet dock walls (Fig 70; Fig 71). Similarity of design suggests that they were built in the same period. Neither features on the 1802 map; the east crane base (S62) appears on the maps of 1858 and 1868. The west crane base (S56, Fig 97; Fig 98) does not appear on any map; it may have been superseded by another two cranes further south on that wall of

the dock, one of them labelled a 'hydraulic crane' on the 1858 and 1868 maps. Like the east crane base, the west one is likely to have been built after 1802, but had been removed by 1858, whereas the east crane base was almost certainly dismantled only after the yard closed in 1869.

Both crane bases were built of two parallel brick walls that formed the long sides, at right angles to the wet dock wall, closed off at the landward end by another shorter wall. The fourth side, towards the dock, stopped short of the internal edge of the dock and was curved internally. Externally this brick rectangle measured 5.00m × 2.20m, and 3.20m × 1.00m internally. The west crane base had been slightly modified.

19th-century 'deadmen'

Two *c* 1.5m square timber platforms (S45, Fig 98) were found buried in the alluvium in the south-west part of the site; these had been made of two thicknesses of oak carvel ship planks

Fig 108 View of square timber platform (S45), possibly a 'deadman', looking south (0.5m scale)

fastened at 90° to each other (Fig 108). Clenched iron bolts (riveted over circular washers), small copper nails and some treenails in the timbers attest the nautical origins of the thick planks. One interpretation of these structures is that they were 'deadmen', that is, a buried anchor point which extended above ground in order to attach cables used to haul heavy objects. Another explanation might be that they were once platforms or pads for removed timber uprights.

The smithy

A pair of bellows in the smithy was reported as worn out and the officers suggested replacing them with 'one of the blowing machines of Messrs Halley and Jefferies' (TNA, ADM 106/3342, 10 October 1820, 55). The replacement was evidently a success as the officers asked for a further five unserviceable bellows to be replaced by these machines (ibid, 7 December 1820, 70). Archaeologically, there appears to have been little change to the smithy in the south-east part of the yard (area 5.2) (B18, rebuilt in the mid 18th century; Chapter 6.3), apart from the construction of a steam hammer, the 1.30m by 1.34m foundations of which in brick and timber were recorded during the excavation (S37, Fig 98). A wall (B34, Fig 98) may relate to a late rebuilding near the smithy.

A make-up layer in the smithy contained a single glass fragment from a wine bottle of uncertain form, while a wall contained a copper-alloy disc brooch with glass setting (<S2>, Fig 185), leather shoe(s) and iron slag. Six copper-alloy nails <614> and five nail shanks <615> were recovered from one of the furnaces. An occupation layer contained a large subrectangular piece of sheet copper alloy with poorly formed, squared lip <206> (perhaps an offcut used as a makeshift aid for pouring), several lengths of irregular, poorly cast copper-alloy

'wire' <202>–<204>, flat strips – possibly also waste – <201> and <205>, and iron slag.

A number of crucible fragments <503>–<507>, probably from the same vessel, were found in two demolition spreads related to the smithy and provide the only evidence of this type of industrial vessel among the pottery assemblage from the site. The vessels display clear evidence of use, being heavily burnt and with internal residues, and it is tempting to link these finds with the operation of the smithy.

Of two destruction layers excavated, one yielded five items of copper alloy that could be machinery components, including a possible lock fitting <670> and a possible machine guard or scraper <673>. Glass from this deposit comprises three fragments from a Hamilton bottle dating to after 1814 and 13 small fragments from five different windows. Further copper alloy waste, comprising two cakes thought to be from crucibles of different sizes, <198> (diameter 82mm) and <200> (diameter 62mm), was found in the other destruction layer, along with a copper-alloy ferrule with opposed rectangular slots on one edge <199>, a stone quern <693> and assorted ironwork. The latter comprises part of a pickaxe <668>, a square socket or ferrule <667> (length 37mm, 50 × 50mm at the top, 30 × 30mm at the base), bulk nails and iron slag. Ten clay pipe bowls and 85 stem fragments were recovered, giving a latest date of *c* 1850–80 for context [5801]. This is based on the presence of types AO29 and AO30 within a group of 19th-century pipes. Taken together, the finds indicate that this building was used for some form of non-ferrous metalworking.

John Rennie and the new wet dock entrance, 1814–19

By the end of 1813, the timber entrance (S9) to the wet dock was 'dilapidated' with a bad foundation. Repairs to the entrance had proved 'abortive, and reduced it to its present ruinous state'. The officers suggested that a new entrance be built that would admit 38-gun frigates which could be repaired in the recently renovated single dock (above, 7.2). An estimate of £14,500 was arrived at, but £2500 could be saved if a 'Floating Dam' or caisson (first introduced at Portsmouth dockyard in 1802 by Brigadier-General Sir Samuel Bentham: Coad 2013, 94–5) was used rather than a pair of gates. The Navy Board forwarded the officers' letter to John Rennie for his opinion (TNA, ADM 106/3185, 16 November 1813). In another letter of the same date, the officers proposed that a storehouse for storing cables be built in the location of the timber entrance to the wet dock (ibid, 16 November 1813).

Rennie estimated that the cost of 'a New Entrance to the Basin [ie wet dock] … a New Wharf Wall from the Middle Slip to the large Slip on the west side and another wall across the present entrance within the Basin and of filling up the said entrance' would be £24,075 (not including the cost of the floating gate). The considerable increase on the estimate made by the yard officers was due to the cost of a cofferdam (TNA, ADM 106/3185, 4 July 1814).

The new wet dock gate was to be wide enough for a frigate (TNA, ADM 106/3185, 7 September 1814, 10; 10 September 1814), built of stone and brick rather than timber and with a more central location in relation to the dock. The Admiralty asked John Rennie to draw up a specification for the work on 6 August 1814 (TNA, ADM 106/3185).

John Rennie (1761–1821) (Fig 109) was one of the leading civil engineers of the early 19th century. He had worked briefly with James Watt before setting up his own engineering business around 1791 based at Blackfriars, London. He was involved particularly in canal construction, including the Lancaster (started 1792), the Crinan (1794) and the Kennet and Avon (1800) canals, but also gained a reputation for building bridges, such as Waterloo Bridge (1811–17) and Southwark Bridge (1814–19) in London. He also designed or rebuilt several docks, including London Docks (1800–5) and Sheerness dockyard (Bissell Prosser 1904, 19).

Jolliffe and Banks were appointed on 5 January 1815 to carry out the work (TNA, ADM 106/3185, 31 December 1816) which was to be completed by 31 October of that year (ibid, 19 May 1817). Edward Banks (1770–1835) had begun his association with Rennie in 1793 when they worked together on the Lancaster and Ulverston canals. He went into partnership with William Jolliffe (1774–1835) in 1807 and their company became a major contractor for public engineering works, operating from Banks's yard at Beaufort Wharf, Strand. Jolliffe's contribution seems to have been principally financial. They made their reputation on projects involving the control of water, particularly their (then) state of the art use of cofferdams. They constructed the Limehouse entrance to the West India Dock in 1811 and in 1817 a new entrance for London Docks and a new river wall and wharf at the London custom house. Outside the capital, they built Rennie's Howth harbour in Dublin Bay in 1809–19 and undertook excavation, piling and walling for his Sheerness naval dockyard in 1812–30. Other important building work of theirs included Rennie's Waterloo Bridge and Southwark Bridge (above), and (with Rennie's son) the new London Bridge (1824–30) (Skempton 2002, 35–7; Port 2008).

The specification was signed by Rennie on 31 August and dated 7 September 1814, subsequently revised (TNA, ADM 106/3185, 10 September 1814). The specification was for 'the masonry brick work, piling, planking etc of a New Entrance to the Basin … and also for the building of a river wall from the said entrance to the Second Slip on the south'. The new entrance was to be 50ft wide (revised later to 60ft). The bottom was to be 2ft (revised later to 4ft) 'under the level of the low water of an 18 feet spring tide or 21ft 6in [revised later to 23ft 6in] under the level of the Wharf at the present entrance and to be carried 1 foot 5 inches above it. It is to be done with an inverted arch having a groove to suit a Floating Gate' (ibid, 7 September 1814, 1; 10 September 1814). The 'floating gate' is also known as a caisson gate; it would have been a boat-shaped, hollow iron structure whose ends articulated with vertical grooves in the dock entrance walls. The gate could be raised or lowered by pumping water either out of or into its central chamber.

One of the important aspects of the work was the use of cofferdams – a speciality of Jolliffe and Banks – which had not been used to this extent previously on such works. Two cofferdams were to be used, one in the Thames, 130ft long, and one in the wet dock itself, 86ft long; both were to be curved (although Rennie says 'circular') and built to the same design. They were to be composed of two rows of piles 5ft apart, each row having 12in square 'gauge or principal piles' 10ft apart. The

Fig 109 John Rennie (1761–1821), painted in 1810 by Henry Raeburn (Scottish National Portrait Gallery, PG 1840)

gauge piles were to be placed opposite each other in the inner and outer rows and connected by screw bolts. They were to be pointed with iron shoes 'of about 18lbs' and driven in 6ft below the lowest part of the foundation of the new entrance. All the piles were to be shod in iron, with hoops at the top to prevent splitting when being driven. The tops of the gauge piles were to stand 2ft above the highest spring tides. Each row of piles was to have 'two double sets of wale pieces not less than 12 inches by 6'; the upper of the wales was to be placed within 1ft of the tops of the piles, the lower as near to low water 'as can conveniently be done'. '[T]hey are to be let into the principal or gauge piles so as to have a clear space of 6½ inches between (to receive the sheet piling)' and screwed to the gauge piles with screw bolts 1¼in square with 'large plates of iron under the heads and nuts' (TNA, ADM 106/3185, 7 September 1814, 1–2).

The sheet piles were to be 12in broad by 6in thick and driven as deep as the gauge piles. Their edges were to be 'planed straight on the edges and close keyed with a key pile between each of the gauge piles so as to make the joints perfectly close … [A]fter the whole is completed they are to be caulked so as to be impervious to water'. The two rows of piles were also to be screwed together with long screw bolts and the space between them 'filled with good clay well puddled until it has become solid' (TNA, ADM 106/3185, 7 September 1814, 2–3; 10 September 1814).

The new entrance was to be excavated 26ft (later revised to 28ft) 'under the level of the Cap Cill of the present entrance'. There were to be three rows of 12ft long, 10in diameter piles under each side, 3ft apart, 'of beech, elm or Norway timber'. Their heads were to be levelled to support a 'fir cill [ie sill]' spiked to the piles. The space between the piles and the sill was to be filled with brickwork, 'after which the whole is to be covered with good fir, beech or elm plank 6 inches thick and spiked down to the cills'. This was to be the foundation on which the walls were to be laid (TNA, ADM 106/3185, 7 September 1814, 3; 10 September 1814).

An elm sill ('oak' is deleted in the original) was to be laid across the new entrance where the floating gate was to be, with a similar piece of wood bolted to it. 'This cill is to have a course of 6 inch grooved sheeting piles drove its whole length no less than 12 feet deep, the heads of these are to follow the course of the bottom and they are to be made perfectly watertight and spiked to the cill' (TNA, ADM 106/3185, 7 September 1814, 3–4).

The base of the new entrance was to be 'an inverted arch' to fit the floating gate, built of 'hard burnt sound made pavoir bricks 3 feet thick at the bottom' set in 'porrolans mortar or Parkes & Co best Roman cement'. The side walls were to stand on the piled foundation, 8ft thick at the base, reducing to 7ft at the top, 'the whole laid in the direction of the radius of the respective courses of which the Entrance is to be formed'. 'Counterforts 3 feet square and 10 feet asunder are to be built behind these walls', except in the location of the floating gate where they were to be 7ft square. The groove in which the floating gate was to rest 'is to be done with Dundee or Craigleith stone in blocks of not less than 20 cubic feet each, but in some places much larger'. This stone was also to be 'laid through the

middle of the wall', with alternate headers and stretchers at the face (TNA, ADM 106/3185, 7 September 1814, 4–5).

The wing wharfs of the entrance were to be built in the same way and joined to the 'new intended river wall' and the 'new intended wall of the Basin' on one side and 'to the Old Wall' on the other. The whole was to be coped with the Dundee or Craigleith stone (TNA, ADM 106/3185, 7 September 1814, 5).

The foundation of the new river wall was to be laid 'at the depth of one foot under the level of an 18 feet tide', and 1ft 5in above the level of the current quay ('2 feet above the top of an 18 feet tide'). The base of the wall was to be 7ft wide, narrowing to 6ft wide at the top, resting on fir sills '12 inches by 6 at least', themselves supported on a course of elm or beech sheeting piles driven at least 12ft deep. Spaces between the sills were to be filled with gravel grouted with mortar, and the whole timber foundation was 'to be covered with 6 inch elm, beech or fir plank spiked to the cills'. The battered face of the wall was to be built 'with best hard burnt sound Marle paviors bricks … backed with hard sound stocks'. Two courses of stone were to run through the wall, the facing of Dundee or Craigleith stone backed with 'Roach Portland' to match the walls of the dock entrance. As with the entrance, the wall was to be coped in Dundee or Craigleith stone. The wall construction work was to be protected by 40ft long cofferdams to a similar design of that mentioned above (TNA, ADM 106/3185, 7 September 1814, 5–7).

'A similar wall is to be built in the Basin across the Old Entrance and joined to the Basin walls', with the same design of foundation. Once the new entrance was built, the old one was to be filled in with earth and made watertight. Rennie was specific about the mortar, which should be 'the best sort for setting in water', suggesting 'Roman cement or Porrolans' (TNA, ADM 106/3185, 7 September 1814, 7–8).

With an eye for detail, he specified the finish of the stones, which were to be 'droved with a chisel for two inches in breadth' round the beds, upper joints and the edge joints, with the space between 'fair punched' (TNA, ADM 106/3185, 7 September 1814, 8). The contractor was to supply all materials and 'a Steam Engine' for the pumps. The navy was to supply the floating gate (ibid, 7 September 1814, 9). In a subsequent letter, the Navy Board said that they had 'no objection to the contract being made' (ibid, 10 October 1814).

The floating – or caisson – gate was designed by a Mr W Stone, and Rennie approved this in July 1815. The design was different from others he had encountered as there was no mechanism for letting water into or out of the dock in the gate itself. Instead, this function would be performed by a culvert in the side walls of the dock entrance (TNA, ADM 106/3185, 19 July 1815).

The work of constructing the new wet dock entrance was hard. The Clerk of Works, a Mr Smith, reported in a letter to Edward Holl at the Navy Office that the whole surface under the new entrance 'is a black running sand (a perfect quicksand)'. Once when 'the piles were driven their heads levelled and ragstone rammed and pointed … in one night a space of about 30 feet square the piles and bottom rose 10 inches'. Part of a wall collapsed. There were 'as many men as could stand with buckets and scoops to clear the sand to a proper depth but the sand was so quick it was impossible'. The clerk asserted that 'the fatigue of body and mind at that job will never be forgotten by me' (TNA, ADM 106/3185, 22 April 1817) – a view no doubt shared by scavelmen since the earliest days of the yard.

The impetus for completing the new entrance was the need to launch the yacht *Royal Sovereign* (278bm-tons), built at Deptford in 1804. Pressure was being brought to bear on Jolliffe and Banks. In May 1816, Rennie stated that the caisson gate would not be ready for the launch of the yacht at the end of the month as envisioned by the Navy Board (TNA, ADM 106/3185, 8 May 1816). The Navy Board was anxious for the caisson gate to be completed as soon as possible. However, the groove in which the gate would travel was not yet built and the officers estimated that at least two months more were needed. '[W]e think that the caisson will be sufficiently compleated to be removed out of its place so as to allow the Royal Sovereign Yacht to pass into the river by the first spring [tide] in July', and once the yacht had been gilded it would be ready to launch (ibid, 16 May 1816). Jolliffe and Banks assured the Navy Board that they would employ 'every exertion in our powers' to complete the entrance so that the yacht could launch by August (ibid, 11 July 1816).

The storehouse on the site of the old timber entrance to the wet dock was being built by April 1816, when the officers asked that the steam engine be removed so that the foundations of the storehouse could be laid (TNA, ADM 106/3185, 25 April 1816). The south side of this east–west aligned storehouse (B55, Fig 97; Fig 98) was exposed in the excavations (the north side lay beyond the trench), east of the wet dock. The 28.10m long storehouse consisted of six bays of roughly the same size, apart from a larger easternmost bay, and was built in red and yellow stock bricks set in sandy mortar. The walls were 0.90m wide with the lower half of a ring of bricks in each – these were used to strengthen the walls of such buildings. Construction of the storehouse truncated a number of land-ties.

The haste in building the storehouse (B55) was to cause a tide dam at the east end of one of the cofferdams to fail and the works to be flooded. Rennie defended the contractors, telling the Navy Board that it was their own decision to lay the storehouse foundations that was the cause. This had 'occasioned a large excavation … consequently when the water got over the Tide Dam, there were neither the firm support behind it nor provision to let the water so quickly out'. He concluded that 'the accident was one of those to which works of this sort are liable and that no blame is imputable'. The Navy Board adopted a resigned tone and concluded that 'the public must bear the expense of repairing the dam' (TNA, ADM 106/3185, 31 May 1816). The storehouse was demolished by 1858, on map evidence (Fig 121).

The balance – presumably for the wet dock entrance – was paid to Jolliffe and Banks on 25 November 1816 (TNA, ADM 106/3185, 19 May 1817), indicating that it had been completed by this date. However, there were problems. That same month, the officers reported that water in the dock was leaking out under the wall adjacent to the old buried entrance. Rennie told

the Navy Board that this was because the foundations of the old wall here were not as deep as those of the new wall to which it was attached. 'It has no sheeting piles in front of it or any other preparation for retaining water.' The dock itself had been deepened 'on an average at least four feet' so (perhaps alarmingly) 'the Basin is deeper than the foundation of this old wall', which was 'much cracked'. The deepening of the dock had taken its base into 'the quicksand' below – presumably a stratum of fine sand within the natural sands and gravels – through which the water in the dock could escape, although the mud deposited by the river would remedy this problem in time, Rennie reassured the Board. A 'small Gun Barrel drain' had also been made under the inverted arch of the entrance to carry off the water from 'a large spring which was found while the foundations of the entrance was putting in'. Rennie concluded that Jolliffe and Banks had fulfilled their contract and should not be held liable for the leak (ibid, 3 January 1817).

The Navy Board pursued the matter and produced a report on the leak by Sir Henry Peake and Edward Holl which they sent to Rennie on 28 April, asking if he had changed his mind. He had not: 'My former opinion was given after a full and due consideration of the subject.' The report tended to confirm his opinion that 'the contractors are not liable'. He added that 'It is well known that the Basin was prematurely opened to admit the launching of the Royal Sovereign Yacht, had this not been the case, it was my intention to have had the work thoroughly examined in all its parts before the cofferdam had been taken away, and to have had the foundations of the walls done with clay where required; but as through the desire to get the Royal Sovereign Yacht out of the Basin this opportunity was lost'. Rennie estimated that 'claying and sheeting' would cost £600 and recommended that Jolliffe and Banks be contracted to do the works (TNA, ADM 106/3185, 3 March 1817). The Navy Board instructed that Rennie's proposal be adopted while continuing to explore who might be liable (ibid, 25 March 1817). A law officer concluded that it was not clear that there had been any breach of contract (ibid, 19 May 1817).

Jolliffe and Banks wrote to the Navy Board in June asking for payment for 'excavation done by us in deepening the Basin and also the front of the New Entrance and a small part near the Mast House … as it is a considerable time since the work was executed'. They wondered whether their original letter of 2 April requesting payment had been lost. The Navy Board directed the officers to 'make out a certificate' for payment (TNA, ADM 106/3185, 23 June 1817).

The Navy Board wrote to the contractors in July 1817, asking them to 'proceed immediately with the work to be done at the Basin'. Jolliffe and Banks replied that this work would have been started, but for 'the bad health of Mr. Banks'. The commissioners were unmoved, 'as the delay in proceeding with this work has occasioned inconvenience already the Basin having filled considerably with mud'. The Navy Board directed that the work be taken in hand immediately: if Banks was too ill it should be supervised by someone else (TNA, ADM 106/3185, 16 July 1817; commissioners' addition dated 18 July 1817).

The work to stem the leak was under way by October, although it had been delayed by neep tides and bad weather. Jolliffe and Banks's men were working on 'the Invert on the inside of the Basin' where they had 'removed a quantity of ragstone from before the front of the sheeting piles', filling it with clay. At the junction of the old and new walls, gravel had to be laid to stop the clay washing away. The contractors asked for 'at least 3 tier of old iron ballast well puddled' to be laid to consolidate their work (TNA, ADM 106/3185, 14 October 1817).

In July 1819, the officers reported that 'the leaks on the river side are effectively stopped, but that the leak on the inside of the basin where the Old and New walls unite, still remains, and they apprehend it cannot be fully prevented'. The Navy Board accepted this and submitted that Jolliffe and Banks should be paid (TNA, ADM 106/3185, 9 July 1819), presumably marking the completion of the work.

Rennie's gateway and walls seen in the excavation

The gateway and walls designed by Rennie were seen in area 2 in the excavation (S32, Fig 97; Fig 98; Fig 110). Both sides of the gateway were nearly identical in construction, with smooth, slightly curved inner walls having corresponding vertical slots in which the caisson gate would have moved. The water-filled, cast-iron caisson gate would have slotted into these recesses at either end, its up and down movement controlled by pumping out or pumping in water. (The iron gate itself was not found, presumably having been scrapped shortly after the yard closed.) The gate piers were constructed mostly in brick with the outside edges built in a rounded stepped construction acting as buttresses on the other side. Both gate piers contained a rectangular stone-lined shaft in the centre (Fig 111). The eastern shaft was sealed by an iron casing and could not be fully excavated while the western shaft continued vertically down for over 3m with a vertical iron rod sticking up from its centre (visible in Fig 111 with its upper section wrapped up). The iron rod was very probably to control culverted water, opening and shutting sluice gates or valves at or near the base of the shaft which formed part of the side wall of the dock entrance here, with a similar arrangement on the other side of the dock entrance (J Coad, pers comm 2015).

Both sides of the gateway curved outwards as they opened up into the dock. The western side connected almost immediately with a brick wall from the previous, 18th-century, phase of construction (cf Fig 59; Fig 60; Fig 70; Fig 71), whereas the eastern side ran along seamlessly as a newly built wall constructed as part of this rebuild. This wall comprised brick and stone blocks supported by a series of buttresses with a series of vertical timber fenders connected by iron fittings to the water side of the wall. Only after some distance did it connect with the 18th-century red brick dock wall.

The new gateway had a depth gauge carved into the stone of the eastern gate pier (Fig 112), similar in location to the depth gauge that was recorded in the timber-lined wet dock (Chapter 6.3). Comparison of the depth gauges revealed that the channel connecting the dock to the river was deeper in the 19th century than in the 18th century by 1.73m. This is also likely to be true of the wet dock itself – in other words the dock would have been excavated deeper over time, as well as getting smaller.

Fig 110 View of the western part of the wall of the 19th-century wet dock entrance, looking east

Fig 111 View of the stone-lined shaft in the gate pier on the western side of the wet dock entrance, with the vertical iron rod partly covered

Fig 112 Views of the eastern part of the stone and brick 19th-century wet dock gate: upper – looking east, note slot for caisson gate and depth gauge, with superseded timber gate in background; lower – detail of the depth gauge

Two truncated oak trestle bases were found in the north-east corner of the brick dock, inside the new walls built for the Rennie-designed gateway. The sills were widest in the middle, tapering towards each end and pierced by several oak treenails, and had thus been reused. The sills' unusual shape and bevelled corners are a form diagnostic of earlier 19th-century anchor stocks (Fig 142; Chapter 9.2). Each sill beam timber was pierced by a central through-mortice for the tenon of a vertical post supported on each side by diagonal bracing. The diagonal braces were set in unpegged sloping mortices.

Early 19th-century wooden slipway roofs

Early in the 19th century, wooden roofs or covers were built over slipways and docks. These saved much weather damage to the wooden ships being built and repaired (sometimes over a long period) and may have extended working time in bad weather. The Admiralty was considering covering slipways and docks by 1812 to prevent rot in the ships under construction, and most of these were designed by Sir Robert Seppings (Coad 2013, 77, 100–3). Plymouth built a roof over a dock in 1812 and by 1814 Deptford, Plymouth, Portsmouth and Woolwich had slip cover roofs; in 1815 money was allocated for dock and slip roofs in all the yards (ibid, 99–101). The wooden slip covers constructed between 1814 and 1841 at royal dockyards consisted of timber-framed roofs covered in a variety of materials, including tarred paper, slates and tiles, and, from 1818, copper sheets (ibid, 101; Hawkins and Butler 2015, 42). Compared to their iron successors, wooden slip roofs were not limited in span or scale (ibid, 42).

A section of the roof of a slip 'proposed by an architect and built at Deptford Yard in 1814' shows a roof truss supported by posts with a secondary over-sailing roof at either side (NMM, ADM/BP/41b; reproduced in Coad 2013, 100, fig 5.14); unfortunately, the below-ground supports for the posts are not depicted. In reply to an order of 13 January 1821, whereby Deptford was to be maintained chiefly as a depot for small work (Oppenheim 1926, 386), the officers sent the Navy Board 'two models for placing paper on the roofs over slips, docks and ships lying afloat' (TNA, ADM 106/3342, 19 January 1821, 81), so the slipway covers may date from very shortly after this. A sketch of *c* 1822 (Fig 113) shows the 3rd-rate, 74-gun, 176½ ft × 48ft *Russell* (1751bm-tons) on the stocks at Deptford under a slip roof; HMS *Russell* was launched on 22 May 1822 after eight years on the stocks (Lavery 2003, 189; Colledge and Warlow 2010).

A series of timber-lined boxes (B45, Fig 97), set below ground level, were excavated either side of slipway no. 1 (S27). These were lined postholes or sockets designed to support the massive uprights for the wooden slip cover roof (cf Fig 113). An unusual broken fragment of metasandstone or siltstone, probably from a quarry in northern England or Scotland, was found underneath one of the timber boxes. The plan evidence suggests that there may have been two phases of these timber post sockets, with the largest socket rectangular and over 1m across, set *c* 10m apart. They were lined with thick sawn plank offcuts of oak and elm, against which wedging chocks could be driven to locate the posts. On some planks the straight saw marks were so regular that they may have been machine-cut using some form of reciprocating (up and down) saw. In others the saw marks were curved and must have been cut by an early power circular saw. A circular saw blade was invented and patented by Samuel Millar of Southampton in 1777, but blades remained small for a number of years, probably capable of cutting to a maximum depth of *c* 8in. Samuel Bentham and Simon Goodrich advanced the technology at the block mills at Portsmouth in the first decade of the 19th century, and Bentham completed a large steam-powered saw mill at Chatham in 1814 (Coad 2005, 19, 44, 50, 123; J Coad, pers comm 2015). Some of the planking was also marked with obscure cursive symbols cut with a timber scribe, but the meaning of these marks is uncertain.

Brick plinths for slip cover roofs (B24, B25, Fig 97) were recorded alongside slipways no. 4 (S30) and no. 5 (S31), some with the base of timber beams surviving centrally placed within the piers to support wooden canopies. A photograph of Deptford dockyard *c* 1871 shows the wooden slip cover roof over slipway no. 5 (Fig 131; Hawkins and Butler 2015, 55, 58,

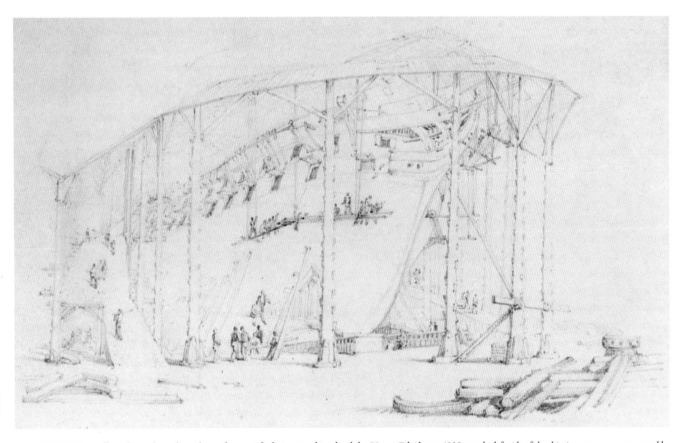

Fig 113 HMS Russell *on the stocks under a slip roof at Deptford, in a graphite sketch by Henry Edridge,* c *1822; on the left side of the ship is an access ramp to enable the upper works to be carried out (National Maritime Museum, Greenwich, PAD8611)*

fig 16). The most complete set of plinths were for the cover roof of slipway no. 5; based on these, the minimum size of the roof was *c* 60m × 19m. Slipways nos 2 and 3, lying within the extant iron cover building (Olympia warehouse), were not investigated (below, 7.4, 'Slipways and iron slip cover roofs in the mid 19th century').

7.4 The final years of the yard, 1830–69: archaeological and historical evidence

Closure of the yard in 1830

The inconvenience of its location on the Thames, problems with silting and other factors meant that by the late 18th century the yard was in decline, a fate shared by Woolwich (see Coad 2013, 11, for the problems of the yards). Ships in need of repair had to make the arduous journey upriver, after removing guns and offloading stores and powder at Northfleet. In 1795, the officers were complaining that there were no ships to work on (TNA, ADM 106/3324, 17 October 1795, 40) and proposed that shipwrights perform work normally done by house-carpenters (ibid, 23 November 1795, 54). The Napoleonic Wars (1802–15) offered some respite, but the focus for navy shipbuilding shifted decisively to Sheerness (Lambert 2012, 82) and Pembroke from 1814 (Banbury 1971, 73). The advent of steam dredgers in the early 19th century eased the situation, enabling the Thames yards to stay open (Lambert 2012, 82). Deptford and Woolwich then worked in tandem, Deptford building the new wooden-hulled screw steamships which were fitted with their machinery at Woolwich (ibid, 85).

However, shipbuilding at the Deptford yard soon ground to a halt and, after the launch of the 114ft × 32ft sloop *Nimrod* (502bm-tons, the renamed former 6th-rate *Andromeda*) in 1828, there would be a gap of 15 years before there was another launch (Banbury 1971, 81; Lambert 2012, 95, appendix 2; Colledge and Warlow 2010).

Facilities were consequently being run down. In 1827 the mast house and adjoining ground of the dockyard were transferred to the victualling yard (Oppenheim 1926, 387). Although the double (dry) dock was falling to pieces as 'large portions of earth detach themselves' from areas opened up for inspection, in January 1829 the Admiralty blocked its repair. By the summer, the officers were particularly alarmed by the 'very precarious situation' of the cover roof. Its piers needed urgent attention 'to prevent any accident occurring to the roof'. The gates of the stern or stem dock and the inner and outer aprons were also in 'a very bad state' (TNA, ADM 106/3346, 18 August 1829, 13).

The yard closed in 1830 (Coad 2013, 34). At the beginning of that year, the officers scrambled to place the yard's workers elsewhere. They sent the Navy Board a list of its shipwrights (TNA, ADM 106/3346, 12 January 1830, 30) and stressed that large families should be taken into account when deciding which of the naval dockyards they should be transferred to (ibid, 14 January 1830, 30). John Gale, a caulker, had '8 children' (ibid, 18 January 1830, 32). The officers asked that four sawyers be transferred 'to Sheerness instead of being discharged as proposed' (ibid, 21 January 1830, 33) and forwarded testimonials for other individuals who should be retained (ibid, 25 January 1830, 34).

The reduction in workers affected ongoing building work. The officers complained that 'the work of the New Barracks will be so much retarded, that we shall not be able to complete them within the scheduled time' unless bricklayers were kept on or replaced (TNA, ADM 106/3346, 27 January 1830, 35). These marine barracks ran along the south-east perimeter of the yard, and the east face of an external wall of the barracks (B58, Fig 98) was seen during the excavations in a trench otherwise obscured by modern services. The wall was built of shallow frogged yellow bricks set in grey cement; an earlier wall of purple-red bricks was the east edge of a culvert.

By March the barracks were almost finished – eight rooms would be ready by the middle of the month and a further six by the end (TNA, ADM 106/3346, 4 March 1830, 40). Lack of workmen meant that 'sheds in the field' (presumably the sailfield in the south-eastern corner of the yard) would not be cleared to schedule (ibid, 11 March 1830, 41). Other repairs were needed to the roofs of the storehouse, including the 'loft containing sails', and to the tiling 'under the Clock House' (ibid, 16 June 1830, 46). The roofs of the 'Cordage sheds', painters' shop, boathouse, mast loft, plank and oakum sheds also all needed attention (ibid, 4 November 1830, 56). The perimeter wall required repair (ibid, 25 March 1830, 42) and since the pavier had been discharged the paving was 'very dilapidated'. For this latter work, the officers had used convict labour but asked for 'proper persons' to repair the roads (ibid, 17 January 1831, 58). The average number of convicts used was 166 a day, divided into 16 gangs (ibid, 6 July 1829, 8).

With no expectation that shipbuilding would return, 1830 was a dismal year for the yard. The death of the king, George IV, in June (TNA, ADM 106/3346, 12 July 1830, 49) and the demise of the Navy Board itself in 1832 (Haas 1994, 3) would have added to the sense that an era had ended. Until 1843, the yard was used only for breaking up ships built during the Napoleonic Wars (*London Journal*, 1 March 1869, 136; MacDougall 1982, 147; TNA, ADM 12/231, 1836).

Ongoing maintenance

Despite the closure, some rebuilding and repair still took place – particularly of some of the yard's most important assets. When part of the head dock of the double (dry) dock collapsed in the summer of 1833 (TNA, ADM 12/291, 27 July 1833) a Mr Guest's tender was accepted, the Admiralty directing that the work proceed at once (ibid, 29 November 1833). New gates for the head dock were to be built at Woolwich (ibid, 6 November 1833). At the beginning of the following year, planking was required for the dock (TNA, ADM 12/299, 25 January 1834) and an advance to Guest of £350 was approved (ibid, 26

February 1834). The sides of the dock were to be reinforced with concrete; 4ft of ground behind the planked sides was to be excavated and concrete put in (ibid, 26 March 1834). Guest had finished his work by May (apart from clearing away soil, for which he was paid an additional £30) (ibid, 14 May 1834).

The stern dock also required repair and the superintendent forwarded a specification for this to Sir John Hill (TNA, ADM 12/299, 7 May 1834). He was instructed to accept the lowest tender for the work (ibid, 17 May 1834) and the repair was under way by May 1835 when payment was authorised to a Mr Ranger for work on the new stone for the piers and entrance of the double dock (TNA, ADM 12/309, 22 May 1835). Despite the work being unfinished and tenders having been received to complete the repairs to the double dock, the Admiralty decided to delay as there was no money in that year's estimate to pay for it (ibid, 15 June 1835).

This delay lasted some years; three years later the Admiralty was considering plans for 'alterations of the Double and Single Docks' and insisting that the original estimate of expense be adhered to (TNA, ADM 12/231, 21 November 1838). Plans by Captain Henry Brandreth RE (1794–1848), the Admiralty Civil Architect, to lengthen the stern dock by 18ft into the river, by substituting a caisson, were rejected in 1839 (TNA, ADM 12/357, 12 July 1839). A tender from Kitt and Elwell for work on the 'wall at the Double Dock' was accepted in early 1839 (three other tenders from MacIntosh, Grissell and Peto, and Plows were unsuccessful) (ibid, 19 January 1839). In 1840, the same company was recommended to repair the 'return wall at the entrance of the Double Dock' and the river wall (TNA, ADM 12/384, 5 April 1840) and won the contract for

'rebuilding the walls and piers of the entrance of the Double Dock' (ibid, 23 April 1840). Kitt and Elwell were 'Admiralty Contractors' and in 1847 successfully tendered to lay the paving of the chain-cable store at Devonport (*Nautical Standard*, 13 November 1847, 701).

Thus the entrance to the double dock had been rebuilt in stone by 1835 and probably by 1802, but the stonework identified in the evaluation is probably that of repairs made *c* 1840 (Hawkins 2015, 94). A 10.40m length of the west wall of the double dock entrance (S26, Fig 97) running north–south across trench 50 (Fig 3) was probably the part built by Kitt and Elwell in 1839–41 (Fig 114). The north part of this wall of the stern dock was built of closely fitting granite blocks. Further south, closely fitting limestone blocks were used and the east face of the wall formed by these blocks curved downwards. The west (landward) face of the upper part of the stern dock wall was built in red brick. Square recesses had been cut on the top of the stern dock wall, perhaps for a capstan. The maximum internal width of the final phase of the double dock as found in the excavation was 15.40m.

The west leaf of the dock gate still survived and its upper parts were exposed during the excavations (Fig 114). The gate consisted of partially decayed oak beams and the uprights of its iron frame. White paint adhering to some of the timbers suggested reuse. The oak was fast-grown and probably of British origin, perhaps surprisingly as in the mid 19th century more rot-resistant tropical timber species were typically used. The gate had become dislodged from the semicircular recess cut into the stone. This is likely to have been one of the gates ordered to be built at Woolwich in 1833.

Fig 114 View of the western wall of the double dock entrance (S26), looking west; note the iron and timber dock gate (lower right)

The south end of the dock west wall was stopped, and a mason's mark or graffito (an 'H', 74mm high and 52mm wide) had been carved into a stone in the end (Fig 115). An area of lime concrete abutted the double dock here, with visible recesses (some of which still contained rotted timber) for a timber land-tie arrangement. A large stone was embedded in the backfill of the dock, where it had fallen – presumably when this early concrete failed or the land-ties rotted. A machine slot was excavated along the double dock wall through to a depth of 1.36m OD to expose the (water side) face of the wall. A number of structures were identified on the west (landward) side of the double dock wall, including a culvert and a well.

The east wall of the double dock was also exposed, although it had been more heavily robbed (Fig 116). A depth gauge, marked in feet in Roman numerals from XVII at the top of the surviving wall to XIII at the base of the excavation, was painted

on the northern part of the wall. The base of number XIIII, visible in Fig 116, lay at 3.18m OD.

The head dock forming the southern part of the double dock was investigated in a number of test pits during the excavation in area 14 (Fig 3). No trace of the head dock was found and it seemed to have been substantially robbed in this area – probably because it was nearer the yard gate. The 1870 Goad map (Fig 129) and a photograph probably dating from c 1880 show a structure covering this part of the dock (Fig 105), and a stone plinth for the east side of this cover building (B21, not illustrated) was identified. The cover roof was probably built in 1839–41 and demolished between 1896 and 1916 (Hawkins 2015, 95).

In 1834, the caisson gate for the wet dock – now some 20 years old – needed to be either repaired or scrapped. The former Navy Board architect, George Ledwell Taylor, inspected it (TNA, ADM 12/299, 6 October 1834) and evidently decided that it was salvageable. A Captain Harrison was instructed to have it towed to Woolwich for repair (ibid, 17 October 1834).

Other building repairs were also identified, costing £350, and the superintendent was instructed to collect tenders for these (TNA, ADM 12/309, 3 June 1835). Some buildings were scheduled to be demolished in 1838 (TNA, ADM 12/231, 4 December 1838).

The slipway 'occupied by Worcester' required repair in 1841 (TNA, ADM 12/397, 30 November 1841). This 4th-rate, 52-gun, 172ft × 44ft ship (1468bm-tons) was 23 years on the stocks (Colledge and Warlow 2010); it had been kept 'under construction' since 1822 to satisfy the lease of Evelyn's land to the Admiralty (MacDougall 1982, 147; Hawkins 2015, 93). The *Worcester* finally launched on 10 January 1843 (Lambert 2012, 95, appendix 2) when the yard reopened. Its slip was the 'No. 1 building slip' according to *The London Journal* in 1869 (*London Journal*, 1 March 1869, 136); although this source is not always reliable, slips were numbered from 1842 and the launch date would fit with the subsequent work carried out in 1844 around single slipway no. 1 (S27) (below).

Fig 115 View of mason's mark or graffito (H 74mm) on the stopped end of the west wall of the double dock

Fig 116 View of the eastern wall of the double dock entrance (S26), looking east; note the painted depth gauge (left)

Plinths for a rectangular structure (B44, Fig 97) were identified immediately west of slipway no. 1 (S27). Two rows, running roughly north–south, consisted of concrete station bases, some still topped with York stone slabs. The bases would have supported timber uprights for a structure that pre-dated the 1844 iron cover roof (B22, below) for slipway no. 1 but could have functioned alongside the wooden slip cover roof structure (B45; above, 7.3, 'Early 19th-century wooden slipway roofs'); this structure is interpreted as a ramp. Typically the bases were 1.13m × 0.75m in size and 0.90m high, not including the 0.15m depth of the stone slab. Five bases survived in the western row and four in the eastern. It seems likely that this ramp on the western side of slipway no. 1 was built when work to complete and launch the *Worcester* was under way in the early 1840s; the substantial character of the foundations for the ramp may be explained by the length of time *Worcester* occupied the slipway.

A similarly sized rectangular structure is shown on the 1774 model and plan (Fig 7; Fig 71) in this position, with others matched by one on the east side of the slip (either side of the other slipways on the 1774 model and plan), confirming that these structures are ramps. Fig 113 shows a wooden ramp providing access to the upper levels of HMS *Russell* on the stocks at Deptford in 1822 under a wooden slip cover.

The yard reopens, 1843

Shipbuilding at the yard began again in 1843 and the *Worcester* finally launched (above). As late as 1856–9 more than 20 acres of ground was bought for future development of the yard (Oppenheim 1926, 386). However, as ships increased in size and iron began to supersede wood, the yard was restricted to the construction of gunboats (Walford 1878, 149). With the end of the Napoleonic Wars, the navy could increasingly utilise steam technology and experiment with steamships, eventually adopting steam propulsion for its battlefleet – ships of the line – from the 1850s (Coad 2013, 25–41).

Ships built or rebuilt after the yard reopened in 1843 included the *Terrible* (1858bm-tons, 1845), the *Termagant* (1560bm-tons, 1847), the *Leopard* (1406bm-tons, 1850), the *Hannibal* (3136bm-tons, 1854), the *Emerald* (2913bm-tons, 1856) and the *Imperieuse* (2358bm-tons, 1862) (Walford 1878, 149; Lambert 2012, 95, appendix 2). *Terrible* (the former *Simoom*) and *Leopard* were wooden paddle frigates. The *Terrible* was the largest and most powerful ship of this type ever built, larger than the last 74-gun ships, but only mounting 19 guns; the *Leopard* was the last paddle frigate built (Lambert 1984, 18–20). *Termagant*, *Emerald* (a former 4th-rate) and *Imperieuse* were wooden screw frigates. The largest ship was the *Hannibal*, a screw-driven, 91-gun, 2nd-rate, 217ft × 58ft (66.14m × 17.68m) vessel; her keel was laid down at Deptford in 1848, she was ordered to be converted on the stocks for a screw (and so to steam and sail) in 1852, and launched from Deptford in 1854 (Fig 117). Her second-hand engine was installed at Woolwich and she was fitted out for sea at Chatham. *Hannibal* served in the Black Sea and Mediterranean fleets; hulked in 1884, she was sold and broken up in 1904 (ibid, 36, 131, 148; Winfield and Lyon 2004, 187; Colledge and Warlow 2010). These ships demonstrate the limitations of Deptford dockyard at the time, but also reflect its convenient proximity to the new steam yard

Fig 117 The launch of the sail and steamship HMS Hannibal *at Deptford, 31 January 1854 (ILN, 4 February 1854) (Illustrated London News/Mary Evans)*

at Woolwich and the various marine engine builders on the Thames who then supplied the navy with most of its steam engines (J Coad, pers comm 2015).

Slipways and iron slip cover roofs in the mid 19th century

The Admiralty had directed in 1842 that all new slip cover roof structures be constructed of iron (cast and wrought), not wood, and corrugated iron sheet (patented in 1829) was widely used for the roofs themselves (Coad 2013, 188–93; Hawkins 2014; Hawkins and Butler 2015, 50). Director of Admiralty Works from 1837 to 1846 was Captain Henry Brandreth (above, 'Ongoing maintenance') of the Royal Engineers who was an advocate of iron construction, motivated principally by the need to reduce the risk of fire in the yards (ibid, 44). The supervisory Royal Engineers officer appointed by Brandreth for Deptford and Woolwich dockyards was William Denison (1837–45). Denison, writing in 1843, made it clear that the Royal Engineers were not familiar with iron roof construction and that he was reliant on civilian roof fabricators and contractors for technical information (ibid, 44–5).

The first iron roofs replacing timber slip roofs were at Pembroke dockyard in 1844, installed by Fox Henderson of London and Birmingham, and the same firm went on to Woolwich in 1845; by the close of 1845 Fox Henderson had erected four iron slip roofs under 'design and build' contracts based on the latest wooden slip covers designed by Sir Robert Seppings (Hawkins and Butler 2015, 45–50). Fox Henderson's roofs were clearly based on the pre-existing wooden slip cover roofs (above, 7.3, 'Early 19th-century wooden slipway roofs').

A different contractor, George Baker and Sons of Lambeth, was commissioned to build the next iron roofs, at Deptford dockyard over slipways nos 1–3 in 1844–5 (Fig 118), and at Portsmouth dockyard over slipways nos 3 and 4 from September 1845. In September 1845, Denison at Portsmouth sent 'drawings of the explanation of this roof and proposed method of closing in the gables and states that Mr Baker's estimates are fair' (Hawkins and Butler 2015, 50). It appears unlikely that the Bakers actually made any of the cast or wrought iron components on their premises (unlike Fox Henderson) but rather sub-contracted (ibid, 50). George Baker and Sons contracted for a number of major government (including dockyard) and other works in the 1830s and 40s, including Deptford and Greenwich stations. They played the leading contracting role in the installation of iron slip cover roofs in the 1840s, contracting for 11, and the design owed much to railway architecture of the time (Skempton 2002, 33–4).

Baker and Sons' roofs differed from the early Fox Henderson roofs in the greater use of cast iron and the wider spacing of the frames (up to 30ft (9.14m) as compared to 12ft 6in (3.81m)), with the load of the corrugated galvanised iron (CGI) sheeting being transferred to the frames through light, trussed purlins (Hawkins and Butler 2015, 51). Furthermore, each pair of Baker roofs cost approximately £1000 less than each pair of Fox Henderson roofs (Cumberland 1847, 65; Williams 1847, 51).

The design of the roofs for slipways nos 1–3 was part of a distinct 'family group', with common design traits and standardised prefabricated parts which helped make the firm cheaper than their competitors such as Fox Henderson. There is little indication of any evolution in design over the two-year period in which they were constructed, or in the extant slip cover roofs of slips nos 4–6 at Chatham and now-demolished examples at Portsmouth, or in the surviving drawings of all their slip cover roofs, including preliminary unexecuted versions (Hawkins and Butler 2015, 56–7, figs 14–15). Despite the considerable alterations to the extant Deptford example, the surviving Baker roofs are recognisable as the work of one civilian design team, although the names of the designers of these roofs are not known (Skempton 2002, 33).

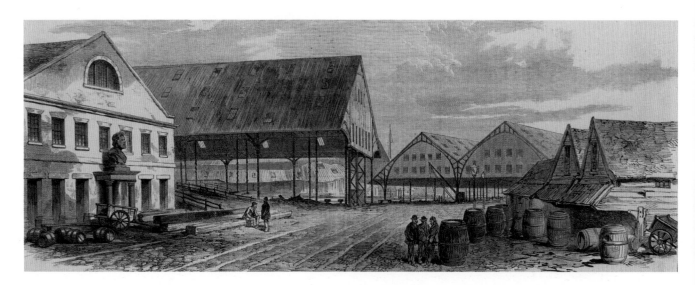

Fig 118 The open-sided slip cover roofs (left) of slipway no. 1 (B22) and (background, centre) of slipways nos 2 and 3 (B23; 'Olympia'), pictured in 1869, looking east-south-east; the buildings in the foreground correspond to those identified in 1858 and 1868 as (left) 'Old Transport Store' or 'Tank Store' and (right) plank/timber sheds (ILN, Supplement, 24 April 1869, 421) (Look and Learn)

The riverside slipways (nos 1, 4 and 5)

The three riverside slipways (S27, S30 and S31; Fig 97), numbered respectively no. 1 slip, and nos 4 and 5 slips, were probably all rebuilt by the contractor George Baker and Sons after 1844. Slipway no. 1 (S27) was given an iron slip cover roof in 1844–5 (Hawkins 2015, 94–6). In 1844, the Clerk of Works was instructed 'to proceed with standard pits for [slip no. 1's] new roof' (TNA, ADM 12/428, 18 February 1844); the roof was completed on 23 May 1845 (TNA, ADM 12/444). This roof was demolished following the closure of the yard but is shown in 1869 in Fig 118. The archaeological evidence for this new cover over the westernmost slip (no. 1) was a series of brick plinths, some with the stubs of cast-iron columns surviving, either side of the slip (B22, Fig 97). A small brass button <522> found in slipway no. 1 (S27) can be dated to 1837–62 (Noël Hume 1969, 90, fig 23); iron short bolts (<225>, <230>), iron, copper-alloy and wooden nails, a wooden wedge and fragments of bottle glass, including the neck of a spa water bottle, had been incorporated into the make-up layers.

The wooden cover roofs (B24 and B25) to slips nos 4 and 5 were retained. Tenders were required for works on no. 5 slip, the easternmost slipway (S31) (TNA, ADM 12/428, 12 February 1844). A make-up layer associated with slipway no. 5 (S31) contained a Victorian farthing <381> of 1839 and a long iron drift bolt with coak of tropical hardwood (<S25>, Fig 190), probably derived from a ship deck beam and dated to the late 18th or early 19th century. The walls of the slipways were replaced in stock brick, buttressed in brick and founded on lime concrete. The lime concrete was of poor quality and appeared to have failed during the life of at least one of the slipways (no. 5, S31). The walls were battered and had a lime cement backing. Poor workmanship by Baker and Sons in slipways and slip cover roofs at Chatham led to their near-collapse. A small, 1.80m × 1.24m, patch of cobbles south-west of slipway no. 5 was identified as part of a path or road (R1, Fig 97).

The wet dock slipways (nos 2 and 3)

In 1844, Baker and Sons' tender for the 'construction of a portion of the Basin [ie wet dock] wall and two building slips' was accepted (TNA, ADM 12/428, 30 September 1844). Baker had worked previously on the victualling yard and the river wall (TNA, ADM 12/299, 25 March 1834). The contract is almost certainly that dated 5 October 1844 between the Admiralty and Baker and Sons, referred to in a drawing related to the contract. The drawing (NMM, ADM/Y/D/11) shows plans to replace the two slipways and single dock on the south wall of the wet dock (shown on the dockyard plans of 1810 and 1813: NMM, ADM/Y/D/6; TNA, ADM 7/593) with two larger slipways, numbered 2 and 3 (Fig 97). The 1.14m wide granite wall of the western slipway, no. 2 (S28), was seen in trenches 21 and 23 (Fig 119; Fig 120). The granite floor of the eastern slipway, no. 3 (S29), was seen in trenches 24 and 22, falling from 1.50m OD to -1.05m OD towards the wet dock. These slipways would have been suitable for relatively small

Fig 119 View of part of the stone and brick wall of slipway no. 2 (S28), looking west

Fig 120 View of part of the stone wall of slipway no. 2 (S28) being excavated inside the surviving Olympia building (B23), looking west; note foundations of a column for the slip cover roof (left)

warships such as sloops and gunboats; Rennie's new wet dock entrance gate 20 years earlier had had to be wide enough for a frigate (above, 7.3). Work was under way by the end of the year when Baker's request to employ five men during the night was approved (TNA, ADM 12/428, 2 December 1844).

Baker and Sons also constructed the slip cover roof (B23, Fig 97) for these new wet dock slipways in 1844–5. The earliest illustration of the structure is an engraving of *c* 1869 (Fig 118). Subsequently, in the 1890s, the roof appears to have failed and been largely rebuilt.

The contract for constructing the iron slip cover roofs over slips nos 2 and 3 appears to have been signed in October 1844 and the structure erected *c* 1844. The foundation of one of the columns of the Deptford cover roof lay within trench 21. The iron column was supported on a series of concrete slabs (with some brick), totalling 0.90m in thickness. Archaeological evaluation trial trenching in 2010 revealed the existing floor level to be *c* 1m (3ft 3in) higher than in 1845.

The building with its arched, iron construction forming two main spans and aisles survives today as the Olympia warehouse, covering an area of some 4672m². The oblong building measures internally 246ft (75m) wide (east to west) by 203ft (62m) deep (north to south), rising to a height of 56ft 5in (17m) at its peak with (now) 33ft 9in (10m) clearance in the main bays and 18ft (5.5m) high at the eaves. The original roof framework was supported on cast iron 'I' columns with flat capitals (totalling 24 in three rows of eight with three columns embedded in each of the end walls). Two wide central bays measuring 91ft 10in × 203ft 5in (28m × 62m) covered the two slipways, together with narrower side aisles measuring 29ft 6in × 203ft 5in (9m × 62m) to the east and west to form covered working areas. The roofs and upper walls of the bays were originally wholly finished in CGI cladding. The vertical upper walls, the two gable end walls, of both the north and south elevations are still clad in this material, although how much, if any, of this fabric is original is uncertain. The engraving of *c* 1869 (Fig 118) suggests that the two bays were lit by 12 windows (five upper and seven lower) in each of the gable end walls in both the south and north elevations, whereas today each bay is lit by ten windows (four upper and six lower) in the south elevation and by nine windows (four upper and five lower) in the north elevation.

A photograph of *c* 1871 shows four upper windows plus a further blocked window and seven lower windows in each bay of the north elevation, and it can be concluded that while the existing windows are probably original, two windows (one upper and one lower) had been blocked in each of the south elevations and three windows (one upper and two lower) blocked in each of the north elevations. This photograph shows a further 14 windows in the lower removable screens of the north elevation; these screens were taken down during ship launches (Hawkins and Butler 2015, 55, fig 10).

The building's roof originally was steeply pitched, as is shown in the engraving of 1869 (Fig 118), the internal photograph of *c* 1871 and the surviving Baker roofs at Chatham (Hawkins and Butler 2015, 53, fig 11). A photograph dating from before *c* 1913 (ibid, 54, fig 12) shows the roof framing of the two central bays replaced by a wrought-iron tied arch roof with riveted plate gussets. The external appearance of the roof as rebuilt is shown in a photograph of 1947 (ibid, 54, fig 13); the roof cover has subsequently been entirely replaced.

The spans of the aisles and longitudinal bracing are, however, largely original and closely match those observed in slips nos 4–6 at Chatham dockyard. The cantilevered trusses of the side aisles are made from single castings with a straight top, curved lower boom and uneven pattern of latticework. These trusses now rest on a steel wall plate supported on steel posts set in the outer walls. Angle/T-sectioned purlins (11) span between the trusses in the central bays and over the side aisles (3). Out of originally 21 haunched longitudinal trusses 14 remain, some 4.0–4.3m high with a ribbed lower flange, cast-iron struts and wrought-iron tie rods.

The four lower sides of the building were completely open originally, as shown in the *c* 1869 engraving (Fig 118). The south, west and north sides were subsequently bricked up (the west perhaps in part by *c* 1913 and the remainder by 1982 but with more recent rebuilds and additions). The east side is clad in a modern profiled sheet-metal fabric; this also now forms the roofing material. Four cast-iron wind braces are attached internally to the north and south walls; these are curved and include wrought-iron elements.

Building work, *c* 1800–1858/69

Archaeological evidence for 19th-century structures

Various structures and buildings for which archaeological evidence was recovered can be identified on 19th-century maps. Two parallel and adjacent timber sheds were built between 1813 (TNA, ADM 7/593) and 1858 (Fig 121) to the west of the wet dock, their main axes approximately north–south; in 1858 they are labelled 'plank sheds', but 'timber sheds' on the 1868 Ordnance Survey map (Fig 128), and 'timber store' in 1870 (Fig 129), while the western building is labelled 'plank shed' in 1878 on an updated version of the 1858 survey.

Remains of the west wall of the eastern shed (B27) and of the east wall of the western shed (B26) were recorded during the excavations (Fig 98; Fig 122). The former wall had been robbed and all that survived was a plank foundation. The latter wall survived only a few brick courses high, 10.50m long and 0.58m wide, also resting on a plank foundation. This wall had subsided where the foundation had rotted. A fragmentary tile surface measuring 1.92m × 0.51m was all that survived of a further building (B41, Fig 98) in the area of the timber sheds.

To the east of the plank sheds, a cobbled road surface (R2, Fig 98; Fig 123) of uncertain date was uncovered (but not excavated). Lines of longer cobbles seemed to form a kerb.

Two brick bases (B36, Fig 98) are likely to have supported the plank store shown on the 1858 map at the western extremity of the small mast dock. They were respectively 1.15m × 1.10m and 1.30m × 1.10m in size and both contained a centrally located vertical drainpipe.

Further fragmentary building remains were identified to the east of the wet dock entrance, south of the storehouse (B55) which was under construction in 1816 but demolished by 1858, apparently (above, 7.3). An east–west aligned thin brick wall measuring 0.83m × 0.35m was all that survived of one building

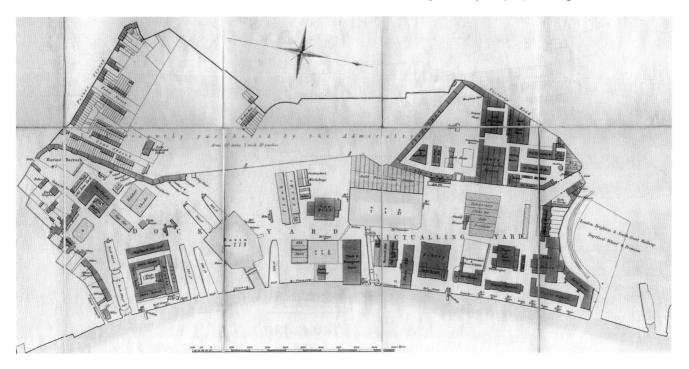

Fig 121 Map of Deptford dockyard in 1858 (ICE, 1858ADMNDP)

Fig 122 View of walls of plank sheds (B26, left; B27, right), looking south

(B38, Fig 98). The second building (B39, Fig 98) survived as a brick wall 1.00m × 0.50m in size. It was unclear what buildings the walls might correspond to.

Sections of the east and west walls of the sailfield in the south-east part of the site were identified in the excavations (respectively B32 and B33, Fig 98). The western timber fence

to the sailfield had probably been replaced in brick by 1722 (TNA, ADM 106/3300, 29 March 1723, 23; /3301, 28 April 1726, 13), and it is likely that the eastern timber fence was also rebuilt in brick around then. However, the excavated lengths of wall appeared to date to the late 18th to 19th centuries and were probably later replacements of the early 18th-century

151

Fig 123 View of cobbled road surface (R2), looking north-east

walls. Both walls were built of red bricks set in grayish-white lime mortar. The eastern wall (B32) was 10.00m long, 0.55m wide and 1.03m high, while the western wall (B33) was 6.25m long, 0.40m wide and 0.71m high. There was no sign of the earlier walls.

Modifications to the small mast dock walls (S38, Fig 98) are likely to date to this period. At the west end of the dock, the earlier brick and mortar walls (above, 7.3) had been heightened by 0.50m through the addition of a wall built of orange bricks set in white mortar-like cement. This wall itself had been heightened by the addition of a 0.15m skim of white concrete. At the west end of the wall, a square stone base with a square recess cut into its upper face was set in the concrete. This was presumably a crane base (S39, Fig 98) associated with the movement of masts. An area of brick masonry at the opposite end of the wall may also have been the base of a crane. This area of masonry was abutted by a later concrete wall. Yellow and red bricks set in white cement had been added to the south face of the small mast dock wall and rendered with cement to create a battered profile. This battering was more complete to the south-east.

The internal faces of the walls at the east end of the small mast dock (S38) were also partly rendered in concrete. A small surviving area of concrete cantilevered over the internal face of the wall in the north-east corner of the mast dock presumably supported the store shown here on the 1858 map (Fig 121).

A large brick structure (S44, Fig 98) may have been part of a building shown on the 1858 map south of slipway no. 5 (S31). The structure was 2.40m wide and built of red brick set in white mortar, and included a buttress-like feature on its east face. The structure appeared to be a large platform rather than a wall, as its south end was stopped and it was only 1.10m deep. The structure may have been a massive base for a crane or other machine. Walls abutting the east face of the brick structure may also have been the remains of the bases for a crane or other

machines. One of the walls was built of yellow and orange brick set in grey cement. An area of flagstones north of this wall may have been the floor of a cellar whose walls, of red brick in white mortar, may also have been a part of this complex.

Buildings constructed along the original perimeter wall on the west side of the yard continued in use even after the new wall had been built to enclose the land acquired from Sir John Evelyn in 1725 (Chapter 6.2). Map evidence shows that the range of workshops (B30, Fig 70; Fig 71) at the north end of this wall, and shown in 1774, was still standing in 1802 (Fig 95) and 1813 (TNA, ADM 7/593) but had been demolished by 1858 (Fig 121); walls of these workshops were exposed during the excavations (Chapter 6.3). The north-east face of the yard perimeter wall was abutted by a red brick wall that was part of one of the workshops. This wall had been removed by a second phase of building consisting of a rectangular building or room. A yard surface (OA18) built of angular stone may have been associated with this later building or room. A complete strap and spike fitting with perforations for attachment (<S27>, Fig 124), a small fragment from the base of a glass phial and leather shoe remains were found in the yard surface. Other finds here included a complete large, domed copper-alloy mount <35>, bulk iron nails and iron slag from a make-up layer, while other deposits also yielded objects also presumably associated with the workshops, including caulking material <40>, an iron forelock wedge <100>, a mid 18th-century pair of iron scissors, the blades slightly open (<S31>, Fig 124), part of a large cast circular disc of copper alloy (<S32>, Fig 192), probably a piece of machinery, more fragments of leather shoe, part of an unidentified wooden object <61>, and fragments of a glass beaker <48> and bottle glass.

The truncated remains of two pairs of large north–south trestles (B49, B54, Fig 98) were identified along the riverfront, to the north of the small mast dock. These comprised a sill beam with a morticed-in post supported by two diagonal braces

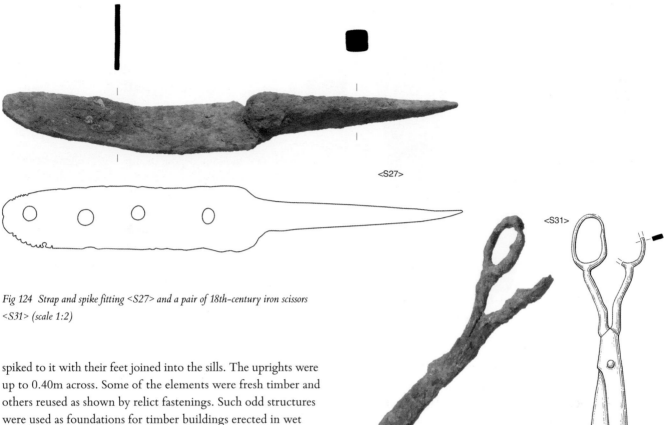

Fig 124 Strap and spike fitting <S27> and a pair of 18th-century iron scissors <S31> (scale 1:2)

spiked to it with their feet joined into the sills. The uprights were up to 0.40m across. Some of the elements were fresh timber and others reused as shown by relict fastenings. Such odd structures were used as foundations for timber buildings erected in wet ground (Heard 2003, 53). The use of the trestle form seems to be employed where a pile driver could not be conveniently rigged. Elsewhere they have been found to have been made using recycled ships' timbers or shipyard offcuts. This was the case here, where a mix of elm, oak and softwood was used.

The date range at other sites for this type of structure is broadly 18th to 19th centuries, and these examples seem to fall in the latter part of this range. The location of the westernmost pair (B49) corresponds to the 'tank and smiths' shop' shown on the 1858 map (Fig 121). The easternmost pair (B54) corresponds to a later, unlabelled building shown on the 1878 map immediately east of the tank and smiths' shop, but not on the 1858 map; however, the two buildings are probably broadly contemporary. A morticed sill beam (B37, Fig 98; Fig 125) running east–west is probably the south wall of this later eastern building. The sill beam must once have supported posts or studs of a timber wall and was made of two pieces of ship false keels of very tough elm, possibly imported rock elm. The timbers had fragments of copper-alloy staples and copper sheathing nails in them. Seven ragged keel dogs <195> (eg <S28>, Fig 126) and <197>, wire <676> and numerous nails (<675>, <677>), all of copper alloy, were associated with the eastern building (B54).

The area bounded to the east by the quadrangle storehouse (B14) and adjacent storehouse (B15) and to the west by slipway no. 5 (S31) was evidently a convenient place to lay drains to the river. The box-drains and timber tank have been described above (7.3, S33; Fig 97; Fig 98). Another drainage feature (S59, Fig 97) in this area consisted of a timber box built in a triangular shape that formed a filtering mechanism for a drain controlled by a sluice gate. The back side of the triangular box fed into the sluice arrangement which comprised a timber gate

Fig 125 View of morticed sill beam (B37), looking west

153

<S28>

Fig 126 Copper-alloy ragged false keel dog <S28> (scale 1:1)

and a plank wall of two planks laid on edge. The other two sides of the triangle were open with copper mesh nailed over them to make a crude filter. The filter was 0.55m high and its sides measured 0.48–0.50m. The sluice gate measured 0.75m × 0.50m and the plank wall behind 2.04m long by 0.60m high in total. The pit in which this structure was built appeared to be rectangular, at least 3.80m × 2.50m in size.

The purpose of this filter mechanism is unclear – the pit which it occupied must have been open for the filter to operate, draining water into the river. The pit may not have been in use for any length of time, since the south, west and east edges were not revetted in timber – or else any revetment did not survive (scattered posts may have supported a crude revetment since robbed or lost). Without a revetment, the sides would eventually have collapsed. Perhaps the pit was a sump that diverted water away from building activities, with the drain carrying the water away at low tide. The sluice gate would have prevented river water flooding in at high tide, while the filter arrangement prevented soil clogging the drain when the water was expelled.

East of this structure, part of a separate timber box-drain (S60, Fig 97) was partially concealed under the west side of the storehouse complex (B15). The exposed west side of the drain was built of planks nailed to vertical posts; a plank was typically 1.70m × 0.30m in size and 30mm thick. The drain lid measured 1.70m × 0.74m. Two fragmentary tie-backs braced the side of the drain. The more complete consisted of a 1.78m long timber, 0.33m thick and 0.46m high, with a slot cut in its far end through which a cross-piece (or 'needle') passed. The needle was braced by posts c 0.12m × 0.08m in size.

In the south-west of the site, within the outer boundary of Admiralty property in the 19th century, the remains of a timber building or buildings (B50, Fig 98) were identified, consisting of a scatter of timber piles driven into alluvium and other timber fragments. There was no readily discernible pattern to the piles.

An extensive demolition deposit of slate may also have related to the building(s). This area lay south of, and outside, the dockyard as shown on the 1802 map (Fig 95). There are no structures marked in this area, 'recently purchased by the Admiralty', on the 1858 map (Fig 98); the 1878 map shows a gasholder and gasworks here inside, and west of, the 'new boundary wall', with workshops and stores south of this. Finds recovered from deposits associated with the building(s) (B50) included copper-alloy nails <513> and a possible offcut <514>, and a small group of iron objects – a large eyelet/collar <224>, possibly from a sail (external diameter 80–85mm, internal diameter c 52mm), two washers <110> and <553>, a wedge <551> and bulk iron nails, as well as lead waste <536> and some tar-like matter <42>.

Finds material from the life of the dockyard

Recovered from across the yard from dockyard-period layers and features was a range of building and industrial materials and items, including earlier, residual, material. Large-scale excavations of naval dockyards are a rarity, and consequently so is the recovery of material which sheds light on the business of, and everyday life in, the yard. The underlying geology had less relevance in this period than in earlier ones, but for consistency the site is divided into the area of the gravel headland (OA16) – in this period, generally the southern and eastern parts of the yard – and the area of alluvium (OA17) (Fig 97; Fig 98) in the first part of what follows.

In the area of the gravel headland (OA16) a posthole yielded a piece of mid 17th-century tin-glazed wall tile featuring the edge of a flower vase design (<T6>, Fig 175) and clay pipe (two bowls and five stems) giving a latest date of c 1800–60. Other building material recovered includes peg tile and pantile roofing, brick and worn floor tile. Another posthole contained lead window cames <682> as well as bulk leather and, more unusually, fragments of moulded blue glass perfume bottle <686>. Make-up layers and construction debris produced copper-alloy nails (<25>, <33>), part of an iron strip/bar <97> and bulk iron nails. Ditches and drains scattered across the gravel headland (OA16) contained iron rods <95> and a strip <96>, the cap of a copper-alloy mount or button <26>, a copper-alloy rivet with lozenge-shaped rove <27>, and nails <28> and <29>. Most of the copper-alloy nails from this area are c 30–35mm in length, but <22> was originally longer (over 40mm).

Recovered from the quadrangle storehouse complex (B14) were two sherds of window glass (posthole [2980]), and part of an iron object with tapering round cross section <137>, probably a stake (posthole [2984]), while a structural feature

[2853] contained copper-alloy nails <168> and <169> and some iron slag, but also a ?pseudo-tortoiseshell hair comb (<S4>, Fig 186), apparently made of an early ?plastic and one of the very few 'female' objects from the site.

Finds from a possible surface in the south-west part of the site included 18 copper-alloy nails (<20>, <22>, <23>), a coiled length of fine copper-alloy wire <21> and three pieces of scrap copper-alloy sheet <24>, lead waste <44> and numerous iron objects – a complete curved ?stake/tool with square cross section and flattened spatulate end <546>, a complete spike/drift bolt with washer attached <93>, five washers (<91>, <92>, <548>, <549>), three wedges (<88>, <89>, <90>), a large lynch pin <772>, a small strip or knife blade <547>, bulk nails and slag.

In addition to these items, many of the finds recovered across the site from structures and features that were part of post-dockyard development and occupation (period 6; Chapter 8) are likely to relate to dockyard use. For example, a make-up deposit [2139] contained a number of items. These include two copper-alloy mounts, one (<191>) of uncertain function but the other (<S16>, Fig 188) a small brass mount or plaque, stamped 'ROYAL NAVY / Nº / Mess' and manufactured in Birmingham by 'JH HOPKINS & SONS' between 1858 and the closure of the yard (discussed further in Chapter 10.6). Also present were an iron threaded pipe cap <233> and two staples <234> and <235>, a lead weight bearing the number '29' (<S20>, Fig 127), bulk iron nails, assorted bottle and window glass, bulk leather and fibre/textile (<712>, <713>).

Elsewhere, unidentified iron objects and nails, iron slag, bottle and window glass were recovered, together with clay pipe (27 bowls and 33 stems were recorded) with a latest date of c 1780–1820, although the pipes cover a wide date range overall, from c 1660–1710 (and residual from the previous period) to the turn of the 18th and 19th centuries. A demolition deposit [5872] associated with the officers' quarters (B10, Fig 98) contained two fragments of glass from the rim/neck and base of a mallet bottle, part of a copper-alloy fitting <196>, probably from a piece of machinery, bulk nails and iron slag.

Final closure of the dockyard, 1869

A government scheme was put forward in July 1864 to concentrate shipbuilding at fewer centres, particularly at Devonport, and an announcement was made in March 1868 that Deptford would close (MacDougall 1982, 155; Fig 128). The closure of Deptford (and Woolwich) was part of a general cost-cutting exercise by the government affecting the army, navy and civil service. The Thames yards were out of date: the huge warships of the steam navy needed vast new basins and docks, and deeper water for launching (Coad 2013, 171–208). The Admiralty ordered that all the warehouses at Deptford should be cleared out by 1 April 1869 and the stores transferred to the royal victualling yard by 1 October 1869. The glimmer of a reprieve lay in the suggestion that the yard could be used by the Military Store Department, but a survey found it to be unsuitable (*London Journal*, 1 March 1869, 136). The last vessel launched at the yard was the 220ft × 36ft wood screw corvette *Druid* (1322bm-tons); this took place on 13 March 1869 in the presence of Princess Louise and Prince Arthur, Queen Victoria's youngest children (Walford 1878, 149; Fig 141). At the end of March 1869, the yard was finally closed and the 800 men at the yard were transferred to other establishments (*London Journal*, 1 March 1869, 136; Walford 1878, 149).

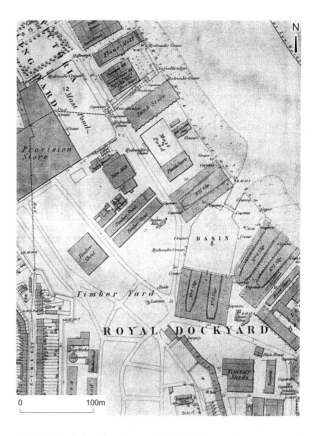

Fig 128 *The dockyard as shown on the 1868 Ordnance Survey map on the eve of closure (drawn at a scale of 1:1056; reproduced here at 1:5000)*

Fig 127 *Lead weight <S20> (scale 1:2)*

8

After the dockyard (period 6, 1869 to the present)

8.1 Historical introduction: the 1870s

The Corporation of the City of London purchased some 23 acres of the yard for about £95,000, as a place to sell and slaughter imported animals, to comply with the Contagious Diseases (Animals) Act 1869. Conversion cost around £140,000 and the yard reopened as the 'Foreign Cattle Market' in December 1871 (Walford 1878, 149).

Other parts of the dockyard were dismembered and sold off. A catalogue of machinery was made in 1870, and an inventory the following year. The machinery included pumps, cranes, hoists, pipes and a weighbridge, from various buildings including 'the Smithery, the Grindstone House, the Fitters Shop, the Engine House, the Fan House, the Tar Boiling House and the Steam Chambers by no. 1 slip and by no. 5 slip' (Fig 128; Fig 129). Building material, including bricks, stone, roof slates, lead and timbers were sold off in June 1872 from 'the Joiners' Shop, Magazine, Smitheries, Fitting Shop, Accountant's Office, Clerks' Office and the no. 23 Store opposite the Smithy'. Successful bidders were instructed that they had to take down the buildings at their own expense. The machinery of the smithy and fitting shop was sold off on 4 June 1872, including a 20-horsepower beam steam engine, a self-acting slotting machine, pumps, a wood sawing machine, fans, 29 wrought-iron smiths' forges, 25 forge cranes, four blast furnaces and other items (LMA, CLA/012/AD/02/002).

Some areas, like the slipways, were repurposed (below).

8.2 Archaeological evidence for the site after final closure, 1869–1914

The former twin slipways were built over as part of accommodating the Foreign Cattle Market. Trestles were built into areas of the floors of the no. 4 and no. 5 slipways (S30 and S31) to support the floors of two buildings (respectively B51 and B52) (Fig 130); these are shown on a plan of the cattle market of 1872 (LMA, CLA/012/AD/02/004 (v)). The trestles for both buildings were similar, consisting of vertical timbers supported by raking timbers, arranged in east–west rows. The uprights were generally a post of reused oak, or softwood in some cases, supported by a single diagonal brace timber on the north side. Some of the braces were of dense tropical timber (Stewart 2013). The braces were spiked into position just below the tops of the posts and set in shallow housings cut into the slipway sleepers; the braces on the north sides of the posts helped to stop them tipping towards the river. These trestles would have supported a series of sill beams holding up a building or buildings set over the infilled slipways. Very similar trestle foundation assemblies have been recorded on two other Thames sites nearby (eg Heard 2003, 28). The trestles were used as alternatives to piled foundations, as piling would not have been possible through the solid oak sleepers of the slipway floors.

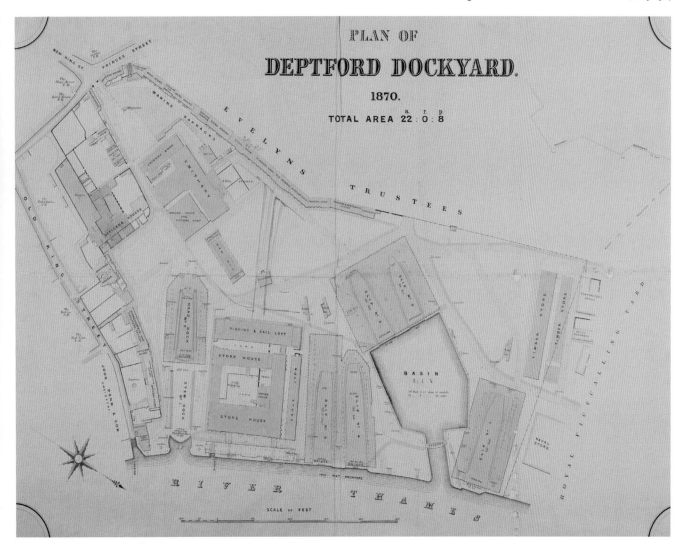

Fig 129 The Goad map of the closed dockyard of 1870 (LMA, CLA/012/AD/02/004 (iii))

Some of the braces and post timbers in these trestles showed signs of reuse. Many of these timbers derived from ships broken or repaired in the former dockyard, possibly after a first reuse in dockyard buildings (detailed in Chapter 9.2, 'Maritime industrial debris').

The cover roofs (B24 and B25) of former slipways nos 4 and 5 were initially retained (Fig 130), although progressively demolished between 1869 and the 1916 Ordnance Survey mapping. The former cover roof (B23, 'Olympia') of slipways nos 2 and 3 (S28 and S29) was also retained.

The cover roofs were linked up with new ranges of substantial and well-ventilated sheds on all three sides of the former wet dock to provide shelter for some 4000 cattle and 12,000 sheep (Walford 1878, 149). Animal pens equipped with water troughs and fodder racks were installed. Fig 131 shows the space beneath the cover roof (B25) over former slipway no. 5 adapted in this way. The former south range of the quadrangle storehouse (B14) and rigging and sail loft (B40) are shown on the 1872 plan of the cattle market (LMA, CLA/012/AD/02/004 (v)) as converted into slaughterhouses for cattle, and the former storehouse (B15) into a slaughterhouse for sheep. Animals were landed at one of three jetties joined by a low-water platform

(Fig 130); this is the loading platform shown in a 1920s photograph (Fig 132).

Walls and culverts were seen south of the former quadrangle storehouse complex (in trenches 25, 27 and 28) (Fig 3) (OA19, Fig 130) and date from this period. Other supports for building floors were seen in the disused wet dock. Evidently the dock had been allowed to fill with mud and been backfilled, and sawn softwood piles had been driven in as supports for a building (B53, Fig 130). In this area there were no underlying solid oak timbers to prevent the use of piled foundations.

A lone brick base recorded in the north-west corner of excavation trench 38 measured 1.15m × 0.75m × 0.60m high, with a central slot in its top measuring 0.64m × 0.30m to accommodate a vertical timber roof support, probably for a late 19th-century warehouse (B48, Fig 130). Other such bases may survive beyond the area of excavation.

The stone slipway Structure 19 that ran into the wet dock along its western edge was closed off with a brick wall ([5867]) supported by stone buttresses made from stones robbed out of the slipway; however, this construction work (shown on Fig 97) appears to relate to post-dockyard use rather than the final remodelling of the wet dock *c* 1844 (Chapter 7.4), based on the

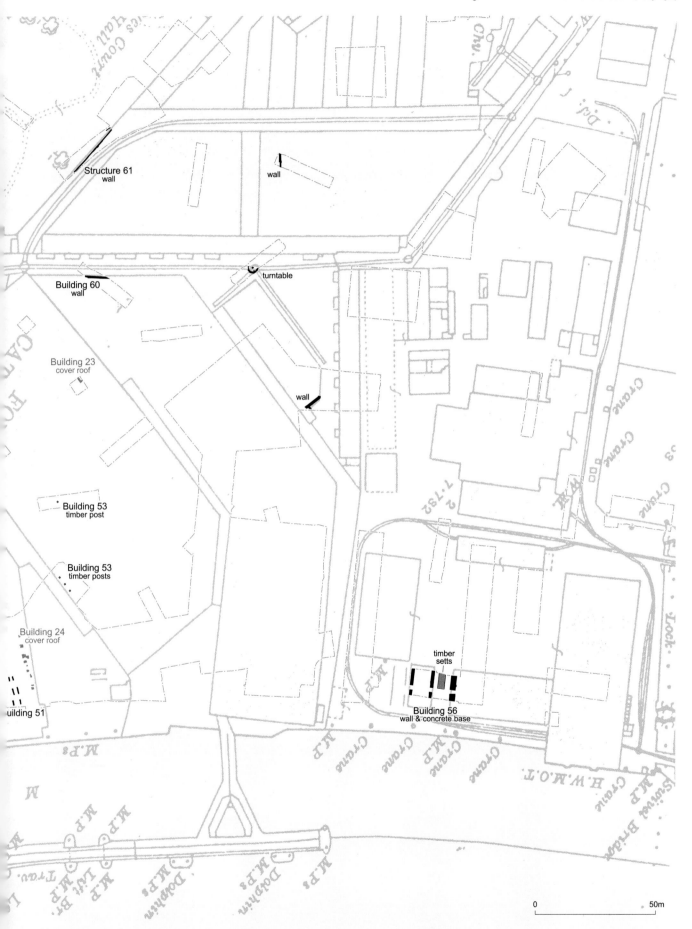

Structure 61
wall

wall

Building 60
wall

turntable

Building 23
cover roof

wall

Building 53
timber post

Building 53
timber posts

Building 24
cover roof

uilding 51

timber
setts

Building 56
wall & concrete base

0   50m

Fig 130 Plan of principal archaeological features post-dockyard (period 6), 1869 to the First World War, overlain on the 1916 Ordnance Survey map (scale 1:1500)

Fig 131 View of slip cover roof (B25) converted into a 'sheep shed' after the closure of the yard, photographed in c 1880 (LLHAC, Thankfull Sturdee Collection PH 71-4158 LS34)

Fig 132 View along the loading platform in the 1920s, photographed from the north-west; the storehouse complex is in the background (right) (LLHAC, A/15/31/4)

finds recovered. A number of datable items were found behind and in this brick wall, principally a Victorian farthing of 1883 (<384>) and an interesting collection of 12 near-complete glass bottles and three jars originating from a pharmacy (Fig 184). Eleven of the bottles bear, or bore, relief-moulded lettering which identifies several of them as products of American companies, either imported or manufactured by London branches (eg <G20>–<G23>); others (eg <G24>–<G27>) are English products (Chapter 10.5, 'Pharmaceutical vessels'). Other items recovered include a small copper-alloy pendant or tag with punched lettering (<S15>, Fig 188), a range of iron structural fittings (part of a ?grille <660>, a possible window latch <661>, a bracket <662>, twisted wire hawser <663> and a large flat mount <664>) and galvanised iron/zinc items (<665>, <666>).

8.3   The site in the 20th century, after 1914

In the 20th century, the south-west corner of the storehouse complex was replaced in yellow stock brick on concrete foundations. Turntables were constructed (visible on the 1916 Ordnance Survey map and identified during the excavation) on a roadway (with rails) built into the centre of the internal yard (Fig 130). These date from the First World War use of the site. Other walls built in yellow stock bricks relate to buildings of this date (B59 and B60, Fig 130); a shell button <188> was found associated with Building 59. A 25m length of thin perimeter wall built of yellow stock brick on a concrete foundation (S61, Fig 130), running north-east to south-west south of Building

60, may date to the early 20th century. Two drains and one yellow brick footing (Fig 130) seemed to relate to a post-dockyard building to the north-west of Building 60 (in the western part of area 12).

A wall by the river, built of yellow brick set in white cement on a concrete foundation, dates from the use of the site in the early 20th century and was possibly associated with a large concrete base that may have been a modern wharf for unloading stores (B56, Fig 130). The concrete base included an area of closely-packed timber setts lying on top of the concrete.

By the 1930s a railway had been built across the site, complete with a railway transit shed and platform, when the site was used as a Supply Reserve Depot. The construction of the railway had a considerable effect on the site, not least on the mid 19th-century terrace of buildings in the south-west part (B57, Fig 98; probably part of Evelyn Row) which was partially demolished (Chapter 9.3). Fig 133 shows a barge loaded with paper rolls (newsprint) berthed in front of the Georgian facade (complete with royal coat of arms) of the quadrangle storehouse c 1930.

The dockyard was bombed in the Second World War. Concrete foundations in the south-west part of the site are likely to have been an air-raid shelter (B62, Fig 134). Three V1 flying bombs fell on or in the vicinity of the site during 1944. For the most part there was only general – rather than structural – blast damage, including to the Tudor storehouse, although there were pockets of more serious damage (Saunders 2005, map 91). The building on the site of Sayes Court was demolished by 1949 (Fig 134). A 1935 plan of the Supply Reserve Depot (LLHAC, A/15/31/10) depicts the former quadrangle storehouse (B14) and rigging and sail loft (B40) as having been substantially modified. The yard's rigging and sail

Fig 133 View of the quadrangle storehouse photographed from the riverfront in the 1920s/30s (LLHAC, A/15/31/5)

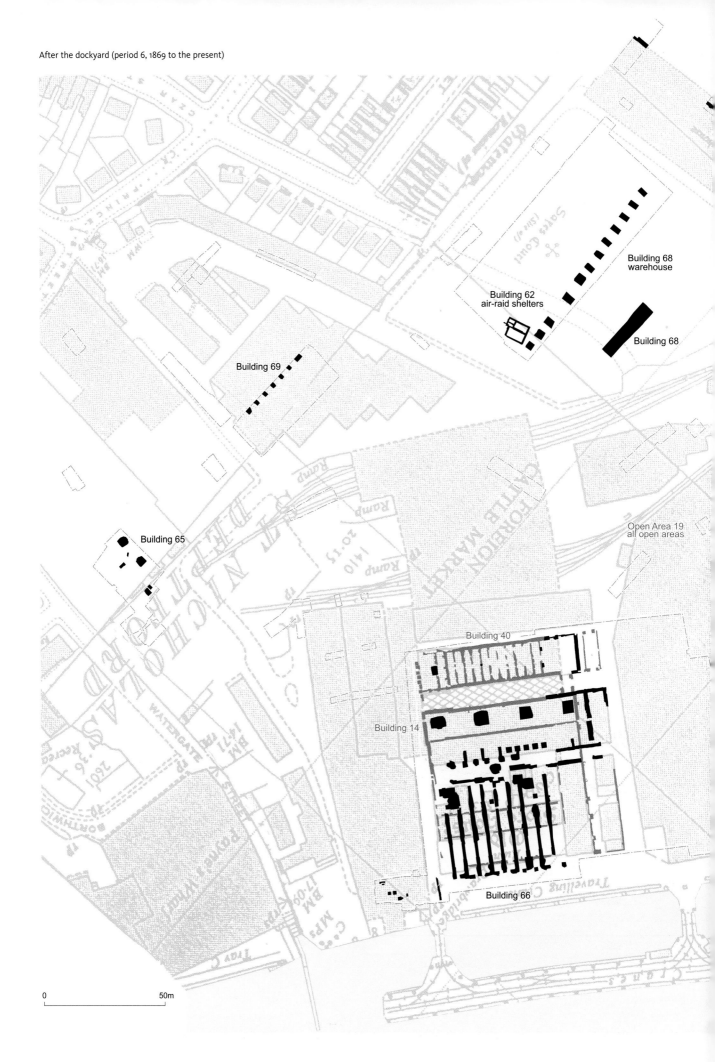

Building 68
warehouse

Building 62
air-raid shelters

Building 68

Building 69

Building 65

Open Area 19
all open areas

Building 40

Building 14

Building 66

0   50m

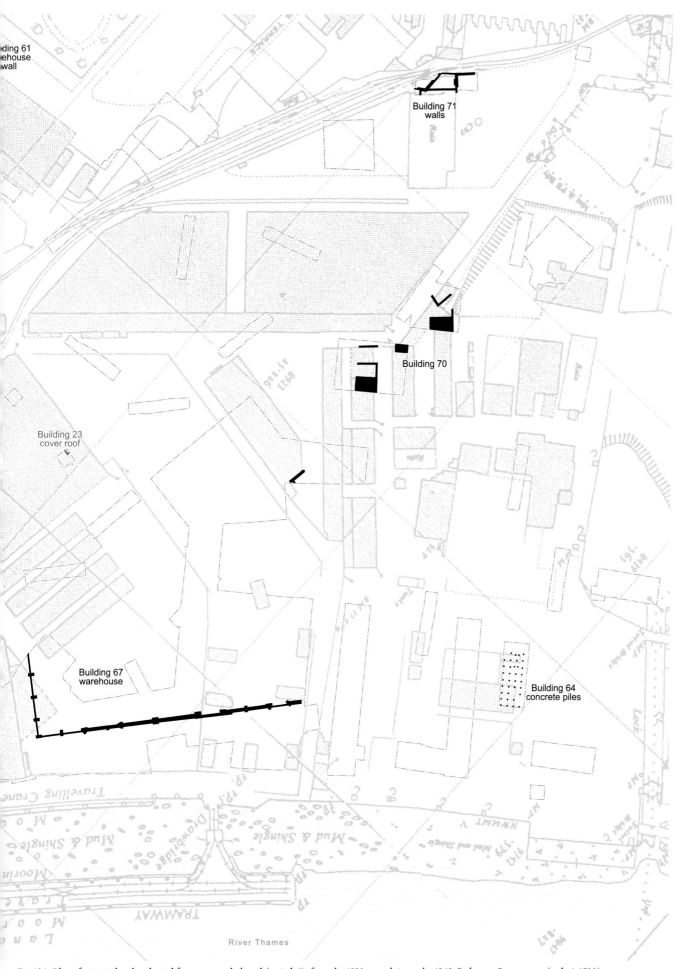

Fig 134 Plan of principal archaeological features post-dockyard (period 6), from the 1930s, overlain on the 1949 Ordnance Survey map (scale 1:1500)

loft and most of the southern part of the storehouse had been converted to 'cold chambers' (Fig 104). The southern part of the building range (B15) to the west of the quadrangle storehouse was demolished, leaving only the northern half intact.

The Tudor storehouse (B1) at this time was a lorry stand and was recorded as a 'ruin' on the 1949 Ordnance Survey map (Fig 134), suggesting that the building was largely out of use by this date. The storehouse, which survived to roof plate level, was revealed during work to remove bomb-damaged buildings in 1952 (*ILN*, 1 March 1952) and demolished shortly afterwards (Fig 15; Fig 16). The flame-headed niche of brickwork (Fig 15), bearing the date of 1513, was eventually installed in the Department of Computer Science at University College London (Mazeika 2007, 129). The quadrangle storehouse (B14) was finally demolished in 1981. The clock cupola was removed by the Greater London Council in 1983 to Woolwich and then two years later to Blackheath for a £60,000 restoration. In 1986 the clock was re-erected at Thamesmead (Steele 1993, 222–3).

Warehouses were built across the site in the 1980s (Fig 2; Fig 4). A concrete ground beam foundation (B67, Fig 134) ran across the front of the former wet dock. Some of the top of the brick and stone wet dock wall had been machined out during the construction of these warehouses, leaving the machine-bucket teeth marks where the walls had been removed. North–south aligned concrete foundations (B66, Fig 134) were inserted across the axis of the Tudor storehouse foundations (Fig 21).

A warehouse (B68, Fig 134) with concrete foundations was built on the site of Sayes Court. Remains of modern warehouses and other buildings post-dating the dockyard were identified elsewhere on the site (B61, B64, B65, B69, B70), as well as a smaller modern building (B71) (Fig 134).

9

Aspects of the Deptford dockyard and conclusions

9.1 Timber supply to the dockyard (16th to 19th centuries)

Damian Goodburn

Introduction

Any multidisciplinary study of a historic shipbuilding and repair site must consider timber supply to the site, as various specific forms and species of timber were the crucial raw materials until the iron shipbuilding boom of the late 19th century. However, the researcher has to be aware that there is also much mythology surrounding this issue, both in detail and in general. One of the popular myths is still that 'the shipyards were destroying the forests'. This has been shown by many researchers to be a great oversimplification and has not yet been systematically examined by archaeologists for the post-medieval or early industrial periods. As the great woodland historian and historical botanist Oliver Rackham has put it, 'The British believe that the history of woodlands has been dominated by the influence of the sea. A nation with a proud seafaring history naturally supposes that the supply of shipbuilding timber has been the reason either for the sacrifice of its ancient forests or the maintenance of its ancient woods' (Rackham 1976, 99). The vast bulk of the timber used to build naval vessels before *c* 1800 was home-grown 'hardwoods', principally our two native oaks and their hybrids, and elm, but also some beech below the waterline. The main local landowner in Deptford, John Evelyn, who was well known as a writer on horticulture and the growing of trees, championed the cause of growing large naval timber as a patriotic duty (Evelyn 1706). It would be difficult to ignore the persuasive effect that living next to the dockyard may have had on him.

The tree-ring study has also shown that the successfully dated oak timbers seem to be derived from trees grown in south-east England or East Anglia (Chapter 10.9). However, long straight, regular trees of softwood (coniferous species) were also bought in for masts and yards, and for later dockyard structures and temporary elements of ships such as outer sheathing. This material had to be imported from Scandinavia and the Baltic region, and even much further away (Morriss 2011, 175–8). Some details emerging from historical enquiries in this field are relevant to the archaeological investigations at the Deptford royal dockyard site and so are flagged up here, such as the comment by Daniel Defoe, writing in the early 18th century, that he had observed that land transport of large Sussex oak to Chatham royal dockyard could take as long as two or three years (Wilcox 1966, 91). If such delays between the felling of timber and its use in the dockyard were more widespread, it is something that might have to be taken account of in interpreting tree-ring dates.

An important factor relevant to discussions of naval timber shortages was the documented practice of the Admiralty, at least by the 18th century, of generally paying the lowest amount for timber it could, so it was often easily outbid by local users

(Rackham 1976, 102). In 1786–7 the Deptford yard purveyor pointed out that if the naval dockyards were experiencing a scarcity of timber, it was mainly because merchant yards set fewer conditions, paid higher prices and paid on time, three months after delivery (Morriss 2011, 176–7).

The dockyards' annual requirement for timber was very substantial even in peacetime. The quantities of oak timber (plank, knees and thickstuff) used in the construction of ships *c* 1780 has been reckoned at 5560 loads for a 100-gun 1st-rate, 4035 for a 90-gun 2nd-rate, 3212 for a 74-gun 3rd-rate and 2601 for a 64-gun 3rd-rate, down to 980 loads for a 28-gun 6th-rate (Morriss 1983, 79, table 7; for the 'load' see below). Admiralty orders required that a stock of oak timber equal to three years' consumption was to be maintained, but at the start of hostilities in 1803 the amount in store, 34,562 loads, was about 1500 loads short. English oak was the most scarce. Every possible source of timber was explored, but the yards were dependent for at least 90% of their timber on contractors. The Napoleonic Wars caused a shortage of hardwoods after 1803 and pushed prices up. St Vincent's refusal to pay the contractors' higher prices precipitated a timber supply crisis in 1803–4; and from 1804 the navy began to build frigates from other woods, fir and eventually teak, and obtained its oak from further afield, in Britain and abroad (Morriss 1983, 77–84; 2011, 170, 177–8; Knight 2013, 369). The dockyards' timber 'crisis' was averted when St Vincent was forced to resign in 1804 and the permitted prices were increased. The total quantity of oak timber in the dockyards was reckoned at 57,998 loads on 1 January 1793 and 34,562 loads on 8 March 1803, but had risen to 80,660 loads by 1 January 1807 (Morriss 1983, 80, table 10).

Historical sources such as Admiralty specifications and dockyard records have been trawled by historians examining these issues, but systematic recording of the sizes, forms and species of the trees actually used in wooden warship building has only very rarely been attempted. A rare example is a pilot study of a representative selection of hull elements of the *Mary Rose* (Goodburn 2009, 66–80). Although that ship appears to have been repaired at the Deptford yard, she was built at Portsmouth and only sheds light on the very beginning of bespoke royal warship building. Most other studies of naval dockyards in Britain rely on two sources, historical records and early pictorial evidence (eg Lavery 1991, chapter 5). While that type of approach clearly yields substantial information and can tackle issues very difficult to address through the material archaeological evidence alone, it still leaves many details obscure. The records may well describe the volume of a parcel of timber bought for the navy but they do not often provide any details as to the form or age of the trees actually used. It is also the case that the precise meanings of some terms for specific types of timber are now difficult to understand. For example, Pepys noted that he 'walked to Deptford to view a parcel of brave knees' (*Pepys diary*, 2 November 1664). While a 'knee', in this context, was clearly a piece of oak timber that had grown to a tight angular curve useful for certain parts of a warship hull, we do not have any record of their form, size or quality.

The key unit of measurement of timber bought by the navy was the 'load', usually reckoned at 50 cubic feet volume (or 50 solid feet), which in fresh home-grown oak was about 1.5 tons in weight (Steel 1805; Lavery 1991, 56). But even then there was debate about that standard value, and in any case irregular, tapering and often curved oak timber is a notoriously difficult natural material to measure accurately (Fig 135). Space does not permit an extended discussion of this complex issue, but it

Fig 135 Irregular curved home-grown timber on a timber wagon (Pyne and Hill 1803–6: V&A, E.2826-1962)

Fig 136 *Detail view of a timber taster's mark (c 1800 or a little later) on the end grain of a small repair timber: an oval engraved hammer mark (Diam c 45mm) with a smaller oval inside containing a small letter 'S' set within a larger letter 'A' or inverted 'V', possibly the timber taster's initials (0.1m scale)*

should be noted that there was much opportunity for corruption in timber sales to the navy between the stages of selection and purchase of standing trees, and partially worked material ready for the shipwrights' use (Wilcox 1966, 90).

We do know that in some large dockyards a specialised clerk was required to document timber coming into the yard. These individuals were known as 'timber tasters [ie testers]' and they often seem to have marked documented timber with a hammer with engraved initials (Lavery 1991, 65). Excavations at the large private dockyard just to the east of the Deptford royal yard provided some evidence of these stamps (Divers 2004, 73), but only one was found during the excavations at the Deptford royal yard, on one late timber offcut used as a repair in slipway no. 1 (Fig 136). 'Timber masters' were additionally introduced to all the yards in 1801 by Samuel Bentham specifically to monitor the quality of timber being delivered by contractors and to reduce waste by shipwrights; the post was abolished in 1827 and revived some 20 years later (Morriss 1983, 77, 89–90; Haas 1994; Knight 2013, 368–9; J Coad, pers comm 2015).

The dimensions and size range of some typical large oak trees used by the navy

Oliver Rackham was really the first researcher to realise that if detailed records were made of the more complete sections of trees used in a historic structure, then they could be used to accurately reconstruct parts of the relevant historic landscape that supplied them (Rackham 1972). The methods developed by Rackham were further refined (by the present writer and others in the MOLA team) based on practical experience of historic woodworking in ancient woodlands and the use of extensive tree-ring sampling. A straightforward stepwise approach was developed for this work, based primarily on detailed scale timber drawings, which has been widely used to examine earlier waterfront and nautical timbers excavated in London and elsewhere (Goodburn 1991b; 1992; 2009). Because the Convoys

Wharf excavation brief did not permit the full excavation and lifting of many timbers, our ability to reconstruct the 'parent trees' of many of the more complete large timbers found is limited, but three worked examples should illustrate the potential of this line of archaeological enquiry into naval timber supply.

The presence of minimally trimmed oak trees with a felled butt end, most branches removed and just two faces hewn flat, that is large 'sided oak timbers', in the slipway bases provided ideal material from which to reconstruct the timbers coming into the yard. Two examples are used here from slip no. 5 (S31): sleeper timbers [2721] and [2727] (Fig 137) lifted from the base of the slipway which was rebuilt in the third quarter of the 18th century (Chapter 6.3).

Slipway sleeper timber [2721] was drawn to scale in detail, showing traces of the fastenings and recesses relating to its slipway use. Other features recorded included the flow of the grain, major knots remaining (which branches once sprang from) and sapwood from just under the bark of the parent oak, together reflecting its standing form closely. The whole sided timber measured 7.50m long with a maximum width of 650mm towards the base and a top width of *c* 270mm. It was hewn to a sided dimension of *c* 300mm (12in). The first major branches of the standing tree would have spread out at a height of just over 3.5m, though none of the lower branches was large (Fig 138). Judging from other, similar sampled timber found in the same slipway base the timber was of medium growth rate. The parent tree clearly had a slight S-curve from about halfway up and a lopsided forking at just under 8m up. Oaks of this form can still be found in what was managed 'coppice with standards' woodland including small underwood trees in the London region today. The woodland was open enough for relatively low branches but not so open that these were heavy boughs like those seen in hedgerow or open pasture oaks. Oak timber trees growing with some underwood typically start to branch out at between 3.5m and 5m in south-east England. This was not the tall, straight tree representing a

167

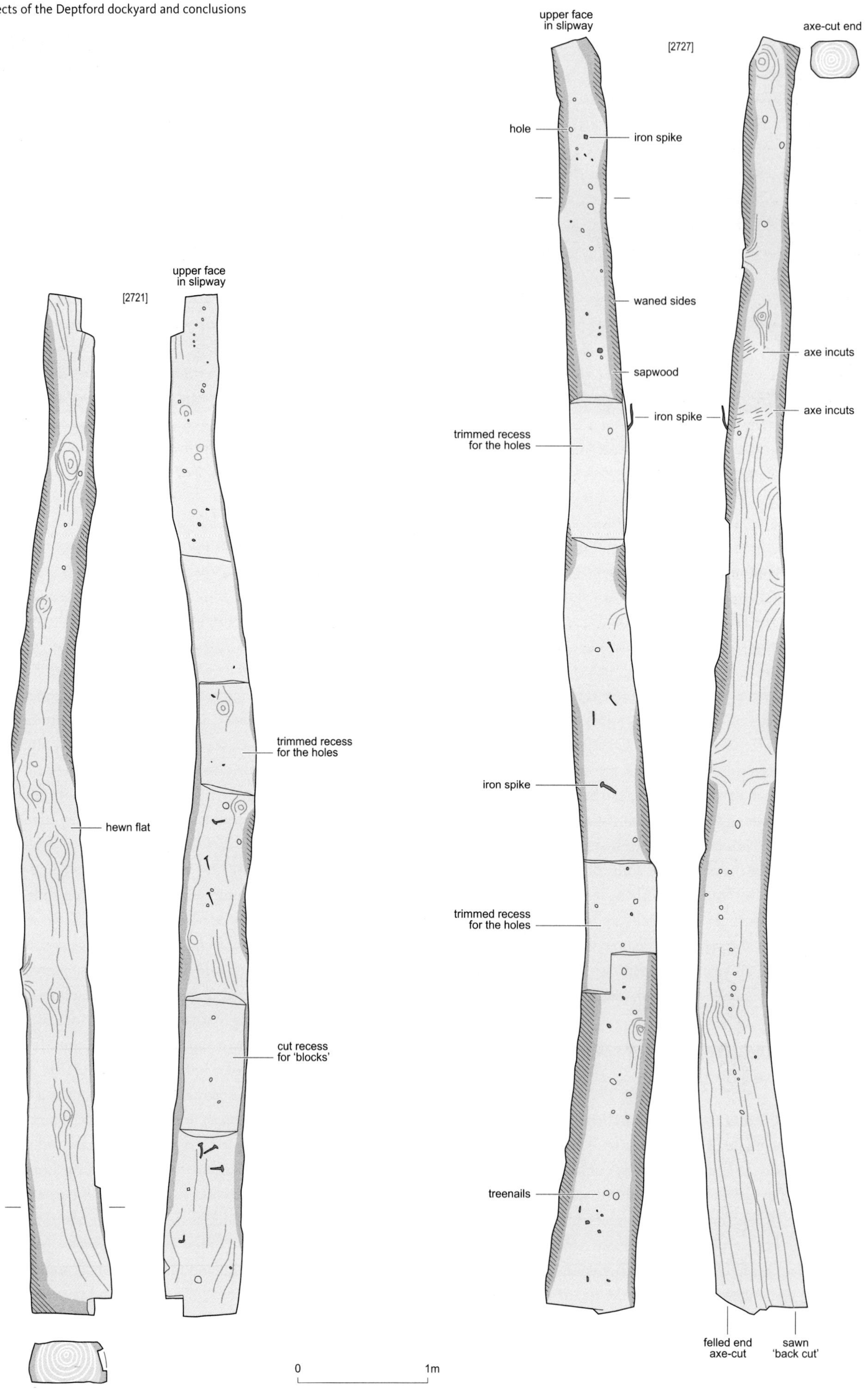

upper face
in slipway

[2727]

axe-cut end

hole — iron spike

waned sides

sapwood

trimmed recess
for the holes — iron spike

iron spike

trimmed recess
for the holes

treenails

axe incuts

axe incuts

felled end
axe-cut

sawn
'back cut'

upper face
in slipway

[2721]

trimmed recess
for the holes

hewn flat

cut recess
for 'blocks'

0   1m

Fig 137 Slipway sleepers or 'sided timbers' [2721] and [2727] as prepared for naval use (scale 1:40)

plantation-grown oak or one from a dark area of virtually natural wildwood.

This would have been a medium to largish oak tree by naval standards of the mid 18th century, but taller, straighter trees and those of greater and smaller diameter were also used. Interestingly, when we calculate the weight of this timber with its two faces hewn off, that is as sided and ready for naval use, it would have been *c* 1.14 tons (here the specific density of freshly felled oak of 1.073 tonnes/m³ is used: Millett and McGrail 1987, 106). However, if we reconstruct it as a whole log, pretty much all that could have been used for naval purposes from the original tree, the approximate weight is *c* 1.496 tonnes. This figure is so close to the standard naval timber volume and weight unit, know as the 'load' of *c* 1.5 tons (above, 'Introduction'), that we may suggest that it was a rather typical, moderately large oak timber coming into the Deptford yard in the mid 18th century. It shows us what a load of naval oak timber actually looked like.

Slipway timber [2727], a slightly larger, sided, oak sleeper timber, even included its felled basal end (Fig 137). The felled base of the tree had one side axe-cut to form the V-shaped 'gob' or 'drop' and the other cut made a little higher up with a cross-cut saw. It appears to be the total length it was when it arrived at the Deptford yard, at 9.35m long by 700mm wide at the butt, tapering to 320mm wide at the upper end and hewn to a

siding of *c* 270mm thickness. The standing tree would have had the first notable branches at *c* 4m up, one of which appears to have rotted off due to shading out (Fig 138). This mid 18th-century tree was rather straighter and a little taller than that described above ([2721]) but overall was broadly similar and likely to have come from the same general type of managed woodland. The weight of the timber sided would have been *c* 1.3 tonnes in fresh condition, but as a whole log it would have weighed *c* 1.8 tonnes, rather more than the typical 'load' of 1.5 tonnes, although the top, very knotty, end may have been rejected by the shipwrights for actual ship use.

The same approach can be used to examine fully shaped, used nautical timbers, particularly large, fairly complete examples. Here the rudder post timber [3720] (Fig 196) has been chosen as an example. This timber survived 5.85m long but must originally have been *c* 7–8m long; it had a maximum width of 530mm and maximum thickness of 490mm but both dimensions tapered in size considerably. Given an original length of *c* 7.5m, this timber would have weighed just over 1 tonne in fresh condition, while the log from which it was sawn would have weighed nearer 2 tonnes. The log used was rather knotty, with knots left by the removal of large boughs along the whole surviving length. Although some of the less knotty basal length may well have been cut off and used for other purposes, we can say that the standing oak was at least 0.70m in

Fig 138 Reconstruction of the parent oak trees of slipway sleeper timbers [2721] and [2727] and (right) of rudder post timber [3720] (scale 1:100)

diameter at chest height and moderately straight with heavy branches (Fig 138). It is most likely that this was a tree growing in a fairly open, parkland-type setting. In darker woodland the branches would have been smaller and sprung higher up.

These three worked examples (and more in the site archive: Chapter 1.5) demonstrate the potential of dockyard and naval timbers for reconstructing historic trees and wooded landscape, as well as something of the logistics of supplying the Deptford royal dockyard. In future this material evidence could be considered alongside documentary evidence in a more systematic approach to the role of the navy in shaping our historic landscape.

The transport of particularly heavy and awkward naval timber

It is clear from some historical accounts that, once trees were bought, the upper parts, branches and bark were often sold locally to help defray costs (Wilcox 1966, 97). Where possible the typically large timber was hauled to the nearest navigable waterway where it could be moved in barges and sometimes then by ship to yards like the Deptford royal yard. As most people today are used to relatively light softwood timber, and the epic tales of lumberjacks in film are almost always set in the coniferous woodlands of western North America, the great weight of freshly felled English-grown oak is something unfamiliar. It has been suggested that sometimes native naval timber was floated down the headwaters of rivers (Lavery 1991,

65) but this is not possible with large, fairly freshly cut, English-grown oak logs which have a specific density of 1.073 tonnes/m³, heavier than water (Millett and McGrail 1987, 106). In practice, generally fairly wide-ringed post-medieval and modern English oak is often heavier than this and will not even float in salt water until it has been dried substantially. It is clear that the supply routes for timber destined for the Deptford yard were often linked to the Thames and its tributaries. Many barges and estuary and coastal trading craft were hired to move the timber to the yard, where they could be unloaded with cranes set on the waterfront quays unencumbered by front bracing timbers (Fig 139).

The selective use of imported timber from Europe and distant colonies

Oak timber, especially in the form of high-quality planks, might also be imported in modest quantities from the southern Baltic countries (sometimes called 'Danzitic oak') in the post-medieval period, continuing later medieval practice. None of this imported oak was clearly identified during the excavations at the Deptford yard, but it was probably used there and has been identified at a large private yard west of the victualling yard, the Grove Street partnership of Barnard, Dudman and Adams (Tyers 1987; Chapter 7.1).

The bulk of imported timber to the London dockyards was coniferous timber which was not native to England, though it is widely planted now. Most of it came from Scandinavia and the

Fig 139 A crane, on the quay between slipway no. 1 (left) and the entrance to the small mast dock (right), unloading timber from a barge, as shown on the 1774 scale model (Fig 7), looking 'south' (National Maritime Museum, Greenwich, L0459-029)

Baltic and was mostly used for rounded straight masts and yards to support the sails of the warships. Offcuts and leftovers of coniferous timber were found in many structures in the Deptford yard, such as in the land-tie assemblies for the brick-walled wet dock of the mid 18th century (period 4; Chapter 6.3). It is also clear that imported softwood timber, mainly pine, was increasingly used in the later dockyard structures, such as the latest wet dock fender posts and the final phase of the large tank (S33) (period 5; Chapter 7.3).

European settlers in the north-east parts of America encountered large quantities of huge coniferous trees very suitable for the largest warship masts, and a trade in them was established from as early as 1609 (Wilcox 1966, 92). By the 1660s there was a well-established bulk trade in softwood mast timber both from the Baltic and – for the largest masts – from New England. Unfortunately, most of this softwood timber, particularly the pines, is very difficult to identify taxonomically beyond genus using standard anatomical microscopy (Hather 2000; Schoch et al 2004). Determining whether these timbers originated in the Old or New World using this technique is therefore not always possible. Here we can briefly cite details recorded by Samuel Pepys, who was keen to develop his knowledge of the timber trade including that in mast timber and baulks and thick sawn planks ('deals'). He was informed in much of this by his friends and colleagues Sir W Batten and W Warren. Pepys's diary entries highlight the importance to the Deptford yard of a trade which the archaeological sources cannot shed much light on. He records that on 3 December 1662 he went to Deptford with Naval Commissioner Pett and Mr Wood and spent the morning measuring his 'New England' masts. These New World masts could be truly enormous and were carried in specially adapted ships: for example, in 1665 W Warren, the imported timber merchant, received two great New England masts measuring 100ft long by 3ft in diameter at the butt (Wilcox 1966, 93). Ships carrying important naval timber were vulnerable to attack and piracy: for example, Pepys records the Dutch interception of one of W Warren's ships carrying part of a 1000-strong Swedish mast order. This trade in exotic conifers also included hewn baulks of timber and sawn plank of standardised dimensions such as the thick Baltic and Scandinavian pine planks or 'deals' like those examined by Pepys at Deptford, which he found 'cheap and good' (*Pepys diary*, 11 July 1662).

In essence, part of the historic landscapes of several areas of distant countries as well as native woodland, park and hedgerow trees in England were extensively exploited by the navy at Deptford and other yards from 1513 to *c* 1869. Indeed, as the British Empire grew and the navy expanded, new timber groups from tropical zones in Asia, South America and Africa started to be exploited from the end of the 18th century. Many of these timber species, new to northern Europeans, were very strong, rot-resistant ones often superior even to oak in some respects. Labour costs must also have been low in many of the new tropical timber-felling zones, which offset the costs of transport. A small amount of such tropical hardwood was found in one capstan base, in late minor repairs to slipway no. 1, and as

late-phase shoring wedges found there from late in period 5 (Stewart 2013, table 1).

The very latest structures found across the Deptford yard, dating to just after its selling-off, were made of second-hand oak naval timbers, imported softwood and noticeably more second-hand tropical naval timbers. The mix of materials used in the trestle foundations built on slips no. 4 and no. 5 (S30 and S31; Chapter 8.2) must have derived from vessels and possibly dockyard buildings of the early to mid 19th century (below, 9.2, 'Maritime industrial debris'). This latest material even included some teak (*Tectona grandis*) (timber [2558]) and tropical timber of African origin (cf *Oldfieldia africana*) (timber [2786]) (Stewart 2013, table 1), identified as what is often known as Eki in modern English waterfront carpentry and shipwrightry. To conclude this section, it may be observed that, even despite the huge urban growth of Greater London, there are still substantial areas of native oak woodland and hedgerow trees just inland of the Deptford yard, such as the famous Oxleas Woods, and Barnet Woods in Bromley, which straddle the River Ravensbourne that becomes Deptford Creek. Shipyards like that at Deptford did not destroy all the woodland in their hinterland.

9.2 Shipbuilding and innovation at the dockyard (16th to 19th centuries)

Changes in the technology and style of shipbuilding in England in the late 15th to 16th centuries

Damian Goodburn

The establishment of the Deptford royal dockyard facilities early in the reign of Henry VIII occurred at a time when a huge change in the technology of building large ships had just taken place in England. This major transition has been illustrated by historical sources and archaeological finds of substantial ship remains such as Henry V's 400/600bm-ton ship *Grace Dieu* of 1418 and Henry VIII's 500bm-ton *Mary Rose* of 1510 (Hutchinson 1994, 31; Adams 2003, 48–99). In the early to mid 15th century large English ships of all types were 'clinker-built', a style of construction originating in the Iron Age of northern Europe. This approach to building boats and ships is based on adding planking to a backbone assembly of the 'keel' (the lowest longitudinal strength member) and various jointed upright timbers at each end, the 'stem' and 'stern' posts (the former at the front or 'bow' and the latter at the back or 'stern'). The planks of the outer shell of a clinker vessel were added, slightly overlapping and fastened with iron rivets ('rove nails') or, less commonly, hooked-over nails or 'treenails' (specialised wedged wooden pegs). The strengthening frame timbers were then added inside the shell of planks, as well as other elements such as deck beams. This style of construction is often described as 'shell-first', or from the outside-in. There was also another tradition of building large vessels in the North Sea region in the late medieval period that involved a shell-first system, where the bottom planks were assembled edge to edge and the sides and ends assembled clinker-style; this is usually termed cog or 'kogge' building. However, even though English monarchs hired such craft it does not seem to have been a significant English shipbuilding tradition by the late 15th century.

During the later 15th century another very different style of shipbuilding was adopted from further south in Europe, now called 'carvel' shipbuilding. In this style of construction, many elements of the framework of a ship were erected first on the backbone assembly of the keel and stem and stern posts. Then the hull outer planking was fitted edge to edge and fastened to the framing with treenails and varying combinations of large iron nails and bolts. The internal planking, deck beams and other structures were then added. The new style of building was quite foreign to English shipwrights at first and it is known that Italian masters and methods were involved in introducing the radically new approach (Barker 1991; Marsden 2009). There is even some archaeological evidence, in the form of the partially excavated 'Woolwich Ship', found in 1912, of clinker-built warships being converted to smooth-skinned carvel-style ships (Adams 2003, 50). The new carvel technology had several advantages: principally, it made it easier to build very large vessels, and as most of the fastenings used for the planking were of wood, the iron saved could be used for other purposes such as guns. It was also much easier to fit gun ports to a hull built in this way, a crucial feature of warship construction in particular. There was an important variation in the procedures used to construct carvel-built ships in the northern Netherlands, which may have evolved out of cog-type construction methods, but currently little clear evidence of this style of construction is documented from England. There was no sign of this method being used at the Deptford yard despite other evidence from the area of widespread trade contacts with the Low Countries.

In some ways the clinker building technique – still used in a modified version for a few small traditional wooden boats in England – was a form of wooden sculpture guided by some traditional 'rules of thumb' and the skilled eye of the boatbuilder. It seems that drawings were not used. However, in carvel shipbuilding, particularly in the building of large royal vessels in England, drawings or 'drafts' were employed at least by the later 16th century. These ship drafts were used to aid the planning and building of vessels to regular, repeatable shapes, and so that they could have more closely measurable capacities.

The best known of the early 'master shipwrights' associated with this new 'drawings-first' approach was Mathew Baker who visited Italy and learned new approaches to ship designing (sets of his drawings and notes made from the 1570s survive and are usually known as the *Fragments of ancient English shipwrightry*: Johnston 2005, 107–65). He carried out ship design work by royal appointment from 1572, using rigorous rules of proportion and accurate scale drawing instruments, and is documented as working at the Deptford yard in particular where he was responsible for designing and planning the

building of several large naval vessels in the later 16th century (Adams 2003, 106).

This senior master shipwright was to become the first head of the new Shipwrights' guild at the turn of the 16th and 17th centuries. John Wells was a younger associate of Mathew Baker who also mainly worked at the Deptford yard. He added to existing advice notes on ship design started by Baker in the 1570s. These included quite complex mathematics in addition to the geometric methods Baker developed, but it is not known how widely such an approach was used. In most of England this new carvel style of shipbuilding was reserved for large ships initially, but began to be used for some medium-sized craft by the 17th century. However, in the London region workers in the old clinker style and builders of upriver barges did not adopt the new technology for centuries. It is clear that there was friction and something of a divide between them and the newfangled carvel shipbuilders working to the east of the City of London; there were no large carvel shipyards in the City itself due to lack of space, nor large dry docks or slipways.

The construction of carvel-built ships in the 17th to mid 19th centuries

Damian Goodburn

Details of how the earliest carvel-built naval ships were constructed during the first half of the 16th century are still the subject of forensic investigation (Adams 2003, 127; Marsden 2009). However, from around the mid 17th century to the end of large wooden shipbuilding on the Thames, the general stages of the work are largely understood and are summarised below.

Following the setting of the specifications and the preparation of drawings for building a particular naval ship, the drawing was extended to full size on a large wooden floor. Very often this was an upper floor by the 18th century and therefore the process is called 'lofting' in nautical English (as in the extant mid 18th-century, first-floor 'mould loft' at Chatham Historic Dockyard: Coad 1973). Light, portable, wooden patterns or 'moulds' were then made of many key timber elements of the ship – particularly the crosswise, curved frame timbers – and used by the shipwrights to find the timbers closest in size and shape to those desired. The naturally curved, 'grown' or 'compass' timber, in which the fibres of wood had grown to a curve, was much stronger and usable with less waste than straight timber. Straighter timbers were also needed for backbone components, hull and deck planking and longitudinal elements. By the late 18th century these straighter, more standardised elements were stored in specialised louvered 'timber sheds' (examples of which survive at Chatham dockyard). This allowed air to circulate around the timber to 'season' or dry it out to some extent, reducing shrinkage and splitting on the finished ship, but was less important for the internal framing. Building ships in the open could take years and left the incomplete hulls vulnerable to all weathers and prey to rot. This was largely solved by the construction of slip roofs in all the royal yards from 1815 (Chapter 7.3 and 7.4).

It is clear that compass timber was often partially shaped to the desired thickness or 'sided dimension', that is, two faces were cut by shaping with axes ('hewing') and/or pit-sawing to be flat and fairly parallel to each other. Compass timber of similar thickness and shape was stacked together in open spaces where the shipwrights could lay their patterns down on the flattened timbers and mark out the various curved edges needed, following the mould's shape. In a large vessel the thickest framing (ie with the greatest siding) was used lowest in the vessel and the thinner timbers were used progressively higher up. Such dispersed stacks of timber can be seen in the 1774 scale model and some of the early pictorial views of the Deptford yard (eg Fig 68; Fig 140). Labourers, junior shipwrights and sawyers would then cut out the curved frame timbers and similar elements for final trimming and smoothing on the ship with adzes (Goodburn 1999). Evidence from other Thameside dockyards and the Deptford yard itself, and comments in some naval treatises, show that by *c* 1800 more of the work of converting logs or imported 'baulks' of timber (squared logs) into planks or slices of thicker timber was being done with the use of various types of pit saws than by shaping or 'hewing' with axes, as in earlier periods. The saw pits are small but key features shown on most of the historic maps of the Deptford yard. Sawyers were the second most numerous craftsmen in the yard after the shipwrights. Pit sawyers normally worked in pairs as generally two workers were required to use the saws – one standing on top of the timber and one (or more) in the pit or below a platform. The steam-driven Brunel sawmill at Chatham did not start operating until 1814 (Coad 2013, 126–7).

Once the framework of the ship was at least partially erected on the backbone of keel and end posts, the shipwrights could start fitting the hull planking and internal strengthening timbers together with the deck framing and the like. Scaffolding and a ramp system of some kind (Fig 7; Fig 113; Fig 140; Chapter 7.4), together with mobile winches, generally of the vertical capstan type, were used with block and tackles to raise up all the heavy timbers. Any planking that had to be bent to a curve was softened first. For this, localised charring was largely superseded by boiling troughs by the early 18th century and the latter, in turn, were replaced by steaming kilns (J Coad, pers comm 2015). Until well into the 19th century, both troughs and kilns operated in most of the yards. The planking was then measured, shaped and fastened with a range of specialised wooden pegs ('treenails'). The gaps between hull and deck planks were next made watertight by driving in rope fibre with pitch poured over it to seal any gaps and waterproof it ('caulking'). Then the hulls were tarred and/or painted, and some sheathed in either thin planking or latterly copper sheet below the waterline (Chapter 4.2; below, 'Large wooden shipbuilding in the late 18th to 19th centuries').

Much of the further fitting out, masting and rigging of the new hulls was carried out afloat. Often this was at the Woolwich yard for Deptford-built vessels, but presumably the large wet dock was also used for this purpose at Deptford. Within as little as a year, wooden ships required regular maintenance, and after a few years of running aground or seeing military action they would have required more extensive repair or even rebuilding. The chief enemies were dry or wet rot. Construction, repairs and alterations were part of the regular work of the Deptford yard, although lighter maintenance was more conveniently carried out at yards less far up tidal rivers. One of the aims of the recording of the woodwork and related finds from the Convoys Wharf site was to examine archaeological evidence for the different stages in these processes and for any changes over time.

Innovations at the yard, 17th to 18th centuries

Antony Francis

Being the closest yard to London and also having the facility of a wet dock, Deptford was frequently used for maritime experiments, of which a selection are outlined here. Perhaps the most famous was John Evelyn's diving bell: 'We tried our Diving-Bell, or engine, in the water dock at Deptford, in which our curator continued half an hour under water; it was made of cast lead, let down with a strong cable' (*Evelyn diary*, 19 July 1661).

Sir William Petty designed a ship with two hulls whose prototype had performed well (*Pepys diary*, 31 July 1663; 22 January 1664). The king attended the launch at the yard in late 1664, naming the sloop the *Experiment* (*Evelyn diary*, 22 December 1664). The vessel was 'lost in the Bay of Biscay in a storm' according to Evelyn (ibid, 22 March 1675).

In 1728, a proposal was made by a Mr Pain 'for mending and preparing iron for building His Majesty's ships'. The officers were dismissive – 'about twenty years since', Ambrose Crowley had provided 'mill'd bolts of several sizes' for merchant and navy ships. At first the idea had seemed 'very good and beneficial', but it turned out not to be – why, we are not told. Nevertheless, the officers were prepared to help 'if the gentleman would try it at his own charge' (TNA, ADM 106/3301, 17 March 1729, 117). Whether Pain's proposal involved bolts, as the officers suggest, or some other use of iron in ships is not revealed.

In August 1752, 'a machine invented by Hans Sybram for working underwater on the bottom of ships' was considered by the officers at the yard. This seems to have been a canvas diving machine, potentially of great importance as it would save ships having to dock for repairs. The officers were unimpressed: '[T]he canvas will by no means keep off the pressure of the water from his body, and … a leather one will be attended by the same inconveniency; we are of the opinion that no person can continue enclosed in such a machine under water to work on the bottom of a ship' (TNA, ADM 106/3309, 8 August 1752, 76).

John Schank, who was an officer at the yard in the 1790s, devised a retractable 'dagger board' keel for added ship stability. The survey brig *Lady Nelson* was fitted at the yard with this type of keel and later undertook a two-year voyage to map the Australian coast; she was destroyed in 1825 off Timor (Colledge and Warlow 2010). Although there was initial enthusiasm for

Fig 140 Panoramic view of the Deptford dockyard c 1794 in an oil painting by Joseph Farington for the Navy Board, showing the yard at work, with (left to right, on the river frontage) the dry (double) dock, the quadrangle storehouse, slipways (nos 5 and 4), the wet dock, slipway (no. 1) and the small mast dock (with the large mast dock behind, far right), together with (top left and right) stacks of timber laid out according to size and form; the officers' quarters are far left, ships at various stages of construction occupy all the docks and slips, and in front of the dockyard's wharfs and jetties are moored a large number of ships in ordinary (National Maritime Museum, Greenwich, BHC1874)

the idea, the problem of water leakage through the hull could not be remedied and the design was abandoned (Drowser 2005, x, 125–7).

In October 1795 the officers were exploring the use of iron knees for two frigates they were building, as they were short of wooden knees. They asked the Navy Board for permission to use 'iron hanging and lodging knees for their Upper and Quarterdecks' which could be supplied by a Mr Gordon, 'the Yard's Smiths being too busy' (TNA, ADM 106/3324, 4 October 1795, 37; 6 October 1795, 33). This was a time when iron was used increasingly in wooden ships.

Large wooden shipbuilding in the late 18th to 19th centuries

Damian Goodburn and Antony Francis

From the mid 17th to the end of the 18th centuries there were relatively few basic changes in naval shipbuilding processes, although copper sheathing to reduce marine borer damage and fouling with weed was widely introduced from *c* 1780, particularly for vessels sailing to warmer waters; sheathing with copper, lead and brass were experimented with between the 16th and 18th centuries, and extra planking was also tried (Cock 2001; Chapter 4.2). In 1811 R Seppings considerably revised the framing systems used in large naval vessels, introducing diagonal strapping for increased strength which allowed longer timber-hulled vessels to be built (Lavery 1991, 83). Other innovations around the same time included the use of straighter, more easily transported timber for cutting into curved oak frame elements, while iron knees increasingly replaced timber ones. Seppings was also behind the settling of ships in dock on a row of iron wedges, rather than directly on the dock bottom (Knight 2013, 155).

Steam power was first used in naval vessels on the Thames in bucket dredgers used to keep open the rapidly silting entrances to the Deptford and Woolwich yards. While initially steam power was used alongside sail to propel large naval vessels, it gradually became dominant, especially when screw propellers replaced paddle wheels and engines became more reliable and efficient. In its last period of operation during the 1850s and 1860s, the Deptford yard specialised in building large wooden-hulled vessels with steam screw power and auxiliary sails. Two of these vessels also had iron armour added over the wooden hull in 1864 ('ironclads') but otherwise the yard carried out relatively little naval iron working, and the steam plant was generally fitted downstream at the Woolwich naval yard (Chapter 7.4, 'The yard reopens, 1843'). The Deptford yard is not documented as converting to the building of iron vessels, and this tends to be corroborated by the lack of diagnostic archaeological finds such as rivets for iron hull plates or plate offcuts, which have been found at some mid 19th-century Thames dockyard sites.

The first practical steam vessel built by the Royal Navy in any of the government dockyards, the 115ft × 21ft, three-gun wooden paddle steamer *Comet* (238bm-tons), was launched at Deptford in 1822 (MacDougall 1982, 144; Colledge and Warlow 2010; Lambert 2012, 95). Another wooden paddle vessel, the 126ft × 23ft, three-gun *Lightening* (296bm-tons), was launched in 1823 and subsequently fought pirates off the Barbary Coast (MacDougall 1982, 147).

The last vessel launched (in the presence of members of the royal family) at the yard was the 220ft × 36ft wooden screw corvette *Druid* (1322bm-tons), a timber-hulled, steam-powered vessel classed as a 'sloop', with a fully laden depth in the water ('draught') of 22ft (Fig 141; Chapter 7.4, 'Final closure of the dockyard, 1869'). The *Druid*'s tonnage was under half that of the very largest naval vessels of the mid 19th century, which were almost all built and maintained closer to deeper water (Lambert 2012, 96).

When the yard closed in 1869, large-scale woodworking did not entirely cease. Features such as the slipways, dry docks and the wet dock were infilled and buildings erected over them. Many new timber foundation structures were created to support the new warehouses, principally trestles and large piles. The trestle foundations incorporated second-hand ship timbers which must have derived from early 19th-century vessels, probably including some built or repaired at the yard.

Maritime industrial debris

Damian Goodburn

The value of targeted archaeological investigations of craft and industrial debris associated with London's post-medieval maritime zone has been recognised for several years and they have been productively pursued as part of some projects (Williams and Brown 1999; Pitt and Goodburn 2003; Divers 2004). It is clear, however, that the Deptford yard was kept unusually tidy, with relatively little diagnostic waste or 'maritime industrial debris' being allowed to build up compared to the practice evident in some other Thameside shipyards. On other sites, some clusters of debris have been found to be diagnostic of particular activities such as rigging block making or removal of underwater sheathing planking and so on (eg Pitt and Goodburn 2003, 204; Divers 2004, 79). Some deposits have also shed light on the details of the gradual mechanisation of shipbuilding from the end of the 18th century.

Although small, the debris samples – such as fastenings, offcuts and tar – taken at the site repay further examination. Most of the fastenings found were large iron nails or 'spikes' but sections of drift bolts and forelock bolts of iron were also found; non-ferrous fastenings included small copper sheathing nails, and copper-alloy false keel dog fragments (Chapter 10.6, 'Objects associated with transport, buildings and services'). Of note too are the tools and fittings that were found, both of metal and oak as well as other timber species, including for example metal dividers (<545>), compasses (<S30>, Fig 191) and chisels (<S29>, Fig 30; <228>) (Chapter 10.6, 'General tools'). Several neatly made oak and tropical hardwood wedges were found (eg <749>) – some of the hundreds in use in the building and repair of vessels in the Deptford yard – and examples of

Fig 141 The launch of the wood screw corvette Druid, *the last ship built at Deptford: Princess Louise releasing the dog-shore* (ILN, *20 March 1869) (Look and Learn)*

fibrous caulking material (<41>, <645>) were also recovered.

Relatively few rigging fittings were recovered during the excavations but several lignum vitae pulley block sheaves were found, such as <S22> (Fig 189), as well as a parrel bead (<S23>, Fig 189) and a rigging cleat fastened to a rounded spar [4439].

Reused in two truncated oak trestle bases in the north-east corner of the brick wet dock, inside the new walls built for the Rennie-designed gateway (Chapter 7.3), were timbers with a double-taper shape in plan and bevelled corners, a form diagnostic of earlier 19th-century anchor stocks (the timber being set crosswise at the top of the iron anchor). They were widest in the middle, tapering towards each end and pierced by several oak treenails. One of these reused oak anchor stocks (timber [481]) was 3.60m long, 400mm wide and 160mm thick, with three through-mortices (Fig 142); another example also had several marks, of uncertain function, cut into its surface with a hooked marking knife. It is possible that some of these timbers were part of an unused stockpile of prepared or second-hand stocks, stored for the use of the anchor smiths.

Another timber ([5128]) was reused in a similar way and proved to be about two-thirds of an oak anchor stock (Fig 142). This timber had a distinctive recess which once housed a timber insert that surrounded the iron shank of the anchor. The pattern of bolt and treenail holes shows how this timber was once one of a matching pair that fitted across the top of the anchor.

Trestle foundation assemblies, comprising uprights and diagonal braces (many reused timber), were built into slipways no. 4 (S30) and no. 5 (S31) to support floors after the closure of the yard in 1869 (Chapter 8.2). Some of the braces showed signs of the previous use of new types of fastenings. In addition to oak treenails and iron spikes, they had large shallow, circular, countersunk holes which may well reflect the early use of machine-made fastenings and clench bolts (large rivet-ended bolts) in the early to mid 19th century, or possibly of wooden 'coaks' (short cylinders of tough timber used to help lock nautical timbers together where they joined or overlapped). Coaks and bolts were increasingly used towards the end of wooden shipbuilding to help make composite assemblies of timber stretch to larger sizes. Surprisingly, some of the bolt-washer or coak holes were neatly filled in with oak cask bungs, possibly before the second-hand timber was sold on for reuse. Many of these timbers showed clear evidence of nautical origins such as relict oak treenails and patterns of paint and even mouldings. For example, several of the post timbers were clearly originally sections of large ship deck beams of oak, with paint and mouldings on the two lower original corners and with the original upper faces marked by original deck plank nail holes. It is likely that many of these timbers ultimately derived from ships broken or repaired in the Deptford dockyard possibly via a first reuse in dockyard buildings. Some may therefore be as old as the mid or late 18th century. A parallel

[481]

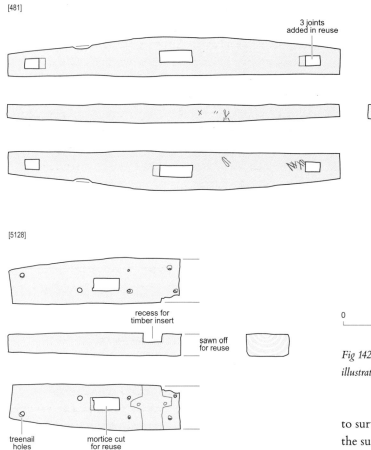

[5128]

recess for
timber insert

sawn off
for reuse

treenail
holes

mortice cut
for reuse

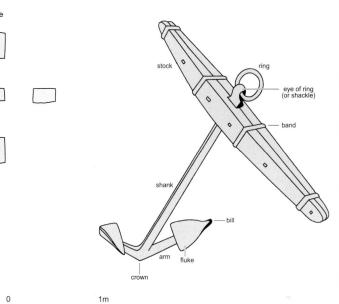

Fig 142 Oak anchor stocks timbers [481] and [5128] (scale 1:40), and (right) illustration of their use in an anchor (after Bowens 2009, 200)

may be the easily visible reuse of large oak ship deck beams as posts in 18th-century naval buildings at Chatham.

Conclusion

Damian Goodburn

Some concluding comments concerning the historic waterlogged woodwork revealed during the excavations at the former Deptford royal dockyard site seem in order and are influenced by recent attempts to summarise key research priorities in maritime, Thames estuary and coastal archaeology research (Williams and Brown 1999; Ransley and Sturt 2013). It must be clearly stated that the project did not furnish data to address the question of how the transition from building large clinker-built ships of the late medieval to early Tudor period to the new carvel-built ships like the *Mary Rose* took place. The material evidence was just a little too late in date. However, some details of the early Tudor naval yard did come to light and have been described, such as the original timber-framed construction of the Tudor storehouse (B1; Chapter 3.2). Small sections of Thames timber frontages of the 16th century and 17th to early 18th centuries were also exposed (Chapters 3.2 and 4.2).

The material evidence for heavy dockyard carpentry, influenced by the shipwrights' work, for the 17th to early 19th centuries was recorded in some detail, and describing aspects of that work, comparing it with other nearby sites and relating it

to surviving documentary evidence has been a central aim of the summary analysis (above, and Chapter 10.7). Elements of construction procedures, tool kits and logistics have been summarised, highlighting some of the effects of early industrialisation in the later structures. These include the widespread use of iron fastenings and reinforcing straps, and eventually the use of brick to replace some of the timberwork and the application of early machine sawing.

9.3   Life outside the dockyard

Through piecemeal acquisition, the royal dockyard expanded over the centuries eastwards towards Deptford Creek, taking in property east of a line from the Master Shipwright's house to the officers' quarters (Fig 6). However, properties outside the yard wall east of Orchard Place and fronting King Street were apparently never acquired by the Navy Board; some time after the closure of the dockyard in 1869 they were acquired by the Foreign Cattle Market and demolished. In consequence, part of the site included areas which had at one time or another lain outside the yard's perimeter wall (Fig 143). The artefact assemblages recovered from this area are examined here for what they potentially suggest of the material culture and lifestyle of those occupying and using these properties in the mid 18th to 19th centuries, that is, overwhelmingly dockyard workers. These assemblages provide a valuable comparison with material from inside the yard.

In the extreme south-east part of the site, the remains of terraced buildings (B57) of mid 19th-century date were

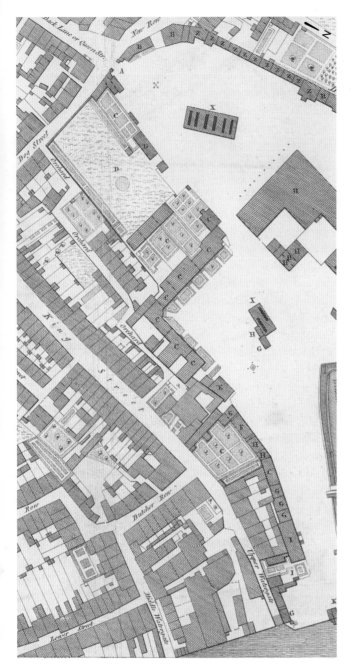

Fig 143 Detail of the east side of the yard on Milton's map of 1753 (Fig 58) (not to scale)

uncovered. This terrace lay outside the original extent of the dockyard and lined up with modern Barnes Terrace outside the site. The buildings were probably part of Evelyn Row shown on the 1858 map (Fig 98).

On the east side of the dockyard: King Street and Orchard Place

Julian Bowsher

The north-eastern corner of the yard, on the riverfront, lay next to the Upper Watergate. This was the northernmost of three such gates, and also gave its name to a short street running southwards for *c* 93m. Here at the junction of Butchers Row

(renamed Borthwick Street in 1937) the roadway continued south under the name of King Street to Lower Road (now Evelyn Street). King Street became Old King Street in the 1840s after the construction of New King Street running parallel to the west, south of the yard. Finally, in 1875, the entire line of (Old) King Street to the river was renamed Watergate Street. Running west from King Street was Dog Street, later Dock Street and, from 1912, Princes (Prince) Street, which formed the south boundary of the yard. However, the eastern boundary was set back from King/Watergate Street itself. As far as can be seen, domestic occupation never encroached on the northernmost stretch, along the original Watergate. At the junction of King Street and Dog Street, houses on the street front were separated from the yard by Orchard Place which zigzagged north-eastwards before rejoining King Street next to the gateway into the yard. The outline of the yard boundary can be seen in the plan of 1698 (Fig 23, 'B' right) with the gateway extending eastwards to the line of King Street. No properties along this side of King Street are shown, although this reflects not their absence but the fact that the royal dockyard did not *own* properties beyond their wall. Despite fears of filth and fire from adjacent properties, the Navy Board resisted all offers to extend its control eastwards. An undated 18th-century map (LMA, COL/PL/01/048/C/219), however, shows that the unencumbered open plot immediately north of the King Street gateway was in the hands of the 'Commissioner of the Navy'. By *c* 1800 most of that stretch, up to the river, was in the navy's hands although it was largely open ground (Fig 143).

Our interest lies in the excavations within a distinct block of properties that fronted King Street to the east, with yards, and possible privies, backing on to Orchard Place to the west. In its final 19th-century configuration, this block measured approximately 37m north–south by 17m east–west. The excavations defined what must be the back walls of the northernmost houses in this block (B9), with cesspits in yards/gardens behind (OA9 and OA8) (below). The excavation area here encompassed not only part of this block and Orchard Place but also the yard perimeter wall and the officers' quarters inside (B10) (Chapter 4.2, 'Rebuilding the officers' quarters, late 17th century'; Fig 40; Fig 41; Fig 144).

Already in 1734 the Navy Board bought six houses adjacent to the yard; these were 'obtained for £749, pulled down and the ground inclosed' (Oppenheim 1926, 368). These properties may have been at the north-western end of Upper Watergate Street where much open ground is seen on Milton's 1753 map (Fig 143) in front of the row of various offices. Of more importance to the location of both Building 9 and Building 10 as uncovered in the excavations are the 'several small tenements situate in a place called the Orchard in the Town of Deptford, belonging to Mrs Wickham, whose chimneys joyn two of the said officers lodgings' described in 1743, which were 'daily lyable to set on fire the whole Range of Buildings, and too probably endanger his Majesty's Magazines of stores, and those ships building in the yard' (NMM, ADM B 123; Oppenheim 1926, 368, citing Navy Board minutes, 28 October 1743). However, 'six tenements adjacent to the officers residence in a place called the

Orchard' were bought in 1744 for £350 (ibid, 368, citing Navy Board minutes, 10 October 1744) are likely to have lain south of the excavation area.

In September 1745 the Navy Board was asked if a brick drain might be built to convey waste water from the scullery of the Globe tavern (also held by Mrs Wickham) to King Street; it was reminded of this request two weeks later (TNA, ADM 106/1006/371, /379). The Globe was of some antiquity, being visited by Samuel Pepys who had dinner there with captains Terne and Berkeley in the winter of 1663 (*Pepys diary*, 18 November 1663). In 1699 payment was demanded by two local women 'for a washhouse built in the yard of the Globe Tavern for the Surgeon of the Dockyard' (TNA, ADM 106/525/283). The Surgeon's house is identified on two plans of 1698 (Fig 40) almost directly behind, or possibly just north-west of, the properties in which the excavations took place. Such proximity makes this part of the site a prime candidate for the location of the Globe tavern. The yard's involvement with the washhouse and drains suggests that the Globe was perhaps under some sort of naval interest, but later documents clearly indicate that it was not actually owned by the Navy Board.

The Deptford dockyard appears to have been particularly prone to fire and outbreaks are recorded in June 1738, July 1739, March 1742 and January 1749 (Oppenheim 1926, 369, 370, 373). The yard authorities maintained that the greatest such threat came from outside the walls, and another 'alehouse' further north was the scene of a fire, potentially dangerous to the yard, in January 1761 (Chapter 6.3, 'Maintenance and repairs, early 1760s'). This was the (old) Red Lyon which abutted the boatswain's house. Another fire started at the Globe in July 1783 and did extend into the yard (NMM, ADM B 227; below).

There were a number of pubs in the area, the oldest of which was the Globe, with the 'old' Red Lyon/Lion further north. From at least May 1747 the latter was known as the Old Red Lion, as William Williams, the landlord, advertised that 'he is removed from the Old Red-lion in King Street, Deptford, to the New Red Lion and City Arms, on the other side of the way' (*Penny London Post*, issue 625), clearly located at the corner of Butchers Row and Watergate Street on late 19th-century maps, including Goad's map of 1870 (Fig 129) and the 1894 Ordnance Survey map. This new Red Lion was only a few doors north of the Red Cow, with both almost opposite our 'block', on the east side of King Street. In the summer of 1770 the officers suggested enclosing two pieces of land at the east end of the yard. One of these fronted King Street and was leased from the City of London, while the other adjoining plot had been 'lately purchased' from 'Mrs Hally and two Miss Lovings'. The officers proposed building a brick wall the same height as the boundary wall around this land, apart from 'the south east side next the ground where the Red Lyon stood' which could be enclosed with a wooden fence. The cost would be £94 5s (TNA, ADM 106/3316, 4 August 1770, 83).

In October 1764 'Three Messuages or tenements (formerly two) with ground & Buildings backwards in King street near the water Gate … and abutting on the King's Yard' were also offered to the Navy Commissioners. The plot was described as 'containing from North to south at the east end fronting King street in Deptford aforesaid thirty eight feet ten inches [11.90m] of assize, and from east to west abutting south seventy one feet six inches [21.80m] of assize, and from south to north at the west end forty one feet [12.50m] of assize and abutting on the King's Yard there, and from west to east abutting north seventy one feet [21.60m] of assize'. However attractive it may be to see this parcel 'near the water gate' in the vicinity of the excavations, the measurements cannot be placed there.

Another offer arose in April 1786 when the Globe was described as 'adjoining to His Majesty's Yard there being long thought an Evil and even dangerous to his Majesty's Premises'. The agent wrote to the Navy Board, noting that it 'is not now used as a tavern but let to a person who lets it out in lodgings which the owners not approving are unwilling to repair it, but have had an offer from a person in Deptford to take it down and build five or six new houses on the ground on a building lease, but before anything is done in the matter the owner has desired that I will make your honours the first offer on it' (TNA, ADM 106/1286/363). On the back of the letter was recorded 'The Board have no occasion on it'.

Further opportunity, in the same area, arose in May 1807 when the Tyrwhitt Drake family were prepared to sell 'some premises contiguous to, and adjoining this Yard', of which the naval surveyor noted that: 'To add the space occupied by these premises to His Majesty's Yard appears to me an object of considerable importance, as well to prevent the danger liable from fire, and the opportunity for fulfilling, as to remove a long standing nuisance to the Yard' (NMM, ADM B 227). The premises were further described by Matthew Ffinch the agent as 'a place called the Orchard which adjoins the Dockyard Wall and which may be purchased by Government, if required'. Two days later the premises were further defined as 'the seven houses with gardens and in the Orchard' which could be had for 800 guineas and 'the premises late the Globe Tavern' for 1200 guineas. The houses at least were occupied by sailmakers, boatbuilders and shipwrights working for the yard. The concluding remarks by the yard surveyor and other officers are worth quoting at length for the state of the King Street properties in 1807, their history and the danger they posed to the yard:

> We beg leave to acquaint you that some houses in King Street are built close to the Yard Wall, and we consider it would be of the most important advantage for the preservation of this arsenal and the stores contained in it that there should be a road quite round it, to prevent the possibility of it being endangered by fire from without; and that if an accident of that nature should happen within the engines might be brought to act in every direction the house in particular known by the name of the Globe Tavern, which abuts close upon the back part of the Commissioner's Office and projects in part into the yard is a common Lodging House, every room containing a family, the windows of which look into the yard, and that it was extremely dangerous was proved when part of it caught fire in the year 1783. The fire penetrated to the Engine House by the Old Gate, the roof of which was entirely

destroyed; the officers lodgings were in great danger and it was found necessary for their preservation to remove the Books & Papers &c from the Clerk of the Cheques office; we beg leave to subjoin a [copy] of the officer's letter to the Board dated 16th July 1783 on the subject.

The old Houses which abut upon the Lodgings late inhabited by the Clerk of the Cheque, run close to the Yard wall, and one or two persons some years ago were discovered to have got from thence into the sailfield and into the Master Attendant's Lodgings; since which a watchman has been placed there in order to guard that part of the yard and the officers lodgings from depredations.

In addition to the premises offered by Mr Ffinch, there is at the lower part of King's Street close to the Water gate a brick Public house, and two very old weather boarded Houses adjoining; the outhouses of which are close up to the Yard wall, and should a fire happen there can be little doubt but the Master Shipwright's Lodgings must suffer from whence it might communicate to the Ships in dock and then to the Storehouse.

The inconveniences and nuisances are too numerous to mention, but may very readily be conjectured when it is known that the windows of the houses overlook the Yard wall and their Privies & are close to it, the filth of which in one or two instances penetrates the earth and rises inside the Yard.

The propriety of keeping buildings at a distance from the Yard were mentioned in the Officers letter of the 2nd and 30th March 1798 which was accompanied by a plan of that part of King's Street; but more particularly so in that which was transmitted to the board by the Officers sometime in the winter of 1804 or early 1805, to which letters we beg leave to refer the Board. (NMM, ADM B 227)

Evidence for the development of this extramural area is fragmentary and there are no detailed maps of it between 1753 (Fig 143) and the 1868 Ordnance Survey map (Fig 128). General maps, however, appear to show buildings along the street front, while dockyard plans continue to show most of the extramural areas blank. The buildings within our 'block' were clearly rebuilt over time and the contents of the cesspits in the back yards of Building 9 (below) suggest changes in the mid 18th century and the 1820s/30s. A late 19th-century photograph of this stretch, with the Bull and Butcher prominently in the middle, shows typical Victorian terraces that might be as early as the 1830s (ODH).

Identifying the function and occupancy of these houses would be important for placing the material remains from the cesspits within a social context. Unfortunately, the rate books for the late 18th and early 19th centuries do not provide sufficient detail to establish which house was which, but they do appear to be mostly tenanted rather than owner-occupied, and although names are given their occupations are not. Census returns, from 1838 onwards, are again difficult to place, particularly for the northernmost stretch containing Building 9. The stretch to the south, down to Princes Street and which included the Bull and Butcher public house in the centre of it, shows multiple occupancies giving the impression that the area was overcrowded. Here, the occupations were, unsurprisingly, dominated by labourers – often specified as dock labourers, stevedores as well as watermen, lightermen and mariners. Other trades included butcher, fishmonger, greengrocer and tobacconist.

It would appear that throughout the 18th and 19th centuries neither the area of the excavated Building 9 nor the properties to the east of it were ever actually part of the yard, as the navy continually declined to expend further funds to increase their property holding in the area despite cogent arguments for doing so. Much of the area was owned throughout the 18th and early 19th centuries by the Tyrwhitt Drake family whose papers survive (LMA, E/TD). After the dockyard closed in 1869 the site was purchased for the Foreign Cattle Market in 1870. The entire street was renamed Watergate Street in 1875, and in 1881 house numbers were made more regular, with the sequence on the west side running from 1 at the southern end to 125 at the northern (Post Office 1881ff). By the late 19th century our 'block', therefore, comprised six houses numbered unevenly 113 to 125 (1894 Ordnance Survey map). The excavation of Building 9 thus covered the sites of house numbers 121, 123 and 125. The Ordnance Survey map of 1916 (Fig 130) shows a large part of the Orchard and King Street area incorporated within the cattle market site. Some time between the 1894 and 1916 Ordnance Survey maps the entire block had been demolished, although the dates of acquisition and final clearance are at present not known (to the present writer), despite searching through the extensive Foreign Cattle Market archives in the London Metropolitan Archives (LMA, CLA/012).

King Street cesspit assemblages and material culture

with contributions by Lyn Blackmore (glass, accessioned finds), Nigel Jeffries (pottery), Jacqui Pearce (clay tobacco pipe) and Alan Pipe (animal bone)

A number of cesspits and other features identified just outside the dockyard wall (OA8, OA9) (Fig 143; Fig 144; Fig 146) provide insights into the life of the residents. Map regression indicates that the brick walls (B9, Fig 144) correspond to the rear walls of properties fronting King Street, now Watergate Street, and locates the cesspits and other features in outbuildings and other structures at the rear of what are shown in 1753 as narrow rectangular properties backing on to the narrow street ('Orchard') running parallel to the east perimeter wall of the yard. The material recovered from the cesspits represents waste discarded by occupants of the King Street properties and customers of the public houses – most likely men employed in the dockyard (above). The filling in the 1820s (dated by the artefacts recovered) of two of the cesspits (apparently in adjacent properties) is contemporary with the closure of the dockyard in 1830, although the dockyard was still occupied and maintenance work continued (Chapter 7.4). The contents of four cesspits – two filled in the mid 18th century ([5994],

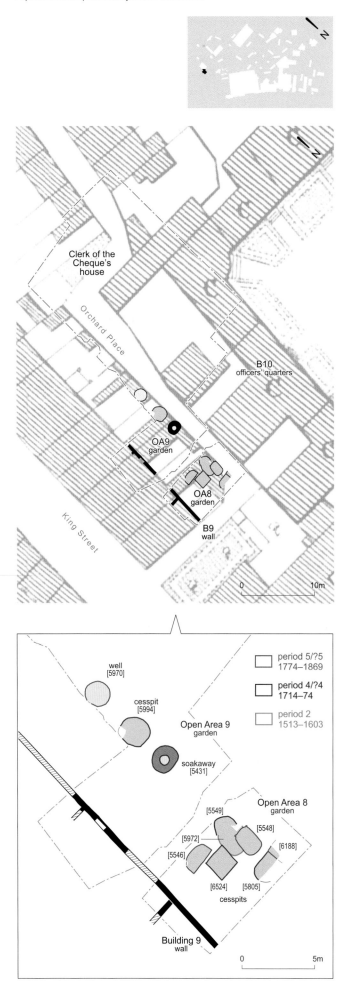

[6524]) and two filled in the 1820s ([5546], [5548]) – are detailed below. Finds from other features are also discussed.

These cesspits were generally brick-lined (Fig 146) and contained faunal remains and artefacts from their last use. The artefacts discarded in these features would typically have been unwanted and/or damaged, and in the main represent dumping to fill in such features when they were abandoned. There is, naturally, a strong emphasis in such discard groups on durable inorganic materials – ceramics, glass, clay pipes – rather than wooden or other organic objects. Household artefacts are generally unlikely to have been of monetary or other – for example, sentimental – value when discarded. If thrown away more or less complete, they may have been perceived as old-fashioned or not of great value and so disposable, for example everyday crockery or personal items (Harward et al 2015, 7–14). The cesspits potentially reflect a particular social context and material culture – the Royal Navy's employees on shore, as opposed to those at sea (cf Colville 2009 for how these distinctions translate to the interwar period, 1918–39). However, much material could occur in accommodation both inside and outside the dockyard (eg cooking vessels) with little differentiation regarding social context.

The household and other items discarded in these cesspits and other features tell an interesting, if partial, story, and one unique in the context of the excavated site: clay tobacco pipe and glassware are only present in large quantities in the cesspits. The substantial amount of imported ceramics (Chinese porcelain (CHPO), Dutch and Portuguese tin-glazed wares (DTGW, POTG)), particularly from the 18th-century cesspits, must reflect the global reach of both the navy and merchant companies (Chapter 10.3). In the 19th century plain creamware (CREA) appears to have been the principal dinner crockery in use, with blue transfer-printed pearlwares (PEAR) providing the bulk of the tea wares, reflecting a general shift to British-made fine wares. By way of contrast, in both periods the clay tobacco pipes were overwhelmingly made locally. The animal bone recovered indicates a diet of beef, mutton, pork and chicken, and occasionally fish, domestic goose, domestic duck (or mallard) and rabbit. The fish eaten were marine/estuarine species, mainly cod and plaice, as one might expect from the yard's Thames-side location; game was extremely sparse and generally represented by rabbit (Chapter 10.8).

It is possible that cesspit [5994] and/or cesspit [6524], filled with mid 18th-century waste, were associated in some way with the Globe tavern which is documented in this area; the Globe had apparently changed function from a tavern to lodgings by 1786 and thereafter may have been demolished and replaced by 'five or six new houses' (above, 'On the east side of the dockyard: King Street and Orchard Place'). The disuse fill of

Fig 144 Plan of principal archaeological features on the east side of the yard (located on inset of the site, see Fig 3), showing remains of the officers' quarters and properties east of the yard, overlain on the 1753 map (Fig 58) (scale 1:500), with (lower) detail of the cesspits and other features (scale 1:250)

the more southern cesspit [5994] contained material dated to
c 1730–60 and that of cesspit [6524] material dated to *c* 1730–80,
including clay tobacco pipe probably dating to after 1764
(below); both contained imported ceramics, including Chinese
porcelain, but [6254] produced a particularly large group of
18th-century Chinese porcelain. The finds from these two
features are typically seen today as suggestive of wealthier
ownership, although they were found outside the yard and are
not directly associated with those of higher social standing who
lived in the officers' quarters. It is known that Chinese porcelain
tea wares were used in some coaching inns by the late 18th
century (eg the King's Arms in Uxbridge: Pearce 2000), and it is
possible that there were rooms in the Globe where more refined
tastes could be catered for in style (J Pearce, pers comm 2015).

Cesspit [5994], filled in the mid 18th century (*c* 1730–60; period 4)

Cesspit [5994] (OA9, Fig 144) was a circular brick-lined pit
2.00m in diameter. It contained three distinct fills, the lowest of
gravelly silt [5935] that was sealed by sand and gravel [5934],
with an uppermost fill of clayey silty sand [5610]. The bulk of
the finds come from the lowest fill [5935] and comprise mainly
pottery, dating to the first decade of the 18th century, and clay
tobacco pipes, ranging in date from the late 17th century to
c 1730–60. The pottery from [5935] survived in a better
condition than that from deposits associated with the Stuart
dockyard (period 3; Chapter 4.2); while some vessels are
represented by single sherds only, the group is characterised by
either whole or reconstructable profiles and joining sherds. This
group dates to *c* 1700–10 and its condition suggests that the
pottery may have continued in use before being discarded in the
mid 18th century, rather than being thrown out earlier. Other
than the four marked clay pipes noted below, this feature
contained no accessioned finds and glass is limited to two
fragments from a small flask (cf Noël Hume 1969, fig 17 no. 9,
dated to *c* 1710), four from different phials, four from a jar and
seven fragments from a window.

This was a particularly rich group of ceramics, with an
emphasis on decorated tablewares and sanitary wares. Tin-
glazed ware – either imported from Portugal (POTG) or plain
and decorated London-made (TGW) – constitutes a significant
proportion (14) of the 31 vessels (90 sherds, 6794g), with the
remainder largely comprising Surrey-Hampshire border white
wares (BORD etc) and red wares (RBOR etc).

The four Portuguese tin-glazed ware (POTG) *pratos* or
dishes (<P3>, <P4>, Fig 145) are decorated in Chinese-inspired
styles with the rim divided into panelled borders displaying
alternating, seated, Chinese figures and stylised foliage. Made in
any one of the up to 28 kilns centred around Lisbon, these
potters were directly influenced by Chinese blue and white
porcelain decorated in the late Ming style and traded at the
same time. Sherds from Portuguese dishes of this type are not
uncommon on riverside archaeological sites in London (Jarrett
2005, figs 23 no. 5, 25 no. 12, 25 no. 14, 26 no. 15, 28 nos
25–31; Meddens 2008, inside back cover, nos 35–7), although

<P3>

<P4>

<P5>

Fig 145 *Portuguese tin-glazed ware
(POTG) dishes <P3> and <P4> and a
London-made tin-glazed ware (TGW
G) capuchine cup <P5> from cesspit
[5994] (scale c 1:2)*

finding a group of them together in one context is most unusual, and collectively these carefully made pieces would have made an attractive table setting. Other decorative tablewares include the profile and a rim fragment of two London-made tin-glazed ware ('delftware'-type) 'cracknel' or lobed dishes, a shape apparently copying silverware (Britton 1987, 119, cat no. 64).

Two tea bowls and a capuchine cup were for hot drinks. The first tea bowl is in Chinese blue and white porcelain (CHPO BW) with an interlinked stylised floral decoration with a chrysanthemum head in the inside of the bowl; the second is a London-made tin-glazed ware, decorated in blue in a (stylised floral) style common in the late 17th century (TGW F). The capuchine cup (<P5>, Fig 145) is painted in the 'polychrome style' of bright reds, green and blue frequently attributed to one of the Lambeth pothouses after the *c* 1690s (TGW G: Orton and Pearce 1984, 56). Evidence for the storage and serving of alcoholic drinks is limited. The Staffordshire brown salt-glazed stoneware (STBRS) tankard with a band of combed decoration under the rim, a common feature of English stonewares during this period (eg from Fulham: Green 1999, 117, fig 94 no. 186), would have been used for drinking beer. A Frechen stoneware (FREC) *Bartmann* jug fragment has a medallion displaying an urn; a similar medallion design is found on pottery from the Dutch East India Company (VOC) ship *Vergulde Draek*, wrecked off western Australia in 1656 (Green 1977, 138, GT 822).

Evidence for diet was minimal from the cesspit. The uppermost fill [5610] produced a mandible (lower jaw) of subadult pig. Dental eruption and wear stages indicate a young animal probably slaughtered early in the second year of life. The mandible had been split along the mid line through the 'chin', probably during splitting of the head to allow access to the brain and tongue.

Also from this pit are a number of sanitary wares, vessels which survived as reconstructable profiles through joining sherds. First are four chamber pots, one a London-made tin-glazed ware with plain white glaze (TGW C) and two in Surrey-Hampshire border red ware (RBOR). The fourth is a Westerwald stoneware (WEST) chamber pot with a flanged rim; a product of the Rhenish stoneware industry, this vessel is atypical in being plain when most examples of this form usually carry applied decoration in the form of lion medallions or the crowned cipher of various English monarchs (Gaimster 1997, 252–3; Hurst et al 1986, 224–5). Also present is a stool pan in Surrey-Hampshire border white ware with clear (yellow) glaze (BORDY). The profiles of two London-area post-medieval red ware (PMR) large rounded dishes, externally sooted from being heated, are examples of other utilitarian vessels.

Smoking of tobacco is reflected in a group of 19 clay pipe bowls, 18 stem fragments and one mouthpiece recovered from the lowest fill [5935] of this cesspit. A latest date of deposition of *c* 1730–60 is indicated by four bowls of type OS11, along with five type AO25 pipes (*c* 1700–70), although there are also four earlier type AO20 and five AO22 pipes (*c* 1680–1710). None of the pipes is decorated and only four are marked, all type OS11, with the maker's initials moulded in relief on the

sides of the heel. Two appear to be marked 'IB' (John Bean, 1764–86) and two have the initials 'WM' with a crown above each. These stand for William Manby (III), recorded in 1719–63 in Green Dragon Alley, near Kidney Stairs, Limehouse (Oswald 1975, 142; Pearce 2013). The Manby family were prominent pipe manufacturers in the 18th century in east London, represented by several generations whose products are widely distributed across the East End, with the largest number so far recorded coming from a site excavated in Aldgate High Street (site code AL74), although these include few 'WM' pipes (Grew and Orton 1984, fig 43 nos 19–21).

Cesspit [6524], filled in the mid 18th century (*c* 1730–80/after 1764; period 4)

Cesspit [6524] (OA8, Fig 144; Fig 146) was a square brick-lined pit measuring 1.70m × 1.65m and 1.70m deep. In addition to a sand bedding [5544] for the brick lining, five further fills were identified. The lowest were a coarse sandy charcoal [5543] sealed by another charcoal-rich sandy fill [5417]; these were overlain by fills [4952], [4951] and [4928], the latter (upper) two containing high concentrations of slag.

Very few artefacts other than pottery and clay tobacco pipe were recovered from this feature, and most are household items with a narrower range than cesspit [5546] (below). Excluding building material and clay pipes, the only finds from the lowest fill [5543] are two small (plus one possible) fragments of window glass (total 7g). No finds were recovered from the next fill [5417], but the overlying deposit [4952] contained a wall tile <764> and both bulk and accessioned glass, as well as a large group of ceramics and a large number of clay tobacco pipes, 14 marked (below). Other activities are indicated by part of a glass inkwell <240> with heavy flanged rim (diameter 46 × 49mm) on a short cylindrical neck with a recessed area for the pen hole; none of the body survives. In addition there are two small pieces (1g) of window glass.

The various groups of clay tobacco pipe, ceramics and glasswares discarded as part of fill [4952] together suggest that disuse and filling-in of the cesspit occurred *c* 1730–80, with the nine clay pipes made by John Bean indicating deposition after 1764 (below). Pottery comprises the largest component, with up to 87 vessels (611 sherds, 7439g) discarded. This material was recovered in a good condition and includes vessel profiles with complete bases or larger joining sherds. Two elements of the pottery in particular – the tin-glazed ware and Chinese porcelain – are suggestive of pots discarded when still usable.

This is one of the largest groups of mid 18th-century Chinese porcelain (406 sherds, 56 ENV, 2447g) recovered from a single feature in over 40 years of archaeological investigations in London. Tea bowls, saucers and slop bowls for hot drinks predominate, with three decorative groups identified. All are typical of standard export wares from the imperial kilns at Jingdezhen and contemporary with the period of deposition. Chinese blue and white porcelain (CHPO BW) tea bowls (21 ENV) and saucers (8 ENV) form the first and largest decorative group and, while each individual piece can undoubtedly be

Fig 146 View of brick-lined cesspits of properties in King Street, east of the dockyard, looking north: clockwise from centre left, cesspits [5548], [6524], [5546] and (bottom left) possible cesspit [5549] (cf Fig 144)

better fitted within a defined style, these designs can be characterised as either similarly themed landscapes displaying combinations of pagodas, figures, mountains, lakeside, riverside and island scenes, or stylised floral sprays, sometimes identified as chrysanthemum, tree peony or bamboo. However, only four tea bowls and one saucer in this group match in terms of the design – a delicate floral pattern in white enamel applied around the base.

A second (but much smaller) component is represented by the three matched tea bowls and three saucers in Chinese Imari porcelain (CHPO IMARI: underglaze blue, overglaze iron-red enamel and gold, with the addition of an iron-dipped rim), presumably originally part of a larger set. The final decorative group is Chinese porcelain with *famille rose* decoration (CHPO ROSE), with floral patterns or figure designs: this comprises a greater variety of vessel types including a fluted milk or cream jug, a slop bowl and a punch bowl, as well as tea bowls (4) and saucers (5). Of note is an armorial piece, with the French inscription 'LAISSEZ MOI FAIRE' ('let me do it') in a wreath surmounted by a coat of arms comprising a lion rampant in the

upper right shield quarter and three fleurs-de-lis in the other three quarters (<P6>, Fig 147).

In addition to the Chinese porcelain, and presumably once used alongside, is a Dutch tin-glazed ware (DTGW) teapot (<P7>, Fig 148). Stylistically, this vessel – fluted, with blue dashes on the handle and decorated in a rich blue on pale blue glaze – appears to be common in the late 17th to early 18th centuries. Although English delftware potters did make tea bowls and handled cups for hot drinks such as chocolate and coffee, as well as posset pots and tea caddies, consumers often looked to other sources for teapots, such as red stoneware. While <P7> might be a well-executed London piece, teapots are not listed in the 1699 inventory of the stock of delftware vessels from the Pickleherring delft- and stoneware pothouse (Britton 1990), unlike stoneware teapots, which are frequently catalogued by Britton, and their rarity in private collections suggests that they were not common products (Ray 1968, 196–97, cat no. 127, pl 66 (bottom); Britton 1987, 156, cat no. 146). The Netherlands therefore is the most likely source for <P7>, as confirmed by Anton Gabszewicz, who comments that

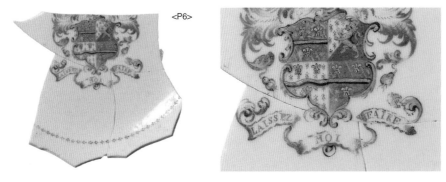

Fig 147 *Chinese porcelain (CHPO ROSE) armorial saucer <P6> from cesspit [6524] (fill [4952]) (scale 1:2, detail, right, 1:1)*

Fig 148 *Dutch tin-glazed ware (DTGW) teapot with maker's mark <P7> from cesspit [6524] (fill [4952]) (scale c 1:2, detail base c 1:1)*

the maker's mark on the base (Fig 148) could be Lambertus van Eenhoorn and that the vessel should be *c* 1730–40 after an exact Chinese original of some 30 years earlier (A Gabszewicz, pers comm 2015).

Three well-preserved DTGW plates display as the central image a leaping hare surrounded by *ju-i* head scrolls. Two have the hare's head cocked and looking left (<P8>, <P9>, Fig 149), whereas on the third plate the hare's head is positioned right (<P10>, Fig 149). All three have a '4' painted on the base in the centre. Like the teapot noted above, these attractive and well-made pieces have design precedents in the Netherlands, with images of animals, notably leaping or jumping dogs, unicorns, horses and hares, frequently central to their delftware products (Korf 1981, 242–6); these potters in turn took their inspiration from Chinese 'Kraak' porcelain of the mid 17th century. The only caveat regarding the suggested Netherlandish source concerns the plate shape (Britton plate shape H: Britton 1987, 194, appendix V) and the applied rim border pattern, both of which are comparable to the products of London's delftware

pothouses. Two other plates found can be confidently attributed to London delftware (TGW) production in terms of design and shape: a plant with a stylised pendent tubular flower and a stylised Chinese garden (ibid, respectively plate shapes G and L). Another plate (ibid, shape G), also contemporary with the period of deposition, has a simple stylised flower as its central design, and polychrome-painted in blue and red (TGWG).

The domestic glasswares include fragments from two wine glasses of colourless lead glass, one (<242>) a goblet with narrow rounded funnel-shaped bowl applied to a multi-knopped stem, with flattened knop at the shoulder and bladed knop at the mid point (cf Bickerton 1971, nos 153–4). Goblet <241>/<735> is represented by much of the base and the lower part of the stem, which is narrower than that of <242>. Both are likely to date from the mid 18th century. Other glass includes a complete base from a small onion bottle dating to between 1680 and 1730, clearly much older than the other finds in the group.

<P8>   <P9>   <P10>

*Fig 149 Dutch tin-glazed ware (DTGW) plates
<P8>–<P10> from cesspit [6524] (fill [4952])
(scale c 1:4, details c 1:2)*

The animal bone from fill [4952] provides some indication of the meat consumed by households in the vicinity. The large group, 84 fragments, is derived mainly from sheep/goat (*Ovis aries*/*Capra hircus*) and pig (*Sus scrofa*), with only a small group of cattle (*Bos taurus*) but a relatively substantial group of poultry: domestic fowl (chicken, *Gallus gallus*) and mallard or domestic duck (*Anas platyrhynchos*). No fish bones were recovered. Game species are represented by a single tibia (lower hind-leg) of juvenile rabbit (*Oryctolagus cuniculus*).

Cattle are represented by fragments of rib and thoracic (chest area) vertebra with single fragments of mandible (lower jaw) and innominate (pelvis). A substantial group of sheep/goat bone was present, derived from vertebrae and ribs with mandible (lower jaw) and limb long bones, particularly lower fore-leg and upper and lower hind-leg from at least two animals, a juvenile and an adult. Dental evidence from a mandible indicates a lamb in the first six months of life. An adult mandible showed severe rodent gnawing. A smaller group of pig bone comprised skull, mandible (lower jaw), upper and lower fore-leg, upper hind-leg and fore- and hind-foot bones, all possibly from the same juvenile animal. Remains of other

domesticates in the animal bone group comprised just two fragments of juvenile cat (*Felis catus*) – humerus and ulna (upper and lower fore-leg) – with no recovery of dog.

The clay tobacco pipes recovered, mostly from context [4952], comprise 20 bowls, 37 stem fragments and four mouthpieces. Seventeen bowls are of type OS12, dating broadly to *c* 1730–80, which is the likely period of deposition, and one bowl of type OS11 (*c* 1730–60). There are also two unmarked type AO18 pipes (*c* 1660–80). None of the pipes bears any form of decoration apart from milling around the rims of the AO18 bowls. However, 14 are marked with the maker's initials moulded in relief on the sides of the heel. Nine of these have the initials 'IB', which stand for John Bean, recorded in 1764–86 in Crane Street, Greenwich (Bowsher and Woollard 2001, 103). There are also five pipes marked 'IL', possibly John Langley, recorded in St Luke's parish in 1721–35 (Oswald 1975, 140). Although it is unclear when John Bean started making clay pipes, the surviving documentary records (parish registers and insurance policies with the Sun Assurance Company) show that the pipes were probably deposited after 1764.

Sanitary wares discarded in the cesspit comprise four pots

made by the London tin-glazed and Surrey-Hampshire border ware industries, of which three are chamber pots. The best-preserved is plain, in tin-glazed ware with pale blue glaze (TGW BLUE), with the second and third being Surrey-Hampshire border red ware flat-rimmed chamber pots with brown glaze (RBORB), characteristic of production c 1650–1750 (Pearce 1992, 69–70, fig 40 nos 331–6), retrieved as upper profiles only. The fourth vessel in this group is a smashed stool pan, also in RBOR.

Possibly connected with health is a two-handled bowl (a porringer) which may have been used as a bleeding bowl (<P11>, Fig 150), a rare identification in London. Another such is the plain white-glazed (TGW C) example with two handles and similarly carinated profile excavated in a 1690s clearance assemblage in a cesspit that served Spittle House in Spitalfields, London, during ownership by Paulet St John, 3rd Earl of Bolingbroke (Harward et al 2015, 131–2). The use of the term 'bleeding bowl' when applied to such porringers is problematic and may not always relate to a bloodletting function (Chapter 10.3). The bulk glass includes part of a small long-necked flask in natural green glass (cf Noël Hume 1969, fig 17 no. 9, dated to c 1710) and fragments of five colourless glass phials (49g), four of small narrow cylindrical form and one slightly larger, all typical of the period c 1780 (cf ibid, fig 17 nos 13–14). These were probably used for medicinal purposes, and the same may apply to a squat square bottle (40 × 40mm) of which the complete flat base was found, although this could possibly be an inkwell.

Cesspit [5546], filled in the 1820s (period 5)

Cesspit [5546] (OA8, Fig 144; Fig 146) was D-shaped in plan, measured 2.00m × 0.90m and was 1.41m deep. Four fills were identified: at the base, brick rubble backfill [5545] and [5255], perhaps relating to a partial collapse of the brick lining and sealed by an organic fill [4880], which itself was sealed by rubble [4879].

The broad range of artefacts found in the two upper fills ([4880] (mainly) and [4879]) of this cesspit constitutes the best-preserved and most significant artefactual group for furnishing insights into the 'domestic' routines of those working in the yard, or servicing those working there, in this case during the Regency period. While pottery is, as in the other cesspits, the most common find (1447 sherds, 186 ENV, 34.1kg), together

with large quantities of clay pipes and glassware, there was also an array of other finds. As a whole the emphasis is on dining and leisure, but dress, grooming and some form of financial transactions are also represented; other finds may be incidental. The overall date range for the filling of this cesspit, based on the clay tobacco pipes, is c 1780 to c 1820, while the ceramics and glass suggest the 1820s (and possibly into the 1830s), but some finds are notably older than this.

DRESS

Items of dress comprise six buttons, of which at least four are of copper alloy (<391>, <397>). Two are c 17mm in diameter, one with a complete attachment loop, while the third is slightly smaller (diameter 13mm). Of the two bone buttons, one is well made with a high polish (<189>); the raised rim and four neatly-spaced holes place it in South type 20, dated to 1800–30 (Noël Hume 1969, 90, fig 23). The other (<S3>, Fig 151) is of the same general type but larger and much cruder, with unfinished edges and four closely-spaced, oversized holes, and would appear to be a do-it-yourself attempt to replace a missing button. Clothing is represented by fragments of leather shoe and knitted garments (<707>), together with two small pieces of textile: <711> (65 × 35mm) is a wine tabby weave (?serge) of greenish-blue colour, and <714> (37 × 19mm) a fine twill with hem (width 9mm) along one of the long sides. None have any obvious form and the cloth at least could have been reused and discarded as 'toilet paper'.

DINING AND DRINKING

This pit contained the best group of cutlery from the site, with complete bone or ivory handles from six knives with iron blades. The knives have straight-sided scale-tang handles that expand slightly towards the terminal (width mostly c 16–22mm). The smallest handle is <S9> (Fig 152), which has the initial 'M' or 'W' carved towards the blade end on one side. The others fall into two groups based on the terminal of the handle. Of the three examples with straight ends, <175> (length 84mm) is possibly of antler and has three rivets, while <176> (length 80mm) and <180> (length 82mm) have only two. All have an oval end plate of iron secured by two centrally placed prongs that splay outwards. Of the three examples with rounded ends, <178> has two rivets and no obvious end plate, while <177> and <179> (length 92mm) are secured by three rivets and have convex oval end plates; that on <177> is fixed in the same way as described above, while that on the longitudinally ribbed handle <179> has two widely-spaced pins that are angled

Fig 150 London tin-glazed ware (TGW) carinated one-handled 'bleeding bowl' <P11> from cesspit [6524] (fill [4952]) (scale c 1:4)

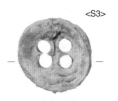

Fig 151 Unfinished bone button <S3> from cesspit [5546] (scale 1:1)

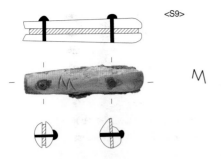

Fig 152 Bone knife handle with iron rivets <S9> from cesspit [5546] (scale 1:2)

inwards. In addition, there are two handles from possible forks, <740> (length 83mm) and <741> (length 87mm), both being straight-sided wooden handles that expand slightly towards the rounded terminal, and with round iron tangs; on <741> this appears to project as a small knop. There is also a large iron disc/vessel <648> that may be from a kitchen. Cutlery is not common in the archaeological record for the period, and these items were presumably only discarded when broken; a comparable London group is that associated with the Reid family, headed by a silk manufacturer, living at 21 Spital Square in 1840s Spitalfields (Harward et al 2015, 223, 266).

As to crockery, the most common constituent among the pottery is Staffordshire-made plain (CREA) and occasionally decorated (CREA PNTD) creamware (670 sherds, 48 ENV, 17kg), in what appears to have originally been a large table setting, along with various pearlware items (564 sherds, 88 ENV, 9287g) – blue (PEAR BW) and polychrome-painted (PEAR ERTH) together with blue transfer-printed (stipple and line) decoration (PEAR TR2) – and bone china (BONE) for tea and other 'hot drinks' (70 sherds, 14 ENV, 435g). A largely mismatched selection of Chinese blue and white porcelain (CHPO BW) plates also feature.

As many as four different dining services could have been in use in the adjacent household(s) during the 1820s and possibly into the 1830s. The first is represented by up to nine PEAR dinner plates with rococo blue shell-edged rims (cf Miller et al 2000 for illustrated examples of shell-edge); a further two have evenly scalloped blue shell-edged rims (eg <P12>, Fig 153) and one green shell-edged example was also found (<P13>, Fig 153). However, the bulk of the tableware is accounted for by the second 'set', of CREA, which overall provided a large proportion of the pottery in this assemblage. Acquired during the 1790s, presumably as part of a large uniform table setting, at least 21 CREA dinner plates (eg <P16>, Fig 153), displaying frequent utensil marks, and two soup plates were found. Five oval dishes (also with cut marks in the glaze), one with a queen's edge rim, survive best, as well as two oval serving dishes. The latter are noted in Spode's 1820 sales catalogue as closely resembling the 'round patty' (Whiter 1978, 114–15, shape no. 291) used for baking (pies, puddings etc) or for transferring vegetables, potatoes and so on from the kitchen to the table. Another contemporary manufacturer's catalogue, for the Staffordshire potters James and Charles Whitehead, illustrates these vessels (Drakard 1973, 30, no. 144) under unlidded 'oval

baking dishes' (ibid, 7). A few vessels in the serving group are overglaze line-painted around the rim edge (CREA PNTD).

While the first two dinner services are largely plain, the third and fourth sets are in pearlware and decorated with two different blue transfer-printed designs (PEAR TR2). The third group comprises seven dinner plates decorated with the ubiquitous willow pattern print (eg <P14>, Fig 153); variously preserved, these nevertheless bear different workmen's marks or ciphers that allow them to be identified as Spode pieces (Copeland 1990, 167, mark no. 10). The other blue transfer-printed group is made up of nine (largely reconstructable) dinner plates with floral basket border (Neale 2005, 108) and central floral basket print (eg <P15>, Fig 153).

In addition to these four dinner services, the less well-preserved and largely mismatched group (in terms of design) of up to nine CHPO plates can be divided into three different design styles. First are three with trellis border displaying different central landscape and water images in what Chinese porcelain literature often describes as the 'willow pattern' (Kerr et al 2003), and which is not to be confused with the blue transfer-printed pattern of *c* 1790 first commissioned by Spode but probably engraved by Minton. Second are two dinner plates with the common tree peony as the central design – the only matching pair in the group – and third are three plates with various landscape designs common to the last quarter of the 18th century.

Tea services are represented by various PEAR and well-curated BONE items. Like the dining crockery, a number of different sets, in varying quantities, can be identified. The first group are in PEAR TR2, all with the chinoiserie 'Two Temples' pattern: four London-shaped teacups and two larger London-shaped breakfast teacups with scalloped rim edges, and a slop bowl (cf Copeland 1990, 53–66). Only one saucer was found with this design, however. Among the rest of the tea wares there is an emphasis on PEAR TR2 Bute-shaped teacups with some saucers and slop bowls with prints of similar British countryside views, for example scenes of cottages with a church, or a ruined abbey, a windmill, or a horse and cart placed in the foreground with two male figures (one standing and one seated) to the left. In terms of their design, these unmarked pieces are in the style of patterns produced *c* 1810–30, in known named series titled 'Rustic Scenes', 'Rural Scenery', 'English Scenery' and 'British Scenery'. A few singular vessels hint at more individual acquisitions, for example the Bute-shaped handled teacup with an overglaze bat print of a British countryside-style view of a lake with a cottage in the foreground.

The lower portions of a few English stoneware (ENGS) bottles which contained beer or ginger beer were the only ceramic vessels linked to alcohol consumption. Glassware was plentiful, however. The upper fill of this cesspit contained 39 glass fragments from up to 32 vessels (1869g), mostly of 18th- and 19th-century date. Wine glasses are the dominant category, with four main types present, of which the first has a bucket-shaped bowl with a relatively short stem and conical foot (between 58mm and 63mm in diameter). No bowls are intact

Fig 153 Dining in the first quarter of the 19th century – examples of plates from each of four different dinner services present in cesspit [5546]: in pearlware (PEAR), with even scalloped shell-edge rim decoration in blue <P12> and in green <P13>; in PEAR, with willow pattern print <P14>; in PEAR, with floral pattern <P15>; and in creamware (CREA) <P16> (scale c 1:4)

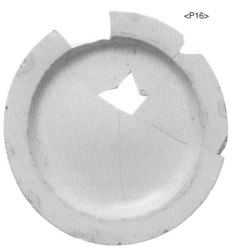

but most have an annular knop at the mid point of the stem (<252>, <G1> (Fig 154), <264>, <278>, <279>); <G2> (Fig 154) has a plain stem, and the same may apply to <276>. Most have a brownish discoloration, but <278> has milky white surfaces. A few rim fragments (<769>) are probably also from this vessel type. An unusual form is <G3> (Fig 154) which appears to be a variation of a thistle-shaped bowl, with low bucket-shaped base and flaring upper body.

A goblet with a funnel-shaped bowl with stepped base and knopped stem (<G4>, Fig 155) appears to be the latest vessel in

the group, possibly of mid 18th-century date. Eight glasses are of plain drawn trumpet form, two with conical feet, including <G5> (Fig 155), and six with folded conical feet, including <G6> and <G7> (Fig 155); no bowls survive intact. One funnel-shaped bowl has an additional collar at its base (<G6>, Fig 155). Four bases are from wine glasses of uncertain form (<254>, <273>, <274>, <275>).

Of interest is a group of five flaring jelly/custard glasses with short stems and very slightly wrythen optic-blown ribs, probably of 19th-century date. In the case of <280> the stem is crudely applied to the foot, and <263> also has an uneven junction at this point, but <G10> (Fig 156) and <259> are more neatly finished (only the lower bowl with upper stem of <267> survives). This 19th-century form appears to be inspired by the pedestal goblets of the 16th century (Willmott 2002, 69, type 13.3) and their early 18th-century successors (cf Thorpe 1969, pl 66; Bickerton 1971, no. 570), but is simpler, with a solid stem and no knop.

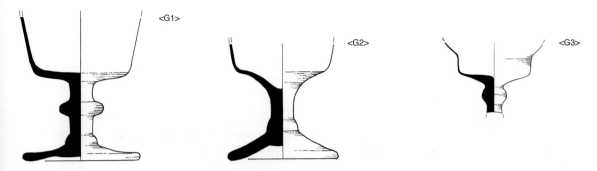

Fig 154 Wine glasses <G1> and <G2> with bucket-shaped bowls and <G3>, a variation of a thistle-shaped bowl, from cesspit [5546] (scale 1:2)

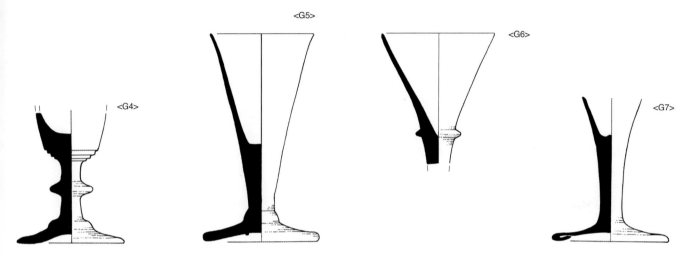

Fig 155 Wine glasses <G4> with a funnel-shaped bowl and <G5>–<G7> with drawn trumpet bowls, from cesspit [5546] (scale 1:2)

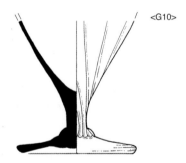

Fig 156 Glass stem <G10> from cesspit [5546] (scale 1:2)

Other glass finds from this cesspit comprise the bases of two small tumblers (<265>, <272>), part of a possible lid (<G12>, Fig 181) and part of an applied trail with reticella decoration from an ornate object decorated in the *façon de Venise* style (<G11>, Fig 181), possibly the earliest item in the group. The remainder of the vessel glass is similar to that from two 19th-century cesspit groups from West Smithfield in the City of London: at Weddell House, thought to be derived from the George Inn, dating to *c* 1810–50 (Blackmore 2006; Cohen 2009, 94–5, fig 11), and from 5–7 Giltspur Street, dated to *c* 1840 (Knight and Pearce 2017).

Fill [4880] also contained a complete French champagne-type bottle (<G15>, Fig 157) with broad base, sloping shoulder and single string below the rim, probably dating to *c* 1780. It also

produced a substantially complete free-blown early cylindrical bottle, represented by the complete base with lower body and the complete rim and neck to the shoulder, but missing part of the body; the overall proportions and the rim form (Haslam 1970, fig 10, type 5a) of this bottle suggest that it dates to *c* 1780–1800. Another rim of the same type is from a much smaller bottle. Also present were three fragments that appear to be from a squat cylindrical bottle.

Fig 157 Glass bottle <G15> from cesspit [5546] (scale c 1:4)

Mould-blown finds include part of a colourless glass bottle with rounded body, narrower flattened oval neck with ribbed moulding on the sides and rounded projection on the front, which may have contained spirits or a condiment, and the base of a small, vertically ribbed, fluted jar or sauce bottle (diameter *c* 44mm). Other finds comprise a complete large base that is probably from a Kilner-type cylindrical storage jar, now milky white in colour, and fragments from two other cylindrical jars or bottles in colourless glass. Fill [4879] of this cesspit contained one fragment (174g) from a larger cylindrical bottle, probably used for lemonade, in aqua-coloured glass.

DIET

Evidence of what was eaten in the property or its vicinity comes from the animal bone from fill [4880], comprising 168 well-preserved fragments, the largest of the cesspit assemblages. The group derived mainly from juvenile cattle (*Bos taurus*) and adult and juvenile sheep/goat (*Ovis aries*/*Capra hircus*), with smaller groups of pig (*Sus scrofa*), fish and poultry, but no recovery of game. Fish remains comprised eight fragments of pleuronectid flatfish vertebrae, probably of plaice (*Pleuronectes platessa*). Poultry remains derived from domestic fowl (chicken, *Gallus gallus*) and goose, probably domestic goose (*Anser anser domesticus*).

The cattle group mainly represented carcass areas of prime meat-bearing quality: rib, thoracic (chest area) vertebra and, particularly, upper fore- and hind- and lower fore-leg of juvenile and infant calves. In addition, there were six complete adult phalanges (toe joints) all possibly from the same foot, possibly indicating consumption of a much cheaper carcass area or perhaps disposal of primary processing waste. One fragment of innominate (pelvis) derived from a foetal or neonate calf. Sheep/goat produced a substantial group derived from at least three animals including an adult and two juveniles, with an emphasis on vertebra, rib, and upper fore- and hind-leg but some recovery of all carcass areas except the skull, maxilla (upper jaw) and horncore. Dental evidence from two sheep mandibles (lower jaws), possibly from the same animal, indicates lamb(s) in the first six months of life. Two stature estimates for sheep/goat indicated animal(s) 0.659m and 0.634m at the withers (shoulder), well within the observed range for contemporary sheep/goat from London sites. The smaller pig group derived almost entirely from juvenile elements of the upper and lower hind-leg, perhaps all from the same animal, with single fragments of skull and hind-foot. A single fragment of innominate (pelvis) derived from a very young infant piglet.

SMOKING

This cesspit yielded the largest collection of clay tobacco pipes found on any part of the site, comprising 157 bowls but only two stem fragments and no mouthpieces. Smoking was banned in the royal dockyard and the officers frequently expressed concern about fire spreading there from outside the yard (Chapter 6.3, 'Maintenance and repairs, early 1760s'; Chapter 7.3, 'Fighting fire and a water tank'; above, 'On the east side

of the dockyard: King Street and Orchard Place'). Most of the clay tobacco pipes came from fill [4880], with only four bowls recorded from [4879]. The great majority of pipe bowls are of type AO27, dated to *c* 1780–1820 (151 bowls). There is also one earlier type (AO25) dating broadly to *c* 1700–70 and three later types: two bowls of type AO28 (*c* 1820–40), one type AO29 (*c* 1840–80) and one type AO30 (*c* 1850–1910). Given the overwhelming emphasis on pipes made at the turn of the 18th and 19th centuries, it seems likely that these later examples could all be intrusive, and that the main period of deposition was between *c* 1780 and *c* 1820.

A high proportion of the clay pipe bowls from the fill of cesspit [5546] had been marked by their makers: 149 examples all carry moulded initials in relief on the sides of the heel (or spur). A total of 125 pipes also bear some form of decoration. Thirteen different pipe makers are represented by two clear, legible initials, although there are 14 more examples in which one or both of the initials are unclear; some of these could have been made by the same makers whose pipes are clearly marked.

There was a marked tendency for clay pipes to be used and discarded within a relatively small radius of their source of production. The majority of pipes recovered from the site will have been made at local workshops, in Deptford, Greenwich and Lewisham, although this by no means rules out the presence of pipes made in other areas of London. Seven pipe makers have been identified with reasonable certainty, all working within the 40-year period during which pipes of type AO27 were made, a time corresponding to the Napoleonic Wars.

The most numerous marked pipes by a single maker bear the initials 'WB' (51, possibly 52, examples). These were made by William Burstow, recorded in Limekilns in 1789–1800, in Blackheath Hill in 1805–12 and in Morden Street in 1822; he died in the workhouse, aged 76, in 1846 (Bowsher and Woollard 2001, 103). In all, 53 (possibly 55) 'WB' pipes are recorded from the site, the great majority of them coming from fill [4880] of cesspit [5546]. All have the initials 'WB' moulded in relief on the sides of the heel, and nine are undecorated. The most distinctive decoration is in the form of a dragon (City of London arms supporter) moulded on the left side of the bowl (facing the smoker), with the three ostrich feathers badge of the Heir Apparent on the right-hand side and moulded wheatsheaf seams at the front and back. Eleven examples were recorded, many of them from the same mould, and some have a long, bowed stem (eg <CP3>, Fig 158). There are also pipes with this decoration that are slightly more elaborate and more crisply moulded, including the 'ICH DIEN' motto of the Prince of Wales below the three feathers. One of these has the pipe maker's name and address 'BURSTOW No 20' moulded in relief along the left-hand side of the stem and, on the right, 'BLACK HEATH HILL' (<CP4>, Fig 158). This gives a very clear indication of production between 1805 and 1812 (ibid, 103). This design continued to be made in London into the second quarter of the 19th century, with further examples known from Greenwich (Le Cheminant 1981, fig 3 no. 29). Use of the Prince of Wales's feathers emblem on clay pipes has a particular association with taverns and public houses. There are several variations of the sign, although 'The Feathers' was used in London as a sign from at least the early 17th century (ibid, 92), with 'The Prince of Wales' or 'Prince of Wales Feathers' also being common. The Burstow pipe from Convoys Wharf almost certainly relates to the Prince Regent's rule in all but name.

Thirty more 'WB' pipes from the cesspit have moulded vertical ribbing around the bowl, 19 of these with alternating thick and thin ribs. Six of the evenly ribbed pipes also have a row of stars or flowers at intervals around the top of the bowl, above the ribbing (eg <CP5>, Fig 158). The remaining decorated pipe bowls with the 'WB' mark simply have moulded leaf or wheatsheaf seams, three of them with a few decorative leaves continuing along the sides of the stem close to the bowl. Moulded leaf seams and vertical ribbing are among the most popular styles of decoration used by pipe makers across London at the turn of the 18th and 19th centuries, bringing affordable 'fancy' pipes to a wide section of the smoking community.

The next most common maker's mark consists of the initials 'RS', which stand for Richard Simmons, recorded in Greenwich between 1764 and 1808 (Bowsher and Woollard 2001, 103). Forty-two examples of this mark were found across the site, with 36 of them coming from cesspit [5546]. Only four are undecorated, although they are incomplete so may originally have been decorated. The rest have moulded vertical ribbing, mostly alternating thin and thick ribs (22 examples), and some of them with leaves extending a short way along the sides of the stem behind the bowl (15 examples) (eg <CP6>, <CP7>, Fig 158).

Another common mark in this cesspit group is 'WG', 23 examples of which are recorded from the site, all of them from fill [4880]. These initials stand for William Gosling of Greenwich, recorded in 1801–2 in London Street, in 1806–13 in Skeltons Lane and in 1813–15 in Roan Street. His son William was born in 1820, and other locations are recorded for William senior beyond the end date of type AO27 pipe manufacture. He died in 1838 (Bowsher and Woollard 2001, 103). Only two 'WG' pipes have no decoration and seven simply have moulded wheatsheaf seams (eg <CP8>, Fig 159). Eleven (possibly 12) pipes have moulded vertical ribs of even thickness, seven of these with wheatsheaf seams and five with leaves part-way along the sides of the stem (eg <CP9>, Fig 159), while two also have flowers at intervals around the top of the bowl (eg <CP10>, Fig 159). Two 'WG' pipes have a moulded thistle on the left-hand side of the bowl and a rose on the right, with wheatsheaf seams (eg <CP11>, Fig 159); this is a relatively common design used by several pipe makers in London, probably in reference to the Act of Union of 1707 and perhaps related to specific public houses.

Other pipes whose makers can be identified with reasonable confidence include two marked 'WS', probably by William Squalfield, recorded in 1799–1805 in Whitechapel (Oswald 1975, 130). One of these has wheatsheaf seams only while the other also has moulded vertical ribbing. Seven pipes (possibly eight) have the initials 'JA' (rather than 'IA',

which would have been more common in earlier years). These stand for Joseph Andrews, recorded in Deptford in 1823–8 (ibid, 130). Two are decorated with vertical ribbing and wheatsheaf seams, and four have moulded rose and thistle decoration, this time with the rose on the left and the thistle on the right (eg <CP12>, Fig 160). There are three pipes marked 'IS' and one 'JS', both of which could stand for John Smith, recorded in 1809–11 in Peckham and who died in 1828 (ibid, 145). Two of the 'IS' pipes have vertical ribbing and leaf or wheatsheaf seams, and the 'JS' pipe has a rose and thistle. Other initials that are legible are 'CR', 'IF', 'WA' and 'WE', although their makers cannot now be identified with any certainty. One pipe marked 'E' or 'C' on the left-hand side of the heel (ie the first name) has 'B' as the initial of the surname; it is decorated with the dragon and Prince of Wales's feathers (<CP13>, Fig 160) seen on the William Burstow pipes in the same assemblage. This could perhaps be Charles James Burstow, recorded in Limekilns in 1802–13 (Bowsher and Woollard 2001, 104), using a mould passed on by William Burstow and altered.

A type AO27 pipe marked with the initials 'CR' has the Prince of Wales's feathers moulded on the back of the bowl, facing the smoker, with the 'ICH DIEN' motto below, garlands to either side and a wheatsheaf seam at the font of the bowl (<CP14>, Fig 161). It has not been possible to identify the maker. A pipe marked 'IF' has vertical ribbing and wheatsheaf seams but again remains unidentified (<CP15>, Fig 161). A single AO27 pipe with the moulded initials 'WA' (unidentified) has close-set vertical ribbing and swags above, and three pipes of the same shape simply have a moulded flower on each side of the heel, so are not traceable to any particular workshop. One of these also has vertical ribbing (<CP16>, Fig 161). A later, type AO28, pipe bowl is marked 'JB', moulded in relief on the sides of the spur and has the name 'BUMBY SHADWELL' stamped incuse within a milled oval on the back of the bowl (<CP17>, Fig 161); again the maker remains elusive, even though the name and location are spelled out. The latest pipe from the cesspit fill is a type AO30 (c 1850–1910) from [4879]; it is decorated with a series of moulded leaf panels around the bowl (<CP18>, Fig 161).

The remaining decorated bowls are all of type AO27, whether marked or not, and mostly have moulded leaf or wheatsheaf seams and/or vertical ribbing. The large assemblage of clay pipes from this pit shows just how popular these particular styles were in London at the turn of the 18th and 19th centuries, and demonstrates the wide circulation of affordable decorative pipes produced on a large scale by many manufacturers across the capital. Completely plain pipes were becoming less common at this time, a trend that is reflected in the large cesspit assemblage. As far as the pipe makers represented are concerned, William Burstow, Richard Simmons and William Gosling dominate, all of them located relatively close to the site. The quantity of pipes recovered from the one feature does suggest the possibility that they were smoked close by, perhaps in a nearby public house, where smoking would regularly accompany social drinking.

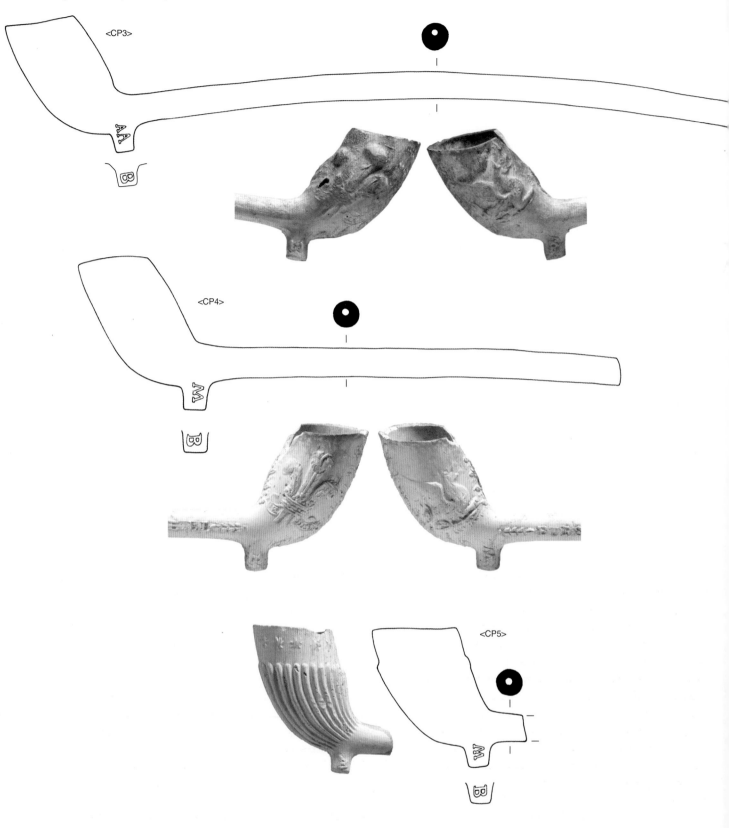

Fig 158 (and facing page) Clay tobacco pipes <CP3>–<CP5> made by William Burstow, and <CP6> and <CP7> made by Richard Simmons, from cesspit [5546] (scale c 1:1)

HOUSEHOLD ACTIVITIES

Domestic routines are reflected by up to three English stoneware (ENGS) blacking bottles, used to contain polish for boots, kitchen ranges and so on, and nine chamber pots, six well-preserved in plain creamware (CREA), two in London-area post-medieval red ware (PMR) and one in pearlware with blue transfer-printed (stipple and line) decoration (PEAR TR2) in the 'Ponte Molle' pattern (Coysh and Henrywood 1982, 287–8). In the same fabric is a wash bowl in the 'Field Sports' series, showing a mounted huntsman with pack of hounds (ibid, 344),

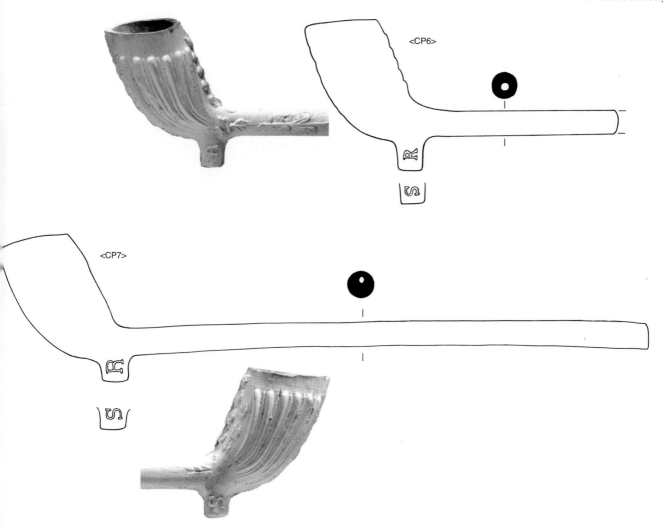

attributed to the Herculaneum pottery near Liverpool; both are done from good-quality copper plates.

Toilet or pharmaceutical vessels are represented by glass phials and a bottle. Fragments from ten free-blown phials (223g) of different sizes were recovered from the pit, of which two are complete and one nearly so; unless otherwise stated, all are of colourless glass. The smallest is a complete lop-sided miniature phial in natural green glass with deep flaring neck, marked shoulder, tapering body and cracked-off pontil scar (<G17>, Fig 162). The two next smallest are of tall, narrow cylindrical form, one complete in natural green glass (<G19>, Fig 162; height 79mm) with the remains of the original contents inside; the other was presumably complete when discarded but is now fragmented (height 81mm, max diameter 18mm). A slightly larger phial is of the same type (<G18>, Fig 162; height 84mm, max diameter 23mm), with a number of horizontal and vertical scratch marks inside the base where the user has tried to extract the last of the contents. The other phials are rather larger, with body diameters of 47mm and 59mm. Fragments from a larger cylindrical bottle of dark blue glass (58g) probably also belong to this functional group. Fill [4879] of this feature contained the base and much of the body of a tall, narrow cylindrical bottle in blue glass (height 144mm, diameter 55mm), probably used for a medicinal preparation.

DOMESTIC ANIMALS

The remains, some 17 fragments, of at least two dogs were recovered, including an adult and a juvenile. Elements of adult dog included mandible (lower jaw), humerus (upper fore-leg), radius and ulna (lower fore-leg), tibia and fibula (lower hind-leg) and metapodials (foot); juvenile dog comprised only a fragment of humerus (upper fore-leg). A fragment of mandible showed loss of the cheek-teeth with considerable bone infilling of the alveolae (tooth sockets), probably indicating an old animal. Measurement of adult limb long bones provided five stature estimates ranging from 0.279m to 0.289m at the withers (shoulder), strongly suggesting that they did indeed derive from the same animal. There was no recovery of cat.

COMMERCE/REGULATION AND BUILDING/NAVAL FITTINGS

Regulation and commerce are represented by half of a probable cloth seal (<527>; diameter 22mm) and 20 corroded copper-alloy discs (<390>–<394>, <528>–<532>) which may be coins, possibly 18th-century pennies. Finds relating to buildings and services include window glass (82 fragments (796g) from some 14 panes from fill [4880] and six fragments (23g) from three different windows from fill [4879]), a copper-alloy nail (<398>; length c 60mm) and a complete but worn wooden parrel bead, used in rigging (<S23>, Fig 189).

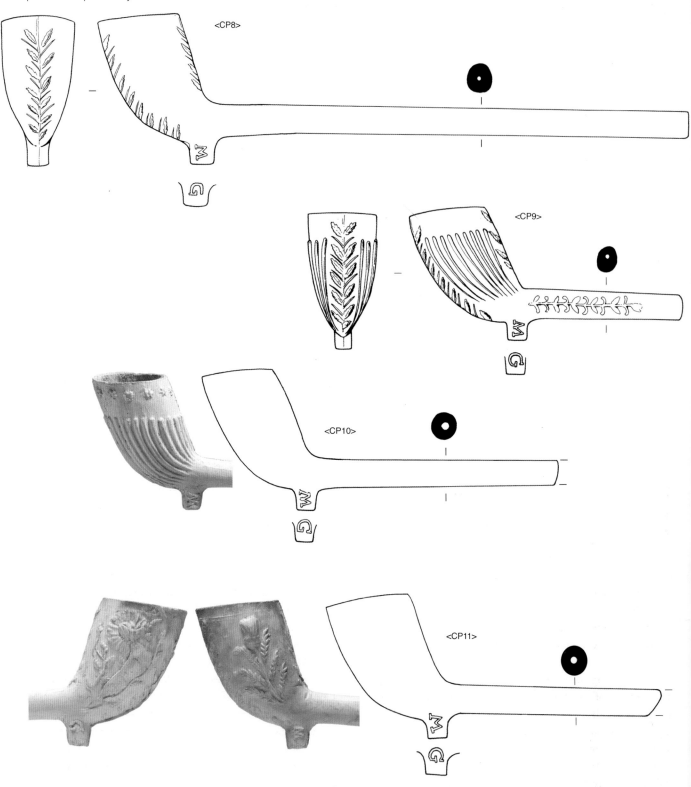

Fig 159 Clay tobacco pipes <CP8>–<CP11> made by William Gosling, from cesspit [5546] (scale c 1:1)

Cesspit [5548], filled in the 1820s (period 5)

Cesspit [5548] (OA8) was a rectangular brick-lined pit with rounded corners, measuring 1.86m × 1.22m and 0.46m deep (Fig 144; Fig 146). A bedding ([5807]) for the brick lining was identified, while of two pit fills, the lower was a greenish-brown silty sand with clay ([5423]) and the upper a silty clay ([5107]).

Like the nearby cesspit [5546], a relatively diverse range of artefacts was found in the upper fill [5107] of this one, including household items and building fittings, again providing insights into the material culture of those working in, or linked in some way to, the dockyard. This fill contained some 19 accessioned objects, and while this group is smaller than that from cesspit [5546] (above), it is no less informative. Items of dress comprise a large disc-type button (<700>) of

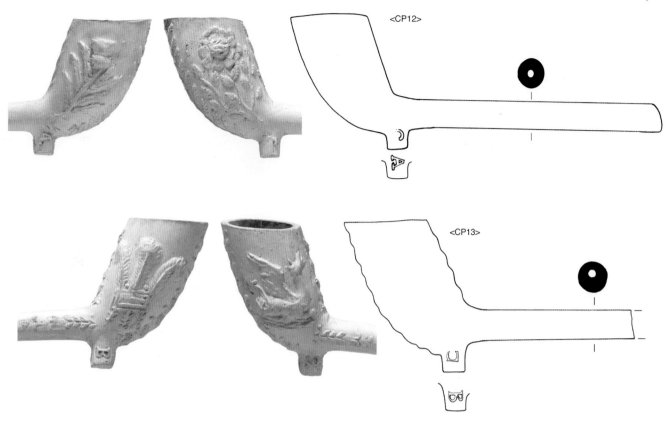

Fig 160 Clay tobacco pipes <CP12>, made by Joseph Andrews, and <CP13>, possibly made by Charles James Burstow, from cesspit [5546] (scale c 1:1)

copper alloy with slightly convex face and loop on the back (diameter *c* 26mm) and a small fragment of textile <710> (26 × 26mm), a herringbone ?twill. Also present were fragments of burnt or calcified leather <768>. Grooming is represented by two joining fragments from a double-sided ivory comb with rounded ends (<S5>, Fig 163), a type in use during the 16th and 17th centuries (Egan 2005, 64) and doubtless later. A small box lid made of bone with copper-alloy rivets (<S6>, Fig 186) may also belong to the category of personal care, although there is no way of knowing what the contents were.

The pottery discarded (508 sherds, 86 ENV, 13,813g) represents a range of vessels of varying preservation and date. The presence of a London-made tin-glazed ware (TGW) plate and porringer dated to the first quarter of the 18th century suggests that some material had escaped the successive removals of nightsoil from the pit. The most common constituents of the pottery assemblage are a selection of Staffordshire-made plain and occasionally decorated creamware (155 sherds, 24 ENV, 4610g), various pearlwares (117 sherds, 15 ENV, 1459g) and well-curated Chinese porcelain (47 sherds, 12 ENV, 524g). Dining and tea drinking wares are therefore common.

Plain or undecorated creamware (CREA) was the most common pottery type in this cesspit, in a variety of plates and serving dishes. Best-preserved are two oval serving dishes, similar to those in the nearby cesspit [5546]. Dining pieces are limited to a few (varyingly preserved) CREA dinner plates, with one example each of a soup, dessert and tea plate. In pearlware (PEAR) are three more dinner plates, with evenly scalloped blue shell-edged rims (cf Miller et al 2000 for

illustrated examples of shell-edge) and six dessert plates decorated with the ubiquitous willow pattern print (Copeland 1990); although variously preserved, the latter also carry the workman's mark or cipher (an 'O') that allows them to be identified as Spode-made pieces (ibid, 167, mark no. 10).

A rather mismatched group of saucers and teacups in pearlware with blue transfer-printed (stipple and line) decoration (PEAR TR2) and variously decorated Chinese porcelain tea bowls and saucers provide the bulk of the tea wares. While the Chinese porcelain with *famille rose* decoration (CHPO ROSE) includes a matching tea bowl (<P17>, Fig 164) and saucer (<P18>, Fig 164), and a handled cup with floral decoration (<P19>, Fig 164), the rest of the Chinese (blue and white) porcelain (CHPO BW) tea bowls and saucers are much more fragmented, reflecting partly the delicate nature of these wares. Saucers are better represented (up to four) in the PEAR TR2 group; two of these have the 'Two Temples' printed pattern (Copeland 1990, 53) but there is just the one (London-shaped) teacup with the 'Two Temples' pattern to go with them. Two PEAR saucers have unprovenanced designs: one has a European landscape of the type common among Staffordshire potters during this period; the other shows a male figure carrying a sack and pole over his left shoulder with a dog by his right side, set against a river in a European landscape. No pattern mark is present on either piece, although the figure in the second print bears a resemblance to that used by the Leeds pottery during the second decade of the 19th century for 'The Wanderer' pattern (Neale 2005, 131). In addition, there are a PEAR teapot lid with a floral pattern and a black basalt

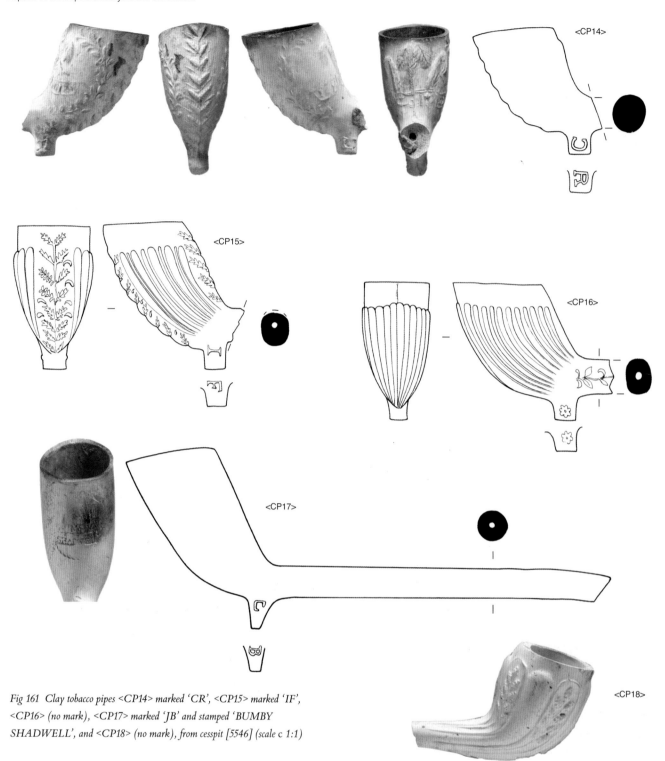

Fig 161 Clay tobacco pipes <CP14> marked 'CR', <CP15> marked 'IF', <CP16> (no mark), <CP17> marked 'JB' and stamped 'BUMBY SHADWELL', and <CP18> (no mark), from cesspit [5546] (scale c 1:1)

stoneware (BBAS) teapot with engine-turned decoration.

A range of household items associated with mealtimes was found. Cutlery was less common than in cesspit [5546], but part of a composite knife (<S10>, Fig 165) was found, with the diagonally ribbed bone scale-tang handle secured by two iron rivets and the remains of a terminal fitting held in place by two prongs.

Glasswares include the remains of a decanter and two wine glasses, one of drawn trumpet form (<G8>, Fig 166), the other more complete with a bladed knop at the mid point, lower merese, and terraced merese at the junction with the ovoid bowl

(<G9>, Fig 166). The decanter (<G13>, Fig 166) has a flat-topped flanged rim and flaring neck with internal ground surface for a stopper and external decoration of three pairs of moulded milled bands. A larger assemblage of bottle glass was found in this pit than in [5546] (above), with the remains of ten early cylindrical wine bottles (33 fragments, 2527g). Most are of standard size (three complete bases measuring 75–80mm). One example has a complete long, tapering neck while two others have much shorter, bulbous necks, but all three mouths are of Haslam type 5a (Haslam 1970). In addition there is one half measure (base diameter 55mm). Free-blown early cylindrical

Fig 162 Glass phials <G17>–<G19> from cesspit [5546] (scale c 1:2)

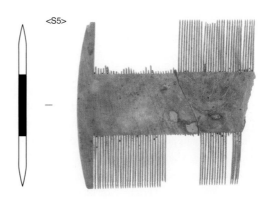

Fig 163 Part of an ivory comb <S5> from cesspit [5548] (scale 1:1)

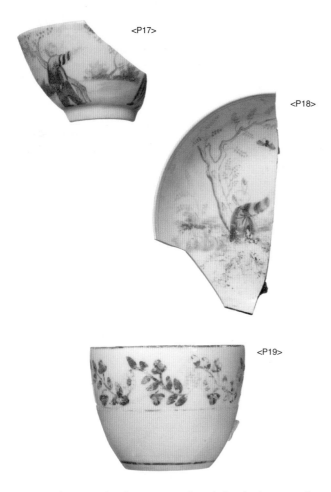

Fig 164 Chinese porcelain (CHPO ROSE) matched tea bowl <P17> and saucer <P18>, and handled cup <P19>, from cesspit [5548] (scale c 1:2)

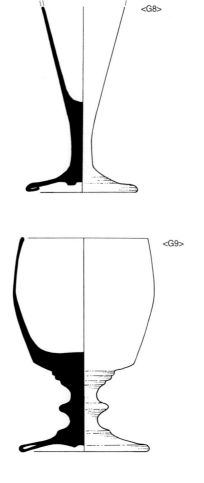

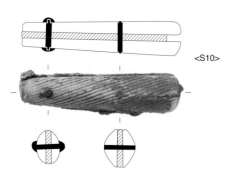

Fig 165 Bone knife handle with iron rivets <S10> from cesspit [5548] (scale 1:2)

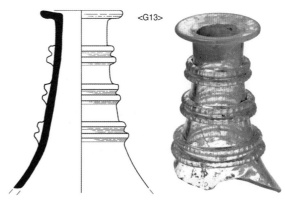

Fig 166 Glass decanter <G13> and wine glasses <G8> and <G9> from cesspit [5548] (scale 1:2)

bottles were made *c* 1735/50–1830, but this group is probably of late 18th-century date. Other finds comprise sherds from two (or three) possible pickle bottles or flasks, probably of 19th-century date. Both have near-flat bases of different sizes and one has a wide cylindrical neck (external diameter 54mm, length 80mm+) with cordon just below the plain rounded rim.

Of particular interest are the 158 fragments of animal bone from the silty clay upper fill [5107], the most species-diverse of the cesspit groups. There was a substantial group, 50 fragments, of fish bone derived largely from head elements of plaice (*Pleuronectes platessa*) with vertebrae of pleuronectid flatfish, probably also plaice, and two head fragments of a cod (*Gadus morhua*) with vertebrae of the cod family (Gadidae) and carp family (Cyprinidae).

Poultry are also well represented, particularly by domestic fowl (chicken, *Gallus gallus*) head, upper wing, thigh, 'drumstick' and foot, with elements of at least two hens, an adult and a subadult. There were smaller groups of goose, probably domestic goose (*Anser anser domesticus*) and mallard or domestic duck (*Anas playrhynchos*) – respectively adult sternum (breast bone) and two upper wings, and fragments of adult head, 'wishbone' and foot. The major domesticates, cattle (*Bos taurus*), sheep/goat (*Ovis aries/Capra hircus*) and pig (*Sus scrofa*), formed the bulk of the context group (66 fragments). Cattle comprised fragments of rib, and single fragments of vertebra, upper fore-leg and upper and lower hind-leg. Sheep/goat were represented by fragments of vertebra and rib, with occasional recovery of skull and upper and lower fore-leg. Fragments of sheep/goat vertebra, rib and ulna (lower fore-leg) showed rodent gnawing ranging from slight to severe. Pig produced occasional fragments of juvenile skull and upper and lower hind-leg.

Game species were represented only by three fragments of rabbit (*Oryctolagus cuniculus*). Other domesticates comprised only ten fragments of adult and juvenile cat (*Felis catus*) head, upper and lower fore-leg, and fore- and hind-foot, with no recovery of dog (unlike cesspit [5546]). In addition, six fragments of black or brown rat (*Rattus* sp) were the only remains of small mammals from any of the cesspit groups.

As regards tobacco smoking, a group of 14 clay pipe bowls and four stem fragments were recovered from cesspit [5548]. All are of type AO27, giving a broad date range of *c* 1780–1820, and come from the top fill [5107] of the pit. The range of pipes present is similar to that from cesspit [5546], with five undecorated pipes marked with the initials 'RS' (for Richard Simmons, 1764–1808) moulded in relief on the sides of the heel and two marked 'WB' (William Burstow, 1789–1846), both with vertical ribbing and one having moulded leaf seams. There is also one pipe marked 'CR' and one marked 'AS' (unidentified). In all, there are seven decorated pipes, all but one of them with moulded vertical ribbing. One example, with wheatsheaf seams and leaves along the sides of the stem, has moulded flowers or stars on the sides of the heel, but also bears the name 'J ANDREWS / DEPTFORD' moulded in relief along the sides of the stem (<CP19>, Fig 167). This is probably Joseph Andrews, recorded in 1823–8 (Oswald 1975, 130), even though the shape of the bowl pre-dates slightly his known period of activity. It may also suggest a possible maker for comparable pipes marked with the same symbol in cesspit [5546] (above).

The pottery assemblage also contained three individual vessels, atypical items for these cesspits. The first is a creamware (CREA) pot lid (<P20>, Fig 168) with underglaze sepia transfer-printed decoration and finished with overglaze brown-painted

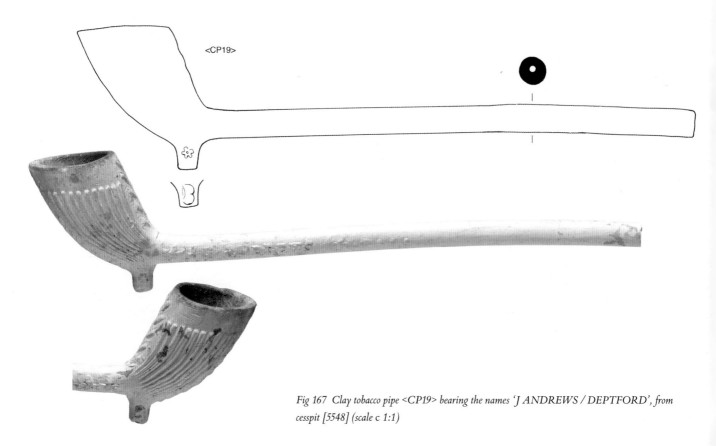

Fig 167 Clay tobacco pipe <CP19> bearing the names 'J ANDREWS / DEPTFORD', from cesspit [5548] (scale c 1:1)

rim and border; the image is neoclassical, of a man and woman in mourning next to a mausoleum bearing a plaque reading 'Iberes[?]/REST/in HEAVEN'. The second is a CREA mug, underglaze transfer-printed and overglaze-painted with a masonic design (<P21>, Fig 168), likely to be the product of one of the Sunderland pothouses which made a range of masonic

wares (eg the Garrison pothouse: Baker 1984, 63, no. 80); it displays the female figure of Justice with a verse taken from the *External prentice* and a range of masonic symbolism such as the crossed keys and the compass displayed in the bottom right of the surviving piece. The third is a CREA underglaze black transfer-printed cylindrical jar (<P22>, Fig 168) advertising as containing Jessamin soap patented by Andrew Johnstone of Lombard Street in the City of London.

Of two English stoneware (ENGS) bottles in this assemblage, one is stamped 'EX/BLACKING/BOTTLE' close to its base, and would have contained a product such as boot blacking, black lead for polishing stoves or Brunswick Black for painted stoves and ironwork (Askey 1998, 102). Serving a similarly mundane purpose is a London-area post-medieval red ware (PMR) flowerpot. Three tall slim glass phials and one larger one dating from *c* 1760 or *c* 1780, represented by five fragments (46g), may have contained pharmaceutical preparations. In addition there are 30 fragments of curved copper-alloy sheet metal (<698>), probably from a fragmented vessel, one with part of a cockle shell adhering.

Games are represented by a complete bone gaming piece or counter in the shape of a fish with a painted red eye (<S14>, Fig 169), dated to the early 19th century. It was probably used for the popular 19th-century numbers game of Loto, a precursor of bingo. This required 24 cards, each with three rows of five numbers, a bag of 90 numbered balls, and a range of counters: 100 counters of one type, worth one unit, 14 counters of a second type, worth 10 units, and 12 of third type, worth 100 units. The counters were often of mother-of-pearl, and the 10-unit counters were commonly fish-shaped (Bell 1969, 114–15, fig 97). Commercial activity is represented by two identical lead tokens (<S18>, <S19>, Fig 169).

The only find associated with transport, other than naval equipment, is part of a horseshoe <565>. Structural items

Fig 168 Creamware (CREA) underglaze transfer-printed and overglaze-painted pot lid with neoclassical imagery <P20> (scale c 1:1), CREA mug with masonic design <P21> and CREA underglaze black transfer-printed jar for Jessamin soap <P22> (scale c 1:2), from cesspit [5548]

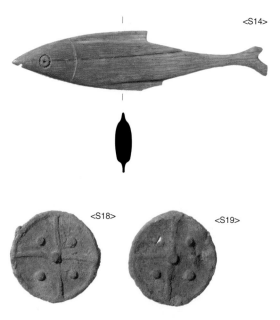

Fig 169 Bone gaming piece <S14>, and two lead tokens <S18> and <S19>, from cesspit [5548] (scale 1:1)

include 25 fragments (183g) from seven different window panes, including two *c* 4–4.5mm thick, and a corner fragment with one straight edge and one curved one. Fittings include a possible hasp/strap distributor <399> of copper alloy (extant length 39mm, max width 17mm), three copper-alloy turn buckles (eg <S38>, Fig 170), swivelling cupboard or locker closures and an associated rod (<171>, <699>), and a possible iron pulley <649>.

At first sight, it might seem that – in some cases – the same sets or pieces of crockery were being discarded in both this cesspit and the nearby cesspit [5546], at the same time and deriving from the same source. However, while it is clear that elements of 'matching' sets were thrown away in this cesspit, most are individual pieces that do not conform to any overall group by form and function. In addition, the fragmented nature of some vessels suggests a mixture of largely already broken and accumulated stockpiled pots related to incidental breakages, or yard and household sweepings, thrown away along with a few more usable pots. A process of more selective disposal can therefore be observed in this cesspit. The suggestion could be made that this feature received less of the material divided between this and the other cesspit close by. Map regression, however, suggests that these two cesspits lay either side of a property boundary, as shown on Fig 143 which employs the map of 1753. The discarded material indicates a date in the 1820s for both cesspit fills; there may have been no physical separation by this date, but the closure of the dockyard in 1830 and hence loss of livelihoods for those living outside the yard could be sufficient explanation for both the disuse of their contents and the similarity of these cesspits.

Finds from other features on the east side of the dockyard

Various features were recorded in the yards/gardens (OA8, OA9) east of the officers' quarters and outside the dockyard, including other possible cesspits, together with wells and other pits (Fig 144; Fig 146).

One feature was earlier than the rest. Pit [5972] (OA8, Fig 144) yielded ceramic vessels (32 sherds, 11 ENV, 1896g) discarded after the foundation of the dockyard (ie after 1513) but no later than *c* 1600 (thus in period 2). There is an emphasis on London-area early post-medieval red wares (PMRE) with a more or less equal representation of vessels used for drinking (pitcher and rounded jug are present), cooking (cauldron and pipkin) and food preparation and serving (carinated dishes). Also present are two imported drinking vessels. The first is a common Raeren stoneware (RAER) mug imported from kilns centred on the Raeren/Aachen region of the Rhineland (Gaimster 1997, 224–50), mainly used for consuming beer and ale. The other is a late Valencian lustreware (VALL) jug (Hurst et al 1986, 49–53) represented by a complete base (sooted) and joining shoulder fragments, with the glaze applied to the shoulder only. Preservation is variable: while the PMRE pitcher survived as a number of large-sized joining fragments – accounting for 1302g of the total 1896g of pottery from this feature – much of the remaining PMRE would have entered the

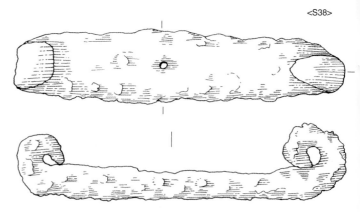

<S38>

Fig 170 Copper-alloy turn buckle <S38> from cesspit [5548] (scale 1:1)

pit in an already fragmented state, with some displaying evidence of being heated. Pit [5972] also contained a possible coin or token of copper alloy <147>, an incomplete scale-tang knife handle of iron and wood <564>, and a (residual) medieval horseshoe <658> of Clark type 3 (Clark 1995, 86–8, 96). This feature with its domestic, perhaps even tavern, assemblage lay east of the Tudor Treasurer of the Navy's house and the Tudor storehouse (Fig 18), and outside the dockyard boundary in the 17th century; some considerable way to its west was the king's slaughterhouse established by the River Ravensbourne (Deptford Creek) in the 16th century, and a storehouse in 'Deptford Strond', and beyond that Greenwich Palace (Chapter 3.1). These and the dockyard all contributed to the growth of Deptford town in the 16th century.

Discarded building materials and assorted more domestic items, ranging in date from the 17th to 19th centuries, were recovered from the fills of the other features excavated in this area. A plain-glazed floor tile was found in a rubbish pit ([5435], OA8) along with brick, peg- and pantile roofing and pre-Great Fire brick, some of which has either a worn upper or lower surface indicating use as brick paving. One clay pipe bowl and four stems were also found in this pit, with a dating of *c* 1660–80. Elsewhere in this area (OA8), iron structural fittings were recovered from a layer of dumped rubbish [5672], including a large rivet/clench bolt <654>, a short, roughly rectangular strip <656> and a complete large stake with hooked shank, corroded on to the lower shank of another <653>. A brick soakaway ([5431], Fig 144), 1.90m in diameter and 1.30m high with a small in-built opening on the north side, was undated (assigned to period 4).

Post-1666 bricks and roofing tiles, and worn stone paving cut from a type of Purbeck limestone, were recovered from the early 19th-century cesspit [5548] (above) and the underlying earlier possible cesspit (cut [5549], Fig 144); the latter also contained two fragments from a glass cup/posset pot or jug <246>, the body made of dark blue glass, with applied footring and handle in opaque white glass (*façon de Venise*), probably 17th-century in date, and a curved iron forelock wedge <652>.

An unlined rectangular pit [5805] (Fig 144) also seems to have served as a cesspit. It measured 1.60m × 0.60m and was 1.12m deep. Its fill ([5806]) contained a small copper-alloy farthing <146> possibly dated to *c* 1613–49, a glass bead or possibly a cane used for glassworking <247>, part of a glass beaker <248>, 46 fragments of bottle and window glass, lead window cames <542>, and bulk nails and iron slag. The bottle glass is mainly consistent with an 18th-century date, deriving from a shaft-and-globe bottle, an onion/mallet bottle, a case bottle and some seven windows; one small fragment, however, is from a cylindrical bottle that appears to be of 19th-century date and so could be intrusive.

Also in this area (OA8), pit [6188] (Fig 144) contained an iron collar with projecting arm <659>, probably used to secure a pipe to a wall, along with bulk iron nails and bottle and window glass. The finds from destruction debris [5254] include a 17th-century token <400> and two buttons, one of bone <183> and one of copper alloy <533>. Also of copper alloy are two 19th-century spoons, <S11> (Fig 171) and <403>, and a small cast bell (<S12>, Fig 171). Other finds include a pencil lead

<634>, window glass, copper-alloy wire <609>, bulk iron nails and iron slag, as well as an 18th-century decorated wall tile showing a figure in a landscape painted in purple on white (<T7>, Fig 175).

In the excavation area to the south (OA9), well [5970] (Fig 144) was infilled in the mid 19th century. Its fill ([6054]) yielded a range of crockery (492 sherds, 184 ENV, 18.5kg), together with smaller quantities of clay pipes, glass bottles and table glass, some bulk leather and a selection of other finds. This material reflects the range of artefacts in circulation in the period shortly before the dockyard closed in 1869, the crockery mostly representing items acquired during the 1850s (<P23>–<P26>, Fig 172). The glasswares include wine glasses <620>, <628> and <687>, lamps <619> and <767>, and 56 fragments of bulk glass (2679g), of which 38 fragments are from 34 bottles. Of these, 12 are wine bottles in dark green glass, while the remainder comprise a range of bottles in colourless, natural blue and natural green glass; some could be sauce bottles but most were probably for pharmaceutical products. Two are complete rectangular bottles with chamfered corners, one plain and long-necked, the other with the words 'WILLIAMS & ELVEY/ HALKIN ST WEST' in relief-moulded lettering, from a chemist's based in or near Belgrave Square which closed in 1862 (*London Gazette*, 22 April 1862). In addition there are four phials, one near-complete with tall, slightly tapering body in colourless glass <813> (height 132mm, base diameter 26mm, rim diameter 17mm), four fragments from one or two pickle jars, and seven pieces of window glass.

A wide range of finds including domestic and structural items was recovered from deposits resulting from the demolition of buildings in this general area of the site. Building material found in the yard/garden (OA8, OA9) includes plain unglazed Low Countries floor tile, pantile, brick, Reigate worked stone, paving and possible roofing cut from fine-grained sandstone, and possible paving cut from Kentish ragstone. Also present were fragments of salt-glazed drainage pipe. Finds from demolition deposit [5241] (B9) include a Victoria halfpenny of 1861 (<145>) and a penny of 1890 (<144>), a copper-alloy and bone button <194>, worked stone <633>, assorted window and bottle glass, and fragments of leather shoe. The bottle glass comprises part of a cylindrical wine bottle and sherds from eight other bottles/storage jars; those that are machine-made include one with a fluted body and two with

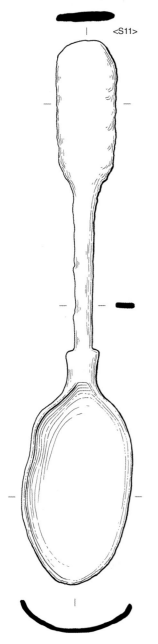

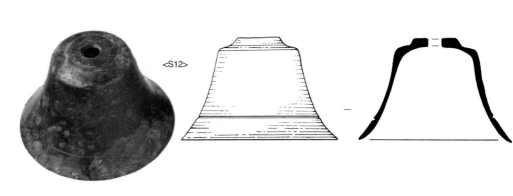

Fig 171 Copper-alloy spoon <S11> and small bell <S12> from Open Area 8 (scale 1:1)

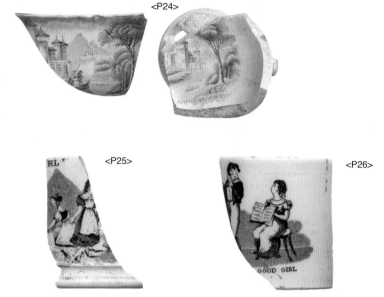

Fig 172 *Refined white wares with underglaze colour transfer-printed decoration (TPW4) with Rhine pattern print <P23> and <P24>, and children's or instructional china <P25> and <P26>, from well [5970] (scale c 1:2)*

relief-moulded lettering on the underside of the base, one cylindrical and the other rectangular. A clearly residual find is a clay pipe bowl of type AO27 found in context [5241], dating to *c* 1780–1820. It is decorated and marked with the initials 'RS', which probably stand for Richard Simmons, recorded in Greenwich in 1764–1808 (Bowsher and Woollard 2001, 103).

Finds from a 19th-century terrace (Evelyn Row)

Demolition deposits in the extreme south-east part of the site associated with the terraced buildings which were probably part of Evelyn Row (B57, Fig 98) included a halfpenny <10> of *c* 1770–5, clay pipes (three bowls, 25 stems and one mouthpiece) with a latest date of *c* 1800–40 (but including residual 17th-century pipes), and a number of household items: a slightly distorted ring <31> (diameter 29 × 34mm) and spoon <30> of copper alloy, an iron fork <124>, a bone needle case (<S7>, Fig 173), an ivory ?knife handle <59>, and bottle and window glass.

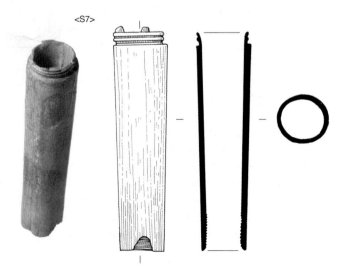

Fig 173 *Bone needle case <S7> from the demolition of the 19th-century terrace (Evelyn Row) outside the yard (scale 1:1)*

Material culture, as represented by ceramics, outside and inside the yard compared

Jacqui Pearce

The finds recovered from the officers' quarters in the royal dockyard, described in Chapter 4.2 ('Rebuilding the officers' quarters, late 17th century'), do not readily offer clues as to the social standing (or occupation) of those who originally owned and then discarded them. When compared with contemporaneous finds from features outside the dockyard described above, it appears that both officers and dockyard workers had access to good-quality ceramics imported from the Continent (Montelupo maiolica), although the larger number of vessels in Portuguese faience from contexts outside the yard (cesspit [5594]) could seem to imply a better standard of living than the smaller quantity of widely available imported maiolicas from inside. This may seem surprising if viewed through a modern lens that equates more 'exotic' decorative pottery with higher social standing, and perhaps should cause us to question such assumptions.

It is clear from waterside finds made at a number of sites along the Thames (on both sides of the river) that imported and overtly attractive decorative pottery (and other finds) was often associated with areas populated by sailors, dock workers and others generally considered to be lower down the social scale, but who had ready access to a constant flow of goods from overseas. A good example of this is provided by the finds from a site excavated in Narrow Street, Limehouse (Killock and Meddens 2005), which included an astonishing collection of imported pottery from various European countries, Turkey, Iran and China. In an area that was far from salubrious, these have been seen as – to a large extent – the results of illicit trade and as booty, and it is not impossible that the Deptford finds were acquired by similar means, at least in part. An interesting overseas example are the finds including Chinese porcelain from the archaeological excavation of houses and a tavern in the

commercial centre of the 17th-century town and naval base of
Port Royal, Jamaica (Hamilton 2000; Coad 2013, 251–6).

This picture is reinforced by the discovery of one of the
largest collections of Chinese porcelain from a single feature
excavated in London (cesspit [6524]), which was found outside
the dockyard walls in an area that appears to have been
inhabited by various dockyard workers. It is possible that these
were used in a nearby tavern (perhaps the Globe), although a
coffee house may be more likely at this date. Unlikely as it may
seem, it should also be considered a possibility that some of
these vessels at least were used in private households, since the
means by which they were obtained are now unknown (and
unknowable).

9.4 Conclusion

The history of Deptford royal naval dockyard spanned much of
the Renaissance, the Age of Enlightenment and the Industrial
Revolution. Sayes Court was home to one of the 17th century's
greatest thinkers and played host to many other figures of that
time. There are records of almost every monarch of the 16th
and 17th centuries visiting the yard, as well as Oliver Cromwell
and, from abroad, Czar Peter the Great of Russia. The yard was
witness to important events in English national life, foremost
among them perhaps the theatrical knighting of Francis Drake,
and there is a close association with nationally important figures
such as Samuel Pepys and John Rennie senior.

Less famous are those who ran and worked in the dockyard.
It is impossible to go back and share their experiences directly,
but it is hoped that this book will have given some sense of
their lives. It is easier to do this for the yard's officers – their
words survive in the letters they wrote and we have the plates
off which they ate. It is less easy for the yard's house-carpenters,
bricklayers, scavelmen and other ranks, although their work is
preserved – in fragmentary form – in the structures they built.
It is hoped that the evidence gathered conveys something of the
day to day challenges in executing the works at the yard. The
same difficulties described by Clerk of Works Smith in
constructing the new entrance to the wet dock in the early 19th
century would have been encountered by John Hopton in
building the wet dock 300 years earlier.

Most of the dockyard – or perhaps dockyards would be a
better description – have vanished. The Tudor dockyard has
largely gone, as have significant parts of the Stuart
establishment, removed by later structures. All that remain of
John Evelyn's famous gardens are his truncated garden walls.
His house may have fared slightly better – a preserved tiled
floor is likely to have belonged to Sayes Court and there are
hints that foundations survive below the walls of the 18th-
century workhouse built on top of them.

The end of the dockyard was brutal. Building work at
the yard almost always reused 'old materials', but at the end
of its life many of the yard's own buildings were pulled down

and their fabric carted away to be used elsewhere. The last use
of the bomb-damaged Tudor storehouse was as a lorry park
and (almost) everything above ground level was demolished,
with everything below buried. In the late 17th century, the
Navy Board ruled against the keeping of pigs at the yard
(TNA, ADM 106/2537, 11 April 1690, np); yet in the late 19th
century, reincarnated as an animal market, the yard was
crammed with livestock and cattle stood where Charles I had
once walked.

It is ironic that the likely reasons for the selection of the site
as a dockyard are the same ones that led to its demise. Probably
one of the principal reasons was the natural pond into which
the *Orfletediche* tributary flowed, which was easy to adapt as a
wet dock, a harbour for ships. However, silting became a major
problem at the yard, especially as ships got bigger and required a
deeper draught. Such silting was probably due more to ground
run-off than deposition by the Thames, and their position at
the base of the *Orfletediche* river system meant that the yard's
wet dock and mast docks were particularly prone to becoming
clogged with silt. Similarly, the Deptford location of the yard is
likely to have been chosen because of its proximity to the palace
at Greenwich, but this upriver situation became an impediment
in later years as ships had to labour up the Thames. The town of
Deptford was of 'none estimation' before the yard was
established, if William Lambarde (1596) is to be believed. The
presence of this huge establishment stimulated the town, which
itself grew as a result, hemming in the yard to the east and
south and preventing further expansion once John Evelyn's
lands had been swallowed up.

History and archaeology are complementary and powerful
tools for understanding the development of a historic site.
Features not shown on the 1774 dockyard model or historic
maps and panoramas, such as the complex timber land-tie
structures supporting the brick wet dock walls, have been
revealed by archaeology. Evidence of the zoning of activities
has been found to add to the information already available from
some of the later detailed dockyard plans. The wet dock was an
innovative feature of the yard, and this project has not only
provided a detailed description of its construction, but a narrow
date range for when it was built. It is hoped that this will be of
help to future researchers elsewhere investigating similar
structures where the historical evidence is less complete.
Archaeological evidence has placed a question mark at least over
the date of the construction of the Tudor storehouse – its first
incarnation may be earlier than 1513, which is generally taken as
the yard's own date of foundation. Conversely, historical
evidence has provided some quite narrow date ranges for
structures identified archaeologically that otherwise could only
be dated with less precision.

In addition, there are important implications for the study
of other Royal Navy dockyards. These establishments were not
closed off from the wider world of civil engineering. Major
works at Deptford – such as the construction of the brick wet
dock, the rebuilding of the wet dock gates, and the Rennie
rebuild – were carried out not by the yard's own workmen but
by independent contractors. Further examination of the records

of how dockyards were built will shed light not only on the work by the yard but also on that of civil engineering contractors on a wider scale.

Inevitably some answers remain elusive. For this project, it was only possible to sample a small part of the available historical resource, and indeed to excavate only some of the archaeology as the project was designed to leave this preserved *in situ*. Future work will discover more of the history of the development of the site. The dockyard was a place of innovation, with many maritime experiments carried out in the wet dock. These experiments – the successes and failures – have only been touched upon in this volume, and will be a fruitful area for future researchers to explore. One of the experimenters was the yard's neighbour John Evelyn, and further research into how the proximity of the Royal Navy dockyard influenced Evelyn's own thinking would be worthwhile. He addressed the problem of timber supply to the navy in his book *Sylva*, and this could provide a starting point.

Regrettably, the scope of the project could not include a more detailed account of the ships built in the dockyard beyond that provided by the secondary literature. If this had been included, the present volume would be twice the size. A wealth of detail still remains untapped in the historical documents of the yard: there are details of the construction of ships, and the officers conducted thorough surveys of ships to be repaired. The latter records include James Cook's discovery ship *Endeavour Bark* (the former *Earl of Pembroke*, 6366bm-tons) and William Bligh's *Bounty* (the former *Bethia*, 4215bm-tons) to name but two of the more famous examples (*Townsville Daily Bulletin*, 14 July 1945, 4; Banbury 1971, 22). This work awaits future researchers.

Nonetheless, these excavations and the material recovered dwarf any previous archaeological investigations of a royal dockyard and should be invaluable in informing future investigations of similar sites. This is perhaps especially so with regard to the more domestic items found at Deptford. Much is known about dockyard buildings and engineering works and the industrial/craft processes of naval shipbuilding and repairing, but very little is known about the ordinary people who worked in the yards, living in some cases within the yards but more often close by. Except for the senior dockyard officials, such people very rarely feature in yard records save for their names. This makes the recovery of 'domestic rubbish' from both inside and immediately outside the dockyard all the more valuable in helping us understand more about the workforce and their living standards, and these excavations provide some of the best artefact evidence yet (J Coad, pers comm 2015).

Beyond this, it is hoped that this project will have led to a greater general appreciation and understanding of the site's development, and that of Deptford itself – and of the potential interaction or disconnection between the yard and the neighbourhood outside. Heightening awareness and increasing understanding of the impact of a naval dockyard on the immediate area, and the relationship between them, can assist local decision making, planning, development and management of the historic environment, as a study of the hinterland of the Portsmouth naval base demonstrates (Hutchings 2016). Some of the conclusions of this book will inevitably be proved wrong, even if based on the best evidence available at the time, and it is hoped that it will act as a spur to further research that will build on what this project has revealed.

10

Specialist appendices

10.1 Building material

Ian M Betts

Stone building material

Most stone was recorded *in situ*, with only a small quantity collected from the site. Occurrences, including roofing and paving stone, are noted in Chapters 2–8 and 9.3.

Of interest is the earliest slate roofing (<775>, Fig 12) which came from demolition fills that apparently pre-date the Tudor storehouse (Chapter 2.3). Most slate roofing used in London before the mid 18th century seems to have come from quarries located in Devon and Cornwall. Also, part of a Portland stone moulding (<754>, Fig 45) was found with material dated *c* 1680–1710 and earlier, associated with the rebuilt smithy (B18) (period 3; Chapter 4.2).

Medieval ceramic building material

Roofing tile

Fabrics 2271, 2586, 2816
A number of medieval and probable medieval peg roofing tiles were found in pre-dockyard contexts: a pit fill (S1), the backfill behind a timber revetment in a ditch or barge gutter (S4) and in Open Area 1 (Chapter 2.3). Splash glaze is present on a number of the tiles, which are of standard two round nail hole type, the holes allowing the tiles to be fixed in place by the use of iron nails or wooden pegs.

Peg tile roofs would have been covered at the top by a line of curved ridge tiles, a glazed example of which was found in the backfill behind the aforementioned timber revetment (S4).

Brick

Fabrics 3043, 3208
Two types of medieval brick were present, both probably imported from the Low Countries. The first (fabric 3208) are pink- and cream-coloured and measure 172–178 × 83–91 × 38–43mm (one brick is 28–30mm high). These were found in a brick drain (S5) and a clay deposit associated with the timber wet dock (S8). There is also a single worn example from a tiled floor associated with the rebuilt Treasurer of the Navy's house (B3), dating from the 16th/17th century to 1684–8 (Chapter 4.2).

Bricks of the second type (fabric 3043) are cream, brownish-cream, pink and brown in colour and similar in size to the first, at 171–187 × 84–90 × 38–43mm. These were found in dumping/make-up, a posthole and floor bedding in the rebuilt Treasurer of the Navy's house (B3) and a tile surface in Building 7 (Chapter 4.2). These bricks may have been used in the original Tudor Treasurer of the Navy's house (B2; Chapter 3.2).

Post-medieval ceramic building material

A concordance of illustrated floor and wall tiles is given in Table 1.

Floor tile

Both glazed and unglazed floor tiles were recovered from the site. Unfortunately many are so worn that it is no longer possible to say whether they were originally glazed or not. Most, if not all, are Low Countries ('Flemish') imports.

LOW COUNTRIES GLAZED

Fabrics 1813, 2850, 2322

A number of glazed and worn Low Countries floor tiles were collected from a tiled surface in Building 7 (?boathouses; period 3; Chapter 4.2). These tiles, which were probably made around 1480–1600, have a plain green glaze above a layer of white slip. It is highly likely that they were used with yellow-glazed examples in a chequerboard pattern. The surviving tiles measure 176–177mm square by 21–23mm thick.

Also present in Building 7 were a small number of larger Low Countries floor tiles measuring 206–208mm square by 31mm in thickness. These have roughly square-shaped nail holes in two diagonally opposite top corners. Most are worn, but there is one example partly covered by brown glaze, although it is uncertain if this was added deliberately. The glaze may have run on to the tile from other glazed items which were being fired in the same kiln.

Another Low Countries floor tile with plain green glaze above a layer of white slip was found with masonry in the smithy (B11) (period 3; Chapter 4.2). This is also of similar size, at 175mm in breadth by 23mm in thickness, suggesting that it is probably contemporary with the floor tiles used in Building 7. The incomplete smithy tile would originally have had two oval (2 × 1mm) nail holes in diagonally opposite corners. A further tile with the same combination of green glaze and white slip was found in Open Area 1, along with brick and roofing tile of similar date, but this must be later contamination. This tile measures 174mm in breadth by 23mm in thickness.

UNCERTAIN SOURCE GLAZED

Fabric 2324

Two highly worn glazed floor tiles were found dumped in Open Area 6 (period 3; Chapter 4.2). These tiles, which are characterised by having their base scraped smooth prior to firing, are over 136mm in length or breadth. The source of these tiles is unknown, although they are probably of similar date to the Low Countries tiles discussed above.

LOW COUNTRIES UNGLAZED

Fabrics 1813, 2318, 2850

Most Low Countries floor tiles from the site are unglazed, including most of the tiles found in the *in situ* areas of flooring. Where present the nail hole is generally square or rectangular. There were probably two nail holes in each tile in diagonally opposite corners. These tiles, which are broadly of *c* 1580–1800 in date, fall into two main size groups.

Smaller floor tiles, measuring around 205mm square by 31–32mm thick, were used in a brick floor in Building 7. Larger Low Countries floor tiles were used in the tiled floors in the rebuilt Treasurer of the Navy's house (B3) (16th/17th century to 1684–8; Chapter 4.2); these measure 246–259mm square by 30–35mm thick. The less worn examples preserve two rectangular nail holes (1.5–3mm in length) in diagonally opposite top corners.

Other unglazed floor tiles, which measure 39–43mm in thickness, were found in the 18th-century yard (OA17), the workhouse building (B13) and east of the officers' quarters outside the yard (OA8).

OTHER FLOOR TILE

An *in situ* tiled floor surface was found in the workhouse building (B13), but may have belonged to part of the earlier Sayes Court house (B12; Chapter 5.2). The upper surface of each tile is very worn, but their size (247–256mm square) suggests that they are also unglazed Low Countries floor tiles of *c* 1580–1800.

TIN-GLAZED FLOOR TILES

Fabrics 2196, 2197, 3078

There are four tin-glazed floor tiles from the site, the earliest of which came from period 3. A worn plain white tile was found

Table 1 Concordance of illustrated floor and wall tiles

Cat no.	Acc no.	Context	Land use	Period	Description	Fig no.
<T1>	<630>	[6013]	OA5	3	floor tile with Tudor rose pattern	174
<T2>	<690>	[5790]	B10	3	medallion floor tile with dog	174
<T3>	<629>	[+]	–	–	floor tile with flower design	174
<T4>	<113>	[2945]	B3	3	wall tile with sea creature	29
<T5>	<112>	[2767]	B3	3	wall tile with ship design	29
<T6>	<502>	[5889]	OA16	5	wall tile with flower vase design	175
<T7>	<501>	[5254]	OA8	5	wall tile with figure in landscape	175
<T8>	<689>	[+]	–	–	shaped brick	176

Fig 174   Tin-glazed floor tiles: with Tudor rose design <T1>; medallion tile with dog <T2>; with polychrome fruit and flower design <T3> (scale 1:2)

in dumps/demolition in the rebuilt Treasurer of the Navy's house (B3; Chapter 4.2). This may be broadly contemporary with a so-called 'Tudor rose' pattern from demolition in Open Area 5 (<T1>, Fig 174). The Tudor rose is the most common design found on tin-glazed floor tiles in London, and this tile was probably made at either the Pickleherring or the Rotherhithe pothouse *c* 1618–50. A complete tile with this design is illustrated by Betts and Weinstein (2010, 111, no. 111).

A so-called medallion tile showing what appears to be a dog surrounded by a multi-circular border (<T2>, Fig 174) was recovered from the backfill of a wall cut in Building 10. The tile is slightly unusual in being painted in blue with just a solitary brownish-yellow circular border, whereas it is more normal for medallion tiles of this type to be painted in polychrome. There are tiles with similar animal designs but these have more elaborate oriental-style 'Wan Li' corner motifs. The brownish-yellow border on this tile suggests that it too was made at the Pickleherring pothouse in Southwark *c* 1618–50. Similar London tiles are illustrated by Betts and Weinstein (2010, 100–3, nos 56–65).

An unstratified floor tile from area 4 (Fig 3) shows part of a well-preserved polychrome fruit and flower design (<T3>, Fig 174). Tiles of this type, although painted in slightly different styles, are known from various London sites (Betts and Weinstein 2010, 108–9, nos 104–6). Again they were probably made at the Pickleherring pothouse in Southwark *c* 1618–50.

Wall tile

TIN-GLAZED

Fabrics 3064, 3067, 3078

Three small fragments of decorated Dutch tin-glazed tile were found associated with the rebuilt Treasurer of the Navy's house (B3), demolished some time between 1684 and 1688 (Chapter 4.2). It seems reasonable to assume that 'delftware' wall tiles were used in this building, and these tiles were probably installed in the mid to later 17th century. In London, the

majority of wall tiles were set in fireplace surrounds. One tile depicts a sea creature and another shows part of a ship, while the third is too small to identify the design. Tiles with a nautical theme would have been fitting decoration for the Treasurer of the Navy's house.

The tile with the sea creature shows possibly a fish or crudely drawn dolphin, painted in blue on white (<T4>, Fig 29). Sea creatures are only found on Dutch tiles, most commonly those dating to the second half of the 17th century, which is probably the date of this example. Blue on white tiles with similar sea creatures are illustrated by van Dam et al (1984, 146–51, nos 182–96). Such tiles are not common in London although they have been found at, among other places, King Edward Street, Laurence Pountney Lane and Lambeth Road (Betts and Weinstein 2010, 168–9, nos 388–92).

The tile showing part of a sailing ship is also painted in blue on white (<T5>, Fig 29). The treatment of the sea is very similar to depictions of mid 17th- to 18th-century coastal vessels illustrated by van Dam et al (1984, 145, no. 181) and van Sabben and Hollem (1987, 52, nos 144, 152). Tiles depicting sailing vessels are not common in London, but this tile bears a close resemblance to two Dutch tiles dating to *c* 1650–80 which are believed to have come from a building in London (Betts and Weinstein 2010, 158–9, nos 343–4).

There are two further fragments of decorated delftware wall tile. From Open Area 16 comes the edge of a blue flower vase design with what may be a blurred blue corner, on a bluish-white background (<T6>, Fig 175). A Dutch tile with a more complete version of this design was found at King Edward Street, London (Betts and Weinstein 2010, 171, no. 402). The Deptford dockyard example measures 12mm in thickness, suggesting a date of *c* 1630–60. From Open Area 8 comes a purple-on-white design showing part of a figure in a landscape set in a circular border, which may be either a biblical or landscape tile (<T7>, Fig 175). This is a Dutch or English tile of the 18th century.

There are also two plain delftware wall tiles from the site, a

<T6>

<T7>

Fig 175 *Tin-glazed wall tiles: <T6> with blue flower vase design, 17th-century; <T7> with biblical or landscape scene, 18th-century (scale 1:1)*

plain white tile from Open Area 17 and a near-complete tile from Open Area 8 with a slightly bluish-tinged white glaze. These tiles could be English or Dutch.

Roofing tile

PEG TILE

Fabrics 2271, 2273, 2276, 2586, 2587, 2816, 3090, 3226, 3204, 3234

Large numbers of post-medieval peg roofing tiles were found on the site, some incorporated into walls and other structural features. A considerable quantity of such tiles was found in demolition and levelling dumps associated with the rebuilt Treasurer of the Navy's house (B3), suggesting that they originally covered the roof of the first Treasurer of the Navy's house (B2) (Chapters 3.2 and 4.2). Many peg tiles were also found associated with the quadrangle storehouse (B14) and smithy (B18) (Chapter 6.2).

These peg tiles are mostly of two round, square or diamond-shaped nail hole type. Most are in London-area fabrics, but there are a number in fabrics (3204, 3234) which originate from tileries located further from London.

Slightly more unusual are two tiles with just a single round nail hole. These are from a dump in Building 18 and post-dockyard backfill in Open Area 19. It is probable that these were meant to have two holes but the second hole was accidentally omitted.

PANTILE

Fabrics 2275, 2279, 2587, 3090, 3094, 3202, 3259

A unique feature of the site is the presence of Dutch brown-glazed pantiles of probable mid to late 16th-century date. Glazed pantiles are relatively rare in London, and those which have been recorded normally have either black or occasionally a dark purple glaze. Brown-glazed pantiles were almost certainly used to cover the roof of the rebuilt 16th- to 17th-century Treasurer of the Navy's house (B3), demolished in 1684–8 (Chapter 4.2). There are also single examples from demolition fill in a pre-dockyard ditch or possible barge gutter (S4), presumably later contamination (Chapter 2.3), and levelling deposits in 19th-century Building 50 (Chapter 7.4).

Documentary evidence indicates that Dutch glazed pantiles were available in Britain by *c* 1700 but are unlikely to have been made in England much before 1748 (Smith 1996). The archaeological evidence from Deptford suggests that the introduction of Dutch glazed pantiles to Britain may have been earlier than previously thought.

Unglazed pantiles were found in modest numbers in periods 3–6. Pantiles rarely survive intact but there are a few partially complete examples from Open Area 8; these measure 333–338mm in length, 221–232mm and 240–242mm in breadth, and 12–14mm in thickness. Another partially complete pantile, measuring *c* 223mm in breadth by 15mm thick, was recovered from the deposits in a timber tank (S33; Chapter 7.3).

Brown-glazed pantiles would almost certainly have been more expensive than unglazed examples. Their association with the rebuilt Treasurer of the Navy's house (B3) suggests that they were seen as prestige products. Hampton Court Palace purchased pantiles in the 1660s (Musty 1990, 417), and black-glazed pantiles were used at Chiswick House during the first half of the 18th century (Betts 2013). However, as the 18th century progressed, pantiles were increasingly seen as an inferior product and their use was commonly relegated to covering sheds, outhouses, industrial and commercial buildings, and lower-status housing stock.

RIDGE TILE

Fabrics 2276, 2586

The crests of both post-medieval peg- and pantile roofs would have been covered with curved ridge tiles. A few were found associated with the rebuild of the Treasurer of the Navy's house (B3) and the demolition of the quadrangle storehouse (B14). Other ridge tiles were found in Open Areas 14 and 17, and in Open Area 8 outside the dockyard.

HIP TILE

Fabric 2271

A rare survival from a pit in Open Area 8, outside the yard (Chapter 9.3), is a complete hip tile. These tiles were required where two roof areas met at an angle. No other hip tiles were identified from the site, although small fragments are very difficult to differentiate from other roofing tile types.

?GUTTER TILE

Fabric 2586

A small fragment of concave-shaped roofing tile from Open Area 7 (Chapter 4.2) could be a gutter tile (or a piece of peg tile which bowed during firing).

Brick

Fabrics 3032, 3033, 3034, 3035, 3038, 3039, 3042, 3046, 3065, 3215, 3217, 3221, 3223, 3224, 3257, 3261, 3274, 3281, 3290, 3307

A large number of bricks were recorded both *in situ* and as brick samples taken on site. The principal aim was to provide dating evidence to help in the interpretation of the large number of brick structures recorded on the site, and full details are available in the site archive (Chapter 1.5).

Initial analysis indicated that the bricks are a mixture of fabric types commonly found in the London area (fabrics 3032, 3033, 3034, 3039, 3046, 3065) and other fabrics which are rarer in the capital (3215, 3217, 3221, 3223, 3257, 3281, 3307). The former were probably made in brickyards in or close to London while the other types likely originated elsewhere, perhaps somewhere in the Deptford area. Most were probably made in temporary brick clamps rather than fixed brick kilns. A number of very fine sandy 17th-century bricks (fabric 3257) used in the construction of Building 6 and Building 10 (respectively, ?tar house and officers' quarters; Chapter 4.2) were probably made at New Cross to the south-west of Deptford. Here a series of brick clamps dating to *c* 1690–1800 produced bricks made from the same distinctive, very fine sandy clay (Proctor et al 2000, 187).

Also present on the site were 19th- to 20th-century yellow London stock bricks (fabric 3035) from north Kent or south Essex, and probable pink Fletton bricks (fabric 3038) from Cambridgeshire. Other bricks were also brought into London during this period (fabrics 3290, 3261).

Some of the earliest brick found on the site comprises a series of red- and orange-coloured bricks of Tudor date used in the walls of the Tudor storehouse (B1) and the Tudor Treasurer of the Navy's house (B2) (Chapter 3.2). Both are very similar in size, at 217–226 × 101–107 × 46–55mm, suggesting that the two buildings were probably constructed around the same time.

Significantly larger bricks (242–252 × 113–120 × 62–63mm) were used in a drain in the vicinity of the Tudor storehouse (OA3, Fig 18). These are also in a different fabric (type 3274), suggesting manufacture at a separate brickyard, and are probably of mid 15th- to mid 16th-century date.

There is little evidence for any elaborate Tudor brick architecture, although a carefully cut brick, perhaps the corner of a decorative plinth (<T8>, Fig 176), may date to this period. It was found in dumping north of a timber revetment (W4; Chapter 4.2).

The site included a large number of brick buildings and other brick structures dating to the 17th century. Pre-1666 bricks are similar in appearance to those used in the preceding century, although they are generally a little thicker (often *c* 60–

65mm). Many bricks made in London after 1666 tend to be dark red in colour, and new types were introduced. These are characterised by the presence of ash and cinders from domestic firing, known as 'Spanish' (fabrics 3032, 3034); this was deliberately added so that the bricks required less fuel to fire. Many of these bricks have a yellowing outer skin (Smith nd). Small fragments of charcoal or coal were also mixed in with the mortar used to bond the bricks.

Many 17th-century buildings seem to have been constructed with walls made of both pre- and post-1666 brick, although it is not always possible to say whether individual bricks were made before or after the Great Fire. This applies to an exceptionally long brick, measuring 292 × 104 × 47–50mm, used in a wall of the smithy (B11) (period 3; Chapter 4.2). This brick, which was made with unusually fine clay (fabric 3224), could be late medieval or Tudor, although other bricks in the same wall are more usual London-made examples (fabric 3046) dating to *c* 1600–66.

Dark red London-made bricks of 18th-century date differ very little in their appearance from the post-1666 examples discussed above. There are few major changes to brick shape during the 18th century, although shallow frogs occur on the base of some bricks and the brick edges tend to become slightly sharper and more defined as the century progressed.

There were also a number of surviving brick structures of 18th-century date on the site, with similar evidence for the reuse of earlier, pre-1666 bricks in the workhouse building (B13), the quadrangle storehouse (B14) and possibly in the 18th-century smithy (B18). Eighteenth-century frogged bricks were relatively rare on the site, but were used in the building range (B15) along the west side of the storehouse complex.

Frogged examples are more common among the 19th-century bricks from the site. A number of Victorian or later bricks have what appear to be letters or numbers impressed in the base of the frog, although these are often very indistinct. They would appear to represent the name of the brickworks owner or the place of manufacture. Some of the most interesting have what may be an anchor symbol. Bricks with the letter 'W' with what appears to be an anchor to the left and others with what appears to be an anchor symbol between the letters 'W' and 'H' occurred in Building 14 (Fig 177). If these

<T8>

Fig 176 Shaped Tudor brick <T8> from Waterfront 4 (scale c 1:2)

Fig 177 Frogged brick with an anchor between the letters 'W' and 'H', photographed in situ *in a wall of the quadrangle storehouse (B14)*

are indeed an anchor then it may imply that the bricks were specially made for the dockyard, perhaps by a brickyard operated by the dockyard itself.

Other frogs have the letter 'M' with a blurred letter or number to the right, while still others appear to show the letters 'C' (or 'V'), 'L', 'S' and possibly 'Y'. More unusual is a yellow stock brick (fabric 3035) with a raised letter 'E'. Other Victorian, or later, bricks have pressure marks on their stretcher face, indicating how they were stacked to allow drying before being fired.

A number of more unusual 19th-century bricks were present. These include a series of bricks made from hard cream firing clay with a scatter of black iron oxide inclusions (fabric 3290). Certain examples have white glaze adhering to either their header or stretcher face. These bricks, which are also slightly thicker than other 19th-century brick types, were probably first used in the second half of that century (T P Smith, pers comm). They were often used in washrooms and lavatories, where an easily cleaned surface was required. Their rather haphazard use at Deptford suggests that they may have been reused from an earlier structure.

Another brick type represented is machine-made bricks with a granular internal fabric (3038) and usually featuring deep frogs. These may well be Fletton bricks which were first made at Fletton, a village near Peterborough, using shale. Later, production expanded into the Bedfordshire area by exploiting the same shale deposits. Fletton's are rather insipid pink-coloured bricks which, although strong, were not very attractive and were often hidden away in walls rather than used as facing bricks. They were first made around the 1870s to 1880s and production continued well into the 20th century (T P Smith, pers comm). There are also some cream and white bricks with the same granular fabric (type 3261), which may be of similar date.

DUTCH BRICK

Fabric 3036

A solitary yellow Dutch brick was recovered from a dump in the rebuilt Treasurer of the Navy's house (B3), demolished in 1684–8 (Chapter 4.2). These small, hard bricks were principally used as paving, although there is no sign of wear on this example measuring 73mm in breadth by 35–38mm in thickness. The earliest small, yellow Dutch paving bricks found in London date to *c* 1480–1550 but they were only common after *c* 1630 and this example is very probably 17th-century.

Drain pipes

The socketed stoneware drainage pipes recorded on the site were probably made in the mid 19th to early 20th centuries by Doulton at their factory situated next to the Thames in Lambeth. A large brown-glazed drainage pipe found associated with the storehouse range (B15) was marked 'DOULTON LAMBETH'.

10.2 Clay tobacco pipes

Jacqui Pearce

Introduction and methodology

The clay tobacco pipes from the site were recorded in keeping with current MOLA practice and entered on to the Oracle relational database. The pipe bowls have been classified and dated according to the chronology of London bowl types (Atkinson and Oswald 1969), with the dating of some of the 18th-century pipes refined where appropriate by reference to Oswald's simplified general typology (Oswald 1975, 37–41). The prefixes AO and OS respectively are used to indicate which typology has been applied.

A considerable number of clay tobacco pipe fragments were recovered from 104 contexts, with several key groups including between 20 and 153 bowls. A total of 517 pipe bowls, 508 stem fragments and 22 mouthpieces were recorded. These include 253 accessioned items, of which 221 are marked by their maker (42% of all identifiable bowls) and 164 are decorated. All pipes are typical of London manufacture and the majority were made in the Greenwich area by local pipe makers. Most appear to have been smoked, some of them heavily.

Twenty-five contexts have been assigned the broad date range of *c* 1580–1910 by the presence of otherwise undatable stem fragments alone. All other contexts span the mid 17th to late 19th centuries. No bowl types earlier than *c* 1640 were identified. Table 2 provides a concordance of the illustrated clay tobacco pipes.

Tobacco pipes from the Stuart dockyard (period 3, 1603–1714)

A total of 141 clay pipe bowls, 160 stem fragments and eight mouthpieces were recovered from contexts dated to period 3

Table 2 Concordance of illustrated clay tobacco pipes

Cat no.	Acc no.	Context	Land use	Period	Description	Fig no.
<CP1>	<725>	[6013]	OA5	3	fleur-de-lis	178
<CP2>	<571>	[4635]	S8	3	no mark	178
<CP3>	<380>	[4880]	OA8	5	WB	158
<CP4>	<448>	[4880]	OA8	5	WB	158
<CP5>	<316>	[4880]	OA8	5	WB	158
<CP6>	<447>	[4880]	OA8	5	RS	158
<CP7>	<465>	[4880]	OA8	5	RS	158
<CP8>	<327>	[4880]	OA8	5	WG	159
<CP9>	<293>	[4880]	OA8	5	WG	159
<CP10>	<371>	[4880]	OA8	5	WG	159
<CP11>	<370>	[4880]	OA8	5	WG	159
<CP12>	<374>	[4880]	OA8	5	JA	160
<CP13>	<343>	[4880]	OA8	5	?EB	160
<CP14>	<328>	[4880]	OA8	5	CR	161
<CP15>	<577>	[4880]	OA8	5	IF	161
<CP16>	<317>	[4880]	OA8	5	flowers	161
<CP17>	<367>	[4880]	OA8	5	BUMBY/SHADWELL/JB	161
<CP18>	<573>	[4880]	OA8	5	no mark	161
<CP19>	<491>	[5107]	OA8	5	ANDREWS/DEPTFORD	167
<CP20>	<588>	[5254]	OA8	5	no mark	179
<CP21>	<596>	[5419]	OA8	5	no mark	179
<CP22>	<589>	[5254]	OA8	5	no mark	179

(Chapter 4.2). Half of these come from the rebuilt Treasurer of the Navy's house (B3), demolished in 1684–8 (70 bowls and 12 stems), and are dated at the latest to *c* 1700–10, with most pipes made between *c* 1660 and *c* 1680 (chiefly types AO13, AO15 and AO18); the latest pipe from Building 3 is a type AO25 (*c* 1700–70) from dumping, context [2024] (the dating of Building 3 is discussed in detail in Chapter 4.2). Most land-use features of this period yielded clay pipes datable between *c* 1660 and *c* 1710, the period from the Restoration to the reign of Queen Anne. A reasonable number of clay pipes (45 bowls, 50 stems and seven mouthpieces) were also recovered from the Stuart period gravel headland (OA5), especially from context [6013] which is dated to *c* 1660–80. Similar dating was obtained for Open Areas 6–8 (Chapter 9.3), with pipes from Building 6 (?tar house) and Building 8 ('sawhouse' or slipway wall), Open Area 9 (Chapter 9.3), Structure 10 (timber ditch revetment), Building 18 (smithy) and Structure 8 (wet dock), all dating to *c* 1680/90–1710.

Overall, there are 68 pipe bowls of type AO15 and 20 of type AO18 (*c* 1660–80), with only ten bowls of types current in the period *c* 1680–1710 (AO19, AO21, AO22). Many of these have milling around the top of the bowl, but none is burnished and none marked with maker's initials. Two examples have some form of mark. A type AO12 bowl from [1993] in Building 3 has a single raised dot moulded in relief on the left side of the heel (<756>) and one other pipe has a single milled line running across the base of the heel (<755> from the same context). Only two decorated pipes were recorded from this period. One of these (<CP1>, Fig 178) has an incuse fleur-de-lis stamped on the heel, with the same device also stamped all over the front of the bowl and on the stem. The other is the only pipe recorded from the site that was probably not made in London; this has a moulded mulberry tree on each side of the bowl (<CP2>, Fig 178).

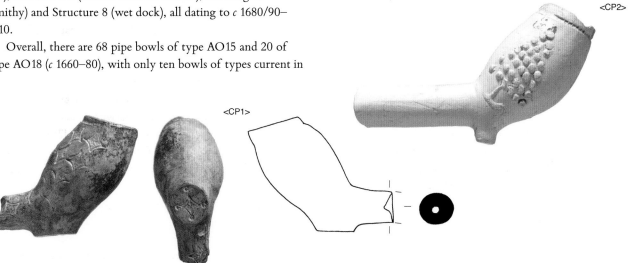

Fig 178 Clay tobacco pipes <CP1> and <CP2> from the Stuart dockyard (scale c 1:1)

Tobacco pipes from the early Georgian dockyard (period 4, 1714–74)

Land-use features assigned to period 4 (Chapters 6.2, 6.3 and 9.3) yielded 92 clay pipe bowls, 180 stem fragments and eight mouthpieces. Excluding undatable stems, these span the period from c 1640 to c 1780. There are only two bowls dated to c 1640–60 (types AO9 and AO10), recovered from boathouse Building 7, and 27 bowls dated to c 1660–80 (types AO13, AO15 and AO18), with 26 bowls of types AO20, AO21 and AO22 found in contexts dated to the turn of the 17th and 18th centuries. The main features in which they occurred were in the quadrangle storehouse (B14), Open Area 14 and Open Area 8,

although examples of type AO25 pipe bowls (c 1700–70) were also found in some of the same contexts. One of the largest groups was found outside the yard in cesspit [6524] in Open Area 8, which included 14 pipes marked with their maker's initials. These are discussed separately (Chapter 9.3), but consist of nine pipes marked 'IB', for John Bean of Crane Street, Greenwich, recorded in 1764–89 (Bowsher and Woollard 2001, 103), and 'IL', possibly for John Langley, recorded in St Luke's parish in 1721–35 (Oswald 1975, 140). The group is dated on the basis of the pipe bowl forms to c 1730–80, and was most likely deposited after 1764. No decorated pipes were recorded in period 4 contexts. Two probable 'IB'-marked pipes were found in another period 4 group, from cesspit [5994] in Open Area 9

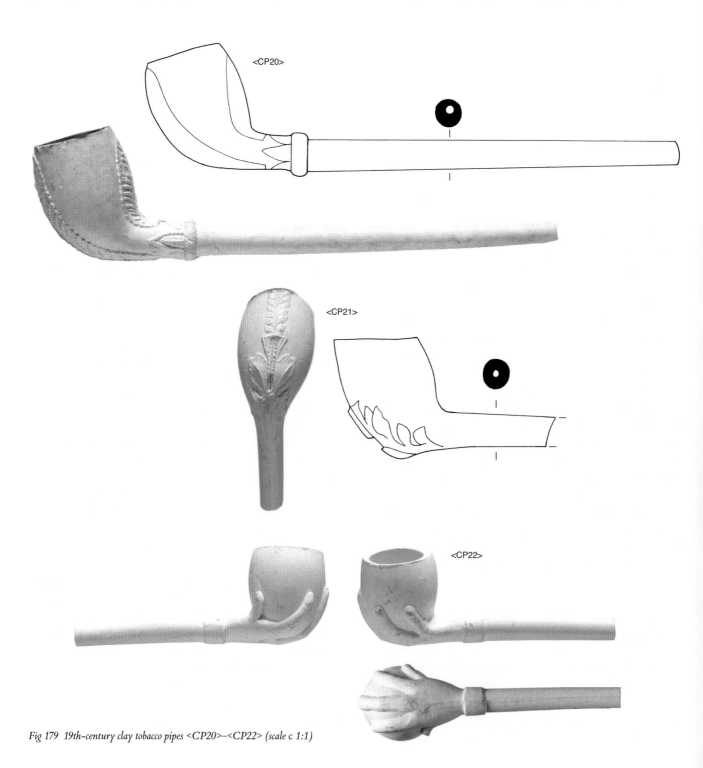

Fig 179 19th-century clay tobacco pipes <CP20>–<CP22> (scale c 1:1)

(Chapter 9.3). The fill of this cesspit is dated earlier, to *c* 1730–60 by the pipes recovered, far fewer in number (19 bowls, eight stems and one mouthpiece), mostly of type OS11 but also including late 17th- to early 18th-century types. Only four marked examples were recorded, possibly made by John Bean of Crane Street (above) and by William Manby of Green Dragon Alley, Limehouse, in 1719–63 (ibid, 142).

Tobacco pipes from the late Georgian to Victorian dockyard (period 5, 1774–1869)

Contexts assigned to period 5 features (Chapters 7.3, 7.4 and 9.3) account for just over half of all clay pipe bowls recovered during excavation (264 bowls, as well as 112 stem fragments and five mouthpieces). The key groups, discussed separately in Chapter 9.3, come from the major cesspit fills in Open Area 8, outside the yard: from cesspit [5548], and the very large group from cesspit [5546]. This last group (contexts [4880] and [4879]) yielded a considerable number of clay pipes, dated at the latest to *c* 1800–40, but mostly consisting of pipes made *c* 1780–1820 (type AO27). The large number of marked pipes includes examples made by local pipe makers William Gosling (1801–2: Bowsher and Woollard 2001, 103), Richard Simmons (1764–1808: ibid), William Burstow (Limekilns, 1789–1800: ibid) and Joseph Andrews (Deptford, 1823–8: Oswald 1975, 140) (Figs 158–61). A total of 121 pipe bowls from this group are also decorated, mostly with moulded leaf or wheatsheaf seams and/or moulded vertical ribbing, although there are also pipes decorated with the Prince of Wales's feathers, dragons or a rose and thistle.

Another major group from Open Area 8 came from the fill of cesspit [5548] (Chapter 9.3), which is dated by the pipes to *c* 1780–1820 (14 bowls, four stems). Twelve of these pipe bowls are marked, by William Burstow and Richard Simmons, as well as Joseph Andrews of Deptford (above; Fig 167). Seven are also decorated, mostly with moulded vertical ribbing.

Seventeenth- and early 18th-century pipes were recorded in several contexts, most being residual (in B10, OA16 and OA17, S27, S31 and S33). Apart from the large Open Area 8 groups noted above, pipes that fall within the date range of period 5 came from smithy Building 18, spanning *c* 1820–80 (types AO29 and AO30). One other feature in Open Area 8 (destruction debris [5254] and [5419]) yielded nine marked pipes in these later forms and type AO27, with the initials 'JD' remaining unidentified, and 16 decorated pipes, mostly with moulded leaf seams (<CP20>, <CP21>, Fig 179). One other late 19th-century pipe from the same area has an egg-shaped bowl held by a modelled hand (<CP22>, Fig 179).

Tobacco pipes post-dockyard (period 6, 1869 onwards)

A relatively small number of clay pipes were found in features associated with period 6 (19 bowls, 54 stem fragments and one mouthpiece) (Chapter 8.2 and 8.3). These date mostly to the 18th to early 19th centuries, so were residual by this date. They come from Building 10 (*c* 1730–80), Building 57 (*c* 1800–40),

Open Area 19 (*c* 1780–1820) and Open Area 9 (Chapter 9.3; undatable stem fragments).

Marked pipes

A large number of the clay pipes from the site carry makers' marks: a total of 221 examples, all of them later 18th- to 19th-century forms (Pearce 2012, table 3). Fifty-three different (or possibly different) marks were recorded, although the number with potential for the identification of their maker is nearer 30, based on the presence of two clear initials or a name given in full. Many of these marked pipes, especially those made after *c* 1780, are also decorated.

A number of pipes are marked with symbols alone, and these cannot be traced to an individual maker.

10.3 Pottery

Nigel Jeffries

The pottery assemblage comprising medieval and post-medieval pottery was recorded by Nigel Jeffries and Lyn Blackmore. The illustrated pottery is summarised in Table 3. With the pottery retrieved from sequences contemporary with the Tudor dockyard (period 2) limited to material from just six contexts, little further can be said about it. The 32 sherds from pit [5972] on the east side of the yard have already been considered (Chapter 9.3), and the pottery in the other five deposits pertaining to the Tudor dockyard sequence was limited to just 13 sherds from 11 fragmentary vessels.

Pottery from the Stuart dockyard (period 3, 1603–1714)

The expansion of the royal dockyard by the end of the Stuart period (period 3; Chapter 4), captured on the 1698 panorama (Fig 23), is reflected in the quantity of pottery found. The significant groups have been presented in Chapter 4.2 and these can be considered as an accurate reflection of the composition in terms of form and function, and the sources of supply, of the remainder of the pottery from this period. Much of the latter material was retrieved from make-up layers and deposits external to any documented buildings or structures and is largely fragmentary.

Taken as a whole, the 332 pottery vessels from features and buildings associated with the Stuart dockyard were derived largely from London and regional sources (Table 4). This serves as a reminder that, despite the focus (below) on the portion of this assemblage from Continental Europe (21.2% ENV, 5576g), London's red ware (27% ENV, 7806g) and tin-glazed ware ('delftware') (23.8% ENV, 2289g) industries remained the most dominant sources of supply to the Stuart dockyard, providing largely utilitarian vessels.

'London-area red wares' describes a group of fabrics and

Table 3 Concordance of illustrated pottery

Cat no.	Acc no.	Context	Land use	Period	Description	Fig no.
<P1>	<779>	[5428]	B10	3	FREC jug	42
<P2>	<623>	[6013]	OA5	3	TGW cat jug	43
<P3>	<780>	[5935]	OA9	4	POTG dish	145
<P4>	<781>	[5935]	OA9	4	POTG dish	145
<P5>	<782>	[5935]	OA9	4	TGW G capuchine cup	145
<P6>	<783>	[4952]	OA8	4	CHPO ROSE armorial saucer	147
<P7>	<784>	[4952]	OA8	4	DTGW teapot	148
<P8>	<785>	[4952]	OA8	4	DTGW plate	149
<P9>	<786>	[4952]	OA8	4	DTGW plate	149
<P10>	<787>	[4952]	OA8	4	DTGW plate	149
<P11>	<788>	[4952]	OA8	4	TGW 'bleeding bowl'	150
<P12>	<789>	[4880]	OA8	5	PEAR dinner plate with blue shell-edge rim	153
<P13>	<790>	[4880]	OA8	5	PEAR dinner plate with green shell-edge rim	153
<P14>	<791>	[4880]	OA8	5	PEAR dinner plate with willow pattern print	153
<P15>	<792>	[4880]	OA8	5	PEAR dinner plate with floral basket pattern	153
<P16>	<793>	[4880]	OA8	5	CREA plate	153
<P17>	<797>	[5107]	OA7	5	CHPO ROSE tea bowl	164
<P18>	<798>	[5107]	OA8	5	CHPO ROSE saucer	164
<P19>	<799>	[5107]	OA8	5	CHPO ROSE handled cup	164
<P20>	<794>	[5107]	OA8	5	CREA pot lid	168
<P21>	<795>	[5107]	OA8	5	CREA tankard with masonic imagery	168
<P22>	<796>	[5107]	OA8	5	CREA 'soap' jar	168
<P23>	<800>	[6054]	OA9	5	TPW4 (Rhine pattern) mug	172
<P24>	<801>	[6054]	OA9	5	TPW4 (Rhine pattern) teacup	172
<P25>	<802>	[6054]	OA9	5	TPW4 children's pattern mug	172
<P26>	<803>	[6054]	OA9	5	TPW4 children's pattern mug	172

Table 4 Statistical breakdown of pottery from the Stuart dockyard (period 3) by major sources

Source	Sherds	Sherds %	ENV	ENV %	Wt (g)	Wt %
Surrey-Hampshire border wares	114	17.6	65	19.6	1894	9.8
London-area red wares	174	27.0	91	27.4	7806	40.6
London tin-glazed wares ('delftware')	154	23.8	63	19.0	2289	11.9
Essex fine red wares	51	7.9	38	11.4	1157	6.0
Imported Continental wares	137	21.2	67	20.2	5576	29.0
Non-local 'earthenware'	5	0.8	3	0.9	196	1.0
Stoneware (British-made)	6	0.9	5	1.5	315	1.6
Total	646		332		19233	

forms manufactured at various kilns in and around the London area from the late 15th century to well into the 19th century. Building on Orton and Pearce (1984), Nenk (1999, 237) best summarises this important and most common source of pottery for the Stuart dockyard (27% sherds, 27.4% ENV). The earliest products of this industry, between the late 15th and mid 17th centuries, are plain or partially glazed red wares (London-area early post-medieval red ware: PMRE) and its slip-coated derivatives with clear (yellow) or green glaze (PMSRY and PMSRG, respectively). These are not, however, particularly common from the site, limited to around a dozen fragmented vessels. Kilns are known in Woolwich dating from the 15th/16th century and earlier (J Pearce, pers comm). London-area post-medieval slipped red ware (PMSR) fabrics and forms begin to go out of fashion by the mid 17th century.

Technological development of this industry at the end of the 16th and in the early 17th centuries resulted in a range of better-fired, more evenly (lead-) glazed, red wares (London-area post-medieval red ware: PMR), also common from the study area. Production is known to have occurred from the late 17th century very close to the dockyard and just downstream at Deptford (Divers 2004) and Woolwich (Pryor and Blockley 1978) in south London, and is further hinted at in north Lambeth, where kiln waste has been found. The first documented example of a potter making red ware in Deptford is dated 1691 (Divers 2004, 91), with 'Deptford' wares recorded in the probate inventories of members of the Glass Sellars' Company from at least the late 17th century (and similarly for 'Hampshire' wares: Pearce 2000, 159). Examples of PMR were recovered from period 3 in a relatively narrow range of utilitarian forms, notably cauldrons or pipkins and a skillet (cooking), storage jars of the type described from make-up layers prior to the construction of the Treasurer of the Navy's house (B3; Chapter 4.2) and bowls. Dishes are infrequent.

Some decorative pottery, largely in the form of London-made tin-glazed ware (TGW: 23.8% sherds, 19% ENV, 2289g) was found. Chinese (blue and white) porcelain (CHPO BW) is restricted to three small-sized cup, saucer and tea bowl fragments, and consequently it is difficult to further characterise it in terms of the various 17th-century decorative traditions (eg the Ming and Kraak styles) this material might have belonged to. Nevertheless, the small quantity of CHPO reflects well its general infrequency in a 'typical' 17th-century London pottery assemblage.

Since Chew and Pearce (1999) published the 17th-century pottery assemblage from Magdelen Street in Bermondsey, similarly dated groups from sites located between Bermondsey and Deptford, notably Bombay Wharf (Pearce 2007) and Chambers Street (Howell et al 2014), in addition to those directly across the River Thames in Limehouse (Tyler 2001; Killock and Meddens 2005), have displayed marked similarities in terms of sources of supply, and have yielded a range of individual and occasionally idiosyncratic vessels from Continental Europe or further afield. These groups – largely dumped in features such as drainage ditches or as part of revetment infilling – are atypical when compared to domestic assemblages of the same date in the City of London. Reflecting instead the geography and topography of sites to the east of the City of London, their proximity to the Thames in neighbourhoods associated with shipbuilding or breaking, mercantile wharfs, trade and so on, has produced a particular ceramic and material signature.

In order to explore whether the character of the pottery from the Deptford dockyard during the Stuart period is similar to the sites noted above, we should first compare sources of pottery supply and, second, how the site's function as a naval dockyard is reflected (or otherwise) in the sources, forms and functions represented, comparing the Deptford material with similarly dated pottery from sites relevant to the Royal Navy during this period. The first is the site of the Royal Navy victualling office or yard (Grainger and Phillpotts 2010), located close to the Tower of London upstream (in East Smithfield), and second is the contents of Henry VIII's flagship the *Mary Rose* (Gardiner 2005) which sank in the Solent in July 1545. While the *Mary Rose* did not yield a large or particularly noteworthy pottery assemblage – beyond the Rhenish jugs that formed part of the barber-surgeon's chest (below) – the composition of the material, with its range of Iberian pottery, does provide a useful parallel.

While the Royal Navy victualling yard lacked well-preserved 'clearance' groups of pottery and other finds that sometimes characterise the archaeology of London during this period (see Pearce 2000, for further definition), an overall picture of pottery use can be achieved by examining the composition of this material from the 1560–*c* 1660 phase (period C1: Grainger and Phillpotts 2010, 9–35). Presuming that the fragmented pottery groups found are related to the use of Ralph Burrow's yard west (ibid, 26–7: OA17) and east (ibid, 27–9: OA18), these can best be characterised as containing a range of domestically sourced pottery (there is no discussion of

form or function) with Rhenish stonewares dominating the imported pottery. The victualling yard yielded more of a spread of Continental pottery than was present in the Deptford yard Stuart sequences, with north German Werra slipware (WERR) and Dutch tin-glazed ware (DTGW) and red earthenware (DUTR) all featuring. Small quantities of Spanish/Iberian olive jars (OLIV) and starred costrels (STAR) are nevertheless found in both yard sequences.

Concentrated in a group of features in the Deptford yard, the 12 Spanish amphora/olive jar vessels found (41 sherds, 3163g) provide a significant proportion of the 67 vessels sourced from the Continent. Whether these vessels are merely reflective of a trade in oils and wine from the Iberian Peninsula or represent a deliberate source of victualling by the Royal Navy can only be surmised, but it should be noted that in the wreck of the *Mary Rose* a number of Iberian jars were found distributed in the stern (Weinstein 2005), suggesting that on at least one Royal Navy vessel these represented a standard provision. The joining sherds found in a posthole that formed part of the Treasurer of the Navy's house (B3) at Deptford suggest that this pottery was reused as packing material in the construction cut. Iberian coins were common in the 17th-century rubbish used to backfill and consolidate a newly constructed wharf in Limehouse (Tyler 2001, 90) and here, involving plots owned by various sea captains, the finds were linked to Britain's expanding global reach (ibid, 90–1), in particular contact with the Spanish empire in the Americas and Caribbean (Killock and Meddens 2005, 16–25).

Ubiquitous Rhenish stonewares from Frechen (FREC) close to Cologne are, however, the most common component of Deptford's imported assemblage from the Continent (57 sherds, 31 ENV, 1948g). An industry best described by Gaimster (1997), durable FREC *Bartmänner*, though shipped empty, served principally as containers of beer or wine for the tavern trade, although their widespread distribution among household assemblages in London demonstrates that such wares should never be viewed as exclusively related to a drinking establishment (cf Jeffries et al 2014). Taken together, the Spanish jars and FREC *Bartmänner* emphasise an imported pottery assemblage that functioned largely as containers for olives, olive oil, wine and so forth. Insights into the pottery used in a 16th-century Royal Navy context can be gleaned from the *Mary Rose* where, in addition to the large quantity of pewter ware found (which had survived well in the silts of the seabed, unlike its near-absence from mainland archaeological sites), the contents of the barber-surgeon's chest included a number of sealed Rhenish stoneware jugs (Gardiner 2005, 471–2) which held a variety of medicinal treatments (ibid, 220).

Dated to the last quarter of the 17th century, the sequence revealed during the excavations at Rotherhithe's Bombay Wharf (Pearce 2007), located close to the Deptford yard, yielded a large quantity of pottery (151 sherds, 83 ENV, 6002g) from the backfill of a V-shaped channel or ditch (ibid, 82). The quantities and percentages of pottery in terms of major sources by estimated vessel count there (ibid, 91, fig 9) correspond well to the assemblage as a whole from the Stuart Deptford dockyard as presented in Table 4.

A clear difference, however, between the Stuart dockyard and the pottery from contemporary sequences from Bombay Wharf and Chambers Street (both domestic sites located just downstream from the dockyard) can be observed in vessel forms. Storage vessels from the Iberian Peninsula and pottery from Frechen rarely feature on these latter sites (Pearce 2007, 85; Howell et al 2014). Deptford ceramic groups, however, display a clear weighting towards olive jars or amphorae from the Iberian Peninsula in addition to Rhenish stonewares. While the production of durable jars served a demand not particularly well met by London's red ware industry and other regional sources of supply to the capital, such as Essex and the Surrey-Hampshire borders, a number of London red ware storage jars are nevertheless present. Among the 332 vessels from the Stuart dockyard there are up to 60 used for drinking or serving drink, with a large proportion (24) of the 33 vessels in the serving category sourced from the Rhineland. The demand for drinking vessels was met by the finely potted and glossy glazed rounded and flared mugs made by the Essex red ware ('earthenware') industry. Vessels for hot drinks such as London tin-glazed ware tea bowls, beakers and coffee cups, or the similar range of vessels made in Chinese porcelain, had at this period yet to make a significant impact on the pottery used in the dockyard. It is worth noting how sanitary wares are also not common, being restricted to a few chamber pots made by London's red and tin-glazed ware industries.

Pottery from the early Georgian dockyard and King Street (period 4, 1714–74)

The early Georgian dockyard and King Street (period 4; Chapters 6 and 9.3) show a marked shift in pottery use and sources of supply in comparison to the Stuart period dockyard (above). Taken as a whole, Table 5 demonstrates that of the 254 pottery vessels (991 sherds, 21,729g) from features and buildings associated with the early Georgian dockyard and immediately outside, the majority were sourced from either London's tin-glazed ware (TGW) pothouses (60 ENV, 23.7% ENV) or imported from the Continent and the Far East (combined: 97 ENV, 38.3% ENV).

The principal resources for understanding the pottery and other material culture from this period are the finds assemblages from two cesspits in the properties east of the yard, fronting King Street, which were filled in the mid 18th century and are considered in detail above (Chapter 9.3, [5994] and [6524]). There is also pottery recovered from various external dumps in the dockyard in Open Areas 15 and 17.

Overall there is a change in the pottery recovered from vessels used for storage and food preparation (jars, bowls, dishes and so on, made by London and regional potteries) in the Stuart dockyard to ceramics for dining (plates) and hot drinks (chiefly tea bowls) in this period. While Portuguese tin-glazed wares (POTG) and London (TGW) and Dutch (DTGW) tin-glazed wares supplied a good proportion of the dinner wares in both cesspits, the contents of the second pit ([6524]) demonstrate that quantities of fashionable porcelain from China had graced tables in the King Street area by this date. During the 17th century, goods from China were acquired by English merchants through the Dutch trading post at Bantam in Indonesia, but from 1699 English ships traded directly with China through Canton, and from 1715 the Chinese government made this city the only port for foreign trade, paving the way for the large-scale export of Chinese porcelain from the imperial kilns at Jingdezhen (Farrington 2002, 80–5).

While the DTGW plates (<P8>–<P10>, Fig 149) and the POTG dishes (<P3>, <P4>, Fig 145) suggest that the acquisition of matching tablewares did feature, the same cannot be observed among the Chinese porcelain discarded in cesspit [6524]. Exactly matching sets of porcelain might have been difficult to obtain at source if the huge cargo of porcelain that went down (in 1752) with the Dutch East India Company (VOC) ship *Geldermalsen* is anything to go by. While it carried only a very narrow range of designs among the 150,000 pieces recovered (Sheaf and Kilburn 1988, 99), the tea wares (two-thirds of the pieces in this cargo) mostly comprised random purchases of bowls and saucers, not the pre-assembled complete

Table 5 Statistical breakdown of pottery from the early Georgian dockyard and King Street properties (period 4) by major sources

Source	Sherds	Sherds %	ENV	ENV %	Wt (g)	Wt %
Surrey-Hampshire border wares	72	7.3	30	11.8	3209	14.8
London-area red wares	85	8.6	38	15.0	4814	22.1
London tin-glazed wares ('delftware')	243	24.5	60	23.7	5797	26.7
Essex fine red wares	34	3.4	10	3.9	1106	5.1
Imported Continental wares	92	9.3	32	12.6	3356	15.4
Imported Far Eastern wares	424	42.8	65	25.7	2610	12.0
Imported other	1	0.1	1	0.4	15	<0.1
Non-local 'earthenware'	5	0.5	3	1.2	196	0.9
British stoneware (fine)	25	2.5	8	3.2	458	2.1
British stoneware	9	0.9	6	2.4	149	0.7
Unknown	1	0.1	1	0.4	19	<0.1
Total	991		254		21729	

sets that VOC archives in 1729 suggest they should consist of, that is a teapot and stand, milk jug and stand, slop bowl, sugar bowl with lid and stand, 12 tea bowls and saucers, six chocolate cups with handles and six without (ibid, 104). The element among the Chinese porcelain in cesspit [6524] that most closely matches this (admittedly) Dutch specification are the *famille rose* (CHPO ROSE) decorated vessels, with tea bowls (4) and saucers (5) more evenly matched, and a fluted milk or cream jug, a slop bowl and punch bowl surviving. Of note is the near-absence of plates in CHPO in this cesspit, but the presence of TGW and DTGW plates. While delftware set the table, there is a clear emphasis on porcelain for hot drinks. One of the disparities of this group is the far higher proportion of tea bowls (21) and saucers (eight) among the blue and white porcelain (CHPO BW).

Although early Georgian contexts continued to yield Iberian Peninsula storage jars or amphorae as found in the Stuart dockyard, albeit in smaller quantities, Frechen stoneware (FREC) is uncommon. This reflects the decreased demand for these wares after the domestic production of glass bottles and stoneware had begun in London in the 1640s and early 1670s respectively. Best-preserved among the pottery sourced from the Continent are the POTG (or faience) dishes from cesspit [5994] (<P3>, <P4>, Fig 145). Sites dated to the 17th century at Chambers Street, Bermondsey, and Bombay Wharf – in addition to those at Limehouse – yielded similar POTG dishes. At Chambers Street, two 'matching' decorated POTG dishes were found discarded in a half cellar and appear to reflect vessels that had been well curated before being discarded alongside a large quantity of clay tobacco pipes and glass bottles during the mid 18th century (Howell et al 2014, 337–8).

Outside the dockyard, it is clear that by the 1750s Deptford strongly reflected the global reach that the eastern part of London had achieved, and had a distinctive maritime flavour in terms of material culture and housing styles. The particular architectural character of the area of what became Deptford High Street has been captured by Guillery and Herman (1998; 1999), with its properties frequently constructed from surplus timbers from the dockyard (Hurman 2006, 46). The inventory from this period of at least one Deptford household, that of the shipwright Joshua Bennett and his wife Elizabeth, shows that they boasted a parlour crammed with a painting of a ship on the stocks, ten paintings of ships at sea and a glass case with a model of a rigged ship, in addition to seven punch bowls, 22 china plates, 15 jelly glasses, 14 blue and white china cups, ten wine glasses and ivory-handled cutlery (ibid, 56).

A note on porringers

When applied to porringers made by the London tin-glazed ware (delftware) industry (eg <P11> (Fig 150), from cesspit [6524]), the use of the term 'bleeding bowl' is problematic (cf Noël Hume 1977, 89, fn1), although there are close parallels between this ceramic form and their pewter equivalents which can be more specifically associated with blood-letting functions. The inventory of the Pickleherring tin-glazed and stoneware

pothouse in Southwark, made upon the death of its manager John Robins in 1699, nevertheless provides some clues as to how tin-glazed porringers were sold and used, with the 'White and Painted Perfect Ware' section differentiating these forms on account of either their shape ('Spanish porringers': Britton 1990, 68), function ('blood porringers': ibid, 68), decoration ('white porringers': ibid, 70) or measure size ('half pinte porringers': ibid, 70; 'half of half pinte porringers': ibid, 71). When the inventory was made, the numbers listed next to Spanish and blood porringers suggest that they did not form a significant output of this pothouse when compared to the larger quantities noted against the other porringers. In his work on this inventory, Britton suggests that 'Spanish porringers' are two-handled porringers (ibid, 89–90), but offers little explanation for 'bleeding bowl'. Noël Hume (1977, 89, fn1), however, wisely cautions against categorising all tin-glazed ware porringers as bleeding bowls when so many are found on domestic sites, while Austin also speculates on the use of this term (Austin 1994, 197, fig 394).

Pottery from the late Georgian to Victorian dockyard and King Street (period 5, 1774–1869)

Dating to this period of postulated slow decline, and temporary closure, of the dockyard is the largest quantity of pottery from any single period on this site (2659 sherds, 78,314g), including two significant pottery assemblages from cesspits in adjacent King Street properties just outside the yard, filled in the 1820s; these discard groups are discussed in detail in Chapter 9.3. While the cesspit fills account for many of the 622 vessels found in period 5, this material was also recovered from other land uses, notably in the adjacent area (well [5970], OA9; Chapter 9.3) and over the wall inside the yard, in demolition spreads over the officers' quarters (B10), in contrast to other pits which contained only small quantities of this rubbish type.

The last quarter of the 18th century marked a well-documented revolution in British pottery production (eg Barker 1999), with a range of these factory-made industrial fine wares (including many of the various common forms and decorative types) found on this site. Table 6 demonstrates how, when compared to the preceding early Georgian assemblage (Table 5), there is a significant difference in the sources of supply to mirror this shift in production and markets, with previously dominant London tin-glazed ware and Continental and (in particular) Far Eastern imports having now dwindled in terms of their frequency on this site.

10.4 Plaster mouldings

Simon Swann, with Ian M Betts

A large quantity of wall plaster was recovered in association, as a group, but unstratified (<WP1>–<WP3>), in addition to which there is a single unstratified plaster moulding (<WP4>). The

Table 6 Statistical breakdown of pottery from the late Georgian to Victorian dockyard and King Street properties (period 5) by major sources

Source	Sherds	Sherds %	ENV	ENV %	Wt (g)	Wt %
Surrey-Hampshire border wares	48	1.8	12	1.9	2917	3.7
London-area red wares	104	3.9	49	7.9	14304	18.3
London tin-glazed wares ('delftware')	33	1.2	33	5.3	517	0.7
Essex fine red wares	8	0.3	5	0.8	206	0.3
Imported Continental wares	22	0.8	11	1.8	828	1.1
Imported Far Eastern wares	132	5.0	33	5.3	2661	3.4
Industrial fine wares	2110	79.4	409	65.8	47030	60.0
Non-local 'earthenware'	106	4.0	29	4.7	4337	5.5
British stoneware (fine)	25	0.9	3	0.5	336	0.4
British stoneware	65	2.4	35	5.6	4413	5.6
Unknown	6	0.2	3	0.5	765	1.0
Total	2659		622		78314	

archaeological recovery of such mouldings is a relatively rare occurrence in London. The plaster was mainly inspected visually, although some fragments were examined at x10 magnification. All material characterisations are based on assumption and not chemical testing; references to 'gypsum' imply plaster of Paris.

Most plaster in the group appears to be *in situ* run moulding, probably a cornice, but with no cast embellishments (eg cornice <WP1>, Fig 180). The plaster materials used in all coats appear to be gypsum-rich mortars, possibly with some lime content, and with some fine aggregates. The assumption about 'gypsum-based material' is based on the qualities of the material sampled, particularly its light weight and the sound the material makes when tapped.

The run mouldings are made up of successive coats of mortar, applied in consecutive coats, possibly 'fresh on fresh' (ie with no drying time between coats), with a fine, 1mm (or less) thick surface finish coat. Trowel marks indented into the surface of initial coats not only push the plaster into the corner but may also have been intended to act as 'plaster keys'. The significant 90° shape and straight surface of the back of the plaster would indicate that the *in situ* run mouldings were applied to already plastered surfaces (ie typically at the junction of wall and ceiling).

There is a trace of possible white/off-white surface decoration on some of the samples' surfaces; this is probably limewash (calcium carbonate, applied as lime, ie calcium hydroxide, and allowed to carbonate) or distemper (calcium carbonate, in the form of fine crushed chalk/whiting applied in a medium of animal glue/size); distemper may also contain pigments as can limewash.

Also present are samples of another flatter moulding, which has been pre-cast and applied to plaster (eg <WP2>, Fig 180). This may indicate that other plaster mouldings were included in the scheme represented by this group.

One section of cornice moulding shows signs of having been applied to plaster rather than *in situ* run; this may be a repair section or a small area that was done in this way to facilitate work. In some cases mouldings were 'bench run' and then applied to walls, rather like 'cast elements' being applied to plaster walls or ceilings, but the process of making these mouldings would be to run the moulding on a bench, rather than *in situ*, and then apply the moulding to the wall. Typically this was done with gypsum-rich mixes, and the technique was probably not used before the 19th century.

There is also a probable 19th-century run cornice of medium quality which is probably not associated with any of the other plaster decoration in the group (<WP3>, Fig 180). Alternatively, it could be just a simple cast ceiling rose.

The unstratified single plaster moulding (<WP4>, Fig 180) is not typical of the other samples but may be of the same date. It comprises a cast scroll or bracket (60 × 140 × 100mm). It is evident that the casting had been applied to a background with adhesive mortar (probably gypsum plaster). There are two sections of narrow wood lath embedded in the back or base of the casting to act as reinforcement or strengtheners. Each measures about 90mm in length and the ends can be seen on the surface of the casting, where they just protrude from the casting as a result of surface erosion. Laths were often used to reinforce or strengthen castings, typically in the 19th but possibly also in the 18th century.

Materials used in the mortar for this cast appear to be a lime-gypsum blend, with a consistently fine texture and air bubbles (surface pitting) apparent on the surface, implying that it was cast as a liquid or semi-liquid material. Significant traces of surface decoration/layers are present, which have been so over-applied as to obliterate or disguise surface detail of casting in places. A thick coating of a grey-blue distemper or similar is visible and this had been overpainted in gloss oil paint, probably with at least three coats.

In conclusion, all the plaster mouldings would appear to be of 19th-century date. The yard closed in 1830 and reopened in 1843 before finally closing in 1869. Most mouldings are relatively simple in design. The group represented by <WP1>–<WP3> may possibly derive from a decorative scheme in the late 18th- to early 19th-century officers' quarters (Chapter 7.2). Moulding <WP4> appears to derive from a different scheme but one of similar date.

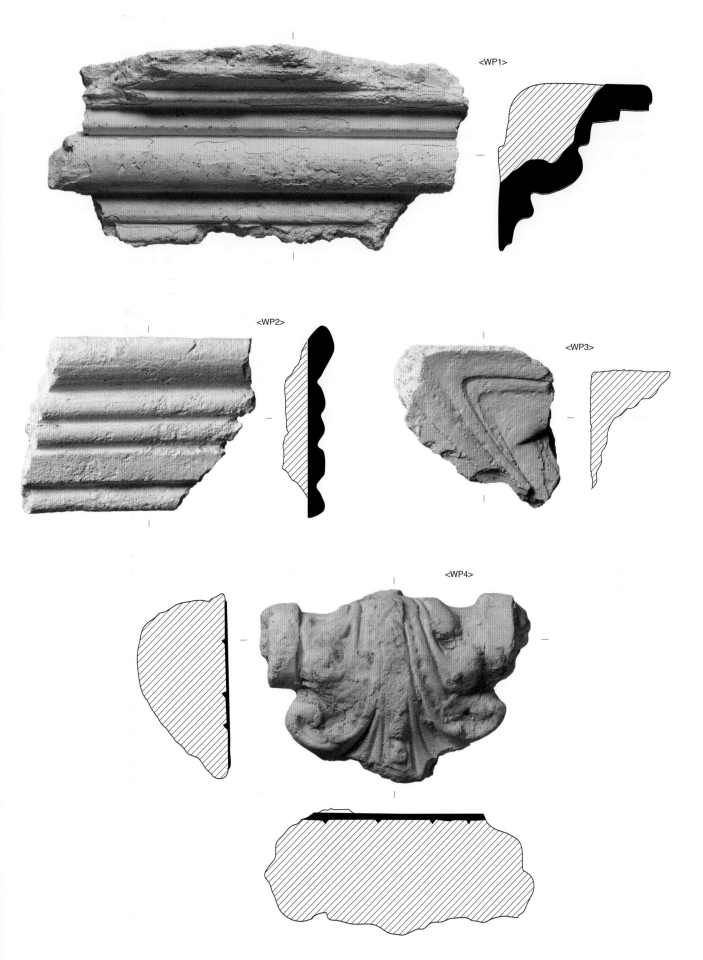

Fig 180 Plaster mouldings <WP1>–<WP4> (scale 1:2)

10.5 Glass vessels

Lyn Blackmore

Introduction and methodology

The following summarises the main functional categories of the glass finds. Catalogue entries were created for most of the accessioned glass finds (70 accessions), while the recorded bulk glass amounts to 631 fragments (270 ENV, 14,318g), of which 588 fragments (244 ENV, 13,357g) are from stratified contexts; time constraints meant that period 6 (post-dockyard) unstratified material and bulk glass could not be examined in detail. Window glass is dealt with below (10.6) under 'Objects associated with transport, buildings and services'. The illustrated vessel glass is catalogued below in typological groups. Also present are fragments from the translucent white glass shade of an oil lamp (<619>/<767>; period 5, OA8) and the stem of a possible glass candlestick in natural green glass (<621>; period 4, B10).

A narrow tube of colourless glass <247> from period 4 (OA8) may be a bead or a cane used for glass working (length 18mm, diameter 4mm).

Vessel glass

Vessel glass was present in 11 phased contexts, the earliest from period 3 (OA5, OA8) including the base of a mug, jug or posset pot in blue glass with opaque white base and handle (<246>). The main groups of vessel glass from cesspits [5546] (fill [4880]) and [5548] (lowest fill [5107]), filled in the 1820s (OA8; period 5), are considered above (Chapter 9.3). Wine glasses dominate (Fig 154; Fig 155) but jelly glasses (eg <G10>, Fig 156), beakers and tumblers are also present, along with fragments of decanter (<G13>, Fig 166) and a ?lid (<G12>, Fig 181). Most are plain, but one reticella rod fragment (<G11>, Fig 181) is from an object in the *façon de Venise* style.

BUCKET-SHAPED BOWL

<G1> Wine glass (Fig 154)
<260>, [4880]; period 5, OA8
Incomplete. Extant H 73mm; foot Diam *c* 63mm; Wt 102g. Complete flat foot, short stem with collar at the base and annular knop at the mid point, and lower part of bucket-shaped bowl. Colourless lead glass.

<G2> Wine glass (Fig 154)
<261>, [4880]; period 5, OA8
Incomplete. Extant H 57mm; foot Diam *c* 60mm; Wt 57g. Complete conical foot, short slightly waisted stem and lower part of bucket-shaped bowl. Colourless lead glass.

THISTLE-SHAPED BOWL

<G3> Wine glass (Fig 154)
<255>, [4880]; period 5, OA8
Incomplete. Extant H *c* 43mm; Wt 43g. Lower part of plain stem with ball knop at the junction with the bipartite bowl (low bucket-shaped base, flaring upper body). Colourless lead glass.

FUNNEL-SHAPED BOWL

<G4> Wine glass (Fig 155)
<277>, [4880]; period 5, OA8
Incomplete. Extant H 66mm; foot Diam 59mm; Wt 82g. Complete low conical foot, plain stem with annular knop at the mid point and collar at the base; lower part of funnel-shaped bowl with three ridges at the base. Colourless lead glass with milky discolouration.

DRAWN TRUMPET BOWL

<G5> Wine glass (Fig 155)
<257>, [4880]; period 5, OA8
Incomplete, but full profile. H 109mm; foot Diam 62mm; Wt 118g. Bowl with small length of rim, short drawn stem and complete thick, low conical foot. Colourless lead glass.

<G6> Wine glass (Fig 155)
<262>, [4880]; period 5, OA8
Incomplete. Bowl Diam 61mm; Wt 61g. Most of bowl, bladed knop at the junction with the plain stem. Colourless lead glass.

<G7> Wine glass (Fig 155)
<266>, [4880]; period 5, OA8
Incomplete. Extant H 77mm; foot Diam *c* 62mm; Wt 56g. Lower part of bowl, short drawn stem and complete folded foot. Colourless lead glass.

<G8> Wine glass (Fig 166)
<245>, [5107]; period 5, OA8
Incomplete. Extant H 98mm; base Diam 59 × 62mm; Wt 73g. Complete low conical base, short stem and thin-walled drawn trumpet bowl. Colourless lead glass.

BOWL OF UNCERTAIN FORM

<G9> Wine glass (Fig 166)
<244>/<770>, [5107]; period 5, OA8
Incomplete; four fragments of bowl and complete base and stem. Total H 116mm; base Diam 72mm; bowl and stem extant H 52mm; combined Wt 171g. Low conical base, short stem with lower merese, bladed knop at the mid point and terraced merese at the junction with the ovoid bowl. Colourless lead glass.

?JELLY GLASS

<G10> ?Jelly glass (Fig 156)
<258>, [4880]; period 5, OA8
Incomplete. Extant H 75mm; Wt 97g. Complete conical foot, short stem and lower part of flaring bowl with slightly wrythen optic-blown ribs. Colourless lead glass.

FAÇON DE VENISE GLASS

<G11> Wine glass/vessel (Fig 181)
<271>, [4880]; period 5, OA8
Incomplete. L 25mm; Diam 7mm; Wt 2g. Reticella trail; double twist of blue and white canes in colourless glass.

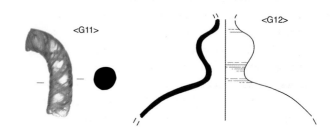

Fig 181 Part of wine glass/vessel <G11> and glass ?lid <G12> (scale 1:1)

OTHER FORMS

<G12> Glass ?lid (Fig 181)
<253>, [4880]; period 5, OA8
Incomplete. Extant H 17mm; Wt 6g. Top of small domed ?lid, possibly optic-blown, with one complete spherical knop and the base of another (or finial). Colourless lead glass.

<G13> Glass decanter (Fig 166) <243>, [5107]; period 5, OA8 Incomplete. Extant H 95mm; rim Diam 45–46mm; Wt 122g. Flat-topped flanged rim and flaring neck decorated with three pairs of applied milled bands. Colourless lead glass. Early 19th-century.

Bottles and flasks

The stratified green wine bottle glass found on the site totals 139 fragments (65 ENV, 7155g) and includes examples dating from the 17th century onwards, although later 18th- and 19th-century types are more common. The cesspit and well groups are discussed in detail above (Chapter 9.3); cesspits [5546] and [5548] were filled in the 1820s and well [5970] in the mid 19th century (OA8, OA9, period 5). The earliest form is the shaft-and-globe bottle, dating from c 1650–80, with two examples including a fragmented bottle from [6013]. Six finds were recorded as shaft-and-globe/onion bottles, while nine were recorded as probable onion bottles (c 1680–1730). One find could be an onion or mallet bottle, while five are probable mallet bottles (c 1725–60). Squat cylindrical bottles (c 1740–1830) are limited to two possible examples. Early cylindrical bottles (dated to c 1735/50–1830) are the most common group, with fragments from up to 19 bottles, of which ten are from cesspit [5548] (fill [5107]) and others are from cesspit [5546] (fill [4880]) and well [5970] (fill [6054]) (OA8, OA9); most are of standard size but one is a half measure with a base diameter of only 55mm. Mould-blown cylindrical wine bottles (from c 1780) are the second most common type, with ten examples, of which nine are from well [5970] (fill [6054]). Other forms include part of an octagonal bottle, probably for wine, found in [6343], a complete French champagne-type bottle (<G15>, Fig 157) from cesspit [5546] (fill [4880]) and part of a hock-type bottle from well [5970] (fill [6054]). There are also a few fragments that could not be assigned to a specific wine bottle form. Perhaps surprisingly, given the status of the site, no sealed bottles were recovered.

Case bottles, mainly used for containing gin, are rare, with only four fragments from four examples in green glass; three others are in natural green and natural blue glass. Of interest is a rim/neck sherd from a large onion-type bottle, possibly a carboy rather than a wine bottle ([1198], period 6). Context [4004] (period 5, S27) contained the rim and upper neck from an imported bottle with flattened round or ovoid body containing spa water, probably imported from Belgium in the later 17th or 18th century (Crismer 1979; van den Bossche 2001, 183–9, pls 133–8). Of more ovoid form is a complete long-necked flask in natural green glass (<G16>, Fig 183), unfortunately unstratified. The original function of this find is unclear. It is not a Hamilton bottle and is too narrow for a urinal; it is probably another form of spa bottle, but could be something quite different, such as an early fire extinguisher. Other finds include fragments from a colourless glass flask/bottle with rounded body, narrower flat-fronted neck with ribbed moulding on the sides and rounded projection on the front, from cesspit [5546] (fill [4880]), and fragments from two colourless glass pickle bottles, probably of 19th-century date, from cesspit [5548] (fill [5107]), alike but not an exact pair. Both have flat bases and one has a wide cylindrical neck with a cordon just below the rim.

<G14> Glass case bottle with lead seal (Fig 182) <219>, [5439]; period 4, OA15 Incomplete. Rim Diam 49mm; bottle c 120mm square; lead collar H 9–12mm, Diam 64mm. Rim and shoulder of large case bottle with lead collar around the neck, probably originally over a cork. Green glass.

<G15> Glass wine bottle (Fig 157) <804>, [4880]; period 5, OA8 Near-complete. H 290mm; base Diam 95mm; Wt 740g. Free-blown champagne-type bottle with high kick, cut rim and single string. Olive green glass. French.

<G16> Glass bottle/flask (Fig 183) <814>, [+]; -, - Complete. H 240mm; max Diam 88mm; Wt 268g. Long-necked bottle or flask with globular body and rounded base. Pale green glass.

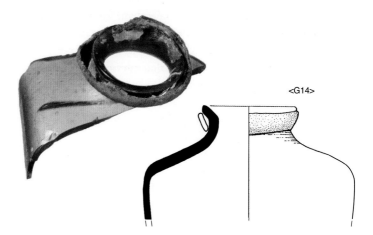

Fig 182 Glass case bottle <G14> with lead collar for the seal (scale 1:2)

Fig 183 Glass bottle or flask <G16> (scale c 1:4)

Pharmaceutical vessels

The complete bottles from well [5970] in Open Area 9 are summarised in Chapter 9.3. In total, there are 51 sherds from 27 phials (440g), including three complete and two near-complete examples, found in seven contexts: Building 6 and Open Area 5 (period 3); cesspit [6524] filled in the mid 18th century (OA8, period 4; Chapter 9.3); layer [2042] (OA18, period 5); cesspits

[5546] and [5548] filled in the 1820s (OA8, period 5; Chapter 9.3); and well [5970] filled in the mid 19th century (OA9, period 5; Chapter 9.3); of these, 21 fragments from nine phials are from cesspit [5546] (fill [4880]). The earliest phials, in natural blue glass, are two 17th-century bell-shaped examples from [6013] (cf Noël Hume 1969, fig 17 no. 8), while the latest are tall slim phials dating from *c* 1760 or *c* 1780 (ibid, fig 17 nos 11, 14), found in cesspits [5546] and [5548] and well [5970]. In addition, there is one very small accessioned phial from cesspit [5546] (<G17>, Fig 162) and part of a moulded blue glass perfume bottle <686> from period 5 (OA16).

Flasks are represented by 35 fragments (365g) from up to six examples, from six contexts, of which eight were small in size. The earliest is of miniature shaft-and-globe bottle form, with base and neck/rim fragments from period 4 cesspit [5994] (lowest fill [5935]), possible body fragments from period 4 cesspit [6524] (fill [4952]) and possible base sherds from [4004] (period 5, S27); examples from Jamestown, Virginia have been dated to *c* 1710 (Noël Hume 1969, fig 17 no. 9). Other hand-blown flasks are represented by fragments from a larger example with a plain neck and flaring rim from [1858] (period 3, OA1), which is very similar in character to a fragment from unphased context [2040].

The main group of medicinal bottles and jars is from the late 19th century (period 6), associated with brick wall [5867] blocking off the stone slipway (S19; Chapter 8.2). This collection of 12 bottles and three jars derives from a pharmacy (Fig 184). Ten of the bottles still have complete, legible relief-moulded lettering. One, of tall cylindrical form (<G20>), reads 'ST JAKOBS OEL / THE CHARLES A VOGELER COMPANY / LONDON ENGLAND', and was produced by a London branch of a company established in Baltimore in 1847; the contents were used for pain relief, including dental pain. Bottle <G21> is of long-necked tall cylindrical form with a recessed panel containing the words 'AUSTEN'S FOREST FLOWER COLOGNE / W J AUSTEN / & CO / OS WE66 NY', probably another American product. Eight bottles are polygonal, of which seven are complete and identical in form but subtly different in size and weight (60g, 65g, 66g (×2), 67g (×2), 80g). The smallest (<G23>) has the words 'SEQUAH PRAIRIE FLOWER' in relief-moulded lettering, while six, including <G22>, bear the word 'SEQUAH' only; the other is incomplete. This identifies them as products of the American Sequah Medicine Company, which was formed in 1887 as the Sequah Medicine Co Ltd selling patented medicines such as prairie flower and Indian oil using travelling salesmen, or quack doctors, known as sequahs. The brand reached England in 1890 but went into liquidation in 1895 (Nurse 2016). Also present is the lower body of a small rectangular bottle (<G24>) with recessed arched panels on all sides. The front panel is left blank for a label while the back reads 'KAY'S COMPOUND / ESSENCE OF LINSEED'. One side reads '[KAY] BROTHERS', the other '[STOCK]PORT' (all lettering from top to base); the underside of the base has an oval recess with the letter 'B' at the centre. Another plain bottle is of octagonal form.

Of the three jars, <G25> is of squat form with angled shoulder and was distributed by Colding Chemist, 42 Upper

Fig 184 Medicinal glass bottles and jars <G20>–<G27> (<G20> H 151mm)

Albany Street. Jar <G26> is a plain squat cylindrical form with the remains of the cork and residues of the dark purple contents, and the only one without relief-moulded lettering. Jar <G27>, of squat cylindrical form with a narrow neck, contained Vaseline made by Chesebrough Co, and dates to after 1859 when the petroleum jelly was first discovered by Robert Chesebrough.

<G17> Glass phial (Fig 162)
<268>, [4880]; period 5, OA8
Complete. H 34mm; body Diam 15mm; ext rim Diam 13mm; Wt 11g. Slightly lop-sided body. Green glass.

<G18> Glass phial (Fig 162)
<815>, [4880]; period 5, OA8
Complete. H 79mm; max Diam 20mm; Wt 14g. Slightly tapering body with remains of the original contents inside. Natural green glass.

<G19> Glass phial (Fig 162)
<816>, [4880]; period 5, OA8
Complete (chipped rim). H 84mm; max Diam 23mm; Wt 43g. Slightly lop-sided, tapering cylindrical body. Colourless glass.

<G20> Glass bottle (Fig 184)
<805>, [5867]; period 6, S19
Complete. H 151mm; base Diam 35mm; rim ext Diam c 23mm; Wt 118g. Made in a two-part mould, with cylindrical body, cylindrical neck, expanded flat-topped rim and the words 'ST JAKOBS OEL / THE CHARLES A VOGELER COMPANY / LONDON ENGLAND', in relief-moulded lettering (reading from top to bottom). Natural green glass.

<G21> Glass bottle (Fig 184)
<806>, [5867]; period 6, S19
Complete. H 145mm; base Diam 35mm; rim ext Diam c 24mm; Wt 85g. Made in a two-part mould, with cylindrical body, concave shoulder, long cylindrical neck and expanded flat-topped rim. Recessed panel with the words 'AUSTEN'S FOREST FLOWER COLOGNE / W J AUSTEN / & CO / OS WE66 NY', in relief-moulded lettering (reading from top to bottom). Colourless glass.

<G22> Glass bottle (Fig 184)
<807>, [5867]; period 6, S19
Complete. H 119mm; base Diam 33mm; rim ext Diam 22mm; Wt 66g. Made in a two-part mould,

with dodecagonal body giving a fluted appearance, cylindrical neck, expanded flat-topped rim and the word 'SEQUAH' in relief-moulded lettering on the body (reading from top to bottom). Natural green glass.

<G23> Glass bottle (Fig 184)
<808>, [5867]; period 6, S19
Complete. H 104mm; base Diam 33mm; rim ext Diam c 21mm; Wt 80g. Made in a two-part mould, with dodecagonal body giving a fluted appearance, cylindrical neck, expanded flat-topped rim and the words 'SEQUAH / PRAIRIE FLOWER' in relief-moulded lettering on the body (reading from top to bottom). Natural green glass.

<G24> Glass bottle (Fig 184)
<809>, [5867]; period 6, S19
Incomplete. Extant H 94mm; body 44 × 27mm; Wt 83g. Mould-blown, rectangular body with rounded corners and recessed arched panels on all sides. Front panel left blank for a label, the others with relief-moulded lettering. Back reads 'KAY'S COMPOUND / ESSENCE OF LINSEED'. One side reads '[KAY] BROTHERS', the other '[STOCK]PORT' (all lettering from top to base). Underside of base has an oval recess with the letter 'B' at the centre and upwardly bevelled corners. Natural green glass.

<G25> Glass jar (Fig 184)
<812>, [5867]; period 6, S19
Complete. H 53mm; base Diam 54mm; rim ext Diam c 31mm; Wt 73g. Made in a two-part mould, with concave base and cylindrical lower body, angled shoulder, short cylindrical neck and expanded flat-topped rim. Relief-moulded lettering reading 'COLDING / CHEMIST' on one side and '42 UPPER / ALBANY ST' on the other. Natural green glass.

<G26> Glass jar (Fig 184)
<810>, [5867]; period 6, S19

Complete, with remains of cork stopper. H 61mm; base Diam 37mm; rim ext Diam c 32mm; Wt 58g. Made in a two-part mould, with cylindrical body, cylindrical neck and expanded flat-topped rim. Recessed base with characters '10 Z' or '1O Z' (? '1 ounce') in relief-moulded lettering on the underside. Colourless glass with purple residue from original contents.

<G27> Glass jar (Fig 184)
<811>, [5867]; period 6, S19
Complete. H 93mm; base Diam 61mm; rim ext Diam c 43mm; Wt 142g. Made in a two-part mould, with concave base, cylindrical body, cylindrical neck and expanded flat-topped rim. Relief-moulded lettering on front reads 'CHESEBROUGH / VASELINE / MANUFACT G,CO'. Natural blue glass.

10.6 Selected accessioned finds

Lyn Blackmore

Introduction and methodology

The following summarises the main functional categories of the finds other than building materials, clay pipes and other ceramics, vessel glass, coins and wood, which are dealt with separately. The illustrated accessioned finds are individually catalogued below, by function and then by period and land use. The bulk of the assemblage comprises nails and structural finds associated with the dockyard and the ships made there, which come under 'transport', 'buildings and services' or 'fasteners and fittings'; the other main category is household equipment associated with drinking and dining. Some objects could belong to more than one category and in such cases have been assigned to the most likely one. A high proportion of the finds discussed below derive from cesspits in adjacent properties east of the yard (cesspit [5546] (fill [4880]), cesspit [5548] (fill [5107]); both OA8, period 5; Chapter 9.3), while other finds of interest are noted in period chapters (above) and the general introductions (below).

Iron is the main material category, with copper alloy second (accounting for 162 and 150 accessions respectively), with additional bulk finds; other materials are poorly represented. Catalogue entries were created for most of the accessioned finds, although due to time constraints finds from period 6 (post-dockyard), unstratified material and the bulk iron (ten shoe boxes and further crates of numerous stakes, bars and nails) could not be examined in detail.

Objects of personal adornment or dress

Items of dress are limited in number, and the earliest is an 18th-century ?shoe buckle from period 4 (<S1>, Fig 185). Buttons are the most common find, with 12 from period 5 and two unphased; eight are of copper alloy, four are of bone, including one with unfinished edges (<S3>, Fig 151), one is of copper alloy and bone (<194>) and one is of mother-of-pearl (<188>). Fragments of knitting (eg <707>, stocking stitch) and textile, including <711>, <714> and <710>, were also recovered from cesspits [5546] and [5548] filled in the 1820s (period 5; Chapter 9.3). Footwear is represented by two lace chapes (period 6) and fragments of leather shoe recovered from contexts assigned to periods 3 (OA6, S8), 4 (OA6, OA14), 5 (B9, B18, OA8, OA16, OA17) and 6 (OA19). Items of personal adornment, possibly 'female', comprise a composite brooch <S2> (Fig 185), while the hair comb (<S4>, Fig 186) may also have been for adornment rather than functional.

<S1> Copper-alloy buckle (Fig 185) <208>, [2217]; period 4, B14 Incomplete. L 32mm; W 46mm; Th 3–3.5mm. Subrectangular frame with flat underside, convex upper side and moulded decoration of two rings at the centre of the surviving long side; pin missing.

<S2> Copper-alloy and glass brooch (Fig 185) <534>, [5525]; period 5, B18 Near-complete. Diam c 22mm; Th 5mm; setting Diam c 9mm.

Copper-alloy disc with raised rim and circular central glass setting in copper-alloy collet; intervening fill (now missing) held in place by a flat-sectioned angled ring. Spring and catch plate on back, pin missing.

<S3> Bone button (Fig 151) <190>, [4880]; period 5, OA8 Complete. Diam 20–21mm; max Th 5mm. Unfinished round disc with four large holes, in very poor condition.

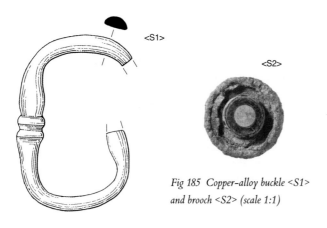

Fig 185 Copper-alloy buckle <S1> and brooch <S2> (scale 1:1)

Toilet, surgical or pharmaceutical instruments

Items used for grooming include a double-sided comb of ivory (<S5>, Fig 163), another of bone (<143>) and possibly the pseudo-tortoiseshell hair comb (<S4>, Fig 186). A small bone ?lid (<S6>, Fig 186) may be from a box that contained toilet items or other personal possessions.

<S4> Pseudo-tortoiseshell (? early plastic) comb (Fig 186) <173>, [2855]; period 5, B14 Near-complete. Back W 53mm; teeth W 43mm at tips, max L 70mm. Pseudo-tortoiseshell comb of dense dark material with eight graduated teeth and slightly arched back, the outside of the side teeth sloping in to the tips. Two small copper-alloy rivets (head Diam 2mm) 9mm apart (centre to centre) at centre of back, with traces of a

subrectangular mount on the front (now lost). ? Decorative rather than practical.

<S5> Ivory comb (Fig 163) <182>, [5107]; period 5, OA8 Incomplete. Extant L 50mm; W 44mm; Th 3mm; teeth L 14mm. Double-sided nit comb comprising two fragments preserving one rounded end and with very fine teeth (13 to 14 per 10mm on both sides).

<S6> Bone box ?lid (Fig 186) <715>, [5107]; period 5, OA8 Complete. ?Lid L 89mm; W 37mm. End plate L 39mm; W 29mm; Th 3mm. Convex ?lid made of half a hollowed long bone, with one concave (?original) edge and one straight edge with

central rectangular notch; pairs of incised lines around each end and three rivet holes on the surfaces of each end; one of two oval end plates with incised groove around edge, secured by three copper-alloy rivets, with a fourth rivet that was originally attached to another.

Objects used in the manufacture or working of textiles

This activity is represented by only one bone needle case (<S7>, Fig 173), which is associated with the demolition of 19th-century terrace buildings outside the naval dockyard in the extreme south-east part of the site (Chapter 9.3), and two pins, of which one is from period 6 and the other unstratified. A pair of scissors (<S31>, Fig 124) is assigned to the category of tools (below).

<S7> Bone needle case (Fig 173) <58>, [1198]; period 5, B57 Incomplete. Extant L 59mm; max Diam c 14.5mm. Tapering

cylindrical body with internal screw thread at narrow end and external screw thread at wider end.

Household utensils and furniture

Cutlery and utensils

Items of cutlery comprise nine (composite) knives, one from period 2 (OA8, <564>), one from period 3 (<S8>, Fig 30), seven from period 5 (<175>–<177>, <S9> (Fig 152), <179>, <180>, <S10> (Fig 165); Chapter 9.3) and two unphased (<186>, <544>); two ?fork handles from period 5 (<740>, <741>; Chapter 9.3) and a fork from period 6 (<124>); and three spoons from period 5 (<30>, <403>, <S11> (Fig 171)). The small knife <S8> resembles a 15th-century glover's knife in the Museum of London collections (Cowgill et al 1987, 105, fig 68 no. 304) but could have served many purposes.

Fig 186 Pseudo-tortoiseshell hair comb <S4> and bone box ?lid <S6> (scale 1:2)

KNIVES

<S8> Iron knife (Fig 30)
<557>, [3263]; period 3, B3
Complete. Total L 118mm. Blade
L c 55mm; W 21mm; Th 5mm.
Blade and centrally positioned tang
from a small knife with binding (W
10mm, Diam 9mm) at the junction
of the handle and the short blade,
which is straight-backed with the
cutting edge curving up to the tip.

<S9> Bone knife handle (Fig 152)
<178>, [4880]; period 5, OA8
Complete. L 65mm; W c 15–18mm;
Th 11mm. Straight-sided bone
scale-tang handle secured by two
iron rivets (head Diam c 5mm),

expanding in width towards the
rounded terminal (damaged) which
has copper-alloy staining. The
letter 'M' or 'W' incised towards
the blade end on one side.

<S10> Bone knife handle (Fig 165)
<716>, [5107]; period 5, OA8
Complete. L 85mm; Th 13–17mm.
Straight-sided bone scale-tang
handle with diagonal ribbing
secured by two iron rivets (head
Diam c 3mm); top (W 15–21mm)
expanding at the rounded terminal
(18–23mm). The oval end plate is
missing but the prongs attaching it
are visible on the X-radiograph.

SPOON

<S11> Copper-alloy spoon (Fig 171)
<402>, [5254]; period 5, OA8
Complete. L 145mm. Bowl L
50mm; W c 30mm. Long oval

bowl and narrow handle with flat
spatulate terminal. 19th-century.
Pair with <403>.

Other

Other items of probable domestic equipment include a possible
curtain ring of copper alloy <404> (period 3, OA5) and a small
bell (<S12>, Fig 171).

<S12> Copper-alloy bell (Fig 171)
<401>, [4642]; period 5, OA8
Near-complete (missing clapper).
H 27mm; Diam at top c 21mm, at

base 42mm. Small bell, concave
wall and ring collar around
opening for clapper.

Objects used for recreational purposes

Objects associated with leisure are limited to two counters,
<S13> (Fig 187) and <S14> (Fig 169), the latter in the shape of a
fish, and the mouthpiece from a musical instrument (<172>,
unstratified).

<S13> Bone counter (Fig 187)
<174>, [3216]; period 3, OA6
Complete. Diam 22mm; Th c 2mm.
Turned disc with concentric
moulding on front and three
angular mandrel marks from the
lathe on the back.

<S14> Bone counter (Fig 169)
<181>, [5107]; period 5, OA8
Incomplete (c 90% present). L
71mm; max W 17mm; Th 4mm.
Fish-shaped gaming piece,
with ring-and-dot eye with red
inlay.

Fig 187 Bone counter <S13> (scale 1:1)

Objects employed in regulation, weighing and measuring

COPPER-ALLOY TAGS

<S15> Copper-alloy tag (Fig 188)
<385>, [5867]; period 6, S19
Complete. Diam 22mm. Disc
pendant with small hole near edge
(Diam 1.5mm) and punched
lettering: 142 / CP [or EP].

<S16> Copper-alloy plaque/mount
(Fig 188)
<192>, [5139]; period 6, OA19
Complete. L 81mm; W 58mm; Th
1mm. Small oval die-stamped brass
plaque, with 'JH HOPKINS &
SONS' around the perimeter at the
top and 'LONDON &
BIRMINGHAM' along the
bottom; in the centre is stamped
'ROYAL NAVY / Nº / Mess'.

Julian Bowsher comments as
follows:

This is clearly a 'tag' or label of
sorts, relating to messing by
different groups from a ship's crew
or, more likely, dockyard workers.
The fact that no mess number
has been stamped on it, and the
absence of any pin or nail holes
or other means for attachment,
suggest that it had not been used
or allocated.

Hopkins was in the japanning
business as Griffiths & Hopkins in
1850, situated in Bradford Street,

Birmingham (Post Office 1850,
25). Within the next eight years
Hopkins established his own
business, for in 1858 we find
Hopkins & Sons, tin-plate
workers and japanners, at 68
Granville Street, Birmingham
(General and Commercial
Directory 1858, 177, 429). In
Peck's circular trades directory (Peck
1896–7), the firm is listed in that
year at the grander-sounding
Granville Works, suggesting an
expansion of the original site;
indeed the company is listed in
a much larger category of
metalworkings, presumably
indicating a successful expansion.
However, Hopkins & Sons was
soon acquired by Joseph Sankey
& Sons (*TNA, Discovery*); the
japanning side of the business
was sold off and Sankey's
concentrated on the stamping
and pressing side. The plaque
clearly dates from some time
between 1858 and (from its
context) the dockyard's closure
in 1869, although the Deptford
victualling yard, west of the site,
continued working after 1869
(MacDougall 1982, 83; Cock and
Rodger 2008, 236).

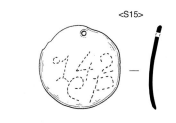

<S15>

<S16>

Fig 188 Copper-alloy tag <S15> and plaque <S16> (scale 1:1)

LEAD ITEMS

<S17> Lead cloth seal (Fig 48)
<217>, [3211]; period 3, B6
Complete. L 50mm; Diam 18mm.
Opened and flattened, one end
disc-shaped, the other ring-shaped;
no obvious design on the outer
face but textile impressions on the
inner face.

<S18> Lead ?token (Fig 169)
<540>, [5107]; period 5, OA8
Complete. Diam 26mm; Th
1.6mm. Obverse with raised border
around the rim and five raised
pellets, one at the intersection of a
raised cross that extends to the rim,
the others at the mid points of the
four quadrants. Reverse plain.
Slightly distorted.

<S19> Lead ?token (Fig 169)
<541>, [5107]; period 5, OA8
Complete. Diam 26mm; Th
1.6mm. As <S18>. Slightly
distorted and slight damage.

<S20> Lead weight (Fig 127)
<220>, [5139]; period 6, OA19
Complete. Diam 91mm; Th
17mm; Wt 872g (1lb 14.8oz).
Discoidal with flat base, number
'29' stamped on the convex upper
face and central perforation (Diam
10mm).

Objects used for or associated with written communication

Fragments of inkwell <240> were found in cesspit [6524] (fill
[4952]) (OA8, period 4) and base fragments (<238>, <239>) that
may be from others came from a crane base (S53, period 5).
Lengths of pencil lead <634> were recovered from [5254] (OA8,
period 5).

Objects associated with transport, buildings and services

Transport – horses and ships

Finds obviously associated with transport include two
horseshoes, one (<658>; period 2, OA8) a near-complete
example of Clark type 3 (Clark 1995, 86–8, 96) and one
fragment (<94>) from period 4 (OA14). Ship-related finds
include two probable sail eyelets, <236> (period 4, S18) and
<224> (period 5, B50), and possibly a length of rope (<712>;
period 6, OA19). Two depth marks (both from period 4,
S9), <704> and <S21> (Fig 80), are thought to originate
from the wet dock gate rather than the hulls of ships, even
though found detached; similar marks were also found at
West India Dock (McCarthy 2005, 206).

Larger items of wood are discussed elsewhere (Chapter
10.7), but included here are a pulley block sheave (<S22>,
Fig 189) and an ?unfinished wooden parrel bead used in rigging
(<S23>, Fig 189). Another fitting included a tropical hardwood
cleat with a hollow base showing that it must have been a
rigging cleat fastened to a rounded spar [4439] (D Goodburn,
pers comm 2014).

DEPTH MARK

<S21> Copper-alloy draught
mark (Fig 80)
<705>, [3639]; period 4, S9
Complete. H 155mm; W 310mm;
Th 1.2mm. Three punched nail
holes (Diam c 5mm) regularly
spaced along both upper and
lower edges. Tidal marker in the
form of Roman numeral 'XIIII'
for the depth of water; found
with a similar mount for 'XI' feet
(<704>).

WOODEN FITTINGS

<S22> Wooden pulley block
sheave (Fig 189)
<743>, [5439]; period 4, OA15
Incomplete. Diam 130mm; hole
Diam c 40mm. Recessed central
hole with letters 'WT' (the
initials of the maker/inventor
William Taylor) on one flat face
and on the other a broad inward-
pointing arrow indicating Royal
Navy ownership (McCarthy
2005, 106). Lignum vitae. Similar
pulley blocks, also of lignum
vitae, and associated pins of
tropical hardwood were found
at West India Dock (Pitt and
Goodburn 2003, 202, fig 9).

<S23> Wooden parrel bead
(Fig 189)
<742>, [4880]; period 5, OA8
Complete. H 90mm; Diam 119
× 111mm. Slightly oval bead
with bun-shaped profile and
central rectangular slot (34 ×
9mm on one side, 23 × 3mm
on the other). Worn. Used in
rigging.

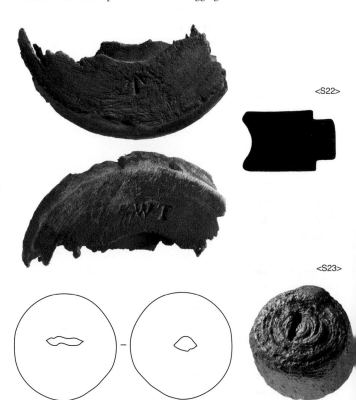

*Fig 189 Wooden pulley block sheave <S22> (scale 1:2) and wooden parrel bead
<S23> (scale 1:4)*

Standing buildings

Finds that can be associated with standing buildings mainly
comprise window glass, with 27 fragments (1615g) from c 25
stratified contexts, although one fragment could be from a case
bottle ([3263]). The largest groups are from cesspit [5805]
(period 4, OA8) and cesspits [5546] (fill [4880]) and [5548] (fill
[5107]); both period 5, OA8; Chapter 9.3); most other contexts
produced fewer than five fragments. One fragment of potash
glass from [5806] could be of medieval date, but the remainder
date to the 17th to 19th centuries. Most pieces are undiagnostic,
but a few are of crown spun glass and broad glass (cut cylinder).
Sheet glass, between 3mm and 45mm thick, is represented by 20
fragments from eight different windows. A few finds have cut
edges with frame marks, but most have no distinguishing
features. Lead window cames were found in period 3 (B3, B6)

and in period 5 (S31, OA8, OA16). The finds from [5867] (period 6, S19) include a possible window bar (<661>), a possible grille from an air vent (<660>) and a ?structural brace (<664>). Some mounts derived from buildings are included under 'Fasteners and fittings'.

Building/dock and ship construction/repair

NAILS AND SPIKES

The bulk of the assemblage comprises iron spikes, nails and other structural items that are less easy to associate with a function, and it was not possible in the time available to measure and classify the bulk finds, although these are only a small sample of those found on the site. That said, given the amount of metalwork used on a ship by the 19th century (Pitt and Goodburn 2003, 207), the vast expanse of the site and the activities carried out, the numbers of finds and the range of artefacts other than nails are remarkably small, suggesting a high degree of recycling and orderly storage of materials for the building and maintenance of ships (ibid, 200), and efficient removal, whether official or unofficial, of metalwork from the site when it was vacated.

Starting with the nails, it is likely that most are related to either dock construction or shipbuilding (Chapter 9.2; Pitt and Goodburn 2003, 194), which required both short bolts and through-bolts and a range of other fittings (for methods of manufacture and problems of terminology see McCarthy 2005, 86–100, 159–87). However, while it can be noted that both round- and square-sectioned forms are present, methods of production (wrought, cast), their relative proportions and the range of combinations of shank and nail head must await a further study. The following comments are thus very general and are focused on the finds from the 18th and 19th centuries (periods 4 and 5).

Nails are generally round-headed; no diamond- or rose-headed forms were noted. Small examples were multi-functional, but where closely spaced they are probably from ships and possibly sheathing nails used to secure a wooden outer hull or false keel (eg <651>). Long tapering square-sectioned nails, either square- or round-headed, are generally termed spikes and were used, countersunk and sealed by pitch or tar, to fasten deck timbers (McCarthy 2005, 73, fig 46). An early example of a large square-headed (and square-sectioned shank) clench nail (<556>) was found in period 3, Open Area 7 (tip missing, extant length 130mm, head c 37 × 37mm). Ring-headed spikes such as <S24> (Fig 39) would probably have held a ring or loop (ibid, fig 63); another unstratified example (<84>) had the washer in situ.

By the late 19th century, dumps or bolt-nails, made of copper alloy, had a uniform cross section to approximately the mid point and a tapering point; they were used to secure timbers to frames as the iron fittings were inserted (McCarthy 2005, 84, fig 58). Screw nails and screw bolts are rare in this assemblage, but part of a large straight-sided blunt-ended screw bolt (<558>; shank and head missing; extant length 88mm, diameter 22mm) from period 3, Building 5, has a spiralling thread at intervals of 5mm and traces of the wood adhering. This must have derived from a construction of some size, whether a building, boat or machinery.

It is likely that the standard nails and spikes were made elsewhere and bought in bulk and finished on site, but others would have been made in the smithy (Chapter 4.2, 'Rebuilding the smithy and other works, late 17th century'; Chapter 6.2, 'The smithy'; Chapter 7.3, 'The smithy'; Pitt and Goodburn 2003, 200, fig 7; for methods of manufacture see McCarthy 2005, 86–100).

Most of the 119-plus copper-alloy nails retained are much smaller and less robust; they may be from buildings or fittings, but were also used as sheathing nails in shipbuilding after 1850 (McCarthy 2005, 91), and in some cases closely-spaced, large-headed examples were used to secure copper sheet sheathing covering the surface of a hull or false keel to protect it from marine contamination (eg <608>; Pitt and Goodburn 2003, 200, 202, fig 7; McCarthy 2005, 102–3).

<S24> Iron ring-headed spike (Fig 39) <136>, [2999]; period 3, B7 Complete. L 121mm, head Diam 33mm; W 9mm; Th 16mm. Flat underside to shank, which tapers from c 15mm to 5mm at the point.

WASHERS, PLATES AND BOLTS

There are also numerous annular washers, or clinch rings, and flat triangular or sub-triangular plates, known as forelock wedges (or keys, tongues, or gibs), that would usually have been used in conjunction with long bolts or through-bolts, a washer being placed against the face of the timber being secured and fixed by the forelock wedge being driven through a slot in the bolt, whether on the inboard or outboard end (McCarthy 2005, 69–70, figs 42, 72). In all 39 washers were retained, of which the eight stratified examples have internal diameters of 25mm (<92a>, <110>), 30mm (<140>), 35mm (<92b>, <548>, <549>, <553>) and up to 40mm (<91>); the wedges vary in length and curvature, but the slots for them were usually a quarter the diameter of the bolt. Forelock wedges are most typical of carvel ships, bolts later being clinched, or burred over the washer or rove on clench bolts or, where they are used at both ends, long rivets (ibid, 70–1, fig 43). Long bolts were mainly used to fasten the different components of a keel or stern, or the scarves and butts of the futtocks and frames (Pitt and Goodburn 2003, 200; McCarthy 2005, 81–2, fig 55). Three long drift bolts, without washers (length 330–380mm, diameter of circular section 20–28mm), each with traces of a central timber flanked by others with a different wood grain, were found in period 5, Structure 34 (<102>, <103>, <104>; cf ibid, fig 47). Another, with a cylindrical wooden coak for keying it into the adjacent timbers to give greater strength, was found in period 5, Structure 31 (<S25>, Fig 190) (cf ibid, 76–8, 81, fig 50). Short bolts are larger than nails and have a fairly uniform cross section (round, square or polygonal) until the tapering tip; an example with washer in situ at the upper end was found in period 5, Open Area 16 (<93>; length 200mm). No iron rag bolts (ibid, 72) were identified among the accessioned finds.

<S25> Iron drift bolt (Fig 190)
<133>, [2742]; period 5, S31
Complete iron bar. L 360mm;
circular-sectioned shank Diam
28mm; broad flattened head Diam
53mm, Th 8mm; a narrower
flattened terminal (Diam 40mm) at
the other end. At *c* 55mm above the
latter is a wooden coak made of a
?tropical hardwood (L 75mm;
Diam 84mm). Traces of oak
planking are also present on other
parts of the bar, aligned laterally
along both sides. Late 18th- to
early 19th-century.

Fig 190 Iron drift bolt with wooden coak <S25> (scale 1:4)

OTHER STRUCTURAL ITEMS

Other structural items include strap fittings (eg <S27> (Fig 124), <662> (period 6, S19)) and two types of staple, of which the earliest is a large U-shaped 'dog' (<S26>, Fig 37) associated with a land-tie beam in period 3 (S8). The three other finds, from unphased contexts, comprise a smaller U-shaped example (<229>) and two broad angular examples with a span of 190mm (<234>, <235>).

Of interest are seven wedge-shaped copper-alloy keel dogs (eg <S28> (Fig 126) and <197>), used to attach a false keel to the underside of the true keel, their shanks ragged to give a better grip. These were presumably lost when the ship keel was being repaired and a false keel being replaced. Copper-alloy keel dogs replaced iron examples when the surfaces of boats began to be galvanised (McCarthy 2005, 93), as iron dogs would speed up corrosion.

<S26> Iron staple (Fig 37)
<647>, [4761]; period 3, S8
Complete. Max L 225mm; max ext W 104mm. Large staple, one side better preserved than the other, the arms *c* 60mm apart (edge to edge, int L *c* 190mm), square in section (max *c* 24 × 27mm).

<S27> Iron strap and spike fitting (Fig 124)
<105>, [2042]; period 5, OA18
Complete. Total L 252mm. Spike L 115mm; square cross section max W 15 × 17mm. Strap L *c* 137mm;

W 43mm tapering to 30mm. Straight-sided strap with rounded end (edge damaged) and four perforations in same plane as back of tang.

<S28> Copper-alloy keel dog (Fig 126)
<195>, [5772]; period 5, B54
L 77mm; max W 23mm; Th 10mm; Wt 81g. Three complete ragged arms from one side of a false keel fitting, tapering with flat rectangular cross section.

General tools

Artefacts of stone are limited to a sandstone quern or knife grinder <693> (period 5, B18), a hone made of Kentish ragstone (<691>, unstratified) and a possible hone made of slate <631> (period 5, S31) – a rather soft stone for this purpose.

There is a noticeable absence of tools related to shipbuilding, suggesting that these had been removed from the site. Among the more likely candidates are a pair of iron compasses (<S30>, Fig 191). Naval compasses tend to be of brass,

and the fact that these are of iron suggests that they were used by ship's carpenters for transcribing lines to aid the cutting of timbers (D Goodburn, pers comm 2014). A mid 18th-century pair of scissors (<S31>, Fig 124; cf Nöel Hume 1969, 267–9, fig 87), pickaxe (<668>; period 5, B18) and L-shaped crank handle complete with tubular socket (<101>; period 5, S34) are the only definite stratified tools; unstratified finds include a bolster chisel (<228>), a file (<221>), dividers (<545>), a plumb bob (<543>) and possibly a knife (<544>). Several wood wedges (eg <749>) and examples of fibrous caulking material (<41>, <645>) were also recovered.

Included here are two small lead weights (<S33>, <S34>, Fig 193) which could have weighted a line or string.

The precise function of a crude oak paddle-like tool, 1.69m long (<S35>, Fig 194), is uncertain: it is too heavy for digging, but it may have been used to stir up silt to clear drains, or for mixing viscous materials, or in the tanning of sails and/or ropes (D Goodburn, pers comm 2014).

Iron tools

<S29> Iron tanged ?chisel (Fig 30)
<126>, [2031]; period 3, B3
Incomplete. Extant L 155mm; tang L 48mm; rectangular cross section max W 7 × 8mm; integral collar Diam 21mm. ?Blade (working end missing, L *c* 50+mm) and round shank (Diam 10mm).

<S30> Iron compasses (Fig 191)
<655>, [5676]; period 4, OA14
Incomplete and obscured by corrosion. Extant L 120mm. The upper arms (W 10mm) are flat, joined by a large round-headed pin at the pivot point; the lower arms are *c* 6mm square, tapering to a point (one near-complete, the other missing the tip). Drawn from X-radiograph.

<S31> Iron scissors (Fig 124)
<231>, [4618]; period 5, OA17
Near-complete. L 140mm. Plain

hafts with solid drawn oval loops, rivet set close to the narrow straight-sided blades (W *c* 12mm), the ends of which curve in to the point. Typical of the period *c* 1740.

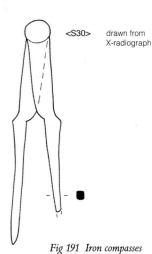

<S30> drawn from X-radiograph

Fig 191 Iron compasses <S30> (scale 1:2)

Copper-alloy ?machine component

<S32> Copper-alloy disc (Fig 192)
<34>, [1864]; period 5, OA17
Incomplete. Max 55 × 34mm;
disc Diam 130mm; Th 6–7mm;
Wt 65g. Part of large disc with

circular perforations (Diam
c 14mm) around the edge; upper
face with engraved concentric
lines and punched dots. ?Machine
component.

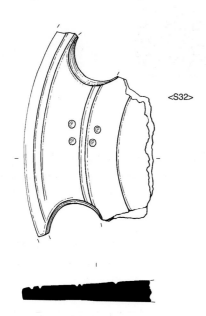

Fig 192 Copper-alloy disc (?machine component) <S32> (scale 1:1)

Lead weights

<S33> Lead weight (Fig 193)
<538>, [1993]; period 3, B3
Complete. H 40mm; Diam at base

c 25mm, at top *c* 50 × 70mm;
Wt 111g. Conical, with unfinished
perforation (for attachment to,
eg, a line or string) through the
flattened top; the flat base suggests
this is not a plumb bob.

*Fig 193 Lead weights <S33>
and <S34> from the demolition
of the Treasurer of the Navy's
house, 1684–8 (scale 1:1)*

<S34> Lead weight (Fig 193)
<539>, [1993]; period 3, B3
Complete. Total L 55mm; L of
body 43mm; max Diam 70–

80mm; Wt 21g. Irregular tapering
body with round cross section, and
flattened head with perforation (for
attachment to, eg, a line or string).

Wooden tools

<S35> Wooden ?stirring paddle
(Fig 194)
<142>, [2997]; period 5, S33
Complete. L 1.69m; paddle
W 145mm; max Th 50mm.

Roughly carved from half
a sawn plank. Oak. Stirring
paddle or possibly tamping
device (D Goodburn, pers
comm 2014).

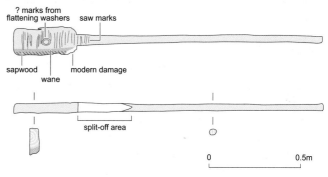

Fig 194 Oak ?stirring paddle <S35> (scale 1:20)

Fasteners and fittings

<S36> Iron ?handle (Fig 195)
<135>, [1887]; period 1, OA1
Complete. L 55mm; W 95mm
(from X-radiograph). D-shaped
loop, possibly a handle, rather
than, eg, a buckle loop; greatest
thickness at centre of bowed side
(*c* 10mm), tapering to 4mm along
straight side.

<S37> Iron fitting and copper-alloy
chain (Fig 195)
<387>, [3216]; period 3, OA6
Incomplete. Extant L 130mm. Six
or more '8'-shaped links, some in
two planes (L 21–23mm, W
10mm); four links attached to an
iron strap with perforated rounded
terminal (hidden in corrosion),

and two detached links, one pulled
open.

<S38> Copper-alloy turn buckle
(Fig 170)
<701>, [5107]; period 5, OA8
Complete. L 86mm; H 17mm; W
at centre *c* 19mm, at ends 13mm.
Slightly boat-shaped strip with small
central perforation coiled under at
the terminals (min W 8mm).

<S39> Iron chain (Fig 195)
<560>, [4642]; period 5, S53
Length of chain made up of oval
links (L 43mm, W 29mm, Diam
9mm), partly folded back on itself
and covered in tar; full length
unknown.

10.7 Archaeological woodwork

Damian Goodburn

Methodology

A tiered approach to recording the structural woodwork
exposed during this unusual and very large-scale urban
archaeological project was developed to fit the work brief.
Essentially a practical compromise was reached, dealing with

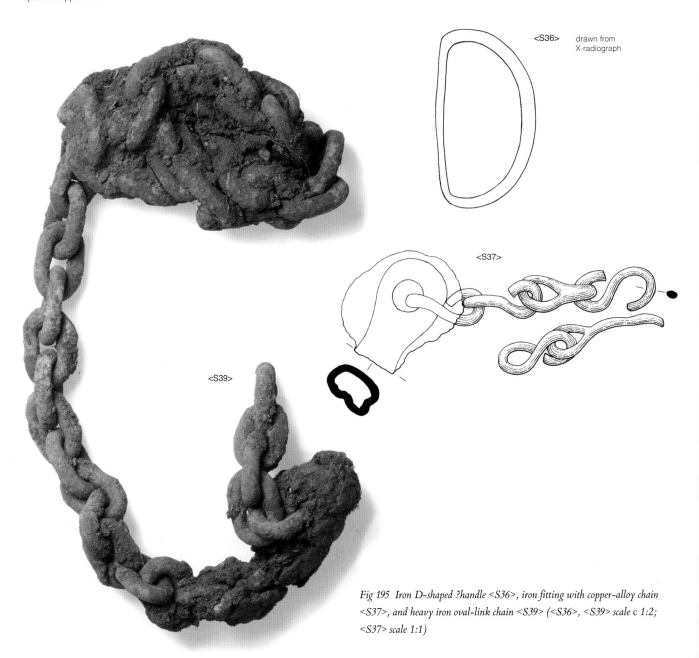

<S36> drawn from X-radiograph

<S37>

<S39>

Fig 195 *Iron D-shaped ?handle <S36>, iron fitting with copper-alloy chain <S37>, and heavy iron oval-link chain <S39> (<S36>, <S39> scale c 1:2; <S37> scale 1:1)*

the huge scale of some areas of excavation and recovering enough detailed archaeological information to address key research aims.

The timber and composite timber and masonry structures discussed here were exposed in plan by a combination of machine and hand excavation followed by careful hand cleaning. The general planning was carried out at a scale of 1:50 with limited, representative, areas drawn in plan and sometimes elevation at 1:20 and key details recorded at a 1:10 scale. The pace of archaeological recording had to vary depending on safety, water conditions and weather as most of the site was very exposed by its position next to the Thames. In a small number of areas of the site, trial trenches could be cut across timber structures such as slipways and drains, which revealed significant structural details not visible initially in plan.

In most cases substantial structural timbers were assigned individual 'timber numbers', but due to the fact that most timbers could not be fully exposed, the vast majority of timber

record sheets were not filled out completely. It is also true that the vast bulk of the woodwork was in fact reburied, still arranged as found, after recording what could safely be exposed. Often, for practical purposes, timbers from discrete timber structures were initially given site 'structure context' numbers. These primary groupings were superseded during the post-excavation procedure for the key structures, buildings and dock or river walls, and that coding ('land use') is used. Extensive and more detailed photography was also widely used, as is common practice in typical standing building recording. Additionally, a small subsample of the numbered timbers were fully exposed and recorded, and for which pro-forma 'timber sheets' and 1:10 timber drawings could be completed.

The MOLA archaeological woodwork specialist was able to attend the site regularly once or twice a week as needed, to provide first-hand advice on targeted detailed recording and sampling and also to identify reused timbers and key woodworking technology features. Typed summary notes and sketches were also compiled after visits to aid the work of excavation staff. These notes have also been drawn on alongside the main site records, principally the plans and elevations.

It is worth noting that the highest surviving top of a timber wet dock upright was at 3.40m OD on its south-west edge, implying an original height of at least 3.50m OD, that is, around 0.4–0.5m higher than at the smaller, privately owned 17th-century shipyard at Rotherhithe (Heard 2003, 48). This may reflect the greater resources available to the navy and their keenness to keep their dockyard rather dry.

Despite extensive efforts on-site to locate suitable samples for tree-ring dating, relatively few were successfully dated (Chapter 10.9). This means that the usual precision of structural dating from London-region waterfront sites with many preserved timbers was not possible here; nevertheless, a skeleton framework of dates was obtained. Subsamples from timbers were taken on-site in order to carry out microscopic wood species analysis (Stewart 2013).

While it is clear that the archive of woodwork records for this project is extensive, though not always easy to compare with those from other sites, it is commensurate with the practical English Heritage (now Historic England) guidelines on waterlogged wood (Brunning and Watson 2010). That is, essential information beyond the simple size and shape of individual timbers was recorded, such as the raw materials, fastenings and joints used. Fine details such as carpenters' and other marks, and some tool marks, were also recorded in written and photographic form as well as diagnostic evidence for the reuse of timbers (principally of ship origin).

Notable reused ships' timbers: complex testaments to the late 17th- to early 19th-century shipwright's craft

The general range of nautical timbers found

At various points in this summary coverage of the woodwork found during the excavations, the reuse of various forms of nautical timbers is described. However, due to the excavation brief's constraint of leaving most of the building and structural remains *in situ*, few of the timbers could be lifted and fully exposed so that the details typically recorded for such material could be recorded; this was possible in just a few cases, and selected, particularly evocative examples are discussed below and in Chapter 9.1 and 9.2. The range of reused ships' timbers found was wide, but surprisingly did not include any timbers from boats or barges that normally dominate assemblages of post-medieval nautical timbers found on other London waterfront sites (Goodburn 1991a; Marsden 1996; Goodburn 2002). However, a very small number of iron rove nails from clinker-built craft were found in the pre-dockyard phase (period 1; Chapter 2.3); as these had been used, they may well have derived from old vessel timbers used as fuel, or from decayed reused timbers. We know that naval small boats were stored and must have been repaired, if not built, on the site, but no archaeological evidence of this smaller-scale work was found.

Such work may have been located in unexplored areas but we might draw two, different, conclusions from this: firstly, that small boat timbers were reused for fuel, kindling and so on and not recycled structurally; and secondly, that very little small boatbuilding and repair actually took place on the site. Boatbuilders (building smaller clinker vessels) and barge builders (working in the distinctive Thames style) and builders of the 'ships royal' would each have had distinct skills.

The most commonly found reused nautical timbers were straighter oak frame timbers pierced with relict oak treenails once used to fasten carvel planking to them; these were particularly widely reused in the extensive repair of the timber wet dock of period 3 (Chapter 4.2). Similar assorted ship frame timbers of oak were also used in the sleeper surfaces of the no. 1 and nos 4 and 5 slipways (S27, S30 and S31), particularly the latter (Chapter 6.3). Several angular ship knees of oak were found reused but rather decayed in the later repairs to the wet dock gateway support structure, but only of moderate size and none particularly diagnostic. Some carvel ship hull planking of oak was also found reused in the timber wet dock sheathing and as sill beam planks under later brick wall foundations, but in general relatively little of this category of material was found. In later contexts fragments of tropical timber ship planking were found reused west of the brick wet dock. The large deck beam timbers were also found in the form of reused sections in the periods 5 and 6 trestle foundations as the main posts (Chapters 7.3, 7.4 and 8.2). A few smaller deck elements were also found such as the smaller beams or 'ledges'. No keel timbers were exposed, but other centre-line elements such as parts of two large composite stern posts and two sections of false keel were found and recorded, and are discussed and illustrated below. Fittings of large ships in the form of the rudder post discussed below and anchor stocks noted above (Chapters 7.3 and 9.2; Fig 142) were also found. Many of the timbers only partially exposed showed traces of relict nautical fastenings such as oak treenails but did not have forms distinctive enough for clear identification of their origins. (A small number of oak treenails were found loose and with a recorded diameter between 22mm and 38mm.) Finally, it is quite possible that some of the reused round softwood timbers were actually sections of ship spars ('yards and booms' used to support the sails), but none were clearly identified.

Large ship stern posts and rudders

Historic Royal Navy specifications for warship construction from the late 17th and 18th centuries indicate that the large vertical timbers, from the back or 'aft' end of the ship, were often joined to another main vertical timber to form a two-part 'stern post' assembly (Godwin 1987, 9). The 18th-century HMS *Victory* has a composite two-part stern post structure, for example. The massive rudders with which such large ships were fitted for steering were hung on the stern post with several heavy iron strapped hinge elements, the male parts being the 'pintles' on the rudder and the female being 'gudgeons' fastened to the stern post. The large rudders were usually made of several vertically set timbers secured to each other with complex joints and carefully fitted iron edge bolting (Dodds and Moore 1984, 104). A nearly complete, though smaller, rudder was found reused in a slipway at the former East India Company yard during excavations there (Divers 2004, 67).

A SHIP RUDDER POST

A ship rudder post (timber [3720]) was found reused as a land-tie beam for the wet dock entrance channel, as part of a repair or rebuild some time after 1700 (Chapters 4.2 and 6.3). This timber was sawn from a whole, rather knotty oak log and trimmed with adzes to a complex rectangular tapering shape (Fig 196); some sapwood was left at the corners of the timber. It also had four recesses for the iron strap hinges or pintles used to support the rudder on the ship by engaging with the gudgeons attached to the stern post. Historic illustrations show that there could be up to seven of these strap hinges on very large ships, which must have been very difficult to align and fit. The surviving length as reused was 5.85m, although the timber was clearly not quite the full original length of perhaps 7–8m or thereabouts. Its cross-sectional dimensions were 520 × 490mm at the larger rectangular end and 260 × 200mm at the smaller surviving end. The larger dimension was used towards the top in the parent ship and the narrower end towards the bottom where the rudder acted like a fine fin turning in the water many feet below the surface. The leading edge of the rudder post was bevelled at the corners to allow it to swing from side to side without its corners hitting the stern post. In some senses this moving part of a wooden warship's structure is a sculptural testament to the skills of the contemporary shipwright.

The great size of the rudders of large warships required that they be made of several separate beams which had to be rigidly joined. Alternate recessed and proud rectangular shapes were cut in the solid timber edges which locked the timbers together once held with large iron bolts. This system of jointing or 'tabelling' was time-consuming to cut out but very secure once bolted and sealed with tarred hair. The depth and height of the tabelling was in this case c 30mm. Tabelling and bolts were also used to add a small extension to the leading edge of the base of the rudder. Interestingly, a similar large rudder post find made at a Rotherhithe ship-breaking yard and reused in the mid 1660s was extended in width without the use of tabelling joints (Saxby and Goodburn 1998, 184). Possibly this elaborate jointing method was either a naval speciality or developed in the later 17th or early 18th centuries.

Three sizes of bolts were used to fasten the rudder timbers together in this case, with diameters of c 25mm (1in), 28mm (1$\frac{1}{8}$in) and 42mm (1$\frac{5}{8}$in). Several of the large iron fastenings in the larger end of this timber were relics of the reuse of the timber, but the large number of small copper nail shanks and small empty nail holes are evidence of the original copper sheathing to reduce fouling and protect the rudder from shipworm.

A SHIP STERN POST

Also found reused as a land-tie beam for the wet dock entrance channel as part of the same repair or rebuild some time after 1700 (above) was a ship stern post (timber [3718]). This timber had distinctive adze-trimmed sloping rebates or 'rabbets' on two opposed faces, showing that it had once been a ship stern post

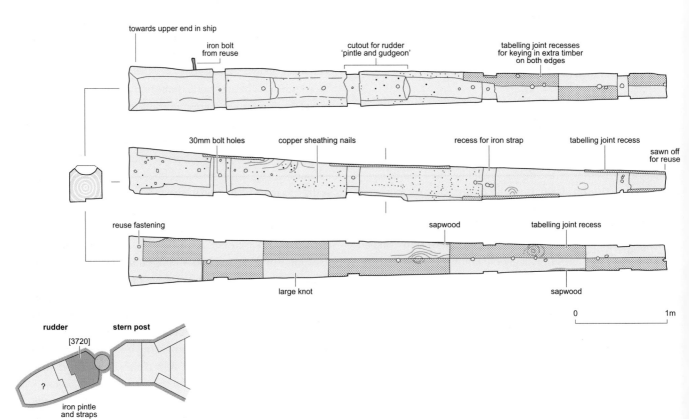

Fig 196 Large 18th-century ship rudder post reused as a land-tie beam (timber [3720]) (scale 1:40)

(Fig 197). The rabbets were for the tapering-in planking of the sharp ship's stern, and traces of tarred hair sealant were noted on-site in the rabbet. The angle of this rabbet changed from sharp at the base where the hull of the vessel was fin-like to wider at the top where it was blunter. Five 20mm deep recesses for the iron strap braces holding rudder hinge elements in place were recorded. This large reused timber survived 6.36m long, with a maximum width of 470mm and thickness of 420mm, tapering down to about half that size at what was the original lower end. It was mainly recorded *in situ* but several sections were also lifted after the sawing out of tree-ring slice samples, when a series of depth or 'draught' marks were found on what was the lower, hidden, face in its reuse. These, from 9ft up to 16ft, were carved in Roman numerals with chisels. The draught implied demonstrates clearly the large size of the parent vessel and shows that it could have visited the timber wet dock when it was well dredged of silt. Again this large timber was sawn out of a whole largish oak to form the taper and trimmed with adzes. However, the timber used was clearly not quite as large as desired and was extended in width using the same form of tabelling and edge bolting described for the rudder post (above). The edge bolt holes were not as centrally located as there, no doubt at least in part because the depth of timber to be bored through in the overall stern assembly would have been very great, and so small inaccuracies in alignment of the holes would have been accentuated.

The best-preserved section of the timber lifted shows several other details of interest, including drift bolt holes *c* 20mm in diameter and oak treenails *c* 34mm in diameter which were used to fasten the ends of the ship planks or 'hoodends'. Many close-set small nail holes *c* 7mm square and a few surviving copper nail shanks show that this timber had also been copper-sheathed.

The Navy Board attempted to set standardised dimensions, called the 'Naval Establishment Lists', for elements of warships. The dimensions for stern posts in the 1719 list of specifications (actually signed at Deptford on 11 November 1719) suggest that this stern post would have been approximately the right size for a 50-gun ship (Godwin 1987, 244).

PART OF A SHIP STERN POST

This stern post timber (timber [5540], period 5) was reused as a vertical post in an assembly (S63) just west of the wet dock brick wall, probably part of a crane base (Fig 107). The surviving one of two braces was a small ship deck beam or 'ledge' [5701]. The stern post timber survived 1.93m long, including the tenon at the recut base, and had a maximum width of 460mm (crosswise in the parent ship) by 440mm. The stern post was reused the same way up as it was used in the parent ship and the section recorded must have derived from towards the top. A slight taper to smaller dimensions was visible at the lower end. The rabbet cut for the stern plank ends shows that the stern of the parent vessel was very sharp even at a high level. The post had two tabelling joint projections on what would have been the aft face of the timber, showing that it was the inner part of a two-timber, composite stern post assembly. The tabelling joint was clearly fastened with iron drift bolts *c* 25mm in diameter and some smaller ones. One of the essential skills of the post-medieval shipwright working on large carvel ships was to bore long and accurate holes for bolts or treenails. In this stern post a major bolt hole only just stayed within the timber and the shipwright was only a hair's breadth away from ruining the work. One recess for the iron braces holding a gudgeon for the rudder hinge survived on each side although it was surprisingly asymmetrically set. A *c* 18mm hole for a drift bolt was found in each side. A small square oak patch or

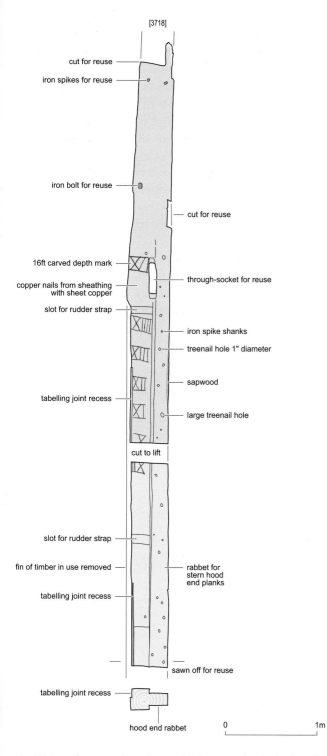

[3718]

cut for reuse

iron spikes for reuse

iron bolt for reuse

cut for reuse

16ft carved depth mark

copper nails from sheathing with sheet copper

slot for rudder strap

through-socket for reuse

iron spike shanks

treenail hole 1" diameter

sapwood

large treenail hole

tabelling joint recess

cut to lift

slot for rudder strap

fin of timber in use removed

rabbet for stern hood end planks

tabelling joint recess

sawn off for reuse

tabelling joint recess

hood end rabbet

0   1m

Fig 197 Reused stern post from a large mid 18th-century ship (timber [3718]) (scale 1:40)

'graving piece' was inserted over a defect in the timber on the internal face.

Chisel-carved draught marks in Roman numerals were clearly visible on one face of this timber, apparently running from 10ft to 12ft (X, XI, XII) but the last figure must have been incomplete and originally read XIII (Fig 107). The reason for this was that the iron rudder brace would have obscured the number. Based on the 1719 Naval Establishment List specifications, this stern post timber probably came from a rather large warship of at least 70 guns (Godwin 1987, 244).

Two false keel timbers

Two false keel timbers were found reused as a morticed building sill beam (from the north end of area 1.2, B54). False keels were intended as a sacrificial element, in the form of a thick plank fastened below the true keel. They served to protect the structural keel and also to deepen the keel to increase the ship's grip on the water for sailing into the wind. To this end they were fastened relatively lightly so that they could be removed in sections once worn or damaged by marine borers or the ship running aground. As all naval warships were copper-sheathed from the late 18th century, the surface fastenings of the false keel would have been in close contact with the sheathing and so they were best fastened with copper-alloy fastenings accessible from the side for easy removal. This was required as the fastenings would have corroded very fast due to galvanic corrosion in salt water if made of iron, and been devoured by shipworm if treenails.

Elm timber [5772] was found reused just north of the small mast dock. However, it had features clearly distinguishing it as once having been a large ship's false keel. It survived 2.30m long, 350mm wide and 180mm thick, and had been sawn out of a whole baulk of elm (Fig 198). Although somewhat damaged by machine excavation, two sets of slots which once held the copper-alloy staples or 'dogs' that joined it to the main keel, and what must have been a smaller additional keel, survived. (Here it might be noted that the famous HMS *Victory* was fitted with two thicknesses of false keel.) The thickness and width of this timber shows that it must have derived from a very large vessel. It was much larger than the broadly contemporary false keels of beech and elm found on a Rotherhithe ship-breaking and shipbuilding site, which were only 75mm thick (Heard 2003, 43). This false keel, and that described below, were also much thicker than any described in the 1719 Naval Establishment List, although the later date may also have been a factor here.

A line of small, close-set, copper-alloy nail shanks *c* 5mm square that once held the lower edge of copper sheathing also survived near what would have been the upper limits of the timber in its original use. In other words, the sheathing does not seem to have covered the whole keel. As the original bottom, lower, corners of the timber were extensively worn, it seems likely that the implied second false keel had been dispensed with before this false keel was removed from the parent ship, probably in the early 19th century.

Elm timber [5895] survived reused 3.44m long by 370mm wide and 150mm thick (Fig 198). Again a false keel of this size

[5772]

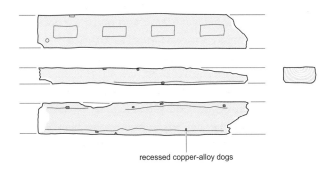

recessed copper-alloy dogs

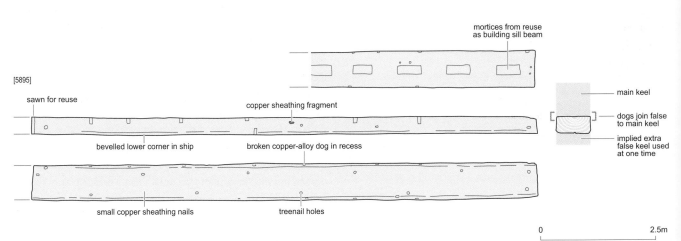

mortices from reuse as building sill beam

[5895]

sawn for reuse

copper sheathing fragment

main keel

dogs join false to main keel

implied extra false keel used at one time

bevelled lower corner in ship

broken copper-alloy dog in recess

small copper sheathing nails

treenail holes

0   2.5m

Fig 198 Reused elm false keel timbers [5772] and [5895] (scale 1:80)

must have derived from a very large vessel. Copper-alloy dogs were found broken off, having originally been fitted into recesses at various intervals of between *c* 400mm and *c* 700mm. A scatter of *c* 25mm square peg holes were also recorded on the faces of the timber, but it seems likely that these were created during an intermediate phase of use as they are more typical of carpenters' rather than shipwrights' work.

Small, *c* 5mm square, copper-alloy nail shanks, very closely set, were recorded running in longitudinal and crosswise lines around the base and sides of the false keel. The multiplicity of nails suggests that there had been two phases of sheathing. As it became worn and corroded through use it would have had to have been replaced. A small fragment of copper sheet even survived attached on one edge, even though it would have been a valuable piece of scrap material. The crosswise lines of sheathing nails coincided with shallow grooves, *c* 1.2m apart, where the copper sheet used must have overlapped with the next sheet. Interestingly, in this example the lower corners of the false keel as used in the parent ship had been bevelled to strengthen them against abrasion but then sheathed with copper sheet. This means that the base of the keel and false keel assembly had this fragile covering as well as the sides, and it is difficult to see how it could have survived the ship running aground.

10.8 Animal bone

Alan Pipe

Introduction

This appendix quantifies, identifies and interprets the hand-collected animal bones recovered from four cesspits in properties immediately east of the yard on King Street (OA8, OA9; Chapter 9.3): cesspit [5994] (fill [5610]) and cesspit [6524] (fill [4952]), both filled in the mid 18th century (period 4); and cesspit [5546] (fill [4880]) and cesspit [5548] (fill [5107]), both filled in the 1820s (period 5). A total of 411 fragments of hand-collected animal bone from these cesspits were recorded on to the MOLA post-assessment database (period totals of 85 fragments for period 4 and 326 for period 5). Preservation was good for all contexts, with surface damage generally insufficient to prevent identification of species, skeletal element, dental wear, epiphysial fusion and modification.

The discussion of these cesspits in Chapter 9.3 provides a description of each context group in terms of species and skeletal recovery, age at death and modification. Where group and context sample size is sufficient to allow further comment, diet, industrial activity and habitat implications are discussed.

Methodology

Animal bones from each context group were described and recorded directly on to the MOLA animal bone post-assessment Oracle database. Whenever possible, each fragment was

recorded in terms of species, skeletal element, body side, age, sex, fragmentation and modification. Interpretations of age at death were made using data cited by Amorosi (1989), Bull and Payne (1982) and Payne (1973). Species and skeletal element were determined using the MOLA animal bone reference collection together with Cannon (1987), Cohen and Serjeantson (1996), Schmid (1972) and Wheeler and Jones (1989). Fragmentation was described using a numerical zone method devised by MOLA. Similarly, butchery, working, burning and gnawing were described using standard codes and conventions in use by MOLA osteology. All fully fused, skeletally adult and well-preserved bones were measured using the techniques of von den Driesch (1976). Stature estimates were calculated using conversion factors. In general, each bone fragment was assigned to species and skeletal element and recorded as an individual database entry; when this was impracticable due to extreme fragmentation and/or erosion, fragments were recorded at an approximate level of identification, particularly as 'cattle-sized mammal', 'sheep-sized mammal', 'sheep/goat' and 'long bone'. Fragments too damaged to be identified to even these approximate levels were not recorded. In general, 'cattle-sized' and 'sheep-sized' long bone and vertebra fragments were only recorded when showing evidence of modification, particularly burning, tool marks or pathological change.

Results

Faunal composition

The assemblage derived largely from cattle (*Bos taurus*) and sheep/goat (including sheep, *Ovis aries*), with smaller groups of fish, poultry, pig (*Sus scrofa*), game and other, probably non-consumed, domesticates: dog (*Canis lupus familiaris*) and cat (*Felis catus*); there was no recovery of goat or horse (Table 7).

Fish mainly comprised marine/estuarine species: cod family (Gadidae) including cod (*Gadus morhua*) and plaice or flounder (Pleuronectidae) including plaice (*Pleuronectes platessa*). Recovery of freshwater fish was limited to three fragments of carp family (Cyprinidae) vertebra from cesspit [5548] (fill [5107]).

Poultry included chicken or domestic fowl (*Gallus gallus*), goose, probably domestic goose (*Anser anser domesticus*), and mallard or domestic duck (*Anas platyrhynchos*), with no recovery of turkey (*Meleagris gallopavo*) or domestic pigeon/rock dove (*Columba livia*).

Associated small mammals comprised occasional recovery of rat (*Rattus* sp) only. There was no recovery of house mouse (*Mus musculus domesticus*) or further small mammals, nor of amphibians.

Meat diet

For all periods, the bulk of the meat weight would been provided by sheep/goat and cattle, and to a lesser extent pig and poultry, predominantly representing consumption of beef, mutton, pork and chicken, with occasional consumption of fish, goose, duck and rabbit. Generally, there was a consistent

Table 7 Animal bone from 18th- and 19th-century cesspits of properties on King Street, immediately east of the yard (OA8, periods 4 and 5), by fragment counts

Common name	Scientific name	Period 4		Period 5		Total
		Cesspit [5994] (fill [5610])	Cesspit [6524] (fill [4952])	Cesspit [5546] (fill [4880])	Cesspit [5548] (fill [5107])	
Cod (family)	Gadidae				3	3
Cod	*Gadus morhua*				2	2
Plaice/flounder	Pleuronectidae			8	8	16
Plaice	*Pleuronectes platessa*				34	34
Carp (family)	Cyprinidae				3	3
Domestic fowl	*Gallus gallus*		7	6	13	26
Goose	*Anser anser domesticus*			2	3	5
Mallard/domestic duck	*Anas platyrhynchos*		9		7	16
Cattle	*Bos taurus*		4	26	8	38
Cattle-size	-		7	15	4	26
Sheep	*Ovis aries*			8		8
Sheep/goat	*Ovis aries/Capra hircus*		19	44	14	77
Sheep-size	-		20	31	31	82
Pig	*Sus scrofa*	1	15	11	9	36
Rabbit	*Oryctolagus cuniculus*		1		3	4
Dog	*Canis lupus familiaris*			17		17
Cat	*Felis catus*		2		10	12
Rat	*Rattus sp*				6	6
Total		1	84	168	158	411

emphasis on adults and juveniles with only occasional exploitation of foetal/neonate and infant animals (Table 8; Table 9). Carcass-part selection emphasised areas of moderate and prime meat-bearing quality, with areas of poorer quality such as head and foot accounting for smaller groups. There was no recovery of cattle or sheep/goat horncore, suggesting removal during primary carcass processing elsewhere. Recovery

of fish was distinctive, with emphasis on marine/estuarine species numerically dominated by two taxonomic groups, cod and cod family (probably all cod (*Gadus morhua*) and particularly plaice (*Pleuronectes platessa*), with a large group of plaice head elements and vertebrae from 19th-century (period 5) cesspit [5548] (fill [5107]) and plaice/flounder vertebrae from 19th-century (period 5) cesspit [5546] (fill [4880]). Both identified

Table 8 Mandibular dental eruption and wear for major domesticates from 18th- and 19th-century cesspits of properties on King Street, immediately east of the yard (OA8, periods 4 and 5) (after Payne 1973; Bull and Payne 1982)

Period	Land use	Feature	Context (fill)	Species	Wear stage (Grant 1982)					Wear stage (Payne 1973)					Age (years)
					dpm4	PM4	M1	M2	M3	dpm4	PM4	M1	M2	M3	
4	OA8	cesspit [5994]	[5610]	pig	0	3	9	7	2						1.5–2.0
4	OA8	cesspit [6524]	[4952]	sheep/goat	12	0	10	3	1	11	0	11	3	1	<0.5
5	OA8	cesspit [5546]	[4880]	sheep	11	0	8	2	0	10	0	8	2	0	<0.5
5	OA8	cesspit [5546]	[4880]	sheep	11	0	7	2	0	11	0	8	2	0	<0.5

Table 9 Stature estimates for sheep and dog from a 19th-century cesspit of a property on King Street, immediately east of the yard (OA8, period 5) (after von den Driesch and Boessneck 1974)

Period	Land use	Feature	Context (fill)	Species	Bone	Greatest length (mm)	Stature (m)
5	OA8	cesspit [5546]	[4880]	dog	humerus	92.0	0.289
5	OA8	cesspit [5546]	[4880]	dog	radius	83.2	0.284
5	OA8	cesspit [5546]	[4880]	dog	tibia	93.3	0.282
5	OA8	cesspit [5546]	[4880]	dog	tibia	92.7	0.280
5	OA8	cesspit [5546]	[4880]	dog	ulna	98.0	0.279
5	OA8	cesspit [5546]	[4880]	sheep	calcaneum	55.6	0.634
5	OA8	cesspit [5546]	[4880]	sheep	humerus	154.0	0.659

species are available from the outer Thames estuary and coastal fisheries on the Kent and Essex coasts (Wheeler 1979, 175–6, 196–7). The game assemblage is extremely sparse, in that it derives only from rabbit (*Oryctolagus cuniculus*) from 18th-century (period 4) cesspit [6524] and 19th-century (period 5) cesspit [5548], and possibly also mallard (*Anas platyrhynchos*) from the same fills, with no evidence for venison or other definite indicators of higher-status consumption.

Non-consumed domesticates

There was no recovery of horse, and dog and cat remains were extremely sparse throughout the assemblage, suggesting casual disposal of the occasional pet carcass. No dog or cat bone bore any tool marks or gnawing, suggesting that their carcasses were not skinned or used to feed other livestock. The group comprised elements of an adult and a juvenile dog from 19th-century (period 5) cesspit [5546] (fill [4880]) only, and small groups of cat from 18th-century (period 4) cesspit [6524] (fill [4952]) and 19th-century (period 5) cesspit [5548] (fill [5107]) only.

Modification

Although clear tool-mark evidence of butchery, with use of saws as well as cleavers and knives, was common on cattle, sheep/goat and pig bones throughout the cesspit group assemblages, other post-mortem modification comprised only occasional rodent gnawing, probably by house mouse (*Mus musculus domesticus*) and rat (*Rattus* sp), and a single example of pathological change.

Evidence of rodent gnawing was seen occasionally on sheep/goat bone from periods 4 and 5 (Table 10), suggesting that waste disposal and hygiene practices allowed some unrestricted access by rats and mice to butchery and post-consumption waste. There was no evidence for gnawing by carnivores.

Evidence for pathological change was limited to a single mandible (lower jaw) of dog from 19th-century (period 5) cesspit [5546] (fill [4880]), showing tooth loss and alveolar (tooth socket) infilling, probably indicating an aged animal (Table 10).

There was no evidence for burning and no tool-mark evidence for working or preparation of horn or bone.

Comparison of cesspit groups

Although the selected cesspit assemblage is quantitatively small, comprising a total of only 411 hand-collected fragments from four fills, some comment may be made on inter-context similarities and differences in terms of species composition, carcass-part selection and modification. With the exception of mid 18th-century (period 4) cesspit [5994] which included only a mandible (lower jaw) of a second-year pig, the remaining cesspit fills – from 18th-century (period 4) cesspit [6524] and 19th-century (period 5) cesspits [5546] and [5548] – included small assemblages (respectively 84, 168 and 158 fragments) derived largely from juvenile and adult cattle, sheep/goat and, to a lesser extent, pig and poultry. Domestic fowl were recovered from cesspit [6524] and cesspits [5546] and [5548], with goose from 19th-century (period 5) cesspits [5546] and [5548] and mallard or domestic duck from 18th-century (period 4) cesspit [6524] only. Very young animals were represented only by single examples of foetal or neonate calf, infant calf and infant pig, all from 19th-century (period 5) cesspit [5546].

For all three of the larger fill groups, carcass-part representation of the major domesticates showed a clear bias towards areas of prime (vertebra, rib, upper limb) and moderate (head, lower limb) meat-bearing quality, with no recovery of horncore and negligible recovery of the foot elements. Fish were recovered from only two fills – 19th-century (period 5) cesspits [5546] (plaice/flounder) and [5548] (cod, plaice, carp family), with the larger group from [5548] comprising mainly head elements and vertebrae of plaice, suggesting preparation, consumption and disposal of at least two fish of this marine species, as well as a few fragments of cod and a freshwater fish of the carp family. Recovery of game was extremely sparse, consisting only of rabbit – a single fragment from 18th-century (period 4) cesspit [6524] and three fragments from 19th-century (period 5) cesspit [5548]. Evidence from species and carcass-part representation thus provides no clear indication that the cesspit groups derived from consumers differing significantly in economic status or social group.

Non-consumed domesticates were also very sparsely represented, with occasional fragments of cat from 18th-century (period 4) cesspit [6524] and 19th-century (period 5) cesspit [5548], and dog from cesspit [5546] only, with no indications of organised large-scale disposal. Evidence of rodent gnawing was noted on sheep/goat bone from cesspits [6524]

Table 10 Gnawing and pathological change on animal bone from 18th- and 19th-century cesspits of properties on King Street, immediately east of the yard (OA8, periods 4 and 5)

Period	Land use	Feature	Context (fill)	Species	Bone	Modification	Description
4	OA8	cesspit [6524]	[4952]	sheep/goat	mandible	gnawing	rodent, severe
5	OA8	cesspit [5546]	[4880]	dog	mandible	pathology	much alveolar resorbtion
5	OA8	cesspit [5548]	[5107]	sheep-size	rib	gnawing	rodent, severe
5	OA8	cesspit [5548]	[5107]	sheep/goat	vertebra, cervical	gnawing	rodent, moderate
5	OA8	cesspit [5548]	[5107]	sheep/goat	ulna	gnawing	rodent, slight

(period 4) and [5548] (period 5) only, with rat bones recovered only from [5548], perhaps an indication that these pits provided easier physical access to scavengers than did cesspits [5546] and [5994].

10.9 Tree-ring dating

Ian Tyers

Methodology

Each dendrochronological sample was supplied as a complete cross section and each sample was assessed for the wood type, the number of rings it contained, and whether the sequence of ring widths could be reliably resolved. Standard dendrochronological analysis methods (English Heritage 1998) were applied to each suitable sample. For this material the sapwood estimates used are a minimum of ten and maximum of 55 annual rings, where these figures indicate the 95% confidence limits of the range. Identifications of wood type are based on the taking of microscopic thin sections of the timber in three planes (radial, transverse and tangential sections). The comparison of these sections with reference slides, or by identification keys, enabled secure identification to be made. Full details are included in the archive report (Tyers 2013).

Results

The submitted material comprised 53 oak (*Quercus* spp) samples, four pine (*Pinus* cf *sylvestris*) samples and one beech (*Fagus sylvatica*) sample. Of the oak samples, 44 contained measurable tree-ring sequences, while the other nine either had too few rings for analysis, or contained aberrant growth characteristics preventing their analysis. The 44 suitable samples were each measured successfully; cross-matching evidence identified eight of these individual series as being of late medieval, post-medieval and early modern dates (Tyers 2013). Two samples ([4885] and [4927]) were found to match but were not dated.

The results are presented in the bar diagram (Fig 199). Seven of the dated samples retained either heartwood/sapwood boundaries or identifiable sapwood, the latter intact to the bark edge in two cases.

The dated series mostly cross-match to datasets from contemporaneous sites in London and the south-east of England, although the geographical distribution of strong reference chronologies is rather uneven during this period. These timbers can be assumed to be mostly derived from trees grown in the London, East Anglian or south-east of England regions.

Discussion

The assemblage presents a number of unusual features for an excavated group of timbers from London. It is of an unusually late date for a large oak assemblage, the vast majority of timbers hitherto excavated in London being either from the 1st century AD or the 11th–13th centuries. There is a very poor dating success rate, and a remarkable absence of internal cross-matching (only two pairs match at a statistically significant level). This aspect possibly suggests that this material is the product of a selection of trees from across a wide area (Chapter 9.1). Typical assemblages of timbers are more similar, perhaps indicating that they were derived from felling within a geographically limited area, or within a few areas, of less extensively managed woodland. There is no dendrochronological evidence for non-native material, which is perhaps surprising given the period.

The material displays unusual rot patterns. This has led to the frequent presence of pale-coloured oak heartwood, resembling sapwood (and possibly mistaken for sapwood during sampling); however, this must be heartwood as it has microscopic tyloses. This rotting may have been caused by tidal fluctuations or other periodic wetting and drying. It is worth noting that if the timbers had been stockpiled by the navy prior to their subsequent use in construction, it is possible that interpretations based on these samples should be treated as a *terminus post quem*. Moreover, many of the timbers used in the dockyard structures derived from ships broken or repaired in the yard, and so were in their first (or a further) phase of reuse (Chapter 9.1).

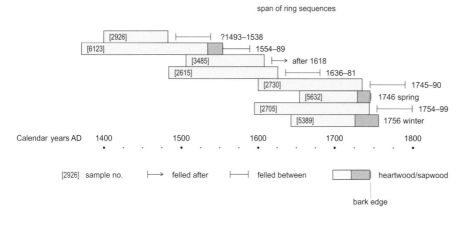

Fig 199 *Bar diagram showing the dating positions of the eight dated oak tree-ring samples; interpretations are shown for each timber based on the minimum and, where appropriate, also the maximum typical amounts of sapwood for London oaks, using a 10–55 ring sapwood estimate*

FRENCH AND GERMAN SUMMARIES

Translated by Madeleine Hummler

Résumé

Cette publication présente les résultats des fouilles les plus étendues jamais entreprises sur un chantier naval britannique. Les recherches ont porté, entre 2000 et 2012, sur une aire d'environ 16,6 hectares dans l'ancienne zone du Deptford Royal Dockyard et de Sayes Court dans le quartier de Lewisham à Londres. Les fouilles conduites par MOLA (Museum of London Archaeology) et autres entreprises furent effectuées avant et après la démolition d'entrepôts et d'autres bâtiments sur le site, alors connu sous le nom de Convoys Wharf. Une vaste quantité de documents écrits et graphiques, de cartes et même une maquette nous permettent de mieux comprendre le complexe de structures et le matériel que les recherches archéologiques ont mis à jour.

Les chantiers navals royaux et un corps de marine permanent avaient été créés par les premiers rois Tudor, en particulier par Henri VIII ; le mouillage de Deptford sur la Tamise et le rivage de Deptford (Deptford Strand) n'étaient qu'à quelques encablures de son palais de Greenwich. Certaines structures, telles un chenal pour péniches, existaient déjà sur le site mais le chantier naval royal vit le jour sous Henri VIII avec la construction d'un entrepôt en 1513. Les bases des murs de ce bâtiment classé monument historique ont été relevées ainsi que celles toutes proches et jusqu'alors inconnues de la maison du trésorier de la marine. D'autres structures anciennes comprennent le double bassin ou grand bassin et la darse aménagée dans un ancien étang. Aucune trace archéologique de ces anciens docks n'a survécu mais un contrat datant de 1517, la commande de construire la darse, est publié ici pour la première fois en entier. Ce contrat nomme certains navires, tel le *Mary Rose*, que la darse allait devoir accueillir. Les fouilles ont par contre retrouvé une série de quais en bois. Les docks de Deptford étaient l'établissement portuaire le plus important de l'époque des Tudors en Angleterre, ce fut la dernière demeure du vaisseau de Francis Drake, le *Golden Hinde*, et ce fameux corsaire y fut nommé chevalier par la reine Elizabeth I.

Les premières cartes du chantier naval datent de l'époque des Stuarts (1603–1714) ; elles illustrent l'envergure qu'a pris le site, avec de nouveaux entrepôts, des bureaux, une forge, des cales pour réparer, construire et reconstruire les vaisseaux et un bassin pour entreposer et stabiliser les mâts. La darse fut reconstruite en 1658–61, ses poutres latérales et la partie orientale de son portail en bois étant exposées et étayées par des attaches fixées sur la terre ferme. Les vestiges d'une cale (la grande cale), ainsi que des hangars à bateaux plus modestes et des structures de stockage de bitume ont été retrouvés.

Vers l'intérieur, dans le secteur sud du site, certains vestiges ont dû faire partie de Sayes Court, la demeure de John Evelyn, auteur d'essais tels *Sylva* et *Fumifugium*, qui y reçut ses amis, dont Samuel Pepys. Aucune trace des célèbres jardins qu'Evelyn avait aménagé n'a pu être identifiée, sauf la base du mur d'enceinte. Le tsar russe Pierre le Grand séjourna ici en 1698, ce qui causa beaucoup de dégâts. Sayes Court fut démoli au milieu du XVIIIe siècle et remplacé par un hospice de pauvres.

Quoique l'importance de l'établissement portuaire ait

décliné au début de l'époque géorgienne (1714–74), ce déclin fut compensé par une augmentation de la demande en navires de guerre dans les guerres que l'Angleterre menait contre la France et l'Espagne. Obtenir un poste à Deptford était encore considéré comme le sommet d'une carrière d'officier de marine. Les conflits du XVIIIe siècle ont contribué à l'essor des travaux dans les docks dans un contexte de réparations et de maintenance permanents des vaisseaux de guerre de la marine.

Les fouilles ont révélé les fondations d'un énorme entrepôt carré à cour centrale construit au début du XVIIIe siècle ainsi que la reconstruction en brique, étape par étape, de la darse. Le plan du chantier naval était largement déterminé par la position des entrepôts et des bassins principaux, mais au sein de ce plan général on ne cessait d'adapter et de transformer les structures existantes et de construire de nouveaux bâtiments. La surface des docks s'élargit, avalant des parcelles de terrain à l'est et au sud, et on construisit un second bassin de stockage des mâts en beaucoup plus grand. Les documents de l'époque nous renseignent sur les problèmes et désastres essuyés par l'établissement portuaire, tels les incendies et l'insuffisance des portes de bassins ; quant aux documents archéologiques, les trois cales sur le rivage constituent les plus frappants vestiges relevés dans les fouilles. Les bases de deux d'entre elles ont été entièrement fouillées. On peut identifier une grande partie de ces structures sur les cartes de l'époque ainsi que sur une remarquable maquette du chantier naval faite à échelle en 1774 sous Georges III.

On peut lire dans un document historique que Deptford n'était de « nulle importance » avant que le chantier naval y fût établi. Par contre, il est certain que l'évolution de la ville était liée à la présence des docks. On pava les rues de Deptford pour la visite du roi Edouard VI. Une partie du site archéologique comprenait une zone en dehors du chantier naval, ce qui nous a permis de relever et d'analyser les objets domestiques jetés par des gens qui avaient accès à du matériel provenant d'outre-mer, soit parce qu'ils étaient directement employés par les docks, soit parce qu'ils tombaient au moins sous leur influence.

Paradoxalement l'essor de la ville a bloqué l'élargissement du chantier naval vers la fin de son exploitation sous les derniers rois géorgiens et la reine Victoria (1774–1869). La position de l'établissement portuaire en amont de la rivière devint problématique car les vaisseaux avaient peine à remonter la Tamise, et sa tendance à s'envaser empêchait le lancement, donc la construction, des navires de plus en plus grands que la flotte exigeait.

Malgré les transformations majeures de la darse effectuées par l'ingénieur John Rennie au début du XIXe siècle, la vie du chantier naval tirait à sa fin. A l'issue des guerres contre Napoléon Bonaparte, l'établissement portuaire devint un entrepôt important mais seuls des vaisseaux modestes y furent construits ; en 1830 on ne l'utilisa plus que pour démanteler des navires. En 1843, un sursis de la dernière minute ne fut que temporaire et en 1869 le chantier naval ferma définitivement ses portes ; on démolit une grande partie de ses bâtiments pour réutiliser ses briques et ses poutres ailleurs. La Corporation de la Cité de Londres acquit le site pour le transformer en marché à bestiaux (le Foreign Cattle Market) en construisant des étables au-dessus des cales remblayées.

Zusammenfassung

Die größte Ausgrabung, die je auf einer Werft der britischen Marine unternommen worden ist, bildet das Thema dieses Berichtes. Die archäologischen Untersuchungen haben eine Fläche von ca. 16,6 ha auf dem ehemaligen Gelände der königlichen Werft von Deptford und von Sayes Court im Bezirk Lewisham in London betroffen. Die Ausgrabungen wurden zwischen 2000 und 2012 vor und nach dem Abbruch von Lagern und anderen Gebäuden auf der ursprünglich als Convoys Wharf bekannte Stätte von MOLA (Museum of London Archaeology) und anderen durchgeführt. Sehr zahlreiche schriftliche und bildliche Quellen, Karten und sogar ein Baumodell haben es ermöglicht, ein besseres Verständnis von archäologisch komplexen Strukturen und Befunden zu gewinnen.

Die königlichen Werften und eine permanente Kriegsflotte wurden unter den zwei ersten Tudor-Königen (vor allem Heinrich VIII.) gegründet. Deptford, ein Ankergrund auf der Themse, sowie Deptford Strand, waren nur eine kurze Bootsfahrt von seinem Palast in Greenwich entfernt. Frühere Strukturen, wie möglicherweise ein Kanal für Frachtkähne, wurden auf der Stätte nachgewiesen. Jedoch wurde die königliche Werft mit dem Bau eines Lagerhauses auf Befehl von Heinrich VIII. im Jahre 1513 erst richtig gegründet. Die Fundamente der Mauern dieses unter Denkmalschutz stehenden Gebäudes und auch diejenigen des danebenstehenden Hauses des Schatzmeisters der Marine (‚Treasurer of the Navy') die bisher unbekannt waren, sind aufgenommen worden. Andere frühe Strukturen umfassten eine doppelte Hafenanlage (das sogenannte Große Dock) und ein Wasserbecken, das einen bestehenden Weiher wiederbenutzte. Es wurden keine archäologischen Spuren dieser frühen Beckenanlagen gefunden, aber ein Vertrag von 1517, der den Bau des Wasserbeckens in Auftrag gegeben hat, wird hier zum ersten Mal völlig veröffentlicht. Dieser Vertrag nennt Schiffe, wie zum Beispiel die *Mary Rose*, die man hier im Becken unterbringen sollte. Eine Reihe von Holzkais wurden auch archäologisch aufgenommen. Deptford war eine der wichtigsten Werften der Tudorzeit in England; sie war die letzte Ruhestätte des Schiffes von Francis Drake, die *Golden Hinde*, und dieser Freibeuter wurde in der Hafenanlage von Königin Elizabeth I. zu Ritter geschlagen.

Die ersten Karten der Werft erschienen in der Stuartzeit (1603–1714) und zeigen, wie sich die Anlage sich erweitert hat: es gab weitere Lagerhäuser, Geschäftszimmer, eine Schmiede, Hellingen, wo man Schiffe bauen, reparieren und umbauen konnte, und ein Becken, wo man die Maste lagern konnte. Das Wasserbecken wurde zwischen 1658 und 1661 umgebaut. Die Holzwände und die östliche Seite des Schleusentors, ebenfalls aus Holz, wurden freigelegt; sie waren mit Spannankern in den Boden verankert. Die Überreste einer Helling (der sogenannte Große Schlipp) und auch bescheidenere Bootschuppen und Strukturen für das Speichern von Pech sind erhalten geblieben.

Im Inneren des Geländes, südlich der Fundstätte, wurden einige Spuren als die Überreste von Sayes Court gedeutet; dieses Gebäude war das Haus von John Evelyn, der Schriften wie *Sylva* und *Fumifugium* veröffentlichte und Freunde wie Samuel Pepys hier empfing. Außer den Fundamenten der Gartenmauer war Evelyns berühmte Gartenanlage nicht mehr erhalten. Der russische Zar Peter der Große war hier im Jahr 1698 auf Besuch und sein Aufenthalt hat viel Schaden verursacht. Sayes Court wurde in der Mitte des 18. Jhs abgerissen und durch ein Armenhaus ersetzt.

Obwohl die Werft in der Frühzeit der georgianischen Königen (1714–74) einen relativen Rückgang erlebte, war dies von einer steigenden Nachfrage nach Kriegsschiffen in den Kriegen mit Frankreich und Spanien ausgeglichen. Eine Stelle in Deptford war immer noch als Höhepunkt des Erfolgs eines Marineoffiziers angesehen. Diese Kriege hatten eine zunehmende Arbeitsbelastung für die Werft zu Folge, mit, im Hintergrund, ständige Reparaturen und Unterhalt der Kriegsschiffe der Flotte.

Die Ausgrabungen haben die Fundamente eines sehr großen quadratischen Lagerhauses mit zentralem Hof freigelegt, das im frühen 18. Jh. errichtet wurde, sowie Spuren des allmählichen Umbaus des Wasserbeckens aus Backsteinen. Der Plan der Werft war weitgehend von der Lage des großen Lagerhauses und der Becken bedingt, aber innerhalb dieser Gestaltung wurden die Gebäude und Strukturen immer wieder umgebaut oder neu errichtet. Die Werft dehnte sich über Land im Osten und Süden aus und ein zweites, viel größeres Mastbecken wurde gebaut. Die schriftlichen Quellen liefern uns Einblicke in die Schwierigkeiten und Katastrophen in der Werft, wie Brände und unbrauchbare Schleusen, und aus archäologischer Sicht sind die drei Hellingen am Ufer der Themse die augenfälligsten Überreste; zwei davon sind in den Ausgrabungen völlig freigelegt worden. Die zeitgenössischen Karten zeigen manche solche Strukturen und es gibt sogar ein maßgetreues Modell der

Werft, das unter Georg III. in 1774 hergestellt wurde.

Es wird in einer historischen Quelle festgestellt, dass Deptford „keine Bedeutung" vor der Errichtung der Werft hatte. Unbestritten ist die Tatsache, dass die Entwicklung der Stadt eng mit derjenigen der Werft verbunden war. Die Straßen von Deptford wurden für den Besuch von Eduard VI. gepflastert. Ein Teil der Ausgrabungsfläche lag außerhalb der Werft, und dies gab uns die Möglichkeit, das Haushaltzubehör der Bewohner freizulegen und zu untersuchen; diese Bewohner konnten Waren aus dem fernen Ausland erhalten entweder, weil sie direkt von der Werft beschäftigt waren oder weil sie mindestens unter ihrem Einfluss lagen.

Paradoxerweise hat die Entwicklung der Stadt die Erweiterung der Werft in der Endphase unter den letzten georgianischen Königen und Königin Viktoria (1774–1869) blockiert. Die flussaufwärts gelegene Lage der Werft ist auch problematisch geworden, da die Schiffe mühsam die Themse hinaufsegeln mussten, und die Verschlämmung des Flusses verhinderte das Ablegen, und deshalb den Bau, von den immer größeren Schiffen, die jetzt erforderlich waren.

Trotz der erheblichen Veränderungen des Wasserbeckens, die der Ingenieur John Rennie im frühen 19. Jh. unternahm, kam das Leben der Werft allmählich zu Ende. Nach den Napoleonischen Kriegen war die Werft ein wichtiges Warenhaus, aber nur kleine Schiffe konnten dort gebaut werden. In 1830 endete auch der Schiffsbau und nur das Abwracken von Schiffen wurde noch weitergeführt. In 1843 gab es noch eine kurze, nur vorübergehende Gnadenfrist und in 1869 wurde die Werft endgültig geschlossen. Manche Gebäude wurden abgerissen und die Backsteine und das Nutzholz wurden wegtransportiert und anderorts wiederverwendet. Die Körperschaft der City of London kaufte die Werft und benutzte sie als ausländischer Viehmarkt (Foreign Cattle Market) und Stallungen wurden über die angeschütteten Hellingen errichtet.

BIBLIOGRAPHY

British Library (BL)

MANUSCRIPTS DEPARTMENT

Add Ch 13686   Blackwall, Middlesex: contracts for shipbuilding at, 1654–87

Add Ch 6289 (1517)   Thomas Howard, 3rd Duke of Norfolk: indenture with John Herone and John Hoptone for making a basin [wet dock] at Deptford, 9 June 1517

Add MS 16945   coloured views of buildings, church monuments, etc, in Deptford and the neighbourhood, co. Kent, 1839–41

Add MS 6693, p 57   letters patent granting the manor of Deptford (inter alia) to Cecilia, Duchess of York, 1461/2

Add MS 78614   Evelyn Papers, vol CCCCXLVII: miscellaneous papers, 1660–1704; consisting of petitions, surveys, correspondence, accounts, articles of agreement, etc, of Sir Richard Browne and John Evelyn and John Evelyn junior

Add MS 78616   Evelyn Papers, vol CCCCXLIX: miscellaneous papers of the time of Sir John Evelyn, 1st Bart, 1706–63; [incl] notes by the steward John Strickland of tenants and rents of houses in Deptford, with drawings in elevation of the houses and the names of occupiers, 1706

Add MS 78621   Evelyn Papers, vol CCCCLIV: Deptford estate accounts of Sir John Evelyn, 1st Bart (receipts and payments, 1735–42, and rental (with notes of payments received and due), 1735–47)

Add MS 78622   Evelyn Papers, vol CCCCLV: Deptford estate accounts (receipts and payments) of Sir John Evelyn, 1st Bart, 1742–59

Add MS 78628 A   untitled plan of John Evelyn's house and garden at Sayes Court, with a detailed key occupying most of the left-hand side of the sheet, linked to the plan by means of 126 numbers, and headed, 'Explanation of the Particulars Referring to the Numbers'; designed by Evelyn (c 1652–4) but probably drawn and written by his amanuensis Richard Hoare c 1654

Add MS 78629 A   map of Deptford by an unidentified cartographer, 1623, with John Evelyn's extensive autograph and annotations … including his sketch of Sayes Court house, c 1698

Add MS 78629 K   'An Actuall Survey of the Lands belonging to Sayes Court in the Parish of Deptford in the County of Kent, being the Estate of John Evelyn Esq: surveyed in the Twelfe year of our Sovereign Lady Queen Ann by John Grove', c 1712 [?1714]

EP   Evelyn Papers [vol no. in arabic numerals] (= Add MSS 78168–78693), 16th to early 20th centuries

Kings MS 43   'A Survey and Description of the principal Harbours [of] the Navy Royall of England … illustrated by generall plans and proper views or prospects of each place … with an account of the emprovements which have been made at each yard since the Revolution of 1688', 1698

KTOP xviii.17.1   Milton's plan of the dockyard and environs, 1753

KTOP xviii.17.2   map of Sayes Court estate by Joel Gascoigne, 1692

Stowe MS 942   chartulary of the hospital of St Thomas the Martyr in Southwark, 16th century

Institution of Civil Engineers Library and Archives, London (ICE)

1858ADMNDP   map of Deptford dockyard in 1858
623.81 (422) M   Admiralty (Hydrographic Office): copies of naval dockyard plans (Chatham, Deptford, Devonport, Portsmouth, Sheerness, Woolwich), 1858 and 1878

Lambeth Archives (LA)

Class VI 67–222; 261   records of the manor of Bermondsey and Deptford Strand

Lewisham Local History and Archives Centre (LLHAC)

A/15/31   Convoy's Wharf Collection: photographs of the former Deptford royal dockyard site
A/15/31/10, /11   Supply Reserve Depot, Deptford (old Foreign Cattle Market), skeleton record plan, scale 10.56ft to 1 mile: sheet 1, 1935; sheet 2, updated layout, stamped 1947
A 66/4   conveyance of manor of Deptford Strand and Rotherhithe, 1556
A88/8/6   different version of the dockyard plan of 1725 (cf TNA, CRES 6/34, fos 80v–81)
PH 71-4158 LS34   Thankfull Sturdee Collection: photograph of slip cover roof converted into a 'sheep shed', c 1880
PT69/62   John Evelyn pays tax on 19 hearths in Sayes Court manor house, 1664

London Metropolitan Archives (LMA)

CLA/007/EM/02/H/019   Bridge House Deeds H19
CLA/007/EM/02/H/077   Bridge House Deeds H77
CLA/007/EM/02/I/018   Bridge House Deeds I18
CLA/012/AD/02   Foreign Cattle Market archives: auction catalogues and plans, 1870–2
COL/PL/01/048/C/219   undated 18th-century map including area adjoining east side of the dockyard
E/TD   Tyrwhitt Drake family papers
O/267/1, 2   map of Sayes Court estate by John Dugleby, 1777

Ministry of Defence, London (MOD)

4153   drawing of a 60-gun ship being launched at Deptford dockyard in 1739; attributed to John Cleveley the elder

The National Archives, London (TNA)

ADMIRALTY

ADM 7/593   minutes of the visitation of the dockyard (with plan), October 1813

ADM 12   digests and indexes, 1660–1974
ADM 106   Navy Board, records: Admiralty in-letters, 1650–1837

CROWN ESTATES

CRES 6/34, fos 80v–81   Constat Books, vol L2: sketch plan of the dockyard, 1725

EXCHEQUER

E 40/6983   Treasury of Receipt: ancient deeds, series A (no title, nd)
E 41/270   Treasury of receipt: ancient deeds, series AA; Dame Jane Sentjohn (St John), widow of John Sentjohn, her title to the manor of Deptford, temp Henry VIII
E 315   Court of Augmentations: miscellaneous books; particulars for the sale of colleges and chantries
E 317/Kent/56   Sayes Court, in Deptford: survey of the manor, January 1649
E 351/3402   Pipe Office declared accounts; works and buildings (miscellaneous): C Brown, repairing the marsh wall and the bank of the Thames adjoining the manor of Sayes Court and Earlsluice (Earl's Sluice), 1627–36

LAND REVENUE

LR 2/196, fos 166–8   miscellaneous books; surveys and rentals, etc: ... Kent ..., vol 16, Eliz I–Jas I: survey of the Crown manor of Sayes Court, July 1608

SPECIAL COLLECTIONS

SC 6/1113   ministers' and receivers' accounts: lands of Richard Duke of York
SC 6/1114   ministers' and receivers' accounts: general series, bundles 740–1124 (incl Deptford Strand, temp Edward IV)
SC 6/HenVIII/6024–6   ministers' and receivers' accounts: manor of Deptford Strand, 1537–40

National Maritime Museum, Greenwich, London (NMM)

ADM B 123   Navy Board, bound out-letters: the yard officers propose the purchase from Mrs Wickham of tenements adjacent to the yard in a place called the Orchard that are posing a fire hazard, 28 November 1743
ADM B 227   Navy Board, bound out-letters: copy letter of agent Matthew Ffinch at Deptford offering for sale premises in King Street and a place called the Orchard owned by Thomas Drake, Tyrwhitt Drake and Rev John Drake, 28 May 1807
ADM/BP/41b   illustration of section of a slip roof built at Deptford dockyard in 1814, dated 7 June 1821
ADM/Y/D/6   plan of the dockyard, 1810
ADM/Y/D/11   plan of wet dock ('basin') with reference to a

contract for Baker and Sons to build two larger slipways, October 1844

BHC1046 painting of the *St Albans* being floated out of her dry dock at Deptford in 1747, by John Clevely the elder

BHC1874 panoramic view of the Deptford dockyard: oil painting by Joseph Farington, *c* 1794

BHC3762 painting of the *Buckingham* on the stocks and ready for launch at Deptford in 1752, by John Clevely the elder

G218:9/22 map of Thames estuary and river by Benjamin Wright, *c* 1606

LAD/11/47 plan of the dockyard, 1774

PAD8611 graphite sketch of HMS *Russell* on the stocks under a slip roof at Deptford, by Henry Eldridge, *c* 1822

The Royal Society, London (RS)

RS.9268 portrait of John Evelyn (1620–1706) by Godfrey Kneller, *c* 1687

Scottish National Portrait Gallery, Edinburgh

Acc no. PG 1840 portrait of John Rennie by Henry Raeburn, 1810 (purchased 1957 with assistance from the Art Fund (London-Scot Bequest))

United Kingdom Hydrographic Office, Taunton (UKHO)

C101a-Ok 'plan of His Majesty's Dock Yard Deptford', signed 'G Tippot', 1802

D4624 map of Deptford dockyard in 1858

Victoria and Albert Museum, London (V&A)

E.2826-1962 plate from *Microcosm* (Pyne and Hill 1803–6) depicting wagons carrying timber

PUBLISHED AND OTHER SECONDARY WORKS

Adams, J R, 2003 *Ships, innovation and social change: aspects of carvel shipbuilding in northern Europe, 1450–1850*, Stockholm Stud Archaeol 24/Stockholm Marine Archaeol Rep 3, Stockholm

Amorosi, T, 1989 *A post-cranial guide to domestic neo-natal and juvenile mammals*, BAR Int Ser 533, Oxford

Archer, M, 1997 *Delftware: the tin-glazed earthenware of the British Isles: a catalogue of the collection in the Victoria and Albert Museum*, London

Ashton, T S, 1955 *An economic history of England: the 18th century*, London

Askey, D, 1998 (1981) *Stoneware bottles, 1500–1949*, 2 edn, Brighton

Atkinson, D R, and Oswald, A, 1969 London clay tobacco pipes, *J Brit Archaeol Ass* 32, 171–227

Austin, J C, 1994 *British delft at Williamsburg*, Williamsburg, VA

Ayling, S, 1972 *George the Third*, London

Ayre, J, and Wroe-Brown, R, 2015a The 11th- and 12th-century waterfront and settlement at Queenhithe: excavations at Bull

Wharf, City of London, *Archaeol J* 172, 195–272

Ayre, J, and Wroe-Brown, R, 2015b The post-Roman foreshore and the origins of the late Anglo-Saxon waterfront and dock at Æthelred's hithe: excavations at Bull Wharf, City of London, *Archaeol J* 172, 121–94

Baker, J C, 1984 *Sunderland pottery*, Newcastle

Banbury, P, 1971 *Shipbuilders of the Thames and Medway*, Newton Abbot

Barker, D, 1999 The ceramic revolution, 1650–1850, in Egan and Michael 1999, 226–34

Barker, R A, 1991 Design in the dockyards, about 1600, in *Carvel construction technique: skeleton-first, shell-first: 5th international symposium on boat and ship archaeology, Amsterdam, 1988* (eds R Reinders and K Paul), Oxbow Monogr 12, 61–9, Oxford

Barnard, J E, 1997 *Building Britain's wooden walls: the Barnard dynasty, c 1697–1851*, Oswestry

Barrow, J, 1832 *A memoir of the life of Peter the Great*, London

Baugh, D A, 1965 *British naval administration in the age of Walpole*, Princeton, NJ

Bedoyère, G de la, 1997 *Particular friends: the correspondence of Samuel Pepys and John Evelyn*, Woodbridge

Bell, R, 1969 *Board and table games from many civilizations: Vol 2*, London

Betts, I M, 2013, Chiswick House building material, unpub Engl Heritage rep

Betts, I M, and Weinstein, R I, 2010 *Tin-glazed tiles from London*, London

Bickerton, L M, 1971 *An illustrated guide to 18th-century English drinking glasses*, London

Birch, W de G (ed), 1887 *Cartularium Saxonicum: Vol 2*, London

Bissell Prosser, R, 1904 *Dictionary of national biography, 1885–1900: Vol 48*, http://en.wikisource.org/wiki/Rennie,_John_(1761-1821)_(DNB00 (last accessed 8 April 2014)

Blackmore, L, 2006 Report on the pottery from West Smithfield (WSI97), unpub MOL rep

Bloice, B, 1971 Norfolk House, Lambeth: excavations at a delftware kiln site, 1968, *Post-Medieval Archaeol* 5, 99–159

Bond, J, 2007 Canal construction in the early Middle Ages: an introductory review, in *Waterways and canal-building in medieval England* (ed J Blair), 153–206, Oxford

Bossche, W van den, 2001 *Antique glass bottles, their history and evolution (1500–1850)*, Woodbridge

Bowens, A (ed), 2007 *Underwater archaeology: the NAS guide to principles and practice*, Oxford

Bowsher, J, and Woollard, P, 2001 Clay tobacco pipes from Greenwich, *J Greenwich Hist Soc* 2, 94–108

Bray, W (ed), 1819 *Memoirs, illustrative of the life and writings of John Evelyn, Esq, FRS: comprising his diary, from the year 1641 to 1705–6, and a selection of his familiar letters, to which is subjoined …*, London, http://archive.org/stream/memoirsillustrat02 eveluoft_djvu.txt

Bray, W (ed), 1879 *Memoirs of John Evelyn, Esq, FRS: comprising his diary, from 1641 to 1705–6, and a selection of his familiar letters*, London

Britton, F, 1987 *London delftware*, London

Britton, F, 1990 The Pickleherring potteries: an inventory, *Post-Medieval Archaeol* 24, 61–92

Brown, D, and Thomson, R, 2005 Pottery vessels, in Gardiner 2005, 462–8

Brunning, R, and Watson, J, 2010 *Waterlogged wood: guidelines on the recording, sampling, conservation and curation of waterlogged wood*, Engl Heritage Guidelines Ser, 3 edn, London, https://content.historicengland.org.uk/images-books/publications/waterlogged-wood/waterlogged-wood.pdf/

Bull, G, and Payne, S, 1982 Tooth eruption and epiphysial fusion in pigs and wild boar, in *Ageing and sexing animal bones from archaeological sites* (eds R Wilson, C Grigson and S Payne), BAR Brit Ser 109, 55–72, Oxford

Burrage, C, 1910 The Fifth Monarchy insurrections, *Engl Hist Rev* 25, 722–46

Cal Cecil P Calendar of the manuscripts of the Most Hon the Marquis of Salisbury … preserved at Hatfield House, Hertfordshire [Calendar of Cecil papers], Roy Comm Hist MSS, 24 vols, 1883–1976, London

Cal Inq Misc Calendar of inquisitions miscellaneous, Public Rec Office, 1916–69, London

Cal Inq PM Calendar of inquisitions post mortem, Public Rec Office, 1904–74, London

Cal S P Col Calendar of state papers colonial, East Indies, China and Japan: Vol 2, 1513–1616 (ed W N Sainsbury), 1864, London

Cal S P Dom [1547–1625] Calendar of state papers, domestic series, of the reigns of Edward VI, Mary, Elizabeth I and James I (eds R Lemon and M A Everett Green), 12 vols, 1856–72, London

Cal S P Dom [1625–49] Calendar of state papers, domestic series, of the reign of Charles I (eds J Bruce and W D Hamilton), 23 vols, 1858–97, London

Cal S P Dom [1649–60] Calendar of state papers, domestic series, of the Commonwealth and Protectorate (ed M A Everett Green), 13 vols, 1875–86, London

Cal S P Dom [1660–85] Calendar of state papers, domestic series, of the reign of Charles II (eds F H B Daniell and F Bickley), 28 vols, 1860–1938, London

Cal S P Dom [addenda 1660-85] Calendar of state papers, domestic series, of the reign of Charles II: addenda (eds F H B Daniell and F Bickley), 1939, London

Cal S P For Calendar of state papers, foreign series, of the reign of Elizabeth I: Vol 8, 1566–8 (ed A J Crosby), 1871, London

Cal S P Spain Calendar of state papers, Spain (Simancas): Vol 3, 1580–6 (ed M A S Hume), 1896, London

Cal Treasury B Calendar of Treasury books (ed W A Shaw), 32 vols in 64, 1904–57, London

Cal Treasury P Calendar of Treasury papers (ed J Redington), 6 vols, 1868–89, London

Cannon, D Y, 1987 *Marine fish osteology: a manual for archaeologists*, Simon Fraser Univ Dept Archaeol Pub 18, Burnaby, BC

Cat Anc D A descriptive catalogue of ancient deeds, Public Rec Office, 1890–1915, London

Chew, S, and Pearce, J, 1999 A pottery assemblage from a 17th-century revetted channel at 12–26 Magdalen Street, Southwark, *London Archaeol* 9, 22–9

Chron Edw VI The chronicle and political papers of Edward VI (ed W K Jordan), 1966, London

Clark, J (ed), 1995 *The medieval horse and its equipment, c 1150– c 1450*, HMSO Medieval Finds Excav London 5, London

Coad, J G, 1973 The Chatham mast houses and mould loft, *Mariner's Mirror* 59, 127–34

Coad, J G, 1989 *The royal dockyards, 1690–1850: architecture and engineering works of the sailing navy*, Aldershot

Coad, J G, 2005 *The Portsmouth block mills: Bentham, Brunel and the start of the Royal Navy's industrial revolution*, Swindon

Coad, J G, 2013 *Support for the fleet: architecture and engineering of the Royal Navy's bases 1700–1914*, London

Cock, R, 2001 The finest invention in the world: the Royal Navy's early trials of copper sheathing, 1708–70, *Mariner's Mirror* 87, 446–59

Cock, R, and Rodger, N A M, 2008 *A guide to the naval records in the National Archives of the UK*, London

Cohen, A, and Serjeantson, D, 1996 (1986) *A manual for the identification of bird bones from archaeological sites*, rev edn, London

Cohen, N, 2009 West Smithfield: the excavation of a site to the west of the City of London, *London Archaeol* 12, 91–8

Colledge, J J, and Warlow, B, 2010 (1987–9) *Ships of the Royal Navy: the complete record of all fighting ships of the Royal Navy*, 4 (rev and updated) edn, Newbury

Colville, Q, 2009 Corporate domesticity and idealised masculinity: Royal Navy officers and their shipboard homes, 1918–39, *Gender and Hist* 21, 499–519

Copeland, R, 1990 (1980) *Spode's willow pattern and other designs after the Chinese*, 2 edn, London

Cordingly, D, 1986 *Nicholas Pocock, 1740–1821*, London

Courtney, T, 1974 Excavations at the royal dockyard Woolwich, 1972–3: Part 1, The building slips, *Post-Medieval Archaeol* 8, 1–28

Cowgill, J, de Neergaard, M, and Griffiths, N, 1987 *Knives and scabbards*, HMSO Medieval Finds Excav London 1, London

Coysh, A W, and Henrywood, R K, 1982 *The dictionary of blue and white printed pottery, 1780–1880: Vol 1*, Woodbridge

Crismer, L M, 1979 *Histoire et commerce des eaux de Chevron au XVIIIeme siecle*, L'Institut Archéologique Liégois Vol 91, Liège

Cumberland, F W, 1847 Iron roofs erected over building slips, no. 3 and no. 4, in Her Majesty's dockyard, Portsmouth, in Royal Engineers 1847, 59–65

Dam, J D van, Tichelaar, P J, and Schaap, E, 1984 *Dutch tiles in the Philadelphia Museum of Art*, Philadelphia, PA

Darley, G, 2006 *John Evelyn: living for ingenuity*, New Haven and London

Dews, N, 1884 *The history of Deptford*, London

Divers, D, 2000 Evaluation of Deptford royal dockyard, unpub PCA rep

Divers, D, 2004 Excavations at Deptford on the site of the East India Company dockyard and the Trinity House almshouses, London, *Post-Medieval Archaeol* 38, 17–132

Dodds, J, and Moore, J, 1984 *Building the wooden fighting ship*, London

Drakard, D B, with Haggar, R, 1973 *Whitehead catalogue, 1798: James and Charles Whitehead: manufacturers, Hanley, Staffordshire*, Bletchley

Drake, H (ed), 1886 *Hasted's history of Kent: corrected, enlarged and continued to the present time …: Part 1, The hundred of Blackheath*, London

Driesch, A von den, 1976 *A guide to the measurement of animal bones from archaeological sites*, Peabody Mus Bull 1, Cambridge, MA

Driesch, A von den, and Boessneck, J, 1974 Kritische Anmerkungen zur Widerristhöhenberechnung aus Langenmassen vor- und frühgeschichtlicher Tierknochen, *Säugetierkundliche Mitteilungun* 22, 325–48

Drowser, G, 2005 *Boats, boffins and bowlines: the stories of sailing inventors and innovations*, Stroud

Dunkin, A J, 1877 *History of the county of Kent: Vol 3, Deptford*, London

Egan, G, 2005 *Material culture in London in an age of transition: Tudor and Stuart period finds c 1450–c 1700 from excavations at riverside sites in Southwark*, MoLAS Monogr 19, London

Egan, G, and Michael, R L (eds), 1999 *Old and new worlds: historical/post-medieval archaeology papers from the Societies' joint conferences at Williamsburg and London, 1997, to mark 30 years of work and achievement*, Soc Post-Medieval Archaeol/Soc Hist Archaeol, Oxford

Ehrman, J, 1953 *The navy in the war of William III, 1689–97*, Cambridge

Ellmers, C, 2013a Gordon & Company, Deptford: discovering a lost London shipyard, in Ellmers 2013b, 43–72

Ellmers, C (ed), 2013b *Shipbuilding and ships on the Thames: proceedings of the 5th symposium, 2012*, London

English Heritage, 1998 *Dendrochronology: guidelines on producing and interpreting dendrochronological dates*, London

Esterly, D, 2013 *The lost carving: a journey to the heart of making*, London

Evelyn, J, 1706 (1662) *Silva, or a discourse of forest-trees and the propagation of timber in His Majesty's dominions*, 4 edn, London

Evelyn diary   The diary of John Evelyn (ed W Bray), 1901, London, http://www.gutenberg.org/ebooks/41218

Field, J, 1980 *Place-names of Greater London*, London

Farrington, A, 2002 *Trading places: the East India Company and Asia, 1600–1834*, London

Francis, A, 2010 Convoys Wharf, Prince Street, London SE8, London Borough of Lewisham: evaluation report, April 2010, unpub MOL rep

Francis, A, 2013 Convoys Wharf, Prince Street, London SE8, London Borough of Lewisham: post-excavation assessment report and updated project design, unpub MOLA rep

Francis, A, and Bowsher, J, 2013 Excavations at Anchor Iron Wharf, Greenwich: Part 2, Industrial and social development in the 17th–19th centuries, *London Archaeol* 13, 217–21

Friel, I, 1995 *The good ship: ships, shipbuilding and technology in England 1200–1500*, London

Gaimster, D R M, 1997 *German stoneware 1200–1900: archaeology and cultural history*, London

Gardiner, J, with Allen, M J (eds), 2005 *Before the mast: life and death aboard the* Mary Rose, Archaeol Mary Rose 4, Portsmouth

General and Commercial Directory, 1858 W H Dix & Co, *General and commercial directory of the Borough of Birmingham, and six miles round; including Wolverhampton, Bilston, Walsall, Westbromwich, &c*, Birmingham

Godwin, P, 1987 *The construction and fitting of the English man-of-war, 1650–1850*, Ann Arbor, MI

Goodburn, D, 1991a New light on early ship- and boatbuilding in the London area, in *Waterfront archaeology: proceedings of the 3rd international conference on waterfront archaeology held at Bristol, 23–26 September 1988* (eds G Good, R Jones and M Ponsford), CBA Res Rep 74, 105–15, London

Goodburn, D, 1991b Wet sites as archives of ancient landscapes, in *Wet site excavation and survey: proceedings of a conference at the Museum of London, October 1990* (eds J Coles and D Goodburn), WARP Occas Pap, 51–3, Exeter

Goodburn, D, 1992 Wood and woodlands, carpenters and carpentry, in Milne, G, *Timber building techniques in London c 900–1400: an archaeological study of waterfront installations and related material*, London Middlesex Archaeol Soc Spec Pap 15, 106–31, London

Goodburn, D, 1999 Echoes of adzes, axes and pitsaws, in Egan and Michael 1999, 171–9

Goodburn, D, 2002 Analysis of ship timbers from the south bank excavation, in Ayre, J, and Wroe-Brown, R, *The London Millennium Bridge: excavations of the medieval and later waterfronts at Peter's Hill, City of London, and Bankside, Southwark*, MoLAS Archaeol Stud 6, 84–9, London

Goodburn, D, 2009 Woodworking aspects of the *Mary Rose*, in Marsden 2009, 66–80

Goodburn, D, Meddens, F, Holden, S, and Phillpotts, C, 2011 Linking land and navy: archaeological investigations at the site of the Woolwich royal dockyard, south-eastern England, *Int J Naut Archaeol* 40, 306–27

Grainger, I, and Phillpotts, P, 2010 *The Royal Navy victualling yard, East Smithfield, London*, MOLA Monogr 45, London

Green, C, 1999 *John Dwight's Fulham pottery: excavations 1971–9*, Engl Heritage Archaeol Rep 6, London

Green, J N, 1977 *The loss of the Veringde Oostindische Compagnie Jacht* Vergulde Draek, *western Australia, 1656*, BAR Int Ser 36, Oxford

Grew, F, and Orton, C, 1984 Clay tobacco pipes, in Thompson et al 1984, 77–84

Grierson, P, 1941 The relations between England and Flanders before the Norman Conquest, *Trans Roy Hist Soc* 4 ser 23, 71–112

Guillery, P, and Herman, B, 1998 Deptford houses: 1650–1800, Roy Comm Hist Monuments Engl rep, http://udspace.udel.edu/handle/19716/2305 (last accessed 1 December 2015)

Guillery, P, and Herman, B, 1999 Deptford Houses: 1650–1800, *Vernacular Architect* 10, 58–84

Haas, J M, 1994 *A management odyssey: the royal dockyards, 1714–1914*, London

Hamilton, D L, 2000 *The Port Royal project: archaeological excavations*, http://nautarch.tamu.edu/portroyal/archhist.htm (last accessed 25 November 2015)

Harward, C, Holder, N, and Jeffries, N, 2015 *The Spitalfields suburb 1539–1860: excavations at Spitalfields Market, London E1, 1991–2007*, MOLA Monogr 61, London

Haslam, J, 1970 Sealed bottles from All Souls College, *Oxoniensia* 35, 27–33

Hasted, E, 1797 Parishes: Greenwich, in *The history and topographical survey of the county of Kent: Vol 1*, 372–420, Canterbury, http://www.british-history.ac.uk/survey-kent/vol1/pp372-420 (last accessed 19 May 2016)

Hather, J G, 2000 *The identification of the northern European woods: a guide for archaeologists and conservators*, London

Hawkins, D, 2000 Archaeological desk-based assessment, Convoys Wharf, Deptford SE8, unpub CgMs rep

Hawkins, D, 2009 Scheme of archaeological resource management (SARM), unpub CgMs rep

Hawkins, D, with Butler, C, and Skelton, A, 2014 The iron slip cover roofs of the royal dockyards 1844–57, in *Treason's harbours: dockyards in art, literature and film: transactions of the Naval Dockyards Society, 2011 conference* (ed J D Davies), Trans Naval Dockyard Soc 9, 65–82, Southsea

Hawkins, D, with Butler, C, Francis, A, Phillpotts, C, and Skelton, A, 2015 Deptford's royal dockyard: archaeological investigations at Convoy's Wharf, Deptford, 2000–12, *London Archaeol* 14, 87–97

Hawkins, D, and Butler, C, with Skelton, A, 2015 The iron slip cover roofs of Deptford and Woolwich royal dockyards 1844–55, *London's Ind Archaeol* 13, 42–61, http://www.glias.org.uk/journals/13-d.html

Heard, K, with Goodburn, D, 2003 *Investigating the maritime history of Rotherhithe: excavations at Pacific Wharf, 165 Rotherhithe Street, Southwark*, MoLAS Archaeol Stud 11, London

Hewett, C A, 1980 *English historic carpentry*, London

Howell, I, Goodburn, D, Jeffries, N, and Richardson, 2014 Development of the Thames waterfront at Bermondsey during the 17th and 18th centuries, *London Archaeol* 13, 333–40

Hurman, B L, 2006 Tabletop conversations: material culture and everyday life in the 18th-century Atlantic world, in *Gender, taste and material culture in Britain and North America 1770–1830* (eds J Styles and A Vickery), 37–59, New Haven and London

Hurst, J G, Neal, D S, and van Beuningen, H J E, 1986 *Pottery produced and traded in north-west Europe 1350–1650*, Rotterdam Pap 6, Rotterdam

Hutchings, J, 2016 Portsmouth Harbour Hinterland Project: historic character assessment (HE project no. 7082), unpub MOLA rep

Hutchinson, G, 1994 *Medieval ships and shipping*, London

ILN Illustrated London News (consulted online at the British Library)

Jarrett, C, 2005 The pottery, in Killock and Meddens 2005, 34–52

Jeffries, N, Wroe-Brown, R, and Featherby, R, 2014 'Would I were in an ale-house in London!': a finds assemblage sealed by the Great Fire from Rood Lane, City of London, *Post-Medieval Archaeol* 48, 261–84

Johnston, S, 2005 Making mathematical practice: gentlemen, practitioners and artisans in Elizabethan England, unpub PhD thesis, Univ Cambridge, http://www.mhs.ox.ac.uk/staff/saj/thesis/baker.htm (last accessed 20 February 2015)

Jones, P E, 1972 Four 15th-century London plans relating to Bridge House property in Deptford, without the Bar of Southwark, without St George's Bar towards Newington, and in Carter Lane in the City, *London Topogr Rec* 23, 35–9

Kemble, J M (ed), 1846 *Codex diplomaticus aevi Saxonici: Vol 4*, London

Kerr, R, Allan, P, and Martin, J, 2003 *The world in blue and white: an exhibition of blue and white ceramics, dating between 1320 and 1820, from members of the Oriental Ceramic Society*, London

Killock, D, and Meddens, F, with Armitage, P, Egan, G, Gaimster, D, Jarrett, C, Keys, L, Phillpotts, C, Sabel, K, Tyson, R, and Willmott, H, 2005 Pottery as plunder: a 17th-century maritime site in Limehouse, London, *Post-Medieval Archaeol* 39, 1–91

Knight, H, and Pearce, J, with Blackmore, L, 2017 Post-medieval development and the local tobacco pipe industry in the late 18th/early 19th century: excavations at 5–7 Giltspur Street, City of London, *London Archaeol* 15, 10–17

Knight, R J B, 1987 *Portsmouth dockyard papers 1774–83: the American War: a calendar*, Portsmouth Rec Ser 6, Portsmouth

Knight, R J B, 1999 From impressment to task work: strikes and disruption in the royal dockyards, 1688–1788, in Lunn and Day 1999, 1–20

Knight, R J B, 2013 *Britain against Napoleon: the organisation of victory, 1793–1815*, London

Knighton, C S, and Loades, D M (eds), 2000 *The Anthony roll of Henry VIII's navy: Pepys Library 2991 and British Library additional MS 22047 with related documents*, Navy Rec Soc Occas Pub 2, Aldershot

Knighton, C S, and Loades, D M (eds), 2011 *The navy of Edward VI and Mary I*, Navy Rec Soc Pub 157, Farnham

Korf, D, 1981 *Nederlandse maiolica*, Haarlem

L and P Hen VIII Letters and papers, foreign and domestic, of the reign of Henry VIII (eds J S Brewer, J Gairdner and R H Brodie), 22 vols in 35, 1864–1932, London

Laird, M, 2003 Sayes Court revisited, in *John Evelyn and his milieu* (eds F Harris and M Hunter), 115–44, London

Lambarde, W, 1596 (1576) *A perambulation of Kent*, 2 edn (ed R Church), 1970, Bath

Lambert, A D, 1984 *Battleships in transition: the creation of the steam battlefleet, 1815–60*, London

Lambert, A D, 2012 Woolwich dockyard and the early steam navy, 1815–52, in *Shipbuilding and ships on the Thames: proceedings of the 4th symposium, 2009* (ed R Owen), 82–96, London

Lavery, B, 1991 *Building the wooden walls: the design and construction of the 74-gun ship Valliant*, London

Lavery, B, 2003 *The ship of the line: Vol 1, The development of the battlefleet, 1650–1850*, London

Le Cheminant, R, 1981 Clay pipes bearing the Prince of Wales' feathers, in *The archaeology of the clay tobacco pipe: VI, Pipes and kilns in the London region* (ed P Davey), BAR Brit Ser 97, 92–101, Oxford

Linebaugh, P, 2003 (1991) *The London hanged: crime and civil society in the 18th century*, 2 edn, London

Loades, D M, 1992 *The Tudor navy: an administrative, political and military history*, Aldershot

Loewenson, L, 1962 Some details of Peter the Great's stay in England in 1698: neglected English material, *Slavonic E European Rev* 40, 431–43

London Gazette Gazette, https://www.thegazette.co.uk

London Journal 17th- and 18th-century Burney Collection newspapers, Gale Cengage Learning, http://gale.cengage.co.uk

Lunn, K, and Day, A (eds), 1999 *History of work and labour relations in the royal dockyards*, London

Lysons, D, 1796 *The environs of London: Vol 4, Counties of Herts, Essex and Kent*, London

McCarthy, M, 2005 *Ships' fastenings from sewn boat to steamship*, College Station, TX

MacDougall, P, 1982 *Royal dockyards*, Newton Abbot

MacDougall, P, 1999 The changing nature of the dockyard dispute, 1790–1840, in Lunn and Day 1999, 41–65

McGowan, A P (ed), 1971 *The Jacobean commissions of enquiry, 1608 and 1618*, Navy Rec Soc Pub 116, London

MacGregor, A, 2004 The tsar in England: Peter the Great's visit to London in 1698, *17th Century* 19, 116–47

Marsden, P, 1996 *Ships of the port of London, 12th to 17th centuries AD*, Engl Heritage Archaeol Rep 11, London

Marsden, P (ed), 2009 *The Mary Rose: your noblest shippe: anatomy of a Tudor warship: Vol 2, The hull*, Portsmouth

Martin, A R, 1927 The alien priory of Lewisham, *Trans Greenwich Lewisham Antiq Soc* 3, 103–27

May, W E, 1999 *The boats of men-of-war*, London

Mazeika, C, 2007 Pearls before swine: a history of the Great Storehouse at Deptford, 1513–1720, *Trans Naval Dockyard Soc* 3, 125–30

Meddens, F, 2008 *Pirates of the East End*, London

Merwe, P van der, 2010 Clevely family (*per c* 1747–1809), *Oxford dictionary of national biography*, online edn, http://www.oxforddnb.com/index/5/101005637/

Merwe, P van der, 2013 Artists and the Thames shipyards, in Ellmers 2013b, 73–100

Milbourn, M, and Milbourn, E, 1995 (1983) *Understanding miniature British pottery and porcelain, 1730–present day*, 2 edn, Woodbridge

Miller, G L, Samford, P, Shlasko, E, and Madsen, A, 2000 Telling time for archaeologists, *NE Hist Archaeol* 29, 1–22

Millett, M, and McGrail, S, 1987 The archaeology of the Hasholme logboat, *Archaeol J* 144, 69–155

Mills, J, 1993 The Benedictine priory of Lewisham: 'Land of St Peter's of Ghent', *Lewisham Hist J* 1, 15–39

Mosley, C (ed), 2003 *Burke's peerage, baronetage and knightage: clan chiefs, Scottish feudal barons*, 107 edn, Wilmington, DE

Morriss, R, 1983 *The royal dockyards during the Revolutionary and Napoleonic Wars*, Leicester

Morriss, R, 1999 Government and community: the changing context of labour relations, 1770–1840, in Lunn and Day 1999, 21–40

Morriss, R, 2011 *The foundations of the British maritime ascendancy: resources, logistics and the state, 1755–1815*, Cambridge

Murphy, G, 1987 *Founders of the National Trust*, London

Musty, J, 1990 Brick kilns and brick and tile suppliers to Hampton Court Palace, *Archaeol J* 147, 411–19

Neale, G, 2005 *Miller's encyclopaedia of British transfer-printed pottery patterns 1790–1930*, London

Nenk, B, with Hughes, M, 1999 Post-medieval redware pottery of London and Essex, in Egan and Michael 1999, 235–45

Noël Hume, I, 1969 *A guide to artifacts of colonial America*, London

Noel Hume, I, 1970 *A guide to artifacts of colonial America*, New York

Noël Hume, I, 1977 *Early English delftware from London and Virginia*, Colonial Williamsburg Occas Pap Archaeol 2, Williamsburg, VA

Nurse, J, 2016 *The rise and fall of Sequah*, http://blog. wellcomelibrary.org/2016/02/the-rise-and-fall-of-sequah/ (dated 24 February 2016; last accessed 24 June 2016)

ODH Old Deptford history, http://www.olddeptfordhistory. com/2012/02/west-side-of-watergate-street-deptford.html (last accessed 25 November 2015)

Oppenheim, M, 1896a *A history of the administration of the Royal Navy and of merchant shipping in relation to the navy: from 1509 to 1660, with an introduction treating of the preceding period*, Hist Admin Royal Navy 1, London

Oppenheim, M, 1896b The navy of the Commonwealth, 1649–60, *Engl Hist Rev* 11, 20–81

Oppenheim, M, 1926 Maritime history, in *The Victoria history of the county of Kent: Vol 2* (ed W Page), 243–388, London

Orton, C, and Pearce, J, 1984 The pottery, in Thompson et al 1984, 34–68

Oswald, A, 1975 *Clay pipes for the archaeologist*, BAR Brit Ser 14, Oxford

Parsons, F G (trans/ed), 1932 *Chartulary of the hospital of St Thomas the Martyr, Southwark, 1213–1525*, London

Payne, S, 1973 Kill-off patterns in sheep and goats: the mandibles from Asvan Kale, *Anatolian Stud* 23, 281–303

Pearce, J, 1992 *Post-medieval pottery in London 1500–1700: Part 1, Border wares*, London

Pearce, J, 2000 A late 18th-century inn clearance assemblage from Uxbridge, Middlesex, *Post-Medieval Archaeol* 34, 144–86

Pearce, J, 2007 An assemblage of 17th-century pottery from Bombay Wharf, Rotherhithe, London, SE16, *Post-Medieval Archaeol* 41, 64–79

Pearce, J, 2012 Convoys Wharf, site code CVF10: assessment of clay tobacco pipes, unpub MOLA rep

Pearce, J, 2013 Clay tobacco pipes made by the Manby family of London, *Journal de l'Académie Internationale de la Pipe* 6, 71–82

Peck, W E, 1896–7 *Peck's circular trades directory and detailed buyers' guide to the manufactures of Birmingham and district*, Birmingham

Penny London Post 17th- and 18th-century Burney Collection newspapers, Gale Cengage Learning, http://gale.cengage.co.uk

Pepys diary The diary of Samuel Pepys: daily entries from the 17th-century London diary, http://www.pepysdiary.com/diary/

Perry, J, 1716 *The state of Russia, under the present czar*, London

Philipott, T, 1659 *Villare Cantianum, or, Kent surveyed and illustrated*, London

Phillips, E J, 1995 *The founding of Russia's navy: Peter the Great and the Azov fleet, 1688–1714*, Westport, CT

Phillpotts, C, 2011 Convoys Wharf: Sayes Court, preliminary documentary research report, with additions 2014 by Mark

Latham, unpub MOL rep

Pitt, K, and Goodburn, D, with Stephenson, R, and Ellmers, C, 2003 18th- and 19th-century shipyards at the south-east entrance to the West India Docks, London, *Int J Naut Archaeol* 32, 191–209

Port, M H, 2008 Banks, Sir Edward (1770–1835), *Oxford dictionary of national biography*, online edn, http://www.oxforddnb.com/view/article/1294 (last accessed 19 February 2014)

Post Office, 1850 *Post Office directory of Birmingham, with Staffordshire and Worcestershire*, London

Post Office, 1881ff *Post Office directories* [1881 onwards], London

Proctor, J, Sabel, K, and Meddens, F M, 2000 Post-medieval brick clamps at New Cross in London, *Post-Medieval Archaeol* 34, 187–202

Pryor, S, and Blockley, K, 1978 A 17th-century kiln site at Woolwich, *Post-Medieval Archaeol* 12, 30–85

Pyne, J, and Hill, J, 1803–6 *Microcosm: or, a picturesque delineation of the agriculture, manufactures &c of Great Britain*, London

Rackham, O, 1972 Grundle House: on the quantities of timber in certain East Anglian buildings in relation to local supplies, *Vernacular Architect* 3, 3–8

Rackham, O, 1976 *Trees and woodland in the British landscape*, London

Ransley, J, and Sturt, F, with Dix, J, Adams, J, and Blue, L (eds), 2013 *People and the sea: a maritime archaeological research agenda for England*, CBA Res Rep 171, York

Ray, A, 1968 *English delftware pottery in the Robert Hall Warren Collection, Ashmolean Museum, Oxford*, London

Rimer, G, Richardson, T, and Cooper, J P D (eds), 2009 *Henry VIII: arms and the man, 1509–2009*, Leeds

Rodger, N A M, 1988 (1986) *The wooden world: an anatomy of the Georgian navy*, 2 edn, London

Rodger, N A M, 1997 *The safeguard of the sea: a naval history of Britain: Vol 1, 660–1649*, London

Rodger, N A M, 2004 *The command of the ocean: a naval history of Britain, 1649–1815*, London

Round, J H (ed), 1899 *Calendar of documents preserved in France, illustrative of the history of Great Britain and Ireland: Vol 1, AD 918–1206*, London

Royal Engineers, 1847 *Papers on subjects connected with the duties of the Corps of Royal Engineers: Vol 9*, London

Sabben, C van, and Hollem, J, 1987 *Antieke tegels*, Rockanje

Sainsbury, S, 2008 *The creation of an English Arcadia*, lot 128, http://www.christies.com/lotfinder/lot/a-london-delft-dated-cat-jug-1659-5097391-details.aspx

Saunders, A (ed), 2005 *The London County Council bomb damage maps (1939–45)*, London Topogr Soc Pub 164, London

Sawyer, P H, 1968 *Anglo-Saxon charters: an annotated list and bibliography*, London

Saxby, D, and Goodburn, D, 1998 17th-century ships' timbers and docks on the Thames waterfront at Bellamy's Wharf, Rotherhithe, London SE16, *Mariner's Mirror* 84, 173–98

Schmid, E, 1972 *Atlas of animal bones for prehistorians, archaeologists and Quaternary geologists*, Amsterdam

Schoch, W, Heller, I, Schweingruber, F H, and Kienast, F, 2004 *Wood anatomy of central European species*, www.woodanatomy.ch

(last accessed 30 April 2012)

Seddon, J, and Moxey, T, 2003 *Queen Elizabeth's Hunting Lodge: a brief history*, London

Sheaf, C, and Kilburn, R, 1988 *The Hatcher porcelain cargoes: the complete record*, Oxford

Sidell, J, Wilkinson, K, Scaife, R, and Cameron, N, 2000 *The Holocene evolution of the London Thames: archaeological excavations (1991–8) for the London Underground Limited Jubilee Line Extension Project*, MoLAS Monogr 5, London

Skempton, A W (ed), 2002 *Biographical dictionary of civil engineers in Great Britain and Ireland: Vol 1, 1500–1830*, London

Smith, T P, 1985 *The medieval brickmaking industry in England 1400–50*, BAR Brit Ser 138, Oxford

Smith, T P, 1996 Pantiles in London, unpub MOL rep

Smith, T P, nd Bricks in 17th-century London, unpub MOL rep

Steel, D, 1805 *The elements and practice of naval architecture*, repr 1997, London

Steele, J, 1993 *Turning the tide: a history of everyday Deptford*, London

Stevenson, J, and Goffin, R, 2010 Accessioned finds, in Grainger and Phillpotts 2010, 108–15

Stewart, K, 2013 Wood species identification of accessioned finds from Convoys Wharf, unpub MOLA rep

Sturdee, T, 1895 *Reminiscences of old Deptford*, Greenwich

Survey of London, 1994 Blackwall yard: development to *c* 1819, in *Poplar, Blackwall and Isle of Dogs* (ed H Hobhouse), Survey of London 43/44, 553–65, London, http://www.british-history.ac.uk/survey-london/vols43-4/ pp553-565 (last accessed 10 March 2015)

Sutherland, W, 1711 *The ship-builder's assistant*, London

Thorpe, W A, 1969 *A history of English and Irish glass*, London

Thompson, A, Grew, F, and Schofield, J, 1984 Excavations at Aldgate, 1974, *Post-Medieval Archaeol* 18, 1–148

TNA, Discovery Joseph Sankey & Sons Ltd (GKN Sankey Ltd), http://discovery.nationalarchives.gov.uk/details/rd/d8addc2f-5797-40f6-bb51-7d13b9a296c1 (last accessed 20 February 2015)

Townsville Daily Bulletin Townsville Daily Bulletin, http://nla.gov.au/nla.news-title97

Trevelyan, G, 2002 *England under the Stuarts*, London

Tyers, I, 1987 Deptford Wharf interim dendrochronological report, in Norton, E, A report on groundworks being carried out at the site of Deptford Wharf, SE8, between 6 and 8 August 1987, unpub MOL rep

Tyers, I, 2013 Tree-ring spot dates from archaeological samples: Convoys Wharf, Deptford, London Borough of Lewisham (site code CVF10), unpub MOLA rep

Tyler, K, 2001 The excavation of an Elizabethan/Stuart waterfront site on the north bank of the River Thames at Victoria Wharf, Narrow Street, Limehouse, London E14, *Post-Medieval Archaeol* 35, 53–95

Tyler, K, Betts, I, and Stephenson, R, 2008 *London's delftware industry: the tin-glazed pottery industries of Southwark and Lambeth*, MoLAS Monogr 40, London

Walford, E, 1878 *Old and new London, a narrative of its history, its people, and its places: Vol 6*, London

Wallenberg, J K, 1931 *Kentish place-names: a topographical and etymological study of the place-name material in Kentish charters dated before the Conquest*, Uppsala

Watson, J, 1987 Domesday Greenwich, *Trans Greenwich Lewisham Antiq Soc* 10, 108–18

Weinstein, R, 2005 Storage vessels, in Gardiner 2005, 460

Weir, A, 2008 *Henry VIII: king and court*, London

Wheeler, A, 1979 *The tidal Thames: the history of a river and its fishes*, London

Wheeler, A, and Jones, A K G, 1989 *Fishes*, Cambridge

Whiter, L, 1978 (1970) *Spode: a history of the family, factory and wares from 1733 to 1833*, 2 edn, London

Wilcox, L A, 1966 *Mr Pepys' navy*, London

Wilkins, C, 2010 *The last knight errant: Sir Edward Woodville and the age of chivalry*, London

Williams, A, and Martin, G H (eds), 2002 *Domesday Book: a complete translation*, London

Williams, J, and Brown, N (eds), 1999 *An archaeological research framework for the greater Thames estuary*, Chelmsford

Williams, M, 1847 Description of wrought iron roofs erected over two building slips in the royal dockyard, Pembroke, in Royal Engineers 1847, 50–8

Willmott, H, 2002 *Early post-medieval glass in England, 1500–1670*, CBA Res Rep 132, York

Winfield, R, and Lyon, D, 2004 *The sail and steam navy list: all the ships of the Royal Navy, 1815–89*, London

INDEX

Compiled by Susan Vaughan

Page numbers in **bold** indicate illustrations
All street names and locations are in London unless specified otherwise
County names within parentheses refer to historic counties

253